FROM THE FIVE GEOGRAPHIC AREAS OF SOUTHERN VERMONT— A CORNUCOPIA OF TRAVELER'S DELIGHTS

The mountain owned by a monastery

Equinox Skyline Drive winds 5.2 miles up the 3,835-foot summit of Mount Equinox, where, on a crystal-clear day, you can watch the sun rise or set over five states and one foreign country. Drive up or hike up. The view is glorious—especially when the foliage is autumn beautiful.

The fabled Battenkill River

Rent a canoe from Battenkill Canoe's fleet of 45 and drift quietly past fly fishermen trying to snag wily trout, glide under bridges, find pastures to picnic in, wade in crystal-clear waters . . . and then be picked up down river and taken conveniently back to your car.

Wonderful Woodstock

Join the locals for an after-work brew in front of the open fireplace at Richardson's Tavern; be pampered at Jackson House, where a harpist strums soft background music while you sip champagne and munch on hors d'oeuvres at no extra charge; or slip away for a horse-drawn sleigh ride over snowy trails at Kedron Valley Stables—what a Christmas treat!

MARGARET BUCHOLT is the former editor of the *Manchester* (Vermont) *Journal* and a contributor to the *Boston Globe* and the *New York Times*. She is the recipient of two Vermont journalism awards and has written extensively about her adopted state since 1976.

An Insider's Guide
TO
SOUTHERN VERMONT

Edited by
MARGARET BUCHOLT

A PLUME BOOK

PLUME
Published by the Penguin Group
Penguin Books USA Inc., 375 Hudson Street,
New York, New York 10014, U.S.A.
Penguin Books Ltd, 27 Wrights Lane,
London W8 5TZ, England
Penguin Books Australia Ltd, Ringwood,
Victoria, Australia
Penguin Books Canada Ltd, 2801 John Street,
Markham, Ontario, Canada L3R 1B4
Penguin Books (N.Z.) Ltd, 182–190 Wairau Road,
Auckland 10, New Zealand

Penguin Books Ltd, Registered Offices:
Harmondsworth, Middlesex, England

First published by Plume, an imprint of New American Library,
a division of Penguin Books USA Inc.

First Printing, June, 1991
10 9 8 7 6 5 4 3 2 1

LIBRARY OF CONGRESS CATALOGING IN PUBLICATION DATA:

An Insider's guide to Southern Vermont / edited by Margaret Bucholt.
    p.   cm.
  ISBN 0-452-26611-4
    1. Vermont—Description and travel—1981—Guide-books.
  I. Bucholt, Margaret.
  F47.3.I57   1991
  917.4304'43—dc20   91-7987
                                                        CIP

Printed in the United States of America

BOOKS ARE AVAILABLE AT QUANTITY DISCOUNTS WHEN USED TO PROMOTE PRODUCTS OR SERVICES. FOR IN-
FORMATION PLEASE WRITE TO PREMIUM MARKETING DIVISION, PENGUIN BOOKS USA INC., 375 HUDSON
STREET, NEW YORK, NEW YORK 10014.

Contents

Acknowledgments

I'd like to thank all the contributors — Connie Fitz, Jo-Anne MacKenzie, Alan Fortney, and Monica Allen — who spent many, many hours compiling the information for this book. As we all discovered somewhat belatedly, this was a bigger project than we initially thought. Without their diligence and perseverance this book would not have been possible. And thanks to artist Karl Stuecklen for his maps and drawings, and to the special section writers — Eric Evans, Mary McKhann, John Merwin, Craig Woods, David Rihm, and Greg Worden — whose expertise is an important component to the success of this book.

A special thank you is also in order to Publisher Thomas Begner and Editor Gordon Hardy for their patience, understanding, and invaluable assistance in getting this book into print.

I'd also like to thank my children, Dan and Maya, and my friends Tom Saltonstall and Jo-Anne MacKenzie for their patience and support during this lengthy project.

Margaret Bucholt

PART I

About the Authors

An Insider's Guide to Southern Vermont was compiled and written by a group of local writers who have lived and worked in southern Vermont for many years.

Margaret Bucholt of Dorset is the Director of Publications at Bennington College. She is the former editor of the *Manchester Journal*, a weekly newspaper in Manchester, Vermont, and the recipient of two Vermont journalism awards. She has written extensively about her adopted state since 1976. Her free-lance writing and photography credits include the *Boston Globe Sunday Magazine* and *Rod and Reel* magazine. She is an avid cross-country skier and tennis player.

Alan Jon Fortney of Bennington, a free-lance writer, is the former editor of *Vermont Summer* (an Eagle Publishing Company weekly supplement). His credits include a stint as copy editor for the *New York Times Sunday Travel Section*, as well as articles and photographs in the *Boston Globe*, *Yankee*, and *Adirondack Life*. He is also the author of several books including *Puppets: Methods and Materials* and the *Vintage Auto Almanac*.

Jo-Anne MacKenzie of Wallingford is the editor of the *Manchester Journal*. She was born and raised in the Springfield – Chester area, which she writes about. She is the recipient of the Mavis Doyle Award from the Vermont Press Association. A graduate of the University of Vermont, she also attended Sarah Lawrence College and interned with poet Hayden Carruth before beginning her journalism career.

Constance Hendren Fitz of Woodstock is a free-lance journalist and a regular contributor to *Woodstock Magazine* and the *Vermont Standard*, a weekly newspaper in Woodstock. Her writing has been published in the *New York Times*, *Film News*, *National Gardening*, and *New England Gardener*.

Monica Allen of Cornwall covered the Rutland area for the *Rutland Herald* daily newspaper in Rutland, Vermont, for four years. A graduate of Brown University, she has won several Vermont and New England journalism awards.

Karl Stuecklen of Sandgate is a well-known illustrator. His credits include the following books: four James Beard cookbooks, *Theme Gardens*, *The Cook's Garden*, as well as several magazines, including the *Country Journal* and the *Boston Globe Sunday Magazine*.

John Merwin of Dorset is the former editor of *Rod and Reel* magazine and has published numerous books on fishing.

Craig Woods of Dorset is the author of several books on fishing and cross-country skiing. His latest book is *The River As Looking Glass*.

David Rihm of Manchester is a golf pro at Stratton Mountain. He is author of *The Games of Golf*.

Eric Evans of Putney is the author of two books, *Mental Toughness Training for Cross Country Skiing* and *Kayaking*. His free-lance work has appeared in *Life*, *People*, *Outside*, *Ultrasports*, and *Cross Country Skier*.

Mary McKhann of Dorset is a copy editor at the *Rutland Herald*, a daily newspaper in Rutland, Vermont. She is the recipient of a sportswriting award from the Vermont Press Association. A former ski instructor, she has been involved in Masters ski racing and the U.S. Ski Writers Association. For summer recreation, she windsurfs.

Greg Worden of Brattleboro is the past president of the Brattleboro Tennis Club. He first began covering the Volvo International Tennis Tournament in New Hampshire in 1972 for the *Brattleboro Reformer* newspaper in Brattleboro, Vermont, where he was the assistant editor for many years. He is a free-lance writer.

Introduction

by MARGARET BUCHOLT

There's something about southern Vermont's lush hills and valleys that never fails to produce a quiet stirring in my heart, a phenomenon that started soon after I moved to the Green Mountain state in 1976.

Like other relocated "flatlanders" of that era, I came with a sense of purpose — to be close to the land. Over the years, I have grown vegetables in its rocky soil, hiked its hills, rappeled its rocky facades, hauled firewood from its forests, and driven its icy back roads with an increasing degree of success. I learned to correctly gauge conditions for cross country skiing, and most recently, I discovered the fun of schussing down mountain trails.

During the lengthy assimilation process, I wrote glowingly, but honestly, of the people, the beauty, and the recreational opportunities. When necessary, I chastised officials who failed to treat the land with the respect it deserved. Those admonishments became more frequent, as southern Vermont began to grow in ways in which locals never dreamed possible. In 1976, there were two women's clothing stores in Manchester, for example, and now there are too many — most of them discount outlets — to count. In the region, tracts of virgin forest land have been cut into "lots" and sold for residential development. Dairy farms, the backbone of the state, are almost extinct. And condominium units, suddenly de rigueur, rudely invaded townscapes.

It was an alarming process to watch, and locals wondered whether the charming villages and pristine hills would be sacrificed in the rite of passage from a rural to an urban state. If that scenario came to pass, southern Vermont would undoubtedly lose its attractiveness to the visitor, who, after all, seeks to escape the unwieldy urban and suburban sprawls for a weekend or longer. Environmental legislation has kept much of the development in check, thanks to a grass-roots movement of locals and natives (the two are not always synonymous), but the direction of Vermont's future continues to be a hot issue.

It was during this era that the so-called resort communities of southern Vermont — Woodstock, Manchester, Wilmington, West Dover, Sherburne, Stratton, to name a few — blossomed into the sophisticated vacation retreats they are today. No longer content with rope tows and double chair lifts, many of the ski areas went high tech — quad lifts, gondolas, pricey stores, gourmet restaurants — and for financial as well as practical reasons, began broadening their scope and focusing on summer visitors. Summer concerts and outdoor recreation and entertainment were added to the growing roster of winter activities.

Development impacted nearby towns that were more accustomed to summer visitors. Long before the first rope tow made its debut outside of Woodstock, southern Vermont was known throughout the region as a summer resort area. Two prominent summer resort communities, Manchester and Woodstock, for example, catered to an affluent summer clientele, prior to the ski area boom of the last twenty years. Before technology made southern Vermont so accessible in the winter, metropolitanites "summered" here and, depending on their economic status, stayed in backwoods "camps" or upscale resort hotels, like the

Equinox in Manchester Village. They fished the fabled Battenkill and the Connecticut River, which separates the Green Mountain State from New Hampshire. Many of those historical resorts have kept up with the times and added such amenities as Jacuzzis, spas, day care, and Nautilus rooms to the tennis courts and golf fairways already in place. Others, like Lake Saint Catherine, choose to remain in a pleasant time warp, which only adds to their charm.

The magnetic pull of southern Vermont is a strong one. Its mystique has lured many a traveler into its fold, some permanently. Besides the average visitor, southern Vermont continues to attract artists and writers as well. Around the turn of the century, Rudyard Kipling found Dummerston to his liking, and in the 1930s and 1940s, *New York Herald Tribune* drama critic Alexander Woollcott bought Neshobe, an island in Lake Bomoseen where he entertained Laurence Olivier and other Hollywood stars. Arlington's locals gained notoriety when famed illustrator Norman Rockwell had them model for his *Saturday Evening Post* covers. More recently actor Michael J. Fox scouted around the Manchester–Pawlet area for a home before he settled on an estate outside of Woodstock, and television producer Norman Lear lives in Shaftsbury, the town poet Robert Frost called home for many years.

What is it about southern Vermont that intrigues visitors and keeps them returning year after year? Perhaps it is the mountain vistas, or quaint villages, villages with a white-steepled church, a post office, and maybe a town office building. Or maybe it's the great outdoors that boasts of hiking the Long and Appalachian trails in the Green Mountain National Forest, fishing in the fabled Battenkill River and pristine ponds and streams, and golfing on courses flanked by lovely hills and meadows. Or, maybe it's the people who are pleasant, friendly, and polite. (Most locals are not impressed by the image of Vermonters portrayed on "Newhart.") More than likely, it's a feeling of a bygone era — nostalgia for a less complex society, a quality of life that is not found in too many places nowadays, which is not to say southern Vermont is immune from the ills plaguing the rest of society. We have our problems like everyone else. The message we hope to convey is that Vermont is a beautiful state with many offerings for the visitor.

In the following pages, we'll attempt to guide you through the southern Vermont area and let you in on some of its best-kept secrets. We'll offer travel tips and suggest lodging places, as well as restaurants and recreational activities.

The guidebook divides southern Vermont into six sections: Bennington, Manchester and the Mountains, Rutland/Killington, Woodstock, Windsor/Ludlow, and Brattleboro/Wilmington. A final section contains special essays on different recreational pursuits: Alpine skiing, cross-country skiing, golf, tennis, fishing, sailboarding, and foliage tours.

Each of the geographic sections is further broken down into locales. Bennington includes Woodford (Prospect Mountain), Arlington and its villages, and Sunderland; Manchester and the Mountains includes Stratton, Magic and Bromley mountains, Dorset, and Poultney; Rutland/Killington includes Killington and Pico ski areas, Hubbardton, and Shrewsbury; Woodstock includes Barnard, Plymouth, Bridgewater, Quechee, and Suicide Six and Sonnenberg ski areas; Windsor/Ludlow includes Bellows Falls, Mount Ascutney and Okemo ski areas, Grafton, and Chester; the Brattleboro/Wilmington area includes Marlboro, Newfane, Jamaica, Mount Snow, and Haystack Mountain. We've not only covered the designated resort communities but those lesser-known villages worth exploring as well.

The geographic sections include listings of lodging establishments, restaurants, entertainment, museums, seasonal events, children's activities, art galleries, craft and specialty shops, antiques stores, golf courses, hikes, foliage vantage points, tennis courts, ski areas, state parks, lakes and swimming holes, and other categories. A word about swimming holes: You have to be responsible for your own safety at areas that do not have a lifeguard. Also, please respect no-trespassing signs on private property.

Our aim is to give you a feel for a particular area by describing towns, year-round events, and recreational activities available. We provide descriptions, phone numbers, and price ranges for restaurants and lodgings. Restaurants are given one of three general ratings: inexpensive (entrées less than $10), moderate (entrées $10 to $18), and expensive (entrées $19 and up). Lodgings are based on double occupancy and have been given one of three general rates: inexpensive (less than $50 a night), moderate ($51 to $99 a night), and expensive ($100 or more a night).

Please note that some establishments may fall between two categories. We have tried to be fair in generalizing; for more specific information we suggest you call the particular lodging or restaurant establishment for details. Due to the nature of the tourist industry, and the many enterprises in the southern Vermont area, there may be omissions and mistakes. We also cannot be responsible for late changes in names, hours, addresses, phone numbers, or descriptions due to our publication deadline. We have done our best, and we hope you enjoy the book.

Travel Tips

by MARGARET BUCHOLT

If you're planning a trip to southern Vermont, there are several pieces of information that might come in handy.

For starters, there is no commercial airline service to the region, although there are several airports where you can land a small aircraft. Commercial carriers have come and gone at some locales when they realized the demand was not large enough to warrant such a service. It was also an expensive proposition for the traveler. At this writing, there was one helicopter taxi service operated by Marilyn George out of West Brattleboro called Southern Vermont Helicopter Service (802-257-4354), which made trips to Hartford, Connecticut, Boston, Massachusetts, and New York City to pick up passengers and ferry them to the Green Mountain state. Since a helicopter needs only a 100-foot-by-100-foot area to land and take off, it literally does become a taxi service because you can almost travel door-to-door. The aircraft holds four passengers plus limited luggage. Ms. George said they always request a landowner's permission prior to using private property for landing and takeoff.

The closest major metropolitan airport is in Albany, New York. Smaller airports that have commercial carriers are located at Hanover and Keene, New Hampshire. And, of course, you can always charter a private plane.

In the railroad's heyday, travel to southern Vermont was easy. In Manchester Depot, the "snow train" from New York City brought skiers to town on a Friday night, and horse and wagons ferried them to local inns and hotels. Today Amtrak no longer serves southwestern Vermont, but it does provide rail service to the southeastern section of the state. From points south, you can take Amtrak to Brattleboro, Bellows Falls, and White River Junction. For more information call 1-800-USA-RAIL. The only commercial carrier that serves all of southern Vermont is Vermont Transit Bus Company. Many bus companies outside Vermont connect with Vermont Transit. During the gas crunch of the 1970s, local lodging establishments reactivated the process of picking up their clients at bus stations and airports. Some resorts may still provide that service.

The best way to get to southern Vermont is by car. We're close enough to Boston, Hartford, New York, and Albany to make it a relatively painless trip. Visitors using other carriers may want to explore renting a car. Aside from the peak times — Friday or Sunday nights on a ski weekend and Columbus Day weekend — there is never so much traffic that you wished you'd stayed home. Everything here is on a much smaller scale than in a major metropolitan area.

Interstate 91 on the eastern side of the state is one of the few interstates to connect with southern Vermont. It makes traveling to southeastern communities a breeze. The southwestern side is not so lucky. Although the Bennington/Manchester/East Dorset area does have the limited access highway Route 7, which runs north to Manchester and East Dorset, that's it. Southwestern Vermont is one of the harder places to get to. Many New York City visitors take the thruway or the Taconic State Parkway and pick up New York's Route 22, which connects with New York's Route 7 into Bennington and beyond. And if you're coming from Boston into southwestern Vermont, it's Route 2 in Massachusetts that will get you here. Or, you can hop on I-91 and pick up Vermont Route 9, an east-west access, or Route 30, which goes north to the Manchester area.

Once you're here, you'll find distances between towns are not far at all. Woodstock, for example, is about forty-four miles from Brattleboro, and Wilmington is forty-five miles from Manchester. What you have to remember is that with the exception of interstate travel, traveling time is a lot slower. The estimated number of miles will take you a lot longer because of the mountains. If you look at a map, you'll see how few state roads there are in southern Vermont. And many of them are all uphill. (Of course, you do get to come down at some point.) That's the bad news, which isn't so bad at all when you figure the scenery will be beautiful and it'll make your trip seem faster. There'll be no ugly billboards to mar the landscape, either. Billboards are outlawed. Instead, there are small, attractive directional signs right on the main roads for businesses located off the highway.

Southern Vermont has two welcome centers — one on Interstate 91 at the Massachusetts border and one on Route 4A at the New York border near Fair Haven. There you can find brochures and help with directions, etc. We suggest you write or call the chamber of commerce at your point of destination beforehand if you're interested in more detailed information than we have provided in this book. Here are the addresses and phone numbers:

Arlington Chamber of Commerce, Box 245, Arlington, Vermont 05250; 802-375-2269.

Bellows Falls Chamber of Commerce, Box 554, 55 Square, Bellows Falls, Vermont 05101; 802-463-4280.

Bennington Chamber of Commerce, One Veterans' Memorial Drive, Bennington, Vermont 05201; 802-447-3311.

Brattleboro Chamber of Commerce, 180 Main Street, Brattleboro, Vermont 05301; 802-254-4565.

Chester Chamber of Commerce, Box 623, Chester, Vermont 05143; 802-875-2709.

Londonderry Chamber of Commerce, Box 58, Londonderry, Vermont 05148; 802-824-8178.

Ludlow Chamber of Commerce, 196 Main Street, Box 333, Jewel Brook Place, Ludlow, Vermont 05149; 802-228-5318.

Manchester and the Mountains Chamber of Commerce, Route 7, Adams Memorial Park, Manchester Center, Vermont 05255; 802-362-2100.

Mount Snow/Haystack Regional Chamber of Commerce, Route 9, Wilmington, Vermont 05363; 802-464-8092.

Quechee Chamber of Commerce, Box 804, Quechee, Vermont 05059 (seasonal, no telephone).

Rutland Regional Chamber of Commerce, 7 Court Street, Rutland, Vermont 05701; 802-773-4181.

Springfield Chamber of Commerce, 55 Clinton Street, Springfield, Vermont 05156; 802-885-2779.

White River Junction Chamber of Commerce, White River Junction, Vermont 05001; 802-295-6200.

Windsor Chamber of Commerce, Box 5, 3 State Street, Windsor, Vermont 05089; 802-674-5910.

Woodstock Chamber of Commerce, 18 Central Street, Woodstock, Vermont 05091; 802-457-3555.

Some other driving tips: You need to be extremely careful driving year-round. Summertime, bicyclists are in the roadway, and many of our thoroughfares are narrow. Don't think twice about giving them the right of way. In winter, when the weather is bad, drive slowly. It might take a little longer, but you'll get there safely. And during foliage, if you want to gaze adoringly at the leaves, please pull over so you don't hold up traffic. Vermont police are always on the lookout for intoxicated drivers, so don't ruin your vacation. Drive sober.

A good way to find out about up-to-the-minute events is to read the local papers, and check those community bulletin boards for church suppers and other events. In small towns, those bulletins are the backbone of the communication network.

Fishing licenses are required for those sixteen years of age and older. Town clerks and local general and convenience stores sell them. Just ask. Don't risk being cited by a Vermont Fish and Wildlife Department official.

If you have any doubt (or even if you don't), don't trespass on private property. Always ask. Vermonters are pretty fussy about their territory.

We're pretty informal here in Vermont. Casual dress is always acceptable. Some restaurants, however, require jackets for men, so you might want to pack one along with a tie in case the mood strikes you for a gourmet meal. During the winter you need to come prepared, particularly if you're interested in outside activities. Bring warm clothing, gloves, scarf, a hat, and, most important, a pair of warm boots that will keep your feet dry. While we're on the subject of winter dress, it's not a bad idea to carry a sleeping bag and chocolate candy in case your car breaks down as you head out for your dream skiing weekend in southern Vermont. Summer evenings are apt to be on the cool side, so be sure and pack sweaters or sweatshirts.

If you need some help with directions or finding a particular restaurant or inn, be sure and ask. Locals are glad to offer assistance. We want you to enjoy your visit to our lovely state.

PART II
Vermont Vistas

The Bennington Area

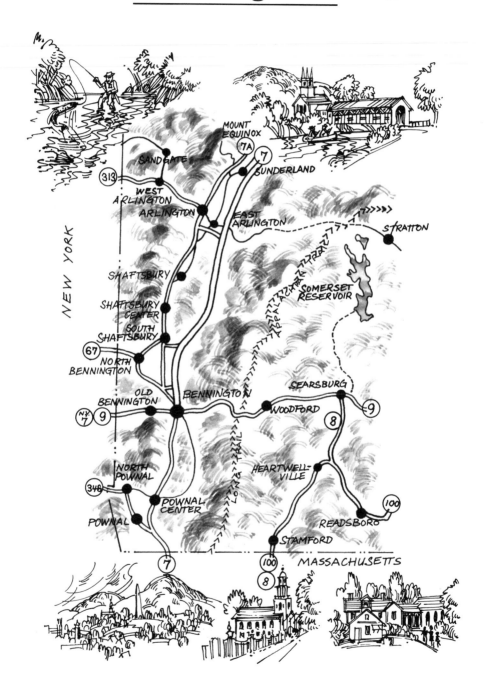

Viewpoints

by ALAN JON FORTNEY

Coming into the lower left-hand (southwestern) corner of Vermont usually means you enter Bennington directly from New York State Route 7. You can tell you are coming into Vermont as you pass Yoshi's Japanese Restaurant on the right, work up a smallish hill, past a "Vermont View" game farm, and hove around a corner that opens suddenly, and breathtakingly, onto a view of Mount Anthony skirted by pasturelands and cornfields, depending on who's rotating what crop when. In one picture that is what Vermont is about: farms and mountains.

Caveat emptor: That New York highway (U.S. Route 7) changes its number right at the Vermont/New York border to become Vermont Route 9. This number change can be confusing, especially since you can also come in from the Berkshires in Massachusetts on U.S. 7 through Pownal. New York Route 7 becomes Vermont Route 9 and crosses U.S. Route 7 at the main intersection in Bennington. Later a "new" U.S. Route 7 turned "old" U.S. Route 7 became "historic route" 7A.

Technically, the countryside we call Bennington Town (like a township elsewhere) starts right there at the Vermont/New York border and contains farms, forests, and mountains as well as the villages of Old Bennington, Bennington, and North Bennington. This community in the southwest corner of Vermont is rich in history and affords the visitor many cultural activities, including the Oldcastle Theatre and the Bennington Museum, which houses many works of Grandma Moses. Bennington Town is famous for its pottery, and North Bennington, with three fine restaurants, is home to the college dubbed the most expensive in the United States: Bennington College. Picturesque Pownal, south of Bennington on Route 7, has Vermont's only pari-mutuel dog racing track, and Shaftsbury, north of Bennington on Historic Route 7A, boasts Lake Shaftsbury, a wonderful state recreation area. Old Bennington, in particular, is a well-preserved village dominated by the Old First Congregational Church where poet Robert Frost is buried.

Old Bennington

Since 1907, the historic section of town has been called Old Bennington, and you'll arrive here first if you come via Route 9 from New York State. Old Bennington has its (mostly) separate government and constabulary. The houses around the Bennington Monument and down the avenue to the top of Elm Street are all white, privately owned, and tend to have dates and historic names on them. Formerly Main Street, this avenue on the hill was where it all began.

Historical Perspective

This Bennington area is chock-full of beauty and legends, in all seasons. Ethan Allen, Ira Allen, Sam Robinson, Tom Chittenden, Jonas Faye. And Sheriff Ten Eyck, of New York, thinking he could come in here and claim Vermont for his state.

Ayup!

"The gods of the valleys are not the gods of the hills," Ethan Allen was said to have roared along about then. When asked what on earth that meant, he bellowed an invitation to the "Yorkers" to "come on up to Bennington and we'll show you."

He wasn't exactly inviting in tourists.

This drama was due to a remarkable deficiency in British King George's understanding of New World geography. In the mid-1700s, George II granted Governor Benning Wentworth, of New Hampshire, the right to sell real estate westward from New Hampshire to about 40 miles short of the Hudson River: To the governor of New York, he granted real estate rights as far east as the Connecticut River. The land thus overlapped almost exactly coincides with the modern state of Vermont.

The drama's first *persona dramata* entered when Sam Robinson, a weary French and Indian War vet, took the wrong fork in 1753 on a river homeward bound to Connecticut, legend has it, and found himself on a lovely hill in these "New Hampshire Grants." He liked the lay of the land so much, in 1761 he led the first actual settlers to the town Benning Wentworth had chartered "on paper" to stake his claim as far west as he dared in 1749. A plaque, next to the Old Academy Library (1821) on Old Bennington's "main street," Monument Avenue, marks where Sam Robinson built his log cabin.

Ethan Allen and the Green Mountain Boys also bought their land from Benning Wentworth about that time. And the Boys had no intention of buying it again, especially at the New York prices. In part because of this quirk, the folks in Albany, New York, called them "The Bennington Mobb" and tried to intimidate and hornswoggle them. But no one had yet met the likes of Ethan Allen. He was bombast personified — amongst other things.

When Vermont's first "tourist," Sheriff Ten Eyck, came with 300 armed men to claim Sam Breakenridge's farm in North Bennington, Ethan and his Green Mountain Boys, pretending to be marauding Indians, administered the "justice of the birches" (they spanked them) and sent them on their way across the Henry Covered Bridge. All other "Yorker" visits (or attempted encroachments) to Bennington, Sunderland, and Arlington were met with noise, tarnation, foxlike wit, and humor-laden threats. No one was hurt, really, let alone killed in these skirmishes, even though the stakes were high and the prizes real (estate).

When circumstance turned Ethan's attention to the revolutionary war, he conquered Fort Ticonderoga without a shot, demanding capitulation in "the name of the Great Jehovah and the Continental Congress." The astonished British captain, who had never heard of the latter, quickly complied and nary a drop of blood was spilled. Only rum. A lot of that, we're told.

Ethan and the Boys, all eventually "wanted" men in New York, planned these larks at the sign of Landlord Fay's Tavern, which was draped menacingly with a stuffed Vermont catamount (wildcat), teeth bared in the direction of New York. God, they had fun! The big cat, permanently memorialized in bronze in 1897, still snarls New-Yorkward but now in front of Art and Kit Robert's genteel Monument Avenue home built on the site of the raucous old tavern (which burned to the ground in 1871).

Ethan devised a daring plan at his tavern headquarters to capture Montreal and nip the British offensive in the bud. It failed because his support troops forgot to cross the Saint Lawrence River when they were supposed to. Even then, Ethan, with about 200 French Canadian farmers armed only with pitchforks, almost succeeded. But only almost.

Ira Allen, his brilliant youngest brother, took up the cause during Ethan's prisoner-of-war years and made Vermont an independent republic rather than knuckle under to the Yorkers. For fourteen years Vermont had its own foreign policy, its own currency and postal system, and a constitution considered far more "advanced" than that of the fledgling United States. Bennington was Vermont's rather ad hoc "capital." Sometimes. Windsor was, too. Or anywhere else the legislature felt like meeting.

Ethan Allen had to have been, in retrospect, one of the most rapscallious revolutionary heroes ever. And we note that Vermont didn't deign to join the union until after Ethan had died. That Vermont exists at all is due to Ethan and Ira Allen and The Bennington Mobb.

Ethan was, as mentioned, in prison during much of the Revolution, so he missed the Battle of Bennington. While the *reason* for the battle was Bennington, it was actually fought in Walloomsac, New York, on August 16, 1777.

British General John Burgoyne heard of storehouses filled with ammunition and supplies in Bennington and a ready supply of farm horses. He sent troops over to "requisition" it all. Burgoyne greatly underestimated these local farmers, who promptly defeated 800 of his trained British, Loyalist, German troops, and Indians at Walloomsac Heights. In fact, the defeat took so much wind out of Burgoyne's offensive he surrendered, following the Battle of Saratoga, a scant sixty-two days later. Burgoyne was known to have referred to Benningtonians thereafter as "the most active and rebellious race on the continent."

The site of the storehouse is now marked by the Bennington Battle Monument, 306 feet, 4½ inches tall, dedicated in 1891 by U.S. President Rutherford B. Hayes, on the highest point in Old Bennington. It is a remarkable way to remember a warehouse/ammo dump, when you think about it.

Two other landmarks are noteworthy in Old Bennington. One is the Old First Church, the "most-photographed" church, right in front of you where Route 9 makes a sharp, and somewhat baffling, turn to the left followed almost immediately by a sharp right to head down the hill into Bennington; the second is the Walloomsac Inn on the opposite corner, built in 1764.

Nearly every visitor stops at the church, at least briefly, to figure out which way to turn. The reason this corner exists is that long ago the main highway went right beside the church and down a too-steep hill. Part of the old road is there, but it dead-ends in a thicket of woods now.

Old First's congregation, first gathered in 1762, is active, though modest in size today. The present building, dating from 1805, was restored to clear-windowed, box-pewed, Colonial splendor by Reverend Vincent Ravi-Booth, who served as minister there in the 1920s and 1930s.

Facing it across a small green festooned with historical markers is the Walloomsac Inn, which first opened its doors in 1764 and looks very much like it has for these several centuries. Among its notable guests were President Rutherford B. Hayes, Thomas Jefferson, and James Madison.

Attractions, Recreational Pursuits

Visible long before you pull up to Old First, the Bennington Monument, and related gift shop, is open April 1 through November 1, 9 A.M. – 5 P.M. For a token admission, you can take the elevator 176 feet up to the observation level (used to have to climb 412 steps), which affords views in all directions. A proud statue of Colonel Seth Warner, a battle leader, was added to the "circle" in 1910. To see the actual battleground in Walloomsac, New York, and the pleasant little park that commemorates the hostilities, take Route 67 about three miles northwest of North Bennington into New York. You'll see signs.

The dead from that battle, and from a lot of the rest of the town's doings, lie in the Old Burying Grounds around Old First Church. And Robert Frost, who lived on various farms in Bennington and Shaftsbury, finally ended his "lover's quarrel with the world" here.

Halfway down the hill from Old Bennington, in what was once the Catholic church, the Bennington Museum has the original "Bennington Flag," which according to legend (not curators) flew over the heroic efforts of the Green Mountain Boys at Bennington's revolutionary battle. Those same curators do claim it is the oldest existing American flag they know of, however.

This museum, open March 1 to December 22 (except Thanksgiving) and most weekends during winter, houses treasures from all time slots on Bennington's two-and-one-half-century historical record. This museum's collections include eighteenth- through twentieth-century military items, Bennington pottery, American glass, and paintings by regional artists. Smack next to the museum is the old schoolhouse Grandma Moses (and her children, grandchildren, and great-grandchildren) once attended. It was moved over from Eagle Bridge, New York, in 1972 and houses some of her paintings and other painterly memorabilia.

Local historian and preservationist, Tordis Ilg Isselhardt, has devised two pleasant, self-guided walking tours — one of Old Bennington and one of Bennington itself. The pamphlets are available at the museum, the chamber of commerce offices, and select shops in town.

Along Vermont Route 9 coming into Old Bennington, you will pass a beautiful old schoolhouse, to which have been appended a number of other buildings to form the nucleus of Hemming's Motor News' publishing enterprises. Usually an antique car (a 1937 something, for some reason) is parked next to the sign. These friendly people have a bookstore there and do welcome old-car hobbyists.

A little closer to the village of Old Bennington is Camelot Village, a complex of stores that pleases many visitors. This complex was once a very important veterinary center, until the racetrack in Pownal stopped running horses, which explains why part of the complex looks like a barn.

On the left, just a few rods farther on, is Old Bennington's finest restaurant, The Four Chimneys. The elegant house the restaurant occupies, which my daughter long ago pointed out has five chimneys, was built on the foundation of a manse that burned in 1910 after having stood there since 1783. Master Chef Alex Koks, trained in the Hague, Netherlands, presides over his kitchen and has turned vast culinary talent into an art form.

Backtracking a bit, another restaurant worth noticing is that landmark mentioned above just back over the border on New York 7. Yoshi's Japanese Restaurant is not the kind of treasure you'd expect to find just on the cusp of Vermont's forests, but Chef Teruo Yoshi, also a master, though trained on the other side of the world in Tokyo, has been serving up smacking-good Japanese foods daily (except Mondays) for more than ten years there.

Bennington, Pownal

People have always come to Vermont for the same reason: it is a beautiful, peaceful place to visit. It is peaceful in summers, spectacular in autumn, and exceptionally good skiing (or sledding) in winter. The same reasons apply to coming to Bennington — with one addition. Bennington is imbued with history, and many of its historical buildings are still standing.

At first, the emphasis in Bennington Town was agricultural, and the industrial activities reflected that. Grist mills, saw mills, even a few wool mills cropped up. Even today people refer to working "in the mills," though the actual mills have all long since vanished; and a peaceful, mostly agricultural feeling prevails in Bennington to this day.

Historical Perspective, Area Attractions

Because of the natural abundance of water for power in the valley below that Old Bennington hill, factories sprang up and workers moved in. In 1810, Giles Olin built a canal (now gone) from the Roaring Branch to the Walloomsac River to power the mills. By the mid-1800s, the emphasis and the center of activity shifted down the east side of the hill into the Bennington Valley. Old Bennington gradually became the home of wealthy "summer people," some of whom, it is said, looking down the hill (or was it their noses?) at the noisy, teeming factories called the "new" settlement "East Bennington" on good days and "Algiers" on most others.

When Henry Bradford turned a woolen mill to the task of making woolen underwear in 1854, he laid the foundations for a "golden age" for an industry that shone between 1860 and 1890. What is called the Holden-Leonard Mill was built in 1865 to make paisley scarves. To stave off failure, it too quickly converted to making woolen underwear and prospered. The owners built additions for the next 60 years until it became known locally as The Big Mill. It served as a magnet to bring in other industries.

When the mill closed its doors in 1938, it put 800 people — a quarter of Bennington's work force — out of work. In a massive project, involving town, state, and federal monies, the buildings were renovated in 1988 – 1989 for light industrial use and can be seen (and leased) on BenMont Avenue.

Olin Scott, whose ancestors had settled the area, became a wealthy industrialist who manufactured gunpowder machinery in several locations in Bennington and exported it all over the world between 1858 and his death in 1913. He gave portions of his wealth back to his community by providing funds and leadership to create that 1910 Seth Warner statue that stands proudly on Monument Circle, the Tudor Revival Masonic Lodge on Main Street, and an Olin Scott Fund to help Bennington youth with college loans.

Another industrialist, Edward H. Everett, who was born here but made his fortune manufacturing bottles elsewhere, returned after his enormous success in time to leave two grandiose monuments to himself: One is the replica of a fourteenth-century English-Norman mansion built in 1911 as a private summer home and now housing 600-student Southern Vermont College on one of the loveliest campuses in Vermont, as well as the Oldcastle Theatre Company, a local professional theatrical company that performs April through October; the other is a slightly scaled-down, though still grand, replica of the Parthenon that houses his and his family's earthly remains in Park Lawn Cemetery, which overlooks his (now Southern Vermont) orchards on the hill.

In a manner of speaking, the fire that destroyed the original courthouse back up in Old Bennington in 1869 graphically illuminated the shift of the focus of activities down into the valley. A new courthouse was built on South Street (the retail stores in town with huge columns) to handle court matters from 1870 to 1936, when an exact replica of that original Colonial Revival courthouse was created a few doors down, as if to prove the center of Bennington was truly, firmly, and finally in the valley. The clock on the facade does keep accurate time.

Pottery has been associated with Bennington since the day in 1793 Captain John Norton built the first kiln in town. He developed a small family business that he passed to his sons, Lumen and John, in 1823. Lumen's son, Julius, and his son-in-law, Christopher Fenton, joined forces in 1840 and ushered in a "golden age" of pottery (1847 – 1858) that glowed brightest at the 1853 Crystal Palace Exposition in New York. The "Monumental Piece" exhibited there is in the museum. After the exposition Fenton closed down his production, though Norton continued until 1894. The 1838 Norton-Fenton House, now the Bennington

County Teachers' Credit Union offices on Pleasant Street, is on the above-mentioned walking tour, as is the (1909) late Gothic Revival Saint Peter's Episcopal Church, along with several other buildings in this section of town.

In 1948, David Gil came to Bennington and, claiming to have never heard of either the Nortons or the Fentons, started Bennington Potters. His factory shop, in what was once H. W. Myers's coal, flour, straw, and grain elevator a half block east of North Street on County Street, he claims, only slightly joshing, is *the* reason people come to Bennington. The Brasserie Restaurant, once the kitchen of Dione Lucas, presents a continental cuisine with a flourish. Before you turn onto County Street, a stop at the Hawkins House, a crafts and art gallery in two beautifully restored, now-joined houses, is also worthwhile.

An antiquarian bookstore, called New Englandiana, buys libraries and accumulations and sells used and antique books from the Big Mill company store on BenMont Avenue and River Street "Mondays and most weekdays," according to owner Roger Harris (company scrip no longer accepted).

Bennington has three other antiquarian booksellers: Now and Then Books on Main Street; Bradford Books, out on Vermont Route 9 west of town across from Fairdale Farms; and Aislinn Books and Research, which is strictly mail order. The Vermont Antiquarian Booksellers Association holds an annual antiquarian fair and publishes a list of some fifty VABA members and where they are in business and how to get in touch with them.

The Bennington Station, which was built of "blue marble" as a railroad station on the Bennington & Rutland Line (1898), is now a very fine, and popular, restaurant. The owner completely renovated it, retaining and restoring as much of the original station as he could while making it attractive as well. In addition to presenting a fine menu daily, it is a gallery of historic photographs from the Weichert-Isselhardt Collection.

Another very popular restaurant is the Publyck House up on Harwood Hill, just north of the town on Historic Route 7A (formerly U.S. 7). It is in a large barn that was moved to the edge of lovely apple orchards in 1971 for the purpose. Various expansions, alterations, and improvements have not changed the fact that this good meal affords one of the most pleasant views in Bennington, no matter the season.

Publyck House owners Dave and Kate Johnson also operate the Main Attraction Restaurant on Bennington's Main Street. Another good restaurant right on Main Street is Alldays and Onions, which serves lunch as well as light dinners.

For those who just want to visit and luxuriate in a weekend of gracious living, an upscale bed and breakfast called The Southshire Inn is in a beautiful old house, built by Luther A. Graves, banker. It, and the adjacent converted carriage barn, house nine elegant, antiques-furnished rooms. The library is richly paneled in mahogany and the dining room suggests the Italian renaissance. Other B&Bs are located in Bennington and nearby towns.

A lovely drive during foliage is south to Pownal, a rural community whose only claim to fame — if you can call it that — is the state's only pari-mutuel racetrack. This village is situated on a knoll just west of U.S. Route 7, which comes out of Williamstown, Massachusetts, and hurries northward to Bennington. The south terminus of the center's main street ends abruptly to overlook the beautiful valley below; the north tip kind of sidles obliquely back into U.S. 7, something like an afterthought. The side street next to the white-clapboard Union Church (1789) comes to an end in a clump of shrubs that mask off the main highway. A dirt road wriggles behind the church and out onto the highway, but it isn't much used. All is quiet here, especially in the Old Cemetery, where huge trees that come ablaze in season shade two and a quarter centuries of local history.

This valley was settled in 1720 by some not-so-hardy Dutch who didn't endure; the permanent settlement started when a group of Rhode Islanders came in 1766. As you look around, you will see why they came. The valley is, quite simply, beautiful. The valley lands are flat and farmable. The Green Mountains in the east, and the Taconics in the west, provide shelter. One sharp, white outcropping of rocks, visible from U.S. 7 and facing west toward the Taconics, is called Kreigger Rocks and is thought to have been part of a natural dam that shored in a glacial lake 10,000 years ago. Indian legend connects them to a tribal tragedy, an entire camp being rubbed out by Iroquois, and calls them the "weeping rocks."

The Green Mountain Race Track, Vermont's first and only pari-mutuel track, was opened in 1963. It went totally to the dogs in 1977, however. Prior to that date, it was harness racing; after that, greyhounds were brought in to chase mechanical rabbits at great speed. About 100,000 fans come between mid-May and mid-October to see if they can turn a $1 or $2 ticket into $200 or $300. If you correctly select first, second, and third place winners in one of these 31- or 39-second races, you could, as one person did in 1989, "hit the trifecta" for $34,000 — on an investment of $1.

People are discovering the pleasures of coming to Bennington to stay while making day (or evening) trips around the area. Bennington is a comfortable drive from such cultural attractions as the Saratoga Performing Arts Center (summer home of the New York City Ballet) to the west in Saratoga, New York; Tanglewood (summer home of the Boston Symphony) to the south in Lee, Massachusetts; Williams (summer) Theatre Festival in neighboring Williamstown, Massachusetts; Marlboro Music Festival to the east in Marlboro, Vermont, to name a few. There are other restaurants in the area to supplement the many that exist in Bennington and North Bennington.

And while many singles insist that it is not a ski adventure unless they stay right at slope-side, many family folks find Bennington quite close enough (and neither as pricey nor as crowded) for sleeping accommodations when they shush down nearby Mount Snow, Haystack, Bromley, or Magic mountains. If you want to come in autumn to see Nature's own light and color show, we suggest you plan well in advance, because all rooms in all the inns fill up during peak foliage season from early to mid-October.

The chamber of commerce offices, located on Memorial Drive (also U.S. Route 7 North), can provide a fuller picture of this community. Just pull in and ask for Mike.

North Bennington, Shaftsbury

Originally called Haviland's Privilege and then Sage City, North Bennington can make a claim most Vermont villages — especially those this size — cannot: It has its own symphony orchestra.

The brainchild of composer/teacher Louis Calabro, who has taught music at Bennington College for several decades, The Sage City Symphony has performed much of the standard orchestra repertoire as well as newly commissioned works. The orchestra members are "amateur" musicians in that they play for the love of it, but the sounds they produce are polished.

History, Attractions

This village got its start in that second wave of growth that turned Bennington from a rural village on the hill to an industrial giant in the valley. The access to additional good water power here meant that factories came out to North Bennington. Despite the fact that a number of the factory buildings are still here, housing different industries today, it still has the feel of a small rural village.

Driving out from Bennington on Route 67A, you will pass three covered bridges and find several large factory buildings along the road just before coming into the village. Some are functional, some a bit rough around the edges, some look strong and useful. A wonderful waterfall spills out of Lake Paran next to the firehouse into Paran Creek. It tumbles over rocks and forms roiling rapids gracing the tasteful condominium complex now called "Haviland's Privilege" and formerly the Stark Paper Company's fieldstone building, with stepped gables and window arches fashioned of halved millstones.

This little village, oddly enough, boasts three restaurants. What was once Percey's News Room has become Percey's Newsroom Café, which emphasizes lunch but serves dinners as well. Just catercorner across the village square (triangle, really) is The Main Street Cafe, which delivers a northern Italian menu every evening, with brunch added on Sunday.

The Villager Restaurant, once a gathering place for the rowdier set from nearby Bennington College, is now all gussied up, refinished, and gentrified by owners Beth and Dan Boepple who offer what they call a "refreshing change in the art of food preparation." The menu is deliciously continental, the walls serve as a fine art gallery displaying the works of many area artists, some widely known, and on Sunday evenings a bistro menu and mellow jazz, live, are presented.

The Park-McCullough House, a 35-room Victorian mansion built by Trenor Park in 1865, seems to boast of his financial success in the California goldfields — without a pan or a pickax. He was a lawyer, not a prospector, and he provided legal services to the likes of John Fremont, whose Mariposa Gold Mines he eventually managed.

The mansion housed the family of John G. McCullough, governor of Vermont (1902 – 04). The 14-foot ceilings, the parquet floors, the elegant central staircase, and the oak and walnut paneling galore speak of gracious turn-of-the-century living. The Hall, Park, and McCullough families saved everything! Never threw anything away! So the place covers a continuous century's history from 1799 to the 1960s. In 1975, the McCullough family turned the care of the mansion over to a private foundation, which keeps it open as a museum and educational facility. In season, art exhibits, outdoor theater and celebrations, garden parties, and weddings are also held here.

It is open to the public late May through October, 10 to 4, for house tours and can be rented for fine social occasions as well. The spacious grounds, which include a grape arbor and Colonial and Victorian gardens, have been beautifully restored by a gardener named Maurice whom some suspect to be at least part leprechaun. The carriage barn has the family carriages and sleighs ready for the horses, who have long since departed.

A cute grace note is the fully furnished playhouse, which is a miniature of the "Big House."

A restored building, the 1880 railroad depot that welcomed Admiral Dewey, whistle-stopping his triumphant way from his heroic actions in the Spanish-American War home to Montpelier in 1898, now houses the village offices.

Although Bennington College's front door more nearly faces Bennington itself (you passed it on Route 67A on the way to this village), its back door, and its heart, is predominantly in North Bennington. There is something in the nature of the college that sets it apart from Bennington and, to a lesser degree, from North Bennington. It was created as a women's college in the 1920s to be a showcase for the educational theories of John Dewey ("learn by doing"), became coeducational in 1969, and has a reputation as the most expensive college in the United States. Its back gate opens into North Bennington, and some students live in this village because it is tree-lined and quiet.

If you continue north on Route 67, it hooks up with Historic Route 7A again. Make a left and a few miles up the road you'll pass through the village of South Shaftsbury at the blinking yellow light.

Off to the west of the main intersection is Stanley Tools, the main industry hereabouts since the 1920s.

When Silas Hawes forged two steel blades together to make the world's first carpenter's squares in 1814, he provided the foundation for what some think is one of Vermont's oldest industries. His partner, Stephen Whipple, built an "old stone mill" to manufacture the squares, which is now a lovely, privately owned home at the junction of Historic Route 7A and Vermont Route 67.

The antique "Carpenter's Square" sign is visible on the wall of Stanley Tools' old stone building (1831) that fronts Route 67, a half mile or so from the 'Whipple mill.' Snugged right up to the highway, the fieldstone building looks old and quaint, but out behind that is a huge, modern Stanley Tools factory.

Going off to the right at that intersection, onto East Street, you can pass the home Robert Frost called his "gully farm," currently owned by television producer Norman Lear, and find your way to Peter Matteson Tavern (it's a few miles, turning northward on East Road).

Peter Matteson Tavern is a museum that is still designated on official Vermont maps as "Topping Tavern." This name came from Lady Gosford who saw it, called it "simply topping," and bought it in 1926. She bequeathed it to the Bennington Museum in 1967, which still owns it. Built in the 1770s as a farmhouse and tavern, it is now used as an educational facility by the museum and, on special occasions, is open to the public.

Other historical buildings of special significance or beauty include the Shaftsbury Historical Museum (1846), which is surrounded by a cemetery because it was originally a church; the Munroe-Hawkins House (1807), now a private dwelling; the Governor Galusha House, still occupied by the descendants of Jonas Galusha who was nine times the governor of Vermont between 1809 and 1820; and the Chocolate Barn and Antiques Shop, for self-evident reasons.

Lovely Lake Shaftsbury State Park has a 27-acre artificial lake to swim in, canoe on, or fish out of, as well as playgrounds, picnic tables, and a large pavilion. Two adjacent group-camping areas are available to bring Boy Scouts, Cub Scouts, and similar groups for relaxing and camping in 101 acres of woodlands.

Arlington, Sunderland

Located about 15 minutes north of Bennington on Historic Route 7A, Arlington is everyone's "hometown." This is the place we all know as Norman Rockwell's America.

The famous illustrator well known for his *Saturday Evening Post* covers lived in West Arlington from 1939 to 1953. Rockwell's was a simpler America, a time when kids played sandlot baseball, when apple pies cooled on windowsills, when the work that men did was as visible as a plow furrow, when machines were simpler and attitudes happier and more optimistic than we now think we have a right to envision. The remarkable thing is that Rockwell didn't make it up; he just moved here and found people — Boy Scouts, moms with apple pies, clear-eyed dads, hometown individualists all — who really lived like that. And many of them still do.

Prior to his moving here in 1939, he painted professional models, and after he left Arlington in 1953, he had begun painting famous people. It was only here that he painted real people.

Henry Hinrichsen, owner of the Arlington Gallery, which houses a "Norman Rockwell Exhibition" and who employs several former Rockwell models there says, "The best-known paintings of Norman Rockwell were painted here. Most people don't realize that Rockwell even lived here. And they certainly don't realize that the image of America they know and love *is* Arlington."

In Arlington and its environs, you'll find the four inns that comprise the Historic Inns of Norman Rockwell's Vermont; the toll road; Equinox Skyline Drive, with its breathtaking views and hiking trails; three covered bridges; and the fabled Battenkill River.

Arlington's Main Street is Historic Route 7A. Those who are in a hurry can take the "new" U.S. 7, a limited access highway that rushes between Bennington and Manchester east of East Arlington (Exit 3).

Arlington is a real place with real people who go to real stores and have real strawberry festivals and game dinners in real churches that are still occupied Sunday mornings.

This village is obviously not a "tourist destination" designed by theme park specialists trying to re-create a bygone era. It is the picture of small-town America we all know and love.

This is a village where white clapboard is the rule of thumb. And where there are almost no sidewalks. A little sidewalk goes from the Arlington Gallery to the Arlington Inn on the east side of Main Street; a remnant appears and vanishes under the road along the west side of the village green. People in villages walk at the side of the road, so drive slowly.

Standing at the corner of Main Street and the East Arlington Road, facing north, a visitor can see most of the village. Immediately on the right is Doc Russell's house. Originally it belonged to Tom Chittenden, a one-eyed giant of a man who became Vermont's first governor in 1778. Russell lived there when he *was* "The Country Doctor" in the Rockwell painting of that name. Marjorie and Larry Brush, the parents who brought Baby Ann in to "the doctor's" in 1947, work in the Arlington Gallery next door. Snugged right next to the gallery is a white-clapboard doghouse. The occupant, according to the sign there, is named "Spot." Of course, he is a Dalmatian.

Just beyond the Arlington Gallery is one of Stewart's Shops — the only thing that resembles a chain store anywhere near here. A little, white-clapboard chamber of commerce information booth, set back from the road, stands between Stewart's and the bank. Beyond that is the white-clapboard post office and town offices, the Arlington Community Center/Martha Canfield Library, a couple of private homes, and The Arlington Inn.

"We're kind of low keyed around here," explained chamber of commerce executive secretary Eleanor Albee. "No factory outlets . . . thank God." She pauses and wonders, "Maybe I shouldn't say that . . . ?"

Historical Perspective, Area Attractions

Dorothy Canfield Fisher left an indelible mark on the community when she deeded her grandmother's handsome 1829 "Brick House," called locally the Canfield House, to the town as a community center. Fisher, a writer who was well known in the 1920s and 1930s for novels and short stories set in New England and France, and who has a children's literary prize named after her, lived here from 1908 until her death in 1958. Her great-great-grandfather, Israel Canfield, was one of Arlington's original settlers in 1764.

Mrs. Fisher felt that at least once in its life a family would have a gathering requiring more dining table and dishes than most have. The Arlington Community House would fill that bill — no charge — in perpetuity. A few rooms are set aside for the Martha Canfield (grandma) Memorial Library. Another room was added on out back for the (Country Doctor) Russell Collection of Vermontiana. But the building's main purpose is to provide the Arlington Community Club and the families of Arlington, Sunderland, and Sandgate a place to party.

In the green tent out front — you can't miss it — the library sells books to passersby. It has sold from its wonderful discards-and-donations inventory for as long as the library has been there (Fridays and Saturdays, 9 A.M.–5 P.M.; Sundays 1–5 P.M.). Believe me, with paperbacks at 20 cents, and hardbounds at 50 cents, and the possibility of stocking all the *National Geographics* missing from your own sporadic collection, even the most self-controlled browser will find something he didn't know he needed.

In addition, Dorothy Canfield Fisher is reputed to have "saved the town" back in the depression. At that time, while farming was still a major occupation, the Arlington Refrigeration Company was the next largest employer. The depression put it out of business and, along with it, Arlington's entire work force.

A town meeting was called with two questions on the agenda: Shall we pack up and go or shall we band together and survive? Mrs. Fisher fervently urged the latter course. The people agreed and soon planted cooperative gardens, developed collective woodlots, and generally showed how much people need what these Vermonters had — an indomitable sense of community.

At the time, Mack Molding, a company in New Jersey, was looking for a place to put a new factory. When the owners — one of whom had grown up in Vermont — heard of Arlington's heroic struggle, they bought the old refrigeration company building and put everyone back to work. Mack Molding is still the major employer in town.

The Arlington Inn, two stories of glorious Greek-Revival pillars built in 1848 beyond the Canfield House on Main Street, was once the private home of Martin Chester Deming, railroad millionaire, Vermont politico. A dozen rooms, named after Deming's children, complement a prize-winning dining room.

Four local inns have joined together to form what they call the Historic Inns of Norman Rockwell's Vermont. These include The Arlington Inn; the West Mountain Inn, on a hill overlooking town; the Hill Farm Inn a half mile off Historic Route 7A in Sunderland; and The Inn at Sunderland, on 7A. The restaurants in the first two are open to public dining.

The 12-room West Mountain Inn is a half mile from Main Street over a steel bridge that leads off Route 313 over the Battenkill River, up a dirt road atop the magnificent hill. It overlooks the town and the hills around and is the home of one Swede, one state senator, and six llamas. You'll have to ask Wes Carlson, the Swede who owns it with his wife (Senator) Mary Ann, why llamas?

Their sense of humor is contagious and the hospitality they serve up there seems to make everyone who visits seem like family. Hope your family likes llamas.

Battenkill River is reputed to be one of the most challenging trout streams in America. But even if you do not want to put on chest-high waders and explore the Battenkill River at the butt end of a fly rod, you can get to know it.

This river forms in Manchester, where the West Branch and the Main Branch join just below Dufresne Pond, and eventually empties into the Hudson River some 55 miles downstream near Schuylerville, New York. Vermont's 21 miles of Battenkill are cold and clear — fed by the sparkling, spring-fed Bromley, Lye, and Mill brooks and the Roaring Branch, which tumble out of the mountains — making the whole stretch an ideal wild-trout river. It meanders under bridges (five of them covered), past white-clapboard houses and churches, skirting cow-studded pastures. They say the river is a challenge to fish, because the brown and brook trout, living as they do so close to human beings, cows, and fishermen, don't take to just any old fly.

You can rent a canoe from Battenkill Canoe's fleet of 45, located on Route 7A in Sunderland, paddle along the Battenkill, find pastures to picnic in (cows bite less frequently than trout), gravel bars to wade near, covered bridges to glide under, and picturesque farms, houses, and villages — not to mention those fly-fishermen trying to snag wily trout — to drift quietly past. Canoe rental includes a shuttle that meets guests at the "take-out" end of their trip at an agreed-upon time and brings them and the canoe back to the put-in point.

Jim Walker, who with his wife, Joanne, owns Battenkill Canoe, says the most traveled stretch of the river is the 30 miles from Arlington to the Rexleigh covered bridge and that they like to stagger the "put-ins" for two reasons: "It lessens the impact on the river and it gives everyone a better time on the river." While the Battenkill is scenic, it is not big and brawling; yet while the river is gentle, it does sometimes have interesting currents here and there. You can canoe it in a few hours or stretch the voyage out over the whole, lazy, autumn day — several days, if desired.

Back in Arlington on the other side of Main Street, looking north of the astonishingly well-stocked Arlington Variety Store, is the newish Family Practices medical building; the Saint James Episcopal Church, built in 1832 of grey fieldstone crowned with crenellated towers; and, enclosed by a stone wall, the old churchyard where Miss Annis Leonard (17 years, 2 months, 4 days) was laid to rest in 1777, along with Mary Brownson, the first wife of Ethan Allen, and many who preceded and followed them in glory. Skirting the churchyard's north wall is Route 313, leading to West Arlington; beyond that a few private homes.

Directly to the right from our vantage on the corner, on the East Arlington Road itself, is Cullinan's, which has been serving the community as a grocery store and butcher shop since 1913. Next to it is the imposing brick building of Mack Molding Company, and a little farther up and off facing sides of the road is the high school and the elementary school, which have a view of the mountains that can only be called breathtaking.

It's 1.4 miles to East Arlington on the road past Cullinan's. East Arlington is on the western hem of Green Mountain National Forest and the Appalachian Trail. There, just one mile before you plunge into wilderness, is the Candle Mill Village.

The story has it that Tom and Barbara Weakley wanted to escape the urban rush and so moved to Vermont. They found the ancient, rundown Lawrence gristmill beside a mountain stream on the site of Remember Baker's mill in a town everyone seemed to have forgotten. Deciding that was remote enough, they bought it and in 1958 began making candles to sell — through the mail. The plan went awry, because people learned about the wonderful gristmill there and began to come over to East Arlington — in droves. The 200-year-old gristmill is now complemented by eight other gift shops situated in a neighboring hay barn and in a rambling house where Tories met in secret during the Revolution. Considering the heat of political sentiments that somehow continue to this day, it's a wonder the Tory meeting place is still standing.

The Happy Cook, in the old hay barn, features countless kitchen gadgets and tasteful ceramic kitchen or house plaques made to order by Rose Anne Hennings. In the gristmill, you can dip your own candles, buy thousands of ready-mades, or be awed by the 248-pound "Jumbo" candle poured in June of 1962. The Music Box Shop, above the candle shop, is guarded by a friendly life-size nutcracker capable of taking on small coconuts. A wonderful window, in the corner going upstairs, affords an ah!-inspiring glimpse of the mountain stream that dashes next to the gristmill.

The crystalline mountain waters hop from rock ledge to rock ledge in a peaceful, pleasant manner in the fall. Some people, usually the youngish, play tag with the water on the ledges. Others sit on benches and drink it all in. Should you have forgotten your picnic lunch, Phyllis' Food Et Cet Era is across the road, and the Stage Coach Take Out, a few doors downstreet, has overstuffed sandwiches and "Mom's own recipe" Toll House pie with hot fudge sauce, vanilla ice cream, and whipped cream.

The Bearatorium is home to hundreds of bears (of the Steif, Gund, and Paddington variety), one of whom would be five feet tall, if he ever stood. Aunt Dudy's fragrances sells a variety of gifts, and Where Did You Get That Hat specializes in Stetsons. The Rosebud Toy Co. is a place "where kids can come in and have a good time." Downstreet a bit, in the East Arlington Antiques Center, the proprietor who sells furniture, rugs, porcelain, and glass also sings in a clear Irish tenor.

While many tourists visit, people still live here, buy stamps at the East Arlington Post Office, take books out of the "free library," shop at a regular IGA grocery store, and hold town meetings at Bailey Hall.

Rockwell once wrote of his Arlington neighbors, "The people were rugged and self contained. None of that sham, 'I am so *glad* to know you!' accompanied by radiant smiles. They shook my hand, said 'How do,' and waited to see how I'd turn out." Those kind of folks still do that here.

Heading farther east from East Arlington on the Kelley Stand Road, which periodically crosses the lovely mountain stream that so wonderfully decorates the Candle Mill downstream, you eventually run into the Long/Appalachian trails and the mostly forgotten boyhood home of Daniel Webster.

The Arlington area has three covered bridges: one in East Arlington, spanning the roaring branch; one in Sunderland on River Road; and the other in West Arlington, which crosses the Battenkill and leads right to Norman Rockwell's old house (now the hospitable B&B "Inn on the Covered Bridge Green"). On a hot summer's day many local youths swim in the river under the bridge.

To get to West Arlington go up to Route 313 in Arlington, turn westward at the cemetery wall, and drive 4.2 miles to the covered bridge. Rockwell lived here from 1943 to 1953, having moved after his first Arlington studio burned to the ground.

Ann Weber, who with her husband, Ron, owns the old (1792) farmhouse, says that people knock on the door and ask expectantly "Is this *his* house?" On some days she teases, "Whose?" She keeps the Rockwell connection pretty low-keyed, she explains, because a lot of her neighbors were his friends and she doesn't want to offend them. The logo for the inn is an artist's palette with the name of the inn and the house's date on it.

She tells many amusing tales about mementos left behind, such as the ancient fire-fighting equipment Norman stationed close to this second Arlington studio (it didn't burn down!); the oddly uncharacteristic signature of "Indian Slim," which Rockwell's son Gerry claims is his father's; the "summer project" tennis court that Rockwell and the boys installed personally; and the triangular dinner gong that Rockwell, leader of the civil defense forces during World War II, was supposed to clang to alert his neighbors should the Germans ever invade Arlington. (He was demoted during a test because he couldn't stop laughing.)

Rockwell's studio out back is rented out to a local family, but guests can play on his tennis court.

There's a lovely picnic area between the river and the 1804 Methodist church. Though the church annex has a "Battenkill 487 Grange" sign, it is still called the *church* hall. The old schoolhouse is a private residence now.

The drive along Route 313 is a picturesque one, especially in fall. The Battenkill meanders along the road against a colorful, rural backdrop. North of Route 313 about three miles on the Sandgate Road, the tiny hill town of Sandgate offers excellent deer hunting, a Methodist church, a game warden's headquarters, and beautiful views from the road that runs along the valley. We know of several artists and writers who have hidden themselves up in there but we don't know their exact whereabouts, or won't tell. The Battenkill that flows through Arlington and past the end of the Sandgate Road offers wily trout for the experienced and determined.

Just north of Arlington on Historic Route 7A is the community named for Ethan Allen's comrade in arms, Peleg Sunderland. It is a curious commercial bump in the road that can be explained by the access there from the highway to Equinox Mountain.

There's not much left to the village of Sunderland, but what there is is off the highway a little. The road that leads to it passes the Hill Farm Inn, which has 50 acres of farmland around it, a mile of frontage on the Battenkill, and views that can keep you spinning slowly and appreciatively in circles all year long. Eleven guest rooms, divided between the main house (1800?) and 1790 guest house, have been serving guests since about 1905.

If you continue past the Hill Farm Inn, you'll come to a one-lane trestle bridge over the railroad tracks. Turn right after you cross it and you'll be on River Road. River Road leads back to East Arlington, via a small one-lane covered bridge a couple of miles down. It's a colorful drive during foliage.

One of the most frequented shops right on Historic Route 7A in Sunderland is Basketville; the original branch of Basketville is in Putney on the other side of Vermont. Right across from Basketville is the Equinox Sky Line Drive, which winds 5.2 miles up to the 3,835-foot summit of Mount Equinox and the Skyline Inn. People may drive it from mid-May to mid-October between 8 A.M. and 10 P.M. Some people climb the trails that lead to the top, others race, on foot or bike, to the summit.

The mountain is owned by the Carthusian Monastery, built behind the mountain in 1960. The dozen or so monks who live there have taken a vow of silence. The profits from the commercial enterprises on the mountain go to the order. Visible from Historic 7A are the new wind turbines on Little Equinox, which generate electricity. The Sky Line Inn on the main mountain is open only when the road is. On a crystal-clear day, the sunsets and sunrises from the top gloriously encompass five states and one foreign country. During foliage, the views are downright spectacular.

Woodford, Searsburg

Just east of Bennington on State Route 9, "Woodford City," as it was once called, is situated at 2,215 feet elevation and therefore claims to be the highest town in Vermont. Not unexpectedly, Woodford State Park claims the statistic for the highest camping. The Union Church, on a hill up on Woodford, overlooking Vermont Route 9, has laid claim to being nearer to God than any other church in the state. This may be true, if God is to be considered in Vermont as "up."

Woodford is home to the Prospect Mountain Ski Area, which offers both cross-country and Alpine skiing. Farther east on Route 9 is Searsburg, another tiny mountain town, and the Sommerset Reservoir, an artificial lake with a boat launch and picnic area.

In Woodford you can get a clear picture of how Woodford Town and Woodford the town differ from each other. As you leave Bennington, you will see a sign along the roadside that has the words Bennington/Woodford on it. That is the town (or township, if you will) line.

A little bit farther on, you can see the two-rooms-and-a-large-closet Woodford Elementary School, then the Woodford Municipal Building and Meeting House. After going up Woodford Mountain, you finally reach the heights that we talked about above. Woodford Town administratively includes all this, not to mention a large tract of forest, while the locals talk about "up on Woodford" only as that part near the peaks and pinnacles. Except when they talk about the school, then it's down. Or the meetinghouse, which is in between. Clear, huh?

The Long Trail crosses Route 9 about 5 miles from the center of Bennington. This is a 260-mile-long "foot path in the wilderness," cared for by the volunteer Green Mountain Club, that extends from the Massachusetts border 17 miles south of Route 9 to the Canadian frontier. This part of the Long Trail is also the Georgia-to-Maine Appalachian Trail, which takes a right at Pico and heads east to its northern terminus on Mount Katahdin. There is a Green Mountain Forest sign and a parking lot to mark the trail.

Two and one-half miles farther up the mountain you will see the sign for Prospect Ski Mountain (2,767 feet). This is a local ski area, which until 1989 depended completely on Mother Nature for snow. The result was that downhill ski slopes, served by a rope tow and T-bar lifts, eventually played second fiddle to the extensive cross-country-ski-trail system, where the snow tended to stick sooner and stay longer. New owners, armed with snowmaking equipment, expect to even the imbalance and provide both Alpine and Nordic skiing in season.

Also on that Prospect Ski Mountain sign is a small AYH symbol and the words "lodging" and "tenting," calling attention to Ed and Ann Shea's American Youth Hostel (AYH) facility called Greenwood Lodge, one of eight in Vermont. The entrance to the grounds is directly off the Prospect Mountain parking lot. They call Greenwood "rustic" and say it includes 120 acres next to the mountain. Since youth hostels are common in Europe and rare in the U.S., this is a find. Open July through Labor Day, they have seven "sleeping quarters," capacities vary from 4 to 14, 20 primitive campsites, one shared kitchen, and three bathrooms. If the place were packed, 2 to a campsite, there could be as many as 95 people lining up at those facilities. The Sheas say they are never *that* rustic.

Woodford State Park, 11 miles east of Bennington (29 west of Brattleboro) on State Route 9, has 102 campsites, 16 lean-tos, a picnic area, and hiking trails that lace through the Green Mountain National Forest all at 2,400 feet, the highest elevation (for campsites) in Vermont. One former employee claimed that the small artificial lake, Adams Reservoir, was named after a beaver named Adam who built his dam where the concrete spillway is now. Whether or not it's true, it's a good story. While there is no lifeguard on duty here, the waters are swimmable, and canoes and boats are available to rent.

There is a commercial center, of sorts, up here. The General Store, whose sign also claims it is the "Woodford Mall," sells beer and mosquito dope, crackers and chips, coffee and sandwiches, and worms and crawlers right next to the beautiful Red Mill Pond. Across the highway is Red Mills Store, which caters to tourists' tastes. During winters, you will see many snowmobiles up here, because they like to take off across the Red Mill Pond and into the National Forest and because the headquarters of the local snowmobile club is right here.

Beyond the Red Mill Pond is a sign proclaiming Green Mountain Forest Campground; Red Mill Brook. There are more than 30 primitive campsites here with an odd twist: They are free. We met a woman here who complained that it was getting crowded since they put that sign up. She preferred primitive camping she said and stepped back into her trailer. The campground was closed for the 1990 summer season, but was expected to reopen in 1991.

The George D. Aiken Wilderness, named for Vermont's special governor/senator, allows you to explore and camp as long as you walk and carry in no mechanical devices. They mean wilderness! Roughing it!

East from Bennington on Vermont Route 9, beyond Woodford, Searsburg is predominantly a wilderness tract with only a handful of houses scattered along the Deerfield River.

This town is situated in the midst of the largest portion of the Green Mountain National Forest — which comprises 630,000 acres in three slightly separated tracts up the middle of the state. The fact that the forest's official border is just east of Bennington and the eastern boundary is at about the tip of Harriman Reservoir just west of Wilmington explains why this stretch of Vermont Route 9 is so beautiful and wild.

Searsburg Mountain is steep enough for State Route 9 to require two gravel "runaway truck ramps" to stop trucks whose brakes burn out on the way down. The largest almost-natural feature in Searsburg (the forest and mountains being natural) is an artificial lake, the four-mile-long Sommerset Reservoir, with its rather remote boat launch and picnic area.

To get to Sommerset Reservoir, turn north off Route 9 at the base of Searsburg Mountain onto a gravel road called Sommerset Road and drive 10 miles on a very remote (read: few houses) backwoods road to the dam that holds the reservoir in place. The NEPCO on the sign pointing the way off Route 9 stands for New England Power Company, not a new Oriental martial art or a graham cracker manufacturing company.

Driving a backwoods road can be unsettling, with 5 miles *feeling* like 20, so set your trip odometer to keep your panic under control. The road does end at the boat launch and picnic area. This artificial lake is a shallow-draft affair, with stumps and rocks lurking close to the surface, so modest boats, sunfishes, and canoes are recommended.

Before arriving at the road's end, the Flood Dam Trail and East Branch Foot Trail start out together east off the Sommerset Road but soon separate and meander through the woods — all at elevations 2,000 feet or above — to a small picnic area where the old flood dam was and to the present dam and boat-launch area, respectively. Very few houses are in these woods because they are owned by NEPCO and cannot be developed. At this elevation, it can get chilly, so think sweater or sweatshirt (even in summers). Mosquitoes consider this to be their home base, too.

Additional trails that girdle either the east or west shore of the reservoir from the boat-launch area afford views of the reservoir and Mount Snow. The East Shore Trail (double yellow blazes) leads five miles to a U.S. Forest Service trail (faded blue blazes) that leads to Grout Pond, a primitive, wilderness camping area that is also accessible, by car, off the Kelley Stand Road out of East Arlington. No camping is officially allowed in the Sommerset picnic area.

The Bennington Area Essentials

Important Information

Municipal Services

Arlington Town Clerk: 375-2332.
Arlington Police: 442-5421.
Arlington Fire & Ambulance:
   375-2500; 375-6313.
Bennington Town Clerk: 442-1043.
Bennington Police: 442-5464.
Bennington Fire & Ambulance:
   442-5555; 442-5464.
Pownal Town Clerk: 823-7757.
Pownal Police: 442-5421.
Pownal Fire & Ambulance:
   823-7200; 447-7911.
Sandgate Town Clerk: 375-9075.

Searsburg Town Clerk: 464-8081.
Searsburg Police: 254-2382.
Searsburg Fire & Ambulance:
   464-3737; 464-5335.
Shaftsbury Town Clerk: 442-4038.
Shaftsbury Police: 442-5421.
Shaftsbury Fire & Ambulance:
   447-7361; 442-5464, 375-6313.
Woodford Town Clerk: 442-4895.
Woodford Police: 442-5421.
Woodford Fire & Ambulance:
   442-6202; 442-5464.

Medical Services

Southern Vermont Medical Center, 100 Hospital Dr. East, Bennington;
   442-6361. Off Dewey St. or Monument Extension.
Vermont Poison Center, Medical Center Hospital, Burlington; (1) 658-3456.
   They will follow through and call back to make sure everything is fine.

Veterinarians

Arlington Veterinary Clinic, Arlington; 375-9491.
Bennington Animal Hospital, White Creek Rd., North Bennington; 442-8714.
Dr. George Glanzberg, Mount Anthony Veterinary Hospital, West Rd.,
   Bennington; 442-4324.
West Mountain Veterinary Animal Hospital, South Shaftsbury; 447-7723.
   Drs. Robert Bergman and Anna Worth.

Weather

Local Weather Phone: 442-3121.

Tourist Information Services

Arlington Chamber of Commerce: Booth on Main St.; Box 245, Arlington
   05250; 375-2269.
Bennington Chamber of Commerce: Office at One Veterans' Memorial Dr.;
   447-3311.

Lodgings

Reservation Services

Vermont Bed & Breakfast Reservation Service, East Fairfield; 827-3827.
Membership or booking fee required.

Inns and B&Bs

ARLINGTON

The Arlington Inn, Historic Rte. 7A; 375-6532. Expensive. Elegant Greek Revival style, Victorian inn, antiques-furnished rooms with private baths. Candle-lit dining rooms.

Arlington's West Mountain Inn, River Rd.; 375-6516. Expensive. Twelve rooms plus one handicapped accessible. One hundred acres and incredible views, shared with llamas.

Eastbrook Bed & Breakfast, RR 2, Box 2215; 375-6509. Moderate. Warmth of an English home.

Four Winds Country Inn, River Rd., Arlington; 375-6734. Moderate/expensive. Surrounded by 50 acres, bordering the Battenkill. Norman Rockwell's first Arlington house.

Hill Farm Inn, north of Arlington off Historic Rte. 7A (RR 2, Box 2015); 375-2269. Moderate. Comfortable, rambling country inn (deeded to Hill family in 1775 by King George III) with mountain views in all directions. Either B&B or MAP. Excellent hiking, photographing, fishing, rusticating.

Inn at Covered Bridge Green, Cross the covered bridge on Rte. 313 (RD 1, Box 3550); 375-9489. Moderate/expensive. A 1792 farmhouse, once owned by Norman Rockwell, is right on the village green. B&B with five rooms. Play tennis on a court Rockwell built. You have to cross a covered bridge to get there. Nonsmoking.

Keelan House, Bed & Breakfast, Rte. 313, Arlington; 375-9029. Moderate. An 1820 Federal Colonial home on 16 acres right on the edge of the village. Children, yes; pets, no.

Shenandoah Farm, Rte. 313 (Battenkill Rd.), Arlington; 375-6372. Inexpensive. An 1820 "Colonial" house is now an antiques-filled B&B five miles west of Arlington. Handicapped accessible.

Whimsy Farm Bed & Breakfast, Box 507, Arlington; 375-6654. Moderate. Large rooms with separate entrances and private baths and an abundant country breakfast. Cross-country skiing on the farm, as well as a whole lot of relaxing. Seven miles north of Lake Shaftsbury State Park (on Historic Rte. 7A), turn right on Old Depot Rd., and right again at the farm.

BENNINGTON

Baker's Bed & Breakfast, Historic Rte. 7A, Bennington; 442-5619. Moderate. In 1859 house at foot of Harwood Hill.

Bennington Hus B&B, 208 Washington Ave., Bennington; 447-7972. Moderate. Scandinavian hospitality in 50-year-old Colonial. Quiet street in historic area. Fireplace for added warmth.

Four Chimneys Restaurant & Inn, 21 West Rd., Bennington; 447-3500. Expensive. Three deluxe rooms in historic setting. Year-round.

Molly Stark Inn, 1067 East Main St., Bennington; 442-9631. Moderate. Cheery fireplace sitting room in 1860 home. Six individually decorated rooms. Nonsmoking.

Safford Manor, 722 East Main St., Bennington; 442-5934. Moderate. Built in 1774, contains Colonial and Victorian decor. Rec room with hot tub and pool table. Some shared baths.

The Southshire Inn, 124 Elm St., Bennington; 447-3839. Moderate/expensive. Nine elegant rooms with private baths, many with fireplaces, in main house and carriage barn. Mahogany paneling and fireplace in library/sitting room, breakfast served in Italianate dining room. AAA diamond rated.

SANDGATE
Evergreen Inn, Sandgate Rd. (Sandgate); 375-2272. Inexpensive. Old-fashioned inn off the beaten path. Family owned for 52 years.

SUNDERLAND
Inn at Sunderland, Historic Rte. 7A; 362-4213. Moderate. Bed and breakfast in a restored Victorian farmhouse. Fireplaces in rooms, high ceilings, comfort.
Ira Allen House, Historic Rte. 7A, Sunderland; 362-2284. Moderate. Inn in a historic 200-year-old building on 12 acres on the Battenkill. Rooms with patchwork quilts and full country breakfast.

Resorts, Hotels, Condominiums

SUNDERLAND
Equinox Sky Line Inn, Historic Rte. 7A, Sunderland; 362-1113 or 362-1114. Moderate. Although the mailing address is in Manchester, the access road to the mountain, a toll road called Sky Line Dr., starts on Historic Rte. 7A in Sunderland across from Basketville. The hotel, which is fairly utilitarian because it is at 3,835 feet above sea level, has a restaurant and overnight accommodations that introduce you to some of the best sunsets in New England.

Motels, Cottages

ARLINGTON
Candlelight Motel, Rte. 7A, Box 363; 375-6647. Inexpensive. Seventeen units, phones, views, fishing, swimming pool, breakfast available.
Cutleaf Maples Motel & Lodge, Historic Rte. 7A, 375-2725. Inexpensive. Coffee pot on all day, cribs free, and breakfasts available. Pets welcome. Low weekly, family, and group rates.
Roaring Branch, Arlington; 375-6401. Inexpensive. Modern or rustic (75-year-old) log cabins in 36-acre pine forest. Rent by week; fireplaces, kitchens, and one to three bedrooms in all. Two clay tennis courts.
Sunderland Motel, Historic Rte. 7A, Arlington; 362-1176. Moderate. Choice of double or king/queen beds. Private baths and steam baths. Color TV. Breakfast available.
Valhalla Motel, Historic Rte. 7A, Arlington; 375-2212. Moderate. Immoderate view of mountains. Look for the rainbow with butterflies.

BENNINGTON
Avalon Motel, Rte. 9 East, Bennington; 442-5485. Inexpensive. Color cable TV, continental breakfast.
Bennington Motor Inn, 143 West Main St., Bennington; 442-5479. Moderate. A/C, color TV, phones.
Best Western New Englander Motor Inn, 220 Northside Dr., Bennington; 442-6311. Moderate. King or queen beds, deluxe accommodations. Nonsmoking rooms available. Restaurant and lounge on premises.
Catamount Motel, 500 South St., Bennington; 442-5977. Inexpensive. Three blocks south of Main St. Sixteen rooms.
Cliffside Motor Inn, Rte. 7 South, Bennington; 442-8547. Moderate. Seven miles north of Pownal's Green Mountain Race Track. Cable/HBO, in-room coffee. Headless Horseman Restaurant & Lounge.
Darling Kelley's Motel, Rte. 7 South, Bennington; 442-2322. Moderate. Twenty-three rooms, large lobby with fireplace. Set 300 feet back from highway for panoramic view. HBO, A/C, phones.
Fife 'n Drum Motel, Rte. 7 South, Bennington; 442-4074. Moderate. Eighteen large rooms and four efficiency apartments. In-room coffee and refrigerators. Two-acre picnic area. Handicapped accessible.
Harwood Hill Motel, Historic Rte. 7A, Bennington; 442-6278. Moderate. Nineteen units with "the million dollar view." Next door to Publyk House Restaurant. Mobil & AAA approved.

Homestead Motor Inn, 924 East Main St., Bennington; 442-3143. Moderate. Thirty-two spacious rooms, 14 of which are efficiencies. Children under 10 free. Coffee in lobby. No pets. Some nonsmoking rooms.

Kirkside Motel, 250 West Main St., Bennington; 447-7596. Moderate. Right next to Saint Francis De Sales Catholic Church. King and queen beds, HBO, individual heat and A/C. Some nonsmoking rooms.

Knotty Pine, 130 Northside Dr., Bennington; 442-5487. Moderate. In-room coffee. Twenty-two rooms, some efficiencies and refrigerators. Pool. AAA and Mobil recommended.

Mid-Town Motel, 107 West Main St., Bennington; 447-0189. Moderate. One-bedroom apartments, daily, weekly. Cable/HBO, Jacuzzi. Picnic area, grills, heated pool.

Monument View Motel, 207 Northside Dr., Bennington; 442-6956. Moderate. Across from Monument View Plaza. Cable TV, picnic and child's play area.

Paradise Motor Inn, 141 West Main St., Bennington; 442-8351. Moderate/expensive. Seventy-six deluxe rooms on 12 landscaped acres, with A/C, direct-dial phones, and cable TV. Restaurant and lounge, clothing and jewelry outlets, pool and tennis courts on premises. Some rooms have saunas, balconies/patios.

Pleasant Valley Motel, Pleasant Valley Rd., Bennington; 442-6222. Moderate. Fifteen rooms and cottages on Rte. 9 at the Pleasant Valley Rd. Open from end of May to end of October. Air conditioning, a pool, and a great view of Mount Anthony.

Southgate Motel, Rte. 7, Bennington; 447-7525. Inexpensive. HBO, color TV, A/C, king and queen beds, pool with spa.

Vermonter Motor Lodge, West Rd. (Rte. 9), Bennington; 442-2529. Moderate/expensive. On the way into Bennington with views of Mount Anthony. Fishing, boating, and swimming in spring-fed pond. Eighteen A/C motel units and 14 cottages, cable TV, restaurant. Some nonsmoking rooms.

POWNAL

Ladd Brook Motor Inn, Rte. 7, Pownal; 823-7341. Moderate. Nine miles south of Bennington. Cable TV, refrigerators, A/C in 27 rooms. Spectacular views of Taconic Mountains westward. AAA 2 diamond. Handicapped accessible.

SEARSBURG

Motel on the Mountain, Rte. 9, Searsburg; 464-8233. Inexpensive. At elevation, 2,400 feet, quite a view westward — especially during early foliage. Fourteen rooms, TV. Halfway between Bennington and Wilmington.

SHAFTSBURY

Bayberry Motel, Historic Rte. 7A; 447-7180. Inexpensive. Complimentary morning coffee. Reservations appreciated. Nine rooms with the same view.

Governor's Rock Motel, Historic Rte. 7A, Shaftsbury; 442-4734. Moderate. Ten rooms out behind the huge rock. Seasonal. Showers, TV, view of mountains.

Hillbrook Motel, Historic Rte. 7A, Shaftsbury; 442-4095. Moderate. Four miles north of Shaftsbury exit from Rte 7. Kitchenettes available. Tub/showers, picnic tables with private tables and grills. Handicapped accessible.

Iron Kettle Motel, Historic Rte. 7A, Shaftsbury; 442-4316. Moderate. Well back from the highway. All rooms with A/C, double beds, color TV, individual thermostats. Coffee in the morning.

Serenity Lodgings, Historic Rte. 7A, Shaftsbury; 442-6490. Inexpensive. Individual motor-court cottages. In-room coffee.

WOODFORD

Lakeview Motel, Rte. 9, Woodford; 447-1831. Moderate. Across from Big Pond. Your basic, small motel on Rte. 9. Snowmobile access in winter, swimming pool in summer.

Peter Pan Motel, Rte. 9, Woodford; 442-3343. Moderate. Recent additions have made this a fine eight-room motel. All rooms with two double beds, coffee in rooms in the morning.

Whispering Pines Motel, Rte. 9, Woodford; 447-7149. Moderate. Seventeen rooms, A/C, TV, queen beds, a two-bedroom kitchenette. Breakfast room.

Campgrounds

ARLINGTON

Camping on the Battenkill, Historic Rte. 7A, Arlington; 375-6663. Moderate. One hundred and three open and wooded campsites. Swimming, tubing, fishing, and some hookups. No motorcycles, minibikes, or mopeds in camping area.

BENNINGTON

Greenwood Lodge & Tentsites, Rte. 9 East, Bennington; 442-2547. Inexpensive. A rustic American Youth Hostel lodge with two dorms and five private rooms; sleeps 50. Twenty tent sites on 120 wooded acres. No pets. Enter through Prospect Mountain Ski Area parking lot from late June to Labor Day.

POWNAL

Pine Hollow Campground, Pownal; 442-4960. Moderate. Twenty-five sites one mile north of Pownal on Jackson Cross Rd. Hot showers, flush toilets, playground. Handicapped accessible.

WOODFORD

Red Mills Campgrounds, Rte. 9, Woodford. Only free camping we know of in the state. Thirty-two wooded sites. Primitive. Closed in 1990, but expected to reopen in 1991.

Dining

ARLINGTON

Arlington Bakery and Pizza, Route 7A, south of village; 375-6973. Inexpensive. Great pizza, baked goods.
Arlington Dairy Bar, Route 7A, south of village; 375-2546. Inexpensive. Hamburgers, hot dogs, ice cream.
The Arlington Inn, Historic Rte. 7A; 375-6532. Expensive. Elegant, candle-lit dining rooms. Award-winning kitchen. Reservations recommended.
Arlington's West Mountain Inn, River Rd.; 375-6516. Moderate/expensive. Ever-adapting menu of fine foods in comfortable candle-lit dining rooms. Reservations recommended.
Cullinan's, East Arlington Rd., Arlington; 375-6466. Picnic fixings.
Edgewood Restaurant, Historic Rte. 7A, Arlington; 375-6604. Inexpensive.
Phyllis' Food And Et-Cet-Era, East Arlington; 375-9990. Inexpensive to moderate. Across from the Candle Mill Village, take-out.
Stage Coach Cafe, Old Mill Rd., East Arlington; 375-6412. Inexpensive. In the same building as the East Arlington Antique Center. Beer, wine, sandwiches, chili, quiches, and "Mom's own recipe" Toll House pie served warm, with hot fudge sauce, vanilla ice cream, and whipped cream. Take-out orders.
Wagon Wheel Restaurant, Historic Rte. 7A, Arlington; 375-9508. Inexpensive. Family restaurant. A local favorite.

BENNINGTON

Alldays & Onions, 519 Main St., Bennington; 447-0043. Moderate. Restaurant, fish market, specialty store, café by day (inexpensive), gourmet restaurant by night. "Flexible menu" means he'll make what you want, if he has the ingredients.
Bennington Station, 150 Depot St., Bennington; 447-1080. Moderate. Pleasant dining for lunch and dinner in the restored 1898 Bennington & Rutland Railroad Station.
Blue Benn Diner, 102 Hunt St., Bennington; 442-9877. Inexpensive. A local favorite. Great breakfasts and lunches. They don't take reservations, but...
Brasserie, 324 County St., Bennington; 447-7922. Moderate/expensive. In the Potters' Yard. Continental cuisine with a theatrical flare. Closed Tues.

Double Crisp Fried Chicken, 201-B South St., Bennington; 442-2060. Moderate. Mostly take-out.

Fortune Cookie Restaurant, 663 Main St., Bennington; 442-5715. Inexpensive. Chin-ese food. Cozy lounge where you can sip exotic drinks while waiting for your take-outs.

Four Chimneys Restaurant & Inn, 21 West Rd., Bennington; 447-3500. Expensive. "Estate dining in elegance" in historic setting. Exquisite continental menu. Reservations appreciated. Closed Mon.

Geannelis' Restaurant, 520 Main St., Bennington; 442-9778. Inexpensive. Good. Friendly. A local mainstay.

Main Attraction, 421 Main St., Bennington; 442-8579. Moderate. In addition to dining and the lounge, they sponsor an electronic trivia game for their patrons, with monitors at tables on request.

Main Street Cafe, 1 Prospect St., North Bennington; 442-3210. Expensive. Northern Italian cuisine. Reservations appreciated. Rather elegant, somewhat formal rendition of a storefront café.

Ming Wah Restaurant, Monument Plaza, Bennington; 442-8168. Inexpensive. Chinese food and take-out.

Mount Anthony Country Club, 17 Bank St., Bennington; 442-2617. Moderate. Lunch and dinner with views out over the golf course.

Occasionally Yogurt, 604 Main St., Bennington; 442-2526. Inexpensive. Used to be "Mainly Yogurt" when it was right in the center of town. Health-food lunches and frozen yogurts.

Paradise Restaurant, 141 West Main St., Bennington; 442-8351. Moderate. Three-hundred-seat restaurant and lounge ("Catamount Tavern") connected to the Paradise Motor Inn. A little bit of everything and at affordable prices. Cozy fireplace in the "Catamount Tavern." Banquet, wedding, and convention facilities.

Percey's Newsroom Cafe, One Main St., North Bennington; 447-2233. Inexpensive.

Publyk House Restaurant, Historic Rte 7A, Bennington; 442-8301. Moderate. A good meal with an extraordinary view: one of the area's most popular restaurants. Twelve different wines by the glass. Set amidst Harwood Hill orchards.

Sugar Maple Inne, West Rd., Bennington; 442-2529. Inexpensive/moderate. Part of the Vermonter Motor Lodge. They serve breakfast and dinners, with a broad range of foods from chicken cordon bleu to roast turkey.

Vermont Steak House, 716 Main St., Bennington; 442-9793. Inexpensive. Open daily. Children's menu always available. Neighborhood lounge.

Villager Restaurant, Main St., North Bennington; 447-0998. Moderate/expensive. Elegant dining in an art-gallery atmosphere.

Your Belly's Deli, 100 Pleasant St., Bennington; 442-3653. Inexpensive. Sandwich shop and deli. Homey. Serves generous deli sandwiches, the "best bite in Bennington." Upstairs, The Daiquiri Factory Lounge opens at 6 P.M.

POWNAL
Jaegger Haus, Rte. 7, Pownal; 823-9377. Inexpensive. German cuisine. It's usually a meal and a half.

Entertainment

Music and Stage

Oldcastle Theater Company, Main St., Bennington; 447-0564. Bennington's resident, professional Equity theater company performs from all parts of the theater repertoire between April and October. Stage at Southern Vermont College, up from Monument Extension. After nearly two decades, it has proven staying power.

Summer Sonatina, 5 Catamount La., Old Bennington; 442-9197. A wonderful piano school in a historic mansion that contains 29 pianos and two organs. Each Thursday, from the last week in June to the second week of August, students perform on the lawn out behind Monument Elementary School.

Nightlife

BENNINGTON
P.T.'s Pub, Depot & River Sts., Bennington; 442-3014. This was a neighborhood bar that was upgraded to a collegiate lounge. Evenings there is live entertainment and dancing.

Movies

BENNINGTON
Cinema 1-2-3, in the Ames Shopping Plaza, Bennington; 442-8179.

Museums and Historical Sites

BENNINGTON
Bennington Battle Monument, Monument Circle, Old Bennington; 447-0550. A 306-foot stone obelisk (almost) with an elevator up to observation level for views in all directions. Open April through foliage.
Bennington Museum, West Main St., Bennington; 447-1571. Contains military memorabilia from the Battle for Bennington; furniture, glass, and pottery collection; and the bones of poor Daniel Redding. Down the hill from the Old Burying Ground. Almost attached is Grandma Moses' schoolhouse. Museum shop.
Park McCullough House, School St., North Bennington; 442-5441. Historic Victorian mansion built in 1865. The properties have been in the Hall-Park and McCullough families since the 1700s. House tours, educational programs, and Christmas parties inside. Concerts, art exhibits, outdoor theater, political rallies, and other festive events are held on the lawns.

SHAFTSBURY
Peter Matteson Tavern Museum, East Rd., Shaftsbury; 447-1571 and 447-2180. Built in the late 1700s as a farm, the main house also served as a local tavern and occasional ballroom (second floor). This is mainly an educational arm of the Bennington Museum but holds various seasonal shindigs as well. On most maps it is still called Topping Tavern.
Shaftsbury Historical Society, Historic Rte. 7A, Shaftsbury; 442-9332. The 1846 Greek Revival Baptist meetinghouse is open weekends.

Seasonal Events

ARLINGTON
Annual Arts & Crafts Fair, on the green, in mid-August.
Annual Memorial Day Raft Race encourages a crazy collection of floating contraptions to compete, slowly and hilariously, on the Battenkill.

BENNINGTON
Annual Bird Conference, held at Bennington College, offers lectures, workshops, and field trips the last weekend in June.
Annual "Dust Off" Car Show held at the Bennington Chamber of Commerce office in late May.
Annual Museum Antiques Show, held at the Monument Elementary School across West Main St. from the museum, offers treasures for sale the second weekend in July.
Annual Renaissance Crafts Faire, held at the high school, is sponsored by the Lionesses in mid-October when their flags fly along Main St.
Annual Road Race, held in early May for those serious runners who keep in shape through the winter. A circumambulation, at your personal best speed, of the Park-McCullough House grounds. Info.: 447-0414.
Annual Triathlon pits triathletes against their clocks swimming, biking, and running on the fourth Saturday in June.

Antique & Classic Car Meet, Willow Park on East Rd., Bennington; 447-3311. For a quarter-century the antique cars have been meeting each other in Bennington. The classic vehicles from the beginning of automotive history up to 1970 get into friendly exhaust, horn-blowing, and beauty contests; the owners parade in costume for a weekend in mid-September. Also an automotive flea market. Arts & Crafts Festival held on the lawn at the chamber of commerce office this same weekend.

Antiques Show & Sale, at the Second Congregational Church, is juried and held the first weekend in October.

Bennington Battle Day Weekend, closest to the August 17 anniversary as possible, features a Sunday parade and much celebration Fri. and Sat., too. The whole town turns out.

Bennington College Writers Workshop, held during July each year at Bennington College, allows neophyte writers to rub shoulders and aspirations with seasoned veterans of the literary wars.

Downstreet Dicken's Weekend/Enchanted Weekend with shopkeepers dressing in Dickensian costume and a weekend of holiday celebrations the first weekend in December.

Mayfest in Bennington, the last weekend in May, closes Main St. so that vendors can vend and entertainers entertain. That same weekend, the Arts & Crafts Festival is held at the chamber of commerce lawn on Veterans Memorial Dr.

Midnight Madness, when all the shops slash their prices and leave their doors open until midnight the fourth Thursday in July. A real social event when nearly everyone in town turns out for a shopping spree.

Museum Week, at the Bennington Museum, offers free admission to the museum the first full week of December. A special exhibition of schoolchildren's art and other events scheduled.

Oldcastle Theater Company, Main St., Bennington; 447-0564. During summer and fall months, Bennington's resident, professional Equity theater company performs on the stage at Southern Vermont College, up from Monument Extension. Moderate.

Old-Fashioned Fourth of July Celebration held at Willow Park with rides, a dunking tank, games, popcorn, music, tae kwon do, eats, entertainment, and fireworks that can be seen all over the valley.

Outdoor, Sports Recreation show is held the first weekend in June at the high school.

Roberts Brothers Circus comes to town in mid-July with its three rings of acrobats, elephants, horses, jugglers, and the works. Benefits the Early Childhood Development Center at Bennington College.

Sage City Symphony concerts. Held in various places, including the North Bennington Grade School gym and Mount Anthony Union High School auditorium. From both modern and classical repertoires.

Summer Sonatina, 5 Catamount La., Old Bennington; 442-9197. A lot of fun. Each Thursday, from last week in June to the second week of August, students perform on the lawns out behind a big house of 29 pianos. Donations accepted.

JAMAICA
White Water Canoe and Kayak Races and the Recreational Water Sports Races held the first two weekends in May at Jamaica State Park.

NORTH BENNINGTON
A *"Victorian Christmas Past"* is held annually at the Park McCullough House the first weekend in December where townspeople gather for punch, cookies, and caroling. The Jolly Old Elf himself usually makes a visit, too.

SHAFTSBURY
Annual Apple and Harvest Festival held at the Peter Matteson Tavern Museum out on East Rd. the fourth Saturday in September. The leaves are beginning to turn about now.

Dressage and Horse Trials held at Doornhoff Farm the first two weekends in June. Info.: 442-4221.

Children's Activities

ARLINGTON

Arlington Recreation Park, on Historic Rte. 7A, just north of Arlington Village, has tennis courts, basketball courts, a nine-hole golf course, soccer field, football field, a swimming pool, and playground equipment for the little ones.

BENNINGTON

Bennington Battle Monument, Monument Circle, Old Bennington; 447-0550. A 306-foot stone obelisk (almost) with an elevator up to observation level for views in all directions. For whole family. Open April through foliage.

Deer Park, Veterans Memorial Dr., Bennington. The kids can visit a herd of deer and run around in a nice little park with a miniature covered bridge while you have a picnic lunch. The small herd of deer stay in winter too.

Sunset Playland, Historic Rte. 7A, Bennington; 442-3555. Miniature golf, go-cart track, batting range, snack bar. On Harwood Hill for the view.

A *"Victorian Christmas Past"* is held annually at the Park McCullough House the first weekend in December where young townspeople get a chance to sit on the best lap in the world when Santa comes for a visit. The week preceding Halloween, the P-M House carriage barn becomes a very haunted house.

Willow Park, East Rd., Bennington. At the light leading up to "Super Seven," turn right onto Kocher Dr., then left up East Hill. Willow Park is at the top of the hill and has a picnic pavilion, playground, horseshoe pitching, and a great hill for rolling down.

SHAFTSBURY

Annual Apple and Harvest Festival held at the Peter Matteson Tavern Museum out on East Rd. the fourth Saturday in September. Kids enjoy the 18th-century fall festival while adults enjoy the views from the 18th-century farm.

Lake Shaftsbury State Park, Historic Rte. 7A, Shaftsbury; 375-9978. Lovely place to picnic. There is a playground here and large playing fields for larger children on its 101 acres. Also nature trails, canoes, rowboats, and paddleboats for rent and a group camping area.

Shops

Art Galleries

ARLINGTON

Beside Myself Gallery, Lathrop La., Arlington; 362-2212. Features regional artists.

BENNINGTON

Bennington Museum and Grandma Moses Gallery, West Main St., Bennington; 447-1571. Contains some of Grandma's lesser-known paintings and many other historically significant regional paintings displayed around the museum's main collections.

The Gallery at Southern Vermont College, in the room right outside the Admissions Office, features changing exhibits of paintings, watercolors, and photography.

Livingston Galleries. Their "Bennington Gallery" is in the Little Red School House at 37 West Rd. (Rte. 9) and features area artists.

Suzanne Lemberg Usdan Gallery, at Bennington College, usually features works of art students at the college.

Craft and Specialty Stores

ARLINGTON

Candle Mill Village Shops, Old Mill Rd., East Arlington; 375-6068. The Candle Mill itself (dip your own candles), The Music Box Shop, The Happy Cook, Bearatorium, Rosebud Toy Co., Aunt Dudy's, and a tumbling mountain brook. Major credit cards accepted.

Cheese House, Historic Rte. 7A, Arlington; 375-9033. In addition to the cheeses, maple syrup, smoked meats, and wines, many other food products, gifts, and souvenirs.

Johnny Hinrichs Studio, Historic Rte. 7A, Arlington; 375-9550. Stained glass custom designs, restorations, repairs, and classes by Johnny Hinrichs, who has been creating heirlooms for 18 years. Studio next to the Cheese House.

Dan Mosheim, Arlington; 375-2568. Cabinetmaker, woodworker. Will customize tables, chairs.

Norman Rockwell Exhibition and Gift Shop at the Arlington Gallery, Main St.; 375-6068. Norman Rockwell's former models still work here. Memorabilia, *Post* covers, reproductions of all kinds for sale.

Scandinavian Country Shop, Warm Brook Rd., Arlington; 375-6666. Slightly-off-the-beaten-path Scandinavian shop located in a delightful Swedish cabin.

Village Peddler, Old Mill Rd., East Arlington; 375-6037. General gift items, plus 21 varieties of fudge in an old wagon shed.

BENNINGTON

Alldays & Onions, 519 Main St., Bennington; 447-0043. Restaurant, fish market, specialty store, café.

Bennington Potters Yard, 324 County St., Bennington; 447-7531. The last vestige of Bennington's long history of pottery manufacturing, Bennington Potters "seconds" store is in the Old Grist Mill along with Terra (South American items). In adjacent buildings are its factory outlet store, Cinnamons (kitchen supplies), the Brasserie restaurant, and John McLeod's Woodworks.

Camelot Village, Rte. 9 (60 West Rd.), Old Bennington; 447-0039. Includes The Antique Center, The Butterfly, Fay Swafford Originals, Marge's Touch of Country, Nancy's Ark, Occasional Flowers, Wrap-it-up, Wine Cellar and Gourmet Shop. In the same compound, in the brick building, is Beautiful Beginnings, a bridal shop.

Hawkins House, 262 North St., Bennington; 447-0488. Fine fabrics, jewelry, woodenware, cards, and other beautiful items you didn't know were necessities.

Hemmings Motor News, Rte. 9, Bennington; 442-3101. Publisher of *Hemmings Motor News,* "the bible of the old car hobby," of *Special Interest Autos,* and *Vintage Auto Almanac.* Special auto-hobby-related bookshop. Visitors are welcome.

Images from the Past, West Main St., Bennington; 442-3204. Photographic prints, cards, posters, and historic house boxes.

NORTH BENNINGTON

Powers Market, North Bennington; 442-6821. While those huge columns make it look like a Greek temple, some say, it was built in 1833 as the only general store in town. It generally has most things you need.

POWNAL

Mahican Moccasin Manufacturing Outlet, Rte. 7, Pownal; 823-5294. Custom-made deerskin, elk, and cowhide moccasins, fleece-lined to order. Also other brand moccasins.

Pownal View Barn, Rte. 7, Pownal; 823-7345. Early American pine and hardwood furniture, decorative accessories, gifts, and gourmet food shop. Seventeen thousand square feet that just keep going. Fun to explore. Usually has some red-flannel, long underwear on the line out front.

The Village Gift Barn, Rte. 7, Pownal; 823-7700. The barn on the way up the hill out of the Pownal Valley. Loft filled with toys and a Christmas shop wherein resides a five-foot-tall troll.

SHAFTSBURY

Chocolate Barn, Historic Rte. 7A, Shaftsbury; 375-6928. Chocolates of all
delicious kinds and rooms and a haymow full of antiques in an 1842 sheep barn.
Elliot Nachwalter's Briar Workshop, Historic Rte. 7A, Shaftsbury; 375-9009.
One mile north of the Chocolate Barn. Elliot Nachwalter and Carole Burns
make fine Briar Workshop pipes for smoking tobacco here. They also blend
tobaccos, including a Vermont Honey Vanilla blend.

SUNDERLAND

Basketville, Historic Rte. 7A, Sunderland; 362-1609. Making and selling baskets
since 1842.

Antiques

ARLINGTON

East Arlington Antiques Center, Old Mill Rd., East Arlington; 375-9607. Specializing in eighteenth- and nineteenth-century furniture, paintings, porcelain, rugs,
and other collectibles. Just down the street from the Candle Mill. Phil Elwell.
Gebelein Silversmiths, East Arlington; 375-6307. Dave Thomas deals in antique
silver, including American eighteenth century, and arts and crafts, Chinese
imports. By appointment.
Gingerbread Antiques, Historic Rte. 7A, Arlington; 375-9455. General line,
specializing in Victorian formal furniture and Orientalia. By appointment.

BENNINGTON

The Antiquarian, 39 West Rd., Bennington; 442-4614. English and continental
period furniture, paintings, and accessories in 1793 Old Bennington Country
Store. On the western edge of Old Bennington.
Camelot Village/The Antique Center of Old Bennington, Rte. 9 (60 West
Rd.), Old Bennington; 447-0039. Antiques, gifts, food shops.
Four Corners East, 307 North St., Bennington; 442-2612. American antique
furniture, paintings, rugs, and accessories.
State-Line Antiques, Rte. 67A, North Bennington; 447-0516. At the Vermont/
New York border.

SHAFTSBURY

Chocolate Barn Antiques, Historic Rte. 7A, Shaftsbury; 375-6928. Rooms and a
haymow in a converted sheep barn full of antiques as well as homemade
chocolates.
Norman Gronning Antiques & Architectural Items, Rte. 7A, Shaftsbury;
375-9607. American antiques, eighteenth- and early nineteenth-century country
and formal furniture, and architectural items like hinges, cranes, flooring, and
complete post-and-beam frames. Call ahead.

Antiquarian Booksellers

Bradford Books, West Rd., Bennington; 447-0387. General; history, biography,
children's books. Across from Fairdale Farms.
New Englandiana, 121 BenMont Ave., Bennington; 447-1695. General stock of
about 10,000 used books; in business since 1961. Libraries and accumulations
purchased.
Now & Then Books, 439 Main St., Bennington; 447-1470. General stock of used
and out-of-print books, cookbooks, and children's books. Upstairs in the Cone
Block. Irregular hours, so call ahead.

Discount Outlets

BENNINGTON

Bennington Potters, Second Shop. Gage St.

CB Sports Factory Outlet Store, 190 North St., Bennington; 447-7651. Discounts from the CB Sports clothes line.

CTC Photo Factory Store, 254 BenMont Ave., Bennington; 442-3114. One-hour developing. Discounts on cameras, lenses. Film mailers at half Kodak prices.

Sports and Recreation

ARLINGTON

Arlington Recreation Park, on Historic Rte. 7A, just north of Arlington Village, has tennis courts, basketball courts, a nine-hole golf course, soccer and football fields, and a swimming pool.

POWNAL

Green Mountain Race Track, Rte. 7, Pownal; 823-7311. Greyhounds race from June to Columbus Day. Vermont's only pari-mutuel track.

Biking

Up & Downhill, 160 BenMont Ave., Bennington; 442-8664. Bicycle and ski equipment experts. Rentals.

Golf

ARLINGTON

Arlington Recreation Park, on Historic Rte. 7A, just north of Arlington Village, has a pleasant little nine-hole golf course, soccer, among other recreational facilities.

BENNINGTON

Mount Anthony Country Club, 17 Bank St., Bennington; 442-2617. Also known as Mount Anthony Golf & Tennis Club. Eighteen scenic holes, par 71, 6,206 yards. Open to the public.

STAMFORD

Stamford Valley Golf Course, Stamford; 694-9144. Nine holes, par 36, 2,715 yards. Open to the public.

Horseback Riding

None open to the public.

Sporting Goods Services

BENNINGTON

Up & Downhill, 160 BenMont Ave., Bennington; 442-8664. The "downhill" part of the season is ski equipment, which they sell, rent, and provide advice about. Uphill has to do with bicycles.

SUNDERLAND

Battenkill Canoe, Ltd., Historic Rte. 7A, Sunderland; 375-5995. The shop, moved from its location on Rte. 313, is now near the cluster of shops at the access road to Mount Equinox. Canoes, clothing, and accessories available, as well as arrangements for canoe trips all over the rivers of New England with the Vermont Canoe Trippers.

Tennis

ARLINGTON
Arlington Recreation Park, on Historic Rte. 7A, just north of Arlington Village. Two hard-surface tennis courts, among other recreational facilities, open to the public.

BENNINGTON
The Bennington Recreation Center, Gage St., Bennington; 442-1053. Four courts and a practice wall.
Molly Stark Elementary School, Willow Rd. off Historic 7A. Two hard-surface tennis courts.

Alpine Ski Areas

WOODFORD
Prospect Mountain Ski Area, Rte. 9, Woodford; 442-2575. Vertical drop 700 feet from 2,767-foot summit, two T-bars and one rope tow, 12 trails. Facilities include base lodge, ski shop.

Nordic Ski Areas

WOODFORD
Prospect Ski Center, Rte. 9, Woodford; 442-2575. Twenty-kilometer set trails through meadows, hills, and national forest. Elevation ranges from 2,150 to 2,767 feet. Instruction, rental, repair.

Fishing

The Battenkill, Route 313 in Arlington on down to the New York border. Canoes and some wading. Trout.
Lake Paran, Grout Pond up on the Kelley Stand, and many ponds and lakes offer up perch, pickerel, trout, bass, and panfish, while the streams, such as the Hoosic River in Pownal and the Walloomsac in Bennington, offer up trout. But the most well known in this area is the Battenkill.

Boating

SHAFTSBURY
Lake Shaftsbury State Park, Historic Rte. 7A, Shaftsbury; 375-9978. Lovely place to picnic. There are canoes, rowboats, and paddleboats for rent on its man-made lake. Canoeing and paddleboating and a group camping area. One hundred and one acres for hiking, swimming, boating, fishing, and picnicking.

SUNDERLAND
Battenkill Canoe Ltd., Historic Rte. 7A, Sunderland; 375-9559. Canoes for day, week, month, or season; guided inn-to-inn trips; flat water and white-water instruction. Guided canoe trips.

WOODFORD
Woodford State Park, Rte. 9 (Woodford Rd.), Woodford; 447-7169. Highest elevation campground in Vermont (2,400 feet). Halfway between Bennington and Wilmington. Four hundred acres, 102 campsites, 16 lean-tos. Flush toilets, showers, fireplaces, picnic tables, Adams Reservoir for canoes and rowboats. No hookups, no motors.

Swimming

ARLINGTON
Arlington Recreation Park, on Historic Rte. 7A, just north of Arlington Village, has tennis courts, basketball courts, a nine-hole golf course, soccer and football fields, and a swimming pond.

Route 313, under the covered bridge, is a local swimming hole.

BENNINGTON

Lake Paran, off Rte. 67A, North Bennington. A public beach. Head north on Main St., turn right on Houghton St., past the Norshaft Memorial Park festooned with playground equipment, over the railroad tracks. Small green and white sign and drive up on right.

SHAFTSBURY

Lake Shaftsbury State Park, Historic Rte. 7A, Shaftsbury; 375-9978. Lovely place to picnic. There is a playground for kids, picnic tables, a lake for canoeing and paddleboating, and a group camping area. One hundred and one acres for hiking, swimming, boating, fishing, and picnicking.

Woodford State Park, Rte. 9 (Woodford Rd.), Woodford; 447-7169. Highest elevation campground in Vermont (2,400 feet). Halfway between Bennington and Wilmington. Four hundred acres, 102 campsites, 16 lean-tos. Flush toilets, showers, fireplaces, picnic tables, Adams Reservoir for canoes and rowboats. No hookups, no motors.

Hiking and Nature Trails

BENNINGTON

The Long Trail, which crosses Rte. 9 about five miles east of Bennington, is also the Appalachian Trail in this neck of the woods. The Long Trail follows mountain ridges and valleys from the Massachusetts to the Canadian borders. The Appalachian Trail continues east and north to Maine and south to Georgia. Many side trails and day hikes are possible on the spur trails that connect to the system.

SHAFTSBURY

The Original Back Road Country Tours, Box 517, Shaftsbury; 442-3876. Niles & Becchi Oesterle take you on four-wheel-drive jeep tours of places most visitors never see and guide you on hikes and snowshoe ventures for the energetic. See deer, fox, wild turkey, and other true Vermont natives.

SUNDERLAND

Skyline Dr. to top of Mt. Equinox. There are several hiking trails up the toll road. Great vistas in fall.

State Parks

SHAFTSBURY

Lake Shaftsbury State Park, Historic Rte. 7A, Shaftsbury; 375-9978. Lovely place to picnic. There is a playground for kids, picnic tables, a lake for canoeing and paddleboating, and a group camping area. One hundred and one acres for hiking, swimming, boating, fishing, and picnicking.

WOODFORD

Woodford State Park, Rte. 9 (Woodford Rd.), Woodford; 447-7169. Highest elevation campground in Vermont (2,400 feet). Halfway between Bennington and Wilmington. Four hundred acres, 102 campsites, 16 lean-tos. Flush toilets, showers, fireplaces, picnic tables, Adams Reservoir for canoes and rowboats. No hookups, no motors.

Foliage Vantage Points

ARLINGTON

Drive out to West Arlington on Route 313, which is off Historic Route 7A. The road follows the Battenkill.

BENNINGTON

On Rte. 9, east of Bennington, on the way up to Searsburg, beyond what the locals call "the eyesore" (a truck body and repair shop), pause and look back toward the west where the mountains spread out like a rumpled, multicolored quilt in season.

POWNAL

On U.S. Rte. 7, heading south out of Bennington, at the Valley View or Pownal View Barn, the view opens out onto the Taconics beyond the Pownal Valley. It can be spectacular.

SUNDERLAND

Skyline Dr., a toll road off Historic Rte. 7A across from Basketville. The top of the mountain has some of the best views in southern Vermont.

But frankly, if the light is right, just about anywhere in southern Vermont is good. That's why so many of you come up here during foliage. Explore. Just pick a spot. Enjoy.

Best of Bennington Area

Country Inn: Arlington's West Mountain Inn, River Rd.; 375-6516.

Breakfast: Blue Benn Diner, 102 Hunt St., Bennington; 442-9877.

Lunch: Your Belly's Deli, 100 Pleasant St., Bennington; 442-3653.

Dinner (Moderately Priced): Villager Restaurant, Main St., North Bennington; 447-0998.

Dinner (Expensive): Four Chimneys Restaurant & Inn, 21 West Rd., Bennington; 447-3500.

Entertainment (Stage): Oldcastle Theater Company, Main St., Bennington; 447-0564.

Museum/Historical Site: Peter Matteson Tavern Museum, East Rd., Shaftsbury; 447-1571 and 447-2180.

Art Gallery: The Beside Myself Gallery, Lathrop La., Arlington; 362-2212.

Craft/Specialty Shop: Scandinavian Country Shop, Warm Brook Rd., Arlington; 375-6666.

Hiking or Nature Trail: The Long Trail (Also the Appalachian Trail hereabouts), accessible five miles east of Bennington on Rte. 9.

Camping: Red Mills Campgrounds, Rte. 9, Woodford.

Children's Activities: Arlington Recreation Park, Historic Rte. 7A, Arlington.

Farm Stand: Shaftsbury Farmers Market, off Rte. 7A, in Shaftsbury Elementary School yard. In season.

Ice Cream: Fairdale Farms Stand, Rte. 9, Bennington. Right next to Fairdale Farms Dairy. Good ice cream, hotdogs, and sandwiches.

Foliage Vantage Points: From the Southern Vermont Orchards road, up on Carpenter Hill, looking northward from just above the packing barn. It spreads out to include the Bennington Monument, the orchards, and a view through the Bennington Valley.

Ski Area (both): Prospect Mountain Ski Area, with its small family oriented Alpine slopes and extensive cross-country trails.

Manchester and the Mountains

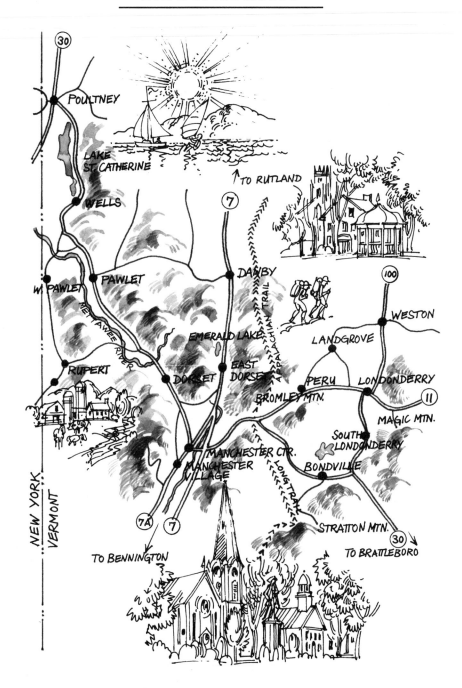

30
POULTNEY

LAKE ST. CATHERINE

WELLS

TO RUTLAND

7

DANBY

W. PAWLET   PAWLET

METTAWEE RIVER

EMERALD LAKE

APPALACHIAN TRAIL

RUPERT

DORSET   EAST DORSET

PERU   BROMLEY MTN.

LANDGROVE

100

WESTON

LONDONDERRY

11

MAGIC MTN.

SOUTH LONDONDERRY

MANCHESTER CTR.
MANCHESTER VILLAGE

BONDVILLE

LONG TRAIL

NEW YORK
VERMONT

7A   7

TO BENNINGTON

STRATTON MTN.

30

TO BRATTLEBORO

Viewpoints

by MARGARET BUCHOLT

Whether you arrive from the south on Route 7A, or the Routes 11-30 east corridor, your first impression of Manchester may be one of surprise. Route 7A into Manchester Village has a delightfully tranquil old-world atmosphere, and Routes 11-30 into Manchester Center create a completely different impression, that of a honky-tonk town with a conglomeration of signs, sights, and shops. Besides the fact that the "village" and the "center" each has their own post office and zip code, as well as a separate form of government, what's most visible to the newcomer is how little they resemble each other.

Manchester Village, a village within the municipality of Manchester, has always been fastidious about preserving its appearance and its history. The main street is on the National Register of Historic Places and strict design control laws govern homes in the village. Stately mansions, marble sidewalks, and the recently revived Equinox Hotel, an impressive 150-year-old landmark, dominate Main Street. Across from the hotel is the picturesque First Congregational Church and the gold-domed county courthouse, which is only used during the summer months. Manchester, as we'll collectively refer to both the center and the village, is a half-shire community; it shares the county seat with Bennington, where court is in session the rest of the year.

During the summer months, huge maple trees and wide, lush manicured lawns adorn these magnificent nineteenth-century homes, and in the winter, with many houses festively decorated with wreaths and lighted windows, you can easily envision a horse-drawn sleigh around the next bend.

If, however, you arrive on what the locals stubbornly refer to as the "new" Route 7, a two-lane highway opened in the 1980s, you'll exit at Manchester Center. A right-hand turn will place you on Routes 11-30 East (called Bromley Mountain Road). This will take you to the ski areas. A left-hand turn onto Routes 11-30 leads you through a commercial corridor, which turns into a three-lane road historically known as the "Flat Road." It becomes more and more congested as it meets up with Route 7A. Lining the road are numerous stores, discount outlets, restaurants, and two shopping centers, all architecturally different.

As you near the intersection where Routes 11-30 connect with Route 7A, a site that has the dubious distinction of being called Malfunction Junction for reasons you will undoubtedly discover, you can either turn right or left onto Route 7A. A left-hand turn heading south will bring you past more stores and restaurants and about a mile or so up the road, the village. A right-hand turn will put you on Manchester Center's Main Street, a cohesive group of charming storefronts.

You have just passed through the new Manchester, a boom town whose year-round population of 3,200 swells to 10 times that number during peak holiday periods, a town whose prosperous economy and low unemployment rates are the envy of many other less fortunate Vermont towns. The problems associated with the rapid growth, however, are not. The most obvious to the naked eye is downtown traffic congestion and the demise of affordable housing. Critics are quick to point to Manchester as an example of uncontrolled growth and what a town can become without stringent zoning and design control. Even Manchester

Village officials voice their disapproval of the center and what they consider as its lack of order.

Manchester is literally a town at the crossroads, and its opposing factions, regardless of whether they live in the town or village, face off during town meetings with little tolerance for the opposition. On one side are those determined to preserve the tranquil Manchester of yesteryear, and on the other are the pro-growth forces who want the best of both worlds — the economic benefits from development and commercialization and the pristine beauty of Manchester, which has drawn tourists to the area for more than 100 years.

While the heated debate is sure to continue — the issues are clearly not black and white and there is no short-term answer to many of the dilemmas — there is one indisputable fact that should not be overlooked, particularly from the out-of-state visitor's point of view. For the sophisticated traveler, Manchester is one of the more commanding places to vacation and explore, rivaling some of the top-notch resort areas in the Northeast. What has emerged after almost a decade of continual growth is a cosmopolitan resort area abundant in old-world charm and the modern amenities so necessary to a successful vacation spot.

Within its boundaries are excellent restaurants, charming inns and bed-and-breakfast establishments, art galleries and antique shops, and special events for every season. Manchester also boasts a luxury hotel and spa and close proximity to three major ski areas — Stratton, Bromley, and Magic — and several ski touring centers. In addition, for the warm weather sports enthusiasts there's golf, tennis, biking, horseback riding, fly-fishing on the fabled Battenkill, and hiking in the Green Mountain National Forest. For those more content to shop, there's no shortage of retail stores and discount clothing outlets, a factor that has earned it the title of "Bloomingdale's on the Battenkill," a phrase coined by a respected ski writer. Aside from its prominent ranking on the shoppers' mecca list, Manchester is known for its scenic beauty, rich cultural history, its dedication to the arts, and its plethora of outdoor recreational activities.

Historical Perspective

What initially earned Manchester a reputation as a recreation area in the mid- to late 1800s was undoubtedly its physical attributes. Nestled at the foot of 3,816-foot Mount Equinox, it is an attractive mountain township that offers pastoral scenes of holsteins grazing in summer meadows as well as magnificent vistas year-round from its ridges and mountains. Lodged between the Green Mountains on the east and the Taconic Mountains on the west, Manchester sits in a picturesque valley punctuated by pristine bodies of water such as the Battenkill, a famous trout stream.

Out-of-state tourists began "summering" in Manchester as early as 1850, according to a bicentennial history called "Manchester, Vermont: A Pleasant Land Among the Mountains," written by residents Nancy Otis and the late Edwin Bigelow. Its reputation as a resort area was established by Franklin Orvis, proprietor of the Equinox House, which grew literally into a block-long luxury hotel catering to wealthy metropolitanites who often arrived with servants and horses for a month's stay in the country. Many traveled via the railroad to what was known as Manchester Depot and were ferried by horse and wagon to the hotel.

Always concerned about the summer residents, a group of prominent locals petitioned the government in 1886 to change the name of nearby Factory Point to Manchester Center because it denoted a manufacturing community, which might deter tourists from the area.

Manchester's reputation as a playground for the rich and famous swelled along with the demand for lodging and recreational activities, and the town and village grew accordingly. Around the turn of the century, Robert Todd Lincoln, son of President Abraham Lincoln, built a summer home called Hildene in the village, as did a host of other dignitaries, diplomats, and wealthy corporate executives. Writers and artists also called this pretty town home during the summer months.

On a midsummer's evening in the 1920s, guests at the Equinox Hotel could be seen leisurely strolling "The Street" or milling around the front porch dressed in evening clothes waiting for dinner and dancing in the ballroom. It was a scene similar to any written by F. Scott Fitzgerald, and the Equinox held its own until changing times and trends forced it to finally shut its doors in the 1960s.

Primarily a summer resort, Manchester didn't acknowledge its potential as a winter vacation spot until 1935, when one of those summer residents, Fred Pabst, Jr., of the Pabst Brewing Company fame, envisioned Alpine skiing in nearby Peru on Bromley Mountain, elevation 3,260 feet. Manchester had its own Winter Sports Club, and with its assistance Pabst built one of the first ski runs on Bromley in the National Forest. The trail was seven miles long and opened in the winter of 1937. A year later, construction began on a 2,200-foot rope tow on the west side of Bromley meadows. The first snow train made its debut at Manchester Depot in January 1938, bringing skiers up from New York City on Friday night. Besides skiing, there was bobsledding, ice skating, and a host of other winter activities sponsored by the Winter Sports Club. It was the beginning of a new era in tourism. White gold had been discovered in the Green Mountains surrounding Manchester.

While the town had always had a small share of Alpine skiing tourists since the sport was born in the United States in the 1930s, those numbers increased dramatically during the 1960s. By the end of that decade, Manchester had become the focal point of what was known as the Golden Triangle, which included the Bromley, Stratton, and Magic ski areas. The second home condominium market was booming, and suddenly Vermont had become the in place to visit. Winter tourism, once relegated to second place, was now rivaling the summer tourist trade.

Manchester also became a hot spot for disenchanted city dwellers who were seeking a better way of life. Many of those urban dropouts who moved to Manchester during this period had skied or summered here. During the back-to-the-land era, they arrived in significant numbers and literally set up shop. And they are, in fact, still coming. These new Vermonters helped turn the community into the sophisticated town it is today. Many of the mom-and-pop-type stores that were plentiful during the 1960s invasion of urbanites have given way to discount outlet chains, although a few family operated businesses, like Mother Myrick's Confectionary, Herdsmen Leathers, and the Northshire Bookstore, can still be found.

But it wasn't until the mid-1980s that the area really boomed. If any one event can be called the catalyst for the growth spurt of recent years, it was the $20 million restoration and reopening of the Equinox Hotel in Manchester Village. With the aid of a $3.4-million federal grant, the grand hotel was refurbished and reopened amid great fanfare. For those of us who had seen the hotel fall into disrepair year after year, it was a thrilling moment. A temporary setback was the devastating fire that consumed the third floor of the south wing while it was under construction. Locals watched in horror as the dream of seeing the hotel flourishing once more literally went up in smoke.

After a flurry of round-the-clock construction, nine months later the refurbished hotel was welcoming its first guests. The revitalization had put Manchester on the developer's map and the area's economy skyrocketed. There wasn't a plumber or a handyman to be found as many were working construction to keep up with the demand. Unemployment dropped to an all-time low. Second home and year-round houses weren't being built fast enough.

Despite a sprinkling of light industry, tourism in Manchester still reigns supreme. In 1976, there were three tourist seasons — summer, fall, and winter — and mud season was the in-between times of the year when browns and grays took over the landscape. No more. The quiet time right after foliage is nonexistent, and the spring mud season is all too brief for many year-round residents. Manchester is now a true four-season resort.

The community has blossomed into a sophisticated suburban type of town, and many homes in the village, once dark during the winter months, are now inhabited year-round. Manchester, scoff the critics, mindful of the many transplanted metropolitanites who now inhabit the town, isn't really Vermont. But they are wrong. It's Vermont, all right, Vermont with a twist.

Manchester Attractions

Summertime in Manchester is spectacular. The hills are lush green, and the weather, except for a brief spell, is seldom humid. Cool nights prevail and air-conditioning is rarely needed. Although there are parades for Memorial Day weekend, the season doesn't really begin until mid- to late June. The highlight of the summer season is the July fourth weekend featuring the Old-Fashioned Fourth festivities at Manchester's recreation park and an outdoor pops concert on the Hildene Meadowlands.

The Old-Fashioned Fourth of July is held every year at the Dana Thompson Memorial Park, otherwise known as the rec area, located just outside of town on Route 30.

If you have kids in tow, don't miss this annual event sponsored by the Manchester Rotary Club. It's well organized with a greased pole climb, bicycle race, three-legged race, pie-eating contest, egg toss, and harness racing, topped off with a splendid fireworks display at dark. It's one of the summer's biggest draws and with good reason. It's an old-fashioned good time with the youngsters' standard banquet fare — hot dogs, hamburgers, and ice cream — and wonderful amusements. Some families park and spend the day carting in chairs, a picnic lunch, and a well-stocked cooler. Others obtain a program ahead of time and limit their children to certain activities. If all else fails, the rec area has the standard playground equipment, and its close proximity to town makes it easy to access, if you're interested in other pastimes.

Traditionally, the Vermont Symphony Orchestra comes to town for its annual concert at Hildene, Robert Todd Lincoln's 412-acre summer estate, which was saved by some civic-minded individuals in 1976 and opened as a nonprofit cultural center. This is truly a gala affair. Some families picnic on the grounds prior to the concert eating leftovers from the fridge out of a wicker picnic basket, while others go all out with a white tablecloth, candles, and a spread fit for royalty. It's your choice. Children are most welcome.

During the summer, the Meadowlands is also home to weekly Sunday afternoon polo matches; a two-day crafts fair complete with jugglers, mime, music, and exotic foods; the Manchester Horse Show; and a reenacted Civil War encampment.

A Saturday in July is usually set aside for a Fair Day on the Hill, an annual event on the grounds of the Southern Vermont Art Center located off West Road. Entertainment abounds with dance groups, puppet shows, and hot air balloon rides. There's food, and in previous years the Marlboro Morris Dancers and the Pipes and Drums of Saint Andrews have performed at the daylong event.

Situated high on a hill overlooking the town, accessible by a mile-long driveway with numerous hairpin turns, the Art Center provides a cool respite on a hot summer's day. The view is magnificent. For nature lovers, the Art Center has the Boswell Botany Trail, which has flowers, trees, and 67 varieties of Vermont ferns identified.

If you're not in town for Fair Day, make sure to visit the Art Center anyway. Its lovely summer quarters "On the Hill" are worth a visit. A cultural centerpiece in the community for more than 50 years, the Art Center has several solo and group shows as well as dance, choral, and classical and instrumental music concerts. In August, there's a Tuesday night movie on the big screen in the Arkyell Pavilion. Luncheon is also served in the Garden Café under a green-and-white-striped awning on the terrace. The salads are great.

Besides the performing arts at the Southern Vermont Art Center, there are other summer musical pursuits, which include the Manchester Music Festival in residence from July to early August and the Third Saturday Series at the Equinox Hotel.

Labor Day weekend or thereabouts, there's the Festival of Fools at the Meadowlands. Check with the Manchester and the Mountains Chamber of Commerce for dates and times for all these events.

Foliage, which runs anywhere from mid- to late September to the middle of October, doesn't need any special events to lure visitors to town. Beginning in September, the air is crisper, and the hills slowly begin to lose their green luster. The bright green leaves give way to vibrant reds, oranges, and golds creating a glorious panorama, a stunning show produced by Mother Nature.

Around every bend a colorful display unfolds. As you can imagine, there are many foliage vantage points in and around Manchester. There's the view from the Hildene Gardens and the one from the Art Center's backyard, high over the town. You can have cocktails on the Wilburton Inn's terrace, which overlooks the Battenkill Valley, or stroll along the recreation area grounds or on the marble sidewalks in Manchester Village. If you're interested in sight-seeing from your car, drive down West Road, which connects Route 7A and Route 30, or North Road, a link between Route 30 and Route 7 North. You can also bike, jog, or walk for a more intimate view of what Mother Nature has to offer.

Hundreds of thousands of travelers make their way to Vermont during foliage, so be forewarned. Traffic is thick, and on the Sunday afternoon of Columbus Day weekend, Route 7 and Route 7A south are backed up from Malfunction Junction a mile each way. One year, a headline in the *Manchester Journal*, the weekly newspaper of record since 1861, admonished, "Don't leave home without one," referring to a most coveted item during Columbus Day weekend: a lodging reservation. This is by far the busiest weekend of the year for everyone — restaurant owners, innkeepers, and shopkeepers.

Locals are well versed on sidestepping the crowds and traffic. We know better than to shop at the Grand Union on a Friday night during the ski season and we avoid the downtown when it rains — regardless of whether it's winter or summer. Daytime inclement weather brings travelers to town to shop, dine, and browse, and inevitably Malfunction Junction lives up to its name. Be patient if you find yourself in gridlock at the infamous intersection.

A rainy day excursion to the Northshire Bookstore located at the Colburn House in the heart of town is well worth any expenditure of energy needed to get there. This remarkable bookstore rivals any big-city counterpart and, as far as we're concerned, supercedes it. The expansive collection and display will surely boggle the browser and delight the purchaser. It is one of Manchester's shining jewels and one of our favorite haunts.

If you have children in tow, the bookstore has a terrific children's section that will occupy them for awhile. Another diversion for a rainy afternoon is the Manchester Cinema, which often has children's matinees on weekends and holiday periods.

Main Street in Manchester Center has a charming collection of boutiques and small shops with high-quality merchandise. Pierre's Gate Gallery is also on Main

Street, and it has a good selection of area artists' work, as do many of the other galleries in town. For variety, there's the Deeley Gallery, Tilting at Windmills, and The Equinox Gallery.

Where to have lunch poses a problem in that there are so many great places, it's a real dilemma. If you're right downtown and want to have lunch at an outside table under an umbrella, try the Gourmet Deli. If you'd like a cocktail with your meal, try Grabber's or the Park Bench. Want health-food fare? Try Molly Coddle's, Rachel's, or the Bagel Works. Super elegant surroundings? Try the Marsh Tavern at the Equinox Hotel. A great spot in summer is the Equinox Sports Club restaurant at the hotel on Union Street overlooking the golf course and the majestic Green Mountains.

If brunch is your thing, try eggs Benedict at Up for Breakfast, a tiny restaurant above Christine's on Main Street. There's also a more standard breakfast fare at the Quality and the Pancake House. A truly decadent brunch is served Sundays at the Equinox Hotel and the Buttery.

Dinner is a tough choice with all the so-called steak/seafood restaurants in town; they're all quite good. Briefly, the best ribs are at Laney's, the best steak at the Sirloin Saloon, and the best nachos at Mulligan's. Many of these restaurants have children's menus.

For a more elegant dining experience, try Mistral's, the Reluctant Panther, the Black Swan, the Chantecleer in East Dorset, and L'Auberge and the Dorset Inn in Dorset.

After dinner, you can listen to Andy Avery and friends belt out those oldies at the Marsh Tavern at the Equinox Hotel. He has a great repertoire, and he interacts well with his audience. The Avalanche Motel often has live rock and roll bands, as does Alfie's, where there is dancing and usually a DJ if there is no live music.

Before deciding where to stay, figure out what it is you want, because most likely you can find what you are looking for in Manchester. Deluxe accommodations abound, but there are simple lodging facilities, too.

If you're looking for an intimate but elegant inn right in town, there's the 1811 House. A country inn about a mile or so out is the Birch Hill Inn on West Road. The Equinox Resort offers many amenities including a pool, tennis courts, and spa. Manchester also has several motels to choose from, many of which have privileges at the Manchester Country Club, where you can play tennis or golf. The splendid Equinox Golf Course is open to the public regardless of whether you stay at the hotel.

During foliage, you'll have to fight the traffic south on Route 7A to the Equinox Valley Nursery, but so will everyone else. Having graced many a magazine cover, the Pumpkin Patch, as it is known, draws visitors from all over to its field of gaily dressed scarecrows, witches, goblins, et al who guard the pick-your-own pumpkins. Be sure and bring a camera.

Church-sponsored turkey suppers and wild-game dinners are usually prevalent this time of year. In the spring and summer it is strawberry festivals, etc., which prompt these wonderful occasions. The food is good and plentiful, and the profits go to a worthy cause.

The Friday after Thanksgiving is traditionally the biggest retail day of the year, and Manchester is usually humming. The trick is to find a legal parking space and walk to your destination. A good bet is near the elementary school on School Street, across from Polly Flinders, a children's dress shop. Another good area is behind the Rite Aid Drugstore on Route 7.

The annual Christmas tree lighting, sponsored by the chamber of commerce, takes place the first week in December. In previous years, horse-drawn wagons brought children from the center to the village where Santa Claus presides over the festivities, the tree is lit, carols are sung, and everyone troops in to the Equinox Hotel lobby for punch and cookies.

The holiday season brings ski races on nearby mountains, Santka Lucia festivals, and Christmas plays and concerts in neighboring communities. And, during Christmas week, Hildene offers its annual candlelight tours of the mansion, which is resplendent in Victorian decorations. January brings the Southern Vermont Art Center's Winter Film Festival, more concerts, and ski races. February is Winter Carnival month, a weekend of skiing events, outdoor volleyball, and a huge bonfire. Come April, it's the Easter parade from the center to the village complete with the Easter bunny.

Recreational Pursuits

Although you'll have to travel outside Manchester for Alpine skiing, that's just about the only sport you can't do in and around town. Manchester has places to cross-country ski, sled, play tennis, golf, jog, hike, fly fish, swim, and bicycle.

Hildene operates a cross-country ski touring center, with rental equipment and a warming hut. The recreation area and the golf courses at the Equinox Hotel and Manchester Country Club are good for skiing, too. For the more adventurous, the U.S. Forest Service on Routes 11-30 will provide a map and directions for some back-country skiing on snowmobile trails. A few minutes from Manchester are the Viking Touring Center in Londonderry and Wild Wings in Peru, two cross-country ski areas with groomed trails that always have snow when Hildene doesn't.

As for sledding, there's Burr and Burton Seminary hill off Seminary Avenue in Manchester Village and the recreation area, which also operates an ice-skating rink.

Located just two minutes from the center of town on Route 30, the recreation area is probably the town's most underutilized resource. The rec area offers basketball courts, swings, slides, a picnic area, volleyball net, and horse ring. Many lunch places offer take-out, which you can bring to the rec area for a picnic. On an autumn or winter's afternoon it is usually sparsely populated, although the fields are great for fitness walking or strolling with your dog. Only in spring and summer does the rec area come alive. In spring, Little League and soccer teams take over the fields, and in summer, the municipal in-ground pool draws a crowd during the week. Lifeguards are on duty, and for toddlers there's a wading pool.

The rec area has three hard-surface tennis courts, where it's first come, first served. Even when the weather is blistering hot, there's always a breeze on the rec tennis courts. Be sure and bring your own water to drink. Check with the Recreation Department at 362-1439 for hourly fees. When you're done playing you can jump into the recreation department's in-ground swimming pool; a fee is charged. The Equinox Hotel also has tennis courts that are rented to the public. Manchester Sports on Route 7A sells rackets and tennis balls, and you can have your racket restrung at Stratton Sports in the Equinox Plaza.

If you have a hankering for a fresh water pond swim and a sandy beach, there's Emerald Lake State Park in East Dorset or Hapgood Pond in Peru. For parents with toddlers, this is a more relaxing atmosphere. Both lakes have roped off areas for toddlers as well as adult swimmers. Lifeguards are on duty.

You can play a round of golf at the 18-hole course at the Equinox Hotel or at the Manchester Country Club on Route 7 North, which was rated the best course in Vermont in 1989 by *Golf* magazine. The views from both courses are breathtaking.

Bicycling in Manchester is also fun. Two bike shops, Pedal Pushers and Battenkill Sports, both located on Routes 11-30, rent touring bikes, helmets, etc. One suggested tour — there are many to choose from — takes you down Richville Road into River Road where you make a right. Watch for geese in the road at Oscar Johnson's farm. River Road winds through some picturesque terrain, past the Hildene Meadowlands, and hooks up with Route 7A. There you make another right and you'll pedal past the stately old village homes and the historic Equinox Hotel. If you bear left instead of continuing on Route 7A toward the center, you'll be on the West Road, another scenic ride. West Road links you to Route 30, where you'll make another right and head back toward town.

If fly-fishing is your sport, stop in at the Orvis Company for some state-of-the-art fishing equipment and tips on the best places to fish. A popular spot on the Battenkill is near the Johnson farm at the intersection of River and Richville roads. For the serious fly-fishermen, Orvis also runs a fly fishing school.

Manchester is home to an office of the U.S. Forest Service, which is located on Routes 11-30, heading up the mountain. Part of the Green Mountain Forest and Lye Brook Wilderness Area are in Manchester, and the Appalachian and Long trails converge just up the road. There are numerous day hiking trips you can take in Green Mountain Forest, and forest service personnel are extremely helpful offering advice and giving directions. They also have brochures about recreational activities in the Green Mountain National Forest, including a small pamphlet on day hikes.

One of our favorites is the Lye Brook Falls Trail. Take Richville Road, which is off Routes 11-30 to the first left, East Manchester Road. Follow East Manchester Road to just under the highway overpass. Be prepared to make a right hand turn, and follow the signs to a parking area. From there the trail is well marked. It's 2.3 miles to the falls. It's an easy trail although it's all uphill.

At Windhall Horses and Tack Shop, Inc. off North Road you can take a horseback riding lesson, rent horses or ponies for trail rides, and rent horse-drawn wagons or sleighs.

Shopping has become a national pastime, and in recent years Manchester has earned the dubious reputation of being a shopper's paradise. With the proliferation of "outlet" stores, it's easy to see why. Outlet stores, women's clothing stores in particular, are opening faster than anyone ever thought possible. Be assured, whatever you're looking for, you'll most likely find it in Manchester. The variety of merchandise will astonish you.

In addition to the wonderful little boutique stores that do not have "seconds" or a "discounted" table, there are outlets where you can get a good quality bargain. Unfortunately, some of the outlet stores are long on shoddy merchandise and short on true, first-quality items. Keeping this in mind, browsing through what Manchester has to offer can be appealing if shopping is your primary interest.

The Mountain Towns: Peru, Londonderry, Weston

East of Manchester on Routes 11-30 are the mountain towns of Peru, Landgrove, Londonderry, and Weston. Because Routes 11-30 east is virtually all uphill, these communities, along with Winhall, Bondville, and Stratton Mountain, are commonly referred to as being "over the mountain."

Recreational opportunities abound in these small towns, which are located on Route 11. Route 30 toward Bondville, Winhall, and Stratton Mountain veers off to the right at the Kandahar Resort after the climb from Manchester. If you continue east on Route 11, you'll hit the Bromley Ski area first and then Peru.

Pristine Peru boasts the Bromley Mountain Ski Area, Hapgood Pond Recreation Area, and numerous trails in the Green Mountain National Forest. Continuing east, Route 11 descends into Londonderry, home to the Magic Mountain Ski Area. Just past the town of Londonderry is Route 100 north, which will take you to Weston, a charming village worth exploring during any season.

Due to the elevation, the weather over the mountain is apt to be different than Manchester's. On a blistering hot, humid summer day, for example, the Hapgood Pond Recreation Area is probably the area's best-kept secret for really cooling off. In winter, rain or sleet in Manchester usually translates to snow on Bromley Mountain and Magic Mountain. Although this is great news for ski enthusiasts, it's bad news for drivers if you're on your way over the mountain where icy conditions on Routes 11-30 east might make driving a little tricky. Although the state highway crews are usually out sanding in a timely fashion, this is a useful bit of information to pocket.

People have been grumbling about the road over the mountain for as far back as anyone can remember. The Peru Turnpike, as it was known until 1917, was one of the last private turnpikes in the country, and it took a lawsuit by the towns of Peru and Winhall for the road to revert into public domain. The old toll booth was near the site of what is now Mistral's Restaurant. According to an account in *The Shires of Bennington*, edited by Tyler Resch, an editorial in a local paper chastised the turnpike owners for the state of disrepair saying tourists had to carry heavy planks of wood with them because the ruts were so difficult to maneuver. This, of course, is not the case today, as the state highway department keeps the paved road in excellent condition.

Peru

If you're expecting an overdeveloped ski town with shops, restaurants, and outlets, you'll be pleasantly surprised when you reach Peru, which is located approximately 10 miles of east of Manchester on Route 11. Despite the fact there is an Alpine ski area within town boundaries, the main area of Peru has remained virtually unchanged for the last 50 years. Most of the condominium development seems to have taken place in and around the Bromley Ski Area, which you passed not long after the paths of Routes 11 and 30 diverged. The "downtown" consists of the post office, J. J. Hapgood General Store, town office building, Congregational church, and the old cheese factory building that is rented to woodcarver Chris Miller. There are an assortment of old houses across from the post office and store, the most noticeable being a rambling, somewhat unkept but nevertheless inviting structure with a sign out front that reads "Russell Inn." A classic Vermont village, Peru was tapped by Hollywood a couple of years back and was featured in the movie *Baby Boom* with Diane Keaton.

The name Peru was not forced on this town when it was incorporated in 1761. It was called Bromley. It was the residents of the community who petitioned the state legislature in 1804 to have the name changed from Bromley to Peru. According to historical accounts, residents felt the original name did not project an affluent enough image and was stifling growth. Peru was a name people could associate with prosperity, the residents claimed. And so the town of Bromley became the town of Peru. In the ensuing years, Peru grew from 72 residents in 1791 to 239 in 1810. By the 1840s, the population was almost 600.

Peru is also home to the Hapgood State Forest, named for a local family whose members served the community. In the 1880s, Marshall Hapgood, an opinionated, outspoken man who was the town's most prominent citizen, was elected to the Vermont legislature, and the Hapgood Pond Recreation Area, completed in 1938, was originally part of his land. Mr. Hapgood donated the Peru Forest to the state for a permanent park, and it eventually became part of the Green Mountain National Forest.

Around the same time that the Hapgood Pond Recreation Area was under construction (1936), Fred Pabst of the Pabst beer brewing family was eyeing land west of the village on Bromley Mountain, elevation 3,260 feet, for a rope tow to accommodate Alpine skiers. His idea took off, so to speak, and Bromley with its south-facing slopes soon became a mecca for skiers. By 1942, the technology included a mile-long ramway and a J-bar lift 2,800 feet long. Bromley boasted seven trails, four open slopes, and two forest slaloms, and a rope tow for Little Bromley, according to a historical account in *Manchester Vermont: A Pleasant Land Among the Mountains*. A new winter sport was making history, and avid skiers began flocking to Peru.

Not long after, the informal ski houses and inns began popping up to serve the market. The earlier mentioned Russell Inn was one. Opened in 1945, the inn still caters mostly to Alpine skiers, providing no-fuss lodging with breakfast and dinner included in the price. The rustic Johnny Seesaw's on Route 11 just before you get to the village is of even earlier vintage and still enjoys a successful following. But the granddaddy of them all, the Bromley House, a three-story inn built in 1822 located just past the Hapgood Store, burned to the ground in the 1970s.

Local Attractions

Right in the heart of town is the J. J. Hapgood Store, a mom-and-pop operation run for more than a decade by Frank and Nancy Kirpatrick. Besides sandwiches and groceries, the Kirpatricks are knowledgeable about the area and can offer advice and information to the visitor. The store, a village focal point since 1827, is decorated with memorabilia, photographs, and a working wood stove that sits in the middle of the room. Outside, there's a bulletin board worth checking for local events. In-between the store and the post office is a hand-carved wooden sign for Peru and room for more posted notices.

Whether the stately maples lining the road are covered with bright green, gold, and red leaves or a thick layer of fluffy snow, the pace in this lovely little hamlet is leisurely and a welcome change from the hustle and bustle of Manchester. Peru is the epitome of a small Green Mountain town, so much so that it was chosen for the movie set of *Baby Boom*, a comedy starring Diane Keaton as a high-powered executive who moves to Vermont and starts her own baby food company. Accordingly, Peru was given the pseudonym of Hadleyville, a more appropriate name for your quintessential Vermont town. Star-struck locals from Manchester, Peru, and the surrounding towns, hired as extras, got to rub elbows with Ms. Keaton and actor Sam Shepard. But after a whirlwind few weeks, the novelty wore thin, and Peru's residents were anxious to have their town back. In late fall, the Hollywood crews finally removed the Hadleyville signs and packed up for home. We're happy to report the town has reverted back into its time warp.

Recreational Pursuits

Sitting on a ridge of the Green Mountains, Peru is a popular resort community for those enamored with the great outdoors. Skiers, snowmobilers, hikers, and campers have discovered the amenities of this wonderful area. In summer, the Hapgood Pond Recreation Area just two miles up the road lures visitors into its fold for camping, swimming, and hiking, and in winter, the Bromley Ski Area, along with the Wild Wings Cross-Country Ski Area, welcomes families for outdoor recreation.

The Bromley Ski Area is looked upon as the hometown mountain by local skiers. Many learned to ski on Bromley's slopes thanks to the late Mr. Pabst who, along with his wife, Sally Litchfield Pabst, pioneered the Junior Instructional Ski Program (JISP), whereby local schoolchildren are given lessons and skied free one afternoon a week. The program is still in effect today, and thousands more area children are becoming downhill ski devotees, as well as avid fans of Bromley.

For those who seek the thrill of downhill when there's no snow and the weather is balmy, the Bromley Ski Area runs the Alpine Slide in spring, summer, and fall. You ride the chair lift up so you get a panoramic view of the area. If you choose the slow lane down (you get a choice of three lanes), you can have a leisurely view of the countryside. Children are more likely to opt for a quick ride down. Bromley also sponsors the Sunday music series during the summer months, and there's an Outdoor Deck Café and a Dairy Bar.

The Long Trail, which runs down the western side of Peru's boundaries, is an easy access for hikers. It's located two miles west of the Hapgood Pond.

There are some tall peaks in Peru, too, namely, Mount Tabor at 3,043 feet; Peru Peak at 3,429 feet; and Styles Peak at 3,394 feet. Styles Peak was named for a prominent Peru family. The well-traversed Long Trail and the Appalachian Trail are located in the Green Mountain National Forest, which accounts for a sizable chunk of Peru's acreage.

In recent years, the tightly knit, year-round community has produced one of the more successful fairs around. The Peru Fair, which has grown in size and popularity since its inception in the mid-1980s, has now become a regular autumnal event. Usually held the last weekend of September, the fair has in excess of 3,000 spectators partake of the festivities. There's live music, crafts, homemade baked goods, and a pig roast.

Fall is a great time to visit Peru. The center of town is gloriously decked out with a multicolored backdrop, and if you're not in the mood to hike, bike, or walk, there are several rides you can take in the area to view the foliage. If you stay on the Hapgood Pond Road past the turnoff for the recreation area, you'll end up in Landgrove, a tiny town located between Peru and Weston. The ride is a pretty one, and it's only about three miles. You'll be riding through the woods, but after a short time the vistas are long and pretty. You'll get to a little bridge with a rusted-out sign. If you turn right here, you'll end up back on Route 11. If you turn left, you'll pass the Village Inn at Landgrove and end up in Weston. This is also a nice drive.

Another picturesque route in autumn is South Road, which intersects in the middle of Peru just after the old cheese house building at the stop sign and before the post office. There's another stop sign at Route 11. Cross over and South Road continues past farms and horse barns. Keep bearing left. When you get to the point when you have to go either right or left, go left and the dirt road will soon turn to pavement. This road will deposit you in South Londonderry on Route 100. You can wind your way back up Route 100 to Peru or explore the Londonderry area.

Londonderry

At the intersection of Routes 11 and 100 is the town of Londonderry, home to the Magic Mountain Ski Area, the Viking Ski Touring Center for cross-country ski enthusiasts, and the remote Lowell Lake and the Winhall Brook area for fishing, hiking, and boating.

In 1775, the first town meeting was held at a gristmill at the mouth of Lowell Lake, the largest lake in town, which prior to the 1880s was known as Derry Pond. According to historical accounts, there were Lowells in nearby Townshend, and it is assumed the name was derived from that family. By 1875, the same spot on the lake was home to the Lowell Lake House, a summer resort community of some renown, which is no longer in existence.

The first post office was opened in Londonderry's main village on Route 11 in 1823, and a second post office opened almost 30 years later in South Londonderry, the village located a few miles south on Route 100. Londonderry's town offices are located in the Town Hall in South Londonderry.

If you travel too fast through Londonderry, you'll pass the post office, a tiny building next to Stoddard's Market. Aside from the Congregational church and the post office, today the heart of Londonderry is comprised of gas stations, two shopping centers, restaurants, and discount outlets.

Local Attractions

The first shopping center you see when you enter town is the Mountain Marketplace where the Derry Twin Cinema theater is located, along with a host of other shops, and a grocery store. Unlike its valley neighbor, Manchester, shopping centers in "Derry," as the town is often called, are more down-home than the posh-looking structures in Manchester.

With the patterned design work on its shingled exterior, the Garden Restaurant complex right off Route 11 has funky appeal. The restaurant has a unique round fireplace visible from all seats in the dining room, and there's an art gallery upstairs usually displaying the works of local artists and craftsmen. Attached to the restaurant is a gift shop with an eclectic collection of fine quality items. Across the way is the local health-food store, which also sells picnic makings.

Along this stretch, too, is Stoddard's Market, which sells fishing licenses, groceries, etc. Be sure to check the huge bulletin board outside Stoddard's for local events, church suppers, etc.

Just a few doors down is the Barn Steakhouse, and at the corner of the Route 11 and 100 north junction where you turn left to go to Weston is a group of discount stores. The Barn is the one that started it all a few years back. It has since been joined by the Barn Annex and the New England Shoe Barn. They have good buys on Rockport shoes for men and women. If you continue east on Route 11, you'll come to the Magic Mountain access road and the turnoff for Lowell Lake.

Recreational Pursuits

The Magic Mountain Ski Area is larger than its sister area, Bromley Mountain, but smaller than neighboring Stratton. In recent years, the owners of Magic purchased Bromley Mountain and tickets between the two areas are interchangeable. Magic has 70 trails, six lifts, and a state-accredited nursery. It also offers ski lessons for beginners and a Diamond Lovers' Workshop for advanced skiers, one of the few in the area.

The access road to Lowell Lake is also off Route 11. The 102-acre Lowell Lake offers fishing, boating, hiking, and swimming. It is managed by the Vermont Fish and Wildlife Department, and boats can be transported close to the lake although there is no trailer ramp. You can fish for yellow perch, chain pickerel, largemouth bass, smallmouth bass, bullheads, and panfish. You can buy your fishing license at Stoddard's Market.

Weston

Route 100 north from Londonderry to Weston is a picturesque drive in any season of the year. And Weston is a pretty little town with several landmarks you don't want to miss including the Farrar-Mansur House, Vermont Country Store, and the Weston Playhouse. Weston is also the spiritual and political haven for the monks of the Weston Priory who made headlines a few years back by sheltering a Guatemalan Indian family who are considered illegal immigrants by the U.S. government.

In 1799, Weston was carved out of the town of Andover because of traveling difficulties to the West Town, as Weston was then called. The reason was Markham and Terrible mountains, which made traveling impossible during the winter months. Almost 20 years later, a post office was established, and the town began to thrive.

The Federal-styled Farrar-Mansur Museum on Route 100 was built in 1797 by Captain Oliver Farrar as a family home and tavern. Route 100 was an important stagecoach route, and weary travelers often stopped for food and drink at the well-established tavern where they were waited on by the Farrar family, which had 13 children. The Farrars and their successors, the Mansurs, lived in the house from 1857 until 1932. In that year, Franklin Mansur's grandson, Frank Mansur, donated the historic landmark to the Weston Community Club, which helps maintain it as a town museum, along with the Weston Historical Society. It is on the National Register of Historic Places.

Weston also has two beautiful old churches — the Old Parish Church built in 1803 and the Church on the Hill built in 1838. Each has been refurbished and is used by area residents. Ecumenical services are held Sundays at the Old Parish Church, and the Church on the Hill is nondenominational. Services are conducted during the summer by visiting ministers. One of the striking features of downtown Weston, population 600, is the town green with its wide lawn and old-fashioned wooden bandstand. Across the good-sized green is the Weston Playhouse, with an imposing facade, and the Farrar-Mansur House on the corner. Once the Congregational church, the playhouse building was refurbished around 1922 by the Weston Community Club, the force behind all the revival spirit in Weston.

In this unique community, every resident is a member of the Weston Community Club, which maintains the Farrar-Mansur House, the Weston Playhouse, Cold Spring Brook Memorial Park, and the Old Mill and Craft Building. Various fund-raising events, like the Weston Antiques Show and the Weston Craft Fair, are held annually to provide revenues to this civic-minded organization. These revenues help keep Weston's downtown one of the most picturesque on record.

Local Attractions

The Farrar-Mansur Museum with its authentic furniture, clothing, utensils, and firearms is must-see on your travel itinerary. Under the direction of the Weston Historical Society, the museum is meticulously maintained and opened to the public from Memorial Day through Columbus Day. The eighteenth-century home is furnished with items donated by Weston families, in addition to the Farrar-Mansur items already on the premises. Each room is furnished accordingly.

An evening at the Weston Playhouse, a summer theater overlooking the West River, which also boasts a lively cabaret after the show, is an enjoyable pastime.

The cabaret's musical review changes with each production. Before the show you can dine Downstairs at the Playhouse. In recent years, the players have been fond of Neil Simon productions (what summer theater isn't) and musicals like the *H.M.S. Pinafore* and *A Little Night Music*. One year, there was a splendid rendition of *Camelot*.

If you desire an elegant gourmet meal, try the Inn at Weston just south of the playhouse. The food is excellent, and on a warm summer's evening you can leisurely stroll through town to the playhouse just before the show begins.

During the day, one of Weston's popular attractions is the Vermont Country Store, a wonderful tribute to the almost extinct general store. A fore-runner in the field of general store reproductions, the Vermont Country Store provides a peek at the days when candy was a penny and a large potbellied stove dominated the only store in town. It's truly a browser's delight. Operated by the Orton family, the Vermont Country Store is a real eye-opener for little ones in the market for sweet treats. In the true Yankee tradition, the store is closed on Sundays.

The Orton family also operates the Bryant House Restaurant next to the Vermont Country Store. The restaurant features an 1885 Mahogany Bar Room with a real soda fountain.

Downtown Weston has many fine stores, including the Weston House Quilt Collection, which has a stunning display of handmade quilts, pillows, wall hangings, folk art, and crafts. There's also the Old Mill Museum, with a local tinsmith hard at work in the 1780 mill built by Ezekiel Pease to power his sawmill, and the Todd Gallery of fine arts and crafts. And the Weston Bowl Mill and Annex has an extensive woodenware collection and a shop with seconds.

Out of town about three miles on Route 155 is the Weston Priory, a spiritual enclave of Benedictine monks who offer daily prayer. The monks are known for their music, and tapes and albums are available at the monastery gift shop, in addition to handwoven items by the Guatemalan Indian family who has resided there for several years. You'll find the monks' services simple, spiritual, and beautiful to hear, regardless of your religious affiliation. They welcome visitors, but call first to make sure they are not on retreat.

Kinhaven, a summer music school in session from June through the first week in August, features concerts by students and faculty on weekends. Check with the school for dates and times.

Recreational Pursuits

The Greendale Campground in the Green Mountain National Forest is approximately two miles north of Weston off Route 100. Take Forest Road 18, a left-hand turn off Route 100, in to the recreation area, which has 11 camping sites. At the end of Forest Road 18 is a beaver pond.

Forest Road 18 turns into Forest Road 17, which winds its way back (keep bearing left) onto Lawrence Hill Road. These Green Mountain Forest trails — Beaver Meadows, Root Beer Ridge — make for some great cross-country ski treks.

Lawrence Hill Road loops around and comes back out onto Route 100. This is a scenic trip during foliage, too. Off Lawrence Hill Road is Trout Club Road where there's a small beach and playground for young children on Wantastiquet Pond. Wantastiquet is the Abnaki Indian name for the head or source of the river. This name is sometimes used for the West River.

Winhall (Bondville) and Stratton Mountain

If you take Bromley Mountain Road (Routes 11-30 east) in Manchester, you'll start climbing into mountain territory. Routes 11-30 split at approximately the 2,000-foot elevation, just after you pass the Long Trail parking lot on the left. If you bear right onto Route 30 south, you'll head downhill into Bondville, a village in the town of Winhall deep in the Green Mountain National Forest, which boasts numerous hiking and outdoors activities. Bondville, a village in Winhall, is located at the bottom of the Stratton Mountain Ski Area access road, and the small community has a few restaurants and shops.

Stratton Mountain Resort, atop Stratton Mountain, elevation 3,859 feet, is located on the town of Stratton's northern boundary. The resort is a citylike enclave with a variety of modern sports' facilities, several restaurants, numerous shops, and condominium developments, none of which is visible from Route 30. In recent years, Stratton has been steadily strengthening its reputation as a four-season resort area. Besides Alpine and cross-country skiing, the resort includes four separate hotels and inns, a fully equipped Sports Center, indoor and outdoor tennis courts, golf course, and a lake for swimming and sailboarding.

Winhall (Bondville)

Roughly one-fourth of Winhall's acreage is located in the Green Mountain National Forest. Winhall boasts more than a dozen peaks over the 2,000-foot elevation mark, including Spruce Peak. The town offers numerous recreational activities including hiking and fishing. For all intents and purposes, the village of Bondville, located right on Route 30, has become the center of Winhall, and you may hear more locals refer to "Bondville" than "Winhall" when describing this area. Prior to the extensive development up on Stratton, Bondville was the closest community for skiers to purchase needed items, so the village grew to meet the demand. It now has a bank, a few shops and restaurants and inns, in addition to the post office (the only one in Winhall), and the Winhall police station and old Town Hall.

Historical Perspective

From its inception in 1761, Winhall has struggled to survive. A wild, mostly uninhabited mountain town, Winhall had several different settlements but only one thrived: Bondville, which was incorporated in 1796. The name Bondville was derived from the first postmaster from the area whose name was "Bond." The village of Winhall's post office was closed in 1880 due to a decline in business, as was the post office at North Winhall. Other Winhall villages like Middletown and Grahamville also did not fare as well as Bondville. Lumber was the primary industry in the area, although at one time there was a blacksmith shop and chair factory.

When Stratton Mountain opened for business on December 22, 1961, the town of Winhall had 245 residents, and Bondville was a sleepy community with a post office, town hall, and a huge old inn, now called Haig's, dominating the main street. In a few years' time, Bondville prospered and became a second-home community for Stratton Mountain. The year-round population is around 325, and it has one of the lowest tax rates in the state.

Local Attractions

One landmark in downtown Bondville is Haig's, an inn and restaurant of substantial size located right on Route 30. Come ski season, this inn is a focal point for drinks and dinner. So is the Red Fox Inn on Winhall Hollow Road, which serves excellent food and has a young bar crowd. Down the road in Rawsonville (which is technically in the town of Jamaica but for all intents and purposes is part of the Stratton ski area), the Bear Creek Sport Hotel and Resort has a good following in winter and summer. It offers tennis, golf, and ski packages, and a good restaurant, Feathers, is right on the premises. For tennis lovers, it has five Har-Tru tennis courts.

There are a sprinkling of eateries and shops off the mountain in the Bondville and Rawsonville area such as the River Café for lunches and light suppers (across from Haig's); and Detail Sports and Equipe Sports, specializing in ski and outdoor wear. The Winhall Market has picnic fixings and a deli counter, in addition to grocery items.

Recreational Pursuits

Heading up the mountain on Routes 11-30 from Manchester, you'll find the parking lot for the Long Trail/Appalachian Trail on the north side of the road just before you reach the intersection where the road splits and Route 30 takes you to Bondville. There is some discrepancy whether the Long Trail parking lot is actually in the town of Manchester or Winhall, but after checking with forest service officials and several maps, we're placing it in Winhall. The parking lot is well marked and is used to access the hiking trails for Bromley Mountain, elevation 3,260 feet, and Spruce Peak, elevation 2,060 feet. In winter, the lot is used for snowmobilers.

The Long Trail runs the length of the state for approximately 265 miles over mountain ridges. In the Manchester Ranger District, the Long Trail is part of the Appalachian Trail, which follows the east coast from Georgia up through Maine.

If you park in the Long Trail parking lot, you have to cross the road to pick up the southern tip of the trail for the 2.2-mile hike. Panoramic views of the Manchester Valley and the Taconic Mountain Range are your reward. The hike to Spruce Peak is rated moderately difficult, according to the forest service brochure "Day Hikes." The Manchester Ranger District Office is located in Manchester on Routes 11-30 about four miles east of the Long Trail parking lot. The office has several maps and brochures about day hikes, camping, and other recreational activities. A helpful receptionist is also on hand Monday through Friday to answer questions and give explicit directions.

Stratton Mountain

If you look at a boundary map for the town of Stratton, you'll see that the Stratton Mountain Ski Area is just over the Winhall line in Stratton, a tiny community that has grown considerably since the ski area opened its doors in 1961. You'll also note that the four-mile access road off Route 30 is in Winhall, not Stratton. In 1961, the town of Stratton had 27 residents; today it has 122, but that figure doesn't take into consideration the second-home owners or how many more vacation on the mountain during the peak ski season. The estimates would more than likely stagger the imagination given the town's history. A drive up the access road will affirm the resort's mammoth size and sophisticated amenities.

In the year 1791, Stratton had a population of 97 inhabitants. Never a densely populated community, Stratton did have a boom time prior to the Stratton

Mountain ski development. According to historical accounts, a 50-year period from 1830 to 1880 saw an upsurge in population thanks to the timber industry. An 1860 census shows Stratton had 366 residents, seven schools, four sawmills, blacksmith shop, and one inn on the Kelley Stand, an important stagecoach road on the town's southern border that led into the heart of Stratton. However, the population slowly dwindled as logging operations ceased. It was during this heyday that Stratton had its moment in the limelight.

The year was 1840, and Martin Van Buren was president of the United States. The ruling party, the Democrats, was being blamed for the sorry state of the economy, and the Whigs were determined to take away control in this presidential election year. A Whig convention was scheduled for the town of Stratton, probably because of its strategic location on the stagecoach road, and the guest speaker was to be Senator Daniel Webster of Massachusetts, a popular and admired speaker. According to historical accounts, a 300-acre site was prepared and a huge log cabin 100 feet long by 50 feet wide was built to accommodate the expected crowds. And the residents of Stratton weren't disappointed. An estimated 15,000 to 20,000 people from both sides of the mountain were reported to have attended this momentous occasion in the wilderness. A road marker on the little-traveled dirt road from the town of Arlington into the heart of Stratton marks the site.

Area Attractions

During the Volvo International Tennis Tournament, an event Stratton hosted for five years, approximately 65,000 people attended the week-long August extravaganza. The professional tennis players on the circuit who have seen tennis facilities worldwide rated the Stratton event as their favorite tournament, and it's easy to see why. The sports' facilities — both winter and summer — are impressive, and Stratton, with its spectacular mountain setting, has been steadily improving its year-round, upscale resort image by providing a plethora of events for all ages.

Besides its 92 trails and 12 lifts, including the high-speed gondola Starship, Stratton offers an extensive skiing program for youngsters and juniors, as well as adults. There are private and group ski lessons, the Little Cub ski program for toddlers and young children, and the Big Cub ski program for older children. For cross-country ski enthusiasts, there are 12 kilometers of groomed trails at the Stratton Mountain Country Club. In recent years, Stratton has expanded its snowmaking capabilities to 65 percent of the mountain and further developed the Sun Bowl with a 350-seat base lodge and 487-car parking lot.

After butting heads with state environmentalists over a condominium complex in the Sun Bowl, Stratton, whose logo is the black bear, a species that has inhabited the mountain since long before Daniel Webster made his impassioned speech, developed an innovative plan to help preserve the bear habitat that would be disturbed by the development. The Indian name for Stratton, by the way, is *Manicknung*, which translates to Home of the Bear.

Staying on the mountain during the ski season has obvious advantages, namely close proximity to the ski lifts. Stratton has built a self-contained resort with several restaurants and a "village" complete with a variety of small shops. Many of them feature ski and sportswear, but there are other shops including an art gallery, home furnishings store, and spectacle shop. The stores are pricey but convenient. Many visitors when they get antsy usually go to Manchester for a change of scene.

Probably the most popular lodging facility on the mountain is the modern, tastefully decorated 125-room Stratton Mountain Inn, which has two restaurants, and Wentworth's piano bar. One of the restaurants, Café Applause, also has live entertainment during the ski season and peak summer weekends. The inn runs a shuttle bus service to the base lodge and has two hard and two clay tennis courts and an outdoor lap pool.

Liftline Lodge prides itself on old-world hospitality and has two restaurants on the premises: Hasenpfeffer's and Victoria's, a café. Birkenhaus, the smallest of the four lodging facilities, also has a restaurant with European cuisine. The Village Lodge, located right above the base lodge, has a microwave, refrigerator, and color TV in each room. And you can just about roll out of bed onto the lifts.

In addition to the above-mentioned eateries, there's A. J. Pimento's, Mulligan's, and Tenderloins at the Stratton Mountain Country Club. Mulligan's and Tenderloins usually have live music and dancing during ski season and summer and fall peak periods. Both the Café Applause and Wentworth's have bands and offer other live music.

In the summer, Stratton has the Arnold Palmer Golf School, which offers weekend and weekday courses on the 27-hole golf course at the Stratton Mountain Country Club. Stratton runs a tennis school with weekend and weekday courses and has outdoor courts and indoor courts, which are also available to Stratton Mountain guests. There are sailboarding lessons on Stratton Lake; horseback riding at Stratton Stables; mountain bikes to rent in the Village Square; and, for guests with children, Stratton offers a children's summer day camp program.

The Stratton Sports Center, available to all guests on the mountain, boasts an indoor pool, racquetball courts, sauna, Jacuzzi, and Nautilus room. All four mountain lodging facilities — the Liftline Lodge, Birkenhaus, Village Lodge, and the Stratton Mountain Inn — have Sports Center privileges. You can also rent condominiums, the Stratton Villas, right on the mountain.

Shortly after the Volvo International Tennis Tourney left Stratton, the Stratton Resort Area Association was created by interested area businesspeople to bring entertainment to the mountain during the summer and fall. In previous years the roster has included Ray Charles and Peter, Paul and Mary. Stratton also hosts the Ladies' Professional Golf Association tournament in August.

Foliage brings a spectacular mountain panorama and the Stratton Mountain Arts Festival, a month-long arts exhibit running from mid-September to mid-October. On weekends, performing artists bring their talent to Stratton. For more than 25 years, local artists have submitted work for the juried show, which has pottery, sculpture, jewelry, furniture, paintings, and fabric art. It's a remarkable event and a wonderful showcase for Vermonters' work.

Other Recreational Pursuits

If a glitzy summer resort just isn't your thing, the town of Stratton has more primitive recreational pursuits that might interest you.

The Grout Pond Recreation Area in the Green Mountain National Forest has campsites, three cabins, and two shelters. You can picnic on the grounds and swim in the 79-acre pond. There are no lifeguards. Canoeing and windsurfing are permitted. Only small boats are allowed in the lake, providing you carry them in approximately 30 feet. There's good bass, pickerel, perch, sunfish, and bullhead fishing. Once owned by the Boy Scouts of America, the land was sold to the Green Mountain National Forest in 1979.

The area has old logging roads and hiking trails, as well as remnants of its previous dwellers, nineteenth-century white settlers who unsuccessfully tried their hand at farming. Logging was the predominant industry in the 1930s and 1940s. In the winter, you can cross-country ski or snowmobile on the relatively flat terrain.

Access to Grout Pond is from the southern boundary of the town of Stratton. The 1600-acre area is 12 miles east of the town of Arlington on the old dirt Arlington-Stratton Road now called Forest Road 6.

You can also pick up the Long Trail/Appalachian Trail on Forest Road 6, which is called the Kelley Stand Road in Arlington, and hike approximately four miles to Stratton Pond. Unlike the easy terrain trails around Grout Pond, this hike to Stratton Pond is rated difficult by the forest service.

For more information, contact the Manchester Ranger District Office in Manchester. They are most helpful about directions, difficulty, and access for all recreational areas.

The Manchester Area: Dorset, Pawlet, and Rupert

Dorset Village, home to the first Vermont constitutional conventions, has a lot to offer the visitor in the way of quiet splendor. Besides an excellent summer theater, well-established country inns, and restaurants in the quintessential Vermont village on Route 30, the town of Dorset has a multitude of outdoor activities and attractions, including the old quarry swimming hole and Emerald Lake State Park.

Farther north on Route 30, the Mettowee Valley towns of Pawlet and Rupert provide a glimpse of working dairy farms and some of the most beautiful terrain in Southern Vermont. Pawlet has its down-home Station Restaurant for hungry travelers, and Rupert is home to the Merck Foundation and Farmland Center on Route 315, a 2,700-acre nonprofit preserve for walking, hiking, cross-country skiing, and outdoor nature programs.

Dorset

Approximately five miles north of Manchester on Route 30 is the pristine little town of Dorset, a well-preserved community with a charming town green. Crisply painted white-clapboard houses with green shutters border this unspoiled expanse of greenery located on Church Street, so-called because of the massive Neogothic Revival Congregational church, the centerpiece of Dorset. Farther up Church Street is the Dorset Pond, and just past the pond, the road connects with West Road.

On the corner of Church Street and Route 30 is the Dorset Inn, built in 1796, called the oldest continuously operating inn in Vermont. Off Church Street is the famous Dorset Playhouse, where amateur and professional thespians provide first-rate productions throughout the year. North Dorset, located on Route 7, on the other side of Danby Mountain, is also home to Emerald Lake State Park. Rich in history, Dorset is a lovely village to explore.

Historical Perspective

Fifteen years after a New Hampshire grant established the town of Dorset, the first Vermont convention was held there in 1776. According to historical accounts, residents itching for independence met several times at the Cephas Kent Tavern in Dorset to draft Vermont's constitution. The Kent Neighborhood Historic District, located a couple of miles from the Dorset green, is listed in the National

Register of Historic Places as the site of the first constitutional conventions. At the intersection of Nichols Hill and West Road, a historic marker recalls the event.

Eight years after Vermont issued its declaration of independence in 1777, Isaac Underhill and Reuben Bloomer opened what is considered to be the first marble quarry in the United States in South Dorset. The quarry on Route 30, now a popular and unusual swimming hole, was later owned by George B. Holley and Spafford H. West. Around 1907, the Norcross-West quarry, as it was called, produced the marble pillars for the New York Public Library. During the heyday of quarrying, Dorset boasted no fewer than 28 quarries. But the marble sources were depleted and quarrying in Dorset became obsolete around the World War I era, according to historical accounts.

A landmark hostelry is the Dorset Inn built in 1796 on the corner of Church Street and Route 30. It is the oldest continuously operating inn in the state of Vermont; leather-bound volumes of guest registers reveal some of its history. The inn, along with 60 buildings in downtown Dorset (including the public library, formerly Gray's Tavern, located across from the inn) are on the National Register of Historic Places. Another magnificent architectural example of a bygone era is the Barrows House Inn, located just south of the village on Route 30.

In the mid- to late nineteenth century, Dorset was discovered by an affluent metropolitan clientele as a wonderful vacation spot and since that time has enjoyed a special status. Generation after generation of these families continue to summer or permanently reside in this sought-after community. The privately owned and operated Dorset Field Club, for example, was established in 1896 and has one of the oldest nine-hole golf courses in the United States.

Dorset has long been known as an artists' and writers' resort. In the 1920s, a group of residents successfully relocated two pre-revolutionary war barns onto Cheney Road, located off Church Street, for the Dorset Playhouse. The theater is owned by the Dorset Players, Inc. and rented each summer to the professional Dorset Theatre Festival. During the year, amateur thespians produce plays for the general public at the rustic structure. The Colony House on Church Street provides housing for the actors during the summer months; at other times of the year, the facility is available to playwrights and writers.

John Patrick Shanley, who wrote the screenplay for the Academy Award winning movie *Moonstruck*, was a writer in residence several years ago when the Dorset Theatre Festival produced one of his first plays, *Gorilla*, an unusual fantasy that revealed some of his talent.

Attractions, Recreational Pursuits

The much-respected Dorset Theatre Festival continues to draw visitors from in and around the Manchester and the Mountains area. Under the auspices of John Nassivera and Jill Charles, the DTF offers high-quality theater during the summer months. Unlike other theater festivals on the straw hat circuit, the Dorset Theatre Festival has a nice mixture of musicals, dramas, comedies, and untested new works. Be sure and catch a performance while you're here.

You can combine your visit to the Dorset Playhouse, which has productions until Labor Day, with deluxe gourmet fare at one of the four fine restaurants this small town has to offer. Fine food is served at the Dorset Inn, Barrows House, L'Auberge, and the Chantecleer in East Dorset. Probably the best-kept secret is the less-expensive tavern fare at the Dorset Inn, which offers Chef Sissy Hicks's fine cooking in addition to the main dining room menu. Reservations are requested at both the main dining room and tavern. Jackets are a must for the dining room.

If you're looking for a quiet getaway that's close to all Manchester and the Mountains amenities, Dorset has several inns worth considering. The 200-year-old Barrows House on Route 30 is a romantic old inn with 28 rooms, outdoor heated pool, tennis courts, and sauna. It has eight buildings on 11 manicured acres. Right up the road is the Cornucopia, a tastefully decorated bed and breakfast with 5 rooms, some with fireplaces, and a cottage suite with a fireplace and loft bedroom. The Dorset Inn has 35 guest rooms all in one building and a sitting room with a mammoth fireplace. Across from the inn is the Dovetail Inn, a modest bed and breakfast that once was part of the Dorset Inn.

All these inns are within walking distance of the green, the library, and Peltier's Market, a pricey convenience store that stocks gourmet wines and cheeses in addition to grocery items. On occasion, comedian Dom DeLuise, who has a home in Dorset, has been seen browsing through the merchandise and bantering with other customers.

Another village attraction is the Dorset Framery, run by Ace and Mary Rita Manley. In addition to custom framing, the Manleys have a small gallery featuring the works of local artists, like Natalee Everett-Goodman, and noted outdoor artists like Ogden Pleissner. The Country Cachet, across from the Dorset Inn, features fine linens, antiques, and accessories.

Dorset has two swimming areas — one regulated in the confines of the Emerald Lake State Park in North Dorset and the other an unconventional rustic spot just south of the village on Route 30 known as "The Quarry." The abandoned West-Norcross quarry is a popular swimming hole during hot weather. It's the local teenagers' hangout. The water is usually icy cold given its marble lining, and it doesn't start to warm up until late in the season (if then). There's a little path around the quarry, but be forewarned. It's not a place to swim for young children, and there's no lifeguard or other amenities. You can't miss the quarry even though it's hidden behind the trees; an abundance of cars parked on either side of the road marks the spot about a mile and a half south of the village.

Emerald Lake State Park is located on Route 7 north of Manchester in North Dorset. This is a wonderful spot. There's a playground for children, picnic tables and fireplaces, a concession stand, and 105 camping sites. There are marked nature and hiking trails around the lake, once known as Dorset Pond, and you can rent canoe and paddleboats. Swimming areas are roped off, and there is a lifeguard on duty. You can also fish for yellow perch, northern pike, smallmouth bass, and panfish.

Bicyclists particularly enjoy Dorset and can often be found sprawled on the green munching on sandwiches and drinks from Peltier's. A picturesque ride during summer or foliage (on a bike or in a car) is the Dorset West Road, which connects Route 30 south in Dorset with Route 30 north in East Rupert. West Road also connects with Church Street. The West Road has some magnificent estates, including the enormous marble mansion called the Manley-LeFevre House, which is privately owned. It was built in 1802 and was featured several years back, along with some outstanding Manchester domiciles, in the posh *Town and Country* magazine.

For adventurous hikers, Dorset has some scenic tours, too. A favorite is to Owl's Head, that mountain you see from the road with a rounded top not unlike the head of an owl. Just beyond the quarry on Route 30, take Kelley Road and follow the signs to the Black Rock condominium project. Just before the development, go right and follow a dirt road that crosses a small brook and then goes southeasterly past a hunting cabin. Here's where you park.

On foot, turn left just short of the camp and continue to a crossroad, once used, according to local lore, for transporting marble from the Gettysburg Quarry. This will lead you to a site near Morse Hill Road near the Dorset Elementary School. Bear left, toward the quarry, but just before it there's a path on the right.

This will take you to another road where you'll travel southeasterly to the top of Owl's Head.

Pawlet and Rupert

A day trip to the villages of Rupert and Pawlet, about 15 miles north of Manchester, is something to look forward to if you're interested in seeing the countryside and some of the working farms that are the backbone of the Green Mountain state. Given its rolling hills and beautiful, unspoiled terrain, it's difficult to believe North Rupert and Pawlet are such a short distance from the commercialized Manchester, a fact that has not gone unnoticed by valley residents.

The growth and development that changed the face of Manchester is spreading up the rural Mettowee Valley, escalating land prices and threatening the existence of rural Vermont. Farms are becoming a vanishing breed in these parts, but there's a staunch movement afoot in Pawlet and the other Mettowee Valley town of North Rupert to preserve the few farms left in the area. The Mettowee Valley Conservation Project is hard at work on an innovative method of land conservation whereby covenants are placed on large tracts of land thereby preserving the open space for posterity.

The rural Mettowee Valley follows Route 30 north of Dorset Village. In about two miles, you'll arrive at the intersection of Route 315 just over the line in East Rupert. If you turn left here, you'll climb Rupert Mountain going west into Rupert and West Rupert. At the top of the mountain are some lovely farms and the entrance to the nonprofit Merck Foundation where you can ski, hike, or enjoy nature programs.

If you continue north on Route 30 to Pawlet, you'll pass through the most picturesque farm country in the Mettowee Valley, named for the Mettowee River that flows north and west into New York State.

Historical Perspective

According to *Vermont Place-Names*, the Mettowee is an Indian name, but its origin is uncertain. The Natick Indians have a similar word that meant "poplar trees," and the Narragansett's meaning was "black earth." Both apply in this case. However, given the fertile valley around the river, we vote for the Narragansett option.

Route 30, by the way, becomes a confusing display of choices when you hit downtown Pawlet; you want to make a sharp (sharp!) left for the Station Restaurant and just about backtrack from the direction you came. The other options include bearing left and continuing north on Route 30 or going north on Route 133 to Middletown Springs. Pawlet's "downtown" consists of several old, three-story buildings; one has a porch for each level.

The Vermont Gazetteer of Vermont Heritage says the town was settled in 1761, and Remember Baker, a Green Mountain Boy, ran a gristmill here in 1768. Known as the "Terror of the Torries," Herrick's Rangers were organized in Pawlet in 1777. Pawlet was also home to Philo Stewart, who invented the cast-iron cook stove. More than a century ago, Pawlet was famous for stove manufacturing.

Neighboring Rupert was also settled in 1761, and one of its first settlers, Reuben Harmon, minted coins for Vermont in East Rupert in 1785. A historical marker on Route 315 recounts the state's only mint, which operated from 1785 to 1788. It was abandoned when the federal government came into being in 1789. The mint building, originally located on Hagar Brook, was moved to the Graf farm in North Rupert. According to *Vermont Place-Names*, Rupert was a populous community; it had 1,034 residents in 1791. At one time Rupert had four post offices, one in each village. Today there are only two left, one in Rupert and the second in West Rupert.

Attractions, Recreational Pursuits

Although there are definite signs that gentrification has already arrived in Rupert and Pawlet given land prices, the stretch of road after the intersection of Route 315 easily dispels that premise. It has some of the most beautiful farm country in Vermont. Traveling along this picturesque stretch is a treat in and of itself, and it's a marvelous experience in any season of the year.

Gentle rolling hills — bright green in summer and somber brown in winter — are dotted with holstein cows freely grazing the fields. Classic farmhouses with too many barns to count, some in a state of disrepair, others immaculately maintained, abut the road, as does the Mettowee River, which meanders under various sections. The Mettowee usually takes a back-row seat to the Battenkill for fishing, but avid fishing enthusiasts claim it is a wonderful river to fish. There's rainbow trout, brown trout, and native brook trout in its waters. There's a parking area about a mile north of Route 315 on the left-hand side of the road. There are no signs, so go slowly or you'll miss it.

The mountain views are long, uninterrupted, and breathtaking. Experiencing this wide expanse of open space is akin to stepping outdoors and taking a large gulp of fresh air after being cooped in a stuffy room. It is particularly impressive at dusk during the summer or winter when the setting sun produces a magnificent display of mauves, reds, and golds or, on a moonlit night, when the barns' tin roofs brilliantly reflect the light.

Occasionally, there'll be a flock of woolly sheep, beige and baaing, instead of Vermont's larger black-and-white trademarks. And inevitably there'll be a farmer on an old red tractor cutting hay or corn or spreading manure in the spring and fall.

The earthy smells wafting in your car window may cause you to wrinkle your nose, but they, too, are part of the experience. After the initial blast, you won't notice them. You'll probably get behind a slow-moving, enormous stainless steel milk truck on its way to or from a dairy barn. Be patient; sit back and enjoy the scenery. This is Vermont's finest.

If at all possible, schedule your trip to Pawlet so you can have breakfast or lunch at The Station. This local hot spot serves dinner only in the summer, but you might want to call ahead to verify this. The Station, as it is aptly named, is literally an 84-year-old railroad station that was moved from South Wallingford to its present location in Pawlet, just up from Mach's General Store, which is at the corner.

The Station, depending on the season, opens at 6:30 or 7:00 A.M., and it is a meeting place for the local farmers as well as celebrities who pop in unexpectedly. Movie star Michael J. Fox has been a patron at The Station and so has William A. Fowler, a Nobel Prize winner for physics who visits his daughter, a Pawlet resident. You're just as likely to see a brand new Volvo station wagon in the parking lot next to a dusty, 10-year-old pickup truck.

Inside, locals trade the latest gossip, and many regulars hang their coffee mugs on the shelf around the top of the counter. Governor Richard Snelling has sampled coffee at The Station several times, and his coffee cup hangs with the rest. There are framed photographs, some of them old black-and-whites, of railroad memorabilia and customers. The decor is early 1950s, with the exception of the original wainscoting, lighting fixtures, and benches.

When you're done with your meal, walk across the street to the Pawlet Potter. Marion Waldo MacChesney has been producing ceramic sculptures and sponge-ware pottery in the lower floor of the impressive corner brick building for more than 15 years. Her work has been written up in *House Beautiful, Town and Country*, and *Country Living* magazines. It's a working studio, so you can view the process firsthand. Upstairs is the Vermont Renaissance Gallery, which features local artists.

If you're in town in the evening, The Barn Steak House has your basic steak menu and sometimes a few specials. Occasionally, there's live music downstairs in the tavern.

Just below this complex back on Route 30 is the Penelope Nelson Collection along with East West Antiques, both housed in a huge barn right on the road. For almost two decades, Mrs. Nelson has been designing natural fabrics such as silk or cotton for apparel. A few years back, Mrs. Nelson collaborated with her husband, Courtney, for East West Antiques, which specializes in huge pieces of scrub pine furniture from Ireland, Indonesian reproductions and antiques, and carved teak pieces from Bali. The juxtaposition of these exotic pieces in an old Vermont barn creates an interesting effect.

If you continue on Route 30 north, the pastoral setting is evident but not as dramatic. You'll also pass Bus Mars's auctioneer barn. In the business since the 1940s, Mr. Mars is a folk hero around these parts. His auctions are always full, and some come just to see the show rather than to buy. Check the local papers and bulletin boards for information on Mars's auctions.

A wonderful Rupert resource to explore is the 2,700-acre Merck Forest and Farmland Center on Route 315 between East and West Rupert. This is the spot for walking, hiking, cross-country skiing, snowshoeing, camping, fishing, swimming, and picnicking. There are Belgian draft horses, turkeys, chickens, and sheep for the youngsters and a small museum with stuffed birds, a table with pelts, skulls, bark and claws, and a butterfly and moth collection. Camping at Merck is of the primitive variety; there are five small cabins and five lean-tos. There are privies but no showers and no length on the duration of your stay.

The Merck Forest and Farmland Access Road is only open during the summer and fall. In the winter, cross-country skiers park at the winter parking lot abutting Route 315 and ski in the access road to the gate where you can pick up a map and make a donation. The foundation has no groomed trails; it's all back-country skiing and you'll find yourself bushwhacking in many instances.

The other times of the year, when the access road is open, you can drive up the parking lot in the woods next to the entrance gate. From there, it's about a quarter of a mile on foot to the Merck Farmland Center, the barn, and visitors' center. When you reach the clearing, the road descends and you can see the building complex ahead of you. Take a minute to turn around for the most spectacular mountain views.

The foundation also runs day camp programs for children during the summer. In addition, it sponsors outdoor nature programs for people of all ages on weekends. During the maple sugaring season, for example, you can watch the sap being boiled (did you know it takes 40 gallons of sap to make 1 gallon of maple syrup?) and sample maple treats.

If you continue traveling past the Merck Foundation on Route 315, there are many signs near barns advertising maple syrup for sale. Most farmers sell maple syrup, although many are not interested in having their operation scrutinized by visitors. If you're interested in watching the process, the Vermont Department of Agriculture prints a brochure available at most chambers of commerce called "Vermont Maple Sugarhouses," which lists sapping operations that welcome visitors.

The Manchester Area North: Poultney and Wells, Danby and Mount Tabor

Two recreational communities are located north of Manchester. One is Lake Saint Catherine in the towns of Wells and Poultney on Route 30, and the other is the towns of Danby and Mount Tabor on Route 7.

The town of Danby, home to one of Vermont's first millionaires and the quarry that produced the marble for the U.S. Supreme Court building in Washington, D.C., is located about 15 miles north of Manchester on Route 7. While Danby is experiencing a renaissance of sorts, Mount Tabor is a tiny town in the Green Mountain National Forest that has numerous recreation sites.

Wells and Poultney are home to Lake Saint Catherine, a summer resort community that's as funky and down-home as Manchester is upscale and pricey. As an added attraction, Poultney has a rich history all its own.

Poultney and Wells

Poultney, a tiny college town of 3,000, is about 40 minutes north on Route 30 out of Manchester. You'll drive through the picturesque Mettowee River Valley, passing the towns of Dorset, East Rupert, Pawlet, West Pawlet, then Wells and Poultney, two towns that share pristine Lake Saint Catherine.

Lake Saint Catherine is a spring-fed little jewel that's approximately seven miles long and about a mile to a mile and a half wide. This body of water is 65 feet at the deepest point, and its natural limestone bottom helps neutralize acid rain. It has a reputation as being one of the cleanest lakes in the state, making it a sought-after haven for water sports and recreation.

Summer cottages line the lake in both Wells and Poultney, and there's a public boat access as well as a public beach in Lake Saint Catherine State Park. Fishermen flock to the lake in spring, summer, and fall for rainbow trout, lake trout, smelt, yellow perch, northern pike, largemouth bass, smallmouth bass, bullhead, and panfish. It's a tranquil setting for a low-key vacation that centers on the basics: swimming, boating, fishing, and windsurfing.

Historical Perspective

Details about the town of Wells's history are sketchy at best. The village has always been sparsely populated. According to *Vermont Place-Names*, a post office was established there in 1824. Lewisville was the only thriving hamlet, thanks to resident Benjamin Lewis who built a cheese manufacturing plant there in 1875. The historical account tells us the factory churned out 80,000 pounds of cheese a year in the late 1880s.

Poultney, on the other hand, is a town with a vibrant history and numerous architectural landmarks.

> "Lookin' for Poultney, y'say?" The old man shuffled closer to the car. "Well, you're in it now. 'Less ya want East Poultney. Which is where Poultney used to be. When Poultney was West Poultney, that is."
>
> I knew I had crossed the line into my home state. This is the kind of conversational web Vermonters delight in weaving.
>
> — Ethel A. Starbird in *National Geographic*

The above anecdote is proudly reprinted in its entirety in the directory provided by the Poultney Area Chamber of Commerce. What the old-timer was referring to is that the present Poultney started off as a tiny village known as West Poultney, which blossomed with the coming of the railroad in 1848 into a full-fledged community. The original town of Poultney, located along the Poultney River a mile or so down the road, then became East Poultney.

Just before the traffic light in Poultney on Route 30, there's a historical marker for Poultney's two famous residents: Horace Greeley, founder of the *New York Herald Tribune*, who lived there during the 1820s and George Jones, cofounder and editor of the *New York Times*, who was born and raised in Poultney. Horace Greeley's residence, the Eagle Tavern, is still standing in East Poultney.

At the end of the main street is Green Mountain College, an imposing complex of brick structures built around 1834. Once a two-year women's college, Green Mountain expanded several years back to include men and four-year baccalaureate programs. One of the more noteworthy buildings is Ames Hall, a replica of the original Troy Conference Academy rebuilt in 1908. Through the generosity of Jane Ames, whose two children graduated from the Troy Conference Academy, the four-story brick edifice was rebuilt on the foundation of the old building, which was destroyed by fire.

Local lore has it that Lake Saint Catherine received its name from a group of Jesuit priests during the French and Indian War. The party was traveling from Connecticut to Quebec and happened to arrive at the lake on Saint Catherine's Day.

According to *Vermont Place-Names*, Lake Saint Catherine was a popular resort community at the turn of the century. Lake View House, a huge hotel on the western shore of the lake, beckoned vacationers into its fold. The onset of World War I hastened the demise of the resort, and it was eventually torn down.

Today, the only lakeside commercial lodging place is the Lake Saint Catherine Inn. Co-owner Pat Endlich said the inn catered to metropolitanites seeking vacation refuge in the country in the 1920s and 1930s. Lake Saint Catherine was also home to the Arrowhead Boys' Camp and the Kinni-Kinnic Girls' Camp, which comedienne Joan Rivers attended and has mentioned in her monologues. If you continue on Route 30 to Poultney, you'll pass a Kinni-Kinnic sign; the site, however, is privately owned.

Attractions, Recreational Pursuits

If you're out for a vacation with upscale resort-type amenities, Lake Saint Catherine is not the place for you. Individual cottage rentals obtained through local real estate agents may afford you the occasional Jacuzzi or hot tub, but more often than not the best-equipped rental cottage will have only a black-and-white TV, if there's one at all. The Lake Saint Catherine Inn, a charming 35-room inn; Sailing Winds, a place to rent boats and sailboards; and Marina Saint Catherine are the only three commercial establishments right on the lake. The lakeside community prides itself on the lack of commercialization. It relies on its natural attributes to lure visitors to the area, and these wonderful qualities are what keeps tourists returning year after year.

The Lake Saint Catherine Inn sits back from the road, a two-story building with an unassuming exterior of natural wood siding weathered gray and brown and an inviting front porch with a bulletin board crammed full of event notices for things to do in the area. Inside, there are cheery gingham curtains and a well-kept entryway with rest rooms on the right. The comfortable living room beckons the weary traveler, and innkeepers Pat and Ray Endlich are accommodating and pleasant.

There's no shortage of things to do, of course. If you tire of water sports, there's golf at the Lake Saint Catherine Country Club and public tennis courts in Poultney. And within an hour's drive, there's all those things you might otherwise miss: shopping, theater, museums, etc.

Driving to the lake on Route 30, you'll hit Wells before Poultney. Unlike Poultney, Wells is a quiet town with few diversions other than the lake. The center of Wells seems to be at the intersection of Route 30 and North Street, which becomes Lake Hill Road. You'll pass the Wells Country Store before hitting the intersection, which boasts Nancy's Country Store on the right north corner, definitely a worthwhile stop. Besides selling hunting and fishing licenses, the store boasts a bulletin board out front with all the information you'll need for your stay. Owners Nancy and Bob Dingman are helpful and friendly, and you can pick up a newspaper, magazine, paperback, or a quart of milk in addition to anything you might have forgotten. Catty-corner to the store is an ice-cream parlor in the old Lewis House, which is open only in the summer and fall months.

Across Route 30 from Nancy's Country Store is a dark brown stained building with royal blue trim. That's the Wells Post Office. You can either make a left at the intersection onto North Street (a.k.a. Lake Hill Road), which will take you past the little lake (a small body of water next to Lake Saint Catherine) and the Lake Hill Farm Gift Shop and the tiny A & S Farm Stand, or you can continue on Route 30 north. At the Lake Hill Farm Gift Shop, you'll have to make a right past the Lake Saint Catherine Marina, which will lead you back onto Route 30, or a left, which skirts around the west side of the lake where there are nice views in summer and fall.

Staying on Route 30 through the intersection where Nancy's Country Store is located, you'll ultimately end up in Poultney but not before you pass the lake and various landmarks you don't want to miss. A few miles up the road, there'll be a sign indicating a summer resort area, so slow down because it is thickly settled. Soon after, you can catch glimpses of the lake on your left. Just before Cones Point, a road that leads to the Lake Saint Catherine Inn, is Cones Point Miniature Golf on your left. This a great way to spend a warm summer's evening with the kids. There's ice cream and soft drinks there, too, as well as a small arcade with whiffle ball and video games. Coming up on the left is the road Cones Point, which has numerous cottages and the inn.

On the way to Poultney you'll pass the Lake Saint Catherine Country Club, with its 18-hole golf course, and Whispering Pines, an informal family eatery with everything from hot dogs to prime rib. It's open all year-round, but the miniature golf course near the premises is only seasonal.

Poultney's Main Street is a broad avenue with a variety of shops and restaurants worth exploring. Poultney, unlike too many Vermont communities, has managed to hold on to its Main Street, a vibrant addition to the community. Too many Main Streets fall victim to changing times and the popularity of shopping centers or malls. But Poultney's Main Street is a busy, thriving thoroughfare, perhaps because Green Mountain College at the end of Main Street has been aggressive in luring students to the community. There's the old Poultney Luncheonette, one of the last strongholds that serves breakfast all day. You can sit at the old-fashioned counter or be served at a table. Incredible Edibles has sandwiches, homemade hot dishes, and baked goods. How refreshing to breeze into Poultney, stop at Incredible Edibles on Main Street for a delicious, hefty sandwich, accompanied by a glass of homemade ice tea, and get quite a bit of change back from your five-dollar bill. Poultney has quite a few stores you'll want to take your time to browse through, like the vintage clothing store Flames and Flowers or Heartstrings on nearby College Street.

Poultney is also home to Lake Saint Catherine State Park, a 117-acre facility right on the lake with 61 camping sites, including 10 lean-tos. Visitors can swim, sailboard, fish, and picnic. There's a playground for the children, nature museum, and trail. The park has a boat ramp, and you can rent boats there as well. Lake Saint Catherine is a popular windsurfing haven for locals.

Danby and Mount Tabor

A 20-minute ride north of Manchester on Route 7 brings you to the sister towns of Danby and Mount Tabor, two communities with an interesting history. Danby, a town where one of Vermont's first millionaires left his mark, is undergoing a revitalization to recapture some of its lost nineteenth-century grandeur. Many of its Main Street buildings on the National Register of Historic Places have been refurbished and turned into posh retail shops and boutiques. And the 17-room Silas Griffith Inn, along with the smaller Quail's Nest Inn, is flourishing. Tiny Mount Tabor remains a quiet, remote Vermont community with 25,000 of its 27,000 acres in the Green Mountain National Forest. It has none of the upscale amenities of its neighbors. Only the primitive beauty of its recreation areas lures visitors to town.

Historical Perspective

What the two towns of Danby and Mount Tabor have in common, besides close proximity and a shared elementary school, is the legacy of lumber baron Silas Griffith who made his fortune from Mount Tabor's terrain. Mr. Griffith started out as a grocery store merchant in Danby in 1861, building a three-story structure innovative in design for the times. The building is still standing and part of the Danby Green development. Eleven years later, Mr. Griffith went into the charcoal and lumber business with a partner and amassed a fortune. When Mr. Griffith died, he left half of his estate to the town of Danby where he resided. Funds built the imposing yellow brick S. L. Griffith Memorial Library on Main Street, and there were endowments to the church and school. Probably the most noteworthy of the lot is the annual Christmas fund, which more than 75 years after his death provides children in Danby and Mount Tabor with a gift, candy, and an orange.

From 1891 to 1905, Mount Tabor was known as Griffith because of all the holdings the lumber baron had in town; most of the mail passing through the Mount Tabor Post Office was for one of Mr. Griffith's many industries. Mount Tabor was incorporated as "Harwich," but in 1803 the residents had the name changed to Mount Tabor, in honor of revolutionary war veteran Gideon Tabor. Mr. Tabor had served as town clerk for 28 years and had an impressive record of public service, according to Vermont Place-Names. He died in 1824.

Marble quarrying has been a solid industry in this community since 1905. The industry enjoyed a boom from 1840 to 1870 in Danby Borough, as the village of Danby was then called, which resulted in the community growing faster than the original town center, Danby Four Corners. However, when Western Vermont Railroad went bankrupt in 1857, it was the beginning of the end for the marble industry, which folded completely in 1870. When marble became a popular building material again at the turn of the century, the Vermont Marble Company purchased the Western Vermont Marble Company and resumed quarrying. Vermont Marble still operates the largest underground marble quarry in the world here.

Attractions, Recreational Pursuits

Many Main Street sites in Danby are listed on the National Register of Historic Places. A few years back summer resident Anne Rothman bought up many of the dilapidated buildings and has been slowly restoring them to prominence. Her vision is the Danby Green, a series of upscale shops she hopes will rival and supercede in popularity bustling Manchester to the south. Not that she envisions Danby becoming the size and scope of Manchester. On the contrary, Mrs. Rothman is optimistic the cozy storefronts of Danby will attract discerning shoppers who prefer small villages.

Mrs. Rothman's predecessor in this regard was none other than Pulitzer Prize winning author Pearl S. Buck, who moved to Danby in 1970 and planned to restore the community to grandeur. According to a magazine interview with Ms. Buck, the simplicity of small-town Danby reminded her of the Chinese villages where she grew up. Like Mrs. Rothman, the author purchased many houses in the downtown area. Unfortunately, the community was skeptical of Ms. Buck's intentions and she never received their support. Ms. Buck died three years after she moved to Danby, and her only legacy was a huge, unfinished 6,000-square-foot addition to her house that still has the black tar paper and metallic insulation for siding.

Besides the Danby Green, other attractions in Danby include the Peel Gallery of Fine Art, a charming little gallery north of town with a magnificent steel sculpture on the front lawn visible from Route 7. The White Dog Tavern, which serves dinner nightly and lunch on weekends, is reported to have good food. Silas Griffith's old home built in 1891 is now the Silas Griffith Inn, a comfortable hostelry with a public restaurant. Up the road, near the Danby Antiques Center, is the Quail's Nest, an intimate inn that is more like a home than a commercial establishment.

Mount Tabor boasts several magnificent recreational sites in the Green Mountain National Forest. Big Branch off Forest Road 10, which intersects with Route 7 just after the Country Garden on the east side of the road, is a terrific spot for a picnic during foliage. You can see down the valley for miles and hear the Big Branch down below. A 0.8-mile trail rated "moderately difficult" by the Green Mountain Forest Service will take you down to the river.

A family excursion on the Long Trail, approximately two miles in length, will take you to Little Rock Pond where there are swimming and camping facilities. If you follow Forest Road 10 from Danby, which runs easterly into the town of Mount Tabor, you come to the Long Trail crossing and parking area where you can leave your car. From here, you can hike northerly on level terrain to the pond.

Another hike in Mount Tabor will take you to Baker Peak, elevation 2,840, and offers a good view of the Dorset Peak marble quarries. Or, you can take the trail to Griffith Lake, which is on the border of Peru. The turnoff is about two miles past Emerald Lake State Park where there is a Green Mountain National Forest sign. Take a right and follow the sign to the parking area. About two miles in, the blue blazed trail takes you to McGinn Brook, where you can either turn left and go another mile to Baker Peak or turn right and hike 1.5 miles to Griffith Lake. The Long Trail/Appalachian Trail has a two-mile connector between the two.

Be sure and stop in the Green Mountain Forest Service office in Manchester on Routes 11-30 for free pamphlets and brochures with detailed maps of the above hikes and others in the area. The rangers in the office are extremely helpful.

Manchester and the Mountains Essentials

Important Information

Municipal Services

Bondville (Winhall) Town Clerk: 297-2122.
Bondville Police: 297-2121.
Bondville Fire & Ambulance: 824-3166.
Danby Town Clerk: 293-5136.
Danby Police: 773-9102.
Danby Fire & Ambulance: 293-5100; 362-2121.
Dorset Town Clerk: 362-1178.
Dorset Police: 362-3639.
Dorset Fire & Ambulance: 362-2121.
Landgrove Town Clerk: 824-371.
Landgrove Police: 824-3915.
Landgrove Fire & Ambulance: 824-3166.
Londonderry Town Clerk: 824-3356.
Londonderry Police: 824-3915.
Londonderry Fire & Ambulance: 824-3166.
Manchester Town Clerk: 362-1315.
Manchester Police: 362-2121.
Manchester Fire & Ambulance: 362-2121.
Pawlet Town Clerk: 325-3309.
Pawlet Police: 773-9101.

Pawlet Fire & Ambulance: 325-3400; (518) 642-1155.
Peru Town Hall: 824-3065.
Peru Police: 824-3915.
Peru Fire & Ambulance: 824-3166.
Poultney Town Hall: 287-5761; Village Office: 287-4003.
Poultney Police: 773-9101.
Poultney Fire & Ambulance: 287-9360; 287-9510.
Rupert Town Clerk: 394-7728.
Rupert Police: 394-7778 or 362-3639.
Rupert Fire & Ambulance: (518) 747-3325; (518) 854-3811.
Stratton Town Clerk: 896-6140.
Stratton Mountain Police: 297-2200.
Stratton Fire & Ambulance: 824-3166.
Wells Town Clerk: 645-0188.
Wells Police: State Police 773-9101.
Weston Town Clerk: 824-6645.
Weston Police: 824-3915.
Weston Fire & Ambulance: 824-3166.
Winhall Town Clerk: 297-2122.
Winhall Police: 297-2121.
Winhall Fire & Ambulance: 824-3166 or (603) 352-1100.

Medical Services

Manchester Medical Center, Rte. 7A, Manchester Center; 362-1263.
Mountain Valley Health Center, Rte. 11, Londonderry; 824-6901.
Northshire Medical Center, Rte. 7 North, Manchester Center; 362-4440.
Rutland Regional Medical Center, Rte. 4, Woodstock Rd., Rutland; 775-7111.
Southwest Vermont Medical Center, Dewey St., Bennington; 442-6361.

Veterinarians

Green Mountain Veterinary Hospital, Rtes. 11-30, Manchester; 362-2620.
Dr. Raymond Koch, East Manchester Rd., Manchester; 362-3570.
Poultney Veterinary Services, 46 East Main St., Poultney; 287-9292.
Rupert Veterinary Clinic, Rte. 153, Rupert; 394-7759.

Weather

New England Weather Associates, Manchester Center; 362-3000, 24-hour weather phone.
Channel 22 Resort Television, Manchester Center; 362-4800.

Tourist Information Services

Londonderry Chamber of Commerce, Box 58, Londonderry 05148; 824-8178.
Manchester and the Mountains Chamber of Commerce, Rte. 7, Manchester Center 05255; 362-2100.
Poultney Area Chamber of Commerce, Box 151, Poultney 05764; 287-9347.

Lodgings

Reservation Services

Area Lodging Service, Box 519, Londonderry 05148; 824-6915 (for Manchester and the Mountains areas).
Emerald Lake State Park, RD, Box 485, East Dorset 05253 (for a minimum six-night stay in campgrounds).
Lake St. Catherine State Park, RD 2, Box 230, Poultney 05764 (for a minimum six-night stay in state park campgrounds).
Magic Mountain, Bromley Mountain, Condominium Reservations; 824-5458 (minimum two nights).
Stratton Mountain Villa Reservations, Stratton Mountain 05155; 297-2200, out-of-state 800-843-6867 (minimum two-night stay).

Inns and B&Bs

BONDVILLE
Alpenrose Inn, Winhall Hollow Rd., Bondville (Winhall); 297-2750. Moderate. Breakfast. Seven rooms furnished with antiques; private baths. Down comforters. Fireplace in lounge. BYOB.
Bromley View Inn, Rte. 30, Bondville (between Stratton and Bromley Mountain ski areas); 297-1459. Moderate. Twelve rooms, private baths, pub, hot tubs, Modified American Plan available.
Red Fox Inn, Winhall Hollow Rd., Bondville; 297-2488. Inexpensive to moderate. Ten rooms, continental breakfast, public restaurant, tavern.

DANBY
Quail's Nest, Main St., Danby; 293-5099. Moderate. Charming little house, circa 1835, nicely decorated with antiques and handmade quilts. Full breakfast. Major credit cards.
Silas Griffith Inn, South Main St., Danby; 293-5567. Moderate. Seventeen-room Victorian inn, comfortable, fireplaces, restaurant. Full breakfast.

DORSET
Barrows House, Rte. 30, Dorset; 867-4455. Expensive. Twenty-eight rooms with private baths; pretty location on 11 acres. Tennis courts, heated pool, sauna, greenhouse dining room, pub.
Christmas Tree Bed and Breakfast, RR-1, Box 582, East Dorset; 362-4889. Moderate. Tiny inn. Full breakfast.
Cornucopia of Dorset, Rte. 30, Box 307, Dorset; 867-5751. Moderate. Delightful inn with five deluxe rooms, some with fireplaces. Cottage suite with loft bedroom, fireplace in living room. Full breakfast.

Dorset Inn, Rte. 30 and Church St.; 867-5500. Moderate to expensive. Breakfast and dinner included. Vermont's oldest continuously operating inn. Charming decor, restaurant, pub. No pets. Children by arrangement. Jackets requested in dining room.

Dorset Marble West Inn, West Rd., Box 847; 867-4155. Moderate. Breakfast. Seven rooms with private baths in country setting.

Dovetail Inn, Rte. 30 and Church St., Dorset; 867-5747. Moderate. Eleven rooms, one with fireplace and small kitchen. Breakfast, afternoon tea.

Inn at West View Farm, Rte. 30, Dorset; 867-5715. Moderate to expensive. (Formerly Village Auberge.) Full breakfast; Modified American Plan available. Ten rooms with private bath, sitting room, library. Gourmet restaurant on premises, L'Auberge, and tavern fare at Clancy's.

Little Lodge at Dorset, Rte. 30, Dorset; 867-4040. Moderate. Breakfast. Small inn right near the green; stenciled walls, cozy, five rooms, antiques, all private baths.

LANDGROVE

Village Inn at Landgrove, RFD Box 215; 824-6673. Moderate. Open fall, winter, and summer. Nineteen rooms, 15 with private baths, 4 with shared baths. Fall and winter, Modified American Plan. Summer rates include only breakfast. More than 15 kilometers of marked cross-country ski trails, all-weather paddle tennis court, two tennis courts, whirlpool spa, outdoor heated pool. Children's play gym, ping pong, bumper pool, pitch and putt golf. Large living room with fireplaces, game tables. No pets. Smoking permitted. Mastercard, Visa.

LONDONDERRY

Highland House, Rte. 100, RFD 1, Box 107, Londonderry; 824-3019. Moderate. Old 1842 white Colonial with 17 guest rooms. Full country breakfast.

Londonderry Inn, Rte. 100, South Londonderry 05155; 824-5226. Moderate. Twenty-five-room inn overlooking West River. Open all year. Outdoor pool, game room, jungle gym for children, shuffleboard, badminton. Bar, nice living room with fireplace. No credit cards. No pets.

Nordic Inn, Rte. 11, Londonderry; 824-6444. Expensive. Five-room inn with lounge, restaurant, game room. Includes breakfast and dinner. Cross-country ski area out the door. Summer, no meals, continental breakfast. Hiking trails.

Swiss Inn, Rte. 11, Londonderry; 824-3442. TV in rooms, game room. Located in ski country near Bromley, Magic, Stratton. Full breakfast. No pets. Major credit cards.

MANCHESTER

Barnstead Innstead, Box 988, Rte. 30, Manchester Center; 362-1619. Moderate. Nicely converted hay barn, in the heart of Manchester. Game room, heated pool. Walk to everything.

Birch Hill Inn, West Rd., Box 346, Manchester Village; 362-2761. Expensive. Lovely location five minutes from town, offers cross-country skiing, trout fishing, and pool in summer. Breakfast included. Home-cooked dinners available. No credit cards, no pets.

Brook-n-Hearth, Rtes. 11-30, Box 508, Manchester Center; 362-3604. Moderate. Small inn, full breakfast, game room, pool, wooded trails. Major credit cards.

1811 House, Rte. 7A, Manchester Village; 362-1811. Expensive. Elegant inn located in heart of village, 14 rooms with private baths, 6 with working fireplaces. Full breakfast, pub with darts and pool table. Major credit cards.

Inn at Manchester, Rte. 7A, Box 41, Manchester Village; 362-1793. Moderate. Old Victorian house, comfortable. Breakfast included. Pool. Major credit cards.

Inn at Willow Pond, Rte. 7 North, Manchester Center; 362-4733, 800-533-3533. Moderate to expensive. Forty-room, beautifully designed inn just north of town. Single rooms or suites with balconies, swimming pool, restaurant (breakfast and dinner), golf and tennis privileges, TV, lounge. Major credit cards.

Manchester Highlands Inn, Highland Ave., Manchester Center; 362-4565. Moderate. Includes full breakfast and afternoon snack. Pool, TV, lounge, game room. Major credit cards.

Reluctant Panther Inn, West Rd., Manchester Village; 362-2568. Moderate to expensive. Located in the heart of the village, 14 rooms, suites, public restaurant, lounge. Light breakfast. Major credit cards.

Seth Warner Bed and Breakfast, Box 281, Manchester Center; 362-3830. Moderate. Includes full breakfast. Five rooms, air-conditioning. Major credit cards.

Skylight Lodge, Rtes. 11-30, Manchester Center; 362-2566. Moderate. On the mountain road, close to Bromley and ski areas. Home-cooked meals, shared baths, bunk beds in doubles, dorms.

Skyline Inn — Atop Mt. Equinox, Rte. 7A, Manchester; 362-1113. Moderate. Fifteen-room inn, public restaurant, lounge, 360-degree views, game rooms. Major credit cards.

Sutton's Place, School St., Manchester Center; 362-1165. Inexpensive. No frills, but clean.

Village Country Inn, Rte. 7A, Manchester Village; 362-1792. Expensive. Includes breakfast and four-course dinner. Lovely decorated inn has single rooms or suites, tennis court, pool, golf privileges, lounge.

Wilburton Inn, River Rd., Manchester Village; 362-2500. Expensive. Includes full country breakfast. Wonderful turn-of-the-century mansion, 30 rooms, tennis courts, pool, public restaurant, lounge, game room. Major credit cards.

PERU

Johnny Seesaw's, Rte. 11, Peru; 824-5533. Expensive. Really rustic inn and cottages (one of first in local ski country) close to Bromley Mountain. Rooms with private baths, game room, pub, low-key. Modified American Plan.

Mountaineer Lodge, Rte. 11; 824-6267. Moderate. Twelve rooms, walk to Bromley Mountain. Outside hot tub, lounge with fireplace, kitchen available, BYOB.

Russell Inn, Main St.; 824-6631. Inexpensive to moderate, depending on the season. Old eight-room inn with shared bathrooms opened in 1945. Open in fall, winter, and early spring. Winter rates include breakfast and dinner. Other times, rates include only breakfast. Living room with fireplace. No credit cards. Clean and basic accommodations.

Wiley Inn, Box 37; 824-6600. Moderate to expensive, depending on the season. Seventeen rooms all with private baths. Family suites available. Winter rates have Modified American Plan; summer rates include only breakfast. Outdoor pool. Smoking in living areas only. Major credit cards.

POULTNEY

Eagle Tavern, on the green, East Poultney; 287-9498. Ethan Allen and his boys met here. New building erected in 1785 on old foundation. Six rooms; two with private baths, two share a bath. Two private rooms are in original ballroom and have domed ceilings. Furnished with antiques. Outdoor heated swimming pool. Smoking permitted in lounge only. European-style breakfast. Closed mid-October to mid-December and mid-March to mid-May.

Lake St. Catherine Inn, Cone's Point, Box 129; 287-9347. Moderate. Modified American Plan. Thirty-five rooms, 16 in main building, 19 in annex. Rural, homey, lakeside inn. Aluminum boats, sailboats, paddleboats, and canoes; free rentals for guests. Special packages for fishermen, families. No credit cards. Cash, personal or travelers' checks only.

Stonebridge Inn, 3 Beaman St.; 287-9849. Moderate. Five rooms with canopy beds, furnished with antiques. Two have private baths, one of them has a sitting room; three with shared bath; continental breakfast for guests only. Three common rooms downstairs, one with 40-inch TV. Major credit cards.

Tower Hall, 2 Bentley Ave.; 287-4004. Moderate. 1895 Victorian with wraparound porch. Three rooms, one with private bath and two with shared bath. Brass beds, rooms furnished with antiques. Sitting room with TV, tables for chess. Expanded continental breakfast. Open all year. Major credit cards. No pets. No children under eight.

WESTON

The Colonial House Inn and Motel, Box 138, Rte. 100 south of village, Weston; 824-6286. Moderate. Great views, carriage house living room, country breakfast and dinners. Cross-country skiing. BYOB. Open year-round.

Darling Family Inn, Rte. 100 north of village, Weston; 824-3223. Moderate. One-hundred-and-fifty-year-old inn furnished with American and English antiques. Fully equipped cottages, swimming pool, full breakfast. Open year-round.

Inn at Weston, Box 56, Rte. 100, Weston; 824-5804. Expensive (includes full breakfast and dinner). Inn circa 1848, walking distance of playhouse. Restaurant, full breakfast. Open year-round.

Inn on the Green, Box 104, Rte. 100, Weston; 824-6789. Moderate. Tiny inn on the picturesque Weston green. Four rooms, two with private baths. Antiques, fireplace, rocking chairs. Homemade full breakfast.

Wilder Homestead Inn, Lawrence Hill Rd., Weston; 824-8172. Moderate. 1827 brick house. Seven bedrooms, both shared and private bath, porch, antique furnishings, stenciling, canopy beds. Full breakfast. Walk to green. Restricted smoking. Open year-round.

Hotels, Motels, and Resorts

DANBY

Bradford at Mt. Tabor, Rte. 7, RFD-1, Box 99, Danby; 293-5186. Basic motel units. Restaurant on premises.

DORSET

Eyrie Motel, Rte. 7 North, RD-1, Box 501, East Dorset; 362-1208. Inexpensive to moderate. Near Emerald Lake State Park. High on bluff, 12 units with full bath, TV, radios, refrigerators. Mature guests. Continental breakfast. Triple A Mobil rating. Fireplace in lobby.

Marbledge Motor Inn and Restaurant, Rte. 7 North, Box 505, East Dorset; 362-1418. Inexpensive. Cable TV, lounge, dining room, home-cooked meals. Ski packages with meals.

LONDONDERRY

Blue Gentian Lodge, Londonderry; 824-5908. Moderate. Full country breakfast. Walk to Magic Mountain lifts. Cable TV, lounge with fireplace, two playrooms. BYOB.

Dostal's, Magic Mountain Access Rd., Londonderry; 824-6700. Moderate. Fifty-room Austrian lodge at the base of Magic Mountain. Outdoor-indoor pool, Jacuzzis, tennis court.

Inn at Magic Mountain, Magic Mountain, Londonderry; 824-6100. Toll-free 1-800-MAGIC IN. Twenty-five-room renovated inn. Color TV, refrigerators. Game rooms. Three hundred feet from slopes. Outdoor pool, sauna, whirlpool. Major credit cards.

Magic View Motel, Rte. 11, Londonderry; 824-3793. Inexpensive to moderate. TV, game room. No pets. Mastercard, Visa.

Snowdon Motel, Rte. 11, Londonderry; 824-6047. Inexpensive to moderate. Alpine chalet motel, AAA and Mobil rated. TV, radio. Close to Magic Mountain.

MANCHESTER

Aspen Motel, Box 548, Rte. 7, Manchester Center; 362-2450. Inexpensive to moderate, depending on season. Color TV, pools, social room, lawn games. Major credit cards.

Avalanche Motel, Box 1261, Rtes. 11-30, Manchester Center; 362-2622. Moderate. On the way to ski areas, ground level, pool, restaurant, lounge. Major credit cards.

Captain's Quarters, Box 925, Rte. 7A, Manchester Village; 362-1033. Inexpensive to moderate. Twelve units south of Manchester, cable TV. Major credit cards.

Carriage House Motel, Box 1263, Rte. 7, Manchester Center; 362-1706. Inexpensive to moderate. TV, pool.

Chalet Motel, Rtes. 11-30, Manchester Center; 362-1622, 800-343-9900. Inexpensive to moderate. On the way to ski areas, TV, movies, phones, free Jacuzzi. Restaurant. Major credit cards.

Equinox Hotel Resort and Spa, Rte. 7A, Manchester Village; 362-4700. Expensive. Deluxe, 144-room, year-round hotel in historic village with everything — tennis courts, pool, sauna, massage, Nautilus, aerobic classes. Two restaurants, lounge with entertainment, golf course. Major credit cards.

Four Winds Motel, Box 1243, Rte. 7 North, Manchester Center; 362-1105. Moderate. Basic motel located two miles north of town.

Kandahar Resort Lodge, Rtes. 11-30, Box 1841, Manchester Center; 824-5531. Inexpensive to moderate. TV in rooms, dining room, lounge with fireplace, sauna. AAA and Mobil Guide rated.

Manchester View Motel, Rte. 7, Box 1268, Manchester Center; 362-2739. Moderate. Four-diamond rating, incredible views, fireplaces, heated pool, close to Manchester Country Club. Major credit cards.

North Shire Motel, Rte. 7A, Box 413, Manchester; 362-2336. Moderate. Cathedral ceiling rooms, located two miles south of town, pool. Major credit cards.

Olympia Motor Lodge, Box 606, Rte. 7 North, Manchester Center; 362-1700. Moderate. Two-story motel, tennis courts, pool, golf privileges at Manchester Country Club. Breakfast seasonally. Major credit cards.

Palmer House Motel/Resort, Rte. 7, Manchester Center; 362-3600. Moderate. Meticulously manicured grounds, walk to town. Heated outdoor pool with Jacuzzi, indoor whirlpool and sauna, two tennis courts, nine-hole pitch and putt, stocked trout pond. Major credit cards.

Red Sled Motel, RR-1, Box 1925, Manchester Center; 362-2161. Moderate. Seventeen-room motel on the way to ski areas, pool.

Stamford Motel, Rte. 7, Box 2320, Manchester Center; 362-2342. Cable TV, golf, tennis privileges at Manchester Country Club, heated pool.

Toll Road Motor Inn, Box 813, Rtes. 11-30, Manchester Center; 362-1711. Moderate. On the way to the ski areas, swimming pool, golf and tennis privileges at Manchester Country Club.

Weathervane Motel, Rte. 7A, Box 378, Manchester Village; 362-2444. Moderate. South of the village, pool, golf and tennis privileges. Four-star AAA rating.

Wedgewood North Motel, Rte. 7, Manchester Center; 362-2145. Inexpensive to moderate. Ten-room motel, pool, TV. Major credit cards.

PERU

Bromley Sun Lodge, Rte. 11, Peru; 824-6941. Expensive. Fifty-room hotel on the slopes of Bromley Mountain Ski Area. Indoor heated pool, sauna, game room, and cocktail lounge. Ski onto the slopes. Best collection of different types of beer. Major credit cards.

STRATTON

Bear Creek Sport Hotel & Condominium Resort, Rte. 30, Rawsonville; 297-1700. Moderate to expensive. European or Modified American Plan, or bed and breakfast. Summer or winter package plans. Mobil three-star rating. Free shuttle service to and from Stratton Mountain. Five Har-Tru tennis courts, outdoor pool, sauna, Jacuzzi, lawn games on premises. Golf privileges at nearby golf courses. Restaurant. No pets.

Birkenhaus, Stratton Mountain; 297-2000. Moderate to expensive. Living room with fireplace, lounge, gourmet food, walking distance from lifts, sports center.

Liftline Lodge, Stratton Mountain, Stratton; 297-2600. Expensive. Walk to lifts, sports center. Cross-country shuttle, apartments, game room, lounge, hot tubs, sauna, New Life Spa gym, ski packages.

Stratton Mountain Inn, Stratton Mountain; 297-2500. Moderate to expensive. Deluxe hotel, 125 rooms, tennis courts, pool, hot tubs, sauna, shuttle bus to ski lifts. Sports Center privileges. Restaurant, lounge, piano bar. Open year-round. Major credit cards.

Village Lodge, Stratton Mountain, Stratton; 297-2200. Expensive. Located right above base lodge. Microwave, refrigerator, color TVs. Sports Center privileges.

WESTON

Friendly Acres Hotel, Rte. 100 North; 824-5851. Full country breakfast, TV, lounge, picnic tables.

Cottages and Condominiums

Note: Many local real estate agencies in all Manchester and the mountain area towns have listings for seasonal rentals (winter or summer) for private houses and condominiums. For summer cottage rentals in the Lake St. Catherine area of Poultney and Wells, call real estate agents in those towns.

DORSET

Emerald Lake Motel and Chalets, North Dorset; 362-1636. Moderate. One-, two-, three-bedroom efficiencies right next to state park. Chalets next to Emerald Lake State Park.

LONDONDERRY

Magic, Bromley Mountain Lodging, Rte. 11; 824-5458. Two-night minimum stay. Condominiums at Magic Mountain or at Bromley Mountain in Peru.

MANCHESTER

Equinox on the Battenkill, Equinox Hotel, Manchester Village; 362-3100. Condominiums, minimum one-month stay.

PERU

Bromley Mountain, Rte. 11, Bromley, Magic Lodging Service; 824-5458. Condominiums at Bromley Mountain. Two-night stay minimum.

STRATTON

Bear Creek Sport Hotel & Condominiums, Rte. 30, Rawsonville; 297-1700. (Close to Stratton Mountain.) Two- and three-bedroom condominiums.
Stratton Mountain. Seasonal condominium rentals; 297-2200 or (out-of-state) 800-843-6867. Two-night minimum stay. Turnkey operations.

WESTON

Darling Family Inn, Rte. 100 North, Weston; 824-3223. Cottages furnished with everything, swimming pool, mountain setting.

Campgrounds

Note: The U.S. Forest Service office in Manchester on Rtes. 11-30, 362-2307, can provide further information about camping facilities within the Green Mountain National Forest for the towns of Peru, Stratton, and Weston listed below.

DANBY

Otter Creek Campground, Rte. 7, Danby; 293-5041. (See Maryville Campground in Dorset.)

DORSET

Dorset RV Park, Rte. 30, RR-Box 180, Dorset; 867-5754. Tent sites, camper sites with water and electric. Horseshoe pits, volleyball net. Pets allowed on leash. Playground, laundry, hot showers, flush toilets. Open April to Nov. 30.
Emerald Lake State Park, Rte. 7, RD, Box 485, North Dorset; 362-1655. One hundred and five sites, including 36 lean-tos. Flush toilets, hot showers, sewage disposal, picnic tables, fireplaces. No hookups.
Maryville Campground, Rte. 7, North Dorset; 293-5041. Fifty sites with and without hookups. Flush toilets, showers, in-ground pool, snack bar, recreation hall, laundry, canoe rentals. Open year-round.

LONDONDERRY

Winhall Brook Campground, Rte. 100, South Londonderry; call Ball Mountain Dam office in Jamaica at 874-4881. One hundred and eight tent sites, picnic tables, fire rings, flush toilets, hot showers, dishwashing stations, amphitheater (weekend programs), old hiking trails. No reservations, two-week limit.

PERU

Hapgood Pond Recreation Area, off Rte. 11, Peru. Maintained by U.S. Forest Service, stay limit 14 days. Twenty-eight tent sites, no hookups, picnic table, fireplace, parking spur, toilets. Early May to late Sept.

POULTNEY

Lake St. Catherine State Park, Rte. 30, RD-2, Box 230, Poultney; 287-9158. Sixty-one sites, including 10 lean-tos, flush toilets, hot showers, sewage disposal, phone, picnic tables, fireplaces, wood.

RUPERT

Merck Forest Foundation, Rte. 315, Rupert; 394-7836. Private, 2,700-acre, nonprofit preserve. Primitive camping. Five small cabins, five lean-tos. Privies. No limit on stay.

STRATTON

Grout Pond, Forest Rd. 6, 12 miles east of the town of Arlington on the Arlington-Stratton Rd. Three cabins, two shelters, tent camping except within 100 feet of the 79-acre pond. Call the U.S. Forest Service in Manchester at 362-2307 for further information.

WESTON

Greendale, Rte. 100. Two miles north of Weston, take Forest Rd. 18 two miles. Eleven campsites. Water, nonflush vault toilets. Contact the U.S. Forest Service in Manchester for more information.

Dining

BONDVILLE

Haig's, Rte. 30, Bondville (just before the Stratton Mountain Access Rd.); 297-1300. Moderate. Steaks, seafood, pasta, poultry. Children's menu. Dinner. Reservations suggested. Lighter fare at the Bridge Café. Inexpensive. Pizza to stay or go, snacks, large TV screen.

Red Fox Inn, Winhall Hollow Rd., Bondville; 297-2488. Charming restored 19th-century barn; veal, fish, chicken, steak. No credit cards. Reservations.

River Café and Restaurant, Rte. 30 (near the Stratton Mountain Access Rd.); 297-1010. Inexpensive to moderate. Lunch, dinner. Continental and American cuisine. Steaks, seafood, Italian specials, soup, sandwiches, desserts.

Winhall Market, Rte. 30 (foot of the Stratton Mountain Access Rd.); 297-1933. Choice meats, wines, cheese, produce, sandwich makings for picnics.

DANBY

Bradford Motel, Rte. 7, Danby; 293-5186. Inexpensive to moderate. Dinner only. Australian cuisine, Chicken Victoria, marinated beef dishes, Indian curries.

Danby Four Corners Store; 293-5316. Sandwiches, ice cream.

Danby Village Café, off Rte. 7, Danby; 293-5620. Inexpensive. Local eatery.

Silas Griffith Inn, Main St., Danby; 293-5567. Moderate. Dinner in a restored carriage house behind the inn.

Nichol's Store, off Rte. 7, Danby; 293-5154. Sandwiches, groceries.

White Dog Tavern, off Rte. 7, Danby; 293-5477. Inexpensive to moderate. Dinner nightly, lunch on weekends only. Chicken, fish, and beef dishes. No credit cards.

DORSET

Barrows House, Rte. 30; 867-4455. Moderate. Good food served in wonderful surroundings. Dinner and breakfast. Also packs picnic lunches to stay or go. Reservations. No smoking in greenhouse or dining room on weekends, holidays. Tavern menu. Inexpensive. Smoking permitted at all times. Major credit cards.

Chantecleer, Rte. 7 North, East Dorset; 362-1616. Expensive. Gourmet dining featuring classic specialties such as chateaubriand. Excellent food, atmosphere, service. Reservations essential. Major credit cards.

Dorset Inn, Rte. 30; 867-5500. Moderate to expensive. A meal you won't forget. Poached salmon, rack of lamb, beef dishes. Consistently excellent. Tavern menu. Inexpensive. Major credit cards.

East Dorset General Store, Rte. 7, East Dorset; 362-1535. Grocery items, sandwiches, soft ice cream.

L'Auberge, Rte. 30; 867-5715. Expensive. Great dining for the discerning palate. Gourmet French cuisine with lamb, fish, and game specialties. Tavern menu at Clancy's. Reservations suggested. Major credit cards.

Marbledge Restaurant and Lounge (Marbledge Motel), Rte. 7, East Dorset; 362-1418. Inexpensive. Home-styled cooking; family restaurant, children welcome. Also serves breakfast.

Peltier's, on the green, Dorset; 867-4400. Sandwiches, groceries.

LONDONDERRY

Dostal's, Magic Mountain, Londonderry; 824-6700. Moderate. Fixed-price dinners, open winter and summer. Visa and Mastercard.

Garden Market, Rte. 11, Londonderry; 824-6021. Health-food store, ready-made sandwiches, quiche, frozen yogurt cones, fresh produce.

Garden Restaurant, Rte. 11, Londonderry; 824-9574. Moderate. Lunches, dinners, brunch. Unique round fireplace, greenhouse. Major credit cards.

Gran'ma Frisby's, Rte. 11, Londonderry; 824-5931. Inexpensive to moderate. Steaks, burgers, chicken teriyaki, family style dining. Children welcome. Lunch, dinners, take-out.

Hearthstone Restaurant, Rte. 100, Hearthstone Village; 824-3019. Moderate. Country cooking, grilled food, seafood. Reservations appreciated. Major credit cards.

Highland House, Rte. 11, Londonderry; 824-3019. Expensive. Shrimp, veal, salmon dishes. Homemade bread, desserts. Dinner. Reservations suggested.

Inn at Magic Mountain, Magic Mountain; 824-6100. Moderate. Steaks, seafood dinners during winter months.

Jake's Market Place Café, Mountain Marketplace Shopping Center, Rtes. 11 and 100; 824-6614. Inexpensive to moderate. Homemade sandwiches, burgers, fresh dough pizza, take-out menu. Breakfast, lunch, and dinner.

Londonderry Inn, Rte. 100, Londonderry; 824-5226. Basic New England fare. Closed April to June. Reservations requested. No credit cards.

Londonderry Pizza, Londonderry Shopping Plaza; 824-6614. Inexpensive. Pizza, grinders, etc.

Mill Tavern, Rte. 11, Londonderry; 824-3247. Moderate. Steak and seafood. No reservations.

Nordic Inn, Rte. 11, Londonderry; 824-6444. Moderate. French cuisine. Fireplaces, solarium. Reservations appreciated. Lunch, dinner, Sunday brunch.

Stoddard's Market, Rte. 11, Londonderry; 824-5060. Ready-made sandwiches to go. Fishing and hunting supplies, groceries. Check bulletin board for events.

Swiss Inn, Rte. 11, Londonderry; 824-3442. Moderate. Swiss continental cuisine. Dinner. Reservations preferred. Major credit cards.

Three Clock Inn, Middletown Rd., South Londonderry; 824-6327. Expensive. Elegant, restored 200-year-old farmhouse, excellently prepared gourmet food. Dinners. No credit cards. Reservations required. Jackets preferred.

MANCHESTER

Alps Restaurant (Avalanche Motel), Rtes. 11-30; 362-2622. Moderate. Family restaurant serving breakfast, 7:30-11:00 A.M., and dinner. Lounge opens at 5:00.

Bagel Works, Rtes. 11-30; 362-5082. Inexpensive. Delicious bagels baked on the premises, toppings of your choice. Frozen yogurt. Great coffee.

Black Swan, Rte. 7A; 362-3807. Expensive. Elegant restaurant serving continental cuisine in brick Colonial in the heart of town. Duck, veal, homemade pâtés. Cocktail lounge. Pub menu. Inexpensive. Major credit cards.

Buttery at the Jelly Mill, Rte. 7A; 362-3544. Inexpensive. Excellent breakfast, lunches, and weekend brunches. Major credit cards.

Cookie House, Corner of Rtes. 11-30-7. Manchester Center; 362-2522. Inexpensive. Frozen yogurt, cookies, and desserts baked on the premises.

Dina's (Inn at Willow Pond), Rte. 7 North; 362-4982. Expensive. American dinners and breakfast in a charming 1780s farmhouse. Major credit cards.

Earth and Sea, Rte. 7A, Manchester Center; 362-1679. Inexpensive. Fresh fish and chips, tiny counter.

Equinox Hotel Restaurants, Main St., Manchester Village; 362-4700. Marsh Tavern: inexpensive, lunch, light dinner. Main Dining Room: expensive, breakfast, lunch, and dinner. Elegant atmosphere, gourmet food. Sports Center Restaurant on the terrace overlooking the golf course: inexpensive, breathtaking views, informal standard sandwich menu. Major credit cards.

Garden Café, at the Southern Vermont Art Center, off West Rd., Manchester Village; 362-4220. Inexpensive. Dine under an awning on the terrace. Open summers. Good salads.

Garlic John's, Rtes. 11-30; 362-9843. Moderate. Italian specialties of veal, seafood, and pasta in an informal atmosphere. Major credit cards.

Golden Royal Dragon, Rtes. 11-30, Manchester Center; 362-4560. Inexpensive. The only Chinese restaurant in town; specializes in Cantonese and Szechuan cuisine. Take-out, too.

Gourmet Café, Factory Point Square, Rte. 7; 362-1254. Inexpensive. Sandwiches. Indoor and outside dining under umbrellas in the heart of the downtown.

Grabber's Restaurant, Rtes. 11-30; 362-3394. Moderate. Lunch and dinner in a restored Victorian decor. Seafood, steaks, salads, etc. Great bar. Major credit cards.

Greenbaum's and Gilhooley's, Rtes. 11-30; 362-4837. Moderate. Mammoth portions, steak and seafood house. Large greenhouse. Major credit cards.

Gurry's, Rtes. 11-30; 362-9878. Moderate. Pizza, burgers, salad. Pool table, video machines in bar. Major credit cards. Outdoor pool, volleyball nets in summer.

Hilltop Pizza, top of Center Hill; 362-0138. Inexpensive. Pizza, grinders, Italian dishes.

Laney's Restaurant, Rtes. 11-30; 362-4456. Inexpensive to moderate. Great ribs, burgers, pizza in a contemporary atmosphere. The kids will love it. Major credit cards.

Manchester Hoagie Company (formerly the Double Hex), Rtes. 11-30; 362-1270. Inexpensive. Hoagies, hamburgers.

Manchester Pancake House, Rte. 7A; 362-3496. Inexpensive. Standard breakfast fare daily.

Manchester Pizza House, Manchester Shopping Center, Rtes. 11-30; 362-3338. Inexpensive. Traditional pizza, grinders, Italian dinners. No credit cards.

Mistral's, Toll Gate Rd.; 362-1779. Expensive. Gourmet cuisine in a spectacular brook-side setting. Rack of lamb, poached salmon. Jackets preferred. Reservations recommended. Major credit cards.

Molly Coddle's Market and Deli, Elm St. and Center Hill; 362-5452. Inexpensive. Gargantuan sandwiches heaped with sprouts, lettuce, tomato. Homemade soups, tabouli, salads. Open for dinner on weekends.

Mother Myrick's Confectionery and Ice Cream Parlor, Rte. 7A; 362-1560. Inexpensive. Sinfully good desserts, ice cream, and handmade chocolates. Major credit cards.

Mrs. Murphy's Donuts, Rtes. 11-30, Manchester Center; 362-1874. Standard coffee shop fare with donuts baked on the premises daily.

Mulligan's of Manchester, Rte. 7A; 362-3663. Moderate. Standard burgers, steaks, nachos fare. Casual dining. Several TVs in large bar area. Major credit cards.

New Morning Natural Foods, Rtes. 11-30, Manchester Center; 362-3602. Manchester's only health-food store. Nuts and healthy snacks to go.

Pam Pam Restaurant, Rtes. 11-30; 362-1622. Inexpensive to moderate. Early bird dinners. Sandwich menu available. Morning breakfast. Full bar.

Park Bench Café, Rte. 7A; 362-2557. Inexpensive to moderate. Lunch and dinner. Country dinners, Mexican, Cajun dishes. Good burgers. Major credit cards.

Quality Restaurant, Main St.; 362-9839. Inexpensive. Country-style breakfast, lunch, and dinners for more than 70 years at the Main St. landmark. Children's menu. Major credit cards. Relaxed atmosphere.

Rachel's, Rte. 7A, Manchester Village; 362-3163. Inexpensive. Sandwiches, soups, fine cheese, and wine to go.

Reluctant Panther, West Rd., Manchester Village; 362-2568. Expensive. Elegant dining featuring continental specialties, seafood. Reservations required. Major credit cards.

Sandtrap, Bonnet St. (Rte. 30); 362-9822. Inexpensive. Tiny restaurant serving lunch during warm seasons.

Sirloin Saloon, Rtes. 11-30; 362-2600. Moderate. The steak house that started it all. Perfectly prepared steaks, fresh seafood. Extensive salad bar. Children's menu. Be prepared to wait for a table. Major credit cards.

Up for Breakfast, Main St., 362-4204. Inexpensive. Tiny restaurant above Christine's clothing store serving breakfast and brunch only. Eggs Benedict and exotic breakfast treats.

Village Country Inn (The Rose Room), Rte. 7A, Manchester Village; 362-1792. Moderate. Continental French menu, patio dining. Also tavern menu. Serves breakfast 8 to 10 A.M. Major credit cards.

Wilburton Inn, off River Rd., Manchester Village; 362-2500. Moderate to expensive. Turn-of-the-century mansion with lovely hardwood paneling serving different chicken, veal dishes. A great place for summer cocktails overlooking the Battenkill River Valley. Spectacular view. Major credit cards.

Ye Olde Tavern, Rte. 7, Manchester Center; 362-3770. Moderate. Restored 1790 tavern, near center of town. Poultry, veal, steaks, seafood, homemade desserts.

PAWLET

The Barn Restaurant and Tavern, Rte. 30; 325-3088. Moderate. Fireside dining; steak, seafood, salad bar. Homemade desserts. Kids' night. Tavern menu.

Blossom's Corner, Rtes. 30 and 149, West Pawlet; 645-0058. Inexpensive to moderate. Family restaurant. Seafood, veal, prime rib. Open all year. Major credit cards.

Mach's General Store, off Rte. 30; 325-3405. Inexpensive sandwiches; general store merchandise, hunting, fishing licenses.

The Station Restaurant, off Rte. 30; 325-3041. Inexpensive. Restored 84-year-old railroad station; serves sandwiches, egg dishes, home-cooked specials, baked items. Open all year; open for dinner in summer; the rest of the year, breakfast and lunch.

PERU

Bromley Market, Rte. 11, Peru; 824-6512. Inexpensive. Ready-made sandwiches to go. Groceries.

Bromley Sun Lodge, Rte. 11, Peru; 824-6941. Inexpensive to moderate. New England cuisine dinner menu. Reservations request. Breakfast daily.

J.J. Hapgood General Store, Main St., Peru; 824-5911. Sandwiches, wine, gourmet cheese. Groceries. Check bulletin out front for local events.

Johnny Seesaw's, Rte. 11, Peru; 824-5533. Moderate. *Skiing* magazine calls it the "best Yankee cuisine in New England." Reservations requested. Major credit cards.

Wiley Inn, Rte. 11, Peru; 824-6600. Moderate. Casual dining. Reservations advisable.

POULTNEY

Incredible Edibles, Main St.; 287-2024. Inexpensive. Family restaurant with homemade hot dishes, sandwiches, and baked goods. Lunch and dinner. Open all year.

Lake St. Catherine Inn, Cones Point, Rte. 30, Box 129; 287-9347. Moderate. Complete five-course meal all-inclusive. Three entrées offered each night (meat, poultry, seafood). Dinner by reservation only. Quaint dining room with gingham curtains overlooking the lake. Immaculate decor. Fish, steak, chicken dishes. Seasonal spring, summer, and fall. No credit cards. Personal or travelers' checks.

Poultney Luncheonette, 84 Main St.; 287-2055. Inexpensive. Breakfast and lunch in old-fashioned diner decor. Take-out. Breakfast all day. Open all year.

Stonebridge Inn, Rte. 30, Poultney; 287-9849. Moderate. Gourmet dining at charming old inn.

Town Pizza, 20 Main St.; 287-9439. Inexpensive. Standard pizza fare, grinders. Open lunch and dinner. All year.

Whispering Pines, Rte. 30; 287-9715. Inexpensive. Family restaurant with hamburgers, prime rib, lobster. Open all year, except for two weeks in January. Informal atmosphere. Smoking permitted.

RAWSONVILLE

Feathers at Bear Creek, Rte. 30, Rawsonville; 297-1700. Moderate. Steaks, seafood. Dinners only. Early bird special dinners. Sunday brunch.

RUPERT

Sherman's General Store, Rte. 315, West Rupert; 394-7820. Inexpensive. Sandwiches, general store merchandise, hunting and fishing licenses.

STRATTON

A. J. Pimento's, Stratton Mountain Village Square; 297-9899. Northern Italian cuisine. Gourmet pizza, burgers. Lunch, dinner. Late-night menu on weekends.

Bear Essentials, off Stratton Mountain Access Rd.; 297-9843. Deli, wine, gourmet food for picnics.

Birkenhaus, Stratton Mountain; 297-2000. Moderate. Continental cuisine. Major credit cards.

Breakpoint at the Stratton Sports Center, Stratton Mountain; 297-2200. Inexpensive to moderate. Breakfast, lunch, or dinner. Deck overlooking tennis courts. Varied menu includes burgers, sandwiches.

Café Applause, Stratton Mountain Inn; 297-2500. Light food, live entertainment. Cabaret and comedy.

Clocktower Café, Stratton Mountain Village Square; 297-2200 (ext. 2613). Deli, breakfasts, light dinners. Beer, wine.

Hausenpfeffer at Liftline Lodge, Stratton Mountain; 297-2600. Moderate. Austrian cuisine. Breakfast, lunch, or dinner. Lighter fare, pastries in Victoria Café. Inexpensive.

Mulligan's Tavern, Stratton Mountain Village Square; 297-9293. Open all day for lunch, dinner, cocktails. Entertainment at night.

Sage Hill at the Stratton Mountain Inn, Stratton Mountain; 297-2500. Moderate. New American cuisine. Nice dining room with fieldstone fireplace. Live entertainment Thursday, Friday, and Saturday.

Tenderloins at the Stratton Mountain Country Club, Stratton Mountain Access Rd.; 297-2200. Inexpensive to moderate. Breakfast, lunch, or dinner. Live entertainment Wednesday nights.

WESTON

Bryant House Restaurant, Main St., Weston; 824-6287. Inexpensive. Lunches. New England fare. Open year-round.

Inn at Weston, Rte. 100, Weston; 824-5804. Moderate to expensive. Continental cuisine, fine wines. Norwegian salmon, duckling, steak, seafood. Reservations requested. Open year-round. Visa, Mastercard.

Weston Marketplace, Rte. 100 North; 824-5818. Deli featuring homemade soups, chili, salads, sandwiches. Vermont cheese, maple syrup. Open year-round.

Entertainment

Music and Stage

DORSET

Dorset Theatre Festival; 867-2223. Box office; 867-5777. Summer stock with Dorset Theatre Festival at the Dorset Playhouse on Cheney Rd. in the heart of Dorset. Other times, local amateur group, the Dorset Players, produces plays, musicals.

MANCHESTER

Manchester Music Festival, c/o Southern Vermont Art Center, Manchester
Village; 362-1405. Summer, fall concerts only. Faculty concerts as well as weekly
chamber music performances. Young artist concert series. Admission charged.

Performing Arts Groups at the Southern Vermont Art Center, Manchester
Village; 362-1405. Summer, fall only. Admission charged. Check with the Art
Center for the changing musical roster.

Third Saturday Series, Equinox Hotel, Manchester Village; 362-4700. This well-attended
classical music event, which runs year-round, features various soloists. Admission.

PERU

Bromley Summer Jazz Music Series, Bromley Mountain, Rte. 11, Peru; 824-5522.
Jazz, country, bluegrass on outdoor deck every summer weekend. No admission.

STRATTON

Stratton Mountain Summer Concert series in the past has included top name
singers, jazz groups. Check with Stratton Mountain information about the summer roster.

WESTON

Kinhaven, Weston; 824-9592. Summer music school performs free classical music
concerts June through beginning of August.

Weston Playhouse, on the green, off Rte. 100, Weston; box office, 824-5288. Summer stock in a delightful theater; dinners available; cabaret after the show.

Nightlife

BONDVILLE

Haig's Restaurant, Lounge, Rte. 30 (bottom of Stratton Mountain Access Rd.);
297-1300. Live rock and roll bands, disc jockey, other entertainment, dancing. Pool
table, pinball. Young ski crowd.

Red Fox Inn, Winhall Hollow Rd., Bondville; 297-2488. Live bands, Foosball, pinball, video games. Young crowd winter and summer.

MANCHESTER

Alfie's, Rtes. 11-30, Manchester Center; 362-2637. Dancing Friday and Saturday
night. Friday night is ladies' night. Admission charged. Proper attire.

Andy Avery and Friends (Normandy), Marsh Tavern, Equinox Hotel, Manchester
Village; 362-4700. Guitarist Andy Avery usually has one or two friends accompany
him on those oldies he sings every Friday and Saturday night. No admission.

Grabber's Restaurant, Rtes. 11-30, Manchester; 362-3394. Occasional pianist,
singer.

Intrada Jazz Quartet, Greenbaum's and Gilhooley's, Rtes. 11-30, Manchester
Center; 362-4837. No admission.

Live Bands, Avalanche Motel, Rtes. 11-30, Manchester Center; 362-2622. Occas-
sional live bands — country, blues, or rock — are presented. Check with the
chamber of commerce or the Avalanche.

POULTNEY

Pub House Tavern, Main St., Poultney. Live bands during the fall and spring
semesters of nearby Green Mountain College.

STRATTON

Applause Café, Stratton Mountain Inn, Stratton Mountain; 297-2500. Live entertainment on Saturdays during ski season, holiday periods. Rock and roll bands,
blues bands. Young crowd.

Mulligan's, Village Square, Stratton Mountain; 297-9293. Live rock and roll bands,
billiards, disc jockey, weekends, holiday periods. Home of the Margaritaville Bar
(on the third floor). The crowd is often young, but on occasion you see all ages
out on the dance floor.

Tenderloins, Stratton Mountain Country Club, Stratton Mountain Access Rd.;
297-2200. Wednesday, live bands, dancing. Entertainment on weekends.
Wentworth's, Stratton Mountain Inn; 297-2500. Piano bar.

Movies

LONDONDERRY
Derry Twin Cinema, Londonderry Shopping Plaza, Rte. 11, Londonderry;
824-3331. Matinees during holiday weekends and holiday weeks.

MANCHESTER
Manchester Cinema, Manchester Shopping Center, Rtes. 11-30, Manchester Center;
362-1229. Two theaters with matinees during holiday weekends and holiday weeks.

Museums and Historical Sites

DORSET
Dorset Inn, Rte. 30 and Church St. The oldest continuously operating inn in
Vermont.
Two historical markers are located here. At the junction of Church St. and Rte. 30,
a marker notes the first conventions held to declare Vermont's independence from
New York and New Hampshire. A second marker is located on Nichols Hill and
West Rd.

MANCHESTER
American Museum of Fly Fishing, Seminary Ave. and Rte. 7A, Manchester
Village; 362-3300. A wonderful little collection for the fly-fishing buff. Crooner
Bing Crosby's rod is on display here.
Equinox Hotel, Main St., Manchester Village. Part of the National Historic Register,
this block-long refurbished hotel was one of the foremost nineteenth-century resorts.
Hildene, Rte. 7A, Manchester Village; 362-1788. Seasonal, mid-May to late Oct.
Robert Todd Lincoln's restored turn-of-the-century 24-room Georgian Revival man-
sion on 412 acres is open for guided tours.

POULTNEY
Historical marker on Rte. 30 and Main St. noting two prominent journalists' ties to
the area. Horace Greeley, founder of the *New York Herald Tribune,* resided here;
and George Jones, cofounder and editor of the *New York Times,* was born and
raised in Poultney.

RUPERT
Harmon's Mint Historical Marker, Rte. 315, East Rupert. Reuben Harmon, Jr.,
made copper coins for the state of Vermont, 1785-1788.

WESTON
Farrar-Mansur House, Rte. 100, Weston; 824-6781. A 1797 tavern, the house has
original artifacts from Weston. Operated by the Weston Historical Society.

Seasonal Events

DORSET
Dorset Antique Show, Dorset green. A biannual outdoor event held in July on
Church Street.
Memorial Day Parade, Dorset green. Church service.

MANCHESTER
Memorial Day Parade, Main St., Manchester Center. A proud local display of
patriotism and talent.
Hildene Antique Car Show, Hildene Meadowlands, Manchester Village. Usually
in June. Antique, classic, and special vehicles. Admission.

Old-Fashioned Fourth of July Celebration, Manchester Recreation Area, Rte. 30, Manchester Center. Sack races, egg toss, greased-pole climb, pet show, etc.; concession stand. Daylong festivities culminating with fireworks at dark. Sponsored by the Manchester Rotary Club.

Wessner's Flea Market, Rtes. 11-30, Manchester Center. Every Saturday morning, spring, summer, fall. Something for everyone.

Church suppers are prevalent during the summer and fall. Usually organized around a theme like strawberries or turkey, they offer good wholesome food at reasonable costs. And the money goes to a worthy cause. In addition, the Lions and Rotary Clubs also sponsor breakfasts and suppers during these seasons. Check the local papers for details.

Vermont Symphony Orchestra, Hildene Meadowlands, Manchester Village. Outdoor pops concert, the weekend of July 4. Bring a picnic supper to have prior to the concert.

Polo Games, Hildene Meadowlands, Manchester Village. Summer Sundays. Polo matches with Vermont teams.

Country auctions are held throughout the summer and fall by different area auctioneers. Check the local papers for details.

Fair Day on the Hill, Southern Vermont Art Center, Manchester Village. A daylong celebration of the visual and performing arts on a Saturday in July. Admission.

Craft Fair, Hildene Meadowlands, Manchester Village. July or August. Two-day event under a yellow-and-white striped tent. Food concession. Admission.

Manchester Horse Show, Hildene Meadowlands, Manchester Village. An equestrian delight.

Festival of Fools, Hildene Meadowlands, Manchester Village. Labor Day weekend or thereabouts. Jesters, mimes, and fun for all. Food concession. Admission.

Lions Club Arcade, Manchester Elementary School, Manchester Center. Early December. Merchants display local wares and Santa Claus's lap is available for the little ones.

Christmas Tree Lighting, Manchester Center and Manchester Village. Early December. Teams of horse-drawn wagons bring children from the center to the village where the tree in front of the Congregational church is lit and Christmas carols sung. Santa presides over the festivities. Punch and cookies after at the Equinox Hotel across the street.

Candlelight Tours of Hildene, Hildene, Manchester Village. Christmas week. Horse-driven sleighs bring visitors to Robert Todd Lincoln's former estate, which is decked out with candles and Christmas ornaments.

Winter Carnival, Manchester Recreation Area, Manchester Center. President's week. Snowmobile rides, races, ice-skating, dog sled demonstrations, food concession.

Easter Parade, Manchester Center and Village. April. Wear your best bonnet. Prizes for hats, best-dressed bicycle. Begins at the Equinox Hotel.

PAWLET

Wild Game Supper, Pawlet. Fall. Exotic wild game dishes. Check local papers, bulletin boards for date.

POULTNEY

Fourth of July celebration.

RUPERT

Wild Game Supper, Rupert Firehouse. November. Bear, raccoon, venison, and other wild game dishes.

STRATTON

Stratton Mountain Summer Concert Series features top-name performers like Peter, Paul and Mary.

Stratton Mountain Fourth of July Celebration includes a street festival with parade, entertainment, performers, food. Stratton provides various kinds of entertainment during the summer months for children and adults. Check with Stratton Mountain.

Ladies' Professional Golf Association Tournament brings the top professionals to Stratton Mountain Country Club golf course. August.

Stratton Arts Festival, Stratton Mountain. Mid-September to mid-October, daily. For more than a quarter of a century the Arts Festival has been a showcase for Vermont artists. Weaving, woodworking, painting, sculpture, ceramics, jewelry. Great food, performing artists every weekend, too. Children's programs. Don't miss it.

Wurstfest, Stratton Mountain. Labor Day weekend. Bavarian music, ethnic food, and music by the Stratton Mountain Boys.

Nor-Ams and other professional ski racing events, Stratton Mountain. Throughout the winter, there are numerous events scheduled, like the Chapstick Challenge for U.S. Disabled Skiers, Snowboarding Championships, etc. Check with Stratton Mountain for dates and details.

WELLS

Variety Day, street dance, flea market, dinner sponsored by Methodist Church first week in August. Check bulletin boards for dates.

WESTON

Weston Antiques Show at the Weston Playhouse, Rte. 100. Late September, early October. A weekend show with many, many dealers.

Weston Craft Show at the Weston Playhouse, Rte. 100. Columbus Day weekend. Quality regional crafts, wood, ceramics, quilts, baskets, weaving, etc.

Children's Activities

DORSET

Annual Fishing Derby sponsored by the Dorset Sportsmen's Club. Spring.

MANCHESTER

Annual Fishing Derby, Manchester Center. Spring. Rod and Gun Club sponsors the event with prizes in different categories.

Old-Fashioned Fourth Activities (see listing under seasonal events).

Manchester Recreation Area, Rte. 30, Manchester Center. Playground, tennis courts, in-ground swimming pool, kiddie pool. Admission to pool. Grounds open all year; pool only in summer months.

Summer Day Camp programs, Manchester Recreation Department. Swimming, arts and crafts, field trips, camping.

Easter Parade, Manchester Center and Manchester Village (see listing under seasonal events).

Christmas Tree Lighting, Manchester Center and Manchester Village (see listing under seasonal events).

PERU

Alpine Slide, Bromley Mountain, Rte. 11; 824-5522. All the fun of downhill skiing without the skis. A controllable sled will take you down the mountain. Adults like it, too.

POULTNEY

Cones Point Miniature Golf, Rte. 30 (near Lake St. Catherine); 287-9811. Seasonal. Miniature golf, video games.

RUPERT

Merck Forest Foundation, Rte. 315, Rupert. Summer environmental camp for youngsters. Nature workshops.

STRATTON

Junior Tennis Academy, Stratton Mountain Tennis School, Stratton Mountain. Summer tennis programs for youth.

Stratton's Wander and Discover Programs. Summer day camp programs for kids only. Swimming lessons, hayrides, nature walks, movies, art classes, magic shows.

Shops

Art Galleries

DANBY
Peel Gallery, Scotsville Rd. (just off Rte. 7), Danby; 293-5230. Paintings, sculpture.

DORSET
Dorset Framery, Rte. 30 (just south of Church St.), Dorset; 867-4494. Charming village gallery with Ogden Pleissner prints, Natalee Everett Goodman primitives. Original oils, watercolors, pastels by local artists.

MANCHESTER
Beside Myself, Lathrop La., off Rte. 7A, south of Manchester; 362-2212. Contemporary paintings in small barnlike structure.
Deeley Gallery, Rte. 7A, Manchester Center; 362-2204. Specializing in old paintings.
Long Ago and Far Away, Factory Point Square, Main St., Manchester Center; 362-3435. Native American art including pueblo pottery, Navajo rugs, paintings, jewelry, Eskimo art.
Pierre's Gate, Main St., Manchester Center; 362-1766. Wonderful gallery with wood carvings, paintings, glass, sculpture. Open all year.
Southern Vermont Art Center, West Rd., Manchester Village; 362-1405. Country estate overlooking Manchester. Open in summer months only with changing exhibits, nature walks, performing arts programs.
Stevenson Gallery, Union St. (across from Equinox Hotel), Manchester Village; 362-3668. Small gallery with fine quality works by local artists.
Tilting at Windmills, Rtes. 11-30, Manchester Center; 362-3022. Prints, posters, original artwork in handsome building. Works by Andrew Wyeth, Gunter Korus, Gerald Lubeck.

PAWLET
Jay Connaway Gallery, Rte. 30, Pawlet; 325-3107. Moods of sea and land. Open mid-March to November, weekends, or by appointment.

STRATTON
Handworks on the Green, Village Square, Stratton Mountain; 297-0900. Contemporary gallery features crafts, woodworking, changing exhibitions.
North Star Gallery, Stratton Village Square, Stratton Mountain; 297-9844. Oils, watercolors, sculpture, lithographs, etc., by artists from the region.

WESTON
Todd Gallery, Main St., Rte. 100, Box 86, Weston; 824-5606. Housed in big red barn near the green. Crafts, original paintings, and limited edition prints by Vermont artists.

Craft and Specialty Stores

BONDVILLE
Detail Sports, Rte. 30, Bondville (bottom Stratton Mountain Access Rd.); 297-9689. European and American skiwear, accessories, sportswear. Major credit cards.

DANBY
Danby Marble Co., Rte. 7, Danby; 293-5425. Marble items made locally.
Gallery of Danby Green, Main St., Danby; 293-5550. A series of shops including the Crafters Coop and the House and Garden Gallery in restored historic landmarks on Main St. Everything from art and pottery to collectors' dolls, hand knits, antiques, quilts, wicker furniture, birdhouses, basketry.
Yankee Vineyard, Rte. 7, Danby; 293-5425. Gift shop next to Danby Marble store. Vermont products, leather items.

DORSET

Cachet, Rte. 30, Dorset; 867-5725. Antique items, linens.
J. K. Adams, Rte. 30, Dorset; 362-2303. Vermont wooden housewares. Seconds shop, too.
H. N. Williams Department Store, Rte. 30, Dorset; 867-5353. Don't let the name fool you; a true general store run by the Rumney family.

LONDONDERRY

Garden Restaurant Gift Shop, Rte. 11; 824-9574. Little shop with a potpourri of fine items; stationery, dried flowers, cards.
Kent Shop, Mountain Marketplace, Londonderry; 824-3555. Men's, women's, and children's clothing, gifts. Major credit cards.
Mountainside Sports, Rte. 11 and Magic Mountain Access Rd.; 824-4003. Skiwear, accessories for adults and children. Major credit cards accepted.

MANCHESTER

After the Gold Rush, Rte. 7A, Manchester Center; 362-4816. Jewelry store with gold and silver bracelets, earrings, etc.
Barbara Anne's, Main St., Manchester Center; 362-4467. Tiny jewelry store; gold and silver adornments.
Bare Elegance, Factory Point Square, Main St., Manchester Center; 362-4477. Fine ladies' underwear, lingerie.
Canedy's Pendleton Store, Rte. 7A, Manchester Village; 362-5466. Classic Pendleton clothing for women and men.
Christine's, Main St., Manchester Center; 362-2677. High-quality women's contemporary clothing, accessories.
Christmas Days, Main St., Manchester Center; 362-2516. Christmas ornaments for tree, hearth, and home. Music boxes.
Clift Collection, Rte. 7A, Manchester Village; 362-3377. Unusual, quality women's clothing and accessories.
Country Furs, Rte. 7A, Manchester Village; 362-4022. Furs and women's summer clothing.
Current Outlook, Rte. 7, Manchester Center; 362-0155. Women's clothing. Visa, Mastercard.
Detail Sports, The Equinox Shops, Rte. 7A, Manchester Village; 362-4922. Men's and women's European and American sport clothing.
Down Outlet, off Rte. 7A next to Bass, Manchester Center; 362-3705. Down-filled outerwear, sportswear, comforters, cold-weather accessories.
Enchanted Doll House, Rte. 7 North, Manchester Center; 362-5464. An unusual doll, toy shop in a 12-room farmhouse you don't want to miss.
Gooseberry, Rte. 7A, Manchester Center; 362-3263. A kitchen shop with everything you can think of, and more.
Harrington's, Rte. 7A, Manchester Center; 362-2070. Gourmet food shop with Vermont cob-smoked hams, etc. Special cheeses.
Heinel's, Main St., Manchester Center; 362-1400. Traditional men's and women's outerwear.
Herdsmen Leathers, Main St., Manchester Center; 362-2751. Quality leather jackets, coats, women's clothing, shoes.
House Works (in the Jelly Mill), Rte. 7A, Manchester Village; 362-3672. Gourmet cookware, home accessories.
Incredible Tree (in the Jelly Mill), Rte. 7A, Manchester Village; 362-3629. Fine jewelry, brass, collectibles.
Irish House, The Equinox Shops, Rte. 7A, Manchester Village; 362-4004. Imported Irish garments, gifts.
Jelly Mill, Rte. 7A, Manchester Village; 362-3494. Huge, four-story renovated barn with different shops on each floor. Unique gifts.
Jewel of the Mill (at the Jelly Mill), Rte. 7A, Manchester Village; 362-1608. Wide selection of silver (and gold jewelry); contemporary styles.
Johnny Appleseed Bookshop, Rte. 7A, Manchester Village; 362-2458. Old stone building next to Equinox Hotel; specializing in new and old regional and sporting books.

Landau's Woolens, Rte. 7A, Manchester Village; 362-3754. Garments from Iceland, Scotland, Canada, Yugoslavia, Austria.

Long Ago and Far Away, Factory Point Square, Main St., Manchester Center; 362-3435. American Indian and Eskimo art, gifts, handmade furniture.

McWayne's Jewelry Store, corner Rtes. 11-7, Manchester Center; 362-1257. Traditional jewelry store.

Manchester Discount Beverages, Rtes. 11-30, Manchester Center. Fine wines, beer. Deli for sandwiches.

Manchester Furniture and Carpet, Memorial Ave., Manchester Center; 362-3444. Oak, pine furniture, beds, wallpaper.

Manchester Sports, Rte. 7A, Manchester Center; 362-2569. Patagonia, Woolrich casual, sport clothing.

Manchester Woodcraft, Rtes. 11-30, Manchester Center; no phone. Wooden products, stools, coatracks, collectibles made on the premises.

Marilyn Forbes, Ltd., Rte. 7A, Manchester Village; 362-4860. Cotton and wool coordinated designer knit sweaters, tops, pants, skirts, jackets, coats, jumpsuits.

Mountain Goat, Rte. 7A, Manchester Center; 362-5159. Outdoor clothing, gear specialists. Patagonia, North Face wear.

Movado, Rte. 7A, Manchester Center; 362-5334. Watches, leathergoods, luggage.

Nina, Factory Point Square, Main St., Manchester Center; 362-4657. Traditional jewelry at discount prices.

Northshire Bookstore, Colburn House, Main St., Manchester Center; 362-2200. An outstanding bookstore with a varied collection of books, records. Great children's section.

Orvis Company, Rte. 7A, Manchester Village; 362-3750. Traditional country clothing for men and women. Gifts, high-quality hunting gear, fly rods, etc.

Pewter and Things, Factory Point Square, Main St., Manchester Center; 362-3673. An eclectic collection of pewter, brass, glass, and collectibles.

Pierre Deux Boutique (Rose Ann Humphrey, Ltd.), Seminary Ave., Manchester Village; 362-1210. Collection of handbags, glasswear, pewter, fabrics.

Pizzaz, Rte. 7A, Manchester Center; 362-4546. A party store with helium balloons, ribbons, paper products, and favors.

Pour Le Bain, Ltd., Manchester Center; 362-1453. A bath boutique, scents, soaps, hand-painted pedestal sinks.

Rachel's, Rte. 7A, Manchester Center; 362-3163. Imported, domestic wines, beers, cheeses. Deli, homemade soup, sandwiches to go.

Red Mountain Coffee, Tea and Spice, Rte. 7A, Manchester Center; 362-4557. Varied selection of flavored coffee beans, coffeepots, handmade jams and kitchen accessories.

Skier's Edge, Rtes. 11-30, Manchester Center; 362-1209. Designer ski outfitters for men, women, children. Ski accessories, equipment.

Sounds Around, Equinox Square, Rtes. 11-30; 362-7073. Tapes, compact discs.

Southwick's Ltd, Rte. 7A, Manchester Center; 362-2401. Traditional high-quality women's country clothing.

Stratton Sports, Equinox Square, Rtes. 11-30; 362-0102. Fine skiwear, clothing by Patagonia, North Face. Downhill, cross-country ski equipment, tennis rackets.

Top Drawer Lingerie, Equinox Square, Rtes. 11-30, Manchester Center; 362-3344. Designer underwear for women.

Valerie's Country Collection and Quilt Shop, Rte. 7 North, Manchester Center; 362-3578. Custom and ready-made quilts.

Village Store at Equinox, Union St., Manchester Village; 362-2599. Vermont products, wines, custom-made gift baskets.

Wildflowers, Equinox Square, Rtes. 11-30, Manchester Center; 362-3850. Dried flowers, plants, fresh-cut flowers.

PAWLET

Beau Monde Studio, Rte. 30; 325-3645. From sheep to shawl. Breeding stock and hand-spun yarns, finished goods. Supplies for spinning and weaving. Lessons. By chance or appointment.

Penelope Nelson Collection, Rte. 30; 325-3466. Originally designed silk or cotton fabric and wearing apparel. Silk-screened and batiked in Indonesia. Visa and Mastercard.

Pawlet Potter, off Rte. 30; 325-3100. Working studio for Marion Waldo Mac-Chesney. Contemporary porcelain in pastel glaze, traditional spongeware. Open daily, or call for appointment.

PERU

The Bromley Shop, Bromley Mountain, Rte. 11, Peru; 824-5522. Downhill and cross-country ski clothing and accessories.

POULTNEY

Cards and Critters, 68 Main St., Poultney; 287-5801. Cards, general gifts, jewelry.
Flames and Flowers, 61 Main St., Poultney; 287-5750. Vintage clothing.
Heartstrings, 27 College St., Poultney; 287-9565. Country items, baskets, candles, tinware, pottery.
Original Vermont Store, 58 Main St., Poultney; 287-9111. Vermont foods, baskets, T-shirts.

RAWSONVILLE

Equipe Sport, Rte. 30 and 100, Rawsonville; 297-2847. Ski and sports apparel and equipment.

RUPERT

Authentic Designs, The Mill Rd., West Rupert; 394-7713. Colonial and early American lighting fixtures.

STRATTON

Bear Essentials, off Stratton Mountain Access Rd.; 297-9843. Gourmet items, hardware, groceries.
Bogner, Stratton Mountain Village Square; 297-2767. Ski fashions from the famous skiwear designer.
CB Sports, Stratton Mountain Village Square; 297-9822. CB ski and sportswear for all seasons.
Country Casuals North, Stratton Mountain Village Square; 297-3264. Active and casual sport clothes.
Finesse Sport, Stratton Mountain Village Square; 297-9644. Luxury ski equipment, clothing.
First Run Ski Shop, Stratton Mountain Village Square; 297-1771. Ski clothes, sports clothes.
Homestead Florist, Stratton Mountain Village Square; 297-2172. Fresh flowers, silk flower arrangements.
Once in a Blue Moon, Stratton Mountain Village Square; 297-3211. Pottery, brass, glassware, baskets, quality, wooden items.
Overland Outfitters, Stratton Mountain Village Square; 297-9887. Sheepskin, leathers, fur clothing, accessories.
Partridge in a Pantry, Stratton Mountain Village Square; 297-9850. Vermont products, European wine, cheese, products.
Resort Interiors, Stratton Mountain Village Square; 297-1224. Furnishings, unique gifts.
Resortworks, Stratton Mountain Village Square; 297-9888. Active wear for men and women.
Spectacles, Stratton Mountain Village Square; 297-2677. Eye wear for skiing, sports activities.
Stratton Sportshop, Sports Center Building, Stratton Mountain; 297-2525. Sport clothing by Nike, Prince, etc. Tennis racquets.
Stratton Village Books and Gifts, Village Lodge Lobby, Stratton Mountain; 297-9709. Apothecary items, newspapers, magazines, stationery, cards, candy.
Sugarplums, Stratton Mountain Village Square; 297-9681. International chocolates, candies, and confections. Vermont products.
Vermont East Indies Co., Stratton Mountain Village Square; 297-3255. Dutch colonial and Indonesian artifacts.

Village Kids, Stratton Mountain Village Square; 297-3115. Skiwear, clothing for older children. Accessories.

Von Bargen's Fine Jewelry, Stratton Mountain Village Square; 297-1975. Jewelry.

Yellow Turtle, Stratton Mountain Village Square; 297-3115. Clothing for newborns, toddlers; toys and dolls.

WESTON

Feather Your Nest, Main St., Weston; 824-3707. Hand-crafted items, furniture, collectors' dolls, Santas. Open year-round.

Mountain Stitchery, in the Weston Village Store building; 824-6431. A complete needlework and yarn shop.

Old Mill Museum, Rte. 100 (just around the corner from Farrar-Mansur Museum). Tinsmith at work in this 1780 mill structure. Traditional lighting designs, tin folk art. Weaving, hand-spinning upstairs. Open June through November.

Todd Gallery of Fine Art and Crafts, Main St., Weston; 824-5606. Functional pottery, crafts, original paintings, limited edition prints by Vermont artists. Open all year.

Vermont Country Store, Main St., Weston; 824-3184. A country store with penny candy, housewares, clothing, and a potbellied stove. Open year-round.

Vermont Craftsmen, Rte. 100, Weston. Display of crafts, demonstrations of stenciling, braiding.

Weston Bowl Mill and Annex, Rte. 100, Weston; 824-6219. Extensive woodenware collection. Seconds available, too.

Weston Fudge Shop, Old Mill Museum complex, Rte. 100, Weston; 824-3014. Freshly made candy, fine chocolate, great fudge. Open all year.

Weston House Quilt Collection, Main St., Weston; 824-3636. Large collection of Vermont quilts, handwoven rugs, patchwork pillows, wall hangings. Open all year.

Weston Toy Works, Main St.; 824-3139. Toy store with fine toys, games, and puzzles. Open all year.

Weston Village Barn, Main St., Weston; 824-5195. Framed prints, photographs, handmade rugs, baskets. Open all year.

Weston Village Store, Main St., Weston; 824-5477. Gifts, collectibles, weathervanes, wine, cheese, syrups, fancy foods.

Antiques

DANBY

The Barn Antiques, South Main St., Danby; 293-5512. Furniture, household items.

Danby Antiques Center, Main St., Danby; 293-9984. American Country Furniture and format, furniture and accessories. Twenty-five dealers. Open April to December, January to March.

DORSET

American Sporting Antiques, Rte. 30, Dorset; 867-2271. Select items from America's "Golden Age" of fishing and hunting.

Anglophile Antiques, Rte. 30, South Dorset; 362-1621. Antique English china, silver, brass.

Antique Quilts, Rte. 30 (across from J. K. Adams); 867-5969. A large selection of all size quilts. By chance or appointment.

Schoolhouse Antiques, Rte. 7, North Dorset; 362-2180. Primitives, folk art, country furniture.

Stonewall's Antiques, Rte. 30; 362-4330. Early American country furniture, chests, commodes, accessories. May to December.

MANCHESTER

Antiques by J. K. Meiers, Rte. 7A, Manchester Village; 362-3721. Country and formal furniture, accessories, linens, hooked rugs, silver, Tiffany. Open all year.

Bellwether Gallery, Rte. 7A, Manchester Center; 362-4811. Importers of eighteenth- and nineteenth-century country furniture and accessories; quality scrubbed pine.

Brewster Antiques, Bonnet St. (Rte. 30); 362-1579. Antique and estate jewelry, sterling, glass, small furniture. Best to call ahead.

Carriage Trade Antiques Center, Rte. 7 North; 362-1125. Country furniture, quilts, rugs, tools, primitives.

Center Hill Past and Present, Center Hill; 362-3211. Nicely done antiques center right in town.

Clock Emporium, Barnumville Rd., Manchester Center; 362-3328. Clocks bought and sold. On display at the Carriage Trade, Rte. 7 North.

Deeley Gallery, Rte. 7A, Manchester Village; 362-2204. Nineteenth- and early twentieth-century American paintings.

1812 House Antiques Center, Rte. 7 North, Manchester Center. Antiques of all shapes and sizes.

Equinox Antiques, Rte. 7A (across from Equinox Hotel); 362-3540. Eighteenth- and nineteenth-century formal American and English furniture and accessories.

Johnny Appleseed Book Shop, Rte. 7A (next to Equinox Hotel); 362-2458. Old and rare books. Great building next to Equinox Hotel.

Mala's Fine Antiques, Rte. 7A, Manchester Village; 362-4595. Decorator accessories, estate jewelry, and paintings.

Old World Antiques, Rte. 7A (Village Mall); 362-2729. Furniture, accessories.

Paraphernalia Antiques, Manchester Village; 362-2421. Antique furniture, accessories. Seasonal.

Stevenson Gallery at the Equinox, Rte. 7A (across from Equinox Hotel); 362-3668. Nineteenth- and twentieth-century American art, folk art. Country antiques. Represents local artists including Arthur Jones, Jay H. Connaway.

Trotting Park Antiques, Rte. 7 North (behind Ye Olde Tavern Restaurant); 362-2374. Country furniture, stoneware. Open all year.

PAWLET

East West Antiques, Rte. 30; 325-3466. Indonesian and Dutch Colonial furniture; Irish scrubbed pine antiques. Monday through Saturday, Sunday by appointment. Visa, Mastercard.

PERU

Peru Village Barn Antiques, Main St.; 824-6336. Country things, furniture, accessories, paintings, textiles. Seasonal, May through October.

POULTNEY

Den of Antiquity, Rte. 30, Poultney; 287-9914. Oak furniture, varied collection. April through December. By chance or appointment during the winter.

Indian Hill Antiques and Collectibles, 110 York St., Poultney; 287-9546. Paintings, prints, glass, china, silver, furniture.

Kay's Corner, 3 Depot St., Poultney; no phone. Antique jewelry, china, glassware. May through mid-December. By chance or appointment.

Lost Moments Antiques and Collectibles, 37 Beaman St. (Rte. 30 North), Poultney; 287-9686. China, glass, postcards, miscellaneous. April through October. By chance or appointment.

Open Cupboard, Rte. 30, Poultney; 287-9680. Varied collection. Open all year.

Picture Window Antiques, 61 Main St., Poultney; 287-2050. Vintage clothing, jewelry, crocks, linens. Open all year.

Raggedy Ann & Andy's Whatnot Shop, 60 Main St., Poultney; no phone. Antiques, but mostly whatnots.

River's Edge Antiques, Rte. 140 on the East Poultney green; 287-9553. Paintings, prints, books, miscellaneous. May through October. By chance or appointment.

Sankanack Antiques, 8 Granville St., Poultney; 287-4030. Oak furniture, primitives, antique car parts. Year-round.

Things of Yesteryear, 63 Main St., Poultney; 287-5202. Varied collection antiques and collectibles.

Town 'n Vill-edge Collectibles, 19 South St., Poultney; 287-5590. China, glassware, books. Closed January and February.

RUPERT

The Country Gallery, Rte. 315; 394-7753. Antiques for contemporary living; night-stands, jelly cabinets, beds, benches, accessories; custom lighting. Open weekdays by chance or appointment. Open some weekends. Call for appointment. Visa and Mastercard.

WESTON

Freight Wagon Antiques and Things, Rte. 100, Weston; 824-6909. Country furniture, accessories, odds and ends. Memorial Day through foliage.

Discount Outlets

LONDONDERRY

The Barn, Rtes. 11 and 100, Londonderry; 824-5000. Discounted men's, women's, and children's clothing.

Barn Annex, Rte. 11 and 100, Londonderry; 824-3858. Children's clothing discounted; gifts, candles, cards.

New England Shoe Barn, Rtes. 11 and 100, Londonderry; 824-3737. Clark's, Rockports, Bass shoes for men and women, all discounted. Major credit cards.

MANCHESTER

Aileen Factory Outlet, Manchester Marketplace, Rtes. 11-30; 362-5575. Women's tops, slacks, and skirts.

Anne Klein Outlet, Battenkill Plaza, Rte. 7, Manchester Center; 362-2958. Sportswear, jeans, dresses at 50 percent discount.

Arlene La Marca, corner Rtes. 11-30-7, Manchester Center; 362-0132. Fine Italian-made leather goods, shoes, handbags, and belts. Shoes by Carlos Falchi.

Bass Shoes, Rte. 7A, Manchester Center; 362-4384. Leather boots, shoes, sneakers for men, women, children.

Battenkill Plaza, Rte. 7A, Manchester Center. Six shops — First Choice, Van Heusen, Fenn, Wright and Manson, Anne Klein, Harvé Benard — under one roof. See individual listings.

Bench Company Outlet Store, Manchester Marketplace, Rtes. 11-30; 362-3063. Men's and women's traditional sportswear discounted 40 to 60 percent.

Benetton, corner Rtes. 11-30-7, Manchester Center; 362-3954. Cotton clothing, shirts from the Italian company.

Boston Trader Kids, Manchester Commons, corner Rtes. 11-30; 362-5060. Children's wear at discounted prices.

Boston Traders, Manchester Commons, Rtes. 11-30, Manchester Center; 362-2910. Active wear for men and women at 20 to 80 percent off retail prices.

Coach Leatherware, corner Rtes. 11-30, Manchester Center; 362-1711. Twenty-five percent or more off bags, briefcases, belts, and small accessories.

Cole-Haan Company Store, Manchester Commons, Rtes. 11-30, Manchester Center; 362-1145. Fine footwear and accessories for men, women, and children at discount prices.

Crystal Factory, Rtes. 11-30, Manchester Center; 362-2850. Vases, glasses, decanters, etc.

Designer Classics, Manchester Marketplace, Rtes. 11-30, Manchester Center; 362-4635. Perry Ellis, J. G. Hook, and John Henry designer clothing.

Designer's Outlet, Rtes. 11-30, Manchester Center; 362-3836. Jones New York, Christian Dior outfits at 30 to 50 percent savings.

Dexter Shoe Factory Outlet, Rtes. 11-30, Manchester Center; 362-4810. Fifty percent discounted shoes for men and women.

Dexter Shoes, Rtes. 11-30, Manchester Center; 362-4810. Shoes, boots, and accessories for the whole family.

Dunham Shoes, Rte. 7A, Manchester Center; 362-4378. Dunham factory outlet; shoes for men, women, and children.

Ellen Tracy of Manchester, Battenkill Plaza, Rte. 7A, Manchester Center; 362-1851. Women's clothing at discounted prices.

Factory Handbag Store, Rte. 7A (next to Dunham's); 362-4955. Wallets, handbags, luggage, belts all at discount prices.

The Factory Store, Rtes. 11-30, Manchester Center; 362-4536. Hardwood tables, chairs, pine buffets, entertainment centers at low prices. Also household accessories.

Fenn, Wright and Manson, Battenkill Plaza, Rte. 7A, Manchester Center; 362-5455. Men's and women's sportswear.

First Choice, Battenkill Plaza, Rte. 7A, Manchester Center; 362-4867. Discounted fashions from Escada, Laurel, Crisca.

Harvé Benard, Battenkill Plaza, Rte. 7A, Manchester Center; 362-4999. Classically tailored clothes.

Hathaway Shirts, The Equinox Shops, Rte. 7A, Manchester Village; 362-3317. Shirts, sportswear, and accessories.

Kids' Depot, Rte. 7A, Manchester Center; no phone. Small designer clothing shop for young children.

Knitwits, Rtes. 11-30, Manchester Center; 362-3848. Name-brand clothing for women, children, men. 40 to 60 percent discounts.

Liz Claiborne, Rte. 7A, Manchester Center; 362-5551. Women's designer clothing.

London Fog Factory Outlet, Manchester Marketplace, Rtes. 11-30, Manchester Center; 362-0134. One-half off regular prices on rainwear, jackets, outerwear, accessories.

Manchester Commons, corner Rtes. 11-30, Manchester Center. Upscale stores including Cole-Haan, Boston Trader Kids, Boston Traders, Samuel Roberts/Joan and David, Polo-Ralph Lauren, Coach Leatherware.

Manhattan Factory Store, Rte. 7A, Manchester Center; 362-3840. Brand-name fashions for men and women discounted 25 to 60 percent.

Northeast Sportswear, Manchester Marketplace, Rtes. 11-30, Manchester Center; 362-5424. Discounted Bugle Boy, Bench clothing for boys, men.

Polly Flinders, Rte. 7, Manchester Center; 362-2445. Lovely hand-smocked girls' dresses discounted 40 to 60 percent.

Polo/Ralph Lauren Factory Store, Manchester Commons, corner Rtes. 11-30; 362-2340. Men's, women's, boys', girls' clothing; towels, sheets, quilts at discount prices.

Samuel Robert Direct, Manchester Commons, corner Rtes. 11-30; 362-4111. Ultrasuede and leather fashions, Joan and David shoes.

Sox Market, Rte. 7A, Manchester Center; 362-5500. Factory discounts on hosiery for men, women, and children.

Sportswear Systems, Battenkill Plaza, Rte. 7A, Manchester Center; 362-5355. Women's clothing.

Timberland Factory Outlet, Rte. 7A, Manchester Center; 362-3210. Discounted sportswear.

Sports and Recreation

Biking

MANCHESTER

Battenkill Sports, Rtes. 11-30, Manchester Center; 362-2734. Children's bikes, 12-speed touring bikes, 18- to 29-speed mountain bikes, accessories rentals.

Pedal Pushers, Rtes. 11-30, Manchester Center; 362-5200. Ten-speed road bikes, mountain bikes, accessories rentals.

STRATTON

CB Sports, Village Square, Stratton; 297-2200. Eighteen- to 20-speed mountain bikes rentals.

Golf

MANCHESTER

Equinox Golf Course, Equinox Hotel, Manchester Village; 362-4700. Eighteen-hole golf course, open to the public.

Manchester Country Club, Rte. 7 North, Manchester Center; 362-3148. Eighteen-hole course. Approximately 15 motels in the area have membership and golf packages.

POULTNEY
Lake St. Catherine Country Club, Rte. 30, Poultney; 287-9341. Nine-hole course, open to the public.

STRATTON
Stratton Mountain Country Club, Stratton Mountain; 297-2200. Vermont's only 27-hole course is opened to the public. Stratton also runs a golf school created by Arnold Palmer and Geoffrey Cornish, which has weekend and week-long programs.

Horseback Riding

MANCHESTER
Village Carriage Co., c/o Equinox Hotel, Rte. 7A, Manchester Village; 447-1769. Horse and carriage rides. Driver in top hat.
Windhill Horses and Tack Shop, North Rd., Manchester Center; 362-2604. Trail rides, pony rides for youngsters. Sleigh rides. New and used English and western equipment and supplies.

STRATTON
Stratton Stables, Stratton Mountain; 297-2200. Horseback trail rides open to the public.

Sporting Goods Services

BONDVILLE
Norse House, Rte. 30 (bottom of Stratton Mountain Access Rd.); 297-1755. Downhill ski rentals by the day, week, or season. Repairs.
Startingate, Rte. 30, Bondville; 297-1213. Custom ski tuning, downhill rental equipment.

LONDONDERRY
Magic Mountain Ski Area, Rte. 11, Londonderry; 824-5566. Alpine skiing rental equipment.
Viking Ski Touring Centre, Little Pond Rd., Londonderry; 824-3933. Cross-country ski rental equipment and shop.

MANCHESTER
Burton Snowboards, Rte. 7 North, Manchester Center; 362-4000. Snowboarding equipment.
Hildene Cross Country Ski Center, Rte. 7A, Manchester Village; 362-1788. Cross-country ski rental equipment.
Manchester Sports, Rte. 7A, Manchester Center; 362-2569. Cross-country ski equipment, tennis rackets, paddle tennis rackets, etc. Also cross-country ski rentals. Sneakers and other sportswear.
Mountain Goat, Rte. 7A, Manchester Center; 362-5159. Camping, rock climbing, backpacking, cross-country ski equipment, kayaks.
Orvis Company, Rte. 7A, Manchester Village; 362-1300. High-quality fishing rods, reels, accessories; guns and accessories. Orvis also runs a fly-fishing school and a shooting school. Call for more information.
Skier's Edge, Rtes. 11-30, Manchester Center; 362-1209. Alpine ski rentals by the day or season. New equipment for sale. Repair service.
Stratton 100 Shop, Equinox Plaza, Rtes. 11-30, Manchester Center; 362-0102. Alpine ski rentals, tennis racket restringing; downhill and cross-country equipment. Repair service.
Vermont Pedal Pushers, Rtes. 11-30, Manchester Center; 362-5200. Cross-country ski equipment, accessories.

PERU

Bromley Shop, Bromley Mountain, Rte. 11, Peru; 824-5522. Alpine ski rentals, snowboards, accessories. Repair service.

Hillside Ski Shop, Rte. 11, Peru; 824-6348. Alpine ski rentals by the day or season. Repair service.

Wild Wings Ski Touring Center, North Rd., Peru; 824-6793. Cross-country ski equipment.

STRATTON

Bear Essentials, off Stratton Mountain Access Rd.; 297-9843. Hunting and fishing licenses.

First Run Ski Shop, Stratton Mountain; 297-2200. Downhill rentals.

Stratton Ski Touring Center, Mountain Rd., Stratton Mountain; 297-1880. Cross-country ski equipment rental.

WELLS

Marina St. Catherine, Rte. 30; 645-0410. Located on west shore of Lake St. Catherine. Canoes, motorboats, paddleboats, pontoon boats for rent.

Tennis

LONDONDERRY

Pingree Park, off Rte. 11 opposite Mountain Marketplace Shopping Center (2/10 mile off Rte. 11), one court. First come, first served.

West River Tennis Center, Rte. 100, South Londonderry; 824-3688. Private, indoor tennis courts but will rent by the hour.

MANCHESTER

Equinox Hotel, Rte. 7A, Manchester Village. Clay tennis courts for rent by the hour.

Dana Thompson Memorial Park (Manchester Recreation Area), Rte. 30, Manchester Center; 362-1439. Three hard tennis courts, first come, first served. No charge.

Wilburton Inn, River Rd., Manchester Village; 362-2500. Three hard-surface courts for rent by the hour.

POULTNEY

Poultney Elementary School. Take a right-hand turn off Main St. at Drake's Pharmacy, follow to end. Across from Marcy's Garage, bear right to school. Two hard-surface courts, first come, first served.

RAWSONVILLE

Inn at Bear Creek, Rte. 30, Rawsonville; 297-1700. Five Har-Tru courts for rent by the hour.

STRATTON

Stratton Tennis School, Stratton Mountain; 297-2200. Weekend or week-long instructional programs. Outdoor and indoor courts for guests or tennis school participants.

Alpine Ski Areas

LONDONDERRY

Magic Mountain/Timber Ridge, Rte. 11, Londonderry; 824-5566. Ski conditions phone; 824-5617. Six lifts, 70 trails, snowmaking, competition training center, state-accredited nursery, half-pipe for snowboarders. Ski school, private and group lessons, advanced skiers workshops. Interchangeable lift tickets with Bromley Mountain.

PERU

Bromley Mountain, Rte. 11, Peru; 824-5522. Beginner, intermediate, expert areas; 35 trails, nine lifts, extensive snowmaking equipment, restaurants, tavern, ski school (lessons by the hour, day, week programs), nursery program, day care, ski rentals. Lift tickets interchangeable with Magic Mountain.

STRATTON

Stratton Mountain, Stratton Mountain; 297-2200. Ski conditions; 297-2211. Skiing on 90 trails; 12 lifts; snowmaking; 12-passenger, high-speed gondola; numerous restaurants. Sun Bowl has base lodge, parking area, quad chair lift. Ski school (group and private lessons), ski packages. The resort also has a 27-hole golf course, 19 tennis courts, golf and tennis schools, sports center. Shopping area.

Nordic Ski Areas

LONDONDERRY

Nordic Inn Ski Touring Center, Rte. 11; 824-6444. Twenty-five kilometers of groomed trails, ski rentals, group lessons. More suitable for intermediate skiers, although there are beginner and expert trails.

Viking Ski Touring Centre, Little Pond Rd., Londonderry; 824-3933. Forty kilometers of groomed woodland trails, lessons, small restaurant, rentals. Inn-to-inn and guided backcountry tours.

MANCHESTER

Hildene Ski Touring Center, Rte. 7A, Manchester Village; 362-1788. Fifteen kilometers of trails; 12 of those groomed. Cross-country skiing right in town. Rentals. Scenic trails for beginner, intermediate, advanced.

PERU

Wild Wings Ski Touring Center, North Rd., Peru; 824-6793. Twenty kilometers, 14 of those groomed and track-set. Low-key cross-country ski area, groomed trails, warming hut with hot soup. Rental equipment, lessons.

STRATTON

Stratton Ski Touring Center, Mountain Rd., Stratton Mountain; 297-1880. Twelve kilometers groomed and track-set for beginner, intermediate, and advanced skiers. Ski rentals, lessons.

Fishing

DORSET

Emerald Lake State Park, Rte. 7, North Dorset. Yellow perch, northern pike, smallmouth bass, panfish.

LONDONDERRY

Lowell Lake, off Rte. 11, Londonderry. Yellow perch, chain pickerel, largemouth bass, smallmouth bass, bullhead, panfish.

MANCHESTER

Orvis Company, Rte. 7A, Manchester Village; 362-3166. Fly-fishing school, retailer of fine rods, reels, and fishing accessories.

POULTNEY

Lake St. Catherine. Rainbow trout, lake trout, smelt, yellow perch, northern pike, largemouth bass, smallmouth bass, bullhead, panfish.

STRATTON

Grout Pond, Stratton. Yellow perch, chain pickerel, smallmouth bass, bullhead, panfish.

Stratton Pond, Stratton. Brook trout, bullhead, panfish.

WINHALL

Gale Meadows Pond. Brown trout, yellow perch, chain pickerel, largemouth bass, bullhead, panfish.

RIVERS IN THE AREA:

Battenkill, brook trout, brown trout.

West branch of the Battenkill, brook trout, brown trout.

Mettowee, brook trout, brown trout, rainbow trout.
Poultney River, brook trout, brown trout.
West River, brook trout, brown trout, walleye, smallmouth bass, panfish.
Winhall River, brook trout, brown trout.

Boating

DORSET
Emerald Lake State Park, Rte. 7, East Dorset; 362-1655. Boat, paddleboat, canoe rentals. No motorboats.

POULTNEY
Lake St. Catherine State Park, Rte. 30; 287-9158. Boat rentals, ramp.

STRATTON
Stratton Sailboarding School, Stratton Lake, Stratton Mountain; 297-2525. Sailboarding instruction on Stratton Lake, open to the public.

SUNDERLAND
Battenkill Canoe Ltd., Rte. 7A, Sunderland. Canoeing on the famed Battenkill. Located about five miles south of Manchester. It offers a pick-up service back to your car.

WELLS
Marina St. Catherine, Rte. 30 (west shore of Lake St. Catherine), Wells; 645-0410. Full-service marina; canoes, motorboats, paddleboats, pontoon boats for rent. Convenience store items available.
North Country Sport and Power, Rte. 30 (½ mile from Lake St. Catherine), Wells; 645-0873. Fiberglass, aluminum and pontoon boats available for rent.

Swimming

DORSET
Dorset Quarry, Rte. 30; no phone. Local swimming hole in old marble quarry. Swim at your own risk. Not suitable for young children.
Emerald Lake State Park, Rte. 7, North Dorset; 362-1655. Swimming, lifeguard on duty. State park fee.

MANCHESTER
Dana Thompson Memorial Park (Manchester Recreation Area), Rte. 30; 362-1439. In-ground swimming pool, children's wading pool, snack bar. Lifeguards on duty. Admission fee.

PERU
Hapgood Pond, Green Mountain National Forest, off Rte. 11; call U.S. Forest Service Office at 362-2307 for information. Swimming, roped-off area for children, lifeguard on duty. Admission fee.

POULTNEY
Lake St. Catherine State Park, Rte. 30; 287-9158. Swimming, roped-off area, lifeguard on duty, boating ramp, sailboarding.

Hiking and Nature Trails

Southern Vermont has numerous hiking trails in the Green Mountain National Forest — too many to mention here. These include the Long Trail, Vermont's extensive hiking system that often hooks up with the Appalachian Trail, an East Coast hiking trail that runs from Georgia through Maine. The Manchester Ranger District Office is located on Rtes. 11-30 in Manchester, telephone 362-2307. Forest Service personnel can provide you with information, as well as maps and brochures about day hikes in the area. Also see the Manchester area essays and listings for parks. The parks —

Emerald Lake in North Dorset, Lake St. Catherine in Poultney, along with the Hapgood Pond Recreation Area in Peru — offer many hiking opportunities, as well.

MANCHESTER
Southern Vermont Art Center, off West Rd., Manchester Village; 362-1405.

RUPERT
Merck Foundation, Rte. 315, Rupert; 394-7836.

Parks

DORSET
Emerald Lake State Park, Rte. 7, North Dorset; 362-1655. Four hundred and thirty-acre park with 105 camping sites, including 36 lean-tos, flush toilets, hot showers (fee), public phone, picnic tables, fireplaces, snack bar, boat/canoe rentals (no motorboats), swimming, fishing, children's playground, market, nature trail, naturalist tours. No hookups. No snack shop. Admission fee.

LONDONDERRY
Memorial Park, Rte. 100, South Londonderry. Call Londonderry Chamber of Commerce, 824-8178, for information. Small swimming area with beach and picnic shelter.
Pingree Park, 2/10 mile off Rte. 11 across from Londonderry Shopping Center; no phone. One hard-surface tennis court, two baseball diamonds.
Winhall Brook Campground and Ball Mountain Dam Recreation Area, Rte. 100, South Londonderry; 824-9509. Hiking trails, camping, picnicking.

MANCHESTER
Dana Thompson Memorial Park (Manchester Recreation Area), Rte. 30; 362-1439. Tennis courts, ball fields, volleyball, winter ice-skating rink, track, grandstand, swimming pool, wading pool, showers, snack shop, children's playground. Admission fee for pool only.

PERU
Hapgood Pond Recreation Area, off Rte. 11, Peru. Call U.S. Forest Service at 362-2307 for information. Seven-acre facility off the beaten path, but accessible, with swimming, fishing, limited boating. Twenty-eight camping units, tent sites, tables, fireplaces. Toilet facilities. Forty other picnic sites. Shelters, playing fields. Admission fee.

WESTON
Greendale Recreation Park, Rte. 100 (one mile north of town); no phone. Camping, swings, small pond. Call Londonderry Chamber of Commerce at 824-8178.

Foliage Vantage Points

MANCHESTER
Lookout on Rtes. 11-30 east heading up the mountain.
River Rd., off Historic 7A in Manchester Village, is a wonderful drive during foliage.
Southern Vermont Art Center's rear garden, off West Rd., overlooks Manchester.

MT. TABOR
Forest Rd. 10 off Rte. 7 just after the Country Garden Shop leads you into the National Forest and the Big Branch Recreation Area. Follow the signs. The views down the valley are truly spectacular, and there are picnic tables and a hiking trail.

PERU
Hapgood Pond Rd. (past the Hapgood Pond Recreation Area) to Landgrove. In
  Landgrove, turn right to get back on Rte. 11 or left to take the back way to
  Weston, which is also a scenic drive.
Peru's Main St., or South Rd. (keep bearing left) into South Londonderry.

POULTNEY
Lake St. Catherine on Rte. 30.

RUPERT
Merck Foundation, Rte. 315, has fantastic views any time of the year.
Rte. 30 through Rupert, Pawlet farm country is great in a car or on a bicycle.

WESTON
The town green in any season of the year is picturesque.

Best of Manchester and the Mountains

Country Inns: Inn at Landgrove, Landgrove; Barrows House, Dorset; 867-4455.
Resort: Stratton Mountain Resort, Stratton Mountain; 297-2200.
Breakfast: Up for Breakfast, Main St., Manchester Center; 362-4204.
Lunch: Molly Coddle's, Center Hill, Manchester Center; 362-5452.
Dinner (inexpensive): Dorset Inn Tavern, Rte. 30, Dorset; 867-5500.
Dinner (Moderately Priced): Sirloin Saloon, Rtes. 11-30, Manchester Center; 362-2600.
Dinner (Expensive): Chantecleer Restaurant, East Dorset; 362-1616.
Entertainment (Casual): Andy Avery and friends, Marsh Tavern, Equinox Hotel,
  Manchester Village (year-round); 362-4700. Bands, jazz groups, Stratton Mountain;
  297-2200 (seasonal).
Entertainment (Stage): Dorset Theatre Festival, Dorset; 867-5777 (seasonal).
Museum/Historic Site: Farrar-Mansur House, Weston.
Art Galleries: Southern Vermont Art Center, Manchester Village (seasonal); 362-1405.
  Pierre's Gate, Manchester Center; 362-1766. Handworks On the Green, Stratton
  Mountain; 297-0090.
Craft/Specialty Shops: Northshire Book Store, Colburn House, Main St., Manchester
  Center; 362-2200.
Antique Shops: Center Hill Past and Present, Manchester Center; 362-3211; Danby
  Antiques Center, Danby; 293-9984.
Discount Outlet: Boston Trader Kids, Manchester Center; 362-5060; Ralph Lauren,
  Manchester Center; 362-2340.
Public Golf Course: Equinox Golf Course, Equinox Hotel, Manchester Village; 362-4700.
Public Tennis Court: Manchester Recreation Area, Rte. 30, Manchester Center; 362-1439.
Hiking or Nature Trail: Southern Vermont Art Center, Nature Trail, Manchester
  Village; 362-1405. Lye Brook Falls, Manchester.
Camping: Hapgood Pond, Peru.
Children's Activities: Manchester Old-Fashioned Fourth of July, Manchester Center;
  Alpine Slide, Bromley Mountain, Peru; 824-5522.
Farm Stand: Dutton Farm Stand, Rte. 7A, Manchester Center; no phone.
Ice Cream: Ben and Jerry's, Main St., Manchester Center; 362-4854.
Foliage Vantage Point: Big Branch Recreation Area, National Forest, Mt. Tabor.
Ski Area (Alpine): Stratton Mountain, Stratton; 297-2200.
Ski Area (Nordic): Viking Ski Touring Center, Londonderry; 824-3933.

The Rutland/Killington Area

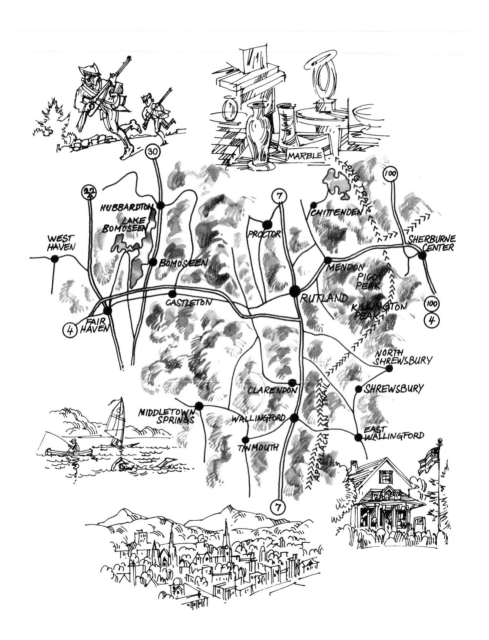

Viewpoints

by MONICA ALLEN

The city of Rutland, and the neighboring small town of Proctor, located a few miles north on Route 7, are two communities with a rich ethnic heritage. Rutland was a focal point during the heyday of the mid-nineteenth century railroad era, which proceeded to shape it into the agricultural and industrial center it is today. Immigrants who worked in the rail yards and marble quarries nearby played an important role in the growth of Vermont's second largest city. Besides being home to the annual Vermont State Fair in September, Rutland is a diverse community with restaurants, galleries, movie theaters, and city parks. It is also the closest city to the year-round resort areas of Killington and Chittenden, located east of Rutland.

Proctor is home to the Vermont Marble Company, which produced the marble used in the U.S. Supreme Court Building in Washington, D.C., and the interior of the United Nations headquarters in New York City. Although the town has no shopping areas or gourmet restaurants, Proctor is a worthwhile side trip to see the Vermont Marble Exhibit, the museum of the marble company where you can view firsthand marble projects in progress.

The City of Rutland

Unlike some of the ski resort towns to the east, or the rural hideaways that surround it, the city of Rutland has a different type of charm. Home to the Vermont State Fair, Rutland has always been more of a Carl Sandburg community, a gritty working town, a center of commercial activity for a farming county, and a community with varied ethnic roots.

Rutland has the largest population in Rutland County, with 18,500 residents, but is the smallest in actual land with 4,300 acres. It is the second largest city in Vermont, behind Burlington. It serves as the county's shire town, housing courts and county government. It is also the commercial and banking center for the region.

Historical Perspective

In pre-Colonial days, the area where Rutland was established was disputed territory for two large, powerful Indian tribes — the Abnakis and the Iroquois. Both wanted to use the land for hunting and fishing. Hunting parties came from Lake Champlain down the Otter Creek to the gentle valley. The land was later controlled by the French until after the British pushed them back during the French and Indian War.

Following the war, a military road was built from Lake Champlain through Rutland to Charlestown, New Hampshire. Rutland became a named community in 1761 when Benning Wentworth, the royal governor of New Hampshire, signed a charter in the name of King George III. One of the grantees was from Rutland, Massachusetts, and it is believed that may have been the reason for the name.

The oldest section of Rutland is the area around Main Street Park. It was here along Route 7 (called Main Street) and around the park that the first village developed in the late 1700s. In 1776, a fort manned by Vermonters was built near what is now the intersection of West and Main streets to protect settlers from British troops and their Indian allies during the revolutionary war. A statue of a Green Mountain Boy stands in the park to honor the role this brave band of early Americans took in the Revolution.

Rutland soon became one of the most important towns in what would later become the Republic of Vermont and eventually the state. As a center for a large farming region, Rutland attracted craftsmen, merchants, ministers, and statesmen. In the early years of Vermont's statehood, the state legislature would often meet in Rutland.

Rutland grew tremendously, nearly tripling in population in the years 1850 to 1880. The simple reason was the railroad. It also became a major manufacturing center and a world center for marble quarrying. The Rutland Railroad, which ran its first train in 1849, pulled the city's development from the hillside of Main Street Park to what is today's downtown business district. This district of proud brick and marble buildings is considered one of the most architecturally significant downtowns in the state.

Due to the railroad, the city of Rutland became an ethnic melting pot. In the mid-1800s, the Irish immigrants attracted by railroad and foundry jobs lived in houses in the southwestern section of town within walking distance of the rail yards. By the turn of the century, there were many Italian families as well. The southwest neighborhood, known affectionately as the "gut," because it girdles the lower half of the city, was and is the most ethnically distinct section of town. Mom-and-pop stores, bakeries, and pizzerias still dot the street corners of the neighborhood.

The Courthouse Historic District on the hillside just above the downtown is where the wealthy railroad officials, foundry owners, merchants, and judges built their homes in the late 1800s as the city boomed. Like the downtown, this area, with its Victorian-styled homes, is listed on the National Register of Historic Places.

Other immigrants have played important roles in Rutland's development as well. The city had an established Jewish community before the Civil War. French-Canadians came to work in local industries at the end of the nineteenth century, later building a cathedral, Immaculate Heart of Mary, on Lincoln Avenue.

West Rutland, which was part of the town of Rutland until it, like Proctor and other neighboring communities, was incorporated as a separate community, was home to many Polish immigrants who came to work in the marble quarries. Mass is still said in Polish at St. Stanislaus Kostka on Barnes Street in West Rutland, located about five miles west on Route 4.

City Attractions

Downtown Rutland, like many of America's central business districts, has struggled over the years to remain alive and interesting. It lost its main reason for existing in 1961 when the railroad went out of business, a victim of the automobile age. The Rutland Shopping Plaza was built on the site of the railroad, but over the years it began to grow dilapidated. There is a great deal of hope in the city as it moves toward the twenty-first century that a new owner of the plaza will bring the 20-acre downtown parcel on Merchants Row to life. That can only help the rest of the downtown.

One of the most striking downtown buildings is the Bardwell House on Merchants Row. This restored four-story building at the corner of Washington Street was built in 1852 as a fancy hotel for travelers who came into town by train. Today, it has been renovated to house elderly and disabled citizens. Standing to the left of the painted-brick Bardwell is the Service Building — considered by locals to be our Daily Planet. Although it does not house the city's newspaper, the *Rutland Herald*, established 1794, it certainly looks like the building where mild-mannered Clark Kent (otherwise known as Superman) might have typed his stories. The 1930-era building is Vermont's only example of an art deco skyscraper.

Besides the historical sites, the city of Rutland has a lot to offer in the way of interesting eateries, galleries, and shops. The Moon Brook Arts Union, a small gallery on the second floor of 21 Center Street run by Bob Dombro, displays a wide variety of work by outstanding professional artists.

Be sure and visit the Opera House on the west side of Merchants Row, across from Woolworth's. Transformed from an entertainment hall to a retail and office complex, it houses Rutland's best modern book shop, Book King, run by Steve Eddy, who works behind the counter daily, and is a good source of information on downtown happenings and books by local authors.

Two of the city's most interesting attractions — the Chaffee Art Gallery at 16 South Main Street and Tuttle Antiquarian Books at 28-30 South Main Street — are located near the courthouse district. Housed in a turn-of-the-century Victorian building, the Chaffee is a private nonprofit organization devoted to bringing art to the community through exhibitions and educational programs. The gallery also hosts two annual "Art in the Park" festivals held in Main Street Park in mid-August and early October. Artists from throughout the country are chosen by a jury to set up displays for this popular weekend event. The Chaffee also offers a variety of shows and educational programs each year. Shows have ranged from modern sculpture by Northeast and Southwest artists to celebrations of flight and airplanes. Susan Farrow, director of the museum, recently brought an early twentieth-century airplane to the front lawn of the museum to display at the airplane show.

Just a block away, Tuttle Antiquarian Books is Vermont's largest old, rare, and secondhand bookshop. The bookstore is located in a Colonial Era building with comfortable reading rooms. There are some 20,000 titles covering such topics as occult, archaeology, Americana, natural history, Vermont and New England, and many travel books as well. In an adjacent building are the offices and display rooms of the Charles E. Tuttle Company, founded in 1832. The grandson of the founder, also named Charles Tuttle, is recognized as America's premier publisher-distributor of books on Asia. Making regular trips to Tokyo, Japan, Tuttle publishes books in both English and Japanese. Many of these books on arts, antiques, travel, haiku, origami, and fiction are on display at his Rutland offices.

Local Eateries

Pappy's restaurant and bar on the first floor of the Service Building in downtown Rutland is a good spot to grab lunch. On a nice day, diners move out to a back patio on what is called Center Street Alley. The most urban-looking part of Rutland, the alley has water fountains, trees, flowers, and summertime lunch-hour concerts on Tuesdays.

Across the alley toward Center Street is the region's only vegetarian restaurant, The Gentle Spirit, serving Middle Eastern dishes and herbal teas.

At 21 Center Street is the Back Home Café, one of Rutland's most distinctive and popular eating spots. Started during the hippie invasion of Vermont to serve natural food lovers, the café, also on the second floor, has gradually evolved into a fine restaurant featuring meat, fish, and pasta dishes, as well as a wide array of desserts including the sinfully famous Aunt Clem's Chocolate Cake. The prices are reasonable and the atmosphere is casual. If you have a table near the window, you get a good view of downtown Rutland. And in the summer, the café opens its back deck where you can dine under the stars.

During the summer and early fall, the Rutland County Farmer's Market is open Saturday and Wednesday. It's held at the center of downtown in Depot Park, the site of the old railroad station. Here you can sample baked goods, buy fresh vegetables, local crafts, and other farm products. There is usually some live folk music.

On Meadow Street in the "gut" is Juliana's Deli, one of the best places in town to get an eggplant parmesan sandwich or a container of cold pasta salad for lunch. It's a favorite among locals. There's no place to sit, so take your picnic to the nearby park.

Vermont State Fair

Rutland is the home of the Vermont State Fair, an annual nine-day agricultural fair that takes over the city's historic and scenic fairgrounds on South Main Street (Route 7 south of the city). Held the first week in September, the 144-year-old fair attracts close to 100,000 visitors each year. There are farm animal exhibits put on by local farmers and 4-H kids, produce competitions, baked goods contests, and horse rides. Each year the midway is filled with carnival games and a number of rides, including a ferris wheel and merry-go-round. There is daily harness racing and betting on the horses. Evening shows feature country and western artists. And one day is called Governor's Day, when Vermont's governor visits the fairgrounds to partake of some of the homemade soups and breads and do a little politicking.

At the fair, the best food can be found in the 4-H building, where homemade chowder and chili are served; in the Dairy Barn, where they will heap your ice-cream cone for a small price with delicious locally produced ice cream; and in the Maple Barn, where you can watch farmers demonstrate how they boil off the water to make syrup as you eat a "maple creaming," a combination of maple sugar and ice cream. And there are other maple delights to buy for later or give as gifts.

Parking can be tricky for the fair, but you can usually find a spot on either of the two roads off Main Street that surround the fair. You will have to pay a local vendor for your spot on Dana Street or Park Street, but the walk will be easy. Traffic is hectic during the fair, so if you're not a country fair lover or country music lover, we suggest you plan to visit Rutland another time of the year.

Recreational Pursuits

Throughout Rutland City there are city parks open to the public. Tennis courts are located at Monsignor Connor on Meadow Street and two other parks. To get to the courts, basketball, and outdoor pool at White's park, take Jackson Avenue off Route 7, an eastern turn a half mile south of Main Street Park. The Olympic-sized pool is open to the public in the summertime. Another park is on North Street. To get there you drive west on West Street from Main Street Park and take your second right onto Lincoln Avenue. Follow this until you reach North Street and take a right. The park, with more tennis courts, handball courts, and a playground, will be on your left. All three parks also have basketball.

The John J. Giorgetti Memorial Park has a skating rink open during the winter. The city recreation department also maintains Pine Hill Park adjacent to Giorgetti.

There is a mile round-trip trail to Rocky Pond in the park. And in the wintertime, indoor skating is also offered to children at the Royce Mandigo Arena on Dana Street. Contact the Rutland Recreation Department at 773-1822 for more information.

Rutland is also home to a number of shopping outlets. Near the fairgrounds is Timberland, a company that sells boots and other outdoor gear. South on Route 7 less than a quarter mile is Ruff Hewn, an outlet with classic men's and women's clothing made of quality natural fabrics. Across the street is the Colonial Sportshoe Center, which offers a large selection of athletic footwear at outlet prices. On Route 4 east of the city, you will find the Dunham and Dexter shoe outlets. On Route 7 north of the city, there is a complex of clothing and leather goods outlets including Van Heusen shirt outlet, the Hathaway Shirt outlet, and a Swank leather goods and jewelry store.

Proctor

This small, quiet town on the banks of the Otter Creek was once the home of the largest marble company in the world. The town still retains the look and feel of a well-planned company town. Many of today's residents live in the still-sturdy duplexes that were built for the immigrant workers. The neat marble sidewalks, churches, schools, and town buildings are also a testament to the glory days.

Historical Perspective

Proctor was created in 1886 by the Vermont legislature and was named for Redfield Proctor, a man who merged a number of small marble companies to form the Vermont Marble Company. The town was created from land that had been part of Rutland. Redfield Proctor, who had served as a colonel in the Civil War, led his new marble company through a period of tremendous expansion and transformed what had been a farming community into one of Vermont's major industrial communities. He brought skilled marble carvers from Italy and unskilled immigrants from Sweden to join with the native Vermont work force.

From the late 1800s to early 1900s, the Proctor family operated a company store, helped workers build homes on the hillsides of the town, and built the community hospital that provided free care to company employees and their families. In addition, they built the town a library.

The Proctor family was not only powerful in the marble industry, but family members also were influential in Vermont politics. Redfield, his son, Fletcher, and two other Proctor descendants, served as governors of Vermont. Redfield Proctor, the older, was appointed secretary of war under President Benjamin Harrison (1889–93) and also served as a U.S. senator until his death in 1903. Vermont Marble received numerous important contracts during these years, including the U.S. Supreme Court Building and the interior of the United Nations headquarters.

Vermont Marble Exhibit

A good place to start your visit to Proctor is at the Vermont Marble Exhibit, the museum of the marble company, located in a long work shed on the banks of the Otter Creek. To get there from Rutland, take Route 4 west three miles, then turn north onto Route 3, which takes you into Proctor. You will then take a left over a marble arch bridge that crosses Otter Creek. Mrs. Emily Proctor, the widow of Redfield Proctor, had the bridge built in honor of her son, Fletcher. Just before you cross the bridge, you will see Proctor Free Library, another marble structure that the Proctor family built for the community. Once over the bridge, drive right down the hill to the marble works.

The museum is inside a long wood and stone building where marble is still cut and shaped by the Vermont Marble Company, now owned by a Swiss company. Inside you will find a hallway of bas-relief sculptures of the nation's presidents, old Italian marble sculptures, enlarged black-and-white photographs of the early days of the marble company, and exhibits describing how marble is geologically formed and how man has extracted it and used it over the years. Take your time looking at the photographs throughout the museum because they contain the faces of the Italian, Swedish, Polish, and Czech immigrants who built the company and were the backbone of the town. While it was the Yankee families that controlled the company, these immigrants are the ancestors of many of the people who populate Proctor today.

Because the museum is part of the working factory, visitors can glimpse some of the work in progress from a balcony above a large cavernous workshop. In addition, inside the museum, a Vermont Marble sculptor chisels away on marble in a small glassed-in studio. You are invited to join the sculptor to watch him work and ask questions. In another section of the museum, you can watch a brief film on the history of the marble company. The museum has an extensive gift shop where you can browse for marble items ranging from small bowls and vases to dining tables and bathroom tiles. There is also an outdoor marble exhibit with larger pieces.

Once you have seen the museum, we suggest you walk through the village just outside the company gates. A luscious grassy park is the perfect spot for a picnic. And across the street are marble town buildings. Proctor has many marble buildings, including its high school and a stately Catholic church on Route 3. To see the homes where the company executives lived in the heyday of the marble company, drive back over the bridge and take Ormsbee Avenue directly across the street from the bridge. The workers' neat, square-porched duplexes can be found on most any back street in town. These houses have weathered the years well and are today considered desirable by many families.

Not a commercial town geared for tourists, Proctor does not have restaurants or shopping areas. Today, it is predominantly a bedroom community for Rutland. The town has just under 2,000 residents living on 4,800 acres of land.

But if you would like a quick bite at a popular local watering hole, the pizza is tasty at Bud's Cannonball Lounge. If you continue driving past the marble museum on your way west to the next landmark, Wilson's Castle, you will pass the lounge.

Wilson's Castle

If you like exploring fancy houses decorated by unusual people from the past, you will enjoy Wilson's Castle on the West Proctor Road. John Johnson, a doctor who went to London, married a noblewoman, and returned with his wealthy wife, had the castle built in the 1880s. The red brick mansion has towers, turrets, arcades, balconies, and extensive porches that overlook the valley. Johnson bred expensive cattle and horses on the property and rapidly went through his wife's fortune and lost the castle by 1890. Over the next few decades, it changed hands a number of times. Colonel Herbert Wilson acquired the house in 1936 and opened it as a museum in 1962. His daughter, Blossom, still lives in a wing of the estate during the summer months, although the colonel has since died. Most of the castle is opened to visitors in the summer. It contains beautiful stained-glass windows, many exotic types of wood furniture, wood paneling, hand-painted ceilings, antiques, and china collected by the colonel during his world travels.

Tour guides give visitors a quick description of the materials in the house. You'll laugh at such funny items as a wooden porch swing designed so girls could partake of the fun without the dread fear their ankles might be revealed. This particular swing rocks horizontally on a plane, rather than tilting slightly up and down like the standard porch swing. Fountains, and a birdhouse with peacocks, adorn the castle grounds.

The Killington Area: Chittenden, Mendon, and Sherburne (Killington)

Just east of Rutland are three resort communities that have become a year-round sporting paradise for the local and visitor alike — Chittenden, Mendon, and Sherburne, home to the largest ski area in the East, Killington.

Chittenden's main attraction is the Mountain Top Ski Resort, an elegant complex that caters mostly to cross-country ski enthusiasts. In summer, the 750-acre Chittenden Reservoir is available for boating and swimming. Little Mendon, sandwiched between Rutland and the town of Sherburne, offers fine restaurants and a gravestone for General Ripley's favorite steed, Old John. And, Sherburne is home to Pico, an intimate Alpine ski area, and mammoth Killington, an Alpine ski resort that also boasts cross-country trails. In the spring, summer, and fall, cyclists, joggers, swimmers, golfers, and tennis buffs round out the roster. Scenic country settings, along with excellent dining and lodging facilities, make this a most attractive resort area for visitors.

Chittenden

Here's a town where you can hide away most any season of the year, yet it's a quick drive to some of the best Alpine skiing in the Northeast, and it's only 10 miles north of Rutland City.

To get to Chittenden, drive north on Route 7 from Rutland. After you leave the city, you will take a right onto the Chittenden Road. There's a small green sign saying Chittenden and East Pittsford. Follow this five miles until you reach a military statue in the center of three roads. You have arrived at the center of Chittenden.

Historical Perspective

This small town of 900 people, chartered in 1780, has been spared development primarily because more than half the town is in the Green Mountain National Forest and the rest is perched on the foothills of the mountains. Initially, Chittenden was a logging community with as many as 12 sawmills. Today, although it has the distinction of being the largest town in land area in Vermont, it is a bedroom community for Rutland and Sherburne. It is also a great place to cross-country ski, hike, horseback ride, bike, swim, and sail.

There are two inns to stay at while visiting Chittenden — the Mountain Top Inn or the Tulip Tree Inn, a green-clapboard inn that was once owned by the prominent Barstow family. It's tucked in the woods off Dam Road and opens eight bedrooms, some with Jacuzzis, to guests. When asked what many of his guests like to do while staying here, innkeeper Ed McDowell said, "They seem to enjoy doing a lot of nothing."

Mountain Top is an extensive four-season resort and offers many recreational opportunities to inn guests as well as the public. Mountain Top runs one of the state's choice cross-country ski areas, which is open to the public for a fee. The 110 kilometers of ski trails include a variety of paths through forests, past grazing horses, and a maple sugar house. The groomed trails lead into open fields that look down the valley.

To reach the inn and ski area, drive to the center of Chittenden as described above and continue up Mountain Top Road, which will be marked near the military statue. The ski area offers ski equipment rentals and a shop where you can purchase everything from skis, poles, and boots to that hunk of red wax you forgot to bring. Mountain Top tends to get more crowded on holiday weekends, but the large number of trails usually can accommodate most crowds. The weekdays are the best time if you like to hear only the sound of your own skis shooshing through the snow. Ski lessons are available, and for a few weeks each winter Olympic champion Bill Koch offers clinics. Mike Gallagher, an Olympic Nordic coach, is also on the teaching staff.

Mountain Top offers horseback riding in the spring, summer, and fall along Chittenden's forested back roads and trails. And in the winter, the horses are hitched up to old-fashioned sleighs for daytime and evening rides over the snowy fields.

The inn has a restaurant open to the public for breakfast, lunch, and dinner. There is also a snack bar at the ski center in the winter.

Summer Recreation

Much summer recreation for both inn guests, locals, and other visitors to the area centers around the Chittenden Reservoir, a 750-acre lake that is framed by the Green Mountains. All the land around the lake is owned by the national forest or the local power company, so there are no houses to interrupt your views of mountains and woods.

The public can reach the lake for boating and swimming at a public access area managed by Central Vermont Public Service Corporation, a Rutland-based power company. To reach the access, drive to the center of Chittenden Village as described above. Take the Dam Road, which is clearly marked, and drive up a hill until the end of the road where there is a sign for the access area. You may put small craft in the lake here.

In order to protect the lake and keep the noise down for those who like to sail, canoe, and fish, motors larger than 15 horsepower are not permitted. On the way to the lake, there's the Mustard Seed Canoe and Boat Rental, a small operation run out of a garage where you can rent a boat for the day. There is no swimming beach at the boat launch, so most people either hike around the lake or boat to a secluded rocky cove for private swimming.

For Mountain Top Inn guests, there is a beach on the lake with sailboats, Windsurfers, and canoes. There is also an outdoor swimming pool and golf course.

For hiking, there is the New Boston Trail a short distance past Mountain Top Inn. The trail is named for an old village and stagecoach stop that once graced these hills, and as you hike, you may see the evidence — cellar holes, old apple trees, and stone walls.

Other points of interest in Chittenden include an art studio run by Al Friedman, which is on a back road above Mountain Top Inn. Friedman spends his days painting watercolors of local landscapes. He also offers art classes to the public. To get to his house/studio, walk past the ski center and take your first left on a dirt road. There should be a sign directing you to the studio.

In autumn, drives or walks down the back roads of Chittenden provide some of the best views of foliage in the area. So just wander up the Dam Road or Powerhouse Road and Sagamon Road, all turns off the Chittenden Road.

Mendon

The town of Mendon is sandwiched between Rutland to the west and Sherburne to the east. Most of the development in Mendon, a town of 1,000 people, is along Route 4, the road that connects the city of Rutland with the ski areas in Sherburne. But if you drive off the main highway, you will find peaceful country roads and excellent gourmet restaurants.

Historical Perspective

Mendon was chartered in 1781 and became a center for logging in the nineteenth century. It was during the early and midcentury that a small village developed. A white meetinghouse and a cluster of houses remain just off Route 4. Across the street from the village is Sugar and Spice, a pancake house and gift shop built on land that was once owned by the town's most famous citizen. Edward H. Ripley (1839–1915) was the general in command of the Union troops that occupied Richmond, Virginia, during the Civil War. During the Civil War, more than half the legal voters in Mendon were in service, many under Ripley's command. In tall grass out behind Sugar and Spice is a quirky reminder of Vermont's Civil War history. A large boulder with a worn-out engraving marks the grave of Ripley's Civil War horse. The engraving reads, "The Grave of General Edward H. Ripley's Old John, A Gallant War Horse of the Great Civil War 1861–1865."

Local Favorites

On Mendon's back roads are some of the finest inns and restaurants in the area. The Red Clover Inn is off Woodward Road, which is a south turn off Route 4. Here you can stay as a guest in a secluded farmhouse or simply dine in a restaurant where the food is delicious and the atmosphere is relaxed. Just behind the inn rises a series of mountain peaks.

Another favorite hideaway is Countryman's Pleasure on Townline Road, south turn off Route 4 just as you enter Mendon. The restaurant specializes in Austrian-style fine cuisine. Other favorite restaurants in Mendon are Little Naples, an Italian restaurant on Route 4, and Churchill's, a steak and seafood restaurant across the street from Little Naples. Both of these restaurants tend to draw many people from the Rutland region as well as visitors.

Mendon also is home to the Mendon Mountain Orchards off Route 4. Here you can buy fresh apples year-round at the country store and pick apples yourself in the autumn. The store sells apple pies and sweet cider.

Recreational Pursuits

For hikers, Mendon has many trails including a pleasant hike to Blue Ridge Mountain. The hike up the 2.4-mile trail makes a 1,490-foot ascent that takes approximately two hours one way. The summit offers good views of Rutland, Killington, and on a clear day as far as the White Mountains of New Hampshire. Drive up Route 4 from Rutland into Mendon. Take a left on Turnpike Road just oppo-site the Killington-Pico Motor Inn. Follow this to a lane on the left where there are signs for Tall Timber Camp and Blue Ridge Mountain roadside parking. From Turnpike Road, the trail follows the lane northwest past Tall Timber Camp buildings and begins to climb the mountain. Refer to a Green Mountain Club hiker's guide for more information on this or other hikes.

Sherburne (Killington)

The drive to Sherburne from Rutland City over the 10-mile stretch up Route 4 is a dramatic one. You climb steadily, passing many shops, and eventually reach Sherburne Pass at the top of the road. From there, you'll descend rapidly to Sher-burne Center. The drive is good psychological preparation for the different world you are about to enter. This is not a quaint Vermont town with a white-steepled church and an old-fashioned country store dominating Main Street.

This is Sherburne, better known as Killington, a sporter's paradise. In the winter, this town grows in population from just under 900 hearty residents to weekend crowds of 60,000. The Killington Ski Area, the largest ski resort in the eastern United States, is known throughout the world for great skiing, great mountain views, and plenty of off-slope dining, lodging, and entertainment. Sherburne is also the home of the Pico Ski Resort, one of the nation's oldest ski areas. The mountain truly hops in the winter, and each year it is becoming more lively dur-ing summer and fall, too, as more people realize the wealth of year-round activ-ities available.

Historical Perspective

Sherburne was established as the town of Killington in 1761. It is believed to have been named for a village in Northumberland, England. The town was re-named Sherburne in 1800, after Benjamin Sherburne, one of the men to whom the town was granted.

Ezra Stiles, one of the founders of Brown University and an early president of Yale University, planned the town's layout from his home in Rhode Island in 1764. However, he ignored the 3,000- and 4,000-feet-high mountains when he laid the town out in a classical manner. Settlers, mostly loggers and farmers, decided to discard these plans when they built their homes, sawmills, and stores in the Ottaquechee River valley. The town remained a sleepy community for more than a century. Too rocky and mountainous for successful farming, Sher-burne became a top supplier of timber. However, from the early days, people appreciated the mountains for their beauty. Prominent Rutlanders built hunt-ing camps and vacation hideaways in the hills.

One such couple, Janet and Bradford Mead, decided to start a small ski area in their backyard in 1937. They installed a rope tow up Pico Peak, elevation 3,957 feet, and founded that ski area, one of the first in the country. Over the years, Pico remained in family ownership. Its slopes became training grounds for Olympic gold medalist Andrea Mead, daughter of the founders.

Just up the road, deep in the woods of Calvin Coolidge State Forest, the Killing-ton Ski Area was started by a 24-year-old man from Connecticut with a passion for the outdoors. Preston Smith, who remains the president of the ski area's parent company, SKI Limited, had planned to go into farming, but after years of skiing in Vermont, he decided to forgo that for a more risky business. His risk paid off.

SKI Limited has grown tremendously in recent years. It has acquired Mount Snow in Dover, Bear Mountain Ski Area in California, and merged with nearby

Pico in the summer of 1989. It has the most extensive snowmaking of any Vermont ski area, and the trails are some of the best groomed in the state.

To reach the Killington Ski Area, drive to Sherburne as described above and take the Killington Access Road near the intersection of Route 100 and Route 4. The Killington Base Lodge and other facilities are at the end of the road, past numerous lodges, shops, and restaurants. You will enter Calvin Coolidge State Forest just before you reach the ski area.

Alpine Skiing

Killington, the big daddy of Vermont ski areas, has had its share of tangles with the state of Vermont in recent years. The testy relationship between Preston Smith and Vermont's officials is well known. Smith wants Killington to be able to grow, while environmental groups have been trying to rein those projects that epitomize uncontrolled development. The ski area and federal government have infuriated some Vermont politicians, environmentalists, and hikers by striking a deal that allowed Killington to build a ski lift and two ski trails across the Appalachian Trail. Despite political controversy, there is no dispute that the six mountains at Killington with their 107 trails provide some of the best skiing in the East.

Each of the six mountains has its own character as do the trails. Mountains range in elevation from Killington Peak, 4,241 feet above sea level, to Sunrise Mountain at 2,456 feet. Killington Peak is Vermont's second highest mountain after Mount Mansfield.

Ski trails range from 48 designated for "easier" skiing to 38 dubbed the "most difficult." There are 18 lifts located among the mountains, including the three-mile Killington Gondola, the longest ski lift in North America. Each mountain has its own base lodge, complete with restaurants or cafeterias, ski rentals, and repairs. The ski area also offers child care.

Killington tends to get crowded on weekends and during holidays, but locals have long avoided these crowds by heading to Northeast Passage, a grouping of intermediate to expert trails that can be reached by driving east on Route 4 to just before where the highway intersects with Route 100, south.

Pico Ski Resort, located on the western side of Sherburne Pass on Route 4, has always been called the "Friendly Mountain." Although a much smaller ski area, Pico appeals to many local families as well as expert skiers. Like the Northeast Passage, it is usually less crowded during the peak ski times of the year.

And Pico earned its reputation as the Friendly Mountain because of its intimate size and long history supporting the Rutland region, with everything from benefit ski races to reasonably priced children's ski lessons.

Pico has four peaks on one mountain and 35 trails served by nine lifts. A single base lodge with cafeteria, lounge, deli, children's center, ski shop, rental, and repair shops serves visitors' needs.

Both Killington and Pico offer lessons for people of all ages and skill levels, and each mountain facility has extensive snowmaking capabilities. Killington is usually one of the last ski resorts to close its slopes in the spring. So if you are interested in a May or June ski complete with T-shirt and shorts, don't necessarily assume it's impossible until you've checked with Killington. They pride themselves on May and June skiing.

Sherburne also is home to Mountain Meadows Ski Touring Center — a cross-country ski area. Take Route 4 east from the intersection with Route 100 and watch for signs to Mountain Meadows on your left. The area has 40 miles of trails, approximately 15 maintained with tracks. Here you can rent, buy, or use your own skis. Cross-country ski instruction is also available.

Other Recreational Pursuits

If the weather turns bad, there is plenty to do in Sherburne. Killington and Pico have health clubs with pools, weight rooms, racquetball courts, and state-of-the-art exercise equipment.

Pico's new Sports Center has a 76-foot lap pool, the largest on the mountain. It's set in a high-ceilinged room with plenty of windows for natural light and views of the woods. Killington's Health Club is in Killington Village off the Upper Snowshed Lodge parking lot near the end of the access road.

Another favorite rainy day activity is to drive down to Rutland City to shop, catch a movie, or try a new restaurant.

The restaurant scene on and off the mountain offers plenty of variety. The bars are lively on rainy days, with skiers flooding popular places like the Wobbly Barn on the Killington Access Road, which features classic rock and roll music, good steak, and salads. Another popular hangout is Mother Shapiro's, also on the access road. The cozy bar is run by Jay Shapiro, a longtime resident of the mountain, who believes there should be a place in Vermont to get good lox, bagels, and cream cheese. Although that's a breakfast or lunch dish, it's available at Mother Shapiro's all day. The bar has a lively evening atmosphere, and other foods are served as well.

If you plan to splurge for at least one meal, we recommend Hemingway's on Route 4. Ted and Linda Fondulas, an exceptionally dedicated husband and wife business team, present diners with a true food and wine experience in an elegant country setting. Given four stars by the Mobil Travel Guide, Hemingway's is the only restaurant in Maine, New Hampshire, or Vermont to receive such distinction. You can choose from a food and wine tasting menu that features four tasting portions of food coupled with four glasses of specially selected wine or order from the prix-fixe menu that includes an appetizer, entrée, salad, cheeses, and dessert. Some of the specialties are polenta with wild mushrooms, scallops with nettles, and grilled duck breast.

Especially during ski season, Sherburne has an active nightlife. Most bars and restaurants have a happy hour and live entertainment. The Pickel Barrel, on the Killington Access Road, is popular among the young singles crowd, which enjoys the light show and rock and roll bands. The Wobbly Barn attracts a broader age range for classic rock and roll music. At the Nightspot, you can dance to taped music played by a disc jockey. The club features a fireplace, sunken dance floor, three bars on different levels, and comfortable seating. Evening entertainment can also be found at Bleachers Restaurant and Lounge in Killington Village. Music as well as comedy acts are featured here.

The Mountain Inn on the access road is the home of Frank Chase, a popular performer with a long history on the mountain. Chase plays New Orleans boogie piano and does comedy. No trip would be complete without taking in his show.

For a little variety, there's the Inn at Long Trail on Route 4 at Sherburne Pass. The McGrath family runs this traditional country inn that has been serving skiers since 1939. The bar has the look and feel of a dark, cozy Irish pub and Guinness is appropriately on tap. On weekends, you will find interesting Irish musicians playing and sometimes storytellers.

Puzant's Restaurant in The Woods at Killington also offers a wide array of fine food served in a rather swanky new resort and health spa. The Woods is located on the Killington Access Road.

Summer, Fall Pursuits

Although winter is the big season for this town, many people visit Sherburne in the summer and fall to enjoy the mountain air, the foliage, and a variety of sports. Killington Ski Area offers a full schedule of summer events including high-quality plays by the Green Mountain Guild, performances by the Hartford (Connecticut) Ballet, and daytime workshops in ballet for children. Another bonus is being able to pull up a chair inside the ballet company's practice tent and watch these professional dancers tune up for evening performances.

The ski area also hosts a bicycle race that brings top cyclists from throughout the country to compete on the steep and breathless hills. And in July, the open grassy fields at the foot of the slopes are used for an annual Equestrian Festival that brings more than 500 top hunters and jumpers to compete for $100,000 in prize money. The Killington Mountain Equestrian Festival takes place for two weekends. In September, Vermont's finest chefs from throughout the state gather at Killington's Snow Shed Lodge for the "Taste of Vermont." This annual competition for chefs is open to the public with admission. If you decide to spend your evening at the Taste, you will join the state's politicos, its chefs, and restauranteurs for a diverse and delicious tasting dinner. Later in the fall, Killington hosts the Annual Foliage Craft Show.

While these events can fill the summer and fall with activities, many local Sherburnites prefer to take advantage of the outdoors. And more and more visitors are recognizing there's more to Sherburne than just winter activities. There is good trout fishing along the Roaring Brook, which runs parallel to the Killington Access Road on the east side, in Kent Pond on Route 100 near the intersection with Route 4, and in Colton Pond, north on 100 a mile. Both ponds are small, so we suggest a canoe, rowboat, or fishing from the shore.

Sherburne also is home to Gifford Woods State Park, off Route 100 across from Kent Pond. The state park has tent sites, lean-tos, showers, picnicking facilities, and a network of hiking trails. Trails take off from Gifford to Deer Leap Mountain, the rocky cliff you see rising up behind the Inn At Long Trail in Sherburne Pass. The hike from Gifford is four miles round-trip and passes over a section of the Appalachian Trail and the Long Trail, which intersect at Sherburne Pass. Check at the Gifford Park gate house for a trail map. If you hike in the other direction on the Appalachian Trail and cross Route 100 heading west, you skirt Kent Pond and walk near Thundering Brook in a beautiful forested valley. There is also another trail to the top of Deer Leap Mountain. You drive to Sherburne Pass on Route 4 and take the Long Trail 1.5 miles north. You will see the rocky cliffs as you climb.

Bicycling can be done throughout the region on main roads, back roads, and logging roads. Because of the many gravel roads and trails, a mountain bike is more versatile, but touring bikes are also fun. Bicycling in Sherburne is for the more athletic soul because of steep terrain.

A popular Killington area bicycle route includes a ride east on Route 4 to where it meets Route 100 south in Bridgewater. Take 100 south toward Plymouth and you will ride through a rural valley with breathtaking mountain views. You might want to stop off for a tour of Calvin Coolidge's old estate. Then get back on Route 100 and head south. The traffic thins out to a trickle on this road. You can continue down 100 to where it meets 20-Mile Stream Road in the tiny town of Tyson. This beautiful mountainous road will take the athletic bicycler east over 20 miles to the town of Reading and Route 106. This is a good day's ride — approximately 40 miles round-trip. To loop back to Killington on a different route, bicycle north on Route 106 to Woodstock and take Route 4 west to Killington.

Killington Ski Area also runs tennis and golf programs during the summer and fall. Killington's tennis school caters to beginners as well as more experienced players. It offers weekend and five-day programs that include extensive playing on either the outdoor clay courts or the indoor courts if it rains. Package deals that include lodging and meals run from $650 to $750 for the five-day program and about half that price for the weekend programs.

Killington also has an 18-hole golf course noted for its hilly and scenic terrain. If you like walking as exercise, this is your place to play golf, not only for the rolling terrain but also for the mountain views. If you prefer to ride, however, there are plenty of golf carts. The area offers morning golf clinics or individual lessons with the golf pro. Package deals are also available for golf weeks and weekends.

Pico offers summer visitors an Alpine slide down the mountain. Ride the chair lift to the top and gaze out over the lush Green Mountains. You can ride inside a blue plastic sled with its own speed-control brake and you're off, roaring down a slippery white track that curls over the grassy ski slope. The well-designed slide is fun for children as well as adults.

For the best and most leisurely views from Killington Peak, even when there's no skiing, we suggest a ride up the gondola or the main chair lift. The gondola, located off Route 4 east of the intersection with Route 100, runs during the summer and autumn on weekends. On a clear day, the 45-minute, seven-mile round-trip ride offers a panoramic view of five states and Canada. Killington also runs a chair lift to Killington Peak daily from the base lodge at the end of the Killington Access Road. This 20-minute ride offers similar spectacular views. The ski area operates a restaurant at the summit for a leisurely lunch and drink overlooking the Green Mountains.

From the peak, you can look north to see Pico Peak. Mount Mansfield rises to the far north. The city of Rutland lies in the valley to the west. Beyond Rutland are the Taconic Mountains and the Adirondacks of New York State. To the east are the White Mountains of New Hampshire. The only prominent mountain to the southwest is Mount Ascutney in the Connecticut River valley. The trip is particularly breathtaking during foliage, so don't miss it.

The Rutland Area South: Shrewsbury, Wallingford, Middletown Springs

Three tiny towns south of Rutland — Shrewsbury, Wallingford, and Middletown Springs — have something for everyone. Shrewsbury, put on the map by a lovesick moose who made national newspaper headlines when he began courting a cow, is home to the W.E. Pierce Store, one of Vermont's oldest operating country stores. This now-famous town has wonderful places to hike, bicycle, and cross-country ski. Wallingford offers interesting shops and some of the best hiking in the Green Mountains, along with a small public beach at Elfin Lake. And Middletown Springs, a pretty town on Route 140, is noted for its Memorial Day parade and its feisty inhabitants.

Shrewsbury

This town was immortalized in the fall of 1986 when a love-struck moose wandered from the woods into a farmer's field and took up with a brown-and-white cow named Jessica. The story of the odd couple's love affair spread round the world, and people stopped for weeks on the back road to get a glimpse of the Shrewsbury moose and Jessica. After a time, the moose returned to the woods.

To get to Shrewsbury from Rutland, you drive south on Route 7 just past the Trolley Square shopping area on your left. Take a left turn on Allen Street at the light. Follow the road until it ends in front of the Rutland Regional Medical Center. Now take a right onto Cold River Road. The road winds along the banks of the rushing Cold River as it takes you out of Rutland, through Clarendon, and into the mountain village of Northam or North Shrewsbury.

The road ends right in front of the W.E. Pierce Store, one of the state's oldest country stores. Run by the same family that founded it in 1835, the store has many of the early furnishings, including a silver cash register, a wooden counter with a glass showcase, and a bay window glazed with Salada tea. Inside the store, you will also find owners Glendon Pierce and his sister, Marjorie Pierce. No two people in town know more about the history of this corner of the state. Locals stop by regularly to pick up a carton of milk and find out what's going on. Just down the road from the store lives James M. Jeffords, Vermont's Republican U.S. senator, who is a former congressman and attorney general. On the wall at Pierce's hangs an old Jeffords' poster as well as clippings about other Shrewsbury notables. There are no other stores in Shrewsbury, so this is the place to stop if you need a cold drink.

Historical Perspective

Shrewsbury was once a farming community, but over the last hundred years the number of farms has dropped as has the population figures. Now it is mostly a bedroom community for the nearby towns of Rutland and Sherburne. Many of its residents are strong environmentalists who have played a prominent role in efforts to slow ski area development throughout the Rutland region. Some of these people fought to keep the town's one-room schoolhouse in business when other local officials were urging a modern complex be built.

Founded in 1761 and named for an English earldom, Shrewsbury has a population just under 900 and a land area of 34,432 acres.

Local Attractions

Shrewsbury is a town to drive through at any time of the year for spectacular mountain views. Before reaching Pierce's Store there is a turnoff for the Upper Shrewsbury Road, which passes rich forest land, a few old farmhouses, and an entrance to the Long Trail, a hiking trail that traverses the state. From this point on, the trail is a half-day's hike to Killington Peak. Along this road you may also see some peacocks, so drive slowly over the gravel lane. A farmer keeps the large birds on his land, but he does not fence them in. Once riding down the road, I was lucky to witness a plump blue and black peacock fly from the lawn to the barn roof.

From Pierce's Store, it is a quick drive to two of the town's sights. For leaf peepers or mountain seekers, drive past the field where the moose fell in love with the cow. Larry Carrara's farm is quiet these days, but the view along his road is one of the most spectacular in the state. When you get to Pierce's Store, take a right and continue to the right when the road forks. This is Hill Road, which will soon pass Carrara's farm on your right. A small sign with L. Carrara printed on it lets you know you're there. Look to the right and you will see a small group of Hereford cows grazing against a backdrop of majestic mountains.

Another stop in Shrewsbury is the Meadowsweet Herb Farm. Facing Pierce's Store, you go right, as if going to Carrara's. Turn left onto Eastham Road, then just follow the sign for Meadowsweet after the store. Polly and Elliott Haynes have created an herbal paradise on this hillside.

Park your car by the horse barn. Then cross the street to the herb barn, a two-story barn with a store on the first floor and workshops on the second. The store is filled with dried flowers, wreaths, herbs, spice concoctions, herbal vinegars, and herbal dip mixes. Everything is grown and made on the farm. Now take a stroll through the gardens and greenhouse. There are theme gardens such as the Medieval, Shaker, Cook's, Bible, and Wedding Garden. The greenhouses overlooking a pond also contain plants, flowers, and herbs. With a "please touch the herbs" sign, visitors are encouraged to feel and smell the aromatic herbs.

Recreational Pursuits

Shrewsbury, because of its mountains and woods, also is a great place to bicycle, hike, and cross-country ski. We suggest in the spring, summer, or fall you hike to Shrewsbury Peak and in the winter, cross-country ski on some of the many logging roads near the Shrewsbury Peak trail. To get to the trail, you drive down what is called the CCC Road, or Mountain Road. It's a dirt road over sometimes rough terrain that connects Shrewsbury with Route 100 in Plymouth. The road itself goes to the left at Pierce's Store and soon turns to gravel. Now drive 2.7 miles and there's a turnoff with a tall stone fireplace in the middle of an old foundation. The trail, which is blue-blazed, is just beyond the fireplace in the woods. You will know you are on it when you see log steps, an old cistern well, and blue blazes. The walk is 1.8 miles to the top. You are now in the Coolidge State Forest, named for Silent Cal, the president who loved Vermont. From the mountaintop you can see as far as New Hampshire's Mount Monadnock and south to Bromley Mountain in Peru.

Along the CCC Road, built by the Civilian Conservation Corps, there are many logging roads. These are great for the adventurous cross-country skier. The CCC Road is closed in the winter, so it's best to park just beyond Pierce's Store and ski in.

Wallingford

Although there is still some small industry and gravel quarrying here, Wallingford is predominantly a bedroom community for Rutland. However, its location in the Otter Creek Valley in the heart of some of the most hikable and picturesque Green Mountains makes it a great place to visit. With a number of inns and bed and breakfasts, it is also a good launching point for bike riders.

Wallingford Village, a wide tree-lined street with a collection of nineteenth-century homes and buildings, is located seven miles south of Rutland City on Route 7. At the heart of the village is a distinctive fountain of a boy in rolled-up breeches holding a boot with a hole in it. The water flows from the hole. It was in this village that Paul P. Harris grew up. He later founded the International Rotary Club.

Local Attractions

In the village, you will also find the Old Stone Shop, a stone building that was once part of the town's main nineteenth-century industry, a pitchfork manufactury. And clustered around the center of the town of approximately 1,800 people, are antique shops, small luncheonettes, general stores, and a Victorian inn.

A quick drive from the village west on Route 140, which intersects Route 7 at the center of town, is Elfin Lake, where the town operates a small public beach. The lake is one of the first ones to warm up in this part of Vermont and makes for a nice early summer swim. But as the summer wears on, it can get a little murky if there is a long hot stretch. But by late summer, the crowds have gone and the lake is again wonderful for swimming. Those who like to stretch can swim easily from one side to the other, about a quarter of a mile. The lake has a picnic area, and the town charges a small fee for use of the beach and picnic area.

If you continue driving up Route 140 you will climb the Taconic Mountain foothills into the small town of Tinmouth. This drive is wonderful in the autumn. If you are traveling on a weekend and have an urge for lunch or a snack, there is a great little country-style restaurant/roadside stand called Tully's in the center of Tinmouth near the firehouse, schoolhouse, and church. From downtown Wallingford, it's about five miles. A favorite among locals for its home-cooked berry pies, Tully's is open all summer, Tuesday through Friday, from 5 to 9 P.M. and weekends from 11 A.M. to 9 P.M. The red-wood restaurant with a patio is open on weekends during the fall.

Recreational Pursuits

For hikers, Wallingford offers two of the most scenic walks in the Green Mountain National Forest, in addition to other hikes. The White Rocks Trail is a 3.2-mile round-trip hike to the top of White Rocks Mountain, a limestone outcropping that can be seen from Route 7 as you drive through Wallingford. On a clear day, the estimated two-hour hike gives you a view that stretches as far as the Adirondacks in New York and south along the valley that divides the Green Mountains from the more irregularly shaped Taconic Mountains on the southwestern edge of the state. To reach the trail drive east from the center of Wallingford on Route 140 and bear right on a side road after two miles. Follow this for 500 feet until you reach the sign for the White Rocks Picnic Area. Follow the blue-blazed Keewaydin Trail at the far end of the parking lot. After one mile, the trail joins the Long Trail, a trail that traverses the state through the Green Mountains. Go right onto the Long Trail, and after more than a mile you will come to a clearing where a blue-blazed trail leads to the cliff. The state recently chose to release peregrine falcons, an endangered species the state is trying to restore, at these remote cliffs.

The other hike in Wallingford is to Little Rock Pond. This is a longer hike at 5.6 miles round-trip. But hikers are rewarded by a pristine mountain lake surrounded by woods and cliffs. No roads for cars lead to the lake. Instead, hikers trek in from Mount Tabor to the south and South Wallingford to the north. The pond is on the southern border of Wallingford, very near the town of Mount Tabor.

The trail is called the Homer Stone Brook Trail, named for a local man. It follows a chatty, crystal-clear brook. To reach the trail, drive south from the center of Wallingford down Route 7 to the village south of the Union Congregational Church onto a side road. You will cross a bridge and find a red schoolhouse on your left. Park here at the Little Red Schoolhouse, a community center. Then walk up the road and you will find the trail begins just behind the next house on the left. No parking is allowed near the house.

The trail is different in every season. We recommend the autumn for good leaf peeping and the summer for swimming. The lake is also good for fishing. The area is a favorite among hunters, so during hunting season it's wise for hikers to stay away or wear very bright clothing.

Hikers may camp at Little Rock Pond. There are two shelters near the lake and limited tenting is allowed. A Green Mountain Club caretaker spends the summer by the lakeshore to manage the area and help hikers.

Lodging, Restaurants

South Wallingford has one bed and breakfast, The Green Mountain Tea Room, a simply decorated 200-year-old house that was originally built as a stagecoach stop in 1792. The Tea Room, located on Route 7, serves delicious and healthful breakfasts and lunches to the public. Also, they serve a wide variety of teas.

For dining in Wallingford, the Wallingford Inn in the center of town serves dinner to the public with a reservation. Menus change daily but include classic continental dishes.

Middletown Springs

The pretty little town of Middletown Springs is a good place to enjoy the peaceful countryside, to view historic homes and exhibits, to search for antiques, and to take long walks down tree-lined country lanes. And if you happen to be in town over the Memorial Day weekend, you'll witness one of the finest parades around.

Townspeople in this community located on Route 140 have traditionally had a feisty, independent streak that is still evident today. Most recently, the feisty streak emerged when the U.S. Postal Service decided to move one of the town's most important meeting places: the post office. Plans called for relocating the post office from the building where it had been since the early 1800s to a new structure. Townspeople protested by holding a demonstration on the day postal workers were to move the office. Local farmers even brought the secret weapon — a manure spreader — to block the move. After much arguing, the postal service agreed to a compromise. The government bought a large eighteenth-century house in the village for the new office.

Historical Perspective

The town was created by a petition to the Vermont legislature in 1784. People living in the upper Poultney River valley decided they needed to form their own town instead of having to travel over the rough mountains to four separate villages. So, the legislature agreed to take corners of the towns of Poultney, Ira, Tinmouth, and Wells to form the new town in the valley. It was named Middletown because it was in the middle. Springs was added to the town's name in the nineteenth century after the mineral springs were rediscovered.

Long before Europeans settled the town, Indians knew of the mineral springs by the river. A major flood in the early 1800s tore up the riverbank and covered the springs. But another flood in 1868 uncovered the springs. A.W. Gray, the owner of a horsepower factory in town, decided to market the springs for their believed healing powers. Gray then built the Montvert Hotel, which attracted travelers from around the country. The mineral water was also bottled and sold. The hotel thrived in the late nineteenth century but began to lose business after the turn of the century when other resorts became more popular. It was dismantled and the wood sold in 1906.

Local Attractions

The Middletown Springs Historic District includes a park on the Poultney River near the village. You can view the springs along with a replica of a Victorian springhouse. The Middletown Springs Historical Society also operates a small museum in the community center on the town green. The museum is open from late June to October, 2–4 P.M. There is no admission. The display includes pictures of the Montvert Hotel, the A.W. Gray Horsepower Factory, and the mineral spring. A walk through the village will give you a chance to see some elaborate Greek Revival and Italianate-style houses.

The village has three antique shops — The Clock Doctor, known for repairing and selling old clocks; The Lamplighter, with antique lamps; and The Old Spa Shop, which specializes in Victorian furnishings.

In the fall, the nearby Burnham Hollow Orchard opens its apple orchards for picking and operates a country store. Drive west of town on Route 140 to find the orchard and store. In the fall, the drive to Middletown Springs from Rutland is also lovely. Take Route 4 west to West Rutland. Turn left onto Route 133 after the Grand Union supermarket. Then follow this through Clarendon to Route 140. Take a right onto Route 140 and you will drive right into town.

If you are in town over Memorial Day, be sure to catch the annual parade through town. You will see floats, antique carriages, school bands, and hear speeches by local officials as well as guests. The spirit of this town is alive and well.

Recreational Pursuits

Middletown Springs and its environs is an ideal place for walking or bicycling down picturesque country roads that abound. Just off the town green area, there are several country lanes just perfect for the walker or the cyclist.

Bicyclists like this area of the state because it has both hilly stretches and flat areas along the river valleys. And the scenery is beyond compare.

The Rutland Area West: Hubbardton, Castleton, Bomoseen (Lake Bomoseen), and Fair Haven

While the eastern side of Rutland County is known for good skiing in the winter, and mountain hiking in the summer, the western side of the county has a different flavor. Here you can visit the rural countryside and the quieter, more old-fashioned towns that surround them, like Castleton, Bomoseen, Hubbardton, and Fair Haven, a slate quarrying mecca in the nineteenth century.

This area west of the city of Rutland is dominated by lakes, the most famous being Lake Bomoseen, a popular summer recreation area for more than a century. Neshobe, an island in the middle of the lake, was a playground in the 1930s and 1940s for the rich and famous. Hubbardtown, a tiny town that was the site of Vermont's only revolutionary war battle, is a must-see for history buffs. Every July there's an actual reenactment complete with authentic costumes and musket fire.

Two state parks, Bomoseen State Park and Half Moon State Park, located in the towns of Castleton, Hubbardton, and Fair Haven, are the focal points of this summer recreation area.

Hubbardton

The peaceful community of Hubbardton's claim to fame is that it was the site of Vermont's only revolutionary war battle. If you are interested in history, or simply want a beautiful mountaintop view of the countryside, take a drive or bicycle ride to the battle site.

To get to the battlefield from Rutland, drive west on Route 4 and get off the highway after about 10 miles at the first Castleton exit. Take a right onto the East Hubbardton Road. There should be a prominent sign for the battlefield. Drive approximately five miles north over a winding back road that leads through lush farm country with green cornfields in the summer and a vivid foliage panorama in the fall. You may visit the battlefield all year-round, but the visitor center is open only from mid-May to mid-October.

Historical Perspective

There's a rolling field that stretches up a hillside to a stone wall as you pull into the driveway of the visitor center. The site does not look particularly unique for Vermont. It is what happened in the field on July 7, 1777, that was unique. If you chance to be in Vermont around the anniversary date of the battle, you can attend the annual re-enactment by the Living History Association. This event — complete with authentic costumes and musket fire — is held on a weekend near the anniversary. Check local papers for details.

The visitor center is open Wednesday to Sunday and is free, has pamphlets explaining the history, prints from early books, drawings of the main participants in the battle, and a diorama of the battle by Vermont artist Paul V. Winters.

In the time of the American Revolution, Hubbardton was a farming community granted by the royal governor of New Hampshire in 1764 and named for Thomas Hubbard, the original grantee of the town. It has grown little since those early days and today has a population of 500 people spread out over the town's 18,000 acres of woods and fields.

Hubbardton secured its place in history when the rear guard of General Arthur St. Clair's American army decided to camp here on the night of July 6, 1777. The soldiers knew that General John Burgoyne's army had followed them in their withdrawal from nearby Fort Ticonderoga in New York State and Mount Independence in Orwell. But the rear guard had a job to do. They were ordered to keep the British from attacking St. Clair's main army.

St. Clair left some 1,000 to 1,200 men at Hubbardton while he escaped southeasterly with his weary troops. The forces remaining in Hubbardton were led by Colonel Seth Warner, who headed a contingent of the Green Mountain Boys. Colonel Ebenezer Francis was in charge of a group from the Massachusetts militia; and Colonel Nathan Hale, a section of the New Hampshire Continental Regiment. This was not the heroic Nathan Hale of Connecticut who was hanged by the British, exclaiming, "I regret that I have but one life to give for my country." He was a lesser-known hero.

Early that morning, the Americans took their positions behind a stone wall at the top of the hill. As expected, the British had followed the retreating American army down a military road that ran from Mount Independence on Lake Champlain to Charlestown, New Hampshire. As the British came within sight, the Americans attacked and retreated to the hilltop. The British, numbering some 850, continued to repeatedly push up the hillside. After about an hour of fighting and heavy casualties on both sides, 200 German mercenaries arrived to assist the British. This ensured a British victory, but by then the Americans had accomplished what they set out to do. They had brought the enemy to a standstill and had given the main force time to move on. Historians say that the losses inflicted on the British were so heavy that they ultimately forced them to give up pursuit and return to Fort Ticonderoga. More than 580 men died in the battle from both sides.

The British plan to separate New England from the other colonies had also been dealt a blow. And by October, Burgoyne had surrendered to the American army at Saratoga, New York. After the battle, the Americans withdrew under the leadership of Colonel Warner; Colonel Francis had been killed and Hale captured.

A tall marble monument stands on the battlefield today in the place where it is believed Francis was buried. According to historical accounts, the leader of the German troops found the young colonel's body on the battlefield and decided to personally see that he received a proper burial out of respect for his bravery.

To take yourself back to revolutionary days, walk from the visitor center up the hillside to the stone wall where the American soldiers squatted as they fired on the British. The exercise will also give you a chance to see three mountain ranges. If you look straight out from the front door of the visitor center, you can see the Green Mountains and parts of the Taconic range. To the west are the Adirondack Mountains, and down the hillside is where the old military road came through the woods.

Standing on the crest of the grassy hill next to the stone wall, you can look down upon the steep western hillside that the British marched up in typical military column formation. Over the years, the wall has become covered with green vines, goldenrod, and other wildflowers. There are also maple trees that would have been helpful to the Americans during that battle. But in those days, it was freshly cleared land. To the south, there is a cellar hole that was the foundation of the house inhabited by the Selleck family at the time of the battle.

Recreational Pursuits

Hubbardton offers more than a revolutionary war site. It is also home to the northern section of one of Vermont's most diverse state parks. The Half Moon State Park, on the western side of town, has lakeshore camping, swimming, and hiking. Half Moon is connected to Bomoseen State Park, and the two parks encompass some 2,000 acres of woods, numerous ponds, marshland, trails, and abandoned slate quarries. The two parks are in the towns of Hubbardton, Castleton, and Fair Haven.

To get to Half Moon, you drive to the end of the East Hubbardton Road to where it meets Route 30. Drive north on Route 30 about 2 miles. Take a left onto Hubbardton Road. There will be a sign for the park. This drive takes you past a number of smaller ponds — Austin, Roach, and Black ponds.

There is some swimming at Half Moon. Hikers are welcome to pick up trail maps and ask for assistance at the gate house. There is a leisurely walk around the pond, and another trail, which is described in this book's section on Bomoseen, takes you from Half Moon to Bomoseen through meadows, forest, and slate quarries. During the summer months, a state naturalist works at both parks to help hikers and campers learn more about the natural history of the area. Feel free to ask for the naturalist program schedules at the gate house.

Castleton

Castleton, home to Castleton State College, is one medium-sized town with a rich history and a strong tradition of education. It was here, at a local tavern about 12 miles west of Rutland, that Ethan Allen and Seth Warner, two of Vermont's most famous Green Mountain Boys, sat down to plan the successful surprise attack of Fort Ticonderoga in 1775.

History, Attractions

Castleton was granted by the governor of New Hampshire in 1761. The name may have come from Castleton, a beautiful section of Ireland that the royal governor knew. The town quickly became a center of education for northern New England. Today, the campus of Castleton State College is just off Main Street, and students fill the downtown during the school year. The Rutland County Grammar School, which would later become the state college, was founded in 1787, four years before Vermont was a state in the union. In 1818, Castleton Medical Academy was started as the first medical school in New England.

The town gained its striking Federal-style houses and municipal buildings on the Main Street in the early 1800s when Thomas Dake, a talented designer-builder from Windsor, Vermont, moved to town. Architectural historians consider Castleton to have some of the most outstanding Federal-style buildings in Vermont. To get to Castleton from Rutland, drive west on Route 4, take the Castleton Corners exit, and turn south on Route 30. Then turn east on Route 4A, which immediately turns into Main Street.

A drive down the wide, stately Main Street gives you a chance to see some of these homes, churches, and commercial buildings that are part of the National Register of Historic Places. Each summer in early August, the town holds an event called Colonial Days, when the private homes are opened to the public for tours. Interiors of these Federal and Greek Revival style buildings feature spiral staircases, molded arches, and vaulted hallways.

The Castleton Historical Society Museum, located in Higley Homestead on Main Street, is another way to delve into the town's rich history. Open during the summer on Sunday afternoons, the 1811 brick house at the eastern end of Main Street contains nineteenth- and twentieth-century furnishings, paintings, costumes, documents, photographs, and military memorabilia. Out behind the house, a long open shed houses a rare collection of carriages including farm wagons, a family go-about, a surrey with a fringed cab, and a doctor's gig.

Today Castleton's economy is based on the college, recreation at the nearby lakes, and some small industry. If you are visiting Castleton during the academic year, you might want to find out about guest speakers and performances. The college, supported by the state, encourages the public to take part in these cultural events. In past years, famous writers, poets, and social activists have spoken to large audiences of students and adults, and traveling off-Broadway shows have entertained packed houses. The college also operates a small lobby gallery in the Fine Arts Center during the school year. The Christine Price Gallery has permanent collections of art objects from Africa, the Philippines, India, New Guinea, Solomon Islands, Sirinam, Sarawak, and Taiwan.

Castleton has a number of villages including Hydeville, which is three miles west of the main village along Route 4A. Here, you will find marinas, a pizzeria, and the southern end of Lake Bomoseen. The other village is Bomoseen.

Bomoseen

The word Bomoseen is believed to have come from an Abnaki Indian word meaning "keeper of the ceremonial fire." Little is known of their lives, but it is believed the Abnakis set up seasonal camps near Lake Bomoseen, perhaps to fish from the lake still known today for trout, bass, and smaller fish.

Historical Perspective

Bomoseen, a village in the town of Castleton about 15 miles west of Rutland on Route 4, was originally settled by farmers, who soon realized there was something more useful in the area than rocky pastureland. They became interested in extracting the valuable slate from the hillsides that formed millions of years ago.

According to geologic history, the northern end of the Taconic range was once the ocean floor where clays and debris had fallen. Millions of years ago, the floor was thrust above sea level to form mountains. Heat and pressure eventually turned the clay and sediment into slate, a metamorphic rock.

The land where Bomoseen State Park is now located was once owned by the West Castleton Railroad and Slate Company. Established around 1850, the slate company at Bomoseen mined surface deposits of slate for roofing tiles, fireplace mantles, billiard tables, and blackboards.

The slate mill closed forever in 1929. Some blamed it on the depression and labor troubles and shortages.

Recreational Pursuits

In 1958, the descendants of the quarry owner gave the land for Bomoseen State Park to Vermont. The park features a wide swimming beach, a grassy lawn, picnic areas, boat and canoe rentals, fishing, marked nature trails for hiking, and 66 camping sites, including 10 lean-tos.

Years before the existence of the state park, however, Lake Bomoseen had etched out a niche as a summer recreation spot. The lake has been popular with summer vacationers for more than a century. In the middle of the lake is an island called Neshobe that was owned in the 1930s and 1940s by Alexander Woollcott, a radio broadcaster and *New York Herald Tribune* drama critic. Famous personalities including Harpo Marx, Lawrence Olivier, Vivian Leigh, and Dorothy Parker stayed in Woollcott's stone house and enjoyed what Lake Bomoseen has to offer.

Cottage rentals around the lake are difficult to get because families have been passing down their cottages and rentals for generations, but each year some are available for rent. Inquire with local real estate agents to learn more about rentals.

At the entrance to the state park, you can pick up information on a half-mile slate history walk that will take you past abandoned quarries, an old railroad bed, and three slate houses built for company officials and to house the company store and post office. These houses sit on a road just behind the park gate.

To get to the park from Rutland, drive west 13 miles on Route 4; take the Castleton Corners exit. Take a left on Route 30, which will take you quickly to Route 4A. Turn west on 4A and you will soon see a sign for Lake Bomoseen. Take a right just before the Bomoseen Inn onto Creek Road. Follow this as it winds around part of the seven-mile-long lake to the park. You will pass clusters of historic cottages with leisurely porches and the state public boat launch.

Just beyond the park is another lake. Although it has no beach, Glen Lake is a favorite swimming hole for locals. The water is clean and refreshing, and you can slip in off rocks near the lake's public boat launch. The launch is on a dirt road just past the state park. You will see the cars parked beside the road on a hot day. Unlike Bomoseen, which is surrounded by camps and cottages, this smaller lake is surrounded by state park land. A scenic hiking trail over steep terrain overlooking the lake starts at the Glen Lake boat launch. The trail was completed by the Vermont Youth Conservation Corps in 1987. Maps and descriptions are available at Bomoseen State Park and Half Moon State Park in Hubbardton. The four-and-one-half-mile trail connects the two parks, which encompass more than 2,000 acres of woodland. The trail follows the lakeshore for one-half mile, and then it detours around a marsh on Said Road. It continues for one-half mile on the lake, crosses a marsh at the north end, and ascends one mile to an overlook, 100 feet above Glen Lake. The trail then continues for another mile along a ridge to Moscow Pond and Beaver Meadow, passing through an oak-hickory forest. It crosses a series of faults and reaches Half Moon State Park. The walk takes four hours one way.

In addition to the state park, the lake also has a privately run campground, Lake Bomoseen Campground, on Route 30. The Bomoseen Golf Club on Route 30 is open to the public and popular with locals and visitors. The course overlooks the lake and is rarely crowded.

Sailing, waterskiing, and even some swimming continues at the lake until the autumn. In the winter, the lake is a favorite among ice fishermen who set up shanties. The perch and smelts are popular winter catches. Fishermen often sell extra perch and smelt to local fishmongers and restaurants.

Local Eateries

A particularly good place to sample deep-fried perch and smelt is the Somewhere Restaurant in Fair Haven. Take Route 4 west of Bomoseen to Fair Haven, about four miles. Then turn south on Route 22A, pass the village, and about a mile south you will find the Somewhere. It's not fancy by any means, but you will eat fish prepared the way Vermonters like it.

There are some pleasant restaurants in Bomoseen including the Trak-In, run by Angie and Dick LaVictoire of Rutland. A chalet-style building, the Trak-In features homemade breads, an extensive salad bar, charcoal-grilled steaks, chops, and seafood from Maine. It is open during the summer and foliage seasons. Down the road is the Dockside, which literally hangs out over the lake. With a decor similar to that of a cruise ship, the restaurant serves a variety of moderately priced meat and seafood. From the lounge there is a panoramic view of the lake.

Fair Haven

Fair Haven is a small, working-class town of 2,800 people located about 15 miles west of Rutland on Route 4, where you can leisurely bicycle on its gentle terrain and take advantage of the charming inns and gourmet restaurants.

History, Attractions

One of the oldest towns in Rutland County, Fair Haven was chartered in 1779 to a group that included many of Ethan Allen's relatives. And today, the descendants of Ethan and his brother, Ira Allen, still live and work in the community.

The town grew in size and importance after slate was discovered in the nearby hills. The first quarries were opened on Scotch Hill in 1839. A drive down Scotch Hill Road will take you past large piles of slate that were left after the quarries were abandoned. That area of Fair Haven was named for the Scotch immigrants that came to work in the slate business. To get to Scotch Hill, simply drive north on Fair Haven's Main Street past Stewart's Shop and the intersection with Route 4A. The road will turn into Scotch Hill. If you continue on the country lane, you will drive past Glen Lake and Lake Bomoseen.

The slate business has continued to the present with a number of companies quarrying the flat, smooth rock and shaping it for roof shingles, floor tiles, and patio stones. Vermont Structural Slate Company on Prospect Street designs elaborate slate roofs for buildings around the world. William Markcrow, the owner, says his company will provide those who are seriously interested in slate quarrying and shaping a tour of the operation. Please call the company two or three days in advance.

Local Attractions

Fair Haven's oldest and most handsome houses encircle a large green near the downtown. Although the green was created in 1798, the homes, churches, and municipal buildings around it were built in the late nineteenth century when the slate and marble businesses flourished. Two of the more striking mansions on the green look as if they could be twins. The two houses are made of a golden marble quarried from nearby West Rutland. One on the south end of the green is a private home today, and the one built by Ira C. Allen, a grandson of Ethan Allen's brother, Ira, is the Vermont Marble Inn, a beautifully restored country inn run by three New Yorkers who have become history buffs since they took over the place. The inn offers dining for the public every evening. If you are staying anywhere in the lake region, this is definitely one of the best restaurants around.

Another popular inn and restaurant rich in Fair Haven's history is located on Adams Street, a small street at the southern end of the green. The Fair Haven Inn, built in 1837 as a travelers' lodge, is believed to have been a stop-off point for escaped slaves traveling the Underground Railroad from the South to freedom in Canada. Innkeeper John Lemnotis says that Chinese refugees were also hidden at the inn when their immigration into this country from Canada was prohibited. Today, the Fair Haven Inn is known for providing diners with scrumptious traditional Greek specialties, as well as fresh seafood and Vermont meats such as lamb. Lemnotis offers guests a wide selection of Greek wines direct from the motherland to liven your meal.

Staying in Fair Haven at either of these inns or a nearby bed and breakfast called the Maplewood Inn, a Greek Revival-style building on Route 22A south of town, can give you a chance to walk by many other historic homes and buildings in town. The architectural styles vary from Greek Revival and Italianate to Queen Anne and mixtures of many styles.

Recreational Pursuits

Fair Haven is also a great town to start your day trips or bicycle through. The land is gentle, not mountainous. And there are many scenic back roads to the nearby lakes. Some routes we suggest are the Scotch Hill Road to Lake Bomoseen, described above; the Sheldon Road, which is off Route 22A north of the village; and Route 22A south, which will quickly take you into rural Granville, New York, another town where the slate industry still survives.

The Rutland/Killington Area Essentials

Important Information

Municipal Services

Bomoseen Police (state): 468-5355.
Castleton Town Clerk: 468-2212.
Castleton Police: 468-5012.
Castleton Fire & Rescue: 468-5560.
Chittenden Town Clerk: 483-6647.
Chittenden Police: call state police at 773-9101.
Chittenden Fire & Rescue: 775-1630.
Fair Haven Town Clerk: 265-3610.
Fair Haven Police: 265-4531.
Fair Haven Fire & Rescue: 265-3322.
Hubbardton Town Clerk: 273-2951.
Hubbardton Police: call state police at 468-5355.
Hubbardton Fire & Rescue: 273-2211.
Middletown Springs Town Clerk: 235-2220.
Middletown Springs Police: call state police at 773-9101.
Middletown Springs Fire & Rescue: 235-2300.

Proctor Town Clerk: 459-3333.
Proctor Police: call state police at 773-9101.
Proctor Fire & Rescue: 775-6664.
Rutland City Clerk: 773-1801.
Rutland Police: 773-1816.
Rutland Fire & Rescue: 773-1812.
Sherburne Town Clerk: 422-3243.
Sherburne Police: call state police at 773-9101.
Sherburne Fire & Rescue: 422-3509.
Shrewsbury Town Clerk: 775-5689.
Shrewsbury Police: call state police at 773-9101.
Shrewsbury Fire & Rescue: 775-4600.
Wallingford Town Clerk: 446-2336.
Wallingford Police: call state police at 773-9101.
Wallingford Fire & Rescue: 446-2121.

Medical Services

Castleton Health Associates, Rte. 4A; 468-5641.
Convenient Medical Care, Inc., 25 North Main St., Rutland; 775-8032.
Rutland Regional Medical Center, Rte. 4; 775-7111.
Sherburne Health Center, Rte. 4; 422-3990.

Veterinarians

Center Rutland Veterinary Services, 409 West St.; 773-7966.
Eastwood Animal Clinic, Rte. 4 east; 773-7711.
Fair Haven Animal Hospital, Washington St.; 265-3822.
Rutland Veterinary Clinic, North Main St.; 773-2779.

Weather

WJJR-FM Weather Phone: 773-7500.
WSYB-AM Weather Phone: 775-1230.

Tourist Information Services

Killington & Pico Areas Associations, Rte. 4; 773-4181.
Rutland Regional Chamber of Commerce, 7 Court St.; 773-4181.

Lodgings

Reservation Services

Killington Lodging Bureau, Rutland Opera House, Merchants Row, Rutland; 773-1330.
Pico Central Reservations, Rte. 4; 775-1927 and 1-800-225-7426.

Inns and B&Bs

CHITTENDEN
Mountain Top Inn and Resort, Mountain Top Rd.; 1-800-445-2100 and 483-2311. Expensive. Comfortable country inn with views of mountains and lake. Numerous recreational activities all year-round including cross-country skiing, sledding, horseback riding, boating, fishing, hiking, tennis, golf, and swimming. Children welcome. Major credit cards.
Tulip Tree Inn, Chittenden Dam Rd.; 483-6213. Expensive. Secluded country inn. Some rooms with private Jacuzzis. Modified American Plan. Mastercard and Visa.

FAIR HAVEN
Fair Haven Inn, 5 Adams St.; 265-4907. Moderate. Four rooms with private baths. Restaurant, lounge. Wonderful Greek food and warm atmosphere. Major credit cards.
Maplewood Inn, Rte. 22A; 265-8039. Moderate. Continental breakfast. No pets and no children under eight. Major credit cards.
Vermont Marble Inn, the green; 265-8383. Moderate, except during foliage season when the rate becomes expensive. Beautifully restored Victorian home made of solid marble. Room rate includes extensive country breakfast and afternoon tea. The inn also has a fine restaurant. Major credit cards.

MENDON
Red Clover Inn, Woodward Rd.; 775-2290. Expensive. Modified American Plan. Gourmet dinner and country breakfast included, fireside dining, intimate pub, and beautiful bedrooms in secluded back-road location. Major credit cards.

MIDDLETOWN SPRINGS
The Heartwood, North St.; 235-2543. Inexpensive. Bed and breakfast in private home. Nineteenth-century house across from the town green. Continental breakfast.
Middletown Springs Inn, The Green; 235-2198. Moderate. Victorian mansion with 10 guest rooms with private baths. Breakfast included and dinner is extra although Modified American Plan is available. Inn has 14 to 18 miles of wilderness cross-country ski trails. Major credit cards.
Priscilla's, South St.; 235-2299. Moderate. Comfortable Victorian decorated with antique music boxes. Bed and full breakfast. Smoking only on porch.

RUTLAND
The Inn at Rutland, 70 North Main St.; 773-0575. Moderate. Distinctive Victorian in the heart of Rutland. Breakfast included. Major credit cards.
Silver Fox, Rte. 133, West Rutland; 438-5555. Expensive. Country inn built in 1768, off the beaten track with on-grounds cross-country skiing, full country breakfast, and public dining. Mastercard and Visa.

SHERBURNE
Grey Bonnet Inn, Rte. 100; 1-800-342-2086 or 775-2537. Expensive. Dinner and breakfast included. Cross-country skiing out back door, indoor pool, whirlpool, and sauna. Major credit cards.
Inn at Long Trail, Rte. 4; 775-7181. Moderate. Breakfast included. Homey guest rooms and Irish pub. Mastercard and Visa.

Killington Village Inn, Killington Access Rd.; 422-3301. Expensive. Small inn serving full skier's breakfast, dinner, and children's menu. Slope-side shuttle. Major credit cards.

Mountain Meadows Inn, Thundering Brook Rd.; 775-1010. Expensive. Casual with large, comfortable rooms, a fireplace lounge, and game room. Complete ski touring center on property. Mastercard and Visa.

Vermont Inn, Rte. 4; 773-9847. Expensive. Gourmet dinner, full breakfast included. Charming farmhouse inn with individually decorated rooms, private baths, sauna, hot tub, tennis court, and outdoor swimming pool. Major credit cards.

WALLINGFORD

Blue Spruce Inn, Rte. 155; 259-2121. Moderate. Modern redwood house on five acres with outdoor swimming pool. Continental breakfast. Public dining. Large barroom. Major credit cards.

Dunham House B&B, Rte. 7; 446-2600. Moderate. 1856 Victorian home with six rooms and full breakfast.

Green Mountain Tea Room, Rte. 7, South Wallingford; 446-2611. Moderate. Full breakfast served in homelike atmosphere. Major credit cards.

Wallingford Inn, Rte. 7; 446-2849. Moderate. Victorian inn with public dining in the heart of historic village. Full breakfast. Mastercard and Visa.

White Rocks Inn, Rte. 7; 446-2077. Moderate. Restored farmhouse inn with canopy beds and views of mountains and meadows, serving full breakfast. Nonsmokers only. Mastercard and Visa.

Hotels, Motels, and Resorts

BOMOSEEN

Edgewater Motel, Rte. 30; 468-5251. Inexpensive. Motel on Lake Bomoseen with outdoor swimming pool. Open year-round. Major credit cards.

Prospect House, Rte. 30; 468-5581. Expensive. No children. Open summers only, primarily for golfers.

CASTLETON

Tag's Motel, Rte. 4A; 468-5505. Inexpensive motel on Main St. Not fancy. Major credit cards.

MENDON

Cortina Inn, Rte. 4; 773-3331. Expensive with moderate off-season rates. Luxurious hotel with indoor swimming pool, fitness center, game room, and fine dining. Major credit cards.

Edelweiss Motel, Rte. 4; 775-5577. Forty-four well-maintained rooms set back from highway, hot tub, sauna, game room, fireplace, lounge, and continental breakfast. Major credit cards.

Grande Finale Motel, Rte. 4; 773-2155. Moderate. Swimming pool, indoor hot tub, and continental breakfast. Major credit cards.

Killington-Pico Motor Inn, Rte. 4; 773-4088. Moderate. Country breakfast included. Major credit cards.

Mendon Mountain Orchards Motel, Rte. 4; 775-5477. Inexpensive to moderate. Economical motel near working apple orchard. Major credit cards.

Pico Manor, Rte. 4; 773-6644. Moderate. Continental breakfast included. Outdoor pool, hearth-side lounge, indoor sauna, and hot tub. Major credit cards.

Tyrol Motel, Rte. 4; 773-7485. Moderate. Outdoor pool, whirlpool, and breakfast included. Major credit cards.

RUTLAND

Comfort Inn, Trolley Square, South Main St.; 775-2200. Moderate. Heated indoor pool, Jacuzzi, sauna, and health center. Modern rooms; near many restaurants. Major credit cards.

Green Mont Motel, 138 North Main St.; 775-2575. Moderate. Modern motel with outdoor pool and some waterbed suites. Major credit cards.

Highlander Motel, 203 North Main St.; 773-6069. Moderate. Bed and continental breakfast motel with indoor hot tub. Major credit cards.

Holiday Inn, South Main St.; 775-1911. Moderate to expensive. Health club with indoor pool, hot tubs, sauna, exercise room. Teens stay for free. Major credit cards.

Howard Johnson's Lodge, South Main St.; 775-4303. Moderate. Heated indoor pool. Children under 12 stay free. Major credit cards.

Nordic Motel, Rte. 4; 773-7964. Inexpensive. Basic motel. Major credit cards.

Royal Motel, 115 Woodstock Ave.; 773-9176. Moderate. Heated outdoor pool, in-room steam baths and kitchenettes available. Major credit cards.

Rutland Lodge, 253 South Main St.; 773-3361. Moderate. Heated indoor pool and sauna. Major credit cards.

Rutland Motel, 125 Woodstock Ave.; 775-4348. Moderate. Basic motel. Major credit cards.

Sunset Motel, 238 South Main St.; 773-2784. Moderate. Waterbeds. Major credit cards.

Woodstock East Motel, 154 Woodstock Ave.; 773-2442. Moderate. Outdoor pool. Major credit cards.

SHERBURNE

Alpenhof Lodge, Killington Access Rd.; 422-9787. Expensive. Skiers' lodge with sauna, whirlpool, and continental breakfast. Open winter and autumn. Major credit cards.

Bear Mountain Inn, Killington Access Rd.; 422-3005. Moderate. Skiers' lodge serving light continental breakfast. Open ski season only. Major credit cards.

Butternut on the Mountain, Killington Access Rd.; 422-9242. Moderate. Contemporary lodge open year-round with indoor pool, game room, whirlpool, and restaurant. Major credit cards.

Cascades Lodge, Killington Access Rd.; 442-3731. Expensive. Contemporary lodge with indoor pool, whirlpool, sauna, and spacious rooms. Open fall and winter. Major credit cards.

Cedarbrook Motor Inn, junction Rte. 100 south and Rte. 4; 422-9666. Moderate. Motel within walking distance of chair lift to Northeast Passage. Open winter, summer, and fall. Major credit cards.

Chairlift Killington, Killington Access Rd.; 422-3451. Expensive. Handsome chalet featuring full breakfast, pub, fireside living room, hot tub, sauna, and game room. Open fall and winter. Major credit cards.

Comfort Inn, Killington Access Rd.; 422-4222. Expensive. Suites with Jacuzzi and kitchenette available. Major credit cards.

Inn at Pico, Pico Ski Area, Rte. 4; 1-800-225-7426 out of Vermont and 775-1927 in-state. Moderate. Suite hotel each with television, phone, and full kitchen within walking distance of Pico chair lift, summer Alpine Slide, and sports center. Major credit cards.

Inn of the Six Mountains, Killington Access Rd.; 422-4302. Expensive. Modern four-season resort inn with indoor lap pool, spa and exercise room, and sauna. Major credit cards.

Little Buckhorn, Killington Access Rd.; 442-3314. Moderate. Cozy ski lodge with fireplace, lounge, pool table, and kitchenette for guests. Hearty breakfasts and dinners. Open winter, summer, and fall. Major credit cards.

Mountainview Resort, Rte. 4; 773-4311. Expensive. All-season resort motor lodge with whirlpool and Jacuzzi. Major credit cards.

Northstar Lodge, Killington Access Rd.; 422-4040. Moderate to expensive. Outdoor heated steam pool. Shuttle to slopes and continental breakfast. Open winter, midsummer, and fall. Major credit cards.

Pike's Lodge, Killington Access Rd.; 422-9782. Moderate to expensive. Skiers' lodge serving full breakfast. Open winter, summer, and fall. Major credit cards.

Red Rob Inn, Killington Access Rd.; 422-3303. Expensive. Newly renovated full-service lodge with indoor Jacuzzi, outdoor Jacuzzi, and sauna. Also home to Jason's Restaurant, serving fine northern Italian cuisine. Off-season discounts. Major credit cards.

Sherburne-Killington Motel, Rte. 4; 773-9535. Expensive. Spacious and well-maintained motel rooms with continental breakfast and one kitchenette. Major credit cards.

Skol Haus Motor Lodge, Killington Access Rd.; 442-3305. Expensive. Motor lodge close to the slopes. Major credit cards.

Summit Lodge, Killington Access Rd.; 422-3535. Expensive. Lodge overlooking mountains and pond complete with racquetball courts, outdoor heated winter pool, massage rooms, fireside lounge, and two on-site restaurants — Maxwell's, serving continental cuisine, and the Grist Mill, serving New England fare. Major credit cards.

Trailside Lodge, Coffee House Rd.; 422-3532. Moderate. Ski lodge just minutes from slopes offering buffet breakfast, hot tub, and complimentary slope shuttle. Major credit cards.

Val Roc Motel, Rte. 4; 422-3881. Moderate. Motel close to Bear Mountain, Gondola, and Northeast Passage skiing at Killington. Spacious rooms, some with kitchenettes. Major credit cards.

The Villager at Killington, Killington Village; 422-3101. Expensive in winter, but major discounts off-season. Killington Ski Area's lodging on the slopes within walking distance of Snowshed and Ramshead lifts. Also complimentary use of Killington Health Club pool, whirlpool, sauna, steam bath, and exercise room. Major credit cards.

Whispering Pines Lodge, South View Path; 422-3014. Moderate. Skiers' lodge specializing in ski weeks for families; full breakfast and dinner offered. Open fall and winter. Major credit cards.

Cottages and Condominiums

MENDON

Hogge Penny Inn, Rte. 4; 773-3200. Expensive with some reduced rates prior to December. Small condominium village with spacious one- and two-bedroom suites, full kitchen, and living room. On-site restaurant and tavern. Major credit cards.

Killington Gateway, Rte. 4; 773-2301. Moderate. Spacious, clean, economical units with kitchen, fireplace, color television, firewood, linens, and towels. Major credit cards.

SHERBURNE

Colony Club, Killington Access Rd.; 773-4202. Expensive. Townhouses with kitchen, bath, bedrooms, firewood, fireplace, color television, and some units with whirlpool bathtub. Mastercard and Visa.

Edgemont Condominiums, Killington Access Rd.; 773-4202. Moderate to expensive. Multibedroom units near lifts and free indoor swimming, sauna, and Jacuzzi. Mastercard and Visa.

Fox Hollow, Killington Access Rd.; 422-3244. Expensive. Condominiums with Jacuzzi-tubs, full kitchen, and washer/dryer. Free use of swimming pool, sauna, and hot tub. Major credit cards.

Glazebrook Townhouse, Killington Access Rd.; 422-4425. Expensive. Townhouses a mile from ski lifts. Major credit cards.

Killington Resort Apartments, Killington Access Rd.; 422-3417. Moderate. Completely equipped units with kitchen, bedrooms, and living areas. Major credit cards.

Killington Village Condominiums, Killington Ski Area; 422-3101. Moderate to expensive. Killington Ski Area owns five separate condominium villages with a variety of one-, two-, three-, and four-room suites located near the base of the slopes. Amenities include swimming pool, sauna, whirlpool, and tanning room. Major credit cards.

Skye Peak Apartments, Killington Access Rd.; 422-3984. Moderate with off-ski season discounts. Fully equipped units half-mile from slopes. Major credit cards.

Spruce Glen, Rte. 4 and Rte. 100 south; 422-3306. Expensive. Convenient townhouses, some equipped with saunas and Jacuzzis. Major credit cards.

The Woods at Killington Resort and Spa, Killington Access Rd.; 422-3100. Expensive. One- to three-bedroom townhouses with oversized Jacuzzi bath, fireplace, VCR, stereo, luxury kitchen, washer and dryer, and sauna. On-site health spa, indoor pool, and cross-country ski trails. Major credit cards.

Campgrounds

BOMOSEEN
Bomoseen State Park, West Shore Dr.; 265-4242. Sixty-six sites including 10 lean-tos, no hookups, flush toilets, hot showers, sewage disposal, public phone, picnic tables, fireplaces, wood, swimming, fishing, boating, boat/canoe rentals, hiking, and snack bar. Open May to Columbus Day.
Lake Bomoseen Campground, Rte. 30; 273-2061. Ninety-five wooded sites on 33 acres bordering lake. Forty full hookups, rest with electric and water, marina, swimming pool, heated rest rooms and showers, full-service store. Open May to mid-October.

HUBBARDTON
Half Moon State Park, Black Pond Rd.; 273-2848. Sixty-nine sites, including 10 lean-tos, no hookups, flush toilets, hot showers, sewage disposal, picnic tables, fireplaces, wood, swimming, fishing, boat/canoe rentals, and hiking. Open May to just after Labor Day.

SHERBURNE
Gifford Woods State Park, Rte. 100; 775-5354. Forty-seven sites including 21 lean-tos, no hookups, flush toilets, hot showers, sewage disposal, picnic tables, fireplaces, wood, public phone, picnic shelter, fishing, and hiking. Open May to Columbus Day.

SHREWSBURY
Note: There's no camping in Shrewsbury, but there is one private campground in the nearby town of North Clarendon.
Iroquois Land Family Camping, East Rd., North Clarendon; 773-2832. Forty-five sites, open and wooded, overlooking mountains. Ten sites with water, electric, and sewer. Tent sites, hot showers, and swimming pool. Open May to mid-October.

WALLINGFORD
Little Rock Pond, Homer Stone Brook Trail in South Wallingford. Call Green Mountain Club at 223-3463. Green Mountain Club (GMC) maintains a limited number of tent sites near the pond for hikers. There is no way to this area except to hike the 2.8 miles from South Wallingford or the 2 miles from Mt. Tabor's Bond Hill Rd. A small fee is charged by the GMC caretaker.

Dining

BOMOSEEN
Dockside, Rte. 30; 273-3334. Inexpensive to moderate. Small restaurant and bar perched on the shore of Lake Bomoseen. Serves seafood specials and Vermont veal.
Ringquist's Dining Room, Rte. 30; 468-5172. Moderate.
Trak-In Restaurant, Rte. 30; 468-5251. Inexpensive to moderate. Overlooking Lake Bomoseen, this restaurant features seafood, steak, and chops and has an extensive salad bar. It serves lunch and dinner from May to October. Closed in winter.

CASTLETON
The Castleton Pizza Place and Deli, Main St.; 468-2911. Inexpensive.
Checkmate, Rte. 4A; 468-5841. Inexpensive. Quick meals.
Jim's Diner, Main St.; 468-5817. Inexpensive.

CHITTENDEN

The Mountain Top Inn, Mountain Top Rd.; 483-2311. Moderate. A wide selection of fine food prepared in a country style. Specialties include sautéed chicken breast baked with a sausage, apple, and Vermont cheddar cheese stuffing and poached salmon in a champagne dill sauce. Reservations are suggested. Guests are asked to refrain from smoking in dining room.

The Tulip Tree Inn, Dam Rd.; 483-6213. Moderate. Delicious and healthful food is served in an intimate dining room. This is primarily an inn for the few guests who stay here, but the public may dine at the same tables as guests if they make a reservation. One meal is served each night and the menu changes often. Some examples of what is served include carrot yogurt soup, baked codling with mustard sauce, and steamed cauliflower.

FAIR HAVEN

Bud's Cannonball Lounge, 35 North St.; 459-6304. Inexpensive. Friendly local bar with pizza and sandwiches.

Fair Haven Inn, 5 Adams St.; 265-4907. Moderate. This fun old Victorian inn offers fine Greek food. Some specialties include grape leaves stuffed with rice and herbs, topped with feta, and avgolemono, a chicken, egg, lemon, and orzo soup. For main courses you can feast on everything from seafood prepared in a Grecian manner to souvlakia, a skewer of lamb to chicken Florentine. Innkeeper John Lemontis also has a wide variety of Greek wines to taste with your meals. Reservations are suggested. The inn also runs a bar and grill with inexpensive burgers and steaks. Major credit cards.

Somewhere Restaurant, 67 South Main St.; 265-3869. Inexpensive. This is a workingman's restaurant that does not pretend to be fancy. It serves deep-fried fish from the seacoast as well as from local lakes. Live country music acts perform in the adjacent barroom. Reservations are not necessary. The Somewhere is open for breakfast, lunch, and dinner.

Vermont Marble Inn, the town green; 265-8383. Moderate. The inn serves exquisite food in a carefully decorated Victorian home of solid marble. Specialties include chilled smoked trout on cucumber with dill-horseradish cream appetizer, braised duckling in port and raspberry sauce, prime rib of beef, and grilled pheasant. Reservations are suggested. Major credit cards.

MENDON

Churchill's House of Beef and Seafood, Rte. 4; 775-3219. Moderate. Fresh seafood and hearty steaks in lively casual atmosphere. Reservations suggested. Major credit cards.

Cortina Inn, Rte. 4; 773-3331. Moderate to expensive. Gourmet continental and New England dishes changing each evening. Popular Sunday brunch buffet that will fill you for a day of skiing. Major credit cards.

Countryman's Pleasure, Townline Rd.; 773-7141. Moderate to expensive. Fine Austrian-style dining in country farmhouse. Reservations requested. Major credit cards.

Grande Finale, Rte. 4; 775-1853. Moderate. Fine dining in Victorian house. German sauerbraten, filet mignon, steak, and veal. Reservations requested.

Little Naples, Rte. 4; 773-4663. Inexpensive to moderate. Well-prepared regional Italian cuisine. Café menu as well. Major credit cards.

Marge & John's Country Breakfast, Rte. 4; 775-3200. Inexpensive. Hearty breakfast and lunch.

Red Clover Inn, Woodward Rd.; 775-2290. Moderate. Country-style cuisine served in small dining rooms at secluded farmhouse inn. Reservations requested. Major credit cards.

Sugar and Spice, Rte. 4; 773-7832. Inexpensive. Gift shop and maple sugarhouse that serves pancake breakfasts and lunches.

T & M Brandy's, Rte. 4; 773-4036. Inexpensive. Chicken dinners.

RUTLAND

Back Home Café, 21 Center St.; 775-2104. Moderate. Popular downtown restaurant for lunch and dinner. Selections include pasta, fish, meat, gourmet pizza, burgers, and wide selection of baked goods. Often there is a live folk or soft rock band performing on weekends at this second-floor restaurant overlooking the heart of Rutland. Can be crowded during holidays but usually no reservations needed. Major credit cards.

Back Home Deli and Bakery, 21 Center St.; 775-1501. Inexpensive. The street-level deli serves hearty New York-style sandwiches for lunch and baked goods all day.

Casa Bianca, 76 Grove St.; 773-7401. Expensive. Rutland's premier fine Italian dining in an old house. Reservations for dinner suggested. Major credit cards.

Clem's Kitchen, 51 Wales St.; 775-6104. Inexpensive. Hearty breakfasts and lunches, homemade breads, and daily specials.

Ernie's Grill and Bar, 37 Main St.; 775-0856. Moderate. Prime rib, seafood specialties prepared for lunch and dinner in a classic New England style. Reservations accepted. Major credit cards.

Gill's Delicatessen, 68 Strongs Ave.; 773-7414. Inexpensive. Great subs and pizza.

Kong Chow, 48 Center St.; 775-5244. Inexpensive. Chinese-American lunches and dinner.

Midway Diner, 120 South Main St.; 773-2366. Inexpensive. A classic 1950s-style diner that serves basic, tasty food round-the-clock.

Murphy's, 31 Center St.; 775-3818. Inexpensive to moderate. Serves Mexican and American food for lunch and dinner. Downstairs bar is popular with locals.

121 West Restaurant; 773-7148. Moderate. Varied menu for lunch and dinner. Major credit cards.

Panda Pavilion, Woodstock Ave.; 775-6682. Moderate. Exquisite presentations of spicy Szechuan, Hunan, and mandarin-style cuisine. Lunch and dinner. Reservations for large parties suggested. Major credit cards.

Pappy's, 128 Merchants Row; no phone. Inexpensive to moderate. Burgers, steaks, and cocktails. Lunch and dinner with patio.

The Rice Bowl, 124 Woodstock Ave.; 775-4336. Inexpensive to moderate. Chinese and American restaurant open for lunch, dinner, and take-out.

Rutland Restaurant, 57 Merchants Row; 775-7447. Inexpensive downtown restaurant with long lunch counter. Open for breakfast, lunch, and dinner. Greek specials served on Saturday evening.

Sal's Italian Restaurant and Pizzeria, 148 West St.; 775-3360. Inexpensive to moderate. Lunch and dinner. Serves veal, shrimp, and chicken pasta dishes and pizza.

Season's Circle Coffee House, 24 Wales St.; 773-3701. Inexpensive. Fruit, meat, and seafood crepes, sandwiches, and omelets. Open for breakfast and lunch.

Sirloin Saloon, 200 South Main St.; 773-7900. Moderate. Southern plantation atmosphere for dinner. Extensive salad bar, homemade breads, and delicious grilled fish, steaks, and chicken. Major credit cards.

South Station at the Trolley Barn, South Main St.; 775-1736. Moderate. Seafood specials and varied menu. Piano bar. Serves lunch, dinner, and Sunday brunch. Major credit cards.

SHERBURNE

Bleacher's Restaurant/Lounge, Killington Village; 422-7442. Moderate. Features pizza, homemade pasta, and grilled foods. Major credit cards.

Café Killington, Killington Access Rd.; 422-3985. Moderate. Twenty-item salad bar and wide array of entrées from seafood to pizza.

Casey's Caboose, Killington Access Rd.; 422-3795. Moderate. Salads, burgers, steaks, chicken, and seafood served in a renovated railroad snowplow car. Open for dinner and Sunday brunch.

Chalet Killington, Killington Access Rd.; 422-3451. Inexpensive. Pub-style lounge with sunken fieldstone fireplace. Soups and chili, sandwiches, and light fare. Open evenings.

Charity's 1887 Saloon, Killington Access Rd.; 422-3800. Moderate. A popular eating and drinking saloon open for lunch, dinner, and Sunday brunch. Well known for French onion soup. Also blackboard specials and Mexican food.

Claude's and Choices, Killington Access Rd.; 422-4030. Two exquisite chef-owned restaurants that are known in the area as the mountain's best-kept secrets. Claude's offers luxurious fine dining with specialties like escargot, rack of lamb, veal, beef Wellington, and salmon; extensive wine list; and elegant decor. Reservations requested. Expensive. Choices features a wide variety of steaks, stews, sandwiches, pastas, and fresh seafood. Moderate. In addition to dinner, Choices serves a Sunday brunch and offers guitar entertainment on Sundays.

Gouchos Mexican Restaurant and Bar, Killington Access Rd.; 422-7887. Moderate. Mexican food and Margaritas.

Grey Bonnet Inn, Rte. 100 north; 775-2537. Moderate. Varied menu open for dinner and breakfast. Steak, duck, rabbit, and veal dishes.

Grist Mill Restaurant, Killington Access Rd.; 422-3970. Moderate. Overlooking a pond, this family restaurant offers a varied menu including steak, prime rib, and seafood. Open for lunch, dinner, and Sunday brunch.

Hemingway's Restaurant, Rte. 4; 422-3886. Expensive. Northern New England's only four-star Mobil Guide restaurant. Menu varies but includes wild mushroom appetizers, succulent lamb, and seafood. Reservations required.

Inn at Long Trail, Rte. 4; 775-7181. Moderate. Serves dinner and hearty skier breakfasts. Spectacular location in Sherburne Pass and great old-fashioned Irish pub atmosphere.

Jason's (at the Red Rob Inn), Killington Access Rd.; 422-3303. Moderate. Fine northern Italian cuisine. Jazz guitar and piano. Reservations suggested.

Killington Bar and Grill, Rte. 4; 422-3301. Moderate. Steaks, seafood, soups, and salads for dinner and weekend lunch.

Killington Village Inn, Killington Access Rd.; 422-3301. Moderate. Varied menu nightly and hearty skier breakfasts.

Maxwell's Restaurant at Killington's Summit Lodge, Killington Access Rd.; 422-3535. Moderate. Elegant cuisine, cocktails, and live entertainment.

Mother Shapiro's, Killington Access Rd.; 422-9933. Inexpensive to moderate. Popular place for breakfast and lunches of soup, salad, and burgers. Lively bar and Monday night comedy acts. It's the one place in the area to get an authentic bagel with lox and cream cheese.

The Mountain Inn, Killington Access Rd.; 422-2311. Moderate. Continental cuisine and fireside lounge entertainment on weekends with Frank Chase, a mountain institution with his piano playing and comedy. Reservations suggested.

Mrs. Brady's, Killington Access Rd.; 422-9760. Moderate. Offering a large menu of pasta, veal, chicken, burgers, and seafood for dinner. Light snacks and cocktails in a fireside lounge.

Pasta Pot, Rte. 4; 422-3004. Moderate. Variety of pasta dishes and vegetarian cuisine. Volleyball pit for summer games. Open for dinner.

Pogonips, Killington's Snowshed Lounge, Killington Access Rd.; 442-7880. Moderate. American and continental cuisine served in restaurant overlooking the mountains. Reservations suggested.

Puzants, at The Woods at Killington, Killington Access Rd.; 422-3100. Expensive. Nutritional and sensory cuisine presented in a fine dining atmosphere. Some specials include Dover sole poached in chardonnay, Great Lake pike sautéed in hazelnuts, and saddle of Vermont rabbit. Reservations suggested.

Season's, Pico Ski Resort, Rte. 4; 773-4033. Moderate. Varied menu; dine overlooking ski slopes.

The Vermont Inn, Rte. 4; 775-0708. Moderate to expensive. Lovely country inn with fine cuisine. Reservations suggested.

The Wobbly Barn Steakhouse, Killington Access Rd.; 422-3392. Moderate. Mesquite grilled steaks and other specials. Live music.

Zorba's Tavern, Killington Access Rd.; 422-3600. Inexpensive to moderate. Pizza, pasta, subs, spaghetti, and salads. Pool table and jukebox. Open for lunch, dinner, and evening snacks.

WALLINGFORD

Green Mountain Tea Room, Rte. 7; 446-2611. Inexpensive. Breakfasts and lunches served in 1792 house with tilting wooden floor. Owner-chef makes wonderful cream cheese and asparagus omelet; menu changes.

Mom's Kitchen, Rte. 7; 446-2995. Inexpensive. Folksy breakfast and lunch counter in the center of Wallingford.

Tully's, Rte. 140 west in Tinmouth; 446-2431. Inexpensive. Home-cooked pies, burgers, and fried seafood served indoors or at take-out window to eat at picnic tables. Open summer and fall.

Wallingford Block Family Restaurant, Rte. 7; 446-2098. Inexpensive. Pizza and hamburgers.

The Wallingford Inn, Rte. 7; 446-2849. Moderate. Fine dining by candlelight for inn guests and the public. Blackboard specials include shrimp, veal, and baked halibut. Reservations requested. Mastercard and Visa.

Entertainment

Music and Stage

CASTLETON

Castleton State College, Fine Arts Center; 468-5611. Frequent plays and concerts; call for information.

RUTLAND

Crossroads Arts Council, 72 Wales St.; 775-1678. Rutland region arts council offers music and theater programs throughout the year. Call for more information.

Grace Congregational Church, Court St.; 773-4301. Church offers classical music and choir concerts at different times of the year.

Rutland City Band. Call the city recreation department for information; 773-1822. Band plays Sunday evening concerts in the park all summer. Recreation department sponsors other bands on Wednesday evenings in Main St. Park.

SHERBURNE

Killington Music Festival, Killington Ski Area; 773-4003. A series of summer concerts by the Vermont Festival Players featuring the work of contemporary and classical composers.

Killington Playhouse, Killington Ski Area; 422-9795. The Green Mountain Guild puts on a number of musical theaters from July to September. There is also a children's theater offered midweek.

Killington Showcase Series, Killington Ski Area; 773-1500. The ski area brings nationally known musicians, dancers, and performers for a summer series of shows. In recent years, the Hartford Ballet has taken up residency in the Green Mountains to perform a number of shows and offer dance classes to local children.

Nightlife

CHITTENDEN

Mountain Top Inn, Mountain Top Rd.; 483-2311. Piano music by a number of local artists throughout the week, all year-round.

FAIR HAVEN

Somewhere Restaurant, 67 South Main St.; 265-3869. Country and western music.

MENDON

Cortina Inn, Rte. 4; 773-3331. Variety of music live and taped in a cozy lounge. Popular hangout during ski season.

RUTLAND

Back Home Café, 21 Center St.; 775-2104. Intimate and friendly bar with occasional weekend music tending toward live folk and soft rock and roll.

Broomsticks, Post and River sts.; 775-7916. Live lowbrow country and western music.

Holiday Inn, South Main St.; 775-1911. Disc jockey spins variety of Top 40 dance tunes.

Howard Johnson's, South Main St.; 773-9501. Live country music and soft rock. Call for more information.

Private Eyes, 87 State St.; 773-9704. Popular hangout for young (20s to 30s) Rutlanders. Disc jockey plays dance music and there are live bands and shows.

The Ritz, 21 Center St.; 775-2944. Disc jockey plays Top 40 with screen. Popular with young set, early 20s.

South Station, Trolley Barn on South Main St.; 775-1736. Piano bar Wednesday to Sunday and other music. Wide range of ages hang out here in casual dining and drinking atmosphere.

Valley Club, 9 Evelyn St.; 775-3474. Rutland's avant-garde, rough and tumble rock and roll bar. Often has interesting bands from around New England.

Whirlaways, Rutland Shopping Plaza; 775-6789. Live, loud rock and roll music and dancing.

SHERBURNE

Bleacher's Lounge, Killington Village; 422-7442. Music, comedy, and other entertainment nightly during ski season. Lively happy hour at this ski area haunt.

Inn at Long Trail, Rte. 4; 775-7181. The only place on the mountain where you might find an Irish musician or IRA supporter telling stories. This old inn with authentic pub decor attracts a nice mix of skiers, hikers, and local music fans.

Mother Shapiro's, Killington Access Rd.; 442-9933. Friendly bar with pool table, mixed crowd, and comedy night. Call for more information.

The Mountain Inn, Killington Access Rd.; 442-3595. Frank Chase, popular musician and comedian, puts on great shows that draw faithful fans regularly to the fireside lounge.

The Nightspot, Killington Access Rd.; 422-9885. Dance club with sunken dance floor, three bars, and disc jockey-selected music.

Pickle Barrel, Killington Access Rd.; 422-3035. Top 40 bands from around New England perform here amid extensive light show. Popular with the younger skiers and well-known pickup place.

The Wobbly Barn Steakhouse, Killington Access Rd.; 422-3392. Variety of entertainment offered in this popular casual dining and drinking atmosphere.

Movies

RUTLAND

Plaza 1 and 2, Rutland Shopping Plaza (downtown); 775-5500.
Studio 1 and 2, Rutland Mall on Woodstock Ave.; 775-1539.
Westway 1-4, West Rutland Mall; 438-2888.

Museums and Historical Sites

BOMOSEEN

Bomoseen State Park; 265-4242. Slate history trail takes visitor on a half-mile walk through this region's history as a slate-producing center. Inquire at the state park.

CASTLETON

Castleton Historic District, Main St. The district includes a collection of outstanding Federal and Greek Revival residences, religious, and commercial buildings.

Castleton Historical Society Museum, Main St.; 468-5328. Nineteenth- and twentieth-century furnishings, paintings, costumes, documents, photographs, and military memorabilia. Old carriages in back garage. The museum is housed in a beautiful homestead built in 1811. Open Sunday afternoons in summer. Not accessible to the handicapped.

FAIR HAVEN

Fair Haven Green Historic District, downtown. Forty-two religious, residential, commercial, and public buildings, including two marble homes, surround this spacious tree-encircled green.

HUBBARDTON

Hubbardton Battlefield, East Hubbardton Rd.; 773-2747. Visitor center has small collection of historical materials, drawings, and an elaborate diorama depicting the Hubbardton battle, the only revolutionary war battle fought in Vermont. The Colonials, led by Green Mountain Boy Seth Warner, brought a successful rear guard action that inflicted heavy casualties on the British. Visitor center open from mid-May to mid-October and guided tours provided. The site is free and open to the public year-round.

MENDON

Civil War Horse Grave, Sugar and Spice Restaurant, Rte. 4; 773-1581. Behind the Sugar and Spice pancake house and gift shop is a boulder marking the site where General Edward Ripley, a native of Mendon, buried his Civil War horse, Old John.

MIDDLETOWN SPRINGS

Middletown Springs Community House, near the green. During the summer and early fall, the Middletown Springs Historical Society opens a small museum with photographs, artifacts, and other exhibits. Here you can learn about the town's Montvert Hotel, the resort that once attracted spring enthusiasts to the area, and the A. W. Gray Horsepower Factory, once the town's main industry. The museum is open from 2–4 P.M. on Sunday. No admission required.

Middletown Springs Historic District, village green. More than 80 predominantly residential buildings constructed in beautiful Italianate and Greek Revival styles during the Victorian era. Also a historic walk on the banks of the Poultney River a short walk from the green. Here you will find a springhouse replica. The original springhouse was used to store spring water that bubbled up from the river and drew hundreds to the community for health reasons.

PROCTOR

Proctor Memorial Bridge, just off Rte. 3 in center of town. The triple-arch marble bridge was built in 1915 by the Proctor family. Designed by New York architect Henry Walker, it passes over the Otter Creek and looks north to Sunderland Falls, the waterfall that has provided hydropower for the Vermont Marble Company since its founding in the nineteenth century.

Vermont Marble Exhibit, 61 Main St.; 459-3311. Dedicated to marble and the marble industry in Vermont, the museum includes a sculpture collection, historic photographs, geologic exhibitions on the formation of marble, sculptor in residence, gift shop, and an outdoor marble exhibit. Admission charged. Handicapped accessible.

Wilson Castle, West Proctor Rd.; 773-3284. Nineteenth-century castle featuring proscenium arches, towering turrets, parapet, stained glass windows, 13 fireplaces with imported tiles, outdoor aviary with peacocks. Open mid-May to late October. Admission.

RUTLAND

Norman Rockwell Museum, Rte. 4; 773-6095. The museum commemorates Norman Rockwell's years in Vermont. Exhibits include magazine covers, advertisements, novel and short story illustrations, movie and war posters. Gift shop. Admission charged.

Rutland Courthouse Historic District, Court St. and Center St. Significant buildings include the county courthouse built in an Italianate style, the Rutland Free Library, and numerous Queen Anne-style residences.

Rutland Downtown Historic District, Merchants Row and Center St. Built during Rutland's railroad era, the downtown includes nineteenth-century commercial buildings often decorated with marble. The downtown is considered one of the most historically significant in Vermont.

SHREWSBURY

W. E. Pierce Store, North Shrewsbury; no phone. This classic Vermont general store has changed little since it was founded by the Pierce family in 1835. It still has an ornate tin cash register, the old wooden shelves and countertop, and many old posters. It is also run by members of the founding family.

WALLINGFORD

Wallingford Historical Society Museum, lower floor of Town Hall, School St.; 446-2831. Permanent collection of costumes, photographs, and memorabilia. Open by appointment and for special events.

Wallingford Main St. Historic District, Main St. The nineteenth-century buildings and homes line a wide, tree-lined street. Buildings include the Old House Stone Shop, original mill of a pitchfork factory built in 1836.

Seasonal Events

CASTLETON

Castleton Colonial Days. Historic houses along Main St. open to the public for tours. Early August, Castleton Historical Society; 468-5328.

HUBBARDTON

Hubbardton Revolutionary Battle Reenactment; 773-2747. On a weekend close to July 7, the 1777 battle date, the Living History Association reenacts the historic battle where Colonials fought a successful rearguard action against the British in a hillside field in this rural town.

MIDDLETOWN SPRINGS

Middletown Springs Memorial Day Parade. This town pulls out all the stops for an old-fashioned parade complete with floats, antique carriages, high school bands, speeches, and singing.

RUTLAND

Art in the Park, Chaffee Art Gallery-sponsored art show and sale in Main St. Park, held two weekends a year in mid-August and October. For information call 775-0356.

Farmer's Market, Wednesday and Saturday, summer and fall, in Depot Park, downtown Rutland. Fresh produce, plants, crafts, natural meats, dairy products, jams and jellies, and live entertainment. Christmas sale in early December at the Unitarian Church on West St.

Festival of Quilts, College of St. Joseph; 773-4143. Held in early May.

Halloween Parade, Rutland Recreation Department; 773-1822. Downtown evening parade includes lively floats and streets full of costumed children and adults.

Vermont State Fair, Rutland Fairgrounds; 775-5200. First nine days of September. Annual fair includes livestock competition, farm products, arts and crafts, poultry, rabbits, week of pari-mutuel horse racing, demolition derby, midway of games and rides, and entertainment.

SHERBURNE

Killington Mountain Craft Show, Northeast Passage Lodge; 422-3783. Late September. Professional craftspeople display work, and annual juried show.

Killington Mountain Equestrian Festival; 422-3333. Hunters and jump horses take over the grassy fields at the base of the mountains during mid-July.

Killington Stage Race. Top U.S. bicyclists compete for cash prizes over the mountainous roads near Killington in late August.

Taste of Vermont. Call the Rutland Regional Chamber of Commerce for information at 773-2747. Vermont's premier chefs compete in a benefit tasting meal that contributes money to the Culinary Arts Scholarship Fund for Vermonters. Held in late September at the Killington Ski Area Snowshed Lodge.

WALLINGFORD

Wallingford Antiques Show. Call the Rutland Regional Chamber of Commerce for information at 773-2747. Featuring numerous country dealers and country cooking. Held on a weekend in late September.

Children's Activities

BOMOSEEN
Bomoseen State Park. Inquire at park or call 265-4242. Swimming and nature programs run by resident naturalist during the summer.

CASTLETON
Pond Hill Ranch, South St.; 468-2449. Pony rides for children, Saturday night rodeos from July 4 to Labor Day, and sleigh rides during the winter.

CHITTENDEN
Mountain Top Inn, Mountain Top Rd.; 483-2311. Horseback riding, sleigh rides, and cross-country skiing and lessons.

RUTLAND
Children's programs at the Rutland Free Library, Court St.; 773-1860. Story hours, puppet shows, and other fun guests.
Crossroads Arts Council, 72 Wales St.; 775-1678. Runs some children's programs throughout the school year.
White's Pool, Ave. C; 773-1822. Olympic-size outdoor swimming pool open to the public all summer.
Winter Ice Skating, Rutland Recreation Department; 773-1822. Both indoor and outdoor.

SHERBURNE
Killington Gondola and Chair Lift; 422-3333. Operates July through September.
Killington Ski Area, Killington Access Rd. off Rte. 4; 422-3333. Lessons.
Pico Alpine Slide, Rte. 4; 775-4345. Open in the summer.

WALLINGFORD
Elfin Lake, Rte. 140. Swimming, picnicking, and snack bar.

Shops

Art Galleries

CASTLETON
Christine Price Gallery, Castleton State College; 468-5611, ext. 323. Changing anthropology and art exhibits, open during school year.

PROCTOR
Proctor Free Library, Rte. 3; 459-3539. Occasional exhibits of sculpture and history.

RUTLAND
Chaffee Art Gallery, 16 South Main St.; 775-0356. Lively and diverse exhibits that change often throughout the year.
Moon Brook Arts Union, 21 Center St.; 775-9548. Multimedia shows by professional artists.

Crafts and Specialty Stores

MENDON
Sugar and Spice, Rte. 4; 773-7832. Vermont gifts.
Sweatertown, U.S.A., Rte. 4; 773-7358. Sweaters, sweatshirts, and T-shirts.

PROCTOR
AR Books, Rte. 3; 459-3344. Used paperbacks and historic, collectible paperback editions.

RUTLAND

Boutique International, North Main St.; 775-1313. Imported gifts, ceramics, jewelry, pewter, crystal, linens, and pottery.

Essential Alternatives, 22 Center St.; 773-8834. Latin American, European, and native American clothing, pottery, crafts, jewelry, and cards. Also sells handmade futons and futon furniture.

La Cuisine, 7 Center St.; 775-0453. China, glassware, coffee machines, and other fine cooking products.

Truly Unique, Rte. 4 east; 773-7742. Gifts, crafts, and antiques.

Tuttle Antiquarian Books, 28-30 South Main St.; 773-8930 or 773-8229. Old and rare books and new books on Japan.

The Wine Cellar, Rte. 7 in shop behind state liquor store; 773-3364.

SHERBURNE

Accents and Images, Killington Access Rd.; 422-3722. Souvenirs, gifts, cards, posters, toys.

Bill's Country Store, intersection of Rte. 4 and Rte. 7; 773-9313. Gifts, syrup, cheese, beer, and wine.

Greenbrier Gift Shop, Rte. 4; 775-1575. Handcrafted items and artwork.

Lothlorien, Rte. 4; 773-3231. Gifts, foods, and Killington souvenirs.

Mountain Wine & Cheese Shop, Rte. 4; 775-6640. Fine cheese and wine.

Pat's Hats, Killington Access Rd.; 422-9896. Variety of hats for warmth and fun.

SHREWSBURY

Meadowsweet Herb Farm, Eastham Rd.; 492-3565. Herb gardens and shop with herbs and crafts.

Vermont Industries, Inc., Rte. 103; 492-3451. Ironworker's shop.

Antiques

CASTLETON

Old Homestead Antiques, Rte. 4A; 468-2425. Furnishings. Clothing and Americana.

Sleigh Antiques, Rte. 4A; 468-8999. Antiques and gifts.

FAIR HAVEN

Foundation Antiques, 148 North Main St.; 265-4544. Specializing in graniteware, kitchenware, earthenware, and art pottery. Large inventory of items including furniture and primitive accessories.

MIDDLETOWN SPRINGS

The Clock Doctor, South St.; 235-2440. Restoration, repair, and retail of antique clocks.

The Lamplighter, South St.; 235-2306. Early lighting instruments from the eighteenth century to the twentieth.

Old Spa Shop, Village Green; 235-2366. Victorian furniture and accessories.

RUTLAND

Antique Center, 67 Center St.; 775-3215. Collectible items, gifts, and accessories.

The Clarendon House, Rte. 4 east; 773-6550. Variety of early American furniture, music boxes.

Conway's Antiques & Decor, 90 Center St.; 775-5153. English and American furniture.

Eagle's Nest Antiques, 53 Prospect St.; 773-2418. China, lamps, dolls, jewelry, silver, bottles, copper, and miniatures.

Park Antiques, Rte. 4 east; 775-4184. Furniture, quilts, folk art, and accessories.

Rutland Antiques and Furniture Shop, Rte. 7 north; 775-6573. Large selection of furniture, dishes, dolls, assorted antiques.

Sugar House Antiques, Woodstock Ave. (Rte. 4 east); 775-0547. Furniture, china, cut glass, country store.

Treasure Chest, 25 Center St.; 775-0310. Furniture and Americana.

WALLINGFORD

Country House Antiques, Rte. 7; 446-2344. American country and formal furniture and accessories.
Wallingford Antique Center, Rte. 7; 446-2450. European, primitive, and country furniture, accessories, dolls, and paintings.
Yankee Maid Antiques, Rte. 7; 446-2463. Early country furniture, baskets, and textiles.

Discount Outlets

MENDON

Dexter Shoe Factory Outlet, Rte. 4; 775-4370.

RUTLAND

All Seasons Factory Outlet, North Main St.; 775-6120. Clothing.
Bass Shoe Factory Outlet, North Main St.; 775-5822.
Colonial Sportshoe Center, South Main St.; 775-4766.
Hathaway Shirt Outlet, North Main St.; 775-7639.
Ruff-Hewn Factory Outlet, South Main St.; 773-7411. Natural fabric classic and casual clothing.
Timberland Factory Outlet, South Main St.; 775-7125.
Van Heusen (shirt) Factory Store, North Main St.; 775-3611.

Sports and Recreation

Biking

RUTLAND

Green Mountain Schwinn Cyclery, 133 Strongs Ave.; 775-0869. Sales and rentals.

SHERBURNE

First Stop Ski Shop, Bridgewater at intersection of Rte. 4 and Rte. 100 south; 422-9050. Bike rentals.

Golf

BOMOSEEN

Prospect House and Bomoseen Golf Club, Rte. 30; 468-5581. Nine holes, open to public.

PROCTOR

Proctor-Pittsford Country Club, Corn Hill Rd.; 483-9379. Eighteen holes, open to public.

RUTLAND

Rutland Country Club, Grove St.; 773-7061. Eighteen holes, open to public.

SHERBURNE

Killington Golf Course, Killington Ski Area; 422-3333. Eighteen holes, open to public.

Horseback Riding

CASTLETON

Pond Hill Ranch, Pond Hill Rd.; 468-2449. English and western, by the hour.

CHITTENDEN
Mountain Top Inn Equestrian Center, Mountain Top Rd.; 483-2311. English or western, by the hour.

Sporting Goods Services

BOMOSEEN
Duda Water Sports, Lake Bomoseen; 265-3432. Rents outboard motorboats for waterskiing and fishing.

CASTLETON
River Road Shop, Rte. 4A; 468-2223. Cross-country skis, new, used, and rentals. Open in winter only. Owner organizes cross-country ski expeditions for children and parents through Castleton-Bomoseen area on old logging roads and state park trails. Ask at desk for information.

CHITTENDEN
Mountain Top Ski Center, Mountain Top Inn; 483-2311. Cross-country ski, bicycling, and other sporting equipment.
Mustard Seed Canoe and Boat Rental, Dam Rd.; 483-6081.

FAIR HAVEN
St. John's Sporting Goods, 55 Main St.; 265-8642. General sporting goods.

MENDON
Highland Ski and Sports, Rte. 4; 773-7194. Ski equipment and gear.
Mendon Mountain Ski Rentals, Rte. 4; 773-4208. Ski rentals.
New England Sailboard Company, Rte. 4; 773-4146. Sailboards.

RUTLAND
Great Outdoors Trading Company, 41 Center St.; 775-6531. Full line sporting goods for skiing, tennis, biking, swimming, golfing, and hunting.
Lindholm Sport Center, South Main St.; 773-6000. Equipment and clothing for skiing, camping, hunting, and fishing.
Mountain Travelers, Rte. 4 east; 775-0814. Cross-country, telemark, snowshoe, and winter camping gear.
Wilson Sports, Rutland Mall; 775-2991. Equipment for skiing, tennis, and backpacking.

SHERBURNE
Aspen East Ski Shop, Rte. 4; 422-3739. Downhill skis.
Basin Ski Shop, Killington Access Rd.; 422-3234. Clothing, equipment, and accessories.
Blue Moon Sports, Killington Access Rd.; 422-8135. Ski tune-ups and repair service.
Carroll Reed Ski Shop, Mountain Green Village Center; 422-3999. Downhill and cross-country equipment and clothing.
The Finish Line Ski Shop, Killington Access Rd.; 422-3008. Downhill skis.
The Forerunner, Killington Access Rd.; 422-3950. Downhill skis.
Green Mountain Woolens Ski Shop and Ski Rentals; 422-4088. Downhill skis.
Killington Ski Shops, Killington Ski Area; 422-3333. Rentals, repair, and tuning. Shops are in Snowshed Lodge, Killington Base Lodge, Northeast Passage, Gondola Base, and Bear Mountain Lodge.
Northern Ski Works, Inc., Killington Access Rd.; 422-9675. Downhill skis.
Ski Shack, junction Rtes. 4 and 100 north; 775-2821. Skiwear.
Southworth's Ski Shop, Rte. 4; 773-6663. Equipment and apparel.

Tennis

Note: All town public courts are on a first come, first served basis.

CASTLETON
Dewey Field, North Rd.; Outdoor town courts, open to the public, no charge.

FAIR HAVEN
Fair Haven, Cottage St.; Outdoor town courts, open to the public, no charge.

MENDON
Cortina Inn, Rte. 4; 773-3331. Outdoor courts and lessons with pro available for fee.

PROCTOR
Proctor High School, Park St. Outdoor town courts, open to the public, no charge.

RUTLAND
Great Expectations-Brookside, Curtis Ave.; 773-9066. Indoor and outdoor tennis courts for fee.
Monsignor Connor Park, Meadow St.; 773-1822. Rutland Recreation Department free public outdoor courts.
Rotary Field, North St.; 773-1822. Rutland Recreation Department free public outdoor courts.
White's Pool Area, Ave. C; 773-1822. Rutland Recreation Department free public outdoor courts.

SHERBURNE
Killington School of Tennis, Killington Ski Area; 422-3333. Lessons given by tennis pro. Weekend and daily packages.
Public Courts, River Rd.; Three courts, no charge.

WALLINGFORD
Wallingford Town Courts, Rte. 140. Two courts.

Alpine Ski Areas

SHERBURNE
Killington Ski Area, Killington Access Rd.; 773-1500. Vertical drop, 3,060 feet, 107 trails, and 18 lifts on six mountains, extensive snowmaking, ski lessons, rentals, and restaurants. Day care available.
Pico Ski Area, Rte. 4; 775-4345. Vertical drop, 1,967 feet, 35 trails, nine lifts, snowmaking, ski lessons, base lodge, and health club. Day care available.

Nordic Ski Areas

CHITTENDEN
Mountain Top Ski Area, Mountain Top Rd.; 483-2311. Fifty-five miles of trails, some with snowmaking; instruction; rentals; moonlight tours; sleigh rides. Adjacent to Mountain Top Inn.

RUTLAND
Rutland Country Club, North Grove St. Rutlanders ski for free at the country club when there is snow. Children also use one of the best hills for great sledding.

SHERBURNE
Mountain Meadows, Thundering Brook Rd.; 775-1010. Forty miles of trails through Killington Basin, rentals, instruction, and tours. Adjacent to Mountain Meadows Lodge.

Fishing

BOMOSEEN
Glen Lake, Scotch Hill Rd. Trout, perch, bass, bullheads, and panfish.
Lake Bomoseen, West Shore Rd. Trout, perch, pike, bass, pickerel, bullheads, and panfish.

CASTLETON
Castleton River. Trout and pickerel.

CHITTENDEN
Chittenden Reservoir, Dam Rd. Trout, smelt, perch, bass, bullhead, and panfish.

HUBBARDTON
Beebe Pond, Rte. 30. Perch, pike, bass, bullhead, and panfish.
Half Moon Pond, Town Rd. Trout, perch, bass, bullhead, and panfish.

MIDDLETOWN SPRINGS
Poultney River, along Rte. 140. Trout.

PROCTOR
Otter Creek, through the center of town. Trout, bass, perch, pickerel, bullhead, and panfish.

RUTLAND
Otter Creek, Creek Rd. Trout, bass, perch, pickerel, bullhead, and panfish.

SHERBURNE
Colton Pond, Rte. 100. Trout.
Kent Pond, Rte. 100. Trout and bass.
Roaring Brook, parallel to the east side of the Killington Access Rd. Trout.

SHREWSBURY
Cold River, parallel to the Cold River Rd. Trout.

WALLINGFORD
Wallingford Pond. Reached by foot. Perch and pickerel.

Boating

BOMOSEEN
Glen Lake, Scotch Hill Rd. Public boat launch on 191-acre lake.
Lake Bomoseen, West Shore Rd. Public boat launch on 2,360-acre lake.

CHITTENDEN
Chittenden Reservoir, Dam Rd. Public boat launch on 674-acre lake. Small craft with no more than 15 horsepower allowed.

SHERBURNE
Colton Pond, Rte. 100. Small lake for small craft.
Kent Pond, Rte. 100. Small lake for small craft.

WALLINGFORD
Elfin Lake, Rte. 140. Small lake for small craft.

Swimming

BOMOSEEN
Bomoseen State Park, West Shore Rd.; 265-4242.
Crystal Town Beach, Rte. 30.
Glen Lake, Scotch Hill Rd. from Fair Haven or West Shore Dr. from Bomoseen. Swim off the rocks near the public boat launch.

CHITTENDEN
Chittenden Reservoir, Dam Rd. No beach; trails around the lake lead to secluded coves where you can swim off rocks.

MENDON
Cortina Inn, Rte. 4; 773-3331. Indoor pool open for fee.

RUTLAND
Centre Sport at Holiday Inn, Rte. 7 south; 775-1911. Indoor pool and health
  club open to inn guests and the public for a daily fee.
White's Pool, Ave. C; 773-1822. City's outdoor public pool. Minimal admission
  charged.

SHERBURNE
Killington Health Club, Killington Village; 422-9370. Indoor 54-foot lap pool,
  health club, and juice bar. Daily rate charged.
Pico Sports Center, Rte. 4; 775-4345. Indoor 76-foot indoor lap pool and full
  health club with weights, racquetball, sauna, and Jacuzzi. Daily rate charged.
Spa de la Foret, In The Woods at Killington complex, Killington Access Rd.;
  442-3100. Indoor pool and other health and exercise equipment. Open to public.

WALLINGFORD
Elfin Lake, Rte. 140 west of the center of town. Swimming, picnicking, and small
  boats.
Little Rock Pond, Homer Stone Brook Trail in South Wallingford. You can reach
  this swimming pond only by hiking through the woods approximately 2.8 miles.

Hiking and Nature Trails

BOMOSEEN
Bomoseen State Park, West Shore Rd.; 265-4242.

CHITTENDEN
New Boston Trail, Blue Ridge Mountain. Trail starts at the end of Mountain Top
  Rd. and climbs up mountains overlooking Chittenden; 4.8-mile round-trip hike.

MENDON
Blue Ridge Mountain Trail. North turn off Rte. 4 onto Turnpike Rd.; 4.8-mile
  round-trip hike.

RUTLAND
Pine Hill Park Trail, Oak St. One-mile round-trip starts behind Giorgetti Skating
  Rink, maintained by Rutland Recreation Department; 773-1822.

SHERBURNE
Gifford Woods State Park, Rte. 100; 775-5354. Hiking trails, camping, and
  picnicking.

SHREWSBURY
The Long Trail passes through this town intersecting Rte. 103 and the Upper
  Cold River Rd. in North Shrewsbury. Many hikes possible along trail.
Shrewsbury Peak, CCC Rd. Take left at Pierce's Store and drive 2.7 miles to turn-
  off; 3.6 miles round-trip to and from top.

WALLINGFORD
Little Rock Pond, South Wallingford. Take the Homer Stone Brook Trail located
  near the Little Red School House on a side road off Rte. 7 in South Wallingford;
  5.6 miles round-trip.
White Rocks Cliff. Side road off Rte. 140 east of Wallingford Village; 3.2-mile
  round-trip hike to white cliff.

State Parks

BOMOSEEN
Bomoseen State Park, West Shore Rd.; 265-4242. Swimming, boating, picnicking,
  fishing, camping, and hiking.

HUBBARDTON

Half Moon State Park, Town Rd.; 273-2848. Swimming, camping, boating, fishing, and hiking.

SHERBURNE

Gifford Woods State Park, Rte. 100; 775-5354. Hiking, camping, boating, fishing, and hiking.

Foliage Vantage Points

BOMOSEEN

Black Pond Rd. The dirt road that connects Bomoseen State Park with Half Moon State Park in Hubbardton.
West Shore Dr. around Lake Bomoseen.

CHITTENDEN

Dam Rd. The road that leads from the center of Chittenden to the Chittenden Reservoir.
Mountain Top Rd. The New Boston Trail at the end of Mountain Top Rd.
Sangamon Rd. The road that leads from Rte. 7 north to Rutland to the East Pittsford Rd. near the center of Chittenden.

FAIR HAVEN

Main Rd. in West Haven. West turn off Rte. 22A. It takes you into the wild town of West Haven where the last remaining rattlesnakes in the state live. The drive can be beautiful and there is little chance of seeing a snake. They are more threatened by humans than we are by them.
Scotch Hill Rd. around Glen Lake.
Sheldon Pond Rd. Small country loop off Rte. 22A west of Fair Haven village.

HUBBARDTON

East Hubbardton Rd. Follow this past the Hubbardton battlefield and you will pass through a lovely tree tunnel.

MENDON

Wheelerville Rd. Left turn off Rte. 4 as you are driving from Rutland to Mendon up the highway. The gravel road leads through lush forest into Rutland City Forest and the Calvin Coolidge State Forest.

MIDDLETOWN SPRINGS

Rte. 140 going east to Tinmouth and Wallingford is beautiful with hilly, numerous vistas. Rte. 140 going west to East Poultney also provides many foliage views.
Rte. 133. Drive south on 133 to Pawlet to view the beginning of the Mettowee Valley, rich farmland protected by the Taconic Mountains that will fill with color in the fall.

PROCTOR

West Proctor Rd. near Wilson Castle; good views from the grounds of Wilson Castle on the hillside.

RUTLAND

Creek Rd., or Dorr Dr. From downtown, drive south on Merchants Row, which turns into Strongs Ave. Take right onto River St. Bridge over railroad tracks. Follow this across another bridge over the silty Otter Creek. Turn left or southbound just after crossing the bridge. After you pass many small houses you will be traveling on a rural road that curves with the creek through beautiful foliage.
North Grove St. Drive out North Grove St. toward Pittsford; stately old homes and lovely colors.

SHERBURNE

Killington Gondola or chair lift provides the ultimate leaf-peeping.
Rte. 4 east of the Killington Access Rd. is a beautiful valley surrounded by high mountains with brilliant foliage.
Rte. 100 north and south.
Take a few detours onto Thundering Brook Rd. or River Rd. Both turns off Rte. 4 near Sherburne Village; less harried views of the foliage.

SHREWSBURY

Eastham Rd. to Bailey Rd. Take a right at Pierce's Store and follow the sign to Meadowsweet Herb Farm. Keep going on what is Eastham Rd. for 1.8 miles. Take a left turn down Bailey Rd., which will take you through a lush tunnel of trees.
Hill Rd. Take a right at Pierce's Store in North Shrewsbury and go a few miles to the farm where the moose and cow fell in love. L. Carrarra is written on the mailbox. Don't disturb the owner, but take a look at the panoramic view of the mountains.
Upper Cold River Rd. Take the Cold River Rd. from Rutland, but get onto the upper road, also called Covered Bridge Rd., for quieter, more dramatic views of foliage.

WALLINGFORD

Homer Stone Brook Trail or Little Rock Pond, see Hiking section for directions.
Rte. 140. Drive east to village of East Wallingford and west toward Tinmouth.

Best of Rutland/Killington

Country Inn: Red Clover, Woodward Rd., Mendon; 775-2290.
Resort: Mountain Top Inn, Mountain Top Rd., Chittenden; 483-2311.
Breakfast: Clem's Kitchen, 51 Wales St., Rutland; 775-6104. Cortina Inn Sunday brunch, Rte. 4, Mendon; 773-3331.
Lunch: Back Home Café, 21 Center St., Rutland; 775-2104. Charity's, Killington Access Rd., Sherburne; 422-3800.
Dinner (Moderately priced): Fair Haven Inn, 5 Adams St., Fair Haven; 265-4907. Little Naples, Rte. 4, Mendon; 773-4663.
Dinner (Expensive): Hemingway's, Rte. 4, Sherburne; 422-3886.
Entertainment (Casual): Wobbly Barn, Killington Access Rd., Sherburne; 422-3392. South Station, South Main St., Rutland; 775-1736.
Entertainment (Stage): None on a regular basis.
Museum/Historical Site: Vermont Marble Exhibit, 61 Main St., Proctor; 459-3311.
Art Gallery: Chaffee Art Gallery, 16 South Main St., Rutland; 775-0356.
Craft and Specialty Shop: Essential Alternatives, 22 Center St., Rutland; 773-8834.
Antique Shops: The Lamplighter, South St., Middletown Springs; 235-2306. Old Spa Shop Antiques, Village Green, Middletown Springs; 235-2366.
Discount Outlet: Ruff-Hewn Factory Outlet, South Main St., Rutland; 775-7125.
Public Golf Course: Proctor-Pittsford Country Club, Corn Hill Rd., Pittsford; 483-9379.
Public Tennis Courts: White's, Ave. C, Rutland; 773-1822. Rutland Recreation Department free courts.
Hiking or Nature Trail: Little Rock Pond, Homer Stone Brook Trail, South Wallingford. Refer to section on Wallingford.
Camping: Half Moon State Park, Black Pond Rd., Hubbardton; 273-2848.
Children's Activities: Pico Alpine Slide, Rte. 4, Sherburne; 775-4345. Rutland Halloween Parade, downtown Rutland; 773-1822.
Farm Stand: Burnham Hollow Orchards, Rte. 140, Middletown Springs; 235-2452.
Ice Cream: Ben & Jerry's, 170 South Main St., Rutland; 775-1134.
Foliage Vantage Point: View from Killington Gondola, Rte. 4, Sherburne; 422-3333.
Ski Areas (Alpine): Killington Ski Area, Killington Access Rd., Sherburne; 773-1500 and 422-3333. Pico Ski Area, Rte. 4, Sherburne; 775-4354.
Ski Area (Nordic): Mountain Top Inn and Resort, Mountain Top Rd., Chittenden; 483-2311.

The Woodstock Area

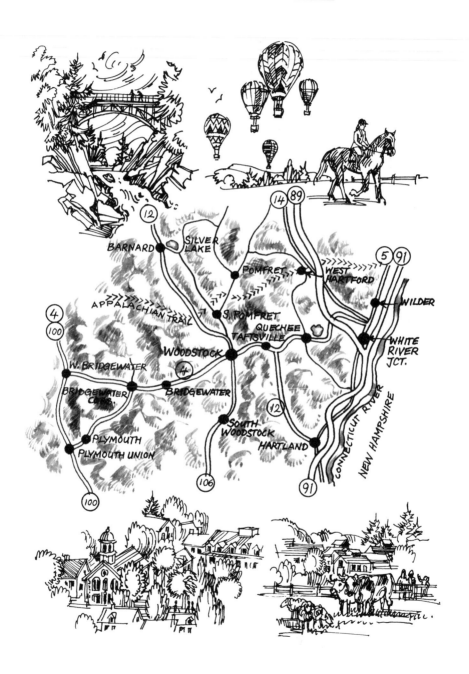

BARNARD

SILVER LAKE

12

14 89

POMFRET

WEST HARTFORD

5 91

WILDER

APPALACHIAN TRAIL

S. POMFRET

QUECHEE

TAFTSVILLE

WHITE RIVER JCT.

4

100

WOODSTOCK

4

W. BRIDGEWATER

BRIDGEWATER CRS.

BRIDGEWATER

12

SOUTH WOODSTOCK

HARTLAND

PLYMOUTH

PLYMOUTH UNION

100

106

91

CONNECTICUT RIVER

NEW HAMPSHIRE

Viewpoints

by CONSTANCE HENDREN FITZ

If Woodstock has the air of a prosperous town, it is well deserved, for Woodstock has been an affluent community for a couple of centuries. As the shire town, or county seat, for Windsor County, Woodstock early attracted a large professional class and all that went with it. This early status shows best in the handsome buildings that line Elm Street and ring the green. Although they give off a self-satisfied air of history and tradition, several are newcomers. Taken together they are a patchwork of New England architectural fashion, and they form an appealing and harmonious whole.

The Woodstock area includes tiny Taftsville, with its much-photographed covered bridge, and South Woodstock, a quiet pretty village on Route 106.

Anyone arriving in Woodstock during one of the town's frequent busy seasons has ample opportunity to take a leisurely look at these buildings. Route 4, mid-Vermont's main east-west traffic artery, goes past the green before cutting through the center of the town's business district. After a weekend spent skiing at Pico or Killington, Route 4 travelers heading back to Connecticut or Massachusetts are destined to join a long patient queue of vehicles — the state's traffic analysts figure more than 12,000 on a peak day — which slowly edge past the elegant buildings. On winter Sundays at dusk, when hundreds of cars loaded with homeward-bound skiers swell the mix, the entire line has halted to allow a young mother pushing a stroller to cross Central Street. It's interesting to imagine the resulting 20-mile chain of brake lights on bumper-to-bumper cars glowing red in sequence, as seen from an airplane.

Improvement in the traffic situation on Route 4 heads the list of desired changes for residents and visitors alike. But in 1988, when consultants hired by the state to find remedies suggested building a four-lane bypass around the town, all hell broke loose, though the idea of a bypass is not a new one. The indignant rejection of plans to skirt the town with a larger highway came not only from NIMBY, or not-in-my-neighborhood types, but from people in Woodstock and neighboring towns who felt that a larger road would only encourage even more traffic.

Another often-heard objection was that a bypass around Woodstock would rip through neighborhoods and landscape features that locals emphatically do not want to lose; historic cemeteries, familiar meadows, and at least one officially designated "Scenic Road."

Plans to build the bypass appear to be on hold for the present. To help upgrade the road's lamentable safety record, parts of the route are slated for spot improvements — passing lanes and the occasional straightening of a tight curve. For the immediate future anyway, little two-lane Route 4 through Woodstock will continue as it has been, a scenic and maddeningly slow drive.

The fact that it can sometimes be a trial to get into the shire town, let alone find a parking spot there, hasn't tarnished Woodstock's reputation as a choice place to visit. Some Woodstockers, having found and settled down in "New England's Prettiest Village," resent the constant crowds, which is not a new sentiment. They are the spiritual descendants of Abby Maria Hemenway, who wrote in 1869 in her *Vermont Historical Gazetteer*:

Let us do all we can to keep up the notion among our city cousins that to live "away up in Vermont" is the American equivalent for being exiled to Siberia. Let us tell them that we like to have them VISIT us during the few fleeting days in mid-summer when we can safely walk about with them in our fields without our buffalo coats and bearskin gowns, but that THEY belong to altogether too delicate a race to think of LIVING THROUGH our severe summers with any comfort. Not that we do not think very highly of our city cousins, especially WHEN WE SEE THEM IN THE CITY.

Those who, having arrived, would pull up the ladder, are in the minority. Visitors are Woodstock's bread and butter. Chief among tourism boosters who can't get enough of visitors at any time of year are local providers of food and lodging, the town's biggest cash cow.

As has happened in most of Vermont's formerly quiet villages that depend largely on tourism for economic survival, Woodstock has undergone changes in the past two decades. To the dismay of many, the town now must wrestle occasionally with the same ills — drug use and alcoholism, vandalism, poverty, and homelessness — that plague the outside world.

Fast action by a consortium of local people working together with the state recently saved the area's only low-cost housing, a trailer park, from upscale development. The land the park is on, in a beautiful river-bend lowland, is now owned cooperatively by its tenants. But as land and housing prices spiral ever upward, the dream of most low-income families to have a home of their own in the town where they grew up, or of older parents to have their children settle nearby, is unlikely to come true. An article in a recent regional magazine recently tagged Woodstock as "the town Vermonters love to hate," and it is true that the town suffers frequent envious jibes as a playground of the rich, which it may well be. State economic statistics show another side of Woodstock not necessarily as a town totally populated by well-heeled inhabitants. Even adding in a few millionaires hidden here and there, Woodstock's $8,114 ranks it only 14th in Vermont for per capita income. It is 44th in Vermont for its median family income of only a little over $18,000, well below the brackets enjoyed by most second-home owners and visitors. As land values, rents, and taxes rise, local shops find they must focus more on the needs of visitors, where the profits lie, and not on the bread and butter stuff. Woodstock, with four art galleries, has no place to buy children's underwear. It boasts several gourmet eating places, but it has a scarcity of spots for a late-night something quick and cheap to eat.

Nevertheless, the posh Woodstock Inn, possessor of Woodstock's largest everything, is a focal point in the community. Perhaps it is because the inn's offerings are all open to the public.

Locals enjoy popping in for an after-work brew in the English-clubby atmosphere of Richardson's Tavern, named for the first public house on this spot built in 1793. The inn's capacious lobby, with its open fireplace and bowls of polished red apples, is a popular meeting place. For those who want only to sit quietly and read, recent renovations carved out a space off the lobby for a real library, with deep chairs, desks to write on, and shelves full of various books, from poetry to travel guides.

Wilderness campers at Silver Lake or Coolidge state parks have been known to stow their bedrolls after a night under the stars, climb into proper duds (no jeans, cutoffs, or collarless or sleeveless shirts allowed), and drive to Woodstock to play a round of golf on the country club's Robert Trent Jones-designed course or a few sets of tennis on the air-conditioned courts at the Sports Center. Both are open to the public.

All of the inn's dining rooms welcome nonguest diners, and breakfast, in particular, is a grand occasion to sample the dining facilities. If you appreciate early morning solitude, a breakfast at the inn will suit you to a tee. It's not prohibitively expensive, and it's well worth the cost to sit on the comfy banquettes in the handsome gray and white dining room with morning sun streaming in through tall windows. You can absorb the quiet atmosphere along with the excellent coffee.

The dining room is open for brunch on Sundays, so that is the one day that breakfast is served in the Eagle Café; lunch and dinners are served there every day as well.

Splendid as the inn may be, not everyone craves the impersonality of a big hotel. Hotels, after all, are city features, and many travelers come to Vermont to savor the unspoiled countryside and small-scale comforts. Bed-and-breakfast establishments build on this preference by custom-tuning their offerings and vying with each other to come up with features to make their place different from — and better than — all the others.

At last count there were 33 lodging providers in an 18-square-mile patch, not even counting local folks who open their homes during peak foliage season.

Beaver Pond Farms provides "lodging for horse and rider," with access to 130 acres of trails and pasture, a dressage ring, and barn stalls for family steeds. The Applebutter Inn, actually a small bed and breakfast on a quiet country road in Taftsville, has genuine down puffs on every bed, an investment that cost the owner thousands of dollars but which pays off in repeat business. Both establishments offer features that set them apart, and guests in such settings tend to remember these fine points.

The inn may be the biggest, but it is not the only luxe game in town and not even, in all cases, the most expensive. Several Woodstock B&Bs concentrate on providing surroundings of absolutely scrumptious elegance, with every detail perfect, from canopied four-poster beds to four-star breakfasts. Charleston House and Canterbury House in the village and Jackson House, west of the village, are in this group. In the nearly seven years that Jackson House has been in operation, its owners have painted or polished every inch of what had been an old farmhouse and furnished each of 10 guest bedrooms in choice antiques of a different period and style. It goes without saying that every room has its own perfect adjoining bath and coordinated linens as well. Besides the obligatory gourmet breakfast featured in all top-notch lodgings, Jackson House guests are pampered even further. Evenings at six a harpist strums soft background music, while champagne and hors d'ouevres are served, at no extra charge. No wonder guests who have experienced such pampering want to return.

Folks undoubtedly have a dozen different reasons for coming to Woodstock, the wonderful New England looks of the place surely being one of them. Since 1972, most of Woodstock Village has been listed as a Historic District on the National Register of Historic Places. Woodstock has aged well and is fortunate to have realized early on that its face is its fortune, so to speak. Despite the village's serene appearance today, grim battles have been fought before planning and zoning committees, as dissenting property owners have tried to make changes unauthorized by the town's plan. The town, however, has always held firm. Except for a few pricey extras like the absence of utility wires — they are underground in the Historic District — a major source of the elegance comes from the absence of jarring elements seen in many American downtown areas. Things that Woodstock *doesn't* have are fast-food emporiums, flashing plastic or neon signs, and traffic lights. What it does have in abundance is a variety of buildings in a mix of architectural styles. Summertime visitors can sign up at the information booth for a walking tour around the village, or you can just stroll around the green; old buildings reveal much of the history of the town.

Historical Perspective

East of the inn on the South Street, Route 106, corner stands a rosy brick 1823 Georgian mansion that was built on the site of an earlier courthouse. This now belongs to the inn and is not yet open to the public. The house next to it, built in 1840, was greatly enlarged a few years back by the addition of a large attached barn imported from England, a feature sure to puzzle future archaeological sleuths trying to decipher origins of the alien nails and timbers. The next house, which you would think had been on the same plot since the mortar between its bricks was still wet, was actually moved here in the 1960s from the lot where the grocery store now stands down on Pleasant Street. Farther down this row was the town jail — Woodstock had to provide one to qualify as a courthouse town — and the white frame "DAR House," originally built to provide lodging and meeting rooms for the Vermont legislature meeting in 1807.

Saint James Episcopal Church guards the end of the green and owns its own little green out front. A huge tent covers this spot each July when the Saint James Fair draws crowds. Inside, beside Tiffany stained glass windows, is a fairly new addition, the Albright Organ, built by David Moore of North Pomfret, an organ maker of national renown.

The white pillared Town Hall, replacing an earlier opera house on the same spot that burned in 1927, houses town offices and a theater operated by Pentangle, the local arts council. West of the Town Hall is the handsome white Unitarian-Universalist church built in 1835, and a few doors west of that, the dark red brick building that housed Woodstock's early medical school.

The Clinical School of Medicine and Vermont Medical College were founded in Woodstock by a Dr. Joseph Gallup in 1827 and operated for nearly thirty years. It was an ambitious and, for its time, advanced teaching institution at a time when most M.D.s still received their training by apprenticing to a preceptor, or practicing physician. Dr. Gallup envisioned an innovative medical school for its day. He planned it as a clinical school, one where physicians in training would actually work with and observe people who were ill. What ultimately did in the small school was the lack of any nearby facility like a hospital or clinic where such training could be provided and the surprising fact that by 1830 the region already had several larger and more successful schools of medicine. The building that first housed the college is built in Greek Revival style, with flat pilasters against the front topped with arches and arches over each window, obviously meant to look imposing. The Medical College later moved to a larger frame building up College Hill, which is no longer standing.

Sculptor Hiram Powers, framed for his daring nude statue "The Greek Slave," was born in Woodstock, as was his friend George Perkins Marsh, author of *Man and Nature*. Published in 1864, the book established Marsh as America's first environmentalist. A small park on Kedron Brook just below street level on Central Street is dedicated to his memory. The George Perkins Marsh Park is across from the post office at the end of a cement bridge.

Many of the comfortable, elegantly maintained houses facing the inn were once shops. One housed a tanning business and one a blacksmith shop. Several of the large brick buildings near the Elm Street end of the green are now offices.

The question most asked by visitors to the staff members of the Norman Williams Library east of the inn is whether it was built to be a church. The answer is, no, it was built to be a library in 1883 and given to the town by Norman Williams, a generous and prosperous merchant whose portrait hangs inside. The annual book sale held on the library lawn in early July brings hundreds of book dealers and bargain hunters and contributes a goodly chunk of the library's budget for new books.

In the 1700s, when Paul Revere was considered *the* man to buy bells from, churches in Woodstock ordered four from the renowned artisan. You can get a close-up look at one on the side porch of the Congregational church on Elm. The Woodstock Historical Society headquarters are in Dana House, also on Elm. It was built in 1807 and furnished with a fine collection of period local furnishings and costumes from the years 1800–1860. Dana House is open May through the end of October and for holiday celebrations at other times.

A short distance beyond the village on Route 12, the Billings Farm and Museum is a must-see for Woodstock visitors. The museum is a working farm, with a complex of buildings designed to enlighten visitors on Vermont's agricultural heritage and earlier ways of country life. An introductory film, tour of a farm manager's 1890s house, and a chance to pet a live cow are all part of the tour. There are also frequent horse-drawn wagon rides around the farm grounds. The special days at Billings Farm all summer and fall include Wool Days, Children's Day, a plowing contest, quilt show, and period crafts demonstrations. The information booth on the green is a good place to find out about these or other local happenings. You may also take the walking tour of Woodstock's Historic District starting and ending on the green. Both Billings Farm and the information booth are seasonal.

Many collectors devoted to realistic art make it a point to visit Woodstock's VINS, or Vermont Institute of Natural Science, on Church Hill Road during the annual Wildlife Art Show each September. The event showcases the work of many nationally known artists, decoy carvers in particular. Woodstock's preeminent decoy artist, Jim Keefer, is always represented, as his lyrical waterfowl interpretations are much in demand. VINS is also home to the Vermont Raptor Center, a large outdoor assemblage of spacious aviaries where injured birds of prey — owls, hawks, falcons — that can no longer fend for themselves in the wild are kept. It is not a zoo. These are teaching exhibits and shelters. They offer a chance to see at close range animals that many of us could never hope to spot in the wild. The aim is to help the public realize the danger that mankind presents to these wild creatures and to sensitize viewers to the need to protect them and their habitat. The Raptor Center is open year-round. A small admission is charged.

Starting in January when the snow season has usually arrived in earnest, both the inn's ski facilities, Suicide Six in nearby Pomfret for downhill skiing and the Ski Touring Center at the country club, are in full swing. Suicide Six is small as ski areas go, but it has an active program of races and special events, and skiing down Six's "Face" is said to be a special event on its own.

The Ski Touring Center at the country club manages 77 kilometers of trails, including those covering the golf course and neighboring Mount Peg, and a maze of beautiful woodland trails that crisscross the ridges on Mount Tom across town. Mount Tom trails can be accessed from Woodstock Village via a trail that leads up from the cemetery on River Street. Open country skiers, or snowshoe aficionados, who may prefer to bushwhack on snowmobile tracks, should follow the nature trails at VINS or try the Skyline Trail down from Amity Pond Natural area in North Pomfret. Folks at the ski touring area can supply directions.

Birders in Woodstock can spot plenty to get excited about, especially when migrations are underway. VINS offers a range of bird-related activities, including a chance to observe bird banding during migration time, and its nature preserve provides good birding locations. Well-stocked feeders ensure that brilliant-colored cardinals and bluejays provide notes of color against winter snow. In summer, swallows, orioles, kingfishers, bright yellow goldfinches, and warblers of an improbable blue swoop over meadows or in light woods at meadow edges. Water-level walks along the river provide close-up looks at many species. When hawks are migrating, their lazy loops over ridges are a sight that stops traffic.

By June, strings of bikers line every road out of town. A 20-mile loop from Woodstock up to Barnard, then back down through Pomfret, is a popular route. In South Woodstock, barns at Green Mountain Horse Association are full, and kids are at pony camp learning how to muck out a stall or pick out a hoof. Kedron Valley Inn hosts summertime inn-to-inn horseback riding jaunts, which begin and end right here in South Woodstock. Less energetic horse lovers can book a leisurely hayride at Kedron Valley Stables, pulled by the same patient critters that provide sleigh rides when the snow flies.

It really can get hot in Vermont, and when dog days come, Woodstock has several super spots to dunk in. The Rec Center on Route 4 has two pools, busy in the morning with lessons, but available in the afternoons for a fee. If you prefer to swim laps indoors, the Sports Center on Route 106 has a beautiful glassed-in pool, with a whirlpool to get the kinks out afterwards. For a country-style dip, park in town and walk across the Ottauquechee River on the metal bridge at the end of Elm Street. To your right, just at the end of the bridge, you will see steps leading down to the rocky river edge. The water is low here by midsummer, and the ledge just under the bridge is a cool shady spot to wade and dip. Large rocks downstream border a deeper swimming hole. On a hot afternoon, the place will be full of kids. Silver Lake in Barnard is a favorite swimming spot, as is the pond at Kedron Valley Inn in South Woodstock. After any dip, an ice-cream cone at the White Cottage west of town is the perfect treat.

When the snow is gone from cross-country trails, walkers cover the paths on Mount Tom nearly around-the-clock. Early in the morning the trails are popular with bird-watchers. Later joggers and dog walkers take over, and on moonlit nights couples find their way to the bench overlooking the small lake called The Pogue. Walking on most of Mount Tom's trails could be dangerous to your health after hunting season starts. Stick to the trails leading up the village side of the mountain, staying close to the town side, which is a village park and is posted.

Woodstock can be hectic in foliage season when tour buses add to the traffic mix. This is the time of year to stroll over the covered bridge near the green, walk straight on (Mountain Avenue), and follow paths to the back of Faulkner Park. There, switchback walkways modeled after the "Cardiac Trails" at Baden-Baden in Germany lead gently to the top, and you emerge onto a broad flat promontory from which you can see up and down the valley for miles.

In any season, when cool mountain air whets appetites, Woodstock has several excellent restaurants to choose from. The inn and Elm Street's Prince and Pauper and Bentley's all got the nod from *Gourmet* magazine when the town was featured a few years back. Spooner's and the Rumbleseat Rathskeller are informal and fun. At lunchtime, winter or summer, folks line up for sandwiches at The Village Butcher's on Elm Street or at the Deli at Woodstock East. The Village Butcher's doesn't have tables, but in summer you can take your lunch out back to the lawns behind the Historical Society and picnic on the banks of the river. The Deli has tables and offers, besides delicious salads, a prime view of meadows across the river.

Taftsville

Driving east out Route 4 from Woodstock, Taftsville, with its eye-catching covered bridge and cluster of old buildings, often brings appreciative travelers to a stop. Winter and summer, the bridge is the centerpiece for vacation snapshots. In summer, anglers duck over the bridge, find a pull-off on the dirt road across the way, and settle down to trout fish in deep water behind the dam.

Taftsville has one of the most attractive covered bridges in the region. Built in 1836, it is also the oldest in the county and, at 189 feet, one of the longest. It cost $1,800 to build. It was the bridge and the cost of its maintenance that brought Taftsville, formerly in Hartland, into the Woodstock fold. The bridge stood at a corner where four towns — Pomfret, Hartford, Hartland, and Woodstock — met, and belonged, in peculiar fractions, to all four towns jointly. Woodstock owned $18/40$, Hartland $3/40$, Pomfret $8/40$, and Hartford $11/40$. In 1851, the state legislature carved 15 acres from Hartland around the bridge and assigned this land to Woodstock. At the same time, they changed the borders of Hartford and Pomfret to place the bridge inside Woodstock's borders with financial responsibility for keeping the bridge and its surroundings in good repair. In the days when horse-drawn sleighs were still commonly used in winter, part of the duties of the covered bridge's keepers was to spread enough snow on the bridge floor to allow folks traveling by horse-drawn sleigh to glide through.

The bridge needs to be sturdy: The river here runs high and full when snow melts in spring, and several previous bridges at this site were swept away. Huge plates of thick ice tumble over the nearby dam when river ice breaks up early in the year. The bridge is supported on stone piers sunk into the riverbed and was raised and braced in 1953, which should keep it in service for a good long while.

On the right, on Route 4 approaching Taftsville, is Tony Farides's small shop selling antiques and collectibles and oak country furniture that he refinishes himself. Asked what he specializes in, Tony answers with a grin, "chickens." Tony is a skilled taxidermist who keeps the shop supplied with an array of startingly lifelike stuffed barnyard fowl. Hens and geese in nesting baskets or boxes are in the majority, but there are pugnacious-looking roosters and lifelike standing geese as well. Tony is bemused by their popularity — stuffed birds don't come cheap — but he has seen his birds in decorating magazines promoting the "country look," and he says they do sell extremely well. He claims some have been purchased for wedding presents, which he thinks is a curious choice for newlyweds in their first home. ("Dear Aunt Millie: George and I thank you so much for your delightful present of a stuffed hen...")

At the Taftsville Country Store you can buy a chunk of cheese and see it cut off of a hefty 40-pound wheel. Cheddar and a Vermont apple make a superior snack. Thus fortified, drive up Happy Valley Road by the store where the Applebutter Inn, a comfortable B&B, and a row of lovely old houses are all that remains of what was once a much busier community. Fraser's Antiques is here, with a marvelous two-story barn out back that invites browsing.

From the Taftsville Store side, and Route 4, cross over the Ottauquechee River on the second bridge. Remember to hold your breath all the way across and make a wish. If no one speaks while you hold your breath, your wish is sure to come true. The Vermont Folklife Center in Middlebury affirms this old tradition. They offer the testimony of one Cleland Selby, who related to one of their interviewers that when he was a youngster he crossed a covered bridge, held his breath, and wished to become governor of the state when he grew up. Unfortunately, while he was holding his breath his grandfather spoke, and the wish was canceled. Instead, Cleland Selby became a well-known rug hooker. What more proof do you need?

At the far end of the bridge you will spot the yellow signs that lead to Sugarbush Farm. Technically, Sugarbush is in Pomfret, but the way up from Taftsville is a scenic one, especially in fall. The road rises up from the valley floor and opens to long vistas through lines of old sugar maples.

The Ayres family started this business in the 1940s selling butternut fudge made from an old family recipe. As business grew, they added maple products and cheese to their wares, and today they sell quantities of their unique smoked cheese, which they prepare using a process they developed themselves. Their bars of cheese, also sold by mail order, keep well as they are coated in wax.

When you drive back down to the covered bridge, turn west just before the bridge where the narrow, dirt river road leads back to Woodstock. In summer and fall, this is a beautiful meander. The Ottauquechee, which roars like thunder in spring, is usually low and placid by then. At every bend it reflects the colors of trees and grasses that overhang its banks. Drive slowly as this road is much used by bikers, joggers, and horseback riders. Taking the river road is not advised in winter, when ice makes it tricky, or in mud season, when parts of the road may be impassable because of ice or washouts.

Fishing and taking photographs create most of the hustle and bustle in Taftsville these days, but it's fun to sit on the riverbank across the way and reflect on the comforting sound of water going over a dam, a constant event for more than 200 years. It will give you a satisfying sense that all's right with Taftsville, if not with the rest of the world.

South Woodstock

Five miles from Woodstock's busy green, South Woodstock seems to be in another, quieter world. You may have already caught glimpses of it. Holiday Budweiser commercials filmed here star hefty Clydesdales puffing through snow beside the Kedron Valley Inn. Depending on the season, there are two routes you can take to this charming village. From Woodstock take Route 106 south in winter; it's a fully paved road. It winds along the valley carved by Kedron Brook. In summer or fall, go by Church Hill Road instead, which is paved in Woodstock but turns into a calendar-pretty, dirt country road out of town, bordered by farms and old sugar maples. It's a lovely back road drive in foliage season. Church Hill starts just to the left of Saint James Episcopal Church in Woodstock at the west end of the green.

Both roads meet at South Woodstock's Country Store and post office. Nearby are large old houses, legacies of times when the South Parish was an important commercial center with its own mills, forges, academy, and hotel. The Kedron Valley Inn next door dates from 1828. If you stay there, you may be booked into the ground floor bedroom that once housed the post office. An imposing metal door on one wall creaks open to reveal the old post office safe, complete with secret drawers.

This room, like all 28 in the inn, is beautifully decorated with family heirlooms of owners Max and Merrily Comins. The beds are decked with handmade quilts from Merrily's extensive collection; other quilts are displayed throughout the inn's public areas. You can go in and browse around, get a cool drink from the tiny bar, and sit and rock a spell on the inn's wide porch. The inn also has a sparkling lake more than an acre and a half in size, with a sandy beach and a lifeguard on duty 11 A.M. to 6 P.M. from mid-June to the end of August. Passes can be purchased at the inn office by day or season. Wide, manicured green lawns surround the swimming area, and it's an ideal spot to spend a peaceful afternoon unwinding after biking or riding. Ask at the desk for a hiking map that will guide you to easy one- or two-mile strolls through the local countryside.

South Woodstock is horse country, and if you didn't bring your own (lots of people do), Kedron Valley Stables, three-quarters of a mile away, can provide one. Hayrides and rides in a horse-drawn surrey, as well as riding lessons and guided trail rides over miles of beautiful back-country paths, are also available. Ask at the stables about its "inn-to-inn" rides, which have been featured in national magazines. These start and end with overnights at Kedron Valley, also a stop on the New England Bicycle Tours itineraries.

One mile south, the Green Mountain Horse Association (GMHA), a membership organization, hosts a busy schedule of events ranging from pony camps for kids to endurance rides for adults. A Fjord Horse Show and the Fall Driving Classic are annual September events. Not to be missed is the Evening of Jazz and Dressage in July featuring formally clad riders on perfectly trained horses going through their mannered paces accompanied by the coolest of cool jazz. The jazz/dressage event charges admission, but other GMHA goings-on are free. Visitors are welcome to lean on the fences and watch the horses in action. Send a stamped self-addressed envelope to GMHA, South Woodstock, Vermont 05071, for a schedule. The season runs from early May through September.

High Brook Horse and Harness next to GMHA is an especially well-stocked tack shop with everything from saddles to Austrian riding smocks. Horse toys, books, cards, videos, and posters all featuring our friend, the horse, are also available.

One-half mile farther on Route 106 is Gambol Hill Farm and the Tog Shop, a charming tack shop in an old barn featuring classic English-style riding gear as well as more contemporary styles. You can order a horse portrait here, a pair of Dehner custom-made boots, or western leather chaps. They also have a "Second Time Shop," which specializes in selling outgrown riding duds.

Kedron Valley Inn is closed the month of April and 10 days before Thanksgiving. In warm weather when the airy, screened patio is open, the dining rooms seat 90. The inn is popular for weddings and get-togethers and is a community watering hole year-round. The inn's special occasion holiday meals are notable. Visitors are welcome at breakfast and dinner; no lunches are served. The food is gourmet and features Vermont ingredients with a continental accent, but the atmosphere is informal. Jeans, shirtsleeves, shorts, or ski duds don't cause a ripple.

The South Woodstock Country Store is crammed with everything from grocery staples and local newspapers to postcards, film, souvenirs, and maple products. You can put together a picnic here, complete with wine from their shelves, or get fresh sandwiches made to order in the tiny adjoining lunchroom. In winter, they offer hearty, warming soups.

South Woodstock has a large and active snowmobile club, which benefits from miles of trails over open country. They maintain excellent relations with local landowners by strict compliance with regulations. Visitors who have a snowmobile with them may join local rides by contacting the club in advance. Ask at the inn or the country store for information. Behind the inn is a gentle hill just right for sledding; sleds are available free to children of guests.

As soon as snow covers the trails, Kedron Valley Stables offers sleigh rides complete with jingle bells. Call the stables to book ahead.

Barnard

From Woodstock, Barnard is about 12 miles north on Route 12. While still inside Woodstock's borders, the road passes the historic marker noting the site of the first U.S. ski tow in Gilbert's meadows to the right of the road. In January 1934, an endless rope tow powered by a Model T Ford engine started pulling people on skis up Gilbert's Hill so they could slide back down, and, as the sign points out, this feat of Yankee ingenuity "launched a new era in winter sports."

The Barnard/Pomfret area has two Alpine ski areas — Sonnenberg in Barnard and Suicide Six in Pomfret. Barnard, an outdoor-lover's haven, is home to Silver Lake State Park, and Pomfret is known for its unspoiled vistas.

An alternate route in summer or fall to Route 12 is the old Barnard Stage Road on the opposite side of the ridge above Clinton Gilbert's hill. This is the road that passes the Suicide Six Ski Area, and it is a pretty country drive. The Stage Road has an unpaved stretch at the Barnard end after about six miles up. It can be tricky to navigate in icy or muddy weather when a four-wheel drive vehicle is recommended. In dry seasons, it's fine. The thoroughfare offers views of valley farms and a stretch of woods that on occasion produces wild turkeys and deer for the traveler.

To reach Barnard via the Stage Road, take the right fork at the gas station just north of Woodstock, then turn left at the Teago Store and South Pomfret Post Office. Keep to the left at all places where the road forks. The Stage Road winds up to Barnard Center and ends where it runs into Route 12 in front of the country store there. The Barnard Country Store, like most of its kind, sells a lot more than six-packs and post cards. It has a skeleton grocery department, heavy on the frozen foods because of two large camping areas nearby. It also has a side room full of souvenirs and T-shirts and, way in the back, an old-fashioned lunch counter with stools. You can get an ice-cream cone, a sandwich, or a full meal. In winter there is always at least one hot dish such as soup, chili, or stew. Sit in the old barber chair in front of the potbellied stove and warm your feet while you wait.

The scenic North Road to Bethel starts in Barnard Center. There is a sign just before the bridge at the end of the lake. Flanked by giant sugar maple trees, it offers some of the most beautiful views of distant hills in this part of Vermont. Past several old vacation homes with interesting trim is the Barnard Town Hall, which is on the left and set back from the road. The building dates from 1837 and served as a church until it was sold to the town of Barnard in 1867 for the grand sum of $500.

Driving into Barnard from any direction is definitely a climb. Route 12 from Woodstock replaces an earlier, dicier one named the Gulf Road that was even steeper and ran through a narrow cut or "gulf" in the rocks. Route 12 still cuts through rocky outcroppings called "The Ledges," and there is no guarantee that the weather at the top will be exactly like that in the valley; weather in Barnard has a mind of its own. However, the trip up is worth it. Barnard Center, a small crossroads village alongside a calendar-picture lake, has the spare white-steepled churches, gingerbread-decked white houses, and an elegant inn and quaint country store that would qualify it for a movie or TV set labeled "New England town." If you drive into town on Route 12, on your right is the magnificent red brick inn built in 1796 that now houses the Barnard Inn, a gourmet restaurant of some renown.

Like many Vermont towns where self-sufficiency became a habit as well as a necessity, Barnard in the days after its 1775 settlement was a beehive of enterprise. According to a town history, early Barnard residents engaged in a variety of commerce, including the manufacture of lime, a potash plant, a shop where felt hats were made, brickyards, and a marble shop that made gravestones.

No trace of these busy industries remains, but to be fair, few of these businesses are still needed. Barnard today is largely a resort town, and the inn, the general store, and a few other commercial ventures serve the town's purposes quite well. Today, the town plan specifies that future land use and development in Barnard be restricted to homes and vacation homes, farming and dairying, year-round recreation, and forest and wildlife preserves. As for distilleries, it's unlikely that Barnard will ever have another. In fact, in 1933, when repeal of the Eighteenth

Amendment, the Prohibition amendment, was considered in Barnard, its citizens, contrary to the rest of the state (which was two to one in favor of repeal) voted to keep Prohibition!

Barnard's fine location and lovely scenery has made it popular with vacationers almost from its inception. The town center once boasted two fairly large hotels — one built in 1830 right in town across from the general store and another on a hillside overlooking Silver Lake. But the crossroads at Barnard is anything but crowded these days. In summer, campers and vacationers enjoy Silver Lake State Park and the nearby, privately operated Silver Lake Family Campground. Bikers making the loop up from Woodstock stop to picnic by the water, and there always seems to be an optimistic angler or two wetting a line.

In winter, skiers who like the comfortable atmosphere of a small well-run resort ski at Barnard's Sonnenberg Ski Area, which has a loyal following, particularly among skiers who remember the glamorous sport skiing used to be. At Sonnenberg, the "Sunny Mountain," there are never lift lines, never crowds. The number of skiers each day is strictly limited. The price of admission covers everything — lessons, all equipment for either downhill or cross-country skiing, or both, and a hearty catered luncheon. To reach Sonnenberg, turn right off Route 12 at the Barnard Store and go 1.2 miles. Sonnenberg is on the right.

The main house at Sonnenberg was built in 1830. Nobel Prize author Sinclair Lewis and his journalist wife, Dorothy Thompson, called it "Twin Farms" when they owned it and lived there in the 1930s. She is buried in the Barnard village cemetery. The Sinclair Lewises were among a group of well-known visitors who have chosen Barnard hideaways. The group includes contract bridge guru Ely Culbertson, manners maven Amy Vanderbilt, and the Baron and Baroness Louis De Rothschild, who came to Barnard after escaping the Nazis in World War II. Television or movie stars may live there now, but chances are locals won't spill the beans and spoil their privacy.

From Barnard Center, a short drive down Route 12 toward Bethel leads to the Different Drummer Antiques, a shop specializing in antique dolls and doll repair. It is located on the right in a pretty old white farmhouse on a knoll. Across the street, on your left and below road level, are the fields of Primavera, a nursery and landscaping business run by Tom DeGiacomo and Jill Anderson. Tom and Jill are noted landscape designers who have created a number of spectacular area gardens and historic restorations including the charming small garden at the Coolidge Homestead in Plymouth and the grounds of the Justin Morrill Homestead in Strafford, which is expected to take several years to complete. Their nursery sells unusual perennial plants. Jill, an expert propagator, has raised many from seed.

Four miles down Route 12 from the Barnard General Store on the right in a house with diamond windowpanes is Porcupine Graphix, well worth the trip for bargain seekers. Despite its modest appearance, Porcupine prints thousands of designer T-shirts every year for customers all over the East, and those that don't look absolutely perfect to eagle-eyed inspectors are sold on racks here for about a fourth of their regular retail price. Depending on recent orders, the selection at Porcupine varies, but they usually have an interesting stock ranging from Woody Jackson's black-and-white cows made famous by Ben and Jerry commercials to shirts bearing the logos of obscure road race sponsors.

All of Barnard is an outdoor-lover's haven. The town center wraps itself around the edge of Silver Lake (a.k.a. "The Barnard Ocean"), and winter or summer the lake is a whirl of activity. Swimming there in summer is delicious. Folks pull up alongside the store, peel to bathing suits, and take an impromptu dip, lolling afterwards to eat lunch on the grassy lawn. Local kids splash there furiously daylong, and the lake is a popular spot for sailboarding. In winter, fishing huts deck the ice and youngsters skate or play hockey. Summer visitors may stay at Barnard's Silver Lake State Park (entrance about .2 miles up the North Road on the right). It offers camping, parking, changing and picnic facilities, and boat rentals. The Silver Lake Family Campground entrance is up a road just behind the country store. It offers tent sites, trailer hookups, and a few rental cabins that are housekeeping units. The wooded grounds with well-tended lawns and a big recreation building look exactly like the private boys' camp (Camp Kitchigamink) it once was.

The Lakota Club, a private club featuring a park and stocked trout lake, is situated on 1,000 acres of land partly in Barnard, partly in Bridgewater. The club and its grounds were used for some scenes in the movie *Ghost Story*, which starred Fred Astaire. It is not open to the public.

East Barnard, about 4 miles from Barnard Center, crowds up against the edge of Pomfret. It no longer has a store or an active school — both are now private residences — but the East Barnard Church, which has services from June to October and Thanksgiving and Christmas, the Grange, and the Broad Brook Fire Association are important to the small community. Almost everyone in East Barnard pitches in to work on the big annual fund-raising event, the October oyster stew supper, an affair that draws crowds from far and wide. The basement of the East Barnard Grange always fills as soon as the doors open around five. Those left outside wait an hour or more for their chance to move in and partake of the famous all-you-can-eat bash. The Grange Hall was originally a cheese factory; it has been a center of East Barnard activities since the Grange bought it in 1908.

Prominent Vermont woodcut artist Sabra Field always helps out at the oyster stew supper. Her studio and galleries, the Tontine Press, are two doors up in an old yellow building that was once an inn. Field's colorful and decorative woodcuts have been on countless magazine covers. One of her prints, a chickadee on an apple tree branch, became the biggest selling U.N. Christmas card of all time. In color and design, Sabra Field's work goes beyond typical woodcut technique. Her range of colors and shading are especially fine, her eye for decorative elements in Vermont landscape — the patterns in plowed fields and overlapping ranks of hills — make her work much appreciated in and outside the state. The Tontine Press Gallery is open to visitors when the Fields are home. Call 763-7092 for directions.

In summer or fall, you can reach East Barnard by a scenic back road that branches off the Stage Road running past Suicide Six Ski Area. To go to East Barnard, keep on the Stage Road 4.5 miles past the Teago Store, then bear to the right at a fork just before the stone-walled Perkins Cemetery on the left ahead. A mile farther on the right and just at road's edge is a large beaver pond backed by high hills. The beavers are active little critters, and if you pull over for a quiet few minutes, they can often be seen swimming near their stick-covered lodges. This pond that the beavers have dammed overflows the road regularly each spring, causing a gnashing of teeth at the state highway department, which is responsible for road upkeep. The bureaucrats would dearly love to dispossess the beavers and drain the pond, but so far the landowner, on the side of the beavers, prefers that the pond and the beavers stay. Past the beaver pond, keep left at the next fork, and just past the cemetery and East Barnard church, turn left at the next intersection. You will see Tontine Press just ahead on the left and beyond a road to the left going up a hill. This road, which is not marked, leads one mile up to the 200-acre Hawk's Hill Demonstration Woodlot, a project of the New England Forestry Foundation, which was developed and protected by the generosity of local ecologist and forester Richard Brett.

As you drive up, you will pass a small sawmill operation. Bear right at the fork and you will see the sign for the Forest Foundation ahead when you get to the end of the road. Trails (unmarked) lead up and into the forest; there is a small pond, a good bird-watching spot morning or evening, and a variety of easy hiking terrain with lovely woods, clearings, old stone walls, and wildflowers. The forest is carefully tended — weed trees are removed and branches are trimmed on hardwoods. The trees are harvested as they mature, and in each section portions of the woodlot are left untrimmed and untended to show the contrast in yield between managed and unmanaged forest areas. In snow season, this trail offers entry to the Skyline Trail, a 10-mile cross-country ski run down to Pomfret for hearty souls who prefer untracked snow and uninhabited scenery when they ski. Skyline Trail starts about 250 paces uphill from the entrance to the forest. An arrow sign to the right marked "Skyline Trail" points the way, along with one of the blue blazes that continue the trail's entire length. Some prefer to pick up Skyline Trail at the Amity Pond Area in Pomfret. Directions are given in the Pomfret essay in this chapter. The Hawk's Hill Nature Trail Guide is available by mail from the New England Forestry Foundation, One Court Street, Boston, Massachusetts 02116.

Remember when hiking in early winter that the woods are not safe to wander in during hunting season. Ask at any country store if in doubt about the dates. Most people come to Barnard for country scenery, outdoor fun, and peace and quiet. Barnard has all of those in full measure.

Pomfret

Pomfret is the only Woodstock area town without a body of water of any great size. There are several energetic brooks and a sliver of both the White and the Ottauquechee rivers, but Pomfret lacks a lake or even a big pond. Instead, Pomfret is known for its wonderful hills and an abundance of unspoiled rural vistas. Pomfret's inhabitants, realizing what treasures they had, made a move to protect the hills a few years back. An ordinance, the first of its kind in the nation, forbids development within a certain distance of the highest point of any Pomfret ridge line, regardless of the height of the hill. Other U.S. locales have protected mountains in a similar fashion. Pomfret's is unique in that the features protected from development are not towering peaks or craggy prominences. Most views inside Pomfret's borders are backed by the town's signature folding hills, and with the new zoning, these vistas will remain pretty much as they were when the earliest settlers arrived from Connecticut more than 200 years ago.

The new rules encourage building sites farther down from hilltops near existing roads or sheltered behind mature trees or similar screens. As a result of this planning, views today in Pomfret are pretty much as they will be for years to come. Unlike other fast-growing areas of the state, Pomfret can make this claim with certainty.

Second home and residential development crowd nearby towns, and some have evolved into busy commercial centers. But almost all of Pomfret would look familiar to a farmer from 100 years ago, though he would find that the style of farming has changed to keep up with the times. Early on, the town was known for its orchards, and today the Pomfret orchards offer a broad variety of fruit and berries and feature pick-your-own harvests. Settlers cleared much of Pomfret's heavily forested terrain into open land and raised livestock. Horse, cattle, and sheep farms still keep acres of land open. The cattle grazing Pomfret Meadows may be Angus, Scottish Highland, or beefalo, a cow-buffalo hybrid. Nowadays, the horses don't pull plows; they are more likely to be saddle horses trained for dressage competition or pleasure riding. Sugar maple trees line Pomfret roads and are tapped each spring for sap to boil down into maple syrup.

In early spring, you still see some trees with old-style covered buckets, but many more are linked with sleek plastic tubing strung from tree to tree, which empties the sap into a vat down the line and saves the busy farmer hours of hauling and emptying sap buckets.

Pomfret has about 900 inhabitants; in 1830 it had nearly twice that number. However, the town never had a bustling commercial center as did most surrounding towns. Pomfret's hill farms and homes remain scattered, and rather than a walking tour, a drive up one of the landmark ridges and back down a valley road is in order. A loop through town along its north-south axis is a good way to start.

From Woodstock, take Route 12 (Elm Street) north out of town toward Billings Farm and Museum. Bear right, leaving Route 12 just past the end of the museum fence where there is a grassy traffic island straight ahead. In a little less than a mile past Billings Farm's parking area, the road crosses a small creek. Past the creek, on the far corner ahead, is an old cemetery enclosed by stone walls. Turn left (the cemetery will be on your right now), and start up Cloudland Road. This lower stretch lies within Woodstock's boundaries, but as the road winds up through wooded areas and then opens up, you'll climb into Pomfret's hills. You can see stretches of sloping farm fields and meadows with wooded ridges beyond that are typical of the local landscape. About two miles up, on the right, is the old red brick Cloudland School, one of Pomfret's former one-room schoolhouses, which is now a residence.

The road keeps on climbing. Woods on either side open again as you near the yellow buildings of Cloudland Farm on either side of the road. It's a busy horse and cattle farm and one of the oldest in the region. Cloudland Road dead-ends three miles from the cemetery. Take a right there, then bear left at the next fork, a short distance beyond. There are wonderful views across open fields from these heights. As you drive down from the ridge, the road goes steeply down to join one of the main roads through town. Technically, the road you are about to turn onto is named "State Assistance Road Number One." There is no sign; the everyday name for this road is Pomfret/West Hartford Road, and here you turn right.

As you come out on the West Hartford Road, at the bottom of the hill straight ahead is an old barn and silo converted into a home. Though the familiar cylindrical shape of a silo says "farm" even to most city folks, silos are fairly recent as farm structures go. Pomfret's earliest farmers would have stored hay and grains inside their barns, probably in squared-off bins built in a corner using upright barn timbers for support. According to a farm history published by the Billings Farm Museum, the very first reported silos in America were noted in the Vermont Agricultural Report for 1869-1870. They became a popular farm fixture, and by 1888, Vermont alone had 100 of them.

Silos reflect a thrifty farmer's need to use everything produced in the region's short growing season to good advantage. When the corn crop was harvested, leaves and stalks were chopped and stacked into silos where they would ferment into a sour, moist fodder that was relished by cattle and kept through the winter. A similar storage system used in area barnyards nowadays piles ensilage, as the chopped material is called, onto the ground where it is covered with heavy plastic. The mounds are often dotted with used automobile tires to hold the plastic down. These may look less picturesque than the old silos, but their function is about the same.

Past the silo house the road bends sharply to the right, passing old farmhouses, into a section of Pomfret called Hewitt's Corners. The second large farmhouse on the left, Moore's Farm, is a good spot to stop in fall for a bag of crisp local apples already picked for you. At this corner, where signs point to Sharon and

I-89, turn left and go downhill past another one-room schoolhouse on the left. On your right, at an imposing high stone wall, lives a herd of shaggy Scottish cattle with ominous-looking horns. This rural-looking enterprise is the headquarters for David and Charles, a company that distributes books from more than 17 Great Britain publishers to the U.S. market.

Take the road to the left, just before the stone wall. A sign on the right says "Sherburne Farm." You can see the farm's buildings across the fields. Drive 2.2 miles from the turnoff, and look for a stone wall on the left and a sign that says "Amity Pond Natural Area." It is yellow, about three inches square, and placed about eight feet off the ground on a tree trunk. There is no formal parking area, so pull off across the road. A two-and-a-half-mile hike that loops through Amity Pond Natural Area is described in detail in the book *Fifty Hikes in Vermont*, published in Woodstock by Countryman Press, and is available in area bookstores. Trails in the Amity Pond Natural Area link up with Sky Line cross-country ski trails from East Barnard Hawk's Hill Forest Area. The Ski Touring Center at Woodstock Country Club (457-2114) can provide maps and directions. It is wise to get local information before starting out alone in strange territory on skis. A trail map and brochure about Amity Pond are available from the Vermont Department of Forest and Parks, 103 South Main, Waterbury, Vermont 05676; 244-8711.

Amity Pond, a choice tract of mixed forest and meadowland, was given to the state in 1969 by the Brett family, who also donated Hawk's Hill Demonstration Forest in East Barnard. They stipulated that except for emergencies, all machinery be forever barred from this stretch of land. It is off-limits to radios and boom boxes, snowmobiles and chain saws.

Amity Pond offers wilderness camping shelters and blazed trails for hiking or skiing. A short walk in from the road, following blue plastic markers on the trees, brings you out into an upland meadow with a spectacular panoramic view of mountains to the south and west. On a clear day, Mount Ascutney to the south and Pico and Killington far to the west are clearly visible. The view in foliage season is breathtaking.

Back out on the West Hartford Road about two miles on the right is the "Harry Harrington Field," Pomfret's recreation area with a Little League diamond, basketball hoop, tennis court, and lots of grassy play areas. Turn here, and retrace the route back to Hewitt's Corners. On the way, you pass the tall white North Pomfret Congregational Church built in 1844 and the North Pomfret Store and post office.

At Hewitt's Corners, follow the road as it bends around to the left, and in about a mile and a half, on the right, is the handsome white wooden Pomfret Town Hall. Built in 1845 as a Unitarian church, the building once had a steeple that was taken down when it had deteriorated past saving. The church was given to the town for use as a town hall in 1872. Here, each year on the first Tuesday in March, Pomfret's citizens gather to decide town affairs on Town Meeting Day. The four pillars that hold up the Town Hall's portico rest securely on four blocks of white granite that a town history insists were "said to come from Oregon." Across the street is the white-frame Pomfret Center School built in 1933 and the red brick Town Clerk's Office.

Pomfret celebrated its centennial in 1870 with ceremonies that included processions, choral singing, and orations. The crowd attending was estimated at "Between 4,000 and 5,000," and 15,000 board feet of lumber was used to make seats and tables for them. Guests were fed in shifts by the Pomfret ladies, "and still there was enough left to feed 2,000 more. To show that the crowd was a cold water army, they consumed 25 barrels of water."

Between Hewitt's Corners and the Town Hall lie the extensive orchards and fields of Moore's Orchards. In berry season (late May, June) and in the fall when apples are ripe, you can stop here and pick your own for a delicious snack. There are signs at the road during picking season.

Continue down this steep winding road that divides at the bottom by the Abbott Memorial Library. The library was dedicated in 1905, a gift to the town from a prosperous citizen who had become a judge in Albuquerque, New Mexico. It is interesting that this library was built almost 100 years after Pomfret's first library, "The Social Library of Pomfret," was formed in 1804. A share in this first library cost $1.50, a hefty amount in a time when cash money was in short supply. Sixty-six men in Pomfret recognized the value of a library in their fledgling community and paid their fee, plus annual dues of 25 cents. When the first books arrived, chances to be the first reader of each volume were sold at auction.

Turn right at the library, and just past a line of houses is a large red-frame building, a former Pomfret school, now converted office space. Across the road is the Pomfret Grange Hall, site of harvest dinners and other community get-togethers. Beyond the Grange, on the fringes of Suicide Six Ski Area parking, is another, more recent Pomfret one-room schoolhouse. This was in use until Pomfret recently built a new consolidated elementary school off the Stage Road.

Suicide Six Ski Area is operated by the Woodstock Inn and Resort. It is much used by locals and other skiers who prefer the small-scale, laid-back atmosphere of this tiny resort to the sometimes frantic surroundings at bigger areas. The base lodge is roomy and comfortable and considerably less boisterous since the Ski Runners program for local youngsters moved into a separate building on the grounds. While not large, Suicide Six has ample snowmaking capability and offers a good assortment of meticulously groomed trails and terrain. "The Face" is a challenge even to expert skiers.

The road past Suicide Six continues up to Barnard, and in dry weather this is a pretty drive. It is not recommended in winter or in mud season, as much of it is unpaved and the top stretch extremely steep. Keep left at all forks in the road to come out by Silver Lake in Barnard.

Turn around at Suicide Six, and go back toward the library. Just across the brook is the Teago Store and South Pomfret Post Office.

Locals drop by Teago all day to pick up mail and the papers, have a soda, and pass the time. There is a registry here for messages to and from hikers on the nearby Appalachian Trail. The store owner is a former chef, and his sandwiches, salads, hot soups, and chili are decidedly beyond the usual country store fare. During hunting or ski season, the Teago Store is a busy spot.

The road running in front of Teago is the Stage Road back to Woodstock. After a stretch of houses, look to the right across an open field for the Smith Covered Bridge. One-half of the bridge is of the town lattice type originally built in 1870 and moved here from Hyde Park, Vermont. In dry weather, you can go in on the unpaved farm track; it offers a great chance to get the whole family in a covered bridge snapshot without cars and trucks to interfere. Kids can wade here in summer, and locals often drive in and park to cross-country ski in snowmobile trails in winter. Sunset in this valley is magical any time of year.

This north/south valley is a flyway for migrating birds each spring and fall. Geese fly over in long straggly V formations, as do hawks, which often whistle as they soar. On the way back into Woodstock, just past a concrete bridge before you reach the gas station, there is a dirt road that runs off to the right and joins with Route 12. Scrubby woods along the creek to the south of this road are a favorite stopping place for migrating songbirds. Early morning is the best time to spot them.

The road from Teago and South Pomfret back to Woodstock is flat, running through the valley where Barnard Brook threads on its way to join the Ottauquechee River. The hills of Pomfret are behind you, with their steep meadows and patches of forest. At dusk, you can see a twinkling of lights from far-spaced farms and houses. The back roads of quiet, spread-out Pomfret remind us of how quiet the Vermont countryside used to be.

Hartford, White River Junction and Quechee

The town of Hartford is populous, as Vermont towns go, with approximately 10,000 inhabitants. It is about the size of Montpelier, the state capital. Hartford's dwellers, though, are spread out among the five villages that make up the town. They are Hartford, West Hartford, White River Junction, Wilder, and Quechee.

In recent years, Hartford has become one of the state's fastest growing regions, a phenomenon reflecting its location at the hub of year-round vacation destinations in nearby Killington, Woodstock, and Mount Ascutney, as well as its prime business site near the Connecticut River in New Hampshire. Each of Hartford's five villages has a distinct flavor, and, in a way, each symbolizes a facet of life in present-day Vermont. White River Junction is a city, albeit a small one, while parts of Hartford and West Hartford have a rural aspect. Wilder represents high technology as it is home to New England Power's massive dam and generator. Quechee, a former blue-collar mill town, has been gussied up as a four-star resort destination with inns, fine restaurants, and facilities for a full range of outdoor activities.

White River Junction has always been a transportation center. It takes its name from the confluence of the White River with the Connecticut River, as well as from its history as a railroad town. You can witness the melding of these historic rivers in Lyman Park behind the Hartford Town Hall on Bridge Street in White River Junction.

History, Attractions

Vermont's first railroad began in White River Junction in 1848 with a train that ran to Bethel, 25 miles up the line. A year later the tracks had been stretched to Burlington; other lines were added, and by the turn of the century five railways with 50 passenger trains a day passed through. Today only a couple of Amtraks run and a few freights rumble by, although an ancient steam engine of impressive bulk sits permanently overlooking Railroad Row, a reminder of the days of steam and White River Junction's heyday.

This engine, "Old 494," was built in 1892 and made its last run in 1938. It was saved by a group of railroad enthusiasts from the Boston area who donated it to the city.

Across from Old 494 the Hotel Coolidge occupies the site of earlier hotels. Built in 1879, and substantially remodeled in the twenties, it has been recently modernized to offer 96 large comfortable rooms and still retains the wonderful flavor of that vanishing breed of lodging, the small-town railroad hotel. The Coolidge Dining Room is decorated with handsome murals painted by Peter Michael Gish, depicting episodes in local history. With uniformed service and sparkling linens, the dining room offers a time warp back to days when eating in a hotel was a special occasion. The Coolidge Dining Room is a favorite with locals, and you need not dress up. The food is excellent. Cashie's, also in the

Coolidge, is less than formal. It is billed as an eatery and pub with hamburgers, sandwiches, or full meals. Weekends feature local musicians, and the scene can get quite lively.

In silent movie days, when famed director D. W. Griffith was making *Way Down East*, the harrowing scenes of Lillian Gish on a cake of ice floating down the river toward the falls were shot here. Then, as now, the Coolidge Hotel houses an opera house, where a resident professional company, the White River Theater Festival, presents plays and musicals in the summer.

Than Wheeler's Coach's Corner downstairs next door to the hotel is an informal pub and restaurant with a sporting theme. The TV here is always tuned to some sporting event, and the dining room has a hoop and basketball in case you get the urge to score while waiting for your meal. Across the way, the Polka Dot, decorated with railroad pictures, is a local fixture. Open every day from 5 A.M. to 9 at night, it features hearty plain food. Pies, muffins, and doughnuts are baked on the premises, and breakfast is available at any hour. The Polka Dot's jukebox was rated one of the area's best by a local paper. You can sit in a booth by a gingham-curtained window overlooking the tracks, drown your sorrows in a bowl of chowder, and listen to Randy Travis singing "I Told You So." Or, you can stave off winter's chill with Polka Dot's hearty pot roast dinner for under five dollars.

Nothing in White River Junction's downtown center is more than a block or two from the hotel, including the Upper Valley Food Coop a few doors away. It's a great place to restock picnic baskets or ski packs when an outing is planned.

Nearby, Briggs, Ltd., is a sportswear store. In back, past racks of men's outdoor duds, is one of the region's best-stocked fishing and hunting gear departments. Briggs's features Orvis fishing equipment, and the staff is all Orvis trained. They can advise on equipment and recommend fishing and hunting locations. They sell licenses, stay current on regulations, and can help you locate guides. They also sell flies tied by local expert Lee Hiscock.

If poking around for old furniture or details to finish a restoration project is your idea of fun, don't miss the Vermont Salvage Exchange near the hotel. Its cavernous rooms are full of enormous items saved from area demolition projects. While an elaborately carved oak mantel might not fit on your luggage rack, smaller items will fit your travel plans. They have bins filled with small hard-to-find items like antique ceramic doorknobs, frosted glass lamp shades, and old brass lock plates. Check out Main Street Furniture, too, (back near the Polka Dot) for smaller items like doll furniture, jugs, and sturdy, country-style picture frames.

Gold, amber, and porter beers are brewed in White River Junction in the tiny Catamount Brewing Company at 58 South Main. Tours and tastings are offered several times a week. Even those who are not fond of beer will find the hourlong walk-through interesting. Beer drinkers will appreciate the chance to sample all three of Catamount's flavors, and everyone gets a free button with the trademark mountain lion on it. Catamount is a microbrewery serving only the New England market. Their plant is a mix of state-of-the-art steel tank and tubing and old-fashioned Yankee ingenuity — their bottling machine, which they adapted themselves, was a secondhand bargain formerly used to fill Pepsi bottles.

Another commercial section of White River Junction has grown up around the intersection of I-91 and I-89, which cross here. A regional Veteran's Administration Hospital crowns a nearby hill with one of the best views in all Vermont. Clustered in the area are a large regional post office center and motels representing several national chains. Across from the Vermont Transit Bus Station is the Junction Marketplace with a small take-out restaurant called Canton House, which serves hot, tasty Chinese specialties prepared without MSG while you watch. In summer, it's fun to pick up an assortment from their menu and drive to a scenic spot to picnic. They are open every day, 11:30 until 9:00, later on weekends. In the same arcaded building there's Athena's Pizza and the Whole Do-Nut, both offering inexpensive take-out food.

Sykes Avenue intersects Route 5 here, and a couple of blocks down Sykes is Astro-Bowl Plaza, a possible rainy day solution to what to do with the kids. There is a video and pinball arcade, and a good-sized bowling alley with both standard and candlepin bowling. Candlepins are a New England tradition, and it might be fun to try the game, just so you can say you did. For little guys who get discouraged at a failure to get the ball right down the middle of the lane, Astro-Bowl can set lanes up for bumper bowling. At the entrance to Astro-Bowl Plaza is A. J.'s Restaurant and Lounge, which opens for dinner at 5 on weekdays, 4 on Sundays. This is a very popular spot. They don't take reservations.

Wilder, up the line on Route 5, has undergone great change in the past few decades with the arrival of the interstate. It has become a bedroom community for the busy Norwich-Hanover area directly north. The town is on the west bank of the Connecticut River, and the location was originally at an area of dangerous rapids called White River Falls. The boat carrying Roger's Rangers of French and Indian War fame broke on the rocks here in 1759.

Besides offering fodder for "What I did on my vacation" essays, the power dam built in 1950 is fascinating to visit. In 1988, the New England Power Company, which operates the facility, built a handsome Visitors Center on the Vermont side, now open from May 15 through Columbus Day weekend. There is no admission charge. The center offers ample parking, spotless rest rooms, and nifty energy-saving drinking fountains that turn on only when a thirsty customer comes near. Exhibits explore area history, energy (including free interactive video games), and information about Atlantic salmon. There is a huge working model of the fish ladder built to allow migrating fish to make their way upstream to home waters.

A guide makes frequent tours to accompany visitors inside the power plant where giant turbines are turned by the roaring water. You can stroll down to the 58 steps of the fish ladder and peer into the tanks on your own. Transatlantic fare on the Concorde is cheaper than the estimated $20 million it costs to accommodate each salmon that has used the ladder so far, but hopes are high that more salmon will find their way back to the upper river. Your chances of spotting one are nil unless you visit in spring migration season.

The Wilder Dam area has picnic tables, a boat ramp, barbecue fireplaces, and plenty of parking. It offers access to the large lake upriver from the dam. Canoes can be rented at Dartmouth College's Ledyard Canoe Club about four miles away. They also give lessons. (Go north on Route 5 three miles to Norwich, the next town up, and cross the river to your right. Turn left just past the bridge on the New Hampshire side.) Fishing is good in the dammed-up river. Perch, walleye, pike, pickerel, bass, bullheads, and a variety of panfish can be taken here. (If you're over 15 years of age, a license is required. Most country stores sell them.) To canoe downstream from Wilder Dam, the portage around the dam is on the New Hampshire side. Follow directions to the Canoe Club, take Route 10 south on the New Hampshire side. Be aware that water is released from the dam without warning, and levels may rise or fall. A boat carelessly pulled onto shore could float off if you are not watching.

Though part of its 100 acres of land lies inside the town of Hartford's borders, the exciting new Montshire Museum three miles to the north of Wilder is only accessible from the town of Norwich. The museum's name was purposely chosen to reflect its function as a regional institution — Ver*mont* and New Hamp*shire*. Today, in a spacious building interesting in itself, the brand-new Montshire offers a wonderful learning atmosphere for kids and adults. Besides extensive outdoor nature trails, the museum's displays include changing theme exhibits and a number of animals, live and preserved, that area kids like to visit over and over. Who could resist a boa constrictor named Victor (really Victoria) or a Rube Goldbergian ant display that gets really busy under beams from the attached flashlight you turn on them? The Montshire also has an abundance of turtles and aquariums, a glass-enclosed elevator, rocks and minerals by the ton, and lots and lots of dinosaur bones.

To reach the Montshire from Woodstock, take Route 4 east to the interstate access road beyond Quechee. Follow signs for I-91 north; get off at exit 13. Keep a sharp eye out at the exit. You have to make a right turn almost immediately at the bottom of the ramp onto Montshire Road, which leads down into the museum grounds. From White River Junction take Route 5 north. Check mileage at the post office on Wilder's Main Street. Three miles past the post office is a stop light. Turn right, and just past the interstate exit ramp is Montshire Road. Turn right into the museum grounds. The Montshire is open year-round, seven days from 10 to 5 and on Tuesdays from 10 to 8.

Heading down Route 5 south in Wilder are two popular informal eating spots. Blood's Seafood is a local institution. They cater far and wide at events that include weddings and political rallies. Their fresh seafood is prepared while you wait, and the prices are reasonable; nobody goes home hungry. Hamburgers are available for those who don't like seafood, but it is a shame to pass up the chance to wrestle a chunky lobster or sample their excellent chowder. They ship fresh lobster anywhere in the U.S. Blood's is decidedly informal, and it's a great place to take youngsters.

Next door to Blood's is The Pizza Factory, run by two Californians who gave up business careers in Hollywood to provide upscale-styled pizza to the area. The Pizza Factory is take-out only.

Quechee, the most tourist-oriented of Hartford's five villages, has had its ups and downs. Which now prevails depends on who you talk to. Tourists and land-owners in the posh resort community like the town just fine the way it is. Some conversationists and planners think the Disneyfication of the Quechee area has gone far enough.

Quechee's natural beauty matches any in the state. It has gentle wooded hills, sweeping flower-dotted meadows, and a chameleon river that changes from a placid stream on one side of town to roaring white water in the course of a few miles. It was the Ottauquechee River and its promise of enormous power that helped create the town and the mills in the first place.

After 200 years of milling prosperity, the bottom fell out for Quechee after World War II. Jobs moved south, and the town was left with empty buildings, a dusty main street, and not much to look forward to. Enter planners with the vision to turn the area into a four-season resort community. Enter Quechee Lakes.

A Rip Van Winkle who went to sleep in Quechee in the forties and awakened in the glittering nineties would not believe his eyes. Snoozing in a rundown, rat infested, down-at-the-heels ghost town, he would awaken to a vacation haven painted and polished as no old-time New England village could ever be. Familiar buildings would greet him — the covered bridge, the mills, and the white-steepled Quechee church. But the bridge today is a brand-new copy. Downer's Mill, no longer dark and dingy, is generously sunlit through huge windows and houses a restaurant, shops, and space for potters and glassblowers. Only the church, dressed in gleaming fresh paint, still serves its original function.

Meantime, development in less-picturesque forms is pressing Quechee from every quarter. Condominium clusters climb the hillsides and crown ridges. The town's lifeline, Route 4, threatens to become a corridor of storefronts. Town planners are hard-pressed to keep up with applications for malls and ever larger commercial structures. Developers are attracted to the area by Quechee's numerous affluent visitors. Traffic at peak tourist seasons can be horrendous. None of this seems to matter to those who come to Quechee for a good time.

The extensive Quechee Lakes sports facilities, which include two championship golf courses, a lake with a beach, ranks of tennis courts, meticulously groomed ski slopes, and indoor and outdoor swimming pools, are reserved for the use of Quechee Lakes landowners and their guests. Guests at nearby Quechee Inn at Marshland Farms or those who rent property from the corporation, whether for a weekend or for a season, may use the facilities for a fee. Everyone else is on the outside looking in, but in a tourist haven like Quechee that doesn't mean sitting on the sidelines.

Fishing is a favored pastime in a region crisscrossed with streams and rivers and dotted with lakes and reservoirs. Equipment can be rented at Marshland Farms if you neglected to bring your own and is provided free if you take lessons in the fly-fishing school there. Bikes, either ten-speed or mountain, and canoes can also be had. In winter, Marshland operates Wilderness Trails Nordic Ski School offering cross-country ski lessons, rental equipment, and 18 miles of trails, including full-moon evening ski tours. Hiking is popular year-round. Quechee Gorge, Vermont's mini-"Grand Canyon," offers a quick down and a puffing climb back up, and, especially in the fall, any road in Quechee can open onto breathtaking vistas.

The small scale of Quechee makes it particularly appealing. Whether you stay at one of the B&Bs, the inn, or camp at Quechee State Park, you can walk to your choice of excellent restaurants. In the village, Downer's Mill, lovingly restored by Simon Pearce, is a fascinating spot to explore. Watch handsome glass blown and shaped by expert craftsmen who swing great gobs of molten glass around with casual ease. Shop in the spacious showrooms for a piece to take home or choose instead from their unique stoneware, also made at the mill, which is decorated with fish, or grape clusters, in splashes of deep blue glaze. The Simon Pearce Restaurant has been featured in *Gourmet* and other magazines. The food is wonderful; a table overlooking the river's a soothing place to settle after a day full of activity.

If you are "horsey," or even if you are not, don't miss the Westminster Equestrian Centre a mile and a half from the village. It welcomes visitors. It may be the only horse barn with red paisley wallpaper that most of us will ever see. You can watch some of its pampered, sleek inhabitants strut their stuff at Quechee's Polo Club grounds most summer Saturdays at 2. Check schedules on posters around town.

And of course, you don't want to miss the annual hot-air balloon festival in mid-June, an event as colorful and appealing as the state of Vermont itself. There's music, entertainment, a juried crafts fair, and balloon rides.

A warning — people visiting Quechee tend to get hooked. Not to worry. There are plenty of real estate people in town who will gladly help you make your dream of owning a part of this nearly perfect village come true.

Hartland

If exploring back-country roads is your pleasure, Hartland is for you. The town is an old one; it dates back to a New Hampshire grant of 1761 and was later rechartered by New York. Both grants were for a town named "Hertford." The fledgling Vermont legislature soon changed the name to Hartland to avoid confusion with Hartford, its neighbor on the north.

To a visitor, there appears to be no town center, but Hartland is a strong community. Each spring the entire town pitches in to produce a spirited musical vaudeville, raising thousands of dollars for local projects.

Three main settlements provide landmarks for travelers in Hartland — Three Corners, Four Corners, and Hartland Green. A good way to see the town for the first time is by driving a loop past all of them.

From Woodstock take Route 4 east and turn right on Route 12 about a half mile past Taftsville. This is not the most scenic route, but it is a good road in all seasons. It brings you to Hartland Four Corners where you turn right. Directly past the lovely old Universalist church is Skunk Hollow Tavern, a local watering hole that houses a gourmet restaurant upstairs and an informal fare of the hamburger and pizza variety downstairs.

Back on Route 12 a mile and a half farther is another hub, Hartland Three Corners, with a country store and Damon Hall, Hartland's seat of government. There is a superior bulletin board here, and it's a good place to check for auction notices, church suppers, contra dances, and other happenings.

In summer and fall, the old Hartland-Quechee Road, which intersects here (turn north between Damon Hall and the War Memorial statue), is a beautiful drive. It returns to Route 4 at the overhead blinker light at Waterman Place in Quechee.

Pick up Route 5 north at Hartland Three Corners. On the right is the brick Hartland Congregational Church in Three Corners, famed for its excellent roast beef suppers.

Vermonters love the outdoors, and Hartland offers four-star attractions for fishing and boating fans. One is the North Hartland Dam and George Perkins Marsh Conservation Center. Signs for the dam are posted at Route 5 where the access road leads in. The recreation area is a large, meticulously maintained park offering spotless rest rooms with handicapped access, barbecue fireplaces and grills, volleyball and baseball fields, nature walks, lawn areas, and a sandy beach. The swimming area is roped off and marked with floats; there's no lifeguard.

Federal dollars are at work here. The dam, a U.S. Army Corps of Engineers facility, is 185 feet high and looms ominously above happy bathers and boaters in summer. Hunting, fishing, and snowmobiling are allowed in suitable seasons. In fall, with the hills ablaze with color, this is a lovely place to put in a canoe and paddle up the lake toward Quechee Gorge. North Hartland Dam is open during daylight hours. For information on camping or reserving picnic shelters, call the Corps's Springfield office at 886-8111. They can also send you the wildflower checklist for the conservation area and a free map, 'Lakeside Recreation in New England.'

If you turn to the right as you leave the facility, you are on a maple-flanked dirt road that winds through lovely farmland with views down the valley. This road intersects with Old Quechee-Hartland Road, where you turn right to reach Route 4 in Quechee. Turn left out of the dam area to get back to Route 5.

Sumner's Falls, North Hartland's exciting stretch of the Connecticut River, is not easy to find. Heading north, the access road is east off Route 5 soon after 5 crosses the interstate. Keep a sharp eye out to your right for the dirt road into the woods. Should you miss it, turn around when you reach Coutermarsh's Country Store and gas station at North Hartland a few miles north, and drive back 2.2 miles. Heading south on Route 5 the road into the falls will be on your left on an uphill grade. The road is not improved; pickups and four-wheel drives are recommended. A sign at one side of the entrance posted by New England Power Company, which owns the land, announces hours. Sumner's Falls are famed for the number and variety of fish that congregate nearby. Though the rest of the river is a warm-water fish habitat, the churning falls attract brook and rainbow trout. Pike and muskie are here, too; the state's record tiger muskie came out of this water a few years back.

Remember, levels rise or fall on the river as the hydroelectric dam at Wilder upstream releases water unpredictably. Don't allow children on the rocks; for boaters the falls are extremely dangerous, as well. The *Vermont Atlas* notes, "*No one in a canoe should attempt to negotiate this highly dangerous stretch of rapids.*" This is a portage for canoe travelers heading either direction. Below the falls is smooth paddling all the way to Bellows Falls. Major Robert Rogers and his Rangers camped overnight by Sumner's Falls after their boat broke up on the White River Rapids near what is now Wilder.

Just north of Coutermarsh's Store on Route 5 is North Hartland Arts, marked by color banners. This gallery and workshop complex is a cooperative venture by six prominent regional artists. Their work for sale here ranges from pottery to painting and jewelry. Exhibits change through the seasons. There is no admission charge, and classes and workshops are held in summer for children and adults.

Just across the small village green is the Catalpa Gallery owned by two former Quebec residents who are artists. They show sculptures in semiprecious stone and unique translucent photographs.

Bridgewater

The distance from the Woodstock green to the town of Bridgewater is about six miles. The road is Route 4 west, and there are no long unsettled stretches, as this route along the Ottauquechee River has always been choice land. While still inside Woodstock, on the left, the road runs past the 1877 Lincoln Bridge, not so old as covered bridges go but unique in that it utilizes the Pratt-type arch first patented by Willis Pratt in 1844. Lincoln Bridge is the only remaining wooden Pratt arch bridge in the U.S. It was extensively renovated in 1947 and again in 1989.

South of Bridgewater, a town dominated by the Ottauquechee River with magnificent vistas and great biking roads, is Plymouth, President Calvin Coolidge's hometown. Neighboring Plymouth boasts the Coolidge Cheese Factory and Coolidge State Park, in addition to the Coolidge Centennial. A few miles farther south on Route 100 is the Echo Lake summer resort area.

On the road from Woodstock to Bridgewater, the river stays in sight almost all the way. The Ottauquechee is an uncommonly interesting river to watch in every season. It is rambunctious and muddy in the spring; placid in summer and fall; and a dormant, broad smooth highway in winter when it often freezes fast and prints of both deer and snowmobiles crisscross its surface. In spring, when the ice breaks up, the force of this small river is astounding. Rising temperatures bring rising water levels that push up slabs of ice. Great chunks, loosened and cracked, get shoved on top of each other as they move downstream, forming giant pileups. The stream, swollen by snowmelt, rolls angrily around and under them. "It is very difficult and dangerous Crossing Water Quechee (an old name for the river) at many times of the year, on account of the heath of the water and the repedicy of the stream," observed a traveler in 1792.

Because of the "heath and repedicy" of the waters during winter and early spring, these are the only times of year when a drive along the Ottauquechee from Woodstock to Bridgewater doesn't pass fishermen in waders standing midstream, hoping to outwit one of the wily rainbow or brown trout that this stretch of the Ottauquechee is known for.

Neither brown trout nor rainbows are native Vermonters. The rainbow trout was introduced from the western United States, and sportfishing groups brought in the brown trout from Germany in the 1800s. The rainbow is esteemed for its fighting spirit, and it is considered a tough critter to successfully play and land. The brown trout is respected as one of the harder fish to hook — it's a clever adversary and an extremely dainty eater that must be tempted with special flies or lures, or with fresh worms, depending on time of day or weather. Both fish found waters here to their liking — a 10-pounder of either variety would not be a record catch — and their abundance keeps anglers coming back each spring.

To many travelers on Route 4, Bridgewater is a town to drive through on the way to Killington or Rutland. This is not a new attitude. In 1779, before the town of Bridgewater had even a single settler, residents of Woodstock petitioned Vermont's general assembly for a road following the river.

In the next few decades, by which time Bridgewater did have settlers, there were frequent petitions from the little town for help to pay for the road and for the many bridges required to cross and recross the river winding along the valley floor. One solution in those days, as today, was to let travelers pay for the road as they used it. In 1825, a toll turnpike operated from the Woodstock/Bridgewater line to where the present-day Route 100 from Stockbridge enters Route 4.

An early act of Bridgewater's first government was to grant to one Richard Southgate and his brother two whole rights of land in 1783 on the condition that they build grist- and sawmills. New settlers were arriving with families, and sawn lumber in great quantities was needed to house them. Richard Southgate's mills prospered, and his own first house, built of logs, was replaced by 1795 with a large and handsome frame dwelling. The restored house, with a fancy lunette window over the front door, stands facing Route 4 and houses Bridgewater town offices and the Bridgewater Library. It can be visited when the library is open. The Southgate House is on the right coming into Bridgewater from Woodstock, a little past the mill.

Attractions

Farther down Route 4, just past the gas station and garage, a sign to the right, pointing up the hill, says "Recreation Center." The Bridgewater Community Center is on the right, just behind the garage, in a restored (1986) red brick building that served in 1803 as Bridgewater's first village school. The original building was one story; the second story was added in the 1840s. The fields maintained by the recreation department in Bridgewater Park are farther along Route 4 on the left and provide a softball field, playground, and tennis court.

Anyone living next to a river recognizes that fortune often depends on events upstream. Bridgewater is no exception. The river has been the town's lifeblood, powering the mill, its largest business and major employer. The river also brought disastrous floods that repeatedly scoured the narrow valley and washed out parts of town. Low water sometimes brought unemployment, when the river in summer ran too meagerly to power a mill at all. But not all upstream menace has been the work of nature. Bridgewater also had to ward off man-made attacks on the stretch of river that is the town's central feature.

In 1910, the Ottauquechee Grab Bill was introduced in the state legislature, an attempt by big upstream lumbering interests in Mendon and Sherburne to gain the right to float enormous volumes of cut timber down the Ottauquechee, a move that would have saved them substantial costs, but Bridgewater feared the move would damage town facilities beyond repair. Representatives from

Woodstock and Hartland farther down the river joined with Bridgewater to fight the plan and it was squashed.

Apprehension ran high again in 1988 when Sherburne, next town upriver, inside whose borders much of the vast Killington Ski Area development lies, asked the state to downgrade the classification of the Ottauquechee on Bridgewater's western boundary from B, which recognizes a river's use as a recreational resource, to C. Now the Ottauquechee has not always been as clean as it might. There is no question that Bridgewater Mills and other industries had no qualms about dumping sewage, dye wastes, and similar discharges directly into the stream over the years. But times have changed, and with increased awareness of the environment, successful cleanup campaigns have reclaimed this once-polluted stretch of river. Now the Ottauquechee is heavily used for recreation: swimming, boating, and fishing. Tourism is gradually replacing defunct industries as a source of prosperity.

Public outcry over proposed downgrading of the river's classification from B to C was gratifyingly loud in downstream towns Woodstock and Bridgewater. Unfortunately for Bridgewater, the Vermont Supreme Court overturned a lower court ruling in 1990 to allow the reclassification of the river. The move may enable the building of many more vacation homes in the Killington area by permitting Sherburne's sewer treatment plant to discharge the anticipated waste increase into the river. If the controversy did nothing else, it brought home to many in Bridgewater how important the river is to the town, even today when it no longer powers mills.

The last flurry of successful industry for the Bridgewater Mill was in blanket making, which started in 1910; but even with milling operations closed, the giant wooden buildings still dominate the small town center as they have for nearly two centuries. It was the rampaging river flooding through town in June 1973 that closed down the mills for the last time, leaving behind heavily damaged buildings choked with mud.

Within two years, renovation had started to change the old buildings into a marketplace of shops and businesses. But, making a commercial success of the project has been tough sledding for a succession of owners. New laws governing public buildings required heavy investment in expensive equipment such as elevators and fire protection equipment, and the lack of high-volume traffic has made it hard for some projected uses, such as outlet stores, to survive.

At this writing, beside a post office serving the local community, there is a clock store, a print gallery, an excellent book store, a Vermont Country gourmet shop selling (and shipping) cheese, condiments, and chocolates, and numerous small boutiques and craft stalls offering a bewildering variety of wares — handmade toys, knitted caps, herbs, and wooden bowls, just to name a few. There is also a new operation in the cellar of the old Mill, Vermont's second microbrewery, Mountain Brewers, Inc. Mountain Brewers make Bear Mountain Gold and Long Trail Ale in several batches each week. Tours, including samples if you are old enough, are available free when the brewery is open. Call 672-5011 for a schedule.

The Mill Marketplace has plenty of parking and it's fun to visit, especially on a rainy afternoon. Besides the shops, there is an assortment of old machinery on display throughout the building including old looms, an ancient movie projector, and a ringy-dingy telephone switchboard that would make Lily Tomlin's heart skip a beat.

History buffs probably know Bridgewater best for the flurry of gold fever that began after prospectors, returning from the California gold rush in the 1850s, found similar quartz-bearing rock in Bridgewater and nearby Plymouth. Gold mines were actually dug in Bridgewater, and at one time there were seven different gold mining companies operating within town borders. As late as 1902, a gold ore crusher plant was being built, but nothing solid ever developed in terms of big profits.

The part of Bridgewater where much of the prospecting took place is the section known as Chateaugay (pronounced Shattigee; the g is hard), once a moderately well-settled part of town but now largely woody and wild. The Appalachian Trail runs through this part of Bridgewater as does the border of Barnard and Stockbridge. At one time there was a community known as "No-town" in Chateaugay, supposedly left out of the survey for each of three towns. Its residents didn't want to pay taxes to any of them.

Driving west about eight miles from Bridgewater's mill is the small community of Bridgewater Corners where Route 100A runs to the left down toward Plymouth Notch. The Junction Country Store is at the corner; nearby are the Corners Inn (on the right just before you reach the store), and behind the store over a metal bridge the Old Grange Hall, the first in Vermont, was built in 1876. The building was dedicated in December of that year. The Sister Grangers fed a celebrating crowd of 200 guests with a repast that included oysters, turkey, chicken, duck, meat, cake, pie, and pastry! Today, auctions are held in the Grange on an irregular basis. Check the front window for signs. Beyond the Grange is the Bethany Mennonite Church, formerly a private home with double facades, one facing north, one south, each with four handsome fluted pillars. Farther down Route 100A, on the right are the seasonal Maple Leaf Farm Stand and the town line of Plymouth.

Steep roads to the right off Route 4 all along this valley offer beautiful views, especially in the fall with blazing red and gold vistas of the mountains on all sides. From Bridgewater Corners to Bridgewater Center (marker on the right .2 miles past intersection of Route 100A and Route 4), the road to Bridgewater Center is two miles from Route 4 but does not, as the name implies, lead to the business district of Bridgewater. That was back near the mill. The small church at the bend of the road is the Oak Chapel, formerly the Advent Chapel, and built by believers in the Second Coming of Christ, which many in Bridgewater, and towns nearby, thought would occur in 1843. The church is still used for worship but not in the original Adventist philosophy. Its small steeple is topped with a finial in the shape of an acorn. The builders of the church were devoted to the practice of baptism by immersion. An item in the *Vermont Standard* for December 4, 1902, notes that neighbors were "fascinated by the sight of Adventists being submerged in the river during winter weather." Another *Standard* item described "curious folk who wanted to watch and climbed onto the roof of the covered bridge and during the actual baptism were known to call out, 'Dip him again, he needs it!'"

For a glimpse of what the less peopled part of Bridgewater looks like, cross the bridge to the left of the Oak Chapel and bear to the right. This makes a good hike or mountain bike ride. It is not recommended in winter or mud season, as the road is not paved. The North Branch, a lively brook, runs beside the road. You can follow it about five miles before it becomes rutted and impassable to vehicles near the summit of a long climb. This road intersects the Appalachian Trail before crossing the Barnard town line and on into Barnard Center. Vermont's last mountain lion, or catamount, was killed in this area in 1881.

From Bridgewater Center, drive the two miles back out to Route 4 and turn right. It is about five miles farther to the intersection of Route 100 with Route 4 in West Bridgewater, a small cluster of businesses right on the edge of the town. Just before this intersection, on the left is Blanche and Bill's Pancake House. If it is not yet 2 P.M. (they serve only from 7 A.M. to 2), and if it's not a Monday or a Tuesday (they are closed those days), and if you are *really* hungry, Blanche and Bill's is a wonderful spot to soak up a stack of pancakes drowning in maple syrup. TC's General Store in West Bridgewater sells ready-made sandwiches to go and the usual country store fare. Behind TC's is the Back Behind, a bar and restaurant.

If you turn back here for the ride back to Woodstock along Route 4 after you go by the mill and leave Bridgewater, keep an eye out for a metal bridge on the right. Cross the bridge and turn left. The dusty country road follows the river most of the way (bear left at all forks) for four miles, going down into Woodstock and Route 4 at College Hill Road leading to the green ahead.

Many Bridgewater folk live on roads not seen by casual visitors. They enjoy their town in isolation from the awful traffic that often clogs Route 4 in the valley below. So far, the town has managed to escape being condominiumized, sanitized, boutiqued, or bypassed, and the town's essential nature as a pleasant, down-to-earth rural community still remains. Plain Vermont river towns like Bridgewater are becoming an endangered type. Drive through today, and you see the shape of a town pretty much as it looked soon after being settled in the 1790s. However, the rumble of bulldozers can already be heard in the background. Driving Route 4 west, through breaks in the hills ahead, you can glimpse broad, snow-covered ribbons of Killington's ski trails that stand out alongside the dark evergreen forest. It is the heavy and, some think, indiscriminate, development brought by the ski areas that offers a role model for relatively undeveloped towns like Bridgewater. Whether that model is one that Bridgewater's citizens want to copy, and whether they can stop development if they choose to, remains to be seen.

Plymouth

To reach Plymouth from Woodstock, take Route 4 west, going through Bridgewater to the intersection with Route 100A south, which dead-ends here, about nine miles from Woodstock green. Turn left at 100A and drive through farming country that gradually becomes more hilly as you go south. About five miles from Route 4, a sign points right to Plymouth Notch and the Calvin Coolidge Memorial.

The town's most prominent citizen, President Calvin Coolidge, dominates this small town. He grew up in tiny Plymouth Notch and, as vice president, was vacationing there when President Harding died in August 1923. His father, Colonel John Coolidge, a notary public, administered the presidential oath of office to his son in the tidy white house across from Plymouth Union Church. Asked later how he knew he could swear in his son to assume the presidency, John Coolidge replied laconically, "I didn't know I couldn't." Actually, a call had been made to the attorney general to determine the form of the oath and its legality.

The Plymouth Notch Historic District is maintained by the state, and a visitor's center was built there for the Coolidge Centennial in 1972. It has rest rooms, a gift shop, and a small museum with presidential memorabilia and portraits. It's open daily, mid-May to mid-October, 9:30 to 5:30. There is a fee to enter the buildings and take a tour, but children under 14 are free. You needn't pay to just walk along the dusty streets of this small village. The old general store and post office are still in operation. The building housing them is attached to the modest little Coolidge birthplace. This part of the building has been restored to its original condition by the state's Division for Historic Preservation, and it contains many of the original furnishings.

The Plymouth Union Church next door dates from 1840, its handsome Carpenter Gothic style interior with pews shaped to center on the pulpit is all of local wood and is worth a visit. It's closed in the winter. Iron thresholds at the doors were forged in the ironworks at Tyson Furnace, a section of Plymouth that lies to the south. Beyond the church is a recently restored historic garden originally planted by the president's stepmother, Carrie Brown Coolidge. Visitors often ask why such a small garden is surrounded by such a sturdy fence. The answer is the meadow beyond was formerly the site of the town blacksmith. If it wasn't for the fence, a steady stream of four-legged creatures would have easily cut through this corner.

Farther down the lane, on the right, is the Coolidge Cheese Factory, still in operation. You can try a sample here or buy a chunk to eat on the road. The original cheese-making equipment, and a wonderful collection of old utensils and vehicles from the region, can be seen in the Wilder Barn near the Visitor's Center.

Calvin Coolidge and his family are buried in the small town cemetery where memorial services are held each year on his July 4 birthday. The spirit of the Vermonter known as "Silent Cal" is most evident in the church where he and his family worshiped. Near the entrance is a granite slab engraved with his familiar "Vermont is a state I love" speech. Compare the simple surroundings at Plymouth Notch with the edifices erected to the glory of more recent American political leaders. In his Plymouth surroundings, Coolidge is revealed as a genuine product of the land that nurtured him, not as a public relations creation. His quiet ways were characteristic of a Vermonter and not due to any lack of wit or deep feelings.

Driving south on Route 100A from Plymouth Notch brings you to the entrance (on the left) to Coolidge State Park. Even if you aren't camping, it's worth a drive up through the park. Trail maps are available free from the ranger station at the summit if you want to hike here from mid-May until the first weekend in October. This is prime bear hunting country so be warned, especially if you have a dog with you, that not every hunter observes the rule of no guns in the state park during camping season. Bear season opens in September.

Bikers call the downhill grade here "Hysteria Hill" and are no doubt thrilled coasting down to the bottom, where Routes 100A and 100 meet at the handsome little Salt Ash Inn. This building has been an inn since the 1800s and was previously known as Union House. Inside, you can still see the old wooden post office boxes and grocery store counter and scales.

Turn right here and take Route 100 about five miles back up to Route 4 for a quick loop through Plymouth. The village of Plymouth Union lies along this stretch with the school library and town offices. On the right, you will pass the Woodward Reservoir, a good fishing lake. The State Fish and Wildlife Department provides a boat-ramp area on Route 100 for access to Woodward, but swimming is not allowed. Farm and Wilderness Camps and five private coed camps are located near the north end of the lake. Just before the intersection with Route 4 is one of the Killington Resort ski lifts on the left.

If you continue south on Route 100 from Saltash, you reach the Hawk Inn and Mountain Resort. You'll pass through the once thriving community of Frog City, which was halfway between Saltash and Tyson at the bottom of Plymouth territory. The main building at Hawk Resort is a handsome Frog City farmhouse built in the early 1800s. Ask here for trail maps for Hawk's extensive system of hiking and nature trails. Hawk is open year-round; its restaurant, swimming pool, boating, ski, and snowshoe facilities are all open to the public for a fee. At this writing, the use of hiking trails was free.

Tyson, formerly Tyson Furnace, is named after a Baltimore man who discovered the rich ore and built an ironworks here in 1837. Iron was made here until 1872, and it is said that the iron plates that armored the Civil War battleship the *Monitor* were produced in Tyson. Echo Lake Inn at Tyson looks like the old resort hotel it is, with a generous front porch lined with wooden chairs. Henry Ford, Thomas Edison, and Harvey Firestone are among the famous people who have signed the register. To get to Camp Plymouth, and the east side of Echo Lake, you cross the fancy little Stickney Bridge here. The former bridge washed away in the disastrous floods that hit the area in 1927, and the new bridge was given by Governor William Stickney in honor of his father.

Camp Plymouth, on Echo Lake near Plymouth's southern border, was first a private camp and then a Boy Scout camp for more than 50 years. Today, as a state park, it provides 300 acres of choice lakeside with plenty of parking and attractive lawns. There are picnic sites under old pines, a sandy beach, clean rest rooms, and snack bars. Camp Plymouth has a nature trail and a boat rental concession. The lake is clear and inviting. It is no wonder most visitors arrive prepared to spend the day with fishing gear, picnic baskets, and blankets. Probably its location far from any large-sized city keeps Camp Plymouth uncrowded. It certainly is a magical spot to spend a lazy afternoon. In early autumn, especially on a weekday, you may have the place to yourself.

It's hard to imagine such a peaceful spot as the scene of gold frenzy, but it was on the Pollard place near here that locals back from the California gold rush spotted telltale glittering flakes in Buffalo Brook. They set off a flurry that left the town no richer in anything other than tales and legends. Buffalo Brook became "Gold Brook," and mining companies promptly arrived. One aptly named "Rook" seemed to have worked a scam, fudging records of how much gold was actually found and making more money on selling paper than on mining gold. That there was gold was never in doubt, and there are still hobbyists who pan today. The original mine shafts are covered by rock slides, however. You are allowed to pan on state land without a permit, but to dredge or dig you need permission from the state.

For a tiny town, Plymouth has many claims to a place in history. Like most area towns, it has considerably fewer people than years ago, and many of its farms and public buildings have either fallen into decay or been turned into vacation homes. Plymouth today is a quiet place, with plenty of woods and open fields to accommodate travelers with the privacy they seek.

The Woodstock Area Essentials

Important Information

Municipal Services

Barnard Town Clerk: 234-9211.
Barnard Police: 234-9933.
Barnard Fire & Ambulance:
234-5253; 911, 728-9600.
Bridgewater Town Clerk: 672-3334.
Bridgewater Police: 457-1416.
Bridgewater Fire & Ambulance:
672-3311; 911.
Hartford Town Clerk: 295-2785
(Hartford includes the towns of
Quechee, West Hartford, White River
Junction, and Wilder).
Hartford Police: 295-3725, 295-7536,
emergency 911.
Hartford Fire & Ambulance:
295-2424, emergency 911.
Hartland Town Clerk: 436-2444.
Hartland Police, Fire, Rescue: 911.
Plymouth Town Clerk: 672-3655.
Plymouth Police: 457-1416.
Plymouth Fire & Ambulance:
228-3434; 457-2323.
Pomfret Town Clerk: 457-3861.
Pomfret Police: 234-9933.
Pomfret Fire & Ambulance:
457-2323, emergency 911.

Quechee Police: 295-3725, 295-7536,
emergency 911.
Quechee Fire & Ambulance:
295-2424, emergency 911.
South Woodstock Police: 457-1416.
South Woodstock Fire &
Ambulance: 911.
Taftsville Police: 457-1416.
Taftsville Fire & Ambulance:
457-2323.
West Hartford Police: 295-3725,
295-7536, emergency 911.
West Hartford Fire & Ambulance:
295-2424, emergency 911.
White River Junction Police:
295-3725, 295-7536, emergency 911.
White River Junction Fire &
Ambulance: 295-2424, emergency
911.
Wilder Police: 295-3725, 295-7536,
emergency 911.
Wilder Fire & Ambulance:
295-2424, emergency 911.
Woodstock Town Clerk: 457-3611.
Woodstock Village Police, Fire,
Rescue: 911.

Medical Services

Alice Peck Day Memorial Hospital, 125 Mascoma St., Lebanon, N.H.; (603)
448-3121.
Dartmouth Hitchcock Medical Center, Hanover, N.H.; (603) 646-5000.
Gifford Memorial Hospital, 44 South Main St., Randolph; 728-4441.
Mt. Ascutney Hospital and Health Center, County Rd., Windsor; 674-6711.
Ottauquechee Health Center (walk-in urgent care), 32 Pleasant St., Woodstock;
457-3030.
Rutland Regional Hospital, 160 Allen St., Rutland; 775-7111.
Statewide Medical Health Care Information Center, 24-hour-phone; 864-0454.

Veterinarians

Lucy MacKenzie Humane Society, Cox District Rd., Woodstock; 457-3080. (Not a veterinary clinic, but check here for lost pets.)
Drs. Lynn Murrell and Heather Hoyns, Rte. 106, South Woodstock; 457-3135.
White River Animal Hospital, Rte. 5, White River Junction; 295-6900.
Woodstock Animal Care, Rte. 4 West, Woodstock; 457-4545.
Woodstock Veterinary Clinic, Rte. 12 North, Woodstock; 457-2229.

Weather

24-hour Weather Phone: 457-4250.

Tourist Information Services

Quechee Chamber of Commerce, Box 804, Quechee, 05059. Rte. 4 at Quechee Gorge, seasonal; no telephone.
Quechee Foliage Season Lodging, Quechee, 05059; 296-7074.
White River Junction Chamber of Commerce, White River Junction, 05001. Rte. 5 near interchange of I-91 and I-89 (across Sykes Ave. from the Vermont Transit Station); 295-6200.
Woodstock Area Foliage Lodging Service, Woodstock, 05091; 457-2389.
Woodstock Area Information Booth, Woodstock Green, Woodstock, 05091. Late June through mid-October; 457-1042.
Woodstock Chamber of Commerce, 18 Central St., Woodstock, 05091; 457-3555.

Lodgings

Inns and B&Bs

BARNARD

Silver Lake House, North Rd.; 234-9957. Inexpensive to moderate. White-gabled house across the road from Silver Lake. Water sports, tennis, hiking nearby. Three rooms, shared baths. Open June to November. No pets. Smoking in bedrooms only. Personal checks.

BRIDGEWATER

Bridgewater Inn, Rte. 4; 672-3876. Inexpensive to moderate. Three guest rooms, private baths, color TV, air-conditioned. No pets, no smoking. Open all year-round. Mastercard and Visa.
Corners Inn, Rte. 4, Bridgewater Corners; 672-9968. Inexpensive. Six rooms share two baths. Closed October. Award-winning restaurant on premises. No pets. Smoking OK. Major credit cards.
Maple Leaf Farm, Bridgewater Corners; 672-3790. Inexpensive. Working 300-acre farm. Four rooms on second floor share one bath. Closed slow season. No pets. Smoking OK. No credit cards.
October Country Inn, Bridgewater Corners; 672-3412. Expensive. Ten rooms, eight with private baths, five on ground floor. Pool and gardens. Dining room. Room rates include dinner and country breakfasts. Closed two weeks in November and two weeks in April. No pets. No smoking. Mastercard and Visa.
Raspberry Hill Bed and Breakfast, Rte. 4; 672-3699. Inexpensive to moderate. Old Vermont home, five bedrooms, one on ground floor, three with private bath, two share a bath. Walk to shopping. Pets OK. Smoking in designated areas. Mastercard and Visa.

HARTFORD

House of Seven Gables, 22 Main St.; 295-1200. Moderate. Renovated century old Victorian mansion. Four guest rooms on third floor, shared baths. Hearty breakfast featuring home baking. No pets. Smoking on ground floor only. Mastercard and Visa.

PLYMOUTH

Echo Lake Inn, Rte. 100; 228-6602. Moderate. Twenty-six rooms, with and without private baths. Two suites, six condo units (minimum two nights). Old-fashioned country inn near Echo Lake. Tennis, pool, boat rentals. Dining room, bar. Closed first two weeks in November and all of April. No pets. Smoking in designated areas.

Saltash Inn, Junction Rtes. 100 and 100A; 672-3746. Moderate. Old country inn, beautifully restored. Fifteen rooms, most have private baths. Four rooms on ground floor. Closed April and first two weeks May. No pets. No smoking in dining room. Credit cards.

Stone Creek Guest House, Rte. 100 (just south of intersection Rtes. 100A and 100); 672-5214. Inexpensive. Log home, one guest bedroom with private bath. No smoking, no pets, no credit cards, no breakfast.

POMFRET

Heartacres Bed and Breakfast, North Pomfret; 457-2621. Inexpensive. Two guest rooms. One, ground floor, has own entrance, private bath. One upstairs shares bath. No pets. Smoking OK. Year-round.

QUECHEE

Abel Barron House, 37 Main St.; 295-1337. Moderate. Victorian house in the middle of Quechee Village, breakfast service in greenhouse addition. Five beautifully decorated rooms, all with private baths. No pets. Smoking in designated areas. Open year-round. All credit cards.

Parker House, Main St.; 295-6077. Expensive. Seven attractive rooms, all with private bath. Restaurant on premises. No pets. Smoking in designated areas. Open year-round. Credit cards.

Quechee Bed and Breakfast, Rte. 4; 295-1776. Moderate to expensive. House dates from 1795, lovely gardens, views. Walk to shops, restaurants. Eight rooms, private baths. Three on ground floor. No pets. Smoking allowed in rooms, no smoking in dining area. Closed November 26–December 21. Mastercard and Visa.

Quechee Inn at Marshland Farms, Dewey's Mill Rd.; 295-3133. Lovely restored historic house. All rooms with private baths. Award-winning dining room. Summer fly-fishing (school and tours), boat, bike rentals. Winter Wilderness Trails Cross-Country Ski facility. Lessons, equipment. Guests at Quechee Inn have guest privileges at sports facilities maintained by Quechee Lakes, including swimming (indoor and outdoor pools), tennis, two golf courses. Downhill ski area.

Sugar Pine Farm, Rte. 4; 295-1266. Moderate. Decorated with owners' collection antique Santas, quilts; featured in national magazines. Shop on premises sells country accessories. Three rooms share two baths. Ask about pets. No smoking. Open year-round. Mastercard and Visa.

TAFTSVILLE

Applebutter Inn, uphill from Taftsville Country Store; 457-4158. Moderate. Twin-gabled Federal-style house. Period stenciling. Five rooms, 2½ shared baths. Down comforters on every bed. Natural foods breakfast. No pets. Smoking in designated areas. No credit cards.

WHITE RIVER JUNCTION

Susse Chalet Inn, Rte. 5; 295-3051, 1-800-258-1980 for reservations. Inexpensive. Ninety-nine rooms, air-conditioning, VCRs. Nonsmoking rooms available. No pets. Outdoor pool. Guest Laundromat. Continental breakfast. Walk to restaurants. Major credit cards.

WILDER

Stonecrest Farm (exit 12 off I-91); 295-2600. Moderate. Charming old farmhouse. Three double guest rooms share three baths. No pets. Smoking in designated areas. Checks. Mastercard and Visa.

WOODSTOCK

Beaver Pond Farm, (4½ miles up Hartland Hill from Woodstock); 436-2443. Moderate. Three large rooms, all with fireplaces, private baths. "Lodging for horse and rider." Georgian house, 130 acres of trails and pasture. Barn stalls, dressage ring. Swimming and canoeing. Open year-round. No pets. Smoking OK. Credit cards.

Canterbury House, 43 Pleasant St.; 457-3077. Moderate to expensive. Beautifully restored village house furnished with Victorian antiques. Cable TV, walk to shops, restaurants. Seven rooms all with private baths, air-conditioning. No pets, no smoking. Mastercard and Visa.

Carriage House Inn of Woodstock, Rte. 4; 457-4322. Moderate. Seven rooms, five with private bath, two share a bath. No pets, smoking OK. Mastercard and Visa.

Charleston House, 21 Pleasant St.; 457-3843. Moderate to expensive. Elegant Greek Revival mansion, handsomely furnished. Seven bedrooms, all with private baths. Cable TV. Bikes provided for local jaunts. No pets. No smoking. Credit cards.

Deer Brook Inn; 672-3713. Inexpensive. Four rooms, private baths in an 1820s farmhouse. Full breakfasts. No pets.

1830 Shire Town Inn, 31 South St., Rte. 106; 457-1830. Moderate. Near the green and across from playgrounds. Walk to shops. Three rooms, private baths. No pets. Smoking in designated areas. Credit cards.

Jackson House, Rte. 4; 457-2065. Expensive. Landmark Victorian mansion, 10 rooms, each furnished in antiques of different period, style. All have private baths. Full breakfasts, complimentary evening wine and hors d'oeuvres buffet. No pets. No smoking. No children under 14. Credit cards.

Kedron Valley Inn, Rte. 106; 457-1473. Moderate to expensive. Rooms in renovated historic inn and surrounding buildings. Twenty-eight rooms, private baths, some with private decks, some ground floor. Open fireplaces, canopy beds, handmade quilts. Swimming lake. Stables nearby. Bar, dining room. Children and pets welcome. Smoking OK. Major credit cards. Closed April and one week in November.

Lincoln Inn at the Covered Bridge, Rte. 4; 457-1255. Moderate. Restored 200-year-old farmhouse. Thirteen rooms, private baths. Dining room, cocktail lounge. No pets. Smoking OK. Major credit cards.

Thomas Hill Farm Bed and Breakfast, 4 Rose Hill; 457-1067. Moderate. Restored Greek Revival house, furnished with antiques. Closed April and November. Three bedrooms, two with private baths. No pets. No children. Smoking not allowed in bedrooms. Mastercard and Visa.

Three Church Street, 3 Church St.; 457-1925. Moderate. Huge handsome brick house, on National Register of Historic Places. Gracious, comfortable public rooms, tennis and swimming pool on grounds. TV room. Closed April. Ten rooms, some with private baths. Pets and smoking OK. Mastercard and Visa.

Village Inn of Woodstock, 41 Pleasant St.; 457-1255. Inexpensive to moderate. Victorian mansion in Woodstock Village, dining room, bar. Eight rooms, six have private baths. Nice garden. No pets, smoking OK. Major credit cards.

Winslow House, Rte. 4 (1½ miles west of the village); 457-1820. Moderate. Comfortable old farmhouse. Four rooms have private baths/showers. Another small extra room is sometimes used for children; shares parents' bath. Open year-round. Children and pets welcome. No smoking. Full breakfast. Mastercard and Visa.

Woodstock House, Rte. 106; 457-1758. Moderate. Renovated farmhouse. Five rooms, three have private baths, two share baths. Full breakfasts. Open year-round. No pets. No smoking. Mastercard and Visa.

The Woodstocker Bed and Breakfast, 61 River St.; 457-3896. Moderate to expensive. Nine rooms, two efficiency suites, all have private baths. Whirlpool available to guests. Breakfast buffet. Open year-round. No pets. Smoking in rooms only. Checks. Mastercard and Visa.

The following are Guest Houses and do not serve breakfast.

1826 House, 57 River St.; 457-1335. Inexpensive. Old farmhouse in town. Two double rooms, one single. All share bath. No pets. Smoking on back porch only. Open year-round. No credit cards.

Olsson's Guests, Rte. 4; 457-3087. Inexpensive. Two guest rooms, both ground floor and share one bath with shower. Open year-round. No pets. Smoking OK. No credit cards.

Hotels, Motels, and Resorts

BRIDGEWATER

Cedarbrook Motor Inn/Suites, junction Rte. 4 and Rte. 100 south. Mailing address: HCR Box 58, Killington, 05751; 422-9666 or 1-800-446-1088. Moderate to expensive. Closed one month after foliage season, one or two months in spring. Modern buildings (converted from condominiums) some ground floor, suites with fireplaces, deck, kitchenettes. Walk across the street to a Killington lift. Pool. No pets, smoking OK.

PLYMOUTH

Farmbrook Motel, Rte. 100A; 672-3621. Inexpensive to moderate. Pleasant little motel overlooks valley view. Nice grounds, creek runs right under main building. All rooms ground level, some with kitchenettes. No pets, smoking OK.

Hawk Inn and Mountain Resort, Box 64, Rte. 100; 672-3811. Expensive. Inn, rooms and suites, condominium rentals. Tennis, skiing, boating, hiking, health club, pool, and restaurant on premises. No pets. Smoking OK. Major credit cards.

QUECHEE

Quechee Gorge Friendship Inn, Rte. 4; 295-7600, 1-800-453-4511 for reservations. Large motel in wooded setting. Open year-round, pets allowed. Outdoor heated pool, Satellite TV. Air-conditioned. Nonsmoking rooms available. Restaurant on grounds. Mastercard and Visa.

Quechee Inn at Marshland Farms Resort, Clubhouse Rd.; 295-3133. Expensive. Beautifully restored historic house. All rooms with private baths. Award-winning dining room. Summer fly-fishing (school and tours) boat, bike rentals. Quechee Inn guests have privileges at sports facilities maintained by Quechee Lakes, including swimming (indoor and outdoor pools), tennis, two golf courses. Downhill ski area.

Quechee Lakes Corporation (Resort), Rte. 4; 295-1970. Condominium rentals. Complete resort with two golf courses, tennis courts, swimming pools, clubhouse. Downhill ski area.

WHITE RIVER JUNCTION

Coach an' Four Motel, Rte. 5 at I-91, I-89 interchange; 295-2210. Inexpensive. Twelve units, air-conditioned, color TV. Walk to bus station (across street). Major credit cards.

Green Mountain Motel, Rte. 5; 295-3695. Inexpensive. Twelve units, open year-round. Swimming pool. Small dogs OK. Major credit cards.

Holiday Inn of White River, at I-91, I-89 interchange; 295-7537, 1-800-465-4329 for reservations. Moderate. Modern, built around a courtyard an acre in size that features a swimming pool and an old caboose. Convention facilities can serve groups to 300. Lounge and restaurant.

Howard Johnson Lodge, Rte. 5 at I-91, I-89 interchange; 295-3015, 1-800-654-2000 for reservations. One hundred and twelve rooms, indoor pool, sauna, game room. Meeting facilities for 250. Exercise room, tennis, racquetball. Restaurant next door. Major credit cards.

Maple Leaf Motel, Rte. 5 (two miles south of interchange); 295-2817. Inexpensive. Motel open year-round (attached campground is seasonal), 24 rooms, cable TV. Pets allowed winter only. Mastercard and Visa.

Pine Crest Motel, Rte. 5; 295-2725. Inexpensive. Twenty units, cable TV. Major credit cards.

Pleasant View Motel, 65 Woodstock Rd. (Rte. 4 west); 295-3485. Inexpensive. Sixteen units, open year-round. In-room phones, air-conditioned. Cable TV. Major credit cards.

Shady Lawn Motel, 89 Maple St. (Rte. 14); 295-7118. Inexpensive. Thirty-five units, cable TV. Some units have waterbeds. Air-conditioned. Efficiency units available. No pets. Mastercard and Visa.

WILDER

Braeside Motel, Rte. 4; 457-1366. Moderate. On Blake Hill overlooking river valley. Open all year-round. Twelve rooms, full baths, color TV, continental breakfast. Outdoor heated pool. No pets, smoking OK. Major credit cards.

Ottauquechee Motel, Box 418, Rte. 4 West; 457-3404. Inexpensive. Inn overlooks the Ottauquechee River. Open year-round. Color TV, 12 rooms all with full baths, 6 air-conditioned. No pets, smoking OK. Restaurant next door. Major credit cards.

Pond Ridge Motel and Apartments, Rte. 4 west; 457-1667. Inexpensive to moderate. Open year-round. Roomy grounds on banks of Ottauquechee River. Twelve air-conditioned units. Seven apartments, fully equipped. (Minimum stay three nights.) Cable TV.

Shire Motel, 46 Pleasant St.; 457-2211. Inexpensive to moderate. In the village, walk to shops, restaurants. Lawns in back down to river. Excellent bird-watching spot. Open year-round. Eighteen air-conditioned units, cable TV. Pets and smoking OK. American Express, Mastercard, and Visa.

Wilder Motel, Rte. 5 north; 295-9793. Nine units, one handicapped equipped. Air-conditioned, color TV, swimming pool, children's play area. Major credit cards.

Woodstock Inn and Resort, 14 The Green; 457-1100, 800-448-7900 for reservations. Moderate to expensive. Built in 1969 and completely overhauled in 1989, the inn offers resort facilities in a small-town setting. One hundred and ten rooms. Air-conditioning. Handicapped access. Conference facilities, dining room, coffee shop, tavern, gift shop. Sports Center complete with indoor pool, exercise rooms, sauna and whirlpool, squash, indoor and outdoor tennis courts, 18-hole golf course, pro shop, fully equipped cross-country ski center. Nearby downhill ski area, Suicide Six. Major credit cards.

Woodstock Motel, Rte. 4; 457-2500. Inexpensive. Fifteen units, cable TV. Air-conditioned. Pool. Major credit cards.

Cottages and Condominiums

BARNARD

Hawk's Hill Demonstration Forest Guest Cottage; 763-7684 for information. The New England Forest Foundation (617) 437-1441, 85 Newbury St., Boston, MA 02116 for reservations. Guest house. Electric heat and hot water. Two double bedrooms, pullout couch sleeps two more. Weekend or week-long rentals. Linens and utensils furnished. At entrance to Hawk Hill Demonstration Forest, East Barnard.

Silver Lake Family Campground. Off Rte. 12, Barnard (behind Barnard General Store), 234-9974. Four housekeeping cabins. Bring your own linens, utensils. Seasonal.

PLYMOUTH

Echo Lake Inn, Rte. 100, Tyson (part of Plymouth); 228-8602. Six condominium units, minimum stay two nights.

Hawk Inn and Mountain Resort, Rte. 100; 672-3811. Condominiums. Two-night minimum stay. Turnkey. Everything furnished.

QUECHEE

Quechee Lakes, Rte. 4 (large red brick building with sign out front); 295-1970. Turnkey accommodations in condominiums and townhouses.

WHITE RIVER JUNCTION

Maple Leaf Motel, Rte. 5; 295-2817. Rents one housekeeping cottage.

WOODSTOCK

Hillside House, Rte. 4 (west of the village between Woodstock and Bridgewater, nearly in Bridgewater); 672-3414. Duplex cottage, two suites, each with private bath, one with kitchenette. Weekly rental. May 15 – November 15. No pets.

Woodstock Inn, 14 The Green; 457-1100. Two townhouses (sleep two couples), one house sleeps eight. No minimum stay. Townhouses have circular stairwells and cannot accommodate children.

Campgrounds

BARNARD

Silver Lake Family Campground, Box 111, 05031. Inexpensive. Ten miles from Woodstock just off Rte. 12 (entrance behind country store across from post office); 234-9974. Twenty-six water, electric, sewer, twelve water and electric. Cabin and canoe rentals. Playground and recreation hall. Seasonal mid-May to Columbus Day. Flush toilets, hot showers. Pets allowed on leashes.

Silver Lake State Park, ten miles north of Woodstock on Rte. 12 to country store, then up North Rd. ¼ mile to camp entrance; 234-9451. Seasonal. Thirty-four acres directly on 100-acre lake. Sandy beach, picnic area for day use. Concession stand, boat rentals. Forty-three sites, one handicapped access, one toilet handicapped access.

PLYMOUTH

Coolidge State Park, Rte. 100A; 672-3612. Five hundred acres, 60 sites (no hookups), 35 lean-tos, flush toilets, hot showers (fee), picnic area. Fee.

QUECHEE

Quechee Gorge State Park, east bridge on Rte. 4 at Quechee Gorge; 295-3725. Thirty sites, no hookups. One campsite has handicapped access. Toilets are handicapped access.

WHITE RIVER JUNCTION

Maple Leaf Campground, Rte. 5, next to motel; 295-2817. Twenty campsites. Flush toilets, hot showers, electric hookups, water, and dumping station. Seasonal.

Pine Valley Resort Campground, just east of I-89 access road off of Rte. 4 across from country store; 296-6711. Discounts for week or month. Twenty-four sites, full water, electric, and sewer hookups. Six with water and electric, 17 tent sites. Dump station. Heated modern bathrooms, metered showers. Fishing in stocked pond. In-ground swimming pool. Playground area. Open mid-May to mid-October.

Dining

BARNARD

Barnard General Store; 234-9688. Inexpensive. Counter lunch stand. Sandwiches, hot dishes daily.

Barnard Inn, Rte. 12; 234-9961. Expensive. Fine dining, continental cuisine prepared by Swiss chef. Dinner only, reservations recommended. Jackets required. Major credit cards.

BRIDGEWATER

The Back Behind Restaurant and Saloon, junction of Rte. 4 and Rte. 100 south, West Bridgewater; 422-9907. Moderate. Dinner daily, lunch Friday, Saturday, Sunday, and holidays. Closed mid-April to mid-June, open Memorial Day weekend. Steaks, seafood, and chef's specialties. Full bar, eclectic decor, includes a train caboose. A local watering hole. Major credit cards.

Blanche and Bill's Pancake House, Rte. 4; no phone. Inexpensive. Open only Monday and Tuesday. Rearrange your schedule or eat your heart out. You'll miss what many consider the best pancakes in the state. Also lunch. "Limited BUT good" as their sign says.

The Corners Inn and Restaurant, junction Rte. 4 with Rte. 100A south; 672-9968. Inexpensive to moderate. Wonderful dining room, Wednesday night buffets, imaginative cuisine. Award winners in "Taste of Vermont." Closed October.

"20's," Rte. 4; 672-1920. Moderate. Bar and restaurant serving informal food — pizza, subs, and take-out orders and full restaurant specializing in Italian food. Mastercard and Visa.

The Village Diner, Rte. 4; 672-5363. Inexpensive. Open 24 hours. Good plain food. Serve yourself coffee to go. Counter, booths, and tables. Full menu and blackboard specials. Typical offerings — three homemade soups, eight flavors of pie, four of pudding, and three kinds of cake. Complaints? Call the owner, home phone number on front of menu! Jukebox.

HARTLAND

M&M Store and Country Kitchen, Rte. 12, Hartland Four Corners; 436-3252. Inexpensive. Country store with lunch counter. Breakfast served at any hour. Hamburgers, sandwiches, and hot daily specials. No credit cards.

Skunk Hollow Tavern, Hartland Four Corners; 436-2139. Inexpensive downstairs in pub, upstairs, moderate. Dinner only. Downstairs pub, informal food. Upstairs continental cuisines, wines.

Vix 50's Restaurant, Jessars Common at Hartland Three Corners; 436-3252. Inexpensive. Breakfast and lunch 6 A.M. to 3 P.M. Monday through Saturday, Sunday 8 A.M. to 2 P.M. Dinner Thursday, Friday, and Saturday nights. Small neighborhood place, informal, booths and counter service. No credit cards.

PLYMOUTH

Echo Lake Inn, in Tyson (a part of Plymouth) south of intersection of Rte. 100 and Rte. 100A; 228-8602. Moderate. Dining room open to the public. Breakfast and dinner. Liquor license.

River Tavern, Hawk Resort, Rte. 100; 672-3811. Moderate to expensive. Open to the public, year-round. Breakfast and dinner. Major credit cards.

Wilder House, Rte. 100A, Coolidge Historic District, Plymouth Notch; no phone. Inexpensive. Seasonal. Lunch only.

POMFRET

Teago Store, Stage Rd.; 457-1626. Inexpensive. Take-out only. Sandwiches, soups, deli counter with salads.

QUECHEE

Dana's By-the-Gorge Restaurant, Rte. 4; 295-6066. Inexpensive to moderate. Restored railroad barn. Seasonal (May–November). Breakfast and lunch. A favorite with locals, old-fashioned, well-prepared home-style food.

Grondin's Deli, on the green in Quechee. Grondin's is in a white Cape Cod house down behind the big red barn on Main; 295-2786. Open year-round (closed Christmas Day). Complete deli with gourmet slant. Sandwiches, salads, picnics, or ski lunches packed to order; call ahead. Continental breakfast, super coffee. Tiny eat-in area. Plenty of lush lawn and a basketball hoop nearby outside.

Isabelle's at the Parker House, Main St.; 295-6077. Expensive. Dining in elegantly appointed Victorian dining rooms or on deck overlooking river. Menu varies with the season, prepared by French master chef. Coats and ties not required, reservations required. Major credit cards.

The Ott-Dog Snack Bar, Rte. 4, Quechee Gorge; 295-1088. Inexpensive. Seasonal (mid-May to late October). Snack bar featuring "Ott dogs." Sandwiches, chili dogs, soft drinks, and desserts.

Quechee Gin Mill, overlooking Rte. 4 just past the crossroads in Quechee; 295-1777. Inexpensive to moderate. Open year-round. Full liquor license, 18 different beers on draft, "pub" cuisine, "lamb-burger" from local lamb. Informal, children welcome. Parties accommodated. Lunch and dinner daily, indoors or on the deck in summer. Mastercard and Visa.

The Quechee Inn at Marshland Farm, Dewey's Mill Rd.; 295-3133. Moderate to expensive. Reservations required. Dinner only year-round. Elegant dining in beautiful surroundings, no jeans. Coats not required, but you will be more at ease if not too casually attired. Extensive menu and wine list. Major credit cards.

Rosalita's Southwestern Bar and Grill, Waterman Pl. Complex; Rte. 4 in Quechee; 295-1600. Inexpensive to moderate. Open year-round. A local watering hole. Decorated in southwestern style, features collection of North American beers, western and Tex-Mex-style food. Mastercard and Visa.

Sevi's, Rte. 4; 295-9351. Inexpensive in lounge, moderate in dining room. Lounge specialty is pizza made on the premises. Fish and chips, chicken in basket, and other snack foods available. Full license, also pizza to go. Informal. Jukebox. Sevi's Dining Room. Moderate. Dinner served year-round. Nonsmoking area. Specializes in seafood and steaks. Informal. American Express, Mastercard, and Visa.

Simon Pearce's Restaurant, Downer Mill Building, Main St.; 295-1470. Moderate to expensive. Check out glassblowing and wheel-thrown pottery operations. Charming restaurant offers excellent and unusual cuisine, Irish-influenced specialties, featured in *Gourmet* magazine. Attractive dining room is air-conditioned, overlooks river and waterfall. Outdoor dining in summer. Full license. Dinner reservations recommended, but at lunch you can usually eat without waiting. A favorite with area residents, especially for lunch. Informal dress OK. American Express, Mastercard, and Visa.

The Whistle Stop Snack Bar and Restaurant, Rte. 4, Timber Village; 296-8182. Inexpensive to moderate. Open year-round; three meals. Snack service and full restaurant.

Wildflowers, Rte. 4 (at Quechee Gorge Friendship Inn); 295-7600. Inexpensive to moderate. Breakfast served 6 A.M. to 3 P.M., plus lunch and dinner. Sit at counter or in dining room. Informal.

WHITE RIVER JUNCTION

A.J.'s Restaurant and Lounge, Skyes Ave. (near Astrobowl bowling); 295-3071. Inexpensive to moderate. Dinner only year-round. Steaks and seafood. Unprepossessing location, locals flock here for the good food. No reservations, crowded on weekends. Informal. Mastercard and Visa.

Athena's Pizza, Rte. 5 Junction Marketplace; 295-9595. Inexpensive. Pizzas, Greek salads, gyros, lasagna. Eat-in or take-out.

Blood's Seafood Market and Restaurant, Taft Ave.; 295-5393. Inexpensive to moderate. Open year-round. Very informal. Bring your own beer or wine. Eat-in or in summer under outside tent with picnic tables or take-out. Mastercard and Visa.

Canton House, Rte. 5 Junction Marketplace; 296-2116. Open year-round. Eat-in (space limited) or take-out. Lunch specials daily. Major credit cards.

Cashie's at the Coolidge, Coolidge Hotel, Main St.; 295-3118. Inexpensive to moderate. A pub and eatery. Railroad theme. Popular lunch spot; dinner, too. Entertainment on weekends. Major credit cards.

Coolidge Hotel Dining Room; 295-3118. Inexpensive to moderate. Lunch, dinner. Comfortable old-fashioned dining room, soft lights, handsome murals, sparkling linens, and uniformed staff. No dress code, but diners will be comfortable if neatly dressed. Very good food. Mastercard and Visa.

Fred Harvey's Restaurant, Holiday Inn, crossroads of I-89 and I-91; 295-7537. Moderate. Lunch and dinner. Sunday brunch in The Patio. Informal. Major credit cards.

Howard Johnson's, at Motel, Rte. 5; 295-3200. Inexpensive. Standard Hojo's. Informal. Counter or restaurant service, good salad bar. Lounge with entertainment. Twenty-four hours. Major credit cards.

The Pizza Factory, Taft Ave. in Wilder; 295-6995. Inexpensive to moderate. Take-out only. New York-style pizza of premium quality. Delivery within seven miles. No credit cards, checks accepted.

The Polka Dot Restaurant, Main St.; 295-9722. Inexpensive. Small diner-type eatery, booths and counter. Over a hundred years old, features good hearty food, informal. Good jukebox.

Than Wheeler's Coach's Corner, downstairs, next to Hotel Coolidge, Main St.; 295-9717. Inexpensive to moderate. Sports-oriented pub and lounge. Informal. Wide-screen TV stays tuned to sporting events. Lunch and dinner seven days. Reservations not necessary.

The Whole Do-nut, Rte. 4 south Junction Marketplace; 296-2606. Inexpensive. Fresh baked doughnuts, muffins, cookies, and deli fare — hearty sandwiches, hot dogs, salad platters, soups, and chili. Eat-in or take-out.

WOODSTOCK

Bentley's, 3 Elm St.; 457-3232. Inexpensive to moderate. Lunch, dinner, and Sunday brunch in multilevel setting filled with Victorian furniture, potted plants, and fringed lamps. Very good food, burgers, imaginative salads, and soups to full meals. Full bar. Major credit cards.

Cole Farm Restaurant, Rte. 4; 672-3419. Inexpensive. Homey old-fashioned place, good plain food, ample portions, specially priced children's plates. Informal, counter and booths. Major credit cards.

The Deli at Woodstock East, Rte. 4; 457-1062. Inexpensive. Informal eating place in big shingle-style building. Eat-in or take-out. Breakfast, lunch, dinner. Eat on deck or inside. Sandwiches, daily hot soups and specials, salads, and deli fare. Good place to take the kids for early supper or put together a picnic. Beer and wine available.

Kedron Valley Inn, Rte. 106, South Woodstock; 457-1473. Moderate to expensive. Comfortable country inn with noted cuisine. Special occasion holiday brunches, otherwise dinner only. Outdoor candlelight dining on screened terrace in summer. Informal, casual dress. Major credit cards.

Lincoln Inn at the Covered Bridge, Rte. 4; 457-3312. Country breakfast, dinner, and Sunday brunch. Fireside dining, continental specialties. Full bar. Reservations recommended. Major credit cards.

Mountain Creamery, Central St.; 457-1715. Inexpensive. Breakfast, sandwiches, homemade soups, salads, and specials. Call ahead for take-out. Ice-cream cones.

The Prince and the Pauper, Elm St. next to historic Dana House; 457-1818. Moderate to expensive. Fine dining in charming, intimate surroundings, recognized in national magazines. Dinner only. Reservations recommended. Mastercard and Visa.

Rumble Seat Rathskeller, Rte. 4; 457-3609. Moderate. Patio dining, seasonal. Several comfortable small dining rooms. Dinner only. European style. Informal. Major credit cards.

The Sports Center, Rte. 106 south; 457-1160. Moderate. Luncheon only. Casual dress. Favorite with locals, open to the public. Delicious sandwiches, salads, full bar. Major credit cards.

Spooner's, Sunset Farms Barn, Rte. 4; 457-4022. Inexpensive to moderate. Chiefly steaks and seafood, well prepared. Excellent salad bar and special low-priced children's menu. Full bar. Lunch and dinner. Informal. Major credit cards.

The Village Butcher, Elm St.; 457-1255. Inexpensive. Take-out only. Great place to put together a picnic. Daily hot specials, sandwiches, salads, brownies, pies to go.

The Village Inn, 41 Pleasant St.; 457-1255. Moderate. Comfortable and elegant dining room, excellent New England fare. Specializing in fresh Vermont turkey, rack of lamb, fresh seafood. Casual dress, full bar, wine. Major credit cards.

Woodstock Country Club, Rte. 106 south at the Golf Course and Ski Touring Center; 457-2114. Fireside lounge and restaurant, lunches only. Casual dress, open to the public. Major credit cards.

Woodstock Inn, 14 The Green; 457-1100. Dining Room. Expensive. Breakfast daily, Sunday brunch. No lunches. Dinner (à la carte). Quiet, formal but comfortable with live piano music, friendly uniformed staff, fresh flowers, very good food. Jackets required for men, anything but blue jeans for ladies. An older three-piece suit and Hermes scarves crowd. Reservations recommended. (If you are not an inn guest, you must give a credit card number to reserve.) Major credit cards. **Eagle Café.** Inexpensive to moderate. Informal dress. Lunch and light lunch for afternoon. Dinner daily. Specially priced "Early Eagle" served 5:30 to 6:30. Good for families as well as concert and playgoers. No reservations. Major credit cards.

Entertainment

Music and Stage

Note: There are dramatic, dance, or musical events in nearby Hanover, New Hampshire, at Dartmouth College's Hopkins Center most weekends when school is in session. Check entertainment pages in local newspapers for listings.

WHITE RIVER JUNCTION

Cashie's at the Coolidge Hotel; 295-3118. Live music on weekends; bands, entertainment, jazz, folk, soft pop.

The Connection Lounge, Holiday Inn, near intersection of I-89 and I-91; 295-7537. Top 40 bands, dancing.

Howard Johnson's, near intersection of I-89 and I-91; 295-3015. Entertainment in lounge.

River City Arts, The Briggs Opera House in the Coolidge Hotel, the Arts Council for the Upper Valley Region; 296-2033. Call or write for information, schedule.

White River Theatre Festival, Briggs Opera House, Hotel Coolidge; 296-2505. Resident, professional repertory theater company. Year-round.

WOODSTOCK

Brown Bag Concerts, Woodstock Library lawn. Thursdays at noon, music, storytelling. Summer.

New Woolhouse Players, Woodstock Recreation Center, Rte. 4; 457-1502. Amateur theater group. Dramatic productions year-round. Stone theater west of the village.

Pentangle Council on the Arts, Central St.; 457-3981. Concerts, plays, film series. Summer outdoor picnic concerts. Winter, coffee house concerts. Street dances. Watch bulletin boards.

Nightlife

WHITE RIVER JUNCTION

Bingo, Mondays, Elks Lodge, Main St., Rte. 4, Hartford. Tuesdays, Hartford VFW, Main St. (behind legion hall), White River Junction. Year-round, no phone.

WOODSTOCK

Bentley's, Elm St.; 457-3232. Live entertainment, dancing.

Bingo, Legion House, Central St.; 7:30 Monday night.

Duplicate Bridge, Parish Hall, St. James Episcopal Church, end of the Green. ACBL sanctioned. Wednesday nights, 7:30, year-round. Bring a partner.

Movies

Town Hall Theatre, Woodstock Town Hall, Woodstock; 457-2620 for schedule.

Museums and Historical Sites

BRIDGEWATER

Bridgewater Mill, Rte. 4. Historic woolen mill, now a shopping mall. Equipment once used in the mill displayed on all floors.

HARTLAND

Hartland has two covered bridges, Martin's Mill over Lull's Brook and Willard Bridge over the Ottauquechee River.

Sculptures at rest areas off Interstate 91 — near exit 7 southbound (Vermont Danby marble, 9 feet × 4 feet × 9 feet, by German-born Herbert Baumann), near exit 12 northbound (Vermont Radio black marble, 4 feet 6 inches × 5 feet 6 inches × 8 feet 6 inches, by Tokyo-born Minoru Niizuma).

PLYMOUTH

Camp Plymouth State Park, east bank of Lake Echo; 228-2025. Old Crown
Military Rd. ran through this area. Site of revolutionary war encampment in 1777.
Later gold discovery near here started "Plymouth gold rush" in 1850s. (A permit
is required for recreational dredging or mining; panning is allowed on state land
without a permit.)

Plymouth Notch Historic District, birthplace of Calvin Coolidge, Rte. 100A;
672-3389. Open daily. Mid-May to mid-October. Visitor's center with lounge, gift
shop, museum, and rest rooms. Fee for guided tour. Visitors may visit the area,
church, garden, general store, and cheese factory free.

POMFRET

Covered bridge in South Pomfret off Stage Rd. (One-half of the 1870 Garfield
Bridge of Hyde Park, Vermont, moved to present site in 1973. The other half is in
Brownsville.)

QUECHEE

Covered Bridge, Waterman Hill Rd. (1970 reproduction. Stringer type.)

Marshland Farms (now an inn) built in 1793, Clubhouse Rd. Home of Vermont's
first lieutenant governor.

Quechee Gorge. "Vermont's Grand Canyon" 165 feet deep at Rte. 4 bridge. Free
maps at nearby information booth, open in summer.

Simon Pearce, Downer's Mill, Main St., Quechee; 295-1470. Free. Watch glass being melted, gathered, blown, and formed by teams of craftsmen at ground level or
from upper balcony. Also hydroelectric turbines that use the falls here to produce
electricity. Huge windows overlook the falls, scenic in all seasons.

Theron Boyd House, Hillside Rd., Quechee. Old 12-room Vermont farmhouse,
virtually unchanged (no water, electricity) since it was built in 1797. Center
chimney. Twelve-over-12 windows with original panes. Surrounded by modern
development, it was saved by a lucky turn of events, now belongs to the state.
Fund-raising to develop the site underway. Just off River Rd. in Quechee. From
Quechee Village, take Main St. past the Quechee Club. At Hillside Rd. turn
right. Boyd house on the right.

WHITE RIVER JUNCTION

Lyman Park (in back of Hartford Town Hall on Bridge St.). Open dawn to dusk.
Large sheltered grassy area with picnic tables. No alcoholic beverages permitted.
Historic marker at site of Indian encampment with captives after 1760 raid on
Deerfield, Massachusetts. Junction of the White River with the Connecticut.

"Old 494." Retired steam locomotive. Centerpiece of downtown plaza in White
River Junction.

WILDER

Montshire Museum of Science is located in Norwich just north of Wilder;
649-2200. Admission charge. Take Rte. 5 north, turn right at traffic light. Museum
to the right next turn.

Wilder Dam Visitor Center, off Passumpsic Ave. in Wilder. Free. Open daily,
Memorial Day through Columbus Day weekend. Exhibits on local history,
salmon, energy conservation. Tours. Free interactive video games.

WOODSTOCK

Billings Farm and Museum, Rte. 12; 457-2355. Seasonal, June–October. Admission fee. Special rates for families, groups. Historic working farm with extensive
exhibits and program on New England rural life. Meticulously restored farm
manager's house furnished in style of the last century. Frequent special events
feature rural skills: children's games, rug making, quilting.

Covered bridges. Woodstock has three — the Middle Covered Bridge (1869, town
lattice type) just off the green; the Lincoln Covered Bridge (1865, Pratt arch type)
on Rte. 4, west of the village; and the Taftsville Bridge (1836, Multiple Kingspost
and Queenspost) on Rte. 4, Taftsville.

DAR House, south side of the green. Not open to the public. Built in 1807 for unicameral Vermont legislature that met in Woodstock that year.

Dana House, The Woodstock Historical Society, 26 Elm St.; 457-1822. Gracious old mansion furnished with Woodstock antiques. Especially rich costume collection. Excellent guides, changing exhibits, programs, events. Herb garden. Admission charged. Museum shop seasonal.

First Ski Tow in the U.S. Historical marker at Gilbert Meadow site, Rte. 12, about three miles north of town.

Green Mountain Perkins Academy, Rte. 106, South Woodstock. Historic school founded in 1848, restored interior. Open Saturday afternoons, July and August. Call Kedron Inn, 457-1473, to arrange tour at other times. Free.

Otis Skinner Commemorative Plaque, Universalist-Unitarian Church, Rte. 4. Terra-cotta plaque in memory of actor Otis Skinner by American sculptor Paul Manship. (If church is locked, ask in minister's residence next door.)

Tours of Historic Woodstock Village. Information booth on the green. Summer only. Fee.

Vermont Institute of Natural Science (VINS), Church Hill Rd.; 457-2779. Statewide organization devoted to study of nature and the environment. Seventy-seven-acre nature preserve with self-guided trails. Frequent programs open to the public; bird and fern recognition walks, travel lectures. Excellent library. Nature gift shop in the visitor's center. Major wildlife art show every fall. (No admission charge.)

The Vermont Raptor Center, on grounds of VINS; 457-2779. Administered by VINS. More than 40 live birds in aviary enclosures. Falcons, owls, eagles that have been injured and cannot be released to the wild. Fascinating look at elusive birds of prey many will never see in the wild. Admission charged.

Norman Williams Public Library, on the green; 457-2295. Red stone building with arched facade overlooking the green. Children's room with lounges, dollhouse, toys. Lots of magazines, newspapers, comfortable sofas. Free paperbacks if you've nothing to read. Japanese articles and local imprints exhibited downstairs.

Woodstock Post Office. Mural by Bernadine Custer, *The Cycle of Development of Woodstock* (1940). Portraits include Woodstock natives Hosea Ballou, Jacob Collamer, and John Cotton Dana.

Seasonal Events

BARNARD
Oyster Stew supper at East Barnard Grange. October.

BRIDGEWATER
Outdoor lobster dinner, recreation field. August.

PLYMOUTH
Fourth of July, Calvin Coolidge Birthday. Memorial ceremony at family cemetery. Plymouth Notch.

POMFRET
Harvest dinners. October.

Pick-your-own strawberries, blueberries, apples. Moore's Orchards, North Pomfret.

Ski races at Suicide Six; 457-1666. Nastar. "Bunny Bertram," "Ironman (and Woman)." Call for dates, times.

Torchlight ski parade followed by dance at Suicide Six Ski Area. February.

QUECHEE
Balloon Festival, Quechee green. Annual, three days, mid-June. Colorful balloon lift-offs at dawn and dusk, music, entertainment, juried crafts fair. Balloon rides. Admission charged. Information, 295-7900 or Quechee Chamber of Commerce, Box 804, Quechee, 05054.

New England Open Golf Tournament and Pro-Am. Mid-September, Quechee Lakes Golf courses; 295-6245 or 295-9356.

Polo, Quechee Polo Grounds, Dewey's Mill Rd. Home games Saturdays, June through Labor Day weekend. Check posters around town for schedule. Admission charged.

Scottish Festival, Quechee Polo Grounds, Dewey's Mill Rd.; 295-5351. Annual, late August. Full day of activities as the clans gather. Music, sheep dog trials, traditional events, dancing, and workshops. Admission charged.

WOODSTOCK

Antiques Show, high school grounds, Rte. 4. Benefit Children's Aid Society. Late July.

Apples and Crafts Fair, Bailey's Meadow east of Woodstock. Columbus Day weekend. Outdoor crafts fair in tents. Entertainment, food. Benefits The Learning Clinic.

Green Mountain Horse Association (GMHA), Rte. 106, South Woodstock. May through end of September. Dressage shows, driving events, special breed shows. Observers welcome, most events free. Special "Evening of Jazz and Dressage" (admission charged) in July. Write for complete schedule.

Norman Williams Public Library Book Sale, on the green; 457-2295. July. Thousands of donated books. Special auction of rare volumes.

Pentangle Summer Festival, Woodstock High School grounds, west of town on Rte. 4, Pentangle; 457-3981. Weekend nearest July Fourth. Juried crafts show, music, performers. Admission charged. Fireworks.

VINS Wildlife Art Exhibit, at the Vermont Institute of Natural Science, Church Hill Rd.; 457-2779. Opens last week in September. Juried. Work by dozens of nationally prominent professional artists. Etchings, decoys, large outdoor sculptures. All works for sale. Benefits VINS. No admission charge.

Woodstock Wassail Week, c/o Woodstock Chamber of Commerce, 18 Central St.; 457-3555 for schedule and information. Early December. Week of special holiday activities; costumed horses and riders, carriages parade through town. Concerts, hand bell choir, Yule log, special dinners, wassail cotillion.

Children's Activities

BARNARD
Silver Lake State Park. Swimming, boat rental. School playground and tennis court.

BRIDGEWATER
Bridgewater Recreation Field, off Rte. 4, west of the mill. Ball field, tennis court. Summer programs.

HARTFORD
Swimming, Hartford Recreation Department; 295-9353. Seasonal. Fee.

Summer story hours at Gates Library, Main St., West Hartford; 295-7992.

Tubing on White River. Tubes at West Hartford Country Store, Rte. 14, West Hartford; 295-5590.

PLYMOUTH
Coolidge Birthplace, Rte. 100A; 672-3389. Charge for tour.

Hawk Inn and Mountain Resort, Rte. 100; 672-3811. Hiking and nature trails. Indoor pool (fee for nonguests). Boat rentals at Lake Amherst. Sailboards, canoes, paddleboats.

Swimming, Camp Plymouth State Park, east side of Echo Lake.

POMFRET
Free J-bar for beginner skiers, Suicide Six Ski Area, Barnard Rd.; 457-1666.

Pick your own berries, apples (in season) at Moore's Orchards, North Pomfret.

QUECHEE

Bike rentals, canoe rentals, fly-fishing lessons, Marshland Farms, Clubhouse Rd.; 295-3133.

Cross-country skiing, snowshoeing, Wilderness Trails, Marshland Farms, Clubhouse Rd.; 295-3133.

Timber Village, Rte. 4; 295-1550. Miniature steam train rides.

WHITE RIVER JUNCTION

Astro Bowl, Astro Plaza, Sykes Ave.; 296-2442. Bowling, "Bumper Bowling" for little ones. Flippers and Joysticks Video Arcade.

WILDER

Montshire Museum of Science is a few miles away up Rte. 5 in Norwich and is well worth a detour. Nature walks, exhibits, programs; 649-2200.

Wilder Dam and Visitor Center. Tour power generator dam and visitor center. Free. Seasonal.

WOODSTOCK

Billings Farm and Museum, Rte. 12; 457-2355. Live animals, wagon rides, exhibits. Admission charged. Children's Day. Games, music, crafts. Late August.

Kedron Valley Stables, Rte. 106, South Woodstock; 457-1480. Hayrides in summer, sleigh rides in winter. Trail rides.

Vermont Institute of Natural Science, up Church Hill Rd.; 457-2779. Self-guided nature trail (free). Raptor Center. Large birds in aviaries. Admission charged. Year-round.

Shops

Art Galleries

BRIDGEWATER

The Print Mint, Bridgewater Mill; 672-3461. Posters, old and new reproductions.

EAST BARNARD

Tontine Press; 763-7092. Gallery and workshops of woodcut artist Sabra Field. Call for times, directions.

HARTLAND

Catalpa Gallery, Rte. 5 (five miles south of Howard Johnson's in White River Junction); 295-5495. Hard-stone sculpture, translucent color photography. Seasonal, April – December.

North Hartland Arts, Rte. 5 (five miles south of Howard Johnson's in White River Junction); 295-7354. Gallery shows work of six artists in many media. Tuesday–Sunday, 12 to 6 or by appointment. Summer workshops, demonstrations.

WOODSTOCK

Caulfield Gallery, 42 Central St.; 457-1472. Gallery devoted to oil and watercolor works by Robert O. Caulfield. Noted for New England landscapes.

Gallery on the Green; 457-4956. Original art, limited-edition prints, decoys. Custom framing. Shipping.

Gallery 2, 43 Central St.; 457-1171. Fine art by Vermont artists. Also, 6 Elm St. has folk arts and prints. Vermont artists, traditional and contemporary. Sculpture, signed art glass.

Northwind Artisan's Gallery, 81 Central St.; 457-4587. Traditional fine workmanship, unusual contemporary crafts, including leather bindings. New England artisans. From small jewelry and ceramics to large wall hangings.

Woodstock Gallery of Art, Gallery Pl., Rte. 4; 457-1900. Large selection of posters, photography, works by local artists. Changing exhibits.

Craft and Specialty Stores

BRIDGEWATER

Bridgewater Mill Marketplace, Rte. 4; 672-3332. Complex of crafts and other shops in restored mill. Many dealers represented by small display booths in open markets on each floor — Rathdowney of Bethel (herbs, potpourri), Weston Bowl Mill (discount wood articles), "The Knitting Lady" (custom-made hats and sweaters), Porcupine Graphix (tees) among them. Sales handled at center desk.

Green Mountain Basket Company, first floor of Mill Marketplace, Rte. 4; 672-3248. Baskets and gifts.

Joyful Heart Boutique, second floor of Mill Marketplace, Rte. 4; 672-5062. Open market of small shops selling women's specialty clothing.

Meadow Mouse, second floor of Mill Marketplace, Rte. 4; 672-5062. Arts and crafts supplies.

Sun of the Heart Bookstore, second floor of Mill Marketplace, Rte. 4; 672-5151. Unusual books, cassettes, Vermont lore, nature, psychology, healing. Tapes, records by Vermont performers.

Vermont Clock Craft, second floor of Mill Marketplace, Rte. 4; 672-3456. Custom-made clocks in hardwood cases.

Vermont Country Gourmet, second floor of Mill Marketplace, Rte. 4; 672-3870. Vermont syrup, cheese, condiments. Gift packs.

QUECHEE

Economy Store, Rte. 4; 295-1881. Inexpensive clothing, scarves, accessories. Here's where you pick up a cheapo sweatshirt when you're freezing in summer or replacement gloves when you've lost one. Lots of T-shirts of the souvenir variety.

Ewe Knit, Waterman Hill Rd., Quechee Village; 295-3400. Small shop, open year-round. Specializes in Vermont wools, no acrylic yarns except Susan Bates's baby yarn. Needles, pattern books, and other essentials for knitters. Custom sweaters. Four shops at intersection of Rte. 4 and Clubhouse Rd.

The Fat Hat Factory, at Tucker Mountain Studios, Clubhouse Rd. and Rte. 4; 296-6646. Unique, informal clothing designed and made on the premises. Soft packable pieces in lush colors, everything goes with everything else.

Flowering Cactus, Waterman Pl., Rte. 4; 296-6611. Full-service florist plus unusual plants.

Gourmet Vermont, at Tucker Mountain Studios, intersection of Clubhouse Rd. and Rte. 4; 296-6656. Vermont food specialties, mustards, syrup, jams. Seasonal (closed end of October to May).

Laro's Farm Stand, Rte. 4 between Quechee and Woodstock; 457-3641. Seasonal, closed cold weather. Fresh produce and plants. Planters, window boxes, porch and patio furniture, Vermont foods. Syrups, honey, cheese, jams. Shipping.

Miranda Thomas Pottery at the Red House, Quechee-Hartland Road; 295-1265. Call for hours and directions. Thomas designs the pottery sold at Simon Pearce. You can watch her complete pieces in her home studio.

Quechee Books, Rte. 4 at I-89 entrance; 295-1681. More than 25,000 books, specializing in history, but anything might be found here.

Quechee Gorge Gifts and Sportswear, Rte. 4; 295-2075. Seasonal, closed cold weather. Clothing for men and women, Vermont foods.

Scotland by the Yard, Rte. 4; 295-5351. Large shop specializing in the fine Scottish imports. Sweaters, tweed jackets, caps, kilts, and neckties in authentic colors; ribbons and tartan materials by the yard. Silver jewelry, books, records, flags. Custom orders for kilts.

Simon Pearce, Main St., Quechee Village; 295-2711. Hugh array of glass and pottery made on the premises (seconds sometimes available at discount) as well as imported wares, lamps, table linens. Imported clothing from Ireland, Australia. Blankets and scarves in melting colors. A shop with mellow country furniture, pale woods, some hand-painted.

The Shop on Main Street, in the Abel Barron and Breakfast, Main St., Quechee Village; 295-1337. Fine art, jewelry, and crafts.

Sugar Pine Farm, Rte. 4; 295-1266. Folk art, American country crafts. Wonderful shop filled with old or "looks old" country accessories. Lambs, pigs, hearts, antique Santas. Accessories, soaps, hand-dipped candles. Sugar Pine has been featured in several national magazines.

Timber Village, Rte. 4; 295-1550. Enormous barn and outbuildings. More than 300 antique dealers, regional crafts outlet, country store, restaurant, rides.

Truffles, Waterman Pl., Rte. 4; 295-1866. Candy shop and gift boutique.

Upper Valley Collection, in the Tucker Mountain Studios complex, intersection of Clubhouse Rd. and Rte. 4; 295-1613. Seasonal. Quilts and handcrafts.

Wear On Earth, Waterman Pl., Rte. 4; 296-6830. Contemporary women's clothing, accessories.

WHITE RIVER JUNCTION

Cloverleaf Jewelry and Gifts (also Vermont State Liquor Store), Rte. 5; 295-2370. Souvenirs, Vermont products.

Coolidge Corner Gifts, in the Howard Johnson complex, Routes. I-91 and I-89; 296-2339. Gift baskets, porcelain dolls, souvenirs.

Forever Yours, 24 South Main St. (Hotel Coolidge); 296-2336. Cards, gifts, candy, Vermont souvenirs.

25,000 Gifts and Woolens, junction Rtes. 4 and 5; 295-3575. Local landmark, knickknacks, maple products. Seasonal, closed Christmas until mid-May.

Upper Valley Food Co-op, 7 South Main St.; 295-5804. Nuts, dried fruits, jams, jellies, T-shirts, candles. Vermont products.

WOODSTOCK

Aubergine, 1 Elm St. (downstairs); 457-1340. Kitchenwares and gourmet cooking supplies.

Christmas Treasures, 71 Central St.; 457-4054. Year-round. Everything for Christmas. Gifts.

The Clover Gift Shop, 10 Elm St.; 457-2527. Gifts, cards, jewelry, collector dolls.

Deertan Leather, Elm St.; 457-2146. Leather clothing and accessories.

Economy Store, 37 Central St.; 457-1327. A town institution, good-looking inexpensive clothing, large selection Vermont shirts, belts, scarves.

18 Carrots, 47 Pleasant St.; 457-2050. Natural foods, books, herbs, and spices.

N. T. Ferro Jewelers, 11 Central St.; 457-1901. Complete jewelry store, gifts, watches, gemstones, on-premise repairs, engraving. Estate jewelry, local charms.

Footprints, 29 Central St.; 457-3395. Light-hearted, informal separates, jewelry, scarves. Fashion shoes.

F. H. Gillingham and Sons, Elm St.; 457-2100 or 1-800-344-6668. Vermont specialty foods, wines, interesting selection house and kitchenwares and gifts. Mail-order catalog.

Jewel Gallerie, 33B Central St. (under Mountain Creamery); 457-4847. Artisan-made jewelry in gold, silver, western and ethnic jewelry.

Kremer & Gallagher, Clothiers, Inc., 24 Elm St.; 457-4255. Upscale weekend wear for men. Trendy, expensive.

Leslie's Loft (upstairs over Recollections), Central St.; 457-3006. Ladies' clothing, offbeat and natural fibers.

The Linen Closet, 55 Central St.; 457-1591. Bath, bed, table linens.

Log Cabin Quilts, 9 Central St.; 457-2725. Large selection contemporary hand-made quilts, pillows. Custom designs and materials.

The Looking Glass, 41 Central St.; 457-3345. Great sweaters, hand-smocked dresses, trendy outfits for fashion-conscious tots. Specializes in Vermont-crafted wear.

Malcolm's, 15 Central St.; 457-3391. Toys, games for all ages from around the world. Cards, kites. Special teddy bears.

Minerva, 61 Central St.; 457-1940. Partnership of eight artisans. Pottery, innovative and attractive handmade sterling jewelry, unusual silky woven clothing.

Morgan-Ballou, Elm St.; 457-1321. Joan and David, Barry Bricken, Joan Vass, and other designer clothing. Distinctive sportswear, unusual sweaters, dressy outfits. Filofax accessories.

Noteworthy Shop, 71 Central St., (upper level; parking and handicapped access up in back of shop off Lincoln St.); no phone as of this writing. Printed and recorded music, compact discs, and tapes.

Patricia's Dollhouse and Miniature World, The Courtyard, 62 Central St. (upstairs); 457-4884. Dolls, dollhouses, miniature materials and fitting to furnish and craft tiny interiors.

Pleasant Street Books, 46 Pleasant St.; 457-4050. Old and rare editions, ephemera, local postcards, baseball cards.

Primrose Lane and Primrose Gardens, Central St.; 457-2570. Two shops, one on either side of the post office. Both sell silk and dried flowers, arrangements, wreaths, baskets, lamps.

Queen Anne's Lace, 20 Central St.; 457-3521. Lingerie, hose, sweaters.

The Red Cupboard, Rte. 4; 457-3722. Vermont-made products, cheese, syrup. Shipping.

Shire Apothecary, 13 Elm St.; 457-2707. Drugstore. Toys, cards, newsstand. Stuffed animals a specialty.

Sugarbush Farm, Rte. 4; 457-1757. Seven Vermont cheeses, smoked cheese, maple syrup.

Town and Country, 16 Central St.; 457-2525. Women's clothing in classic styles. Accessories. Bargain basement.

Unicorn, 15 Central St.; 457-2480. Unusual and imaginative jewelry, crafts, greeting cards, adult toys. Owner a specialist in knives.

Vermont Workshop, 73 Central St.; 457-1400. Three-level shop (parking available on upper level). Antiques, handmades from picture frames to imported mohair blankets. Needlepoint studio — patterned canvas, kits, wool, books, help.

The Whippletree, 4 Central St.; 457-1325. Everything for knitting — wool, directions, hand-knit hats, sweaters for sale. Artist's, philatelic, and sewing supplies.

Woodstock Florist, on the green; 457-4996. Full-service florist specializing in unusual plants, flowers. Containers, dried, and silk flowers. Stained glass.

Woodstock Inn Gift Shop, in the Woodstock Inn; 457-1100. Vermont-made souvenirs, toys, clothing.

Woodstock Pharmacy, Central St.; 457-1306. Drugstore. Magazines, perfumes, cards, souvenirs. Well-stocked toy department in basement.

Woodstock Potters, Mechanic St. (behind Economy Store); 457-1298. Studio workshop. Stoneware, porcelain, and jewelry.

Woodstock Rug Gallery, Rte. 4, Gallery Pl.; 457-1252. Handmade rugs from around the world. Antique rugs a specialty.

Yankee Book Shop, Central St.; 457-2411. Shop crammed with everything from best-sellers to children's storybooks. Vermont books a specialty.

Antiques

BARNARD

The Different Drummer, Rte. 12; 234-9403. Specializing in antique dolls, doll repairs.

QUECHEE

Decklebaum and Creech's Antiques East of Woodstock, Waterman Place on Rte. 4 at blinker lights; no phone as of this writing. Antiques in more than a dozen shops.

Farides' Antiques, Taftsville, Rte. 4; 457-3037. Specializing in oak furniture and stuffed barnyard fowl, chicken, geese, etc., in lifelike poses.

Fraser's Antiques, Taftsville (three miles east of Woodstock on Rte. 4 then .1 mile up Happy Valley Rd. on left); 457-3437. Country antiques and collectibles.

Simon Pearce, Main St.; 295-2711. Country furniture.

Peddler's Attic, Rte. 4; 296-2422. Farm items, country pieces, advertising signs, sleds.

Sugar Pine Farm, Rte. 4; 295-1266. Folk art, quilts, pictures.

Timber Village, Rte. 4 (near Quechee); 295-1550. Antique mall, more than 300 dealers.

WOODSTOCK

Church Street Antiques, 4 Church St.; 457-2628. Porcelains, silver, and furniture.
Country Woodshed, Rte. 12; 457-2490. Country antiques and collectibles.
Recollections, 20 Central St.; 457-2879. Antiques, gifts, and accessories.
Who is Sylvia? 26 Central St.; 457-1110. Large selection period and antique
  clothing; linens, hats, accessories.
Wigran and Barlow, 29 Pleasant St.; 457-2453. Extensive collection fine furniture,
  silver, tableware. Specializing in garden seating, urns, accessories. Seasonal (closed
  December 1 – April 1).
Windsor Galleries, 47 Central St.; 457-1702. Interior design shop, selected fine
  antiques, reproductions. Orders taken for one-of-a-kind hooked rugs.

Discount Outlets

BARNARD

Porcupine Graphix, Rte. 12; 234-9692. Seconds of designer and commercial
  T-shirts printed here.

BRIDGEWATER

Dunham Factory Outlet, first floor of Mill Marketplace, Rte. 4; 672-3566. Sturdy
  shoes at discount prices.
Northern Ski Works, first floor of Mill Marketplace, Rte. 4; 672-3636. "Largest
  selection of sunglasses in Vermont" plus seasonal sportswear.

QUECHEE

Fall River Knitting Mills, at Quechee Gorge; no phone. Sweaters, tees at 40% to
  60% off retail prices.

Sports and Recreation

Note: The following organizations have sports activities throughout the year: Hartford Parks and Recreation, Hartford Town Hall, Bridge St., White River Junction,
  295-9353 (24-hour Recreation Hot Line, 295-3236); Woodstock Recreation Center,
  54 River St., Woodstock, 457-1502. Call for more information.

Biking

QUECHEE

Marshland Farm, Clubhouse Rd.; 295-7620. Bike rentals, ten-speeds, adults' and
  children's sizes. Mountain bikes.

WOODSTOCK

Note: A free Woodstock area cycling map is available at the information booth on
  the green.
Bike Vermont, Box 207, Woodstock, VT 05091; 457-3553. Inn-to-inn bike touring.
  Early May to end of October. Tours start in many areas of the state. Equipment
  rentals.
The Cyclery, Rte. 4; 457-3377. Bike and helmet sales, rentals, repairs. Maps and
  guides, accessories, racks, and trailers. Open year-round.

Golf

QUECHEE

Two 18-hole courses, Clubhouse Rd. For Quechee Lakes' members, guests, and
  guests at Marshland Farms. Not open to the public.

WOODSTOCK

Woodstock Country Club, Rte. 106 south; 457-2112. Championship Robert Trent Jones designed. Eighteen holes, par 69, 6,001 yards. Pro shop, lessons, repairs, rentals. Driving range, practice green. Open to the public. Dress code.

Horseback Riding

PLYMOUTH

Hawk Mountain Inn and Resort, Rte. 100; 672-3811. Trail rides.

QUECHEE

Quechee Equestrian Centre at Westminster Meadows. One and a half miles past Quechee Village on Quechee-West Hartford Rd. (with Simon Pearce on your left, take Main St. in Quechee Village and where this road bears left you keep straight ahead up the hill); 296-6000. Visitors welcome. Lessons, clinics, boarding. Accommodations for 36 horses. Tack shop. Indoor arena.

SOUTH WOODSTOCK

Green Mountain Horse Association (GMHA), Rte. 106 south; 457-1509. Seasonal. Information on horse-related events in area. Trail information.
High Brook Horse and Harness, Rte. 106 south (near GMHA); 457-4677. Lessons, boarding, tack shop.
Kedron Valley Stables, Rte. 106; 457-1480. Trail riding, hay and sleigh rides. Lessons.

WOODSTOCK

Rivendell Stables, River Rd.; 457-3088. Lessons and boarding.

Sporting Goods Services

BRIDGEWATER

Vermont Ski and Sport, first floor of Mill Marketplace, Rte. 4; 672-3636. Ski equipment sales and rental.

HARTLAND

North Country Flies; 436-3211. Evenings and weekends. Handmade streamers, wet, dry, and other varieties of flies by Lee Hiscock who ties for L. L. Bean among others. Extremely small sizes a specialty. Custom orders welcome.
Ottauquechee Tackle Shop, Rte. 5; 295-5539. Fishing tackle including ice-fishing gear. Archery equipment and supplies, licenses.

QUECHEE

Barrows Point Trading Company; 295-1050. Every conceivable need for area hunting and fishing, including licenses and snowshoes. Archery supplies and information a specialty.
Henderson's Ski Rental Systems, Rte. 4; 295-1973. Equipment for Alpine and cross-country, sales and rentals. Tune-ups, repairs, and assorted gear.
Ski Shop, Quechee Club Base Lodge, River Rd.; 295-1000. Alpine and cross-country rentals. Clothing and gear. Ski tuning, repairs.
Wilderness Trails, Marshland Farms, Clubhouse Rd.; 295-7620. Bike, canoe, fly-fishing school and equipment in summer. Cross-country ski trails, equipment rental, and sales in winter. Lessons. Full-moon evening ski tours.

POMFRET

Suicide Six Ski Area, Stage Rd. (take Rte. 12 north from Woodstock. Bear right at gas station just outside town); 457-1666. Ski equipment rentals.

WEST HARTFORD

West Hartford Trading Company, Rte. 14 just past metal bridge; 295-5590. Inner tube rentals.

WHITE RIVER JUNCTION

Briggs, Ltd., Main St.; 295-7100. Clothing and equipment for hunting, fishing, camping. Orvis tackle. Guide information.

Norm's Gun Shop, 203 Woodstock Rd. (Rte. 4); 295-3364. Large stock new and used guns, fishing, archery equipment.

WOODSTOCK

Gambol Hill Farm, Rte. 106, South Woodstock; 457-2503. English and contemporary riding gear. "Second Time" shop, used riding clothes.

High Brook Horse and Harness, Rte. 106, South Woodstock; 457-4677. Complete clothing, equipment, books, supplies for all styles riding.

Woodstock Country Club, Pro Shop, Rte. 106 south; 457-2114. Clubs, repairs, clothing, rentals, lessons, driving range.

Woodstock Sports, 30 Central St.; 457-1568. Clothing and equipment for all area sports. Ammo and fishing gear. Ski sales, rental, repair. Snow-board rentals.

Woodstock Sports Center, Tennis Shop, Rte. 106 south; 457-1160. Tennis duds, equipment, rentals, lessons.

Tennis

Note: All town courts are first come, first served. Quechee courts are for members and guests only.

BARNARD

Tennis court at elementary school, Rte. 12.

BRIDGEWATER

Tennis court at Recreation Field, Rte. 4.

HARTFORD

Four tennis courts at Hartford High (from intersection Rtes. 5 and 14, take Rte. 5 up hill to end of metal fence. Hebard Ave. Turn left, sign ahead for Hartford High). One at town-owned Clifford Park (entrance off Hartford-Quechee Rd. You can see Clifford Park from Rte. 14 in West Hartford, but access at end of metal bridge over White River at Hartford-Quechee Rd. is blocked. Drive up hill, take first left. Park is between housing development and river).

PLYMOUTH

Tennis court at Echo Lake Inn, Rte. 100, Tyson; 228-8602. Fee.

POMFRET

Court at North Pomfret's Harry Harrington Field. From Woodstock go out Rte. 12 north, right at Texaco, right at Teago store and post office. Follow this road (North Pomfret-West Hartford Rd.), which bends around to the right. Recreation field is on the right about seven miles from Woodstock.

QUECHEE

Tennis courts available only to Quechee members. Pro shop; 295-3929.

WOODSTOCK

Public courts. Four all-weather courts, Vail Field. Rte. 106 south; 457-1502. Open as late as weather permits. Night play Tuesday, Thursday, Saturday until 9:30. Practice area.

Woodstock Sports Center, Rte. 106 south; 457-1160. Ten outdoor courts, two indoor (air-conditioned). Also paddle, squash, and racquetball. Pro shop, lessons. Equipment rentals.

Alpine Ski Areas

BARNARD
Sonnenberg Ski Area, from Rte. 12 turn right at country store, keep left, Sonnenberg is about a mile on the right; 234-9874. Only open weekends and holidays. Two Poma lifts, 11 downhill runs. No snowmaking. Five or six miles of groomed cross-country trails, "unlimited" natural trails. Call ahead, number of skiers each day limited to 100. Fee includes lunch, equipment, lessons, all facilities. Call for information.

POMFRET
Suicide Six, Barnard Rd., South Pomfret; 457-1666, snow phone; 457-1622. Expert to novice. Free J-bar in beginners area. Two double chairs, 18 trails. Snowmaking, lessons, rentals, packages.

QUECHEE
Quechee Lakes Ski Area; 295-3929. Snowmaking. (Only open to landowners, their guests, and guests at Marshland Farms.)

Nordic Ski Areas

BARNARD
Sonnenberg Ski Area; 234-9874. Six miles groomed trails, "unlimited" wilderness trails. Area links with other area trail systems. Number of skiers each day limited to 100. Only open weekends and holidays. Rentals, lessons.

PLYMOUTH
Hawk Inn and Resort, Rte. 100; 672-3811. Twenty-five kilometers groomed trails. Equipment rental. Groomed and wilderness trails. (Also snowshoes rentals and trails.)

QUECHEE
Wilderness Trails Nordic Ski Center, Quechee Inn, Marshland Farms, Dewey's Mill Rd.; 295-7620. Eighteen kilometers; 12 of them groomed. Lessons, equipment, rentals.

WOODSTOCK
Woodstock Ski Touring Center, Woodstock Country Club, Rte. 106 south; 457-2114. Seventy-five kilometers of trails. Golf course, Mt. Peg and Mt. Tom areas. Links with Suicide Six and Skyline Trail. Five-kilometer snowshoe trails. Sales, rentals (including snowshoes), guided picnic tours, lessons, repairs. Warming lounge, showers, dining room.

Fishing

BARNARD
Brook and rainbow trout in local streams.
Silver Lake. Yellow perch, northern pike, largemouth bass.

BRIDGEWATER
Ottauquechee River. Brook, brown, rainbow trout.

HARTFORD
White River. Smallmouth bass, brook trout.
Connecticut River. Brook, rainbow, brown trout. (In Sumner Falls area and tributaries.) Yellow perch, walleye. Pike, pickerel, bass, bullheads, panfish, and other warm-water species in rest of river.

HARTLAND
Brook trout in local streams.

Connecticut River. Brook, rainbow, and brown trout. (In Sumner Falls area and tributaries.) Yellow perch, walleye, northern pike, chain pickerel. Large- and smallmouth bass, bullheads, and panfish in warmer river areas.

North Hartland Dam. Boat ramp. Above dam, trout. In dam, lake bass, trout, panfish.

PLYMOUTH

Amherst and Echo lakes off Rte. 100A. Three boat ramps with parking provided by Vermont Fish and Wildlife along these waters.

Amherst Lake. Rainbow trout, lake trout, smelt, yellow perch, chain pickerel, large- and smallmouth bass, panfish.

Echo Lake. Rainbow trout, lake trout, smelt, yellow perch, chain pickerel, large- and smallmouth bass, panfish.

Woodward Reservoir, Rte. 100. One State and Wildlife boat ramp off Rte. 100 near north end of lake. Rainbow and brown trout, smelt, yellow perch, chain pickerel, large- and smallmouth bass, panfish.

POMFRET

Barnard Brook running through Pomfret from Barnard has brook trout but is posted along much of its length.

QUECHEE

Mill Pond. Ottauquechee River. Bass, panfish.

Ottauquechee River. Brook, rainbow, and brown trout.

Vermont Fly-Fishing School, Marshland Farm, Dewey's Mill Rd.; 295-7620. Seasonal. Equipment rental (equipment furnished free as part of lessons), trips arranged.

TAFTSVILLE

Deep water behind Taftsville Dam, Ottauquechee River. Rainbow trout.

WILDER

New England Power Company Dam Lake (Connecticut River). Perch, walleye, northern pike, chain pickerel, bass, bullheads, panfish. Boat ramp above dam.

WOODSTOCK

Ottauquechee River. Brook, brown trout, and rainbows.

Boating

BARNARD

Silver Lake, boat rentals at Silver Lake State Park; 234-9451. Boat rentals: rowboats, paddleboats, and canoes.

PLYMOUTH

Camp Plymouth State Park; 228-2025. East side of Echo Lake. Rte. 100 south to end of lake, then cross bridge at bottom end of lake, turn left across bridge, look for entrance on left. Boat rentals: paddleboats, canoes, rowboats.

Hawk Inn and Mountain Resort, Salt Ash Marina, Scout Camp Rd. off Rte. 100A; 672-3811. Access from west side Lake Amherst. Paddle- and rowboats, canoes, sailboards, and boats. Lessons. Open to the public. May to October. Dawn to dusk.

Plymouth Village Canoe Rentals, north of intersection of Rte. 100 and Rte. 100A in Plymouth Village; 672-3708.

QUECHEE

Canoe Rental, Marshland Farm, Dewey's Mill Rd.; 295-7620.

Swimming

BARNARD
Silver Lake, grassy area across from country store, State Park nearby (fee); 234-9451. Beach, dressing rooms, toilets, picnic tables.

HARTFORD
Public pool at Hartford High. Open mid-June to Labor Day. Fee. Dressing rooms. (From intersection Rte. 5 and Rte. 14 in Hartford, take Rte. 5 north up steep hill. At end of metal fence on left, turn left, Hebard Ave. Turn left on Hebard, sign ahead on right for Hartford High. Swimming pool is behind building marked "gym."

HARTLAND
North Hartland Dam and Recreation Area. Sign on Rte. 5 going south marks access road. Free. Lawns, restrooms, sandy beach, roped-off area of lake for swimming.

PLYMOUTH
Echo Lake, Camp Plymouth; 228-2025. East side of lake. From Rte. 100 south, cross bridge at bottom of Echo Lake, keep left on other side. Town Rd. 42 leads into campgrounds. Fee. Beach, dressing rooms, concessions.
Echo Lake Inn, Rte. 100; 228-8602. Outdoor pool. Open to the public. Fee.
Hawk Inn and Mountain Resort, Rte. 100; 672-3811. Indoor pool and health club. Open to the public. Fee.

QUECHEE
Ottauquechee River. Use caution, current can be swift. Swimming hole beneath covered bridge in Quechee Village in popular spot. Public parking near bridge, paths lead to water.
Quechee Club (outdoor and indoor pools and private beach at Lake Pinneo only available to landowners and their guests or guests at Marshland Farm).

SOUTH WOODSTOCK
Kedron Valley Inn, Rte. 106; 457-1473. Lake, sand beach, lifeguard. Fee, by day or season.

WHITE RIVER
Many locations, especially along Rte. 14 north. Look for other swimmers. Area near metal bridge over White River at Hartford-Quechee Rd. is popular with local kids.

WOODSTOCK
Ottauquechee River. Stone steps to swimming hole just to the right of northeast end of Elm St. Bridge. No parking nearby, park in village lot and walk over bridge. Unattended.
Recreation Center, Rte. 4. Outdoor pools. Mid-June to Labor Day. Fee. Dressing rooms.
Woodstock Sports Center, Rte. 106 south; 457-1160. Indoor pool, sauna, whirlpool. Year-round. Open to the public. Fee.

Hiking and Nature Trails

Note: The Appalachian Trail runs through Bridgewater, Pomfret, and Hartford. It crosses Rtes. 12 and 14, which are easy access points for hiking a short stretch. North of Woodstock, about four miles on the right, is the beginning of the Dartmouth Outing Club (DOC) section of the trail. DOC is responsible for the next 70 miles of the trail and employs eight students to maintain it.
You can enter the trail here and hike 2.2 miles to Stage Rd. in Pomfret and other side of the ridge. That's about one mile straight up and another mile straight

down. The trail is marked with white blazes. For information call (603) 646-2428. The Teago Store on Stage Rd. in South Pomfret (just before Suicide Six Ski Area) keeps a logbook where hikers can sign in or leave messages.

BARNARD

Hawk's Hill Demonstration Forest, New England Forestry Foundation project, East Barnard. Trail (unmarked) into forest links (250 paces on the right) with Skyline Trail (blazed) to Pomfret. From East Barnard, on road to Barnard, take left fork up hill, keep bearing right. A large sign is on the left just beyond beginning of trail. Forest is one mile from bottom. No vehicles allowed on trails.

BRIDGEWATER

Appalachian Trail runs through Bridgewater near the Barnard line.

For a pleasant hike from Bridgewater Center (two miles north of Rte. 4 just past Junction Country Store), cross bridge at Oak Chapel, bear right across bridge. Dirt road offers woods, meadows, steep climb after about five miles into wild Chateaugay section of Bridgewater/Barnard.

HARTFORD

Hurricane Hill Refuge Area, near Veteran's Administration Hospital, North Hartland Rd., White River Junction; 295-9353 for directions.

HARTLAND

North Hartland Dam and George Perkins Marsh Conservation Area, one mile off Rte. 5, North Hartland. Marked trails. Wildflower checklist available. Hunting permitted.

PLYMOUTH

Camp Plymouth State Park, east side of Echo Lake (take Rte. 100A south to Rte. 100, continue to end of Echo Lake, follow signs); 228-2025. Echo Lake Vista Trail. Nature trail, 1.5 miles, marked.

Coolidge State Park, 4.2 miles south of Rte. 4 off Rte. 100A; 672-3612. Trails in park, maps at office. Open mid-May to mid-October. The Slack Hill Trail is 3.1 miles.

Hawk Inn and Mountain Resort, Rte. 100; 672-3811. Eleven trails, varying levels of difficulty. Guide to nature preserve and trail map available at desk of administration building.

POMFRET

Amity Pond Natural Area (Skyline Trail). Take Rte. 12 north out of Woodstock, bear right at gas station, right at Teago Store to North Pomfret. Round bend to right, then turn left at sign "To I-89 and Sharon." Just before farm with high stone wall on right, turn left, go past Sherburne Farm (on right) about two miles, looking for stone wall on left and blue-blazed trail markers. Sign for Amity Pond Natural Area is yellow, about three inches square and is about eight feet off the ground on a tree. Winter information on cross-country skiing Skyline Trail — John Wiggen, Woodstock Ski Touring Center; 457-2114. Amity Pond Natural Area trail map and brochure available from Vermont Department of Forest and Parks, 103 South Main, Waterbury 05676; 244-8711.

QUECHEE

Bird-watching: Birds abound in area of Dewey's Mill Pond across from Marshland Farms in a waterfowl sanctuary. Riverbanks and gorge especially lively during spring and fall migrations.

Quechee Gorge. One hundred and sixty-five feet deep. Marked trails to river level. Free maps at information booth and at Quechee Gorge State Park nearby. Seasonal. Do not attempt to hike or climb the gorge walls off marked trails. Continuing cost of rescuing stranded climbers has resulted in levy of steep fines for rescue by town of Hartford. Several climbers have been killed here by ignoring marked trails. Quechee Gorge hike is 1.5 miles.

WILDER

Marked nature trails and nature activities at Montshire Museum of Science in Norwich (next town north); 649-2200. From Wilder village, take Rte. 5, go three miles north from Wilder post office on Main St., turn right at traffic light, right again onto Montshire Rd. into Montshire grounds.

WOODSTOCK

Jogging and Mt. Tom Hiking Trails, Woodstock area. Map free at information booth on the green open in summer or at Woodstock Inn desk. Guided walks from inn (free) Tuesday and Friday mornings. Public invited. Call 457-1100 to sign up.

Mt. Tom trails. Mt. Tom lies north of Woodstock Village. From Faulkner Park on Mountain Ave., easy switchback trails modeled on the "Cardiac Walks" at Baden-Baden up to the summit. Other trails lead up from track alongside east side of River St. cemetery. Or drive out Rte. 12, take first road to the left (Prosper Rd.), and pull in at entrance to ski trails (green metal barrier gate) or park along road. Miles of ski trails make pleasant hiking, bird-watching in summer and fall. (Not posted in hunting season.) Reserved for skiing in winter, and hiking on the ski trails is forbidden. Skiers must purchase trail pass at Woodstock Country Club; 457-2114.

Vermont Institute of Natural Science, Church Hill Rd.; 457-2779. Self-guided nature trails through 77-acre preserve. Frequent programs, guided walks.

State Parks

BARNARD

Silver Lake State Park, North Rd.; 234-9451. Thirty-four acres. Forty-three sites, no hookups, flush toilets, hot showers (fee). Picnic tables, playground. Day use with swimming, boat rentals, fishing. Public phone.

PLYMOUTH

Camp Plymouth State Park, east side of Echo Lake; 228-2025. Take Rte. 100A south to Rte. 100, continue to bottom of Echo Lake in Tyson. Cross concrete bridge, one mile to crossroads, turn left, then north one mile. Three hundred acres. Swimming, picnic area, concessions, boat rentals, restrooms. Marked nature trail. Group camping area.

Coolidge State Park, Rte. 100A; 672-3612. Sixty sites, no hookups. Flush toilets, hot showers (fee). Picnic tables. Hiking, trails, snowmobile trails on 16,165 acres.

QUECHEE

Quechee Gorge State Park, Rte. 4 at Quechee Gorge; 295-2990. Thirty sites, no hookups. Flush toilets, hot showers (fee). Hiking trails on 612 acres.

Foliage Vantage Points

BARNARD

Take Rte. 12 to Barnard. Instead of staying on 12, go straight on the North Rd. (Silver Lake will be on your right). Gorgeous mountain vistas.

In Barnard, from Rte. 12, turn between the lake and the general store, follow signs to East Barnard. At East Barnard turn right, and, keeping right, follow road down into Pomfret and Woodstock.

BRIDGEWATER

The entire valley is a blaze of color in the fall the length of Rte. 4.

HARTLAND

Any back road in Hartland is heart-grabbing in fall color. One such road runs up behind Skunk Hollow Tavern in Hartland Four Corners. Follow road into Woodstock. Beautiful views.

POMFRET
At Teago Store in South Pomfret, take the right fork. This winds up into North Pomfret, past orchards, lovely farms, and old buildings.

QUECHEE
At the blinker light on Rte. 4, turn south and drive down Old Hartland/ Quechee Rd. to Hartland Three Corners.

WOODSTOCK
Hike the trail up through Faulkner Park in the village (off Mountain Ave.) and enjoy a panorama from the top of Mt. Tom.
Leave Rte. 4 and go through the covered bridge in Taftsville, take the dirt road back to Woodstock. Comes out on River Rd. and intersects with Rte. 12 at Billings Farm. (This is also a nice hike or bike jaunt.)

Best of Woodstock

Country Inns: Echo Lake Inn, Plymouth; 228-8602. Kedron Valley Inn, South Woodstock; 457-1473.
Resort: The Woodstock Inn and Resort, Woodstock; 457-1100.
Breakfast: Dana's By the Gorge, Rte. 4, Quechee; 295-6066. Blanche and Bill's Pancake House, Rte. 4, Bridgewater; no phone.
Lunch: Simon Pearce Restaurant, The Mill, Main St., Quechee; 295-1470.
Dinner (Moderately priced): AJ's Lounge, Sykes Ave., White River Junction; 295-3071.
Dinner (expensive): The Prince and the Pauper, Elm St., Woodstock; 457-1818, 457-1648.
Entertainment (casual): Look for the names Dick McCormack and Al Alessi (not a team). Regional performers, their talent and wit light up the stage wherever they appear.
Entertainment (stage): The White River Theatre Festival, Briggs Opera House, White River Junction; 295-2813 (professional, year-round). New Woolhouse Players, Woodstock; 457-1502 (amateur group, year-round).
Museum/Historical Sites: Plymouth Notch Historic District, Plymouth; 672-3389. Billings Farm and Museum, Rte. 12, Woodstock. The Montshire Museum of Science, Norwich; 649-2200.
Art Galleries: All the Woodstock galleries offer excellent opportunities to see serious work by regional artists. (See individual listings under Woodstock.)
Craft Specialty Shop: Who Is Sylvia? 26 Central St., Woodstock; 457-1110.
Antique Shops: For quantity, the Antiques Mall on Rte. 4, Timber Village, outside Quechee; 295-1550. For quality, The Antique Center at Hartland, Rte. 5, Hartland; 295-2441.
Discount Outlets: When available, "Seconds" at Simon Pearce's Quechee shop; 295-2711. Porcupine Graphix in Barnard for cheap designer T-shirts.
Public Golf Course: Woodstock Country Club, Rte. 106, South Woodstock; 457-1160.
Public Tennis Courts: Woodstock Sports Center, Rte. 106, South Woodstock; 457-1160.
Hiking or Nature Trail: Hawk Inn and Mountain Resort, Rte. 100, Plymouth; 672-3811.
Camping: Silver Lake State Park, Barnard; 234-9451. Coolidge State Park, Plymouth; 672-3612.
Children's Activities: Summer: Wading or tubing in any of the area's lakes and streams. Winter: Montshire Museum in nearby Norwich; 649-2200.
Farm Stand: Laro's, Rte. 4, Quechee.
Ice Cream: The White Cottage, Rte. 4 west of Village, Woodstock.
Foliage Vantage Points: The North Rd., Barnard. Top of Mt. Tom, Woodstock. Quechee Gorge.
Ski Area (Alpine): Suicide Six, Barnard Rd., South Pomfret; 457-1666, snow phone; 457-1622.
Ski Area (Nordic): Cross-Country Ski Touring Center at Woodstock Country Club, Rte. 106 south; 457-2114.

The Windsor/Ludlow Area

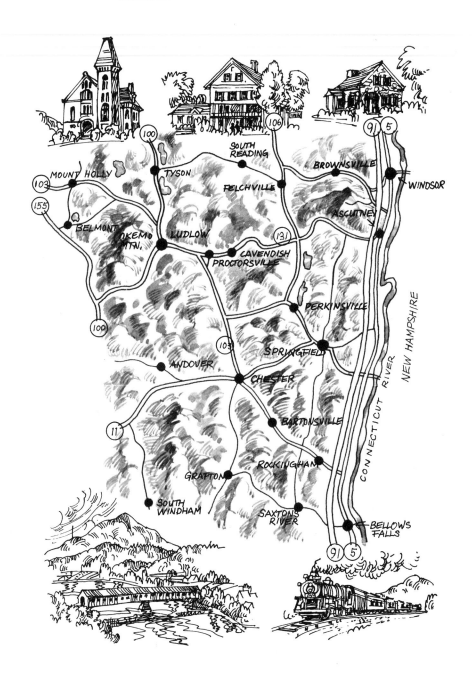

Viewpoints

by JO-ANNE MACKENZIE

If Vermont history is what interests you, mark Windsor in red on your itinerary. Known as "the birthplace of Vermont," Windsor is bursting with early Vermont history, and the village itself, a National Historic District, boasts many fine examples of both eighteenth- and nineteenth-century architecture.

The Ascutney Mountain Resort in nearby Brownsville offers visitors year-round recreational opportunities, and two state parks provide plenty of hiking, camping, fishing, and boating.

Windsor is only four miles off I-91; take exit 8. You'll come into town on Route 5 and will see Mount Ascutney towering some 3,144 feet above you. If you take the Back Mountain Road one mile out, you'll come to the stone caretaker's house at the entrance to this mountain park, established in 1935 and covering nearly 2,000 acres.

The Civilian Conservation Corps built a two-lane, paved road nearly to the summit of the mountain in the 1930s. Stop at the parking overlook halfway up for some great views. The road leads almost to the summit, and there's a short hiking trail from the parking area to the top of the mountain. Stop for a picnic lunch at the stone shelter, or just go up and eat up the view.

You can camp and picnic in the park and hike as much of the mountain as your legs are up to. There are trails for snowmobiles and cross-country skiers in the snowier months. One popular trail, known as the Windsor Trail, starts out 1.5 miles from the park entrance, farther down Back Mountain Road.

This is a real hike — it will probably take you four hours for the round-trip — and there are some steep sections. From the pasture entrance the trail climbs up, passes a waterfall with lots of ledges for resting those tired calf muscles, then brings you to a frigid, freshwater spring. From the spring you can choose an older branch of the trail and stop in at the log shelter or climb up to Blood Rock, the surface of which is actually white. The two forks rejoin before climbing to the summit.

There are several other well-marked trails to the summit. The first U.S. hiking trail was opened on Mount Ascutney back in 1825. This is a nice way to start your Windsor visit and get a view of the historic area from above before you descend and explore. Some choose to fly off the mountain — quite literally — it's a popular spot for hang gliding enthusiasts.

Historic Windsor

Even before hikers were scaling Mount Ascutney, history was being made down in the village of Windsor. More than 200 years ago, Vermont's constitutional convention was held in Windsor and created the state as an independent republic, changing its name from New Connecticut to Vermont. This historic convention took place in Elijah West's tavern — Vermont's earliest existing building.

Built in 1772, the Constitution House — as it's now known — was moved twice from its original site. A small park on Main Street marks the original site of the building. After the tavern ceased operations in the middle of the nineteenth century, the building was operated as a rooming house. It was moved about 22 years later and housed shops and light-manufacturing operations.

In the early part of the twentieth century an association was formed to protect and preserve the building. Through the efforts of this group, the house was moved once again, this time to its present location at the northern end of Main Street. The association was responsible for the building's restoration and operated it as a tea room and historic site. In the early 1960s, the title was transferred to the state of Vermont.

The building is now the site of a museum, operated by Vermont's Division for Historic Preservation. The permanent collection includes the table around which the convention delegates sat, eighteenth- and nineteenth-century furnishings, paintings, and many other historical items. It was here that Vermont's first constitution was drafted and adopted. That constitution, signed on July 8, 1777, made Vermont the first state to abolish slavery and establish universal suffrage.

Also on Main Street is the historic Windsor House. Flags fly from the two-story porch, supported by six white columns. Built in the nineteenth century as an inn, this restored Greek Revival brick building houses one of Vermont's two State Craft Centers in the former lobby and mezzanine areas.

The work of some of the state's finest artisans is on display in this sales and display gallery setting. Offerings include everything from wooden toys to pieced quilts, from delicate porcelain to beautifully crafted furniture. The building is also home to the offices of Vermont Public Radio and the Windsor Area Chamber of Commerce.

Another fine example of Greek Revival style architecture is Saint Paul's Episcopal Church on Dunham Street. Built in 1821, it is the oldest church still in use in the diocese of Vermont.

Many fine Federal houses line the downtown streets of historic Windsor. The district encompasses nearly 50 significant buildings. The Old South Church on Main Street, chartered in 1768, is a four-columned, white-clapboard building designed by Asher Benjamin.

The Windsor Post Office, also on Main Street, is Italianate in style and was designed by Ammi Young. The post office was established seven years before Vermont was admitted to the Union as the fourteenth state. The present post office and courthouse building, built in 1857, dominates one side of Main Street — the towering brick structure is topped with a golden eagle.

Another historic Windsor structure is of an entirely different ilk. The Windsor-Cornish covered bridge was built in 1866 and its 460 feet span the Connecticut River, connecting Vermont and New Hampshire. The only remaining one of three such covered bridges built across the river, this is now the longest covered bridge in the country.

The two-lane, lattice truss structure was restored in 1989, and a barge was built solely for the restoration process. In the mid-eighteenth-century, travelers going from one state to the other had to cross by ferry. A bridge was built in 1796, and the present bridge replaced that late eighteenth-century structure. The bridge was designated a National Historic Engineering Landmark in 1970.

There is an old superstition that says you should hold your breath whenever you pass through a covered bridge — try doing that when you travel through this one and you may pass out before your tires strike New Hampshire soil. Whether you choose to hold your breath or not, do cross the bridge into Cornish to gear up for some river paddling or bike pedaling.

Recreation and Attractions

North Star Canoe/Bike Rentals is just on the other side of the river and offers rentals and a variety of canoe and bicycle trip packages, some with overnight stays at an inn or campground. They also offer fall hayrides and winter sleigh rides.

Some of North Star's packages include a stay at the Juniper Hill Inn in Windsor. The inn was built around the turn of the century as the private residence of attorney Maxwell Evarts. High above the river, the inn offers 15 tastefully furnished guest rooms, some with fireplaces. Some of the 13 other rooms in this converted Colonial Revival mansion include parlors for relaxing after a day on the river or back roads and a dining room where guests are treated to a full breakfast and dinner.

If you prefer to stay on terra firma and stand on your own two feet, the Windsor Country Club might be the place for you. The nine-hole course is located on Route 5 just north of town. This club was established back in 1921 and offers a clubhouse with a porch for viewing the greens and food and bar service.

If you'd rather take a golf cart apart than ride in one, Windsor has a museum just for you. The American Precision Museum has an extensive collection of hand and machine tools. Located on Main Street in a building designated as a National Historic Landmark, the museum chronicles the importance of tool manufacturing in Windsor's history.

In addition with being credited as the birthplace of Vermont, Windsor is also known as the cradle of the American tool industry. The coffee percolator, sewing machines, the ratchet wrench, hydraulic pump, and glazier points are some examples of what Windsor inventors contributed to modern society.

The Robbins, Kendall, and Lawrence Plant, built in 1846, now houses the tool museum but was formerly an armory and machine shop. The three-story brick structure once bustled with the production of repeating rifles and early Sharps rifles. Windsor produced large quantities of guns and gun parts during both world wars.

Among the museum's collection of typewriters, generators, measuring tools, and steam engines, visitors will find some Thomas Edison tools and Henry Ford products.

Windsor's machine production even went behind prison walls. The Vermont State Prison opened here in 1809, and one enterprising warden set up a hydraulic water pump company inside the walls of the correctional facility. The prison closed several decades ago, but the state still operates a minimum security facility on a working farm outside town.

If you prefer your history in the form of furniture and accessories from centuries past, stroll down Main Street to the Windsor Antiques Market. Housed in a Gothic Revival building that used to be a church, the market offers a wide range of antiques from a number of dealers. Included in the offerings are folk art pieces, military items, early American furnishings, and Orientalia.

If all this history and healthy activity has given you one very healthy appetite, head down Depot Street to the restored 1900 Windsor railroad station. The traditional brick building now houses the Windsor Station Restaurant, serving lunch and dinner in a Victorian atmosphere.

Just across the way, in Depot Square, you'll find the Rib Room, a delicatessen, and a bakery. Up on Main Street, the English Muffin Coffee Shop is a good morning stop and their bakery items are too tempting to pass up.

For extra early risers, the funky Brunch Bar Restaurant — glistening red and chrome — opens up at 5:30 A.M. every weekday. You don't have to miss out if you don't get up with the cows; the restaurant also serves lunch and dinner.

Pie lovers — Italian ones, that is — should check out Pizza Chef on Main Street and Pizza Plus on State Street. The latter also offers a pub. Downstairs from Pizza Plus is The Representations of New England gift shop, with some interesting gifts to choose from.

Walk up a small hill on State Street and take a breather in the small park at Court Square. Benches line the sides of this hillside park, and there's a band-stand for the youngsters to conduct an imaginary orchestra.

There was orchestration of a different kind when Hollywood came to town a few years ago. Chevy Chase and company moved into Windsor for the filming of *Funny Farm*. Some of the footage was shot on 70-acre Mill Pond, and an exception was made to the no-motorboat rule for the starry crew.

The town operates a municipal beach on the pond in the summer months, with lifeguards, and there is access for nonmotorized fishing boats on trailers. Paddle a canoe around the wooded shoreline or tote your rod and try to hook a few brookies or rainbow trout.

A luxurious condominium village has sprouted on one side of the pond and prospective home buyers are enticed with all kinds of recreational opportunities — an Alpine ski area minutes away, cross-country skiing on the premises, swimming, hiking, skating, tennis.

If you are in the mood for tennis and haven't quite made up your mind about purchasing a condo in Windsor, don't despair. The Fairgrounds Recreation Area on Ascutney Street has two public courts, plus a basketball court for a quick game of Horse, fields for a pickup softball scrimmage, and a playground to amuse the smaller members of the party.

Late September is a good time to visit Windsor — the weather is generally cool and crisp, the leaves have begun their annual color show, and Windsor residents turn out in full force for a three-day celebration.

The Windsor Festival is the best kind of fall celebration. There are gastronomic delights that range from a pancake breakfast to snack-as-you-walk fare from street vendors, a parade featuring Windsor school bands, lots of fire engines, and some floats, a pet show, jugglers, games, and an abundance of community spirit.

Windsor really suits everyone — it teems with recreational opportunities for the athletically inclined, has enough museums and historical sites to please any history buff, the architecture of its many fine buildings will fill a photographer's album, and the shops and restaurants will satisfy those who like to spend their vacations buying for themselves or the unlucky ones left at home.

Ascutney Mountain Resort

The Ascutney Mountain Resort lies in the tiny village of Brownsville, a village in West Windsor with a population of less than 800. Brownsville is a few minutes drive out Route 44 from Windsor.

The town this four-season resort calls home first separated from the rest of Windsor in 1814, only to be rejoined in 1816 and separated finally in 1848. West Windsor is the town, Brownsville, the village. But avoid confusion and use Brownsville when talking about the area — it's the only village of any consequence in the town and is home to all municipal activity.

Most people come to Ascutney for the Alpine skiing, but there's plenty to do in the other three seasons as well. The resort is tucked on one side of this 3,144-foot peak, and its buildings are not visible from Route 44.

Drive up the curving road to the resort area and the first thing that will strike you is the New England village atmosphere of the resort buildings. No Swiss chalets here. The exteriors are traditional clapboard and blend in nicely with the surrounding mountainside.

For aerial leaf peeking, hop aboard Ascutney's chair lift in prime foliage season and take a ride to the top of the ski area. Stop there or climb the rest of the way to the mountain's summit. If you time this right, you could take the chair for fall viewing and hit the annual ski sale and swap at the resort.

For hikers who really want to test their stamina, skip the ride and hike up the Brownsville Trail. This trail starts off Route 44 and follows an old quarry road. Ascutney was once home to four granite quarries, but the stone did not prove to withstand the wages of weather well and the quarries were abandoned in the early 1920s. This trail first climbs North Peak and then joins the Windsor Trail for the trek to the summit.

If going downhill is what recreation is all about for you, Ascutney offers more than 30 trails down a 1,530-foot vertical drop. Snowmaking is extensive, covering some 70 percent of the mountain. Skiers travel to the top of the resort via three triple chairs and a double lift. Instruction, equipment sales and rental, and child care are all available at the resort.

Cross-country ski enthusiasts will find everything they need at the Ascutney Nordic Center. The 20 kilometers of trails suit skiers of every ability level, from novice to expert. Nordic ski instruction and rental equipment are available.

Those who prefer Vermont with its mountains green and its road free of ice and snow will still find plenty to do at the Ascutney Mountain Resort in the warmer months. This area of Vermont, bordering the Connecticut River as it does, is a bicyclist's dream — rolling hills, beautiful scenery, and plenty of places to stop for a picnic near the water or a tour of a general store.

Suggested routes are available at the resort's Activities Center when you pick up your rental touring or mountain bicycle. Pedal east toward the river and Route 5 or head up Route 106 north to Woodstock.

Racquet sports fans will enjoy a workout at the resort's Sports and Fitness Center. This relatively new complex offers two racquetball courts and seven outdoor tennis courts. There are also both indoor and outdoor pools, a weight room, and a whirlpool and saunas for relaxing after you test your tendons.

The Ascutney Resort Hotel offers luxurious suites and some 240 hotel rooms for those who wish to stay right on the mountain, and the Ascutney Harvest Inn serves three meals daily. After your meal, stroll over to the second floor of the Windham Building and browse through the Gallery on the Mountain, featuring rotating exhibits of local artists' work.

The resort is certainly the main attraction in Brownsville, but the village itself is very separate from the activities on the mountain. The Brownsville Post Office shares quarters with a hair salon. The Brownsville General Store is a good bet for a cold drink and some local gossip.

The West Windsor Historical Society is headquartered on the second floor of the municipal building and open Saturdays in July and August. Although there are no permanent displays, the museum does offer an interesting thematic approach to its displays. Residents and schoolchildren get involved in building a different display each year. The Historical Society is probably best known for its annual Brownsville Bean Suppers, which draw people from thousands of miles away.

Weathersfield

Weathersfield, just a few minutes south of Windsor on Route 5, was booming in the 1800s — booming and baaing, that is. In 1811, U.S. Consul to Portugal William Jarvis imported some 3,500 merino sheep from Spain to Weathersfield Bow. Thirty years later there were more than 10,000 woolly residents.

Today, Weathersfield is spread out over five separate villages, none of which are particularly busy or noteworthy but all terrific for bicycle touring or leaf peeking.

Attractions

Just minutes off I-91, in the village of Ascutney, is a beautiful state park. Wilgus State Park was established in 1931 on 100 acres of land along the Connecticut. There are campsites, including some with lean-tos, a picnic area and shelter, a children's playground, nature trails, and plenty of fishing opportunities on the river. You can rent a canoe and explore the shoreline or cast your line for some bass, perch, trout, or panfish.

Travelers will find restaurants, stores, motels, and a campground all within minutes off exit 8 on I-91. Those who prefer to travel a bit off the beaten path should explore the villages of Weathersfield Center and Perkinsville.

Weathersfield Center

At the junction of Routes 5 and 131, take Route 131 west. Go under the interstate overpass and continue on for approximately 2.5 miles. Look for a small sign reading Weathersfield Center. Take the left and begin the climb.

This road is a definite pick for foliage season — it climbs up to Weathersfield Center and then descends into Springfield. About three miles off Route 131 you'll find the village of Weathersfield Center. If you're in the area any time from June through October, stop at the Reverend Dan Foster House.

The house's ell was built in 1785, the main house in 1825. First built as the town's first minister's residence, it later served as an inn. During the second half of the nineteenth century, the building was a farmhouse and the Weathersfield Center Post Office. Today the Weathersfield Historical Society operates its museum here. Displays include postal equipment, blacksmith tools, Civil War items, maps, photographs, and local history documents.

Next to the Foster House is the Old Forge, a replica of an earlier blacksmith shop, which now contains a working forge and bellows.

Just across the road is the First Congregational Church of Weathersfield and Meeting House, an imposing brick building with Palladian windows. The original meetinghouse was a wooden structure, built in 1775; the brick building was constructed in 1821.

You can continue on the Weathersfield Center Road into Springfield or turn around and head back down to Route 131. When you get back down to 131, turn left and continue on until the road intersects Route 106, about seven miles.

Perkinsville

Follow Route 106 south to Perkinsville. Before you get into the village itself there is a road to your left, marked Stoughton Pond Road, and it's well worth the detour.

The first thing you'll come to is the Vermont Soapstone Company. This company has been mining soapstone and manufacturing products from it for nearly 150 years. Visitors may tour the mill and browse through the outlet shop. Soapstone griddles are a terrific addition to any kitchen, and a soapstone bed warmer can really come in handy during Vermont's colder months.

Just down the road is the Stoughton Pond Recreation Area — a beautiful spot for swimming, picnicking, boating, or fishing. This 65-acre pond is a good bet for rainbow and brown trout, and there is a boat ramp. The beach is great for kids.

Continue down Stoughton Pond Road, if camping is your thing. The Crown Point Camping Area sits just above Stoughton Pond in a pine plantation. You can rent canoes, rowboats, paddleboats, and bicycles here and explore the water and surrounding countryside. The kids will enjoy the neat playground and the sandy beach.

To explore the village itself, turn back down and get onto Route 106. The small village green is triangular, and the Perkinsville Community Church sits at the base of the triangle. The Perkinsville General Store and Post Office share quarters on one side of the green.

Just past the Weathersfield Elementary School, south of the green, sits the elegant Inn at Weathersfield. This lovely inn was built in the eighteenth century as a stagecoach inn. Today guests can relax on the sweeping veranda or stroll through the English garden. Many of the guest rooms have fireplaces and the decor throughout is charming. If you aren't spending the night, at least go for dinner. The food is highly acclaimed and deservedly so. This is definitely a place to visit.

If you stay on Route 106 you'll come into North Springfield and can opt for a trip to Springfield in one direction, Ludlow in the other.

Ludlow

Ludlow is a combination that works — a major ski area, which is quickly becoming one of the Northeast's favorite family mountains, and a town nestled at the bottom, which has successfully transformed itself from a fading mill town into a four-season destination point.

Easily accessible from metropolitan areas, Ludlow lies on Route 103, along the Black River. Apart from the recreational activities offered on Okemo Mountain, the area boasts a chain of three beautiful lakes, a winery in nearby Proctorsville, cheese and candle factories in neighboring Mount Holly, and plenty of shopping.

Okemo Mountain is an exception among Alpine ski areas in that it is not a real village in itself. There are a few restaurants and condominium units on the mountain, so skiers must come down into Ludlow for shopping, dining, and lodging choices.

History, Recreation

Located in southwestern Windsor County, Ludlow is easily accessible. Most travelers exit I-91 in Rockingham, exit 6, and head north on Route 103. The town sits on the Black River, the source of power for the many mills that once dominated the town. It also lies at the end of the string of so-called Plymouth lakes, the largest of them — Rescue — is in the town of Ludlow, as is tiny Lake Pauline.

The Okemo State Forest, more than 4,500 acres, lies in Mount Holly and Ludlow and was acquired by the state back in the mid-1930s at an amazing price of four dollars an acre. A Civilian Conservation Camp was located there and built the road to the summit of Okemo. It's paved, two lanes wide, and leads to an astonishing view of the valley below. The road ends several hundred feet short of the summit and there are several lookouts on the way up, with room enough to pull over and park. Hike to the summit, a short and easy walk from the end of the road, and picnic atop Vermont's fourth highest peak. Several of Okemo's ski trails cross the summit road.

Back during Civil War days, Ludlow was known not for its recreational facilities but for its textile mills. The Civil War seriously depleted the Northeast's wool supply and led to the development of shoddy mills. Shoddy production was an early form of recycling — wool cloth was reworked into shoddy.

The long, multiwindowed brick textile mill, with its tall clock tower and chimney, still dominates Main Street. After the decline of textile production, many of Ludlow's blue-collar workers were employed by General Electric. The company leased many of the mill buildings and produced aircraft engine parts there for about 25 years.

When General Electric moved out of town in the mid-1970s, the town of Ludlow acquired what could easily have become a hulking, downtown eyesore. Fortunately, an architectural firm bought the property in 1981 and transformed the former mill into an attractive place.

The clock tower and chimney remain, and walkways, decks, and stairways now break up the facade of the huge building. Known as the Mill, the former industrial center now houses luxury condominiums, Arthur's — a good place for breakfast and lunch — and Christopher's, the sports bar and restaurant located in the bottom of the Mill.

The Mill Condominiums offer one-, two-, and three-bedroom units, all with full kitchen, living, and dining areas. They are equipped with telephones, cable TV, and working fireplaces. You can even get free firewood for a cozy evening of relaxation following a day on the slopes. Maid service is also offered, and the decks at the rear of the building overlook the Black River.

The Black River originates from the Plymouth Lake chain, just a little way from the junction of Routes 103 and 100. Then it winds its way along 103, curving along behind the Mill and on into Proctorsville and Cavendish. It is believed to have been named the Black River by Indians, because its banks are often heavily shaded by overhanging trees.

Swimming in the Black River in Ludlow is not especially recommended, but a stream that runs into it, just north of town, is one you don't want to miss. Take Route 103 north, past the junction with Route 100, and turn right at the Ludlow V.F.W. Follow this road to the end; it's the old road that the present Route 103 replaced. It's a short drive and there is a reward at the end. Buttermilk Falls is a natural gorge area with cold, rushing water and slippery rock slides into the pools. It is not a recommended swimming hole for young children.

Kids will be happier at Echo Lake — Lake Rescue does not offer public swimming — or at the town recreation area. Take West Hill Road, off Route 103 in town where it curves near Benson's Garage. A short drive will lead you to the West Hill Recreation Area. Lifeguards are on duty at this swimming pond, complete with bathhouse, and there's a nice picnic area. A small admission fee is charged.

Although you can't swim in Lake Rescue, you can fish there. The state has a public fishing access area on the eastern side of the lake. Take the dirt road off Route 100 past the Red Bridge. Motorboats are permitted on the 180-acre lake, and it's a very popular fishing lake.

Lake Rescue, as well as Echo and Amherst, is under the management of the state's Water Resources Department, which stocks all three lakes every year with rainbow and lake trout. The lake is also known for its perch, pickerel, and large- and smallmouth bass fishing. Fishing for smelt is a popular winter sport on the lake. Remember to buy a fishing license before casting a line — you can get one at the town clerk's office on Depot Street.

You might want to explore the lake region by bicycle — Echo Lake Inn is a favorite with touring groups. Originally built in 1799, the inn was reconstructed in the mid-1800s. Former visitors include Presidents Calvin Coolidge and William

McKinley. The inn offers year-round lodging and dining, tennis, a swimming pool, and a wonderful porch with rocking chairs in which to rest those stretched calf muscles.

Ludlow has another recreation area. On Pond Street you'll find three tennis courts, a skateboard area, swings, ball field, and room for volleyball. Sports equipment may be signed out at the rec center there. Jewell Brook runs along one side, a nice place for a brook hike or just sitting on the bank.

Another popular summer activity is golfing at Fox Run. Just north of town on Fox Lane off Route 103, you'll find a pleasant nine-hole golf course, open to the public. The clubhouse offers lunch during the golfing season.

You may go back to Fox Run in snow season, because they also offer a cross-country touring center, complete with instruction and rentals.

There are several ski rental shops in downtown Ludlow, offering both Alpine and Nordic equipment. Two of them, George Dunnett's Ski Rentals and the Totem Pole Ski Shop, stay open until midnight every Friday to serve lost late arrivals who don't want to waste valuable slope time in the morning.

O-K Ski Rentals, in the Jewell Brook Marketplace, rents only Alpine equipment, but they also rent bicycles in the off-season. Route 100, to the lake area, is a terrific bike route and doesn't require a lot of stamina to complete.

Okemo Mountain

Of course, the real ski center of Ludlow is Okemo Mountain. If you're looking for a ski area with lots of nightlife, forget Okemo. It is most definitely a family mountain, geared to the novice skier but with plenty of trails for intermediates and experts, too.

There are 10 lifts on the mountain, including 2 quad chair lifts and 3 triple chairs. Of the 70 trails, about 50 percent of them are for beginners, 30 percent for intermediate skiers, and 20 percent for expert skiers.

Okemo has been working hard on its snowmaking equipment and can now cover some 95 percent of its terrain with man-made snow. There's a Ski-Wee program, with poma lift, a base lodge nursery, ski school, equipment sales and rentals, and the Sitting Bull Lounge in the base lodge. The Sitting Bull is a bar with typical tavern snacks.

Priority's, a restaurant near the base lodge, completes the food and spirits offerings on the mountain. Priority's is a casual place, offering light meals and entertainment. The entertainment is mellow — a solo guitarist or singing duo or a nightclub routine. There are three condominium clusters on the mountain — the Okemo Trailside units front on Little Satchem trail.

Fireworks, an Easter celebration, and a Spring Spree Bump Contest are a few of the activities sponsored by the mountain. Unlike ski areas like Killington or Stratton, Okemo depends heavily on Ludlow's restaurant, shop, and lodging offerings. In return, Ludlow gets the business from the thousands of skiers who flock to Okemo every winter.

Dadd's, on the access road, is probably the closest you'll come to typical ski mountain dining and entertainment. Dadd's offers a menu featuring burgers and steaks on three floors of a barnlike building and has somewhat of an evening bar scene.

Attractions

Chuckles, at the base of the access road, has live music on weekends and the menu features nightly specials like Italian night, Cajun night, and seafood specials. Summer dining on the deck overlooking the pond in this converted barn is nice, too.

The Sunshine Marketplace, at the foot of Okemo, is home to Nikki's — good pasta and dessert — and Sweet Surrender Bakery. Also in the marketplace are Mountain High Jewelry, specializing in handcrafted gold and silver, and Darwin's Country Store, a good place for Vermont gifts. Or stop at PotteryWorks for stoneware and dried flowers.

Across Route 103 is another collection of businesses in the Pond Meadow Marketplace. Boggles, a bar and restaurant, is a good bet for lunch, dinner, or a drink and snacks. Northern Ski Works is right next door. There is also a drugstore and hardware-variety store in this marketplace.

Just up the road from Pond Meadow is the Ludlow Fire Department. They have an annual auction on the Saturday of Labor Day weekend that is lots of fun. Eat barbecued chicken and bid on a treasure to bring back home.

The older sections of town are south of the access road. The buildings on Main Street are closely packed, many of them connected. Brick is big here, and the buildings often tower three stories in height. There are lots of shops and eateries, all within an easy stroll of one another.

There's a small park, with benches, on the corner of Depot and Main streets, and the Ludlow Police Station and Town Hall are adjacent, on Depot Street. Next door to Town Hall is Depot Street Delicatessen, an inexpensive bet for a good breakfast sandwich or hearty soup and sandwiches for lunch.

Continue up Depot Street, don't bother with the car, and stop in at Pat's Porch — an interesting shop with antiques and prints. There is a reason for the street's name — the Ludlow Railroad Station, a small yellow building, is at the end, just under the stone railroad overpass. Green Mountain Railroad in Bellows Falls offers a fall foliage ride in a vintage passenger train that stops in Ludlow. Passengers may choose to stop off for an hour or so of shopping and eating or continue on with the train up to the summit in Mount Holly.

Depot Street intersects with Pleasant Street, the site of one of the many bed-and-breakfast inns Ludlow has to offer. The Andrie Rose, named for the woman who first opened her home to skiers back in the 1950s, has eight wonderful guest rooms, all complete with either a whirlpool or claw-foot bathtub. Dinner is a five-course affair on Saturday and Sunday evenings, with equally as tasty but less involved meals other nights.

Back on Main Street, shoppers can browse through a quilt shop, antiques, kitchenware, stuffed animals, and dried flowers and baskets. The Main Street Book Stop, selling both new and used books, is a good place to stop and stock up on reading material, be it for an evening by your inn's fireplace or along the banks of the river.

The Black River Inn, Jewel Brook Inn, and the Governor's Inn are all good places to stay. The Governor's Inn is outstanding. This elegant Victorian Main Street house was built in the late nineteenth century by Governor William Wallace Stickney as a wedding gift for his bride. The guest rooms are beautifully furnished, attention is paid to every detail, and the food is extraordinary. The public may dine — gourmet six-course meals are offered — but reservations are a must. The inn also is noted for its sumptuous picnic baskets, packed and ready for you to take on a back-road exploration or lakeside setting.

Ludlow has motels, too — the Inn Towne, the Ludlow Colonial Motel, the Timber Inn Motel, and the Hide-Away. Condominium offerings include the luxurious Birch Landing on Echo Lake, with beach, pool, and tennis, and the Brookhaven, with tennis and saunas.

If you'd like to explore some of the history of the town and its buildings, stop in at the Black River Academy Museum on High Street. The three-story brick building was completed in 1889 and is listed on the National Register of Historic Places. The building's own claim to fame is the fact that President Calvin Coolidge graduated from the academy.

The building served as the town school until 1938 and now houses Coolidge memorabilia, local photographic history, Finnish and Italian cultural exhibits, and a turn-of-the-century schoolroom display. The museum is open from late May through Labor Day.

Ludlow's village green is triangular and sports a lovely gazebo. Band concerts are held on the green on Sunday evenings throughout the summer. The Ludlow Baptist Church, which dominates one end of the green, has been spied through many a camera lens. The public library also faces the green.

If golf and biking are interests, the Okemo Inn on Route 103 north of town will cater to your needs. The inn, built in 1810, sits back up off the highway with a view of the Black River. It has a rural atmosphere. In addition to a swimming pool and winter sauna, the inn has special packages for cyclists and golfers.

For family fun, head out Route 100 to the Green Mountain Sugar House on the edge of Lake Pauline. Maple syrup and candy are made on the premises, and one sugarhouse is open to visitors during the production months. Green Mountain also has fields of strawberries, and you may pick your own in the early summer. The cider mill starts up in September and you can watch it being pressed daily.

Just across Route 100 you can buy an inexpensive lunch at The Café on the Farm — burgers, steaks, chicken wings, and a bar, too. Souvenir shopping is handy at the Mountain View Country Store in the same area — it bulges with T-shirts, wooden animals, food products, and more. To stay in Ludlow lake country, take a right over the bridge at the bottom of Lake Rescue. The Combes Family Inn is secluded, comfortable, and offers cross-country skiing.

Before you leave Ludlow, take a trip to the small cluster of businesses south of the village on Route 103. The Ludlow Antique and Gift Center features rotating exhibits by antique dealers and gifts. Across Route 103 at the Wayside Store you'll find more souvenirs, thick sandwiches, and low prices on their delicious deli items.

Continue down Route 103 to the Fletcher Farm School for the Arts & Crafts on your left. The school was established in 1948, and most of the activity takes place in its 200-year-old barn. Weaving and spinning workshops are in an old sugarhouse down back, and there is a retail shop on the premises. The school is open from June to September and also hosts a crafts fair on the Saturday of July 4 weekend.

If you're visiting the farm school, walk down Route 103 a few hundred yards to the south. A sign marks the site of Fletcher Spring, discovered by Jesse Fletcher in 1783. Steps lead down to the stone trough the cold, clear spring water runs through.

You can take a long way back into town. Heading back on Route 103 north, you will notice a large mill at the base of the hill to your left. That's a talc processing plant belonging to Cyprus International Minerals Corporation — they also own the quarries up on top of the mountain. Take East Hill Road to your left before the Antique and Gift Center. The road is paved for about two miles and then becomes a dirt surface. Bear right on the dirt and keep bearing right if it looks like you have a choice. It will bring you back onto South Hill in Ludlow but first gives you a wonderful view of the town from above and Okemo from a different perspective.

There are so many places to eat in Ludlow you could spend a week sampling menus and still not hit them all. Michael's Seafood and Steak Tavern, just south of town, is moderately priced and a good choice for family dining. The salad bar is good, desserts — especially the Fudge Fantasy — worth the calories, and steak lovers will be in heaven.

Up the road near the school is the Winchester Inn, with a tennis court of its own and pool. The Winchester is open to the public for dining and does a nice job with traditional fare.

DJ's on Main Street is terrific for steak and seafood lovers and is renowned for its prime rib special. The salad bar is good, too. Reservations are suggested.

If you're visiting in the fall, a nice side trip to Weston will take you onto one of southern Vermont's best foliage drives. Take Andover Street, which will turn into Route 100. This will bring you out north of Weston and is a highly recommended way to exit when your visit is complete.

Mount Holly

Mount Holly, just a short trip up Route 103 from Ludlow, is worth a visit, but be advised that it's a trip best taken when the roads are bare.

If you see it spitting snow in Ludlow or Rutland, you can be fairly certain it will be snowing like crazy in Mount Holly. Anyone who regularly travels Route 103 between the two towns knows enough to anticipate the possibility of more severe weather when passing through Mount Holly. And you can be almost as certain, when you describe your winter driving adventure — in an awestruck voice — to someone else, the response will be, "Oh, it's always like that in Mount Holly."

Historical Perspective

There is a good reason for this, of course. Mount Holly itself has an altitude of 1,540 feet and two of its villages — Belmont and Healdville — have altitudes of 1,820 and 1,432 feet, respectively. In fact, statewide, Belmont's altitude is topped only by the tiny Windham County town of Somerset and then only by 180 feet.

Its height makes Mount Holly the site of some pretty spectacular views, but it's an interesting place for other reasons, too. One of those reasons is the manner in which it was established.

When Wallingford and Ludlow were chartered in 1761, there was a 10,669-acre gore left over, according to Esther Swift in *Vermont Place-Names*. When Mount Holly was incorporated in 1792, Wallingford gave up an additional 3,000-plus acres and Ludlow contributed nearly 12,000 more acres.

When passing through, visitors see very little of Mount Holly from Route 103. The flashing yellow light on the highway, about eight miles north of Ludlow, is a good landmark if you're up for exploring the hills of Mount Holly. If you turn left at the light, heading north, the Mount Holly Country Store will be on your left. It's a sight hard to miss at holiday time, when the store owners string the entire building with Christmas lights.

Back 100 years, Mount Holly was quite the commercial center. There was a toy factory, a chair factory, sawmills and blacksmith shops, a rake factory, and a cheese manufacturer. Today, the cheese factory is still in operation and there's a new manufacturer, The Candle Factory.

Attractions

About four miles north of Ludlow on Route 103, you'll see the Crowley Cheese Shop, a retail outlet for Crowley Cheese that also sells maple syrup, gifts, and baked goods. There is a small sugarhouse next to the gift shop, and you can watch maple syrup being made there in season.

About one-half mile north of the Cheese Shop, turn left onto Healdville Road. Go up this road for 1.5 miles and you'll see a sign for The Candle Factory on your right. Turn at the sign and tour the factory and create a candle of your own. The candles come in every imaginable configuration and color and they sell a unique candle-making kit, suitable for young children.

Another half mile up Healdville Road, the Crowley Cheese Factory sits on the left-hand side of the road. Built in 1882, the factory is listed on the National Register of Historic Places and is believed to be Vermont's oldest cheese factory. Visitors are welcome and will watch cheese being made in very much the same way it was back in Winfield Crowley's day.

Cavendish and Proctorsville

If you'd like some wine to go along with your Crowley cheese, head south on Route 103 again, back through Ludlow. Cavendish and the village of Proctorsville lie just south of Ludlow on Route 131. Proctorsville boasts a winery and bakery; Cavendish offers two campgrounds and some scenic routes.

Historical Perspective

If you have driven up Route 103 from Chester, you will probably remember a narrow, steep, and winding three-lane road through a ravinelike area known as Proctorsville Gulf.

The road was built through the gulf in the eighteenth century by one Captain Leonard Proctor, according to Esther Swift in *Vermont Place-Names*. A toll road already existed between the towns of Cavendish and Ludlow, and the story goes that Proctor wanted to avoid paying for the privilege of traveling it.

Two lanes were put in for travelers heading north because dump trucks and milk tankers have slow going up through the gulf. The banks rise steeply from the sides of the road and it's not unusual to see snow slides there, some of which end up in the roadway. Watch, too, along the 1.5-mile stretch of road for falling and fallen rock.

Right at the junction of Routes 103 and 131, high atop a knoll, sits the massive stone Castle Inn. A former Vermont governor, Allen M. Fletcher, built the mansion as his home back at the turn of the century. The stone walls are 18 inches thick, the interior glows with polished carved oak and mahogany, and be sure to crane your neck a bit for a look at the sculptured ceilings.

You can stay in one of the inn's comfortable guest rooms, all with private baths and sitting areas. Guests may enjoy using the pool, tennis courts, or hot tub and sauna. Or you might choose just to dine. Cocktails are served in the library before the candlelit dinner in elegant, and intimate, surroundings. Roast duckling is the house specialty, and at least one person in the party should try it. Reservations are strongly recommended.

Opposite the Catholic church on Route 131 in Proctorsville is a road leading up the hill — Twenty Mile Stream.

Twenty Mile Stream was named by militia during the French and Indian Wars who used to travel through the area from Fort Number 4 in Charlestown, New Hampshire. The headwaters of the stream was a favorite campsite of these soldiers and is approximately twenty miles from the New Hampshire fort.

If roughing it is more your style, head five miles up Twenty Mile Stream to Meadow Brook Farm. Open from mid-May through mid-October, depending on the weather, this campground has thirty sites spread out over the 190-acre farm. There's a pond for swimming, stocked trout brook for fishing, and lots of room for hiking.

Continue up the road another two miles and you will be on Kingdom Road. Turn left and it will lead you into Tyson; turn right and you'll travel down the mountain into Felchville. Twenty Mile Stream is a highly recommended foliage route.

Vermont's first Republican governor, Ryland Fletcher, was born in Cavendish, as was Redfield Proctor, the founder of Vermont Marble and General Ulysses S. Grant's secretary of war. But the winner of the prize among former Cavendish residents for taking the most unusual place in history must go to Phineas Gage.

Gage was a construction worker on the Rutland Railroad in 1847, and he had the grave misfortune of having a steel bar blown through his head. The bar is believed to have passed directly through his brain. Miraculously, Gage survived the freak accident and willed his head to Boston Medical College.

No one in recent history has made quite such an impression, but Cavendish is home to Aleksandr Solzhenitsyn. However, don't journey to Cavendish just in the hopes of catching a glimpse of the Russian author — he doesn't hang out in the post office and residents are very respectful of his wish for privacy and won't reveal anything about his residence or habits.

Attractions

Proctorsville has one business that is a bit unusual for the Green Mountain State — a winery. The Joseph Cerniglia Winery is located just off Route 103, up the road a bit from the junction with Route 131. Window boxes line the bridge over the Black River that takes you to the winery.

Cerniglia produces fine Vermont apple wines, wine coolers, and excellent hard cider. You can tour the facility and sample their products in the wine-tasting room. After you've tested it, make your selection and shop for wine accessories and gifts in the on-premise shop.

The highways and byways of Cavendish and Proctorsville are well suited to biking. Route 131 east toward Ascutney is a beautiful road. It follows along the Black River, with a few good swimming holes, and can take you all the way to Ascutney and the Connecticut River.

The expansive, and somewhat expensive, Golden Stage Inn on Depot Street is popular with bicycle touring groups. This sprawling white clapboard inn was built in 1788 as a stagecoach inn, and the rooms' decor will remind you of those earlier days. Dinner is a five-course affair and is served in an airy sun room bursting with plants.

Proctorsville also offers a discount store — Wild Bill's Country Discount — with terrific buys on ski apparel, electronics, and gifts.

Right in front of the discount store is Singletons' Store, a country store in the truest sense with an impressive selection of cheese, wine, and their own cob-smoked ham and bacon.

At the corner of Route 131 and Depot Street in the 1895 Pollard Block is the Baba Louis Bakery, producers of some of the finest bread baked in Vermont. You'll see their loaves in stores all around the state, but if you're in Proctorsville you should definitely stop in at the bakery.

Just down Route 131 from Proctorsville Village you'll come into Cavendish. Situated along the Black River, Cavendish's main street is dominated by the town's major employer — Mack Molding. Just next door is the general store, a Civil War memorial, and the Cavendish Historical Society Museum.

The museum is housed in a stolid brick building, which served as a Baptist church in the last century. Exhibits include a historical collection of Cavendish textiles, photographs, weaving equipment, utensils, and farm tools. The museum is open Sunday afternoons, May through October.

A popular Cavendish spot with those who prefer to get closer to nature is the Caton Place Campground. The campground is a little more than two miles off Route 131, up Tarbell Hill, on the historic Crown Point Road. This 77.5-mile-long trail was established by Captain Stark and his troops back in 1759. The trail leads from Fort Number 4 in New Hampshire all the way to Lake Champlain. The trail is well marked in this section and an excellent hiking choice.

Caton Place Campgrounds opens Memorial Day weekend and closes November 1, with special arrangements made after that for deer hunters. It's a true family campground, with a playground for the kids, swimming pool, horseshoe pits, and shuffleboard court.

Springfield

Springfield, an industrial center in the eighteenth and nineteenth centuries, now offers visitors an abundance of recreational and cultural activities. Built along the banks of the Black River and into the surrounding hillsides, Springfield has adjusted well to the sharp decline in the machine tool industry over the past few decades and presents a pretty face for the visitor who wishes to relax and soak up some small-town atmosphere.

Neighboring Chester is one of those Vermont villages that often grace the pages of full-color travel magazines; its center is marked by a pristine village green and the surrounding streets and back roads are chock full of shops, country inns, and antique havens. Close to many of southern Vermont's major ski areas, the Springfield area boasts two golf courses of its own and a small Alpine area in nearby Windham.

The Black River wends its way through the heart of Springfield, its banks shaded with overhanging trees, its waters relatively peaceful. But when the river reaches Comtu Falls, it drops 110 feet in one-eighth of a mile. The Abnaki Indians gave the falls the name Comtu, meaning "great noise."

Today, the falls are the site of the Black Dam Hydroelectric Project. If you turn off Main Street and park your car, take a walk across the Park Street Bridge and take a look over at the breathtaking sight. If you drive along Mineral Street, you'll be able to pull over and look back up the river at the hydroelectric project.

In the eighteenth and nineteenth centuries, factories sprung up along the river; many of those buildings still stand. Most noticeable when you drive down River Street into the center of town is the former Fellows Gear Shaper building. A steel bridge — pedestrians only — crosses the Black River and leads to the huge old brick factory. Today it's used as a small business incubator space, operating under the auspices of the Precision Valley Development Corporation.

Precision Valley — that's the familiar name for the Springfield area and it certainly earned it. Springfield has been called home by numerous inventors and a number of businesses involved in the machine tool industry. Fellows Corporation, Jones & Lamson Machine Company, Lovejoy Tool Company, and Bryant Grinder Corporation still remain, but Springfield has had to adjust to pretty dramatic declines in the industry over the past decade.

The home of one of the former machine tool magnates is now a popular inn and restaurant. James Hartness was the president of Jones & Lamson Machine Company and also served as the state's governor from 1921-23.

Hartness was an inventive and industrious man — he became one of Vermont's first licensed pilots rather late in life, at age 55, and the state-owned airport in North Springfield bears his name. Hartness also is credited with inventing the turret lathe, a number of telescopes, and cofounding the Amateur Telescope Makers Association, an organization founded in 1920 and still meeting today.

When Charles Lindbergh came to visit his friend Hartness, he stayed in the turn-of-the-century mansion that was Hartness's home. Now you can stay there, too, in one of the 42 guest rooms in this charming inn, listed on the National Register of Historic Places.

Tall hardwoods overhang the inn, a sprawling clapboard building with some interesting stonework on its facade. It sits on thirty-two wooded acres in the heart of Springfield and has gardens worth strolling through. The rooms are cozy and decorated with period pieces.

Dining may take place in the large main dining room or in the more intimate surroundings of the porch or living room areas. The woodwork here is worth noticing.

Guests have plenty of recreational opportunities right on the inn grounds — swim in the heated pool, work on your backhand on the lighted clay tennis court, hike through the peaceful wooded surroundings or strap on your cross-country skis and explore the winter hillscape.

An interesting feature of this hilltop inn is the working Turret Equatorial Telescope on the front lawn. Even more unusual is a tunnel, almost 250 feet long, which leads from the main building to a five-room underground apartment, which Hartness used as a private observatory. Today the Stellafane Society uses the space to display a telescope collection.

The amateur Springfield Telescope Makers have their own observatory on a hill southwest of town — take Stellafane Road off Route 103 before you come into Springfield from Chester. A stellar feature of this site is the Porter Turret Reflecting Telescope, built in 1930. Telescope makers from across the country gather in Springfield every summer for a convention and lots of sky watching.

Although for most of this century it has been the machine tool industry, and an interest in astronomy, that has brought outsiders to Springfield, this town of nearly 11,000 is now beginning to attract tourists as well. A number of historic sites and recreational activities are two of the drawing cards that are credited with making Springfield a town worth getting off the interstate to visit.

Attractions

If you do arrive via I-91, you'll enter town on Route 11, heading northwest. Howard Johnson's Motor Lodge sits just off the interstate ramp and is certainly one of the nicer chain motels you can stay at. An indoor pool, exercise room, sauna, whirlpools, and a pleasant lounge and restaurant all add up to a good choice for the whole family.

Just up Route 11, on your right, is a historic site the whole family will enjoy. A covered bridge and one-room schoolhouse have both been moved to a spot along the Black River and are open to the general public.

The Eureka Schoolhouse was built around 1785 and was in continuous use until 1900 in a section of Springfield known as Eureka. The schoolhouse is Vermont's oldest remaining public school building and has been carefully restored.

The historic building saw its share of hard times — following its closure, the school was the target of vandals and a victim of neglect. That all changed in the late 1950s, when a group of local residents organized and had the building disassembled and moved to its present location, where more visitors could view it.

The Vermont Historic Sites Commission aided in the reconstruction, which was completed in 1968. Features of the building include 24-pane windows, scored pine planking, and an interior complete with desks and period antiques. The schoolhouse is also a good place to pick up some area brochures and is open and staffed daily from mid-May through Columbus Day.

Another historic building, the Baltimore Covered Bridge, was also moved from another section of town and resited near the schoolhouse. This bridge is an example of a lattice truss covered bridge and used to cross the Great Brook in North Springfield. It was moved in 1970, 100 years after its original construction.

Just off Route 11 is an interesting restaurant — The Paddock. In a converted horse barn, the restaurant offers casual dining and does not take reservations. The Sunday brunch is a good buy — try a stack of pancakes dripping with Vermont maple syrup.

If you're in this part of town and anything of a history buff, take a side trip across the toll bridge over the Connecticut River to Charlestown, New Hampshire. About one mile north of the village is The Fort at Number 4. The site is an authentic reconstruction of the fort that overlooked the Connecticut during the mid-1700s, the age of the French and Indian Wars.

It was from this fort that Captain Stark and his men traveled across Vermont to the fort at Crown Point on Lake Champlain. The reconstructed settlement includes a lookout tower, houses, barns, and a working blacksmith shop. Costumed guides man the exhibits and there are several special annual events on site, including an antique show, craft fair, and Militia Muster Days.

For scenic foliage viewing or a pleasant spring or summer drive along the Connecticut, take Route 5 north or south from the Vermont side of the river. Head north and you'll follow the river past cornfields along a winding route to Weathersfield and Ascutney. Choose the southern route and catch glimpses of the river on your way to Rockingham. Both of these stretches of Route 5 are great bicycling routes as well.

Recreational Pursuits

Fishermen may choose to stay near the toll bridge for some good angling. Just before you cross the toll bridge from Springfield, turn right. The state of Vermont has provided fishermen with a beautiful fishing access and boat ramp right on the shores of the Connecticut.

Hoyt Landing is a pretty spot for a quiet afternoon of casting or just sitting along the bank on one of the benches provided for a relaxing few hours of river watching. If you do cast your line, you might pull in trout, perch, large- and smallmouth bass, or panfish.

Just down Route 5, heading south, there's a nice spot for hiking above the river. Less than one-half mile down on your left, look for a wooden sign that says Bryant Farm Nature Trail. It's a self-guiding trail and well marked. The Bryant Recreation Area in Springfield is summer home to a local YMCA camp.

A superb hiking spot is located north of Springfield, above the North Springfield Reservoir. Here there are 55 acres of woods and fields, dotted with shallow lakes and brooks, to explore. The Springweather Nature Area has opened a nature trail to the public.

The North Springfield Reservoir covers 290 acres and holds a healthy population of large- and smallmouth bass. The reservoir is the site of a huge and impressive dam. Operated by the U.S. Army Corps of Engineers, the project is a flood control area. There is a federally regulated fishing access, with a boat launch.

Those with a taste for the outdoors may want to check out the year-round camping at the Tree Farm Campground. Located in a pine plantation on

Skitchewaug Trail, the campground offers a playground, bicycle rentals for campers only, hiking trails, and cross-country skiing.

The Crown Point Country Club is a popular spot with those whose ideal afternoon includes some time on the greens. It is located on Crown Point Road, and a marker on the fifth tee indicates where a section of the historic military route crosses the golf course. The 18-hole course is also open for some pretty terrific cross-country skiing in the winter months.

Younger golfers will delight in the 18-hole miniature golf course at the Abby Lyn Motel in North Springfield. The course is open to the public, but motel guests get a discount. Located at the junction of Routes 106 and 10, the motel has 24 units, some with kitchenettes. It's close to town but far enough out to make you think you're in the country.

There's a neat playground for the younger family members, a heated swimming pool, an area for cooking out and picnicking, and a nature trail on the motel's 27 rolling acres.

Another recommended motel in a similar close-to-the-village but out of the center of things location is the Pa-Lo-Mar, just off Route 11 from the Chester end. They also offer a heated pool, picnic area, and some units with kitchenettes.

After you've burned up all those calories, stop in at Sweet Temptations Bakery on River Road and check out the Polish rye bread.

For some more exercise, this time of the indoor variety, stop at the Springfield Racquet Club on River Street. It's open to the public and has four racquetball courts and plenty of exercise equipment.

For a little autumn exercise, and plenty of eating pleasure, head for Wellwood Orchards on the road by the same name and pick a few bags of McIntosh, Cortland, Delicious, or Northern Spies, while taking in the view of Mount Ascutney.

If you would rather have someone else do the picking, stop at their retail stand where you can also pick up a pumpkin ready for carving, Indian corn to hang by the front door, or a Vermont gift to take back home.

The Double Four Orchard, off River Street, produces apples destined to be made into wine, wine coolers, and cider at the Joseph Cerniglia Winery in Proctorsville.

Springfield goes for apples in a big way. Riverside Junior High School is the site of an annual apple festival, held in early October. The light posts along Main Street sport large wooden apples in the weeks before the festival, and the crispy fruit is definitely the food of the day at the fall festival.

You can enter your apple pie in the baking contest, or leave the baking to someone else and try your mouth at the pie-eating contest. Sip freshly pressed cider, or enter the paring contest and see if you can produce the longest peel. There is also a display of antique engines, and a guess-where-the-cow-will-do-her-business event.

Riverside is also home to the municipal swimming pool and four public tennis courts. The Black River runs behind the park, peaceful in its passage above Comtu Falls, before it joins the Connecticut south of town.

Trout habitate the waters of the Black River, and a lucky angler may hook a smallmouth bass. There are plenty of bullhead and panfish waiting to be pulled in from along the river's banks.

The town's Parks and Recreation Department does an excellent job of providing residents and visitors with year-round activities. Riverside Park is just one of the places where you can test your ice-skating ability. Town parks at the Commons — high atop Springfield's downtown area — and the North Springfield park both offer ice-skating rinks and warming huts.

Picnickers would do well to go up Woodbury Road to the town's Hartness Park. There you will find tables provided and trails to explore.

Going up a hill is not an unusual experience in Springfield; although it lacks any real mountains, the town's residential section is built on the steep hillsides that surround the river valley and commercial center.

Down in town, off Main Street just across the Park Street Bridge, you'll find Park Street Bowl, an upstairs, candlepin bowling alley.

After a few games, stop for lunch or dinner at Penelope's, on the village square. Mexican food is the specialty on Wednesday evenings; the regular menu includes seafood, steak, and prime rib for dinner. Lunch features homemade soups, great sandwiches, quiche, and salads. The onion soup is excellent.

Springfield is also home to a Chinese restaurant, pizza parlors, family-style restaurants, and one fast-food outlet. There are several antique shops for browsing pleasure, as well as several gift and specialty stores.

On the cultural side, Springfield has theater, concerts, and a historical museum. The Springfield Art and Historical Society building sits high above the village square on Elm Street. Four towering white columns front the brick building, and the roofline is broken up by four chimneys.

Permanent exhibits include Bennington pottery, Richard Lee pewter, and nineteenth-century paintings. Trace some of Springfield's history by wandering through the local historical exhibit. There are also rotating exhibits of Vermont artists' work. The museum is open from May through October.

Just down the hill, standing guard over the village square, is the imposing stone United Methodist Church, built in 1834. Farther down Main Street sits the town library, housed in the brick Spafford Library Building, built at the end of the nineteenth century and listed on the National Register of Historic Places.

Pop in for a look at an oil portrait of James Hartness or listen to some local oral history on cassette. The library has a wonderfully inviting children's room, and some interesting historic photographs are on display.

For music lovers there are summer concerts by the Springfield Community Band, comprised of local musicians of all ages with a surprisingly professional flair. Their marches will definitely set your toes to tapping.

The Springfield Community Chorus performs at Christmas and in the spring, and the Vermont Symphony Orchestra comes to town occasionally.

For stage lovers, the Springfield Community Players have been in existence for more than 60 years and usually offer a few performances a year.

A nice way to exit Springfield is out Valley Street, which will bring you into Weathersfield Center and eventually to Route 131 near Ascutney. For many years, Valley Street was one of several Polish neighborhoods in town. There is still a large segment of the population of Polish and Russian ancestry, exemplified by the Holy Trinity Orthodox Church on Park Street.

Before you leave, stop at the summer farmer's market on River Street or Neil's Stand on Route 11 for some local produce. If you visit in the spring, plan a trip to Lookaway Farm on Barlow Road. The Barlow family produces maple syrup and cream and invites visitors to watch the steamy production process at their sugarhouse.

Chester

Four state highways and one town highway lead into Chester. The least logical but prettiest way in is on Route 35 from Grafton. Seven miles of winding, paved road lead down the hills into Chester, depositing the traveler at the intersection of Grafton Street and the junction of Routes 11 and 103.

On your left at this intersection is the local True Value, an unassuming wooden building that is a fairly recent addition to the town and an improvement over the weedy lot that preceded it. A gas explosion in the 1960s shook the whole main street and destroyed the general store that had held court over the corner for years, as well as the gas station next door.

Nothing that explosive has happened since. In fact, Chester is one of those fortunate small Vermont towns that has eased gracefully into the last decade of the twentieth century. Its population has remained stable, around 2,800, and it has neither faded away nor dramatically changed its face with rapid, unplanned development.

Chester certainly attracts its fair share of visitors; a dozen or more lodging places and almost as many restaurants attest to that. But the maintenance of a quiet and attractive facade is what draws a lot of people to it. There are no shopping malls, no fast-food restaurants, no condominiums dotting its hillsides.

Bed and breakfasts, antique and gift shops, and art galleries abound, but these relative newcomers are, for the most part, in preexisting buildings. And those buildings have been upgraded or preserved.

Historic Village

A stellar example of such upgrading is the Inn Victoria at the end of the village green. This mid-nineteenth-century home operated for years as a slightly seedy lodging house and changed hands a number of times before finally sitting vacant for several years. The five-columned, three-storied building now houses the Inn Victoria, a small bed and breakfast with period antiques and accessories. The Inn Victoria Collection is an on-premise antique shop, offering furniture and accessories.

The Inn Victoria, with its distinctive purple shutters, marks the commercial end of Main Street and the village National Historic District. Two doors down is Carpenter's Emporium, an oddly painted country store whose paint job unfortunately makes it stand out from the rest of the stately and sedate buildings on the street.

The street used to be an archway of tremendous, leafy elms, but those trees went the way of most of that species, and the narrow village green is now dotted with younger trees. Chester had an impressive tree planting program in the 1960s, and those replacement trees are now beginning to come into their own.

The green is dominated, as it has been seemingly forever, by the Inn At Long Last. The broad, pillared porch, complete with rocking chairs, offers a relaxing view of the rest of the world passing by. The inn has some 30 guest rooms, only one of which the owners claim is haunted, and a fine dining room. There is a bar and a soloist appears on Saturday night with guitar, banjo, and some humor. Stay at the inn if you want to be in the heart of Chester, but be prepared to pay extra for that luxury.

Directly across the green is the Chester Academy building, now home to the Chester Art Guild and Chester Historical Society. This staunch brick building, complete with bell tower, was originally a private academy, once the town high school, and, finally, the junior high school. The Art Guild occupies the two downstairs rooms and has a rotating exhibit and sales gallery. It is open to the public at no charge. The Historical Society's collection upstairs is comprised of hand-pieced quilts, nineteenth-century furnishings, photographs, and early typewriters.

It still feels like an old schoolhouse inside, with only two main rooms on each of its two stories. The wide staircase treads have been worn smooth by years of students' feet passing up and down to classes, and the cloakroom hooks look as though they may just recently have held slickers and baseball caps. The view from the windows at the building's rear is of Stewart's Hill, private property but a longtime favorite evening feeding ground for whitetail deer.

Next door to the academy is the Hugging Bear Inn & Shoppe, a place no kid will pass by and probably very few adults. Huge bears usually sit on the front porch or are seated on the front lawn in a wagon or sleigh. One of those big bears disappeared a few years ago and remained at large for a few anxious days before the bear-nappers returned him to his rightful spot.

The inn promises a bear in every bed and then some. More than 3,000 bears and other cuddly creatures fill every nook and cranny of this bed and breakfast and gift shop. Bear books, bear jewelry, bear T-shirts, bear greeting cards, the list is endless. The bears' house, built around the middle of the nineteenth century, is a charming Victorian with a wraparound porch.

The next building is an elegant bed and breakfast, the Chester House. Built at the end of the eighteenth century, the building is listed in the National Register of Historic Places. Some of the rooms have fireplaces, one even has a whirlpool, and all are decorated in an Early American motif.

The village green is the site of craft sales, art exhibits, and the traditional tree lighting at Christmastime. The cohesiveness of the community, and the desire to put its best face forward, are dramatically evidenced during the holiday season. The majority of homes and businesses in this historic district decorate with small white lights, and Main Street is truly a sparkling wonderland during the month of December.

Next door to the Inn At Long Last is Misty Valley Books. For years, the bookstore building was home to the local IGA store, but Misty Valley is a definite improvement and has to be considered one of the better bookstores in southern Vermont. It's a bookstore for browsing, sitting, and skimming and offers a tremendous selection of books — the children's section is good, as is the selection of Vermont books.

You can stop for lunch at the nearby Village Green Deli or Chester Pizza. Beverly's, at the west end of the green, offers good dinner food and a super salad bar.

Before leaving the village green, it's worth a trip back across Main Street to the old cemetery. Not too many towns could manage to make a midtown cemetery a plus, but Chester does it. The wide entrance to the cemetery is marked with a broad stone wall, a favorite place for teenagers to cool their heels. A Civil War monument, cannon, and the stone public tomb complete the entrance. The cemetery dates back to revolutionary days, and it's easy to spend an hour or two reading the epitaphs of some of the town's earliest residents. The stately, brick Baptist church next door is the site of delicious strawberry festivals in season.

Attractions

Take a walk down School Street at the eastern end of the green. The street dead-ends for vehicles at the suspension bridge over the west branch of the Williams River, but pedestrians may cross. On the way to the bridge you'll pass the National Survey on your left. The survey, established in 1912, is famed worldwide for its maps. Check out the ones in your glove compartment; chances are good they were produced in Chester.

Just to your right, before you cross the bridge, is a nice example of one of Chester's many stone buildings. Once a noisy hub of activity when it housed the Chester Volunteer Fire Department, the building is now an electrician's headquarters.

The bridge has a story of its own. For many years it was wooden and known locally as "the swinging bridge." That's because you could terrify anyone stuck in the middle of it by bouncing on either end and starting it to sway, high above the rocky riverbed. The river itself saw fit to eliminate the wooden structure — a tree floating downriver at high water in the mid-1970s took the bridge out.

Fortunately, the town replaced it with the present cable structure, and it's still possible to get a bit of a swing out of it. Pocket a few rocks before you step on; who can resist chucking stones into water?

The path on the other side of the bridge will lead you onto High Street. Turn left and follow it to the end, where you again turn left onto Grafton Street. You'll cross the river again, but this time on the more traditional highway bridge, and soon find yourself back at the True Value.

It might be a good time to cross over the street and visit the Christmas Village Gift Shop, where it feels like December every day. Continue back up Main Street, past the Chester-Andover Elementary School, and you'll be back at the village green.

If you still feel like walking or, better yet, have a bike along, keep going up Main Street. Soon you'll come to the Congregational church. Its steeple dominates that end of the street, and you can check the time on any of the four sides. The clock bell has a deep and resounding ring, which will mark every hour of your Chester visit. The upper end of Main Street has some nice homes, many with slate roofs, gingerbread trim, and well-kept lawns and perennial beds.

If you stay on the same side of the street, you'll pass two stone houses and then come upon Buttonwood Farm. The original barns, one with an indoor riding ring, are still there, but the beautiful house burned in a devastating fire in the 1960s. The farm used to house stablefuls of elegant quarter horses, but the present out-of-state owners don't have any in permanent residence.

Across the street is Allen's Garage. You can gas up if you've decided to drive or inflate your tires if you're biking. Just past Allen's, on the opposite side of the street, is the turn into Lovers Lane Road. Whatever else the name might imply, the road leads to the Chester Recreation Area.

There you'll find a municipal swimming pool, tennis courts, baseball field, and an area used for local horse shows. Lifeguards are on duty in season and there is a small admission charge. Behind the pool is a hill known locally as the pinnacle. It's a good place to hike or strike off on cross-country skis, on no particular trails, but downhill skiing and sliding are what the pinnacle is really all about.

The town runs a rope tow up a few gentle slopes, and those with sleds are almost as frequently on line as the skiers are. It's a superb sliding hill and a great place for novice skiers to gain some confidence.

Ambitious walkers or those with a bike might want to continue out Lovers Lane. The road soon changes its surface to dirt, and it's an easily accessible yet quiet back road. The road follows a brook on the left, a good place for kids to fish, and there are a number of old logging roads for exploration — in summer or winter.

If you're ready for more history, turn around and head back down Main Street. Take the other side of the street this time and you'll come to the Whiting Library, just below the village green. It's worth stopping to take a look. It's a gorgeous brick structure with unusual, large windows and, if it's open, step in. It smells just the way a town library should. In July and August there is evening entertainment on Tuesdays on the library lawn. Entertainment may range from a folksinger to a puppet show.

On one side of the library is the Charthouse, a retail store for the National Survey. The Charthouse, a favorite with photographers, is loaded with three stories of gingerbread trim. Inside, in addition to maps, you'll find art craft supplies, books, and gifts.

Chester Depot

When you get to the now familiar foot of Grafton Street, turn left past the American Legion and curve up over the hill down into Chester Depot. You'll pass more bed and breakfasts and several antique shops on Depot Street. On the hill to your left, just before the crest of the hill you're walking up, sits the former Chester High School. It's set back from the street, and a tree-lined walk leads to the imposing brick building, which now serves as an apartment complex.

You'll know you're in Chester Depot when you cross the railroad tracks. To your left is the Chester Depot Station, built in 1872 and recently restored. This is the passenger depot for Green Mountain Railroad. The railroad operates a passenger excursion train between Chester and Bellows Falls, a 26-mile round-trip.

A bay window caboose is on display next to the station and there are picnic tables on the side lawn. The diesel-powered train runs during the summer and early fall months and is well worth taking. You'll chug through the river valley, past cornfields, covered bridges, and a natural gorge. A special foliage run will take you from Bellows Falls to Ludlow.

Just over the tracks is Cummings Hardware, a Depot landmark, selling everything from wood stoves and bib overalls to engineers' caps and Vermont souvenirs.

Chester Town Hall, built in 1884, dominates the center of the Depot. For many years Chester had three post offices, and the Depot Post Office was located in the bottom of Town Hall for much of that time. It closed in the late 1980s, less than twenty years after the closure of Chester's third post office, in the village of Gassetts on Route 103 north.

Stay on Route 103 north, past town hall, and take a look at the historic Yosemite Fire Station on your right. The red-and-white clapboard building sits almost in the road, and its hose-drying tower has been the object of many a photographer's lens and artist's canvas. You'll soon cross the Williams River. This is the bridge where the Memorial Day parade stops for a rendition of taps and the tossing of a memorial wreath into the water.

Just below the bridge and its dam is the Dawson Mill Gallery. It's not open very often but worth a try and the building is unique. One of Chester's more infamous former residents, Clarence Adams, received what most would consider his just desserts at that very spot, back in the late 1800s when the building was an operating gristmill.

Adams was a town selectman for many years and, for almost as many years, was apparently burglarizing local businesses with alarming regularity. Local history has it, in a number of different versions, that the gristmill owner was fed up with the brassy burglar and set a trap one night, complete with a loaded shotgun. The story goes that Adams triggered the trap during one of his felonious forays and got what he deserved.

Some versions of the tale of the gentleman burglar have it that Adams fled town and was never seen again. Others say that he was injured, apprehended, and confined to the state prison in Windsor until the time of his death.

Leaving the scene of the crime, continue on Route 103 into Chester's second historic district, the Stone Village. North Street is a quiet, shady street lined on both sides with beautiful stone buildings. The buildings were constructed of locally quarried stone at the beginning of the nineteenth century by a family of masons.

One building, now a private home, served as the local kindergarten for years. The house still has the look of a one-room school, bell tower intact. The buildings are all private, with the exception of the Old Stone Church. The church is home to both the Universalist congregation and the Christian Science Society.

The church is also the site of the Women's Review Club's annual book sale, for four days in the fall. It's a wonderful sale, down in the church basement, but get there early because there will be a line and a lot of dealers.

You can stop in and watch handmade, stuffed dolls in production at Bonnie's Bundles on North Street. The stuffed dolls appeal to both squirmy young arms with hugs to spare and doll collectors. Bonnie Watters, the dolls' designer, is a designer for Butterick patterns.

Just across the street is a large white house, built in the eighteenth century. Once a stagecoach shop known as Kelly's Tavern, it has been a private home for years. If you wonder about the size of the home, there is a spring floor ballroom (the floor actually bounces) on the second floor to accommodate.

At the end of Depot Street you can turn left onto Church Street, follow it up over the hill and down, and find yourself back at the Congregational church on Main Street. If you continue on Route 103, you'll pass a large farm on your right. Directly in front of the farmhouse, right on the highway with no real room to pull a vehicle over, is a marker, designating the spot as the site of the first courthouse, built around 1766.

Chester doesn't have a courthouse today, but back in 1766 it was the shire town of Cumberland County. Chester was first granted as Flamstead. When the governor of New York made most of southern Vermont into Cumberland County in 1766, the town's name was changed to Chester, and it became the county seat.

Chester lost that honor when the Vermont legislature created Windsor County and passed the county seat title on to the town of Windsor. Not many people know that Chester was ever a county seat, but they do know about Flamstead; a section of town is still known by that name.

If you head back down North Street, when you get back to the blinking light near the Dawson Mill go straight. You'll come upon a steep, left-hand turn onto Flamstead Road, although many locals refer to it as Crow Hill Road. The views from the hill are nice, and you can also visit Crow Hill Gallery.

Artist Jeanne Carbonetti, who works mostly in watercolor, has established a beautiful art gallery on the hill. Walk through the outdoor sculpture garden and stroll through the gallery.

When you come back down Flamstead Road, turn left at the bottom. This short dirt road will bring you onto Route 11. Cross Route 11 with caution, it's a dangerous spot, and you will be on the Green Mountain Turnpike. To the dismay of those in the business of promoting the town, many residents refer to this road as the Dump Road, because that's where it used to lead.

Now it leads to the Henry Farm Inn. The inn was a stagecoach stop and tavern in the 1700s and has been restored and converted into a bed and breakfast well worth checking out. Seven guest rooms, eight fireplaces, two common rooms, and a quiet ambience beckon those who find even the relative peace of Chester Village too noisy.

Pass the Henry Farm and continue south. When you reach Chester Dairies you have a choice to make — turn left and head for Bartonsville and two covered bridges or keep straight and come out on Route 103 in Rockingham. Either route is a good choice.

Another nice back road not too far from the village is the Reservoir Road. Take Route 11 west out of town. You'll pass the Stone Hearth Inn — a good bet for lunch or dinner — and the Motel in the Meadow. Just past the motel and the U.S. Army Reserve Center, a narrow dirt road turns off to the right — that's Reservoir Road.

Not too far up the road look for a small sign on the right-hand side that says "Dogpatch," which marks a private drive, so keep going, but slow down. About 100 feet past that sign, stop and look for a little footpath on the same side. It will lead you to some of the coldest, clearest springwater you could ever hope to find.

Suitably quenched, continue up the road, being careful to take it slowly and keeping to your own side. You'll pass Chester's water supply on your left — a massive, enclosed structure that looks like it may have dropped down from another galaxy. You're heading up this tree-lined, dirt road to the old town water supply, the Chester Reservoir. It's about one-half mile beyond the new one and has been opened to the public for canoeing and picnicking.

When you come back down Reservoir Road, turn right on Route 11 and you'll be heading for Londonderry, Andover, and Weston. Turn right and go straight through town, staying on Route 103, and you'll go to Rockingham and Bellows Falls. If you turn left onto Route 11 south of town, you'll reach Springfield.

If you want to go to Ludlow or Rutland, turn left onto Church Street, go over the hill, and get onto Route 103 north. If you go that way, stop at Kendall's Barn. They're open from April 1 through October, and you can find furniture, old books, bicycles, canning jars, pumpkins in the fall, and the kitchen sink.

Route 103 now follows the Williams River and winds and bends with the stream bank. On your left, you'll notice two more stone houses and a number of one-lane bridges leading to homes on the other side of the river. The river along this stretch is often the site of spectacular, and potentially very damaging, ice jams in the spring when the river starts to break up.

You'll know you've come into the village of Gassetts when you hit the junction of Route 103 and Route 10. You can turn onto Route 10 to get to North Springfield. Gassetts is little more than a skeletal village today, with a gas station and convenience store and bingo in the Grange Hall on Saturday nights.

About four miles out of Chester Depot, notice the Chat & Chew on your right. It may not look like much, but the fare is hearty and inexpensive. Right across the road is the 1828 House Antiques and the entrance to Smokeshire. In *Vermont Place-Names*, Esther Swift suggests the name may have come from the fact that a charcoal kiln in the area produced a lot of smoke.

For a truly scenic drive in summer or foliage season, turn onto Smokeshire Road. You'll still end up in Ludlow, but you'll see a part of the area few people discover. If you have a fishing pole along, there are some hungry trout in holes all along the Williams River, which the road follows closely for several miles.

As on all back roads, it's important to stay far over to the right and take it slowly; you'll cross a few bridges and some places in the road where two vehicles have a tight squeeze. If it looks like you have a choice, stay right over the bridges; some driveways may look like the main road.

A few miles out you'll see a sign pointing rather vaguely to Andover and Ludlow — that means you're going in the right direction. About 7.5 miles out the surface changes to pavement. Just before that, look for a small cemetery on your right. It has some interesting old markers.

If you're clocking it, at almost the nine-mile mark pull over. Even if you're not measuring miles, you'll know where to stop. You're actually in Ludlow now and have a breathtaking view of Okemo Mountain and the town of Ludlow down below. The grade is steep here, and you'll quickly descend into the center of Ludlow, via South Hill.

Andover and Windham

Andover and Windham are both barely recognizable as towns but worth exploring for several reasons. Andover, a tiny town nestled in the mountains between Chester and Weston, offers several nice places to stay and some breathtaking views. Rowell's Inn and The Quilted Cat are both recommended — the former for its historic ambience, the latter because it offers rural accommodations without sacrificing comfort.

If you're traveling on Route 11 toward Londonderry, you could easily miss Windham altogether, but if golf, tennis, or skiing are for you, take the time to find your way. A town that doesn't even have its own post office, Windham, oddly enough, boasts two resorts. Tater Hill offers golf, tennis, swimming, and cross-country skiing, and Timber Side is an Alpine ski area.

Route 11, from Londonderry or Chester, is the easiest way to access both resorts. Tater Hill is 10 miles west of Chester, 4 miles east of Londonderry. Turn off Route 11 onto what is known as both Hitchcock Hill Road and Popple Dungeon Road, and take your first right to find Tater Hill.

Tater Hill is so named because back in the eighteenth century there was a potato farm on the site. The resort is open to the public year-round and is also accessible by air. A 2,500-foot airstrip is nearby but closed in the winter months. The golf course is nine holes, and there is the Tater Hill Pro Shop for instruction, equipment, and rental golf carts.

During the golfing season there is also swimming at Tater Hill in the pool, which overlooks part of the golf course. Lunch is served daily in the clubhouse, and there is a full bar. There's live music and dancing on a marble floor on some summer and winter weekends.

Tater Hill also offers tennis on red clay courts and holds a junior tennis camp in June. The courts and golf course both open in May.

During the winter you can cross-country ski on the club's 43 kilometers of trails. There is some machine grooming of the trails, which wind through open meadows and in the forest. Night touring is one special feature of the ski touring center, and instruction is available. The ski shop offers both sales and rentals.

The easiest way to access Timber Side is down Route 11, a few miles closer to Londonderry. From Londonderry, turn right onto Route 121. The ski area is about two miles out. When the area was first developed in the 1960s, it was operated under the name of Glebe, the mountain on which it is located. It later changed hands, and names, and was known as Timber Ridge.

Timber Side is now part of Magic Mountain in Londonderry, and the two ski areas are connected. You can ride the lift to the top of Timber Side and ski down Magic, then take the lift up to the top of Magic and ski back down to Timber Side. It's a small mountain, with 32 trails and two lifts. It does have its own base lodge with food available and a ski shop that handles sales and rentals, but if you need instruction or babysitting, the ski school and nursery are both located on Magic's side of the mountain.

There are no public lodging facilities at Timber Side, nor are there any in the entire town of Windham. Don't despair, both Londonderry and Chester offer a wide range of lodging options, and both are within an easy drive of Timber Side and Tater Hill.

Rockingham, Grafton

Ask almost any Vermonter where Rockingham is and they'll probably tell you it's a small town along the Connecticut River, just north of Bellows Falls. Well, it is along the river, but Rockingham is actually the town that includes Bellows Falls, Saxtons River, Bartonsville, Cambridgeport, and the village of Rockingham.

Covered bridges dot the area, fishing and boating opportunities abound, and nearby Grafton has to be one of Vermont's most picturesque villages.

Rockingham

Rockingham itself used to be the center of activity — town meetings and church services were held there and the town offices were located there. Today little remains of that municipal hub — the post office closed in 1908, after more than 100 years of operation.

The fact that the railroad completely missed the village of Rockingham contributed to its demise. Bellows Falls's proximity to the Connecticut River and the power of the falls there both led to its further development.

The village of Rockingham is something that's easy to miss — the only real building of note is the Rockingham Meeting House, and you have to turn off Route 103 to see that.

The meetinghouse was built in 1787 and was the site of town meetings until 1869. It is one of the finest examples of early church architecture. The two-story frame building is unique in several ways.

The main entrance of this Federal-style building is on the side, the only one located that way in the entire state, according to Herbert Congdon in *Old Vermont Houses*. The building features a gable roof, seven bays, a high pulpit, and box pews. The adjacent cemetery is full of old slate markers and makes an interesting side trip for those inclined to learn some local history by visiting early grave sites.

The meetinghouse is available for weddings and there is an annual pilgrimage, open to the public, on the first Sunday in August.

It's difficult to tell when you are actually in Rockingham, but there are a few places of interest along, or just off, Route 103.

The Vermont Country Store, founded in the 1940s by Vrest Orton in Weston, has a branch on Route 103 in Rockingham. There's a 42-foot covered bridge on the property that was originally built in West Townshend in 1872 and moved to Rockingham in 1967. Just beside the stream is a reconstructed water-powered gristmill.

The store itself is packed, quite literally floor to ceiling, with old-fashioned merchandise in a country store atmosphere. You can buy what used to be penny candy — take a bag and step back a few decades to Mary Janes and chocolate babies. There are garlic presses, Cross crackers, chamois shirts, silk-screened aprons, Vermont cheese, balsalm bags, and much, much more. The store is open seven days a week, year-round.

Just across Route 103 from the Vermont Country Store is the entrance to the Bellows Falls Country Club — a nine-hole, 2,865-yard golf course.

About one-half mile up Route 103 north look for a road to your right and a small sign reading Brockway Mills. You'll drive down a hill, cross some railroad tracks, and cross a bridge. After the bridge, turn right or left and find a place to pull over.

Walk back to the bridge, take a look, and be prepared for your stomach to do a few flip-flops. The Williams River does something rather spectacular here — there's a small hydroelectric dam below the bridge and then the river swirls and churns madly as it falls deep into the chasms of a natural gorge.

If you look to the southwest, you'll see where the railroad bridge crosses high above the gorge. Please watch your footing carefully here and be content with the view from the bridge or roadside; the drop is dramatic. There is a small footpath from the western end of the bridge for those so inclined.

If you turn left after the bridge over the river, you'll be heading north, basically running parallel to Route 103. Approximately one mile from where you turned after the bridge, you'll come to a covered bridge. You'll be in Bartonsville now, but it doesn't really matter if you realize it because Bartonsville is nothing more than a residential village in Rockingham.

This covered bridge was built in 1871 and spans 87 feet of the Williams River. Cross it, and in less than one-half mile you'll be back on Route 103. Turn right toward Chester or left to Bellows Falls. If you like covered bridges, turn right.

Less than one-half mile up Route 103 watch for another road to the right — this one is marked by a sign for the Rockingham Veterinary Clinic. Less than one mile down this road you will come to Bartonsville's second covered bridge. This is a one-span (single lane) bridge across the Williams River, built in 1870. Make sure your tires are in the right places when you enter or you'll rough up the sides of them.

Once you've passed through the bridge you can turn around and go back to 103 or stay to the left and take a dirt back road all the way up to Chester, entering on the Green Mountain Turnpike. This road follows the railroad tracks pretty closely, and you might catch glimpses of the passenger train chugging by. This is not a recommended winter or spring route.

If you're heading for Bellows Falls from Route 103, southbound, and you want to spend some time on the Connecticut River, watch the road after you pass under the I-91 overpass. To your left you will see Route 5, which can take you on a pretty ride all the way to Springfield.

Go down the hill and watch for a dirt road on your right, about .8 mile out on Route 5. You may think you have the wrong road — it's a narrow, dirt one that appears to be going through someone's cornfield. Actually, you're heading for the New England Power Company picnic area and boat landing at Herrick's Cove.

This is a beautiful spot — there are many, many picnic spots to choose from — all complete with tables and grills and a landing for launching your small boat or canoe. There's also a tiny beach near the boat landing for anyone who wants to take a dip.

The Connecticut River is 345 miles long and forms a natural boundary between Vermont and New Hampshire. Remember that if fishing is your sport, please. An out-of-state Vermont fishing license entitles you to fish only on the Vermont side of the river.

And there are certainly enough fish on this side to keep even the pickiest angler happy. The Connecticut is prime fishing water, and you may pull in brook, rainbow, or brown trout, perch, walleye, pike, pickerel, large- and smallmouth bass, bullhead, or even a feisty pumpkinseed.

If you left your boat behind and want to test the waters, Green Mountain Marine on Route 5 — known locally as the Missing Link Road — is a full-service marina and also rents canoes and fishing boats. They supply the life preservers and oars and some useful information regarding fishing spots or scenic routes for those just out for pleasure.

Bellows Falls itself is just three miles down from the I-91 overpass. Route 103 ends here and becomes Route 5. On the way there you'll pass some places to stay and eat.

Spoon's is a small, diner-type restaurant that serves hearty food in a pleasant atmosphere and is just the kind of place a lot of travelers are looking for after a long drive on the interstate. It's a friendly place, the coffee is good, and you can fuel up before you continue on.

Almost across the road is Leslie's — a good choice for dinner after you've settled somewhere and are ready for something a little more formal. You can dine in style on European and American cuisine in a renovated late-eighteenth-century house. The service is good, the prices reasonable, and the food delicious.

Just down Route 5 are two places to spend the night. The Rockingham Motor Inn is just off exit 6 of I-91 and has 30 units. There's an outdoor pool and a nice big lawn. The lawn is the site of a summertime fiddlers gathering.

The restaurant, open to the public, features a menu of seafood and prime rib, and there's also a lounge to relax in or dance to oldies music on Friday and Saturday nights.

Just down Route 5 on your right, on the crest of a small hill, sits Whippowill Gifts and Cabins. These are the kind of cabins you thought all disappeared in the 1960s. Set back off the road in the woods, these tiny cabins come complete with those funky metal lawn chairs that spring when you rock them. If the kids can live without a pool, this is a neat place to check out.

As you get closer to Bellows Falls you'll begin to see more of the Connecticut. Down the hill from the Whippowill, you'll notice some setbacks on your left. This is a popular spot for ice fishing.

High atop a knoll overlooking the river is the Joy Wah. The view from the dining room, with its many windows, is a pleasant one, and you can eat your fill of Szechuan and Cantonese cuisine.

Bellows Falls

The roadside becomes more populated now, an indication that Bellows Falls has truly become the center of the town of Rockingham. The Hetty Green Motel will be on your right just before you come into the center of Bellows Falls. It's clean and it's inexpensive.

Hetty Green was one of Bellows Falls' more illustrious residents. She was known as the "Witch of Wall Street," probably because of her enormous success on Wall Street. She was a wealthy woman, a millionaire several times over, and commuted by train from her Bellows Falls home to New York.

Her home is no longer standing — the First Vermont Bank is on the site at the corner of School and Church streets — but there is a small park named in her honor on School Street. The curious may visit her grave in the Immanuel Episcopal Church Cemetery.

The church itself is well worth a visit — its bell tower is home to a bell cast by Paul Revere. It was first hung in 1819 and still peals today on Church Street. The towering stone church was designed by Richard Upjohn and is a shining example of Gothic Revival architecture.

Bellows Falls was named for both the impressive falls of the Connecticut River and Colonel Benjamin Bellows. Bellows actually lived across the river in Walpole, New Hampshire. Despite the river that divides them and the state line, Bellows Falls and Walpole are closely connected.

Bellows Falls is a town of many firsts. The first bridge across the Connecticut was built here in 1784 by one Colonel Enoch Hale. The first canal in the United States was built here in 1802 — it took some 10 years to construct. Paper was first made from wood pulp in Bellows Falls in a mill established in 1869 by William A. Russell. Russell went on to become the first president of International Paper Company.

Long before white settlers ever came to this part of northern Windham County, the Abnaki, Pennacook, and Pequod Indians used the Connecticut as one of their main routes. Even after white people had settled the area, the Abnakis returned every summer to see the great falls in the river. One old Abnaki chief came back in the mid-1860s to that sacred spot in the river and chose to stay there until his death. He lies in an unmarked grave in a local cemetery.

Some Pennacook petroglyphs are still visible on the steep rocks that line the sides of the river. These early carvings are visible about 50 feet below the Vilas Bridge. Rock hounds are attracted to this area because of the presence of sillimanite crystals.

New England Power Company has a hydroelectric plant on the river, below the 62-foot drop of the falls. Below the dam there is some shad fishing and some future hopes for salmon. A fish ladder at Bellows Falls was constructed to allow the fish free passage to the spawning grounds of the White River. The hope is that someday in the not-too-distant future, anglers will once again be able to fish the Connecticut for Atlantic salmon, as the Indians did when they traveled the river north.

There is a visitor center at New England Power's hydroelectric project and fish ladder. Open Wednesday through Sunday, the center allows visitors the opportunity to try to spot fish swimming through the ladder, and a taped lecture explains something about the project.

The tremendous effort that went into constructing the canal to bypass the falls did not result in a surge of steam traffic through Bellows Falls. Although Samuel Morey was steering his steamboat along the Connecticut in 1793, nearly 15 years earlier than Robert Fulton and the *Clermont* made history, steam traffic around Bellows Falls just never made it. The canal's nine locks were removed around the middle of the nineteenth century.

As mills and manufacturing operations sprouted alongside the Connecticut in the latter half of the nineteenth century, the demand for water power increased and the canal played an important role in providing that power.

The canal was both widened and deepened in response to the demand for power. A second enlargement took place in the early part of the twentieth century. Following the conversion from water power to electricity in most mills, the canal was enlarged to its present width of 100 feet.

To get an idea of what those mills were like in their heyday, visit the Adams Old Stone Gristmill Museum on Mill Street. The mill was in operation for 130 years, until it closed in 1961. This summertime museum is operated by the Bellows Falls Historical Society.

The original milling equipment remains intact, and other exhibits include machinery, farm tools, railroad items, and household furnishings.

Green Mountain Railroad

The railroad played an important role in Bellows Falls' history. The beginning of serious rail construction and travel in the 1840s peaked in the following decade when four different rail lines served Bellows Falls. One unique feature of this railroad construction is a 40-plus-foot railroad tunnel that runs under the village square. This is one of only two tunnels of this kind in the state.

The railroad continues to play a role in Bellows Falls today. Green Mountain Railroad operates the Green Mountain Flyer, a vintage passenger train powered by a diesel locomotive.

From weekends in mid-June through the fall foliage specials in September and October, the Flyer takes passengers through the river valleys between Bellows Falls and Chester — a 26-mile round-trip. You'll chug past covered bridges, farmland, and a natural gorge. Be sure to pack your camera for this trip.

Union Station on Depot Street is the place for tickets and a visit to the Depot Square Gift Shop. The shop offers all kinds of railroad memorabilia and plenty of postcards. There's also a small park nearby with benches provided for passengers awaiting the next trip.

Fall foliage specials include a longer trip from Bellows Falls to Ludlow. Passengers may opt for a 90-minute layover in Ludlow to explore that town or continue on an additional seven miles to the summit. Reservations are accepted for these special excursions.

Above the railroad tunnel sits Bellows Falls' commercial core — known as the square. Large brick buildings line the sides of the square, the most notable being the massive Centennial Block. This was originally constructed as a bank building and is an example of High Victorian Italianate style architecture.

The first floor of the block contains storefronts, whose facades have been dramatically altered from their original construction. An extensive interior fire in the late 1970s caused considerable damage, but the storefronts have been restored.

Across the street looms the Rockingham Town Hall building. Another towering brick building, this building was erected in 1926 to replace the structure destroyed by fire the previous year. The building's tower, with town clock, is a village focal point. The New Falls Cinema is also in the building.

Another interesting architectural example is the Polish-American Club. The baked enamel facade stands out from the surrounding brick, and the curved glass and rounded ends of the front window will catch your eye.

Just across the street rests the Miss Bellows Falls Diner — listed on the National Register of Historic Places. The diner was built by the Worcester Lunch Car Company in the 1920s. Sit at the marble counter and enjoy some hearty diner fare and local gossip.

Next door is the Express Café & Deli — the place to stop for soup, a sandwich, or a salad. Next door is The Real Scoop — a must for ice-cream lovers. This Vermont-made ice cream will please the pickiest of palates — try the sweet cream or red raspberry.

The square is the site of many of Rockingham's community events. The tree-lighting ceremony in early December is a good way for visitors to peek into community life — sing some carols and snack on cider and doughnuts. Other annual events include a three-day Home Show in April, with rides for the little ones; a circus every summer; Fall in the Falls on Columbus Day weekend; and Rockingham Old Home Days.

You have some choices if you want to stay right in Bellows Falls. Horsefeathers Bed & Breakfast at 16 Webb Terrace is a good choice for Nordic ski enthusiasts, with cross-country ski trails of its own. There's also the River Mist Bed & Breakfast on Burt Street and The Blue Haven on Route 5 south of Bellows Falls.

Billing itself as the state's largest farm stand, Allen Brothers Farm Stand on Route 5 is an exception in a couple of ways — it's open year-round and you can buy fresh produce, baked goods, maple syrup, ice cream, and freshly pressed apple cider. This is a good choice for pumpkin picking, Christmas trees, and sweet corn.

Bellows Falls offers architectural buffs a variety of styles and examples of different period construction. If you're visiting the square, you can walk up the 44 stairs that connect downtown with the residential district.

Saxtons River

Travel writers have used a variety of words to describe Saxtons River — quintessentially Vermont, a quaint country village, picturesque, and so on. All of them are on target, but don't get the idea that this is a restored village like nearby Grafton or popular Woodstock.

Telephone and utility lines still get in your way when you try to photograph some of the village's more impressive architectural offerings, kids hoot and holler down Main Street on their bikes and skateboards, and there are plenty of pickup trucks with gun racks parked in front of the general store.

Saxtons River is an incorporated village in the town of Rockingham, with a population wavering around 600. It sits, not surprisingly, along the Saxtons River on Route 121, in between Bellows Falls and Grafton. If you had to pick the prettiest village from Rockingham's quintet, Saxtons River would probably be the unanimous choice.

The drive from Bellows Falls along 121 is not particularly pretty from the eastern end, but the closer you get to Saxtons River, the nicer the scenery becomes. Just before you come into the village, look for a covered bridge on your right.

The Hall Bridge, spanning 117 feet over the Saxtons River, was built in the early 1980s as a replacement for the original structure, built in 1867. The replacement bridge was built in a nearby meadow and moved into place by a team of oxen.

The first commercial enterprise you'll see is the Café 121, open for dinner Tuesday through Sunday — good food at moderate prices. The village's Main Street is lined with trees, nicely kept homes, and the businesses blend in with residences.

The village is a National Historic District and offers many examples of a variety of architectural styles — Greek Revival, Italianate, Federal, Colonial Revival, and Queen Anne. Main Street is dominated at the far end by the former West Church and its towering white steeple.

The church's ground floor is presently occupied by the Saxtons River Historical Society Museum. Open on Sunday afternoons during the summer and foliage season, the museum's permanent exhibit includes local historical photographs, household utensils from the eighteenth and nineteenth centuries, tools, and local artifacts.

For a tiny town, Saxtons River is a surprisingly busy place. It was a busy place in the nineteenth century, too. The river provided the power for the many mills that sprung up along its banks.

Today one of the most unusual businesses in town, and a neat place to visit, is Rubber Stamps of America. If you're the kind of person who likes to stamp their bills with a skull and crossbones or adorn letters to the folks back home with an erupting volcano or a border of hearts, this is the store for you.

Located on Academy Avenue, the company does a lot of its business via mail order, but there's plenty to choose from on the premises. An inflatable dinosaur growing out of an oversized stamp back greets visitors on the front porch. Whether you want to add to your existing collection, start a new one, or pick up some nifty stocking stuffers, there's a stamp to suit every personality here.

If you're not part of an organized tour or didn't pack your two-wheeler, you still don't have to miss out on pedaling through the surrounding countryside. Fuller's Hardware on Main Street rents bicycles.

If local crafts are of interest, check out the Jelly Bean Tree, also on Main Street. Here you'll find quilts, wooden toys, jewelry, baskets, stained glass, and lots more.

All that biking can give a person an appetite, and Katie's Kitchen has good food at low prices in a casual setting right on Route 121. Pizza lovers and punsters won't be able to resist Pizza, Paul & Mary on Main Street.

Food for the soul is available in the summer in the form of productions by the Saxtons River Playhouse. One summer's offerings included *Amadeus*, *The Fantasticks*, *Arsenic & Old Lace*, and *Snoopy*. There are special shows for children every Friday afternoon during the season. Main Street Arts is an active place with a wide range of cultural activities throughout the year.

You might find something unusual to take home at the Sign of the Raven on Main Street. This antique shop and gallery specializes in early country furniture, china, tin, brass, paintings, and old books. Like some marriages, the months are May to December, by chance or appointment.

You can take the taste of Vermont back with you in the form of huge, juicy blueberries that you can pick for yourself at Kibbe's Vermountain Farm on Leach Road, just west of town off Route 121. It's good picking here, and they do sell them already off the bushes if you don't want to get quite that close to nature.

A little later in the year you can pick some of Vermont's sweetest, crispest fruit right from the trees at the Saxtons River Orchards, just off Route 121. Again, you can do your own picking and choose the ripest McIntosh, Cortland, Macoun, or several other popular Vermont apples right from the tree, or stop at the retail stand and select a bushel or two already picked.

The Saxtons River offers recreation of its own. You can follow the riverbank and find yourself a good fishing hole and match wits with the indigenous brook and brown trout. Or pick up the fixings for a picnic lunch at the Village Market on Main Street and cool your toes from an overhanging tree. The town does have a municipal swimming area on Pleasant Valley Road, complete with lifeguards.

You can leave Saxtons River on a number of roads, most of them pretty and winding, so let your destination be your guide here. A great foliage route that will plant you near the Rockingham Meeting House starts out on Pleasant Street. The surface switches from pavement to dirt and then back again before the seven-mile route brings you out just behind the meetinghouse.

Route 121 west to Route 35 north to Grafton is highly recommended, both for motorists and cyclists; you follow the river all the way.

Grafton

If you look at Grafton on a map, you'll see that it is smack in the middle of the four-way intersection of Routes 35 and 121. Now look again and take note that Route 121 from the west is an unpaved road. Now look at it a third time and see where those roads originate — Windham, Townshend, Chester. You're not going to find any all-night gas stations and diners in Grafton where, in fact, one of the first things visitors notice is the noise or, rather, the lack of it.

If a town could be a museum, Grafton might be a good candidate — most of the buildings have been carefully restored and maintained, there are two covered bridges within walking distance of the center of the village, and the streets are hushed and shaded. But don't let this pristine exterior lull you into thinking you've stepped into a time warp. Grafton is very much a thriving and active community.

Back in the nineteenth century, there was a period of some 60 years when Grafton was in less than terrific shape. Grafton was just one of a number of Windham and Windsor County towns that suffered badly from the importation of foreign wool following the Civil War.

In its heydey, around 1830, Grafton was a virtual boom town, with a human population of nearly 1,500 and some 10,000 sheep. There were mills all along the Saxtons River between Grafton and Cambridgeport, and the town was bustling with production — woolen mills, soapstone manufacturing from 11 quarries, gristmills, sawmills, a carriage and sleigh factory, a butter churn factory, and a cheese factory.

The Civil War claimed some Grafton residents — some were killed, others relocated — and then the bottom dropped out of the wool market, destroying a mainstay in Grafton's economic base. A major flood in 1869 did even more damage to the faltering community, and then began a long period of dormancy.

The fact that Grafton is so well maintained and has a healthy economy now is due, in large part, to the largess of a New Jersey banker. Grafton could well have gone the way of the neighboring towns of Athens and Cambridgeport when its economy basically collapsed in the late 1860s, but, fortunately for Grafton, approximately 100 years later, Dean Mathey established the Windham Foundation.

Mathey's intentions were to revitalize Grafton's economy, restore its many fine buildings, initiate projects and programs that would benefit the state and its citizens, and give financial assistance to private charities and educational programs. Mathey died in the early 1970s and left the bulk of his estate to the foundation.

Attractions

The foundation has accomplished a lot since its inception. It now owns, and has restored, more than half the village's 50-plus buildings and operates three Grafton businesses — the Old Tavern, the Grafton Village Cheese Company, and the Grafton Village Nursery.

The Old Tavern is the one business that did survive Grafton's leaner days; it has been in operation for more than 180 years. When it was built in 1801, it was a stagecoach inn. When the foundation acquired the property in the mid-1960s, it underwent a complete renovation.

Four stories high, the tavern dominates the village center. The broad porches that run along two sides of the main building on the first two floors are lined with rocking chairs and flower boxes that overflow with color in the summer months. The tavern's exterior is traditional New England white clapboards with black shutters, fronted by a lawn that looks like it doesn't have a blade of grass out of place.

The 70 guest rooms are furnished with antiques — four-poster beds a specialty — and are clean enough to pass the most finicky white-glover's test. You could get to stay in the room where General Ulysses S. Grant spent a night or two in 1867. Grant was just one of the inn's more illustrious guests — Daniel Webster, Woodrow Wilson, Teddy Roosevelt, Rudyard Kipling, and Paul Newman are among the others. The tavern is surprisingly not too expensive, a room can be had for a moderate price — rates vary according to the room — and they offer midweek discounts.

Guests may spend a quiet evening reading in the Kipling Library off the main lobby or sneak off to the TV room for a doubleheader or walk down to the pond for a swim. The tavern also has tennis and paddle tennis courts.

A local man and his team of horses are often parked out front with a fringed surrey, and you can ride around the village in true style. The same horses will pull you in a sleigh out at the ski touring center in the winter.

Dining at the Old Tavern is an experience — lunch and dinner are open to the public, jackets required for dinner. Dinner is on the expensive side, but most people think it's worth it. Start out with the Grafton Sage Cheddar Tart or the Tavern's Cheddar Soup. New England Lobster Pie and Colonial Quail are recommended entrées.

If you eat often at the tavern, you'll probably need to do some walking, and there couldn't be a place better suited to it than Grafton. Almost everything in the village is accessible by foot. The Grafton Historical Society has published a brochure of nine historic walking tours, some more ambitious than others, but you'll see some historic sites walking that are inaccessible by car.

The Historical Society also operates a museum in the Sumner Mead House. The seven-room house and barn-annex house are an impressive collection of local history. The collection includes Civil War memorabilia, soapstone products manufactured in Grafton, inkwells, fire-fighting equipment, samplers, textiles, photographs, and more. The museum is open from Memorial Day to Columbus Day, Saturday afternoons and Sundays in July and August.

Just up the street, on the second floor of the town clerk's office, you'll find the Grafton Natural History Museum. It opened in 1989, the result of efforts by several local residents. Kids will like this museum — there's a fascinating live bee display where they can watch the bees come and go and work their comb and a respectable collection of fossils, dinosaur eggs, and bones. The museum sponsors field trips and lectures throughout the year but is only open from May through mid-October.

Another place the whole family might enjoy is the Grafton Village Cheese Company, out on Townshend Road. Grafton had a cheese factory back in the nineteenth century, but it was destroyed by fire in 1912. The foundation built the present factory in 1966. The factory produces cheddar cheese and sells it at the retail shop in the factory.

On the cheese factory's grounds there's a covered bridge of fairly recent construction, over the south branch of the Saxtons River. It's for pedestrian traffic only and leads to a footpath worth trying. It's a short walk out to the Grafton Ponds, owned by the foundation, and there are benches provided so you can take a breather and watch for birds.

In the winter you can ski around the ponds and surrounding area at the Grafton Ponds Cross-Country Ski Center. There are 30 kilometers of groomed flat and tracked ski trails through the meadows and into the woods at the foot of and up around Bear Hill. Instruction is available, as is rental equipment. Discounts are given to Old Tavern guests.

If you're not on skis and you've walked into the ponds from the cheese factory, take the footpath north and you'll come down the hill onto the Kidder Hill Bridge, a covered bridge that is not open to through vehicular traffic.

You'll almost be at the Hayes House, a bed and breakfast in a home built just after the turn of the nineteenth century. Other lodging options include historic Eaglebrook on Main Street and the Inn at Woodchuck Hill Farm on Middletown Road.

Another point of interest on Middletown Road is a bronze marker that lists 12 historic sites in the vicinity. On the opposite side of the dirt road from the bronze marker, walk down through a meadow to a grove of pine trees. If enough people have visited before you, you should be able to follow their tracks; if not, try anyway. Go into the pines and see if you can find the massive serpentine rock, believed to be the largest deposit of precious serpentine on the continent.

Although there are many historic sites to see within a few miles' walk of the village, you can see a lot of historically significant buildings right in town. Just up Main Street from the tavern is the White Church, built in 1858, and just up from that, on the opposite side of the street, is the Brick Church, built in 1833 and listed on the National Register of Historic Places.

One congregation, by the name of the Grafton Church, uses the two buildings. The congregation is Unitarian Universalist and American Baptist. If you happen to be in Grafton in mid-July, you won't want to miss the Annual Grafton Church Fair. It's held on a Saturday at the Brick Church and goes on no matter what the weather decides to do. The fair consists of an antique and craft fair, a band concert, bake and rummage sales, and games for the younger set.

If the idea of an antique show excites you and you're not going to be in Grafton in July, don't despair. Pickle Street Antiques, Gabriels' Barn, Woodshed Antiques, and Grafton Gathering Place Antiques offer hours of browsing pleasure.

If fine art interests you, the Gallery North Star on Townshend Road features the work of professional Vermont artists — oils, watercolors, and sculpture. The foundation owns the gallery building, which was constructed around 1877. Plaques are mounted on all buildings the foundation owns.

In addition to the gallery building, the foundation owns but does not operate the Grafton Village Store, the Grafton Village Garage — probably the prettiest garage you'll ever see — and a working dairy farm. The foundation's own offices are on Townshend Road, and there are some displays of interest in the old horse barn out behind the administrative offices.

The story of the sheep's place in Grafton's history is one display. An explanation of the foundation's current sheep project is another. The foundation holds workshops, clinics, and demonstrations for sheep breeders. "The Windham Foundation Sheep Project hopes to demonstrate that sheep farming can be profitable," states the display copy.

A turn-of-the-century general store is another display, as are a carpenter's workshop, wheelwright and cooper's workshop, old carriages and sleighs, and tools. There is no charge for the horse barn display.

A few more Grafton sites are of agricultural or horticultural interest. The foundation's Grafton Village Nursery on Pleasant Street has a half acre of perennials in raised beds. The best garden viewing takes place in June and July. The nursery has a gift shop, and plants are dug at the time of sale.

Take Route 121 east out of the village for 1.5 miles and you'll come to the Grafton Village Apple Company. The retail operation is open year-round and features McIntosh, Cortland, and Empire apples. Other Vermont food products, including maple syrup, are also sold.

Before you come to the apple company you will notice a small pond on the left-hand side of the road. This is Grafton's town swimming pond, a tiny one but with a nice sandy beach at one end and a picnic area under the trees.

Route 121 east follows the Saxtons River all the way to Cambridgeport. There are any number of nice fishing holes along the way. Brook and brown trout are both indigenous to the river.

There's not a lot going on in Grafton, or anywhere else in Vermont, at the end of winter and early spring, with one major exception — sugaring season. When the sap starts to flow, sugar makers all over the state fire up their evaporators and begin the arduous process of making maple syrup. Plummer's Sugarhouse on Townshend Road welcomes visitors and sells maple syrup and maple cream.

Grafton is one of those towns that you can easily drive right through and never really notice. If you take the time to stop and stretch those leg muscles a bit, you'll find Grafton has enough to keep you walking for at least two days.

The Windsor/Ludlow Area Essentials

Important Information

Municipal Services

Andover Town Clerk: 875-2765.
Andover Police: 875-2112.
Andover Fire & Ambulance:
875-3200; 875-2233.
Ascutney Town Clerk: 674-2626.
Ascutney Police: 674-2185.
Ascutney Fire & Ambulance:
1-885-4545; 542-2244.
Bellows Falls Town Clerk: 463-4336.
Bellows Falls Police: 463-4528.
Bellows Falls Fire & Ambulance:
463-3131; 463-4223.
Brownsville/West Windsor Town
Clerk: 484-7212.
Cavendish Town Clerk: 226-7292.
Cavendish Police: 226-7295.
Cavendish Fire & Ambulance:
226-7283.
Chester Town Clerk: 875-2173.
Chester Police: 875-2233.
Chester Fire & Ambulance:
875-3200; 875-2233.
Grafton Town Clerk: 843-2419.
Grafton Police: 1-875-2112.
Grafton Fire & Ambulance:
1-603-352-1100; 463-4223.
Ludlow Town Clerk: 228-3232.
Ludlow Police: 911 or 228-4411.
Ludlow Fire & Ambulance:
228-3434; 228-4411.
Mt. Holly Town Clerk: 259-2391.
Mt. Holly Police: 773-9109.
Mt. Holly Fire & Ambulance:
259-2700; 775-3133.

Perkinsville Police: 674-2185.
Perkinsville Fire & Ambulance:
885-4545; 1-603-542-2244.
Proctorsville Police: 226-7295.
Proctorsville Fire: 226-7283.
Reading Town Clerk: 484-7250.
Reading Fire: 484-3322.
Rockingham Town Clerk: 463-4336.
Rockingham Police: 1-875-2112.
Rockingham Fire & Ambulance:
1-603-352-1100; 463-4223.
Saxtons River Town Clerk:
463-4336.
Saxtons River Police: 1-254-2950 or
1-875-2112.
Saxtons River Fire: 1-603-352-1100.
Springfield Town Clerk: 885-2104.
Springfield Police: 885-2113.
Springfield Fire & Ambulance:
885-4545.
Weathersfield Town Clerk:
674-2626.
Weathersfield Police: 674-2185.
Weathersfield Fire & Ambulance:
885-4545; 1-603-352-1100.
Windham Town Clerk: 874-4211.
Windham Police: 875-2112.
Windham Fire & Ambulance:
824-3166 or 875-3280; 824-3166.
Windsor Town Clerk: 674-5610.
Windsor Police: 674-2183.
Windsor Fire & Ambulance:
674-2112.

Medical Services

Mt. Ascutney Hospital and Health Center, County Rd., Windsor; 674-6711.
Rockingham Memorial Hospital, Hospital Court, Bellows Falls; 463-3903.
Springfield Hospital, 25 Ridgewood Rd., Springfield; 885-2151.

Veterinarians

Rockingham Veterinary Clinic, Pleasant Valley Rd., Bartonsville (Rockingham); 875-3985.
Springfield Animal Hospital, Rte. 106, Springfield; 885-2505.
Windsor Animal Clinic, North Main St., Windsor; 674-2070.

Weather Information

Okemo Mountain Ski Report: 228-5222.

Tourist Information Services

Bellows Falls Chamber of Commerce (Greater Falls Chamber of Commerce), Box 554, 55 Square, Bellows Falls; 463-4280.
Chester Chamber of Commerce, Box 623, Chester; 875-2709.
Ludlow Area Chamber of Commerce, 196 Main St., Box 333, Jewel Brook Pl., Ludlow; 228-5318.
Springfield Chamber of Commerce, 55 Clinton St., Springfield; 885-2779.
Windsor Chamber of Commerce, Box 5, 3 State St., Windsor; 674-5910.

Lodgings

Reservation Services

Ascutney Mountain Lodging Service, Brownsville; 1-800-243-0011.
Okemo Mountain Lodging Service, Ludlow; 228-5571.

Inns and B&Bs

ANDOVER
Hillside B&B, Cobb Rd.; 875-3844. Inexpensive. At the end of a back road, there are some nice views to be seen from the Hillside. The guest living room has a large fireplace. No smoking.
The Quilted Cat, East Hill Rd.; 875-3658. Expensive. Eight rooms with private baths in a restored, circa 1810, farmhouse. Offers a beautiful mountain view, sauna, swimming pool, and cross-country skiing. No smoking.
Rowell's Inn, Rte. 11, Simonsville; 875-3658. Expensive. This former stagecoach hotel is listed on the National Register of Historic Places. Built in around 1820, the inn has been carefully restored and decorated with antiques. Major credit cards.

BELLOWS FALLS
Blue Haven Bed & Breakfast, Rte. 5, 1.6 miles from exit 5 off I-91; 463-9008. Moderate. Three guest rooms with period pieces and canopy beds in an 1830 schoolhouse building. Fireplace in common room; great homemade muffins for breakfast. No smoking.
Horsefeathers Bed & Breakfast, 16 Webb Terr.; 463-9776. Moderate. Six guest rooms, four with private baths. Country decor in the 1897 house. Cross-country skiing.
River Mist Bed & Breakfast, 7 Burt St., 463-9023. Moderate. Three guest rooms in a large Victorian home, filled with a combination of "antiques and today's comforts." Flower-filled porch.

BELMONT
The Parmenter House, Church St.; 259-2009. Moderate. Four guest rooms, all with private bath, breakfast.

BROWNSVILLE
Ascutney Mountain Resort, Rte. 44; 484-7711. Moderate. A luxury resort in the tiny town of Brownsville. More than 200 hotel rooms and "condominium-style" suites available. Major credit cards.

The Mill Brook, Rte. 44; 484-7283. Inexpensive. Across from the Mt. Ascutney
Ski Area, the Mill Brook invites guests to afternoon tea. Three rooms with private
baths, five with shared facilities.

The South View Bed & Breakfast, Roe Hill Rd.; 484-7934. Moderate. Private,
yet close to Mt. Ascutney. This B&B is in a Vermont log home, with spectacular mountain views. Some guest rooms offer a view of Mt. Ascutney. Covered bridge within
easy walking distance. Full breakfast, afternoon refreshments. Major credit cards.

CAVENDISH

Cavendish Inn, Main St.; 226-7329. Moderate. Victorian setting, six rooms, two
with private bath, full breakfast.

CHESTER

Chester House B&B, Main St.; 875-2205. Moderate. Situated across from
Chester's lovely village green, the restored late-eighteenth-century inn is listed on
the National Registry of Historic Places. The four guest rooms, all with private
baths, are furnished with antiques.

Greenleaf Inn, Depot St.; 875-3171. Moderate. There are five large guest rooms, all
with private baths, in this restored 1850 home. It's a pleasant stroll from the
Greenleaf up to the village center. Full breakfast.

Henry Farm Inn, Green Mountain Tpk.; 875-2674. Moderate. The inn served as a
stagecoach stop and tavern back in the 1700s. The restored inn is located on a
quiet dirt road and surrounded by wooded hillsides. All seven rooms have their
own baths and a full breakfast is served. There are eight fireplaces, two sitting
rooms, and beautiful wide pine floors.

Hugging Bear Inn and Shoppe, Main St.; 875-2412. Moderate. Bears, all stuffed,
abound and there's one in every bed. Located on the village green, the inn serves
a full breakfast and afternoon refreshments. Guests are given a discount in the
on-premise shop, which features more than 3,000 bears. No smoking.

The Inn at Long Last, Main St.; 875-2444. Expensive. This inn has dominated
the village green for many years. Of the 30 guest rooms, the owners claim only
one is truly haunted. Each of the guest rooms is named for individuals the innkeeper admires — George Orwell and Currier & Ives are two examples. Swimming
pool and tennis court. Closed for the month of April and two weeks in
November. Major credit cards.

Inn Victoria, Main St.; 875-4288. Moderate. Seven guest rooms, furnished with
period antiques. Antique shop on premises.

Night With A Native, Rte. 103; 875-2616. Inexpensive. This small bed and
breakfast is brimming with antiques — there's an antique shop on the premises.
The two hand-stenciled bedrooms share a bath. A full, home-cooked breakfast is
served.

Old Town Farm Inn, Rte. 10; 875-2346. Moderate. This 1860s farmhouse served as
Chester's town farm in the middle of this century. Located on 36 rural acres, the
inn offers guests the use of a canoe and pond. Full breakfast.

Quail Hollow Inn, Rte. 11 east; 875-3401. Moderate. The guest rooms in this
restored farmhouse and barn all have private baths. Full breakfast. No smoking.

Stone Hearth Inn, Rte. 11 west; 875-2525. Moderate. Built as an inn around 1810,
the Stone Hearth has been nicely restored and features exposed beams and wide
pine floors. Located west of Chester Village, the inn has a licensed pub and
public dining. Pool table, games, and whirlpool in the attached barn. Full
breakfast.

Stone Village Inn, Rte. 103; 875-3914. Moderate. Located in the Stone Village in
Chester Depot, the inn has five guest rooms with private baths, a swimming pool,
and billiard table. Full breakfast.

GRAFTON

Eaglebrook, Main St.; 843-2564. Expensive. Built in 1831 with an identical house
across the street. First and second floor hallways feature stenciling by Moses
Eaton, Jr., circa 1840. Three rooms, one with private bath. Full Continental
breakfast. No children.

The Hayes House, Bear Hill Rd.; 843-2461. Inexpensive. This house was built in the early part of the nineteenth century and has three guest rooms. Continental breakfast.

The Inn at Woodchuck Hill Farm, Middletown Rd.; 843-2398. Moderate. Most of the 12 guest rooms have private baths. The eighteenth-century farmhouse is situated on 200 gorgeous acres. Antique shop on premises. Closed during winter months. Continental breakfast.

The Old Tavern, Main St.; 843-2231. Moderate to expensive. Built in 1801 as a stagecoach inn, restored in 1965, the inn has been in operation for more than 180 years. Tennis court, paddle tennis court. Major credit cards.

LUDLOW

The Andrie Rose Inn, 13 Pleasant St.; 228-4846. Expensive. All eight guest rooms have private baths and are furnished with antiques. Bicycles available for touring back roads. Built in 1829, the inn is named for a former owner who ran her home as a guest house in the 1950s. Full breakfast. No smoking. Major credit cards.

Black River Inn, 100 Main St.; 228-5585. Moderate. Ten guest rooms, most with private baths. The inn is situated on the bank of the Black River and is across from the town green. Polished marble fireplaces.

The Coombes Family Inn, two miles off Rte. 100; 228-8799. Moderate. On a dirt road that winds around one end of Lake Rescue, the inn is not far off the beaten path but far enough to get you into the quiet countryside. Colonial decor in the 1850s building. Full breakfast.

The Governor's Inn, 86 Main St.; 228-8830. Expensive. This Victorian inn, built in the late 1800s, offers eight guest rooms with private baths and furnished with period antiques. Full breakfast. Major credit cards.

Jewel Brook Inn, 82 Andover St.; 228-8926. Moderate. Comfortable rooms, tavern, and dining. Small pond on the premises. Lots of porches for outdoor relaxation.

The Okemo Inn, Rte. 103 north; 228-8834. Expensive. The inn offers 13 rooms, most with private baths. Special packages include golf passes and bicycle rental. Full breakfast. Major credit cards.

Trojan Horse Guest House, 44 Andover St.; 228-5244. Inexpensive. A century-old carriage barn has been converted into sleeping quarters — twin bunk beds. A lounge with a TV and wood stove is open to guests.

The Winchester Inn, 53 Main St.; 228-3841. Moderate. A village inn for more than 40 years, the inn has a swimming pool and tennis court. Guest rooms are all stenciled. Fireplace in common lounge.

MT. HOLLY

Hortonville Inn, Hortonville Rd.; 259-2587. Moderate. In a rural setting just a few minutes off Rte. 103, north of Ludlow, the inn was built in the mid-nineteenth century and offers five guest rooms. Full breakfast.

PERKINSVILLE

Amoroso's, Main St.; 263-5248. Moderate. Pleasant and quiet. Close to Stoughton Pond, Mt. Ascutney, Okemo.

PROCTORSVILLE

Allens' Inn of Proctorsville, Depot St.; 226-7970. Inexpensive. Furnished in a country motif, the inn has eight guest rooms, one with a private bath. Comfortable common room. Full breakfast.

The Castle Inn, junction of Rtes. 103 and 131; 226-7222. Expensive. This massive stone mansion, which sits up on a hill overlooking Rte. 103 and the Black River beyond, was built in 1904 by Governor Allen M. Fletcher. It has 18-inch-thick stone walls, stone fireplaces, and a carved oak and mahogany interior. The inn offers nine guest rooms, each with private bath and sitting area. Outdoor pool and tennis court. Closed April, May, November. Major credit cards.

The Golden Stage Inn, Depot St.; 226-7744. Expensive. A beautiful inn built in the late eighteenth century, the Golden Stage has 10 guest rooms and a public dining room.

Okemo Lantern Lodge, Main St.; 226-7770. Moderate. Ten guest rooms in a Victorian home. Swimming pool. Full breakfast.

READING

Greystone, Rte. 106; 484-7200. Moderate. A bed and breakfast in an 1830s stone house, furnished with antiques. A short drive to Woodstock and Mt. Ascutney. Continental breakfast.

ROCKINGHAM

Hazeltine House Bed & Breakfast, Rte. 5, 3.5 miles from turn near I-91 entrance; 463-2270. Moderate. Two guest rooms with working fireplace in 1789 farmhouse. Cross-country ski on the 38 acres or fish in the two brooks on the property. Perennial and herb gardens; sun room.

Rockingham Motor Inn, Rte. 5, exit 6 on I-91; 463-4536 or, outside Vermont, 1-800-255-4756. Moderate. A 30-unit motel with swimming pool. Dining facilities on premises. "Oldies bands" on Friday and Saturday nights in the lounge. Major credit cards.

SAXTONS RIVER

Red Barn Guest House, Hatfield Ln.; 869-2566. Moderate. Four guest rooms in this homey, turn-of-the-century bed and breakfast. Continental breakfast.

SPRINGFIELD

Bull Run Farm, 903 French Meadow Rd., North Springfield; 886-8470. Inexpensive. Bed and breakfast in a homey farmhouse.

Hartness House Inn, 30 Orchard St.; 885-2115. Moderate. Built in 1904 as the home of Governor James Hartness. Cross-country skiing on 32 wooded acres. Swimming pool and clay tennis court. There is an abundance of fireplaces in this lovely inn, a Registered Historic Place. The Turret Equatorial Telescope, designed and built by Hartness, remains in working order on the front lawn.

TYSON

Echo Lake Inn, Rte. 100; 228-8602. Expensive. This beautiful inn was built in 1799 and reconstructed in 1840. The inn offers 26 guest rooms and suites, a swimming pool, and tennis court. Major credit cards.

WEATHERSFIELD

The Inn at Weathersfield, Rte. 106, 263-9217. Expensive. There are 12 guest rooms, all with private bath, in this lovely eighteenth-century inn, which was built as a stagecoach stop. English garden and pillared veranda. Many of the guest rooms have working fireplaces.

WINDSOR

The Gingerbread House Bed & Breakfast, 5 Court St.; 674-2322. Moderate. This Carpenter Gothic home offers a furnished apartment that will sleep four adults. Full bath and kitchen, private entrance. Cable TV. Continental breakfast. No smoking.

Juniper Hill Inn, Juniper Hill Rd.; 674-5273. Moderate. Fifteen guest rooms, all with private bath and some with fireplaces. Furnished with antiques. Formal gardens on grounds. Full breakfast.

What Not House, Rte. 5; 674-5574. Inexpensive. Guest rooms.

Hotels, Motels, and Resorts

ASCUTNEY

Yankee Village Motel, exit 8 on I-91, Rte. 5; 674-6010. Moderate. Coffee shop, HBO, close to Mt. Ascutney.

BELLOWS FALLS

Hetty Green Motel, Rockingham Rd.; 463-9879. Inexpensive. Color TV.

Rockingham Motor Inn, Rte. 5; 463-4536 or, outside Vermont, 1-800-255-4756. Moderate. A 30-unit motel with an outdoor pool. Oldie bands play every Friday and Saturday night. Public dining. Air-conditioned, in-room phones, TV. Major credit cards.

Whippowill Gifts & Cottages, Rockingham Rd.; 463-3442. Inexpensive. Small cottages set back from the road in the woods, the kind of cottage you thought had disappeared.

BROWNSVILLE

Ascutney Mountain Resort, Rte. 44; 484-7711. Moderate to expensive. Downhill and cross-country skiing, 240 hotel rooms and suites, a sports center, and day-care facility. Major credit cards.

CHESTER

Motel in the Meadow, Rte. 11 west; 875-2626. Moderate. In a quiet, rural setting just minutes from Chester Village, the motel offers 12 units and is open year-round.

LUDLOW

Best Western Ludlow Colonial Motel, 93 Main St.; 228-8188. Moderate. The motel, located in the heart of Ludlow, is connected to a nineteenth-century home. Swimming pool. Family units with one and one-half baths. Kitchenettes. Air-conditioning and HBO. Major credit cards.

The Hide-Away Motel, Rte. 103; 228-7871. Moderate. Minutes from Okemo Mountain and Ascutney Mountain. Motel rooms with private baths and HBO; three-bedroom cottages.

Inn Towne Motel, Main St.; 228-8884. Moderate. Pool, HBO, kitchenette units. Porches run along both stories, giving guests a view of the downtown area.

Timber Inn Motel, Rte. 103 south; 228-8666. Moderate. Located on the bank of the Black River, just east of Ludlow village. Swimming pool, children's playground, HBO, sauna, and Jacuzzi. Major credit cards.

SPRINGFIELD

The Abby Lyn Motel, junction Rtes. 106 and 10, North Springfield; 885-2223. Moderate. Swimming pool, miniature golf, nature trail.

Howard Johnson Lodge, Rte. 11, just off I-91; 885-4516, 1-800-654-2000. Moderate. Indoor heated pool, sauna, exercise room, Jacuzzi. Restaurant and lounge. Major credit cards.

Pa-Lo-Mar Motel, Rte. 11; 885-4142. Inexpensive. Outdoor heated pool, picnic area, some units with kitchenettes.

WINDSOR

Country Vista Motor Lodge, Rte. 5; 674-5565. Moderate. Overlooking the Connecticut River, the Country Vista offers eight motel units and two rooms in the main house. Nature trail. The 1797 main house also houses a gift shop.

Windsor Motel, Rte. 5; 674-5584. Inexpensive. Ten-unit motel with two cottages. Swimming pool. Small pets allowed.

Cottages and Condominiums

LUDLOW

Birch Landing on Echo Lake, off Rte. 100 in Tyson; 228-4844. Expensive. Lakefront townhouses deep in the woods but still just minutes from Okemo Mountain. Swimming pool and tennis court. Major credit cards.

Ludlow Colonial Condominiums, 93 Main St.; 228-8188. Moderate. Daily, weekly, and monthly rentals. In two locations, both within easy walking distance of Ludlow Village. Efficiencies, one- and two-bedroom units available.

The Mill Condominiums, 146 Main St.; 228-5566. Moderate. These one-, two-, and three-bedroom units are located in a renovated nineteenth-century mill in downtown Ludlow. Each unit has a fireplace — free firewood provided — kitchen, color TV, and telephone.

Okemo Trailside, off West Hill Rd.; 228-8255. Expensive. Located just off Okemo's Sachem ski trail. Swimming pool, tennis courts, saunas, whirlpools. Major credit cards.

Strictly Rentals, Jewel Brook Pl.; 228-3000. Handles rentals on the mountain, in town, in the lake region, and in the country. Short- and long-term rentals.

Campgrounds

ANDOVER

Horseshoe Acres, Andover-Weston Rd.; 875-2960. Open year-round, except month of April. Pond and swimming pool, hiking, and cross-country skiing. Fireplace lounge and heated rest rooms in winter. Recreation room and convenience store. One hundred and six sites.

ASCUTNEY

Running Bear Camping Area, Rte. 5; 674-6417. Open May 15 through October 15. Ninety-eight sites, showers, pool, playground, camp store, recreation room.

CAVENDISH

Caton Place Campground, Crown Point Rd.; 226-7767. Hot showers, swimming pool, wooded and open sites. Hunting and hiking. Open Memorial Day through November 1; hunting season by reservation. Children's playground, horseshoe pits, shuffleboard court.

CHESTER

Hidden Valley Campground, off Rte. 10 about three miles from Gassetts; 886-2497. Fishing, swimming, 33 sites. Open May 1 through October 15.

LUDLOW

Hideaway "Squirrel Hill" Campgrounds, off Rte. 103; 228-8800. Free hot showers, 24 sites, playground. Winterized hookups with cable TV for RVs.

PERKINSVILLE

Crown Point Camping Area, off Rte. 106; 263-5555. Thirty-eight acres in a pine plantation, overlooking Stoughton Pond. Open May through November 1. Swimming, boating, fishing. Children's playground.

PROCTORSVILLE

Meadow Brook Farm, Twenty Mile Stream Rd.; 226-7755. Thirty rustic sites on 190 acres of quiet. Hiking, pond, fishing. Open Memorial Day through November 1.

SPRINGFIELD

Tree Farm Campground, Skitchewaug Trail; 885-2889. Open year-round. Eighty sites on 40 acres of a pine plantation. Bicycle rentals, playground, hiking, cross-country skiing, hunting. Heated lodge.

Dining

ANDOVER

Rowell's Inn, Rte. 11, Simonsville; 875-3658. Moderate. Good food in a beautiful country inn setting.

ASCUTNEY

Alice's Restaurant, Rte. 131; 674-2137. Inexpensive. Serves breakfast, lunch, and dinner.

Max's Country Village Store, Rte. 131; 674-6902. Inexpensive. Good sandwiches.

BELLOWS FALLS

Allen Brothers Farm Stand, Rte. 5; 722-3395. Inexpensive. On-premise deli features pie, soup, sandwiches on homemade bread.

Athens Pizza House, 41 Square; 463-9495. Inexpensive. Pizza, salads, grinders.

The Express Café and Deli, 92 Rockingham St.; 463-4143. Inexpensive. Casual dining, soup, salads, sandwiches.

Joy Wah, Rte. 5; 463-9761. Moderate. Open seven days a week. Take-out orders also available. Szechuan and Cantonese cuisine.

Miss Bellows Falls Diner, 90 Rockingham St.; 463-9800. Inexpensive. Listed on the National Register of Historic Places — it's one of the last Worcester Lunch Cars still in use. One of the last diner holdouts — food traditional, atmosphere friendly.

Spoons, Rockingham Rd.; 463-9882. Inexpensive. Breakfast, lunch, dinner. Open seven days. Good, diner-type fare.

BROWNSVILLE

Ascutney Harvest Inn, off Rte. 44; 484-7711 or 1-800-243-0011. Expensive. Special Sunday brunch, complete wine list, excellent desserts.

CHESTER

Beverly's Restaurant and White Parrot Lounge, on the green; 875-2400. Moderate. Good salad bar, nice atmosphere. Major credit cards.

Chat & Chew, Rte. 103, Gassetts; 875-3943. Inexpensive. Don't let the exterior fool you; good home cooking at low prices. Homemade soups, hearty sandwiches.

Chester Pizza, on the green; 875-2908. Inexpensive. Breakfast served from 5:00 A.M. to 10:30 A.M. daily. Pizzas and hot grinders served from 10:00 A.M. daily.

Delaney's Country Girl Diner, Rte. 11; 875-2650. Inexpensive. Traditional diner fare.

The Inn at Long Last, Main St.; 875-2444. Moderate. Traditional New England cuisine; full bar. On the village green in the middle of Chester. Major credit cards.

Kalico Kitchen, Rte. 103; 875-3484. Inexpensive. Diner food, good homemade soup.

Karin Anne's Delicatessen, North St.; no phone. Inexpensive. Good deli sandwiches.

Murray's, junction of Rtes. 11 and 103; 875-3474. Moderate. Breakfast and lunch. Great muffins. Sunday buffet.

The Stone Hearth Inn, Rte. 11 west; 875-2525. Inexpensive. Hearty fare — lasagne, shepherd's pie, chili, stuffed peppers.

The Village Green Deli, on the green; 875-3898. Moderate. Light food in a pleasant setting.

GRAFTON

The Old Tavern, Main St.; 843-2231. Moderate. Fine dining. The Grafton Sage Cheddar Cheese Tart is terrific. Specialty entrées include Vermont lamb and chicken; traditional selections include lobster pie and colonial quail. Reservations, please. Major credit cards.

LUDLOW

Arthur's, in The Mill; 228-2150. Inexpensive. Breakfast and lunch only. Good place for breakfast.

Black River Inn, 100 Main St.; 228-5585. Moderate. The menu changes daily at the inn, and dinner includes five courses. Seating is at 7 P.M. in this 1835 inn. Reservations must be made by 2 P.M.

Boggles, Pond Meadow Marketplace; 228-7447. Moderate. A saloon and restaurant, serving lunch and dinner. Lunch menu features sandwiches, burgers, and salads. Cozy atmosphere. Friday and Saturday night entertainment and dancing.

Café on the Farm, Rte. 100; 228-8700. Inexpensive. Charcoal burgers, wings, soups, steaks, Sunday breakfast buffet. Casual dining.

Christopher's Sports and Spirits, downstairs in The Mill; 228-7822. Inexpensive. Steaks, burgers, sandwiches. Pool tables.

Chuckles, Rte. 103; 228-5530. Moderate. Located in a renovated nineteenth-century barn. The regular menu features beef, chicken, seafood, and veal. Children's menu available. Dancing and entertainment. Major credit cards.

Clockworks at Okemo, on the mountain; 228-2800. Moderate. Lunch and dinner. Sunday brunch. International cuisine specials every night. Children's menu and bar menu available. Major credit cards.

Common Crossing, Ludlow Plaza; 228-8495. Inexpensive. Good for breakfast. Dinner served all day. Lots of sandwiches, hot platters, salads, and burgers. Children's menu available. Casual dining.

Dadd's, Okemo Access Rd.; 228-9820. Moderate. Definitely a mountain restaurant, for those out for a good time. Menu features burgers and steaks. Major credit cards.

DJ's Restaurant, 146 Main St.; 228-5374. Moderate. Menu features steak and seafood, with a special prime rib dinner served Thursday through Sunday. Good salad bar. Reservations suggested.

Depot Street Delicatessen, Depot St.; 228-4210. Inexpensive. Open daily 7 A.M. to 7 P.M. Breakfast. Sandwiches, homemade soups, and desserts.

The Fox Run Club House, Rtes. 100 and 103; 228-8871. Moderate. Lunch during the golfing and winter seasons. Dinner served on weekends during the ski season.

The Governor's Inn, 86 Main St.; 228-8830. Expensive. Six-course gourmet meals in an elegant setting. Reservations a must. Major credit cards.

The Hatchery, Main St.; 228-2311. Moderate. Breakfast and lunch. Try the homemade muffins for breakfast. The lunch menu includes homemade soups, great salads, hefty sandwiches, and omelets.

Jewell Brook Inn, 82 Andover St.; 228-8296. Moderate. Tavern and public dining on Thursday, Friday, and Saturday evenings, from 6 to 9 P.M. Good food.

Ludlow Village Pizza, Rte. 103; 228-5618 or 228-9842. Inexpensive. Pizza, spaghetti, hot grinders, and salads. Ice-cream shop adjoins.

Michael's Seafood & Steak Tavern, Rte. 103; 228-5622. Moderate. Dinner. Tavern opens at 4 P.M. Sirloin served in a variety of ways and seafood. All meals include unlimited trips to the salad bar. Reservations suggested. Major credit cards.

Nikki's, The Marketplace, Rte. 103; 228-7797. Moderate. Dinner served from 5 P.M., Sunday brunch. Dinner menu features steak, seafood, and excellent fresh pasta. Wine bar and good selection of California and imported wines.

The Pot Belly, Main St.; 228-8989. Inexpensive. Try the Pot Belly Ribs or their Buffalo wings. Cuisine wanders from Italian to Mexican. Good wine list.

Priority's, on Okemo Mountain, near the base lodge; 228-2800. Bar, casual and light dining.

Sitting Bull Lounge, Okemo Mountain Base Lodge; 228-4041. Bar, Mexican snacks.

Valente's Italian Restaurant, 190 Main St.; 228-2671. Inexpensive. Healthy portions, good Italian food.

The Wayside Store, Rte. 103; 228-8934. Inexpensive. Delicatessen offering grinders, sandwiches, homemade soup, and baked goods.

The Winchester Inn, 53 Main St., 228-3841. Moderate. The traditional menu includes steak, lamb, and seafood. Nightly specials. Reservations suggested.

Harry's, Rte. 103, four miles east of Ludlow; 259-2996. Moderate. A cozy restaurant worth the short drive. Specials include Thai Night, and ribs.

PERKINSVILLE

The Inn at Weathersfield, Rte. 106; 263-9217. Expensive. Fine dining in a gorgeous country inn. Excellent fare in beautiful surroundings. Reservations. Major credit cards.

PROCTORSVILLE

The Castle Inn and Restaurant, junction Rtes. 103 and 11; 226-7222. Expensive. Fine dining. The menu features veal, beef, and seafood. Reservations. Major credit cards.

Sisters' Restaurant, Rte. 103, near the junction of Rte. 131; 226-7768. Moderate. Casual dining, lunch, dinner. Steak, seafood, burgers.

ROCKINGHAM

Leslie's, Rte. 5; 463-4929. Moderate. Dine in a renovated late-eighteenth-century building on European and American cuisine. Reservations suggested.

Rockingham Motor Inn, Rte. 5; 463-4536. Moderate. Prime rib and seafood. Lounge. Major credit cards.

SAXTONS RIVER

Café 121, 121 Main St.; 869-2907. Moderate. Prime rib specialty. Lounge with big-screen TV.

Katie's Kitchen, Rte. 121; 869-2383. Inexpensive. Basic fare.

Pizza, Paul and Mary, Main St.; 869-2222. Inexpensive. Pizza, grinders, salads.

SPRINGFIELD

Alibi's, Springfield Shopping Plaza; 885-5466. Moderate. Casual dining, lunch and dinner. Good salad bar.

Athens Pizza III, 371 River St.; 886-8383. Inexpensive. Pizza, grinders, fried chicken.

Gaslight Lounge and Restaurant, Springfield Plaza; 885-5466. Inexpensive. Basic fare.

The Hartness House, 30 Orchard St.; 885-2115. Moderate. Elegant dining room in the former house of a Vermont governor. Serving breakfast, lunch, and dinner.

KAHA Diner, 20 Valley St.; 885-2856. Inexpensive. Breakfast and lunch. Good diner variety food. Ice cream.

The Lookout, Clinton St.; 885-5554. Inexpensive. Seafood, Italian and American cuisine.

The Paddock, off Rte. 11, exit 7 on I-91; 885-2720. Moderate. Traditional fare, hearty servings. Dining in a renovated barn with unusual, but nice, interior.

Penelope's, on the square; 885-9186. Inexpensive. Serving lunch and dinner. Features homemade soups, quiche, salads, huge sandwiches, seafood, steak, ribs.

Riverside Restaurant, River St.; 885-9231. Inexpensive. Traditional New England fare.

Shanghai Gardens, 129 Clinton St.; 885-5555. Inexpensive. Eat in the unusual pink diner or take out.

The Subway, 85 Clinton St.; 885-2022. Inexpensive. Pizza, grinders, good shakes.

TYSON

Echo Lake Inn, Rte. 100 north; 228-8602. Moderate. Fine dining in a beautiful lakeside setting.

WEATHERSFIELD

Country Creemee, Downer's Four Corners; 263-5677. Inexpensive. Open summers only. Burgers, clams, scallops, chicken, shakes, and soft ice cream.

WINDSOR

The Brunch Bar, 135 Main St.; 674-6557. Inexpensive. This silver-and-red diner-type building perches on the side of Main St. Open at 5:30 A.M. and serves three meals daily, Monday through Friday.

Cattleman's Restaurant and Lounge, Rte. 5; 674-2032. Moderate. Dinner, Sunday brunch, lounge.

Depot Square Deli and Bakery; 674-2675. Inexpensive. Eat lunch here or take out — good salads, cheese, meats, baked goods.

The English Muffin Coffee Shop, Main St.; 674-5597. Inexpensive. Features Nowland Farmhouse Bakery products.

Pizza Chef, Main St.; 674-6861. Inexpensive. Good pizza.

Pizza Plus, State St.; 674-9366. Inexpensive. Rathskellar pub and pizza.

The Rib Room, Depot Square; 674-2675. Moderate. Victorian decor, features prime rib. Seafood, lamb, and pasta offered on Friday and Saturday nights.

Sala Thai, Rte. 5; 674-5574. Moderate. Thai food.

Stub & Laura's, Rte. 5; 674-5715. Inexpensive. Fast-food and ice cream.

Windsor Station Restaurant, Depot Square; 674-2052. Moderate. Built as a railroad station at the turn of the century, the station building now houses a Victorian-decorated restaurant.

Entertainment

Music and Stage

SAXTONS RIVER
The Saxtons River Playhouse, Main Street Arts, Main St.; 869-2960. Summer theater productions run from late June through August. Children's programs every Friday afternoon.

SPRINGFIELD
Southeast Council on the Arts. Presents an annual series of dance, chamber music, and the Vermont Symphony Orchestra. Check local listings.
Springfield Community Players, the state's oldest continuous amateur theater group, gives performances annually — check local newspapers for information.

Nightlife

ASCUTNEY
Mogul's, Rte. 5; 674-9965. Nightclub — entertainment and dancing.

LUDLOW
Boggles, Pond Street Marketplace; 228-7447. Friday and Saturday night entertainment and dancing.
Chuckles, Rte. 103; 228-5530. Weekend dancing and entertainment.
The Pot Belly, Main St.; 228-8989. Live bands and dance area.

WINDHAM
Priority's, at the Clocktower on Okemo Mountain; 228-2800. Live music and entertainment Friday and Saturday nights.
Tater Hill, Popple Dungeon Rd.; 875-2517. Live music and dancing on Saturday night.

Movies

BELLOWS FALLS
New Falls Cinema, on the square; 463-4766.

SPRINGFIELD
Ellis Theatres 1 & 2, Main St.; 885-2929.

Museums and Historical Sites

BELLOWS FALLS
Adams Old Stone Grist Mill and Museum; 463-3706. Local history. Open Saturday and Sunday afternoons in July and August.
Bellows Falls Canal, between the town square and the Connecticut River. Constructed over a 10-year period to bypass the Great Falls, this is believed to have been the first canal built in the nation.
Boston and Maine Railroad Tunnel, built underneath the village square. One of only two such railroad tunnels in the state.
Indian petroglyphs about 50 feet downstream from the Vilas bridge on the rock walls of the Connecticut River. Faces carved in the rock by members of the Pennacook tribe.

Rockingham Free Public Library and Museum, 65 Westminster St.; 463-4270.
The Historical Society operates a second-floor museum in the Carnegie Library
building. Collection includes local historical photographs and documents, tinware,
tools, and Hetty Green's writing desk.

BELMONT

Belmont Historical Society Museum; 259-2283. This tiny museum is located
just behind the library and is open by appointment. Special summertime events.

BROWNSVILLE

Benjamin Blood birthplace, turn left off Rte. 44 just before the town hall.
Granite marker commemorating birthplace of Blood, who gave the town its
library and left bequests to local churches and schools.
West Windsor Historical Society, Rte. 44; 484-7474. A second-floor space in
town hall that has no permanent display. Area schoolchildren and residents
collaborate on annual, thematic displays.

CHESTER

Chester Academy, Chester Art Guild and Historical Society Museum, on the
green. Originally built as a boarding school, this building has also served as the
town high school and junior high school.
Stone Village, Rte. 103, Chester Depot. A church and a number of private homes
constructed of locally quarried granite in the early nineteenth century.
Whiting Library, Main St.; 875-2277. This lovely brick building is an outstanding
example of Art Nouveau and Queen Anne styles — a photographer's dream.

GRAFTON

Grafton Historical Society Museum, Sumner Mead House. Seven-room house
and barn annex with soapstone articles, Civil War memorabilia, nineteenth-
century toys and clothing, photographs, fire-fighting equipment.
Grafton Museum of Natural History, in the village center, over the town clerk's
office. Displays include local minerals, galls, birds and nests, mammals, fossils. Gift
shop.
Kidder Bridge, a covered bridge on Water St.
Soapstone Quarries. Walk through Kidder Bridge, take trail .5 mile up hill, take
trail to left for about 2 miles. Old quarries that were once among the nation's
largest.
Windham Foundation Horse Barn, Townshend Rd.; 843-2211. Grafton historical
displays, including history of sheep farming, cooper's workshop, general store
display, and tools. Open Memorial Day through mid-October.

LUDLOW

Black River Academy Museum, High St.; 228-5050. Founded in 1835, the present
academy building was built in 1888 and its most famous alumnus was President
Calvin Coolidge, an 1890 graduate. The museum is listed on the National Register
of Historic Places. See a turn-of-the-century schoolroom, ethnic exhibits, tools,
photographs, memorabilia. Summer and early fall.
Fletcher Spring, across from Fletcher Farm School on Rte. 103. Steps lead down
to fresh spring, discovered in 1783.

PROCTORSVILLE

Historic Site Marker, just past Golden Stage Inn and before the railroad tracks.
Marks the site of the birthplace of Edward H. Williams, Jr., the founder of Tau
Beta Pi.

READING

Indian Stones, Rte. 106. Historic site marking the birthplace of Elizabeth Johnson,
who was born nearby to parents who were being held captive by Abnaki Indians.
Reading Historical Society, Rte. 106, Main St.; 484-7271. Built in 1761, this tiny
collection is often mostly by chance.

ROCKINGHAM
Bartonsville Bridge, just off Rte. 103. A 151-foot covered bridge built in 1870.
Rockingham Meeting House, off Rte. 103. Built in 1787, this building is considered one of the finest examples of early New England church architecture. Old cemetery with slate headstones adjoins.
Worrall Bridge, off Rte. 103 in Bartonsville. Built in 1871, the 87-foot bridge spans the Williams River.

SAXTONS RIVER
Hall Bridge, Rte. 121. A covered bridge built in 1982 to replace an 1867 structure.
Saxtons River Historical Society Museum, Main St., located in the former Congregational church; 869-2657 or 869-2328. Open late May to mid-October. Furnishings, decorative arts, toys, and tools from the eighteenth and nineteenth centuries.

SPRINGFIELD
Baltimore Covered Bridge, Rte. 11, next to the Eureka Schoolhouse. A 37-foot-long bridge built in 1870 and moved to its present location in 1970.
Eureka Schoolhouse, Rte. 11, east of Springfield. Vermont's oldest schoolhouse, built in 1795, authentically reconstructed.
Hartness-Porter Museum, 30 Orchard St.; 885-2115. Housed in a five-room underground apartment, joined to the Hartness House by a 240-foot tunnel. The museum is run by the Springfield Telescope Makers and displays include telescopes and paintings.
Springfield Art and Historical Society, 9 Elm St.; 885-2415. Local history, Bennington pottery, nineteenth-century American paintings, Richard Lee pewter. Open May through October.
Springfield Town Library, 43 Main St.; 885-3108. Listed on the National Register of Historic Places, this library building was built at the end of the nineteenth century. Collection includes historic photographs, sculpture, oral history tapes, and watercolors.

TYSON
Plymouth Kingdom Cemetery. Turn right at Echo Lake Inn to Felchville, 1.5 miles up on left, turnout. The burial spot of Deacon Daniel Clark, who was a leading businessman in Tyson in the early 1800s. The other 20 graves are of revolutionary war victims and early settlers.

WEATHERSFIELD
Covered Bridge. Take Rte. 131 west from Downers Four Corners .2 mile, turn left onto Upper Falls Rd.
Reverend Dan Foster House and Old Forge, Weathersfield Center Rd.; 263-5230. Museum run by Weathersfield Historical Society and including displays of tools, furniture, photographs, and books.

WINDSOR
American Precision Museum, 196 Main St.; 674-5781. Open mid-May through November 1. Admission. The museum houses an impressive collection of hand and machine tools, engines, typewriters, and computers. A Registered National Historic Landmark.
Historic marker on Main St. marks the original site of the Constitution House. A small park surrounds it, complete with benches.
The Old Constitution House, Main St.; 828-3226. Known as the "Birthplace of Vermont," the Constitution House was the site of the drafting and signing of Vermont's first constitution in July 1777. The Vermont Division for Historic Preservation now operates the site as a museum. Free admission.
Vermont State Craft Center, Windsor House, Main St.; 674-6729. Sales gallery and rotating exhibits by Vermont artisans.
Windsor-Cornish, N.H., covered bridge. Built in 1866, this is the longest covered bridge in the state and was designated a National Historic Engineering Landmark.

Seasonal Events

BELLOWS FALLS

Rockingham Old Home Days; 463-3543. Early August. Craft fair, fireworks, entertainment, 5K road race.

Sidewalk Sales. Two days in late May local merchants reduce prices and display sale items on sidewalk.

Fall in the Falls. Columbus Day weekend. Midway, games, rides.

Christmas tree lighting, in the square. Early December. Tree lighting, caroling, cider and doughnuts.

BROWNSVILLE

Annual Country Antique Show, Ascutney Mountain Resort; 674-6752. Two days in late July.

Brownsville Baked Bean Suppers. Saturday nights in July and August.

Mountain Music Festival, at the Ascutney Mountain Resort; 484-7711. July.

Annual Ski Sale and Swap, Ascutney Mountain Resort; 484-7711. October.

CAVENDISH

Annual Fire Department Chicken Barbecue & Fair. Two days in mid-August. Barbecue, bingo, flea market, pony and carnival rides.

Annual Cavendish Historical Society Flea Market. Usually first Saturday in September.

CHESTER

Chester Rotary Penny Sale, at Green Mountain Union High School. Early September. Fifty chances to win new merchandise for every ticket you purchase.

Sale on the Green. Labor Day weekend. Arts and crafts, refreshments, music.

Annual Book Sale, at the Stone Church in Chester Depot. Four days in early October. Get there early.

Harvest Fair, St. Joseph's Parish, Main St. Early October. Food sale, crafts, plants, white elephants.

GRAFTON

Annual Grafton House Tour. Mid-August. Tour of historic homes.

Town Fair, at the town ball field; 843-2436. Usually held in mid-July. The day of festivities usually includes a crafts and antiques fair, a barbecue, and town band concert.

Annual Fall Foliage Festival, held at the Grafton Firehouse. Crafts, food, fun.

Plummer's Sugarhouse, Townshend Rd.; 843-2207. This sugarhouse produces maple syrup and cream and welcomes visitors to its sugarhouse.

LUDLOW

Band concerts on the village green. Every summer Sunday evening at 7 P.M.

Annual Ludlow Elementary Parent-Teacher Group Harvest Fair. Early October. Craft fair, games, food, cider press.

Ludlow Antique Show, Ludlow Armory. Late September.

Okemo Mountain Ski & Spring Fling Weekend and 1950's Night Beach Party. By mid-March cabin fever has set in and everyone is ready for something to boost their flagging winter spirits. This could be it — if wild and wacky are your style, head for Okemo. For information call 228-4041.

Easter. Okemo Mountain celebrates Easter with races, hunts, bunnies, and more. For information, call 228-4041.

Annual Fletcher Farm Craft Fair, Fletcher Farm Craft School, Rte. 103; 228-8770. Usually held the first Saturday in July. Craftsmen from around Vermont and the Northeast exhibiting and selling their products. Demonstrations. Participants usually include quilters, woodworkers, weavers, potters, basket makers.

Annual Firemen's Auction, Ludlow Fire Station. Usually Labor Day weekend, 9 A.M. to 6 P.M.

Green Mountain Sugar House, Rte. 100; 228-7151. Visitors get a free sample taste of freshly produced maple syrup. Visit in the fall for some freshly pressed cider.

PERKINSVILLE

Weathersfield Historical Society's Fall Frippery, at the Hawks Mountain Grange on Center St. Usually mid-September. Rummage and bake sale.

PROCTORSVILLE

Venjbars Farm, Heald Rd.; 226-7657 or 226-7429. Visitors are invited to stand near the two large wood-fired evaporators and watch maple syrup production.

READING

Jenne Farm, Jenne Rd.; 484-7855. Floyd Jenne sets out about 3,500 taps and produces 1,000 gallons of syrup. Visitors are invited to watch.

ROCKINGHAM

Annual Pilgrimage to the Rockingham Meeting House, early August.
Vermont Championship Old Time Fiddlers Contest, held in September at the Rockingham Motor Lodge on Rte. 5.

SAXTONS RIVER

Fourth of July Festivities. Many towns have activities around this holiday, but Saxtons River's is one of the best. Parade, art show and sale, firemen's water polo.
Annual Organ Recital, Historical Society Building. Mid-August. For information, call 869-2328.

SPRINGFIELD

Moonlight Madness, downtown and Springfield Plaza areas. Mid-August. Street dancing, barbecue, arts and crafts fair.
Windsor County Agricultural Fair, Barlow's Field; 885-4920. Late July. Livestock competition, horse pulls, craft show.
Springfield's Annual Vermont Apple Festival, Riverside Junior High School. Columbus Day weekend. Food, cider, crafts, contests involving apples — award for the longest peel — entertainment. For information, call 885-2779.
Lookaway Farm, 222 Barlow Rd.; 885-4904. Visitors may come and watch maple syrup being produced. This is a fairly large operation, producing 5,000 – 7,000 gallons of syrup each season.

WEATHERSFIELD

Annual Antique Show and Sale, Weathersfield Meeting House. Late June. A two-day event, with displays inside and outside. Snack bar open all day.
Dana Farm, Bowen Hill Rd.; 436-2068 or 885-3688. This roadside sugarhouse welcomes visitors to watch maple syrup production. The Danas produce syrup, cream, and sugar.

WINDSOR

Annual Hike up Mt. Ascutney. May.
Annual Old Home Days Horse Show. Late June. For information, call 457-1792.
Historic Windsor's Annual Country Antiques Show and Silent Auction, Ascutney Mountain Resort. Two days in late July. Silent bidding on antique items. Call Historic Windsor at 674-6752.
Festival Windsor. Late September. A street fair atmosphere with crafts, food, entertainment. For information, call 674-5910.

Children's Activities

BELLOWS FALLS

Bellows Falls Fish Ladder, below railroad station. Built to allow free passage for salmon to the White River for spawning. Displays and recorded lecture.
Green Mountain Flyer, Green Mountain Railroad, One Depot Square; 463-3069. Take a 26-mile round-trip ride through the river valley to Chester Depot aboard a restored, vintage passenger train. Runs summer and fall. Union Station houses the Depot Square Gift Shop with souvenirs for railroad buffs. Foliage special in late September and early October, weekends only. Train runs from Bellows Falls to Ludlow for fall specials.

CHESTER

Bonnie's Bundles, in the Stone Village; 875-2114. Visit a doll workshop and watch handmade dolls in production. Closed January.

Green Mountain Express; 875-2760. Horse-drawn wagon rides through Chester.

Green Mountain Flyer, Green Mountain Railroad; 463-3069. A 26-mile ride in a diesel-powered, vintage passenger train between Chester and Bellows Falls. The nineteenth-century Chester Depot Station has been restored and offers a picnic area, and a bay window caboose is on display.

GRAFTON

Horse-drawn surrey rides and sleigh rides, Harry Wilbur; 875-3643. Tour the town in style. You can usually find Wilbur parked near the Old Tavern in summer and fall or ride in the sleigh out at the cross-country center once snow flies.

Grafton Natural History Museum, over the town clerk's office. Exhibits include dinosaur bones, a live bee exhibit, fossils, Indian artifacts, local birds and mammals. Small gift shop.

HEALDVILLE

The Candle Factory, Healdville Rd., Mt. Holly; 259-2483. Watch candles being made at the factory and create your own. Candle-making kits suitable for children.

The Crowley Cheese Factory, Healdville Rd.; 259-2340. The nation's oldest cheese factory, listed as a National Historic Place, has been open since 1882. The factory is open to the general public Monday through Friday, 8 A.M. to 4 P.M. and is open year-round. Crowley produces Colby cheese in wheels and bars and special spiced varieties.

LUDLOW

The Fletcher Farm School for the Arts and Crafts, Rte. 103. A converted farmhouse and outbuildings serve as a bustling crafts center in the summer. Special classes for children.

Green Mountain Sugar House, Rte. 100; 226-7151. Watch maple syrup being made, usually March and April. Watch cider being pressed starting in September.

PROCTORSVILLE

Joseph Cerniglia Winery, off Rte. 103; 226-7575. Tour the winery, sample the apple wines, wine coolers, hard cider, and nonalcoholic beverages.

ROCKINGHAM

Vermont Country Store, Rte. 103; 463-3855. Kids will lose themselves in the shelves of penny candy and toys.

SAXTONS RIVER

The Saxtons River Playhouse, Main St. Arts, Main St.; 869-2960. Summer theater, special children's programs every Friday afternoon.

SPRINGFIELD

Miniature golf, The Abby Lyn Motel, junction Rtes. 106 and 10; 885-2223. Eighteen-hole course, open to the public.

Park Street Bowl, 11 Park St.; 885-5384. Candlepin.

Plaza Bowl, Springfield Plaza; 885-5087.

Wellwood Orchards, Wellwood Orchard Rd.; 263-5200. Pick your own apples. Usually mid-September through October.

WINDSOR

American Precision Museum, 196 Main St.; 674-5781. This museum, housed in a National Historic Landmark, documents the history of tools, machines, and engines.

Shops

Art Galleries

BROWNSVILLE
The Gallery at the Mountain, Ascutney Mountain Resort; 484-7711. Local artists, who work in a variety of mediums, exhibit monthly.

CHESTER
American Renaissance Gallery, on the green; 875-4143. Paintings, photography, sculpture, stoneware, weaving.
Chester Art Guild, on the green; 875-3767. A consortium of more than 100 local artists and friends. Gallery in the Chester Academy building open from late June to mid-October.
Country Tidings, Rte. 103; 875-2241. Photography and fine art.
Crow Hill Gallery, Flamstead Rd.; 875-3763. Watercolors and limited-edition prints by Jeanne Carbonetti and several regional artists. Sculpture garden.
Dawson Mill Gallery, in the old gristmill at the corner of Rte. 103 and the Green Mountain Tpk. Local artists. Irregular hours.
Gallery T.C., at Carpenter's Emporium, on the green; 875-3267. Paintings, drawings, prints.
Highland Ponds Gallery, Flamstead Rd.; 875-4085. By appointment. Watercolors, prints, wrought ironwork.

GRAFTON
Gallery North Star, Townshend Rd.; 843-2465. Features work of Vermont artists.

LUDLOW
Fletcher Farm School, Rte. 103; 228-8770. Work of members of the Craftsmen Society. Craft shop.

SAXTONS RIVER
The Gallery at Sign of the Raven, Main St.; 869-2500. Rotating exhibits of area artists' work.

SPRINGFIELD
Springfield Art and Historical Society, 9 Elm Hill; 885-2415. Permanent collection includes Bennington pottery, nineteenth-century art, and Richard Lee pewter. Monthly displays include local artists' work.

WINDSOR
Vermont State Craft Center, Windsor House; 674-6729. Features Vermont artists and craftsmen.

Craft and Specialty Stores

ANDOVER
The Red Sleigh Gift Shoppe, Rte. 11 west; 875-2555. Country crafts and Christmas shop.

BELLOWS FALLS
Arch Bridge Bookshop, 142 Westminster St., second floor; 463-9395. Nonfiction and rare books, specializing in WW II, Civil War, the American West.
The Big Red Barn, exit 5 on I-91, Rte. 5 south. Souvenirs, gifts, Vermont products.
Depot Square Gift Shop, Depot St.; Railroad memorabilia and souvenirs.
Old Cottage Heirlooms, Rte. 5; 463-9008. Fine art and the work of Connecticut River valley artisans.
The Rock and Hammer, 30 Square; 463-2289. Fine handcrafted jewelry.

Sam's Army and Navy Department Store, on the square. Sporting goods, footwear, apparel.

Strictly Vermont Store, 115 Rockingham St.; 463-4818. Hardwood furniture, quilts, candles, slate art.

CHESTER

Andover Designs, Rte. 11 and Elm St.; 875-4056. Stainless steel and glass, wood and marble tabletops and desk consoles. Factory showroom.

Bonnie's Bundles, in the Stone Village; 875-2114. Doll workshop and retail sales. Handcrafted, stuffed dolls. Bonnie Watters designs patterns for Butterick.

Carpenter's Emporium, Main St., on the green; 875-3267. A nineteenth-century country store with Vermont and imported gifts, apparel, fabric, gourmet food, pottery.

The Charthouse, Main St.; 875-2121. National Survey maps, artist and craft supplies, globes, gifts.

Christmas Village Gift Shop, Main St.; 875-2210. Christmas items and gifts.

Country Treasures, on the green; 875-4377. Quilts, folk art, crafts.

Daniels Dried Flower Shoppe, Rte. 11 west. Dried flower arrangements, wreaths, baskets.

The Hugging Bear Shoppe, Main St.; 875-2412. More than 3,000 teddy bears, stickers, books, T-shirts, puzzles, cards, "bearaphernalia."

Kendall's Barn, Rte. 103; 875-3469. Open April through October. Antiques, collectibles, and everything else you can imagine.

Misty Valley Books, on the green; 875-3400. Excellent bookstore.

Stone Village Antiquarian Books, Flamstead Rd.; 875-2297. By appointment. Leather bindings, Vermont books, Polish paper cutouts.

Vermont Forgings, Trebo Rd.; 875-3801. Hand-forged ornamental ironwork; shop on premises. Chandeliers, gates, pot racks, and more.

GRAFTON

The Gift Shop at Eaglebrook, Main St.; 843-2564. Woven and printed textiles, soaps, jewelry, brass, china reproductions.

Grafton Village Apple Company, Inc., Rte. 121; 843-2406. Vermont food products including apples, cider, wine, maple syrup, honey, jams, and preserves.

Grafton Village Cheese Company, Townshend Rd.; 843-2221. Cheddar cheese made and sold.

Grafton Village Nursery; 843-2442. Perennial plants in raised beds, bulbs, dried flowers, gift shop.

LUDLOW

The Cook's Cupboard, Main St.; 228-2005. Kitchen items.

Cuddly Critters, 136 Main St.; 228-2175. Plush and stuffed animals of all kinds.

Green Mountain Sugar House, Rte. 100 north; 228-7151. Maple syrup and candy made on the premises. Gift shop features maple products, Vermont cheese, smoked meats, crafts.

Handcrafts & Gifts Unlimited, Jewel Brook Pl.; 228-3045. Vermont souvenirs and handcrafts, maple products, Christmas shop.

Lamps & Shades by Alice, 47 Depot St.; 228-5630. Custom-design lampshades, supplies.

Main Street Book Stop, 196 Main St.; 228-2665. New and used books, Vermont books, cards.

The Penny Scale, Main St.; 228-5610. A jam-packed store that sells rugs, candles, baskets, wreaths, and much more.

Pottery Works, Sunshine Marketplace; 228-8743. Stoneware, dried flowers, wreaths.

The Quilt Patch, 160 Main St.; 228-4830. Quilts, quilting supplies, and books.

The Wayside Store, Rte. 103; 228-8934. Vermont food products, T-shirts, crafts, and gifts.

MT. HOLLY

The Candle Factory, 160 Healdville Rd., turn off Rte. 103 about six miles north of Ludlow; 259-2483. Watch candles being made and make your own right at the factory. Seasonal, carved, figurative, hand-painted, scented candles. Seconds.

Crowley Cheese Shop, Rte. 103, Healdville, five miles north of Ludlow; 259-2210. The shop sells Crowley Cheese products, maple syrup, bakery items, jams, and preserves.

Vermont Sampler, Hortonville Four Corners, turn at the blinking light on Rte. 103, go 2.2 miles; 259-2033. Open weekends early July through mid-September; open daily mid-September to just before Christmas. Demonstrations of wreath and garland making. Straw, grapevine, and evergreen wreaths. Christmas shop. Mail order, too.

PERKINSVILLE

Perkinsville General Store, Rte. 106; 263-5474. Gifts, groceries, T-shirts.

Vermont Soapstone Company, Stoughton Pond Rd., off Rte. 106 north; 263-5404. This company has been mining and manufacturing soapstone products since the middle of the nineteenth century. Visitors may tour the mill. Gift shop features soapstone products.

PROCTORSVILLE

Singleton's Store, Rte. 131; 226-7666. A real general store — a specialty is cob-smoked ham and bacon.

ROCKINGHAM

Vermont Country Store, Rte. 103; 463-3855. Country store, bakery, Cross Cracker factory. Covered bridge, gristmill, 1885 soda fountain.

SAXTONS RIVER

Jelly Bean Tree Crafts, Main St.; 869-2099. Juried crafts including quilts, baskets, jewelry, wooden toys, stained glass.

SPRINGFIELD

Hermit Thrush Kitchen Shop, 15 Main St.; 885-4320. Vermont specialty foods, gourmet cookware, and Vermont crafts.

J & B Balloon Company, Main St.; 885-5510. Balloons, gifts, cards, jokes, kites. A fun place to visit.

Pastimes, 218 River St.; 885-5819. Country and Vermont-made gifts.

Wee Too Shop, 163 North Main St., North Springfield; 886-2722. Dollhouses and miniatures.

Welcome Friends Craft Shoppe, 43 River St.; 885-5540.

WINDSOR

Cider Hill Farm, Hunt Rd.; 674-5293. Herbs, perennials, wreaths, herbal products.

The Representations of New England Gift Shop, State St.; 674-2529. An interesting gift shop collection.

Antiques

ANDOVER

Grafton Gathering Place Antiques at Rowell's Inn, Rte. 11; 875-3658. Furniture, quilts, primitives, lamps.

ASCUTNEY

Ascutney Country Store and Antique Center, junction of Rtes. 5 and 131; 674-2623. Country furniture, primitives, oak furniture.

BELLOWS FALLS

Gae Managan's Store, 29 Westminster St.; 463-9656. Antiques and crafts.

BROWNSVILLE
Schoolhouse Ten Antiques, Brownsville-Hartland Rd.; 484-3396. Open May through October, 10 A.M. to 5 P.M., by chance or appointment. Varied antiques.

CAVENDISH
Sigourney's Antiques, Rte. 131; 226-7713. Children's books and toy soldiers, English copper and brass, variety of antiques. Open April through November, by appointment only.

CHESTER
Antiques at New Horizons, Andover-Weston Rd.; 875-4144. Specializing in Victorian pieces.

Karen Augusta, Depot St.; 463-4958. Open Friday through Sunday, noon to 4 P.M. Antique laces, textiles, vintage clothing, and jewelry.

Austin's Antiques, corner of Rtes. 11 and 103 north; 875-3032. Country furniture and accessories, oak.

Brick Cottage Collectibles, Rte. 11 east, Chester Depot; 875-3431. Antiques, books, used furniture.

1828 House, Rte. 103 north; 875-3075. Open May 15 through October 15, 10 A.M. to 5 P.M., daily. English eighteenth- and nineteenth-century country furniture and accessories.

Inn Victoria Collection, on the green; 875-4288. Antique furnishings and decorative accessories.

GRAFTON
Gabriels' Barn, at the Woodchuck Hill Farm Inn on Middletown Rd.; 843-2398. Open May through October, 10 A.M. to 5 P.M., daily. Country furniture, crocks, jugs, primitives.

Grafton Gathering Place Antiques, Sylvan Rd.; 875-2309. Period furniture, country pieces, accessories.

Pickle Street Antiques, Grafton Village Center; 843-2533. Irregular hours. Country furniture, nineteenth-century quilts, primitives.

Woodshed Antiques, Rte. 121, east of village; 843-2365. Open daily May through October. Country furniture, tools, phonographs, ox yokes, primitives, glass.

LUDLOW
Black River Antiques Center, Rte. 103 north; 228-8908.

Ludlow Antique and Gift Center, Rte. 103; 228-7335. Changing selection from a group of dealers, including furniture and accessories. Open daily, year-round.

Red Clover Antiques, 119 Main St.; 228-4333.

Village Barn Antiques, 126 Main St.; 228-3275. Open weekends and holidays.

READING
Liberty Hill Antiques, Rte. 106; 484-7710. Open May 15 through October. Country furniture and accessories, woodworking tools.

Mill Brook Antiques, Rte. 106; 484-5942. Open daily year-round, call ahead if traveling a long distance. Furniture, primitives, stoneware, china, country store collectibles.

Yellow House Antiques, Rte. 106; 484-7799. Open year-round by chance or appointment. Features eighteenth- and early nineteenth-century Americana — furniture, art, and Shaker.

SAXTONS RIVER
Schoolhouse Antiques, Rte. 121; 869-2332. Open year-round by chance. Country furniture and accessories.

Sign of the Raven, Main St.; 869-2500. Open May through December, by chance or appointment. Early country furniture, glass, china, tin, paintings, old books.

SPRINGFIELD
Chair By The Fire, Pleasant Valley Rd.; 885-4640. Formal and country furniture, lamps, glass, china. Open year-round, by chance or appointment.

Murray's Antiques, 10 Royal St.; 885-3046.
Pastimes, 218 River St.; 885-5819. Open Monday through Saturday, 10 A.M. to
  5 P.M. Furniture, crocks, butter churns.
The Summer Hill Shop, 80 Summer Hill; 885-3294. Open May through
  November, by appointment only. Dolls, toys, and related articles.
Upper Crust Gallery, 2 Valley St.; 885-8097.

WINDSOR
Patterson Mountain Antiques, 53 North Main St. at the Windsor Antiques
  Market; 674-9336. American furniture, art, and folk art.
Windsor Antiques Market, 53 North Main St.; 674-9336. Open 9:30 A.M. to
  5:30 P.M., May through October; open Thursday through Monday, 10:00 A.M. to
  5:00 P.M., November through April. Located in Gothic Revival church and featuring American furniture, folk art, paintings, Orientalia, American Indian, military,
  textiles.

Discount Outlets

CHESTER
Vermont T's, Main St., across from Jiffy Mart; 875-2091. Silk-screened T-shirts,
  sweatshirts, and caps. Outlet store.

LUDLOW
Karl's Kasuals, Grand Union Plaza. Men's and women's clothing, shoes, and
  accessories at 25% to 50% off. Open daily.

PERKINSVILLE
Vermont Soapstone Company, Stoughton Pond Rd.; 263-5404. Gift shop offers
  20% discount on soapstone products.

PROCTORSVILLE
Wild Bill's Country Discount, Depot St.; 226-7500. Clothing, records, skiwear,
  books, VCRs.

SPRINGFIELD
Dunham Factory Shoe Outlet, Rte. 11.
Karl's Kasuals, Springfield Plaza. Men's and women's clothing, footwear, and
  accessories at 25% to 50% off.

WINDSOR
Ernie's Discount Store, Rte. 5; 674-5441. Greatly discounted prices on everything
  from toys to tools to clothes and more.

Sports and Recreation

Biking

BROWNSVILLE
Ascutney Mountain Resort; 484-7711. Touring and off-road bike rentals.

CHESTER
Neal's Wheels, Rte. 11; 875-3627. Bicycle rentals, sales, and service.

LUDLOW
O-K Ski Rentals, Jewell Brook Marketplace; 228-2125. Bicycle rentals by the hour
  or by the day.

SAXTONS RIVER
Fuller's Hardware, Main St.; 869-2284. Bicycle rentals.

WINDSOR
North Star Canoe and Bike Rentals, Rte. 12A, across the river in Cornish, N.H.; 603-542-5802.

Golf

LUDLOW
Fox Run Golf Course, Fox La., Rte. 103; 228-8871. Nine holes.

ROCKINGHAM
Bellows Falls Country Club, Rte. 103, turn opposite the Vermont Country Store; 463-4742. Nine holes.

SPRINGFIELD
Crown Point Country Club, Weathersfield Rd.; 885-2703. One unique feature of this 18-hole course is the fact that the Crown Point Military Rd., built as a connector between Fort No. 4 in Charlestown, N.H., and Fort Ticonderoga in N.Y., passes the 10th green. The course also offers nice views of Mt. Ascutney.

WINDHAM
Tater Hill, Popple Dungeon Rd., off Rte. 11; 875-2517. Nine holes.

WINDSOR
Windsor Country Club, from exit 9 on I-91, take Rte. 5 south for two miles; 674-6491. A nine-hole course located just north of Windsor.

Horseback Riding

MT. HOLLY
Holly Hills Trails, Summit Rd., off Rte. 103; 259-2650. Open daily at 9 A.M. Guided trail rides.

Sporting Goods Services

BELLOWS FALLS
Rte. 5 Citgo, Rte. 5 north. Bait and tackle.

BROWNSVILLE
Ascutney Mountain Resort, off Rte. 44; 484-7711. Alpine and cross-country rentals, repairs, sales.
Carroll Reed, at Ascutney Mountain Ski Resort, off Rte. 44. Sales and rentals.
Sitzmark Ski Shop, Rte. 44; 674-6564. Sales and rentals.

LUDLOW
Fox Run Ski Touring Center, Fox La.; 228-8871. Cross-country rentals and sales.
George Dunnett's Ski Rentals, off Rte. 103 in the village; 228-7547. Cross-country and Alpine rentals, tune-ups, and repairs. Open until midnight on Friday.
Northern Ski Works, Pond Meadow Marketplace; 228-3344. Sales and rentals.
O-K Ski Rentals, Jewell Brook Marketplace; 228-2125. Alpine ski rentals, tune-ups.
Okemo Mountain Ski and Rental Shops, Base Lodge; 228-4041. Rentals, sales, repairs.
Totem Pole Ski Shop, 16½ Pond St.; 228-8447. Ski sales, tune-ups, and rentals. Open until midnight on Friday.

MT. HOLLY
Ralph & Joan's Place, Rte. 103, about four miles north of Ludlow. Tackle, bait, licenses.

ROCKINGHAM
Green Mountain Marine, Missing Link Rd.; 463-4973. Canoe and fishing boat
  rentals.

TYSON
Echo Lake Inn, Rte. 100; 228-8602. Rowboat and canoe rental.

WINDSOR
North Star Canoe & Bike Rentals, Rte. 12A, across the river in Cornish, N.H.;
  603-542-5802. Canoe rentals and organized trips.

Tennis

Note: Most public town recreation courts are first come, first served unless otherwise
  indicated. Call the town clerk or recreation department for more information.

BELLOWS FALLS
Memorial Field, four courts. For information, call 463-3944.
Village Playground, two courts.

BROWNSVILLE
Ascutney Mountain Sports and Fitness Center, on the mountain; 484-7711.

CHESTER
Chester Recreation Area, Lovers Lane Rd., four courts.

LUDLOW
Recreation area, Pond St., three courts.

SPRINGFIELD
Riverside Park, four courts. For information, call 885-2727.

WINDSOR
Fairgrounds Recreation Area, Ascutney St., two courts.

Alpine Ski Areas

BROWNSVILLE
Ascutney Mountain Resort, Rte. 44; 484-7711. The mountain has a 1,530-foot
  vertical drop, four lifts, over 30 trails, snowmaking over 70 percent, ski shop,
  instruction, rental, child care.

LUDLOW
Okemo Mountain Ski Resort, off Rte. 103; 228-4041. Some 70 slopes on a mountain with a 2,150-foot vertical drop, Vermont's fourth highest. Ten lifts, snowmaking over 95 percent. Nursery, Ski Wee, ski school, full-service ski shop, rentals,
  base lodge.

WINDHAM
Timber Side; 824-5566. Owned and joined with Magic Mountain in Londonderry,
  this small mountain offers 32 trails and two lifts. You can ski over the mountain
  and back. It has its own base lodge and ski shop, but the ski school and nursery
  are on the Magic side.

Nordic Ski Areas

BROWNSVILLE
Ascutney Nordic Center at Mt. Ascutney, Rte. 44; 484-7711. Novice to expert
  trails, instruction, rentals, repairs, child care.

GRAFTON

Grafton Ponds Cross-Country Ski Center, Townshend Rd.; 843-2234. Open and wooded trails, 30 kilometers. Tracked and flat skiing. The trails start at the foot of Bear Hill and wind around and up it. Open 9 A.M. to 5 P.M., daily. Ski instruction, rental, repair, and sales.

LUDLOW

Fox Run Ski Touring Center, Fox La., off Rte. 103 north; 228-8871. Golf-course trails, some machine grooming. Instruction, equipment rental, and repair.

MT. HOLLY

Holly Hills Trails, Summit Rd., off Rte. 103 north; 259-2650. Cross-country skiing on trails through fields and woods.

SPRINGFIELD

Crown Point Country Club, Weathersfield Rd.; 885-2703. Cross-country skiing is permitted on the golf course.

TYSON

Camp Plymouth State Park, off Rte. 100. Skiing permitted on park land; no marked or maintained trails.

WINDHAM

Tater Hill Club, Popple Dungeon Rd.; 875-2517. Trails run through open meadows and woodlands, some machine grooming. Night touring, instruction, equipment sales and rental.

Fishing

ASCUTNEY

Wilgus State Park, 100 acres, fishing on the Connecticut River, rental canoes.

BELLOWS FALLS

Below Bellows Falls dam, some shad fishing in the Connecticut River.
Connecticut River setbacks, ice fishing for perch and walleye.
New England Power Company boat landing. Take Rte. 103 north out of Bellows Falls, turn onto Rte. 5 just before entrance to I-91. Take right turn at bottom of hill. Boat landing, picnic area. Brook, rainbow, and brown trout, pike, pickerel, perch, walleye, large- and smallmouth bass, bullhead, panfish.

CHESTER

The Williams River. Take 103 north through Gassetts, four miles from Chester, turn left on Smokeshire Rd., across from Chat & Chew. The next four miles of dirt road offer lots of nice fishing holes. Brook and brown trout.

LUDLOW

Lake Rescue, public fishing access on east side, dirt road off Rte. 100, past Red Bridge. Trout, perch, pickerel, bass. Ice fishing for smelt.
West Hill Recreation Area. Turn off Rte. 103 at Benson's Garage, continue on for about two miles, pond fishing.

MT. HOLLY

Lake Ninevah, off Rte. 103. Ask locally for directions. State fishing access on 237-acre lake. Rainbow trout, perch, pike, pickerel, bass, panfish.

READING

Knapp Brook Ponds, state-owned access. Brook and rainbow trout, panfish.

SPRINGFIELD

Hoyt Landing, Fish and Wildlife access with boat ramp. On Rte. 5, on the right just before the toll bridge. Perch, bass, trout, panfish.

North Springfield Reservoir, Rtes. 11 and 106. Two hundred and ninety-acre lake with boat ramp for small boats. Good largemouth bass fishing. Yellow perch, panfish.

TYSON
Colby Pond. Turn right off Rte. 100 at Echo Lake Inn, continue for about 2.5 miles. State-owned boating access on small, 20-acre pond. Brook trout.
Echo Lake. State-owned boat launch on Rte. 100, about one mile north of Echo Lake Inn. Trout, pike, pickerel, bass, and perch in 96-acre lake. Ice fishing for smelt and lake trout.

Boating

ASCUTNEY
Wilgus State Park, Rte. 5; 674-5422. Rental canoes on the Connecticut River.

TYSON
Camp Plymouth State Park, off Rte. 100; 229-2025. Rental boats on Echo Lake.
Colby Pond, Fish and Wildlife boating access on small, 96-acre pond. A good choice for canoeists.

WINDSOR
Mill Pond, Ascutney St. Municipal access, no motors. Rainbow and brown trout in 70-acre pond.

Swimming

BELLOWS FALLS
Meeting Waters YMCA, 66 Atkinson St.; 463-4769. Sponsors swimming nights at an indoor pool at the Kurn Hattin Home in Saxtons River. Call for specific days and hours.

BROWNSVILLE
Ascutney Mountain Sports and Fitness Center, on the mountain; 484-7711. Indoor and outdoor pools.

CHESTER
Chester Recreation Area, Lovers Lane Rd. Municipal pool.
Downers Four Corners. Turn left off Rte. 106 north at the intersection with Rte. 131. Look carefully. About .2 mile on 131, there is a dirt road leading off and down to the left, Upper Falls Rd., to a covered bridge. Good swimming hole in the Black River there.

GRAFTON
Grafton Town Pond, Rte. 121 east. Small beach and picnic area.

LUDLOW
Buttermilk Falls. Turn right at VFW on Rte. 103. Natural gorge and sliding rocks. Not for young children.
West Hill Recreation Area. Turn off Rte. 103 at Benson's Garage. Pond swimming, bathhouse, shelters.

MT. HOLLY
Star Lake, in the center of Belmont. Municipal beach on small lake.

PERKINSVILLE
Stoughton Pond Recreation Area, Stoughton Pond Rd. Nice beach and picnic area.

READING
Swimming holes in north branch of Black River on Kingdom Rd. Turn off Rte. 106 north at Reading General Store; river is on your left as you climb up the hill. A number of good spots between Rte. 106 and the intersection with Twenty Mile Stream Rd.

SAXTONS RIVER
Saxtons River Recreation Area. Swimming pond, lifeguards.

SPRINGFIELD
Springfield Municipal Swimming Pool, Riverside Park. Lifeguards.

TYSON
Camp Plymouth. State-owned, lifeguards, bathhouses, concession, picnicking.

WINDSOR
Mill Pond, Ascutney St. Municipal beach on 70-acre pond.

Hiking and Nature Trails

ASCUTNEY
Wilgus State Park, Rte. 5. Marked nature trails.

BROWNSVILLE
Brownsville Trail, from Rte. 44 to the top of Mt. Ascutney. Trail passes former granite quarries.

GRAFTON
Grafton Village Park, in the village. Seventy acres of woodland to explore on defined trails, some benches provided for relaxation.
Walking tours. The Grafton Historical Society has a booklet outlining nine walking tours of the area — both scenic and of historical interest.

SPRINGFIELD
Bryant Farm Nature Trail, Rte. 5. Self-guided nature trail near the Connecticut.
Springweather Nature Trail, just north of the North Springfield Dam. A nature area developed by a local Audubon Society and the U.S. Army Corps of Engineers.

TYSON
Camp Plymouth State Park, off Rte. 100; 228-2025. Marked trails through 300 acres of state parkland.

WINDSOR
Ascutney State Park, off Rte. 5 on Back Mountain Rd.; 674-2060. Marked trails.
Windsor Trail up Mt. Ascutney, 1.5 miles from state park entrance on Back Mountain Rd.

State Parks

ASCUTNEY
Wilgus State Park. From exit 8 on I-91 go 1.5 miles south on Rte. 5. Located on the Connecticut River, Wilgus offers 22 campsites, 6 with lean-tos; flush toilets; hot showers; picnic tables; fireplaces; picnic shelter; playground; canoe rental; and group camping on 100 acres. Nature trails to explore, the river to fish or boat on.

TYSON
Camp Plymouth State Park; 228-2025. Cross concrete bridge off Rte. 100 in Tyson, go one mile, turn left, and go one more mile. Beach, nature trails, hiking, fishing, boating, and group camping on 300 acres. Open Memorial Day through Columbus Day.

WINDSOR
Ascutney State Park; 674-2060. From exit 8 on I-91 go two miles north on Rte. 5, turn onto Back Mountain Rd. and continue on for one mile. Open Memorial Day through Columbus Day. Forty-nine camping sites, including 10 lean-tos, flush

toilets, hot showers, fireplaces, picnic shelter, and group camping on 1,984 acres. Hiking, picnicking, mountain toll road, snowmobile trails.

Foliage Vantage Points

ANDOVER
Take the Andover-Weston Rd., detour near the summit onto Andover Ridge Rd. — a breathtaking view of the Green Mountain Forest north of Weston.

BELMONT
Turn toward Belmont at the blinking light on Rte. 103 in Mt. Holly. The road is arched with hardwoods and will take you into the center of Belmont, then down over the mountain onto Rte. 155 north of Weston.

BROWNSVILLE
Ride the chair at the Mt. Ascutney Resort to the top of the ski trails — hike the rest of the way to the mountain's summit.

CHESTER
Take the Smokeshire Rd. off Rte. 103 north of Gassetts. This is a dirt road, which follows the Williams River for quite a while. If in doubt, always bear right. This will lead you to the top of South Hill in Ludlow — stop for a terrific look at Okemo and the valley below.

GRAFTON
Take Rte. 35 north to Chester. Seven winding miles of woodland.

LUDLOW
Take the Okemo Toll Rd. to the summit. A beautiful view of the valley.

PROCTORSVILLE
Take Twenty Mile Stream Rd. up the mountain to Kingdom Rd.

READING
Turn off Rte. 106 south of Felchville Village onto the road to Knapp Ponds — continue straight and you'll end up on Rte. 131 in Cavendish — a very scenic route.

ROCKINGHAM
Follow Rte. 121 from Saxtons River, through Cambridgeport — this follows the Saxtons River. Turn right onto Rte. 35 to Grafton.

SPRINGFIELD
Take Rte. 5 north to Windsor — the road follows the Connecticut River and lots of farmland.
Follow Valley St. out — it will turn into the Weathersfield Rd. and take you right through Weathersfield Center, ending up on Rte. 131 near Ascutney.

TYSON
Cross the concrete bridge near the Echo Lake Inn. You'll climb the mountain, first overlook and then pass pristine Colby Pond, pass through South Reading Village, and end up in the center of Felchville.

WINDHAM
Take Rte. 121 off Rte. 11 three miles out of Londonderry. At the corners you have two great choices. Take the road slightly to the left and follow the Saxtons River down into Grafton; turn right and descend steeply into West Townshend.

WINDSOR
Take the Mountain Rd. past the Ascutney State Park entrance. Park and hike the Windsor Trail to the summit of Mt. Ascutney for some outstanding viewing.

Best of Windsor/Ludlow

Country Inns: Chester House Bed & Breakfast, Main St., Chester; 875-2205. Echo Lake Inn, Rte. 100, Tyson; 228-8602. Juniper Hill Inn, Juniper Hill Rd., Windsor; 674-5273. The Okemo Inn, Rte. 103, Ludlow; 228-8834. Rowell's Inn, Rte. 11, Simonsville; 875-3658.
Resort: Ascutney Mountain Resort, off Rte. 44, Brownsville; 484-7711.
Breakfast: Depot St. Delicatessen, Depot St., Ludlow; 228-4210. The English Muffin Coffee Shop, 74 Main St., Windsor; 674-5597. Murray's, junction of Rtes. 11 and 103, Chester; 875-3474.
Lunch: Boggles, Pond Meadow Marketplace, Ludlow; 228-7447. The Express Café and Deli, 92 Rockingham St., Bellows Falls; 463-4143. Penelope's, on the square, Springfield; 885-9186.
Dinners (Moderately priced): DJ's Restaurant, 146 Main St., Ludlow; 228-5374. The Inn at Long Last, Main St., Chester; 875-2444. The Old Tavern, Main St., Grafton; 843-2231. The Rib Room, Depot Square, Windsor; 674-2675.
Dinners (Expensive): The Castle Inn, Rtes. 103 and 11, Proctorsville; 226-7222. The Governor's Inn, Main St., Ludlow; 228-8830. The Inn at Weathersfield, Rte. 106, Perkinsville; 263-9217.
Entertainment (Casual): Chuckles, Rte. 103, Ludlow; 228-5530.
Entertainment (Stage): Saxtons River Playhouse, Main St.; 869-2960.
Museum/Historical Site: Black River Academy Museum, High St., Ludlow; 228-5050. Grafton Historical Society Museum, Main St., Grafton; 843-2344. Old Constitution House, Main St., Windsor; 828-3226.
Art Galleries: Crow Hill Gallery, Flamstead Rd., Chester; 875-3763. Gallery North Star, Townshend Rd., Grafton; 843-2465. Springfield Art & Historical Society, 9 Elm Hill, Springfield; 885-2415.
Craft/Specialty Shops: Misty Valley Books, Main St., Chester; 875-3400. The Vermont Country Store, Rte. 103, Rockingham; 463-3855. The Vermont State Craft Center, Windsor House, Main St., Windsor; 674-6729.
Antique Shops: Inn Victoria Collection, Main St., Chester; 875-4288. Sign of the Raven, Main St., Saxtons River; 869-2500. Windsor Antiques Market, 53 North Main St., Windsor; 674-9336.
Discount Outlets: Ernie's Discount Store, Rte. 5, Windsor; 674-5441. Vermont T's, Main St., Chester; 875-2091. Wild Bill's Country Discount, Depot St., Proctorsville; 226-7500.
Public Golf Course: Crown Point Country Club, Weathersfield Rd., Springfield; 885-2703. Tater Hill, off Rte. 11, Windham; 875-2517.
Public Tennis Court: Ascutney Mountain Sports & Fitness Center, off Rte. 44, Brownsville; 484-7711.
Hiking or Nature Trail: Ascutney State Park, Back Mountain Rd., Windsor; 674-2060.
Camping: Horseshoe Acres, Andover-Weston Rd., Andover; 875-2960. Crown Point Camping Area, Stoughton Pond Rd., Perkinsville; 263-5555.
Children's Activities: The Candle Factory, Healdville Rd., Mt. Holly; 259-2483. Grafton Natural History Museum, Main St., Grafton. Green Mountain Flyer, Depot Square, Bellows Falls; 463-3069.
Farm Stand: Allen Bros. Farms and Orchards, Rte. 5, Bellows Falls; 722-3395. Grafton Village Apple Company, Rte. 121, Grafton; 843-2406.
Ice Cream: The Real Scoop, 94 Rockingham St., Bellows Falls; 463-3522.
Foliage Vantage Points: In Ludlow, take Rte. 100 over the mountain to Weston — a truly beautiful route. In Saxtons River, take Rte. 121 west through Cambridgeport along the Saxtons River. Turn right onto Rte. 35 north to Grafton. In Springfield, take Valley St. out — it will turn into the Weathersfield Rd. — into Weathersfield

Center. You will then descend and end up on Rte. 131 between Ascutney and
Amsden. In Windsor, hike the Windsor Trail off the Back Mountain Rd. to the
summit of Mt. Ascutney.

Ski Areas (Alpine): Ascutney Mountain Resort, off Rte. 44, Brownsville; 484-7711.
Okemo Mountain Ski Resort, off Rte. 103, Ludlow; 228-4041.

Ski Areas (Nordic): Fox Run Ski Touring Center, Fox La., Ludlow; 228-8871. Grafton
Ponds Cross-Country Ski Center, Townshend Rd., Grafton; 843-2234. Tater Hill
Club, off Rte. 11, Windham; 875-2517.

The Brattleboro/ Wilmington Area

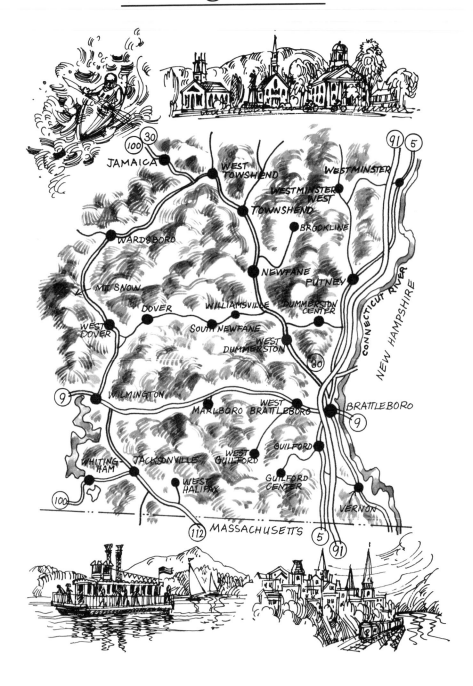

Viewpoints

by ALAN JON FORTNEY

If you come into Vermont from Massachusetts on Interstate 91, Brattleboro is off exits 1 and 2. That's why locals call Brattleboro the gateway to Vermont, or "Where Vermont Begins."

Before you even get to that exit, you can visit the Guilford Visitors' Center, which is about a half mile in from the Massachusetts/Vermont border on I-91. Considered the busiest in the state, the center has brochures by the dozens and advice from pleasant people who are here to answer questions. Even when the parking lot is full outside, the pace inside seems unrushed.

The Brattleboro-Marlboro area has much to offer the visitor. Brattleboro boasts a wonderful selection of cultural offerings, including the Brattleboro Music Center and the Brattleboro Museum and Art Center. The School for International Training is located in this thriving town near the Massachusetts border, and the community has more than 24 fine restaurants to choose from as well as an abundance of shops and discount outlets. For sports enthusiasts, Brattleboro has a winter carnival that includes ski jumping on the 70-meter Harris Hill, one of five jumps that size in the United States. Next door in Marlboro, a small town on Route 9, is Marlboro College and the world-famous Marlboro Music Festival, where musical greats such as Pablo Casals have come on retreat.

The area has three state parks — the Molly Stark State Park in Marlboro, Fort Dummer State Park in Guilford, and Dutton Pines State Park in Dummerston — and a small ski area, Maple Valley, located in Dummerston, a tiny town with a picturesque covered bridge located about 7 miles north of Brattleboro on Route 30.

Brattleboro, West Brattleboro

Sometimes referred to as a college town without a college, Brattleboro, population approximately 12,000, is a popular town with visitors. Besides the rich and far-reaching cultural offerings, Brattleboro has good restaurants and varied seasonal activities, and its location at the junction of I-91 and Route 9 makes it easily accessible.

Historical Perspective

From a historical point of view, Brattleboro can claim to be where everything got started in Vermont, due to the establishment of the first permanent foothold, a military fort, that opened the way for later settlements.

As early as 1724, Fort Dummer was built along the Connecticut River as an outpost for trading with the local Indians and to protect the settlers in neighboring Northfield, Massachusetts, when those original inhabitants began to object to the presence of the white settlers. By 1752, the area was considered secure enough to attract nonmilitary settlers who cleared about 200 acres around the fort, about one and a half miles from the present-day Brattleboro's business district. The fort, 486 feet in circumference and containing eight buildings, was no longer necessary in 1760 and was thought to have been demolished before the end of the eighteenth century, according to historical accounts. The site of the fort sank under the Connecticut River when the Vernon Dam went in in 1908. All that remains to be seen is a historical marker at the corner of Vernon Drive and Vernon Road.

Brattleboro is named for the man to whom it was officially chartered in 1753, one William Brattle, Jr., a colonel in King George's militia, a Harvard graduate, a politician, a doctor, a lawyer, and a land speculator who never once set foot in the town that bears his name. He died in Nova Scotia.

The people of this town had a reputation during the Revolution for being Tories. This trait did not endear them to the organizers of the Independent Republic of Vermont. While there were doings at that time, most of this community's life was devoted to scratching a living out of the soil. Tourism was not primary on the Colonial settlers' minds.

The idea did eventually occur, of course. When Dr. Robert Wesselhoeft developed the Brattleboro Hydropathic Establishment along the banks of the Whetstone Brook in 1846, Brattleboro became known as a resort town where people flocked to take the fashionable "water cure." This cure really involved refraining from excessive use of alcohol and tobacco; taking healthy, quieting walks in the woods; and taking the waters. It put Brattleboro on the tourist maps all over the East. People have been discovering Brattleboro ever since.

The one widely known industry to have developed here in Brattleboro, also starting in 1846, was the Estey Organ Company. Jacob Estey's company reached prominence in 1855, by which time it was considered de rigueur to have a handsome, black-walnut Estey organ in every parlor. At its height, the company employed 500 people and sold its products around the world. Estey continued to be a viable company for a century after its founding. The 1869 flood destroyed the factory, and eight new plants were constructed on Birge Street. Four of these buildings are still standing today.

A name of international consequence that is associated with this area is that of Rudyard Kipling. His home for three years, which he named Naulakha, was built in 1893. During that time he wrote *The Jungle Book*, *The Second Jungle Book*, poems included in *Seven Seas*, and *Captains Courageous*. The home, privately owned and not open to the public, is located just over the Brattleboro line in Dummerston.

Attractions, Recreational Pursuits

The business district is a point of pride with some locals, who say we have "no shopping malls, to speak of. Instead, we have a Main Street." While there are a few shopping centers that could be considered malls, and a commercial strip on Putney Road, most of the business activity in Brattleboro takes place on Main Street, giving it a centralized character and focus that many a town is now trying to recapture after having lost it to the malls. Brattleboro has kept its Main Street. It, along with Eliot Street and High Street, is where people come to shop, to eat lunch and dinner, to take in a concert or a movie. It's as it has been for a long time. It's the way many a small town wishes it still were. In this case, the Main Street area is also the cultural hub of Brattleboro.

The Brattleboro Museum and Art Center, in the old Union Railroad Station at the foot of Main Street, has sponsored ever-changing exhibits in its four galleries, as well as lectures, workshops, and performances such as the ceremonial drummers of Japan. The Gibson-Aiken Center, located on Main Street, specializes in athletic and cultural events. The Brattleboro School of Dance teaches classes

in ballet, jazz, and modern dance and performs some of the classical dance repertoire. And the Brattleboro Opera Theatre offers opportunities for young singers
to perform in workshops or master classes where scenes from grand opera can
be performed.

Cultural opportunities are not only relegated to the downtown. The Brattleboro
Music Center on Walnut Street offers Blanche Moyse's Bach Chorale Festival
and a Chamber Concert Series all through the spring and summer. The Community Chorus invites community members to join together in song, with performances held at Christmas and in the spring. The Brattleboro Brass Band,
founded in 1981, has joined the community in celebrating dances, parades,
weddings, and parties. It even has an album, "Black Cat Quadrille."

With more than two dozen fine restaurants in the town and the area, it is a
bit hard to single one or two out. Shin Li is Brattleboro's only Korean restaurant,
and it is quite popular especially at lunchtime. Another favorite for lunch, and
dinner, is Walker's on Main Street. The Common Ground, known usually as
the "hippy" restaurant in town, offers poetry readings and folk music and jazz
on various occasions. The shops along Eliot Street and Main Street include
bookstores, jewelry stores, arts and crafts stores, and carry work, much of it locally
produced, of the highest calibre.

South of the business district of Brattleboro is a shoppers' haven where there
are 12, one even dozen, factory outlets under one roof. Given the size of discount outlets, this one is rather modest, but it's got a lot of what someone wants,
or it wouldn't have been there as long as it has, nor would it stay open seven
days a week.

If you come at Brattleboro from the west, from Bennington (or from the Mount
Snow/Haystack region), there's a lot to see on Route 9.

Coming down the first hill from Hogback Mountain and the 100-mile view, you
will pass The Longwood, a lovely building set back from the road a ways, neatly
set behind a stone wall. In this building is a nine-room inn, with four studio
apartments in the adjoining barn, and a restaurant that overlooks the expanse
of lawn that is punctuated by a half-acre pond. Among those who have enjoyed
eating their meals and taking in the view have been noted economist John Kenneth Galbraith and former secretary of defense, Robert McNamara. The building
dates back to 1790 and is reputed to have been the site of Marlboro's first wedding.

Going around a curve in the road, farther downhill, is one of our favorite farms.
It has a little pond, usually populated with a duck or two (some years, there
were great blue herons of imperturbable plastic), which overlooks the perfect
pastures on the other side of the road. The Colonial farmhouse and barns on
this wonderfully cleared expanse in a declivity between mountains would be a
wonderful place to live.

The large horse pastures, with the white board fences that line the road farther on, after the nursery, is the Brattleboro Veterinary Clinic, not a misplaced
bluegrass horse farm.

As you come down the hill from Marlboro to Brattleboro, there are some amusing tourist places to stop, if you're in search of the ultimate Vermont gift. You
might find it at the Molly Stark Sugar House and Gifts or a place that calls
itself Unique Vermont Gifts. The latter is the yellow gift shop that is strung along
the side of the road and is fascinating to browse through. Along about here,
three miles west of Brattleboro's exit 2, is the Molly Stark Motel.

As you drive down the winding road into the flats of West Brattleboro, you
will see the Jolly Butcher, The Country Kitchen, The Fitness Barn, and other
signs (all self-explanatory) of the nightlife strip of West Brattleboro. There are
a couple of places along the road that sell Page's ice cream, a local product of
high quality, which keeps these places busy during warmer months.

After you pass Stockwell's, which claims in large P. T. Barnum-type letters to be a "One-Stop Convenience/General Store/Coin Laundry/Village Restaurant," you know you are in the heart of West Brattleboro. There you will find, besides Stockwell's, a volunteer fire station, a small triangular village green, and a deli/convenience store, Dalem's (if you think to look up behind the church).

Dalem's Chalet sits on a hill up behind the First Congregational Church and it overlooks West Brattleboro. Although there are a couple of those state signs pointing the way, the way to find it is by turning south at the firehouse, which is right across from Stockwell's, and taking the road that diagonals up the hill right behind that firehouse. The road spills into the Dalem's Chalet parking lot. Not only is this a 30-room motel built in a manner that reminds you of Swiss Alpine lodges found in the Alps today, it is a 50-seat restaurant that serves *echte* (genuine) Austrian, German, and Swiss cuisine.

Ursula Dalem started this business in 1965 with her late husband, Oscar, whom she had met on a brief visit here from Bavaria. Because of Oscar, she never went home again, except for visits. They actually built it, with the help of three carpenters. She boasts of one 80-foot beam in the main dining room that was put in place by three people — "my husband, a carpenter who was working with us, and me."

Also up from that little triangular green is the West Village Meeting House, where people gather for lectures, for demonstrations of Japanese tea ceremonies, for opera workshops, and the like. It is a lovely, modern building with a cultural mission.

Some visitors wonder why one house, on the north side of the highway, has all those deliberately derelict cars in the yard. The neighbors have been wondering the same thing for the past 20 years. The man who lives here is an erstwhile and somewhat eccentric politician who has employed alternative parties and original political methods for years. Apparently, one of his political statements has to do with cars. We know this because when his neighbors complained that he didn't have the right to junk up the neighborhood, the law clearly stated that as long as he did it on his property only, he could. He did. And still does.

West Brattleboro is not quite as well kept as Brattleboro, but all other homes and businesses we know are in better shape than this man's. Politics make strange junkyards.

Although there is an overlap, we think of getting into Brattleboro itself after crossing over Interstate 91 as it soars along the highlands overlooking the Connecticut River valley. There is something comforting about driving along High Street, with its lovely homes, most of them restored and/or turned into law offices, down the hill to the light that marks Main Street.

Vermont State Route 5 (called the Calvin Coolidge Memorial Highway, at least part of the way) and Interstate 91 thread the same needle in these parts, crossing back and forth over one another all the way up to Lyndonville, way north, where they finally sort things out and go their separate ways. In Brattleboro, Route 5 becomes Putney Road, which is where the commercial strip is. After crossing Route 9, which heads for Keene, New Hampshire, Route 5 becomes rural again, for the most part.

Before leaving Brattleboro on Route 5, you can find the Brattleboro common on the west side of Putney Road at Park Place. This eighteenth-century common comprises three acres and has heard the political orations of such presidents as William McKinley and Theodore Roosevelt. It is also where the chamber of commerce has a booth. The other is on the west side of town, on Route 9, next to the covered bridge.

Beyond the common, heading northward on Route 5, the Connecticut River Safari offers a way to explore the Connecticut and West rivers by canoe or kayak.

They are located at the bridge Putney Road uses to cross the West River, before it gets into the commercial strip.

Off that commercial strip, up the Black Mountain Road past the Brattleboro Reformer offices, is the School for International Training. An offshoot from the Experiment for International Living, this school offers masters degrees in subjects relating to international living through language and linguistics courses, teaching English as a second language, and the like.

Another special school in Brattleboro is the Austine School for the Deaf, founded in 1904. The elementary and secondary core is language instruction through reading, writing, signing, and lipreading.

If you take Main Street, which is also U.S. 5, south three miles, you'll reach the town of Guilford where Fort Dummer State Park is located.

The park has 61 sites, including 10 lean-tos, on its 217 acres. Amenities include hot showers, flush toilets, picnic tables, fireplaces, a playground, trails, hiking, and a small picnic area. There are no hookups.

To get there from I-91, take exit 1 for one-tenth of a mile north on U.S. Route 5, then a half mile east on Fairground Road, then one mile south on Main Street and the Old Guilford Road.

Vermont's first, southern-approach welcome center located out on Interstate 91 just a half mile north of the Vermont/Massachusetts border has a Guilford address and is locally called the Guilford Information Center, though it does not appear to be in the village itself. This is another example of the mysterious "town" concept in Vermont.

Back on the west side of Brattleboro is the Living Memorial Park, which has a swimming pool, two softball diamonds, basketball court, tennis courts, playgrounds, a 15-meter ski jump, and some cross-country ski trails.

The Brattleboro Outing Club has more than 20 kilometers of cross-country skiing on the Brattleboro Country Club off Upper Dummerston Road. The Ski Hut has rest rooms and refreshments available.

Harris Hill is a 70-meter ski jumping hill in Brattleboro, one of the only five actively used hills of that size in the country. The February meet is used as a kind of kickoff for the annual winter carnival here in Brattleboro.

Up Route 30 in the town of Dummerston is the Maple Valley Ski Area, a small family ski area opened in the 1963–64 winter season. The ski slopes can be characterized as smaller than Bromley's and larger than Prospect Mountain's. Two double chair lifts and a T-bar bring skiers up to the top to ski the 13 trails, covered by 100 percent snowmaking, that drop 1,000 feet to the base lodge. The south chair lift is 4,000 feet long. The base lodge is open for rental for social occasions during the off-season, so you might find parties and wedding receptions going on. The mountain has its own ski school and night skiing.

Just south of the ski area is the Dummerston covered bridge, which crosses the West River. While it is open to (slow) automobile traffic, trucks are not allowed. It is a very long span and as you drive through it, it begins to feel like a long, dark tunnel. Some drivers turn on their headlights to see better, and two cars can, in fact, pass in opposite directions on the bridge itself, though it feels tight.

At the opposite end of the bridge is the East/West Road T-1. This is, as it appears to be, a relatively remote country road. As you climb up the hills on the gravel roadbed, the views of the landscape are extraordinarily beautiful, as usual.

Dutton Pines State Park, located just south on U.S. Route 5, is in the town of East Dummerston. It was established in 1937 on 13 acres and offers a place to picnic in a small pine grove. This little picnic area has a shelter and requires no fee.

The best overview of Brattleboro, particularly in the fall, is from New Hampshire's Wantastiquet Mountain. After crossing the island bridge at the end of

Main Street, take the first dirt road on the left (south) to the parking lot. This is at the base of an access road for the cable company, and it is a good trail, if a somewhat rough road. A 40-minute walk to the top of the mountain affords a wonderful view of Brattleboro and the Connecticut River.

Marlboro

Marlboro is off the beaten path — a half mile off, to be exact, if you consider Vermont Route 9 the beaten path. You turn south from Route 9 and head past a cemetery along a country road and come to a cluster of white-clapboard buildings, including the church, the post office, a bulletin board, and the Whetstone Inn. This is Marlboro, home to the world-renowned Marlboro Music Festival.

Historical Perspective

Molly Stark is a name you'll see often in these parts. Route 9 is often referred to as the Molly Stark Trail. The roadway was first chartered in 1796 as the Vermont Turnpike and then completed as the Windham Turnpike. It was the first serviceable road over the Green Mountains.

What did Molly Stark do to achieve such lasting, if highly localized, fame? She didn't sleep a widow on August 18, 1777. That's all.

She was married to John Stark, a military man who had fought in the French and Indian Wars; had been at the Battle of Bunker Hill; and was called in to lead the combined New Hampshire, Massachusetts, and Green Mountain boys against General Burgoyne's expeditionary forces at the Battle for Bennington on August 16, 1777. When General John Stark espied the enemy troops he declared, "There stand the Redcoats, and they are ours or this night Molly Stark sleeps a widow."

Stark won; Molly did not become a widow that night; and schools, roads, motels, and other businesses have borne her name ever since.

The big frontier excitement of Marlboro Town occurred even earlier than Molly's fame, in 1748. So the folks around here have all had a little while to settle back down again.

At that time, Sackett, an Abnaki leader who was trying to reclaim territory the Abnaki once owned, attacked a company of 40 soldiers from Fort Number 4 over in New Hampshire under the command of Captain Humphrey Hobbs. Both Sackett and Hobbs had reputations for fearlessness and tenacity in battle, so the pitched battle lasted hours and hours. Sackett shouted his demand for Hobbs to surrender, or he would rub out the whole contingent. Hobbs is said to have roared back, "Come on in and get us! If you're afraid, send your red dogs of hell in after us." The inconclusive battle ended when Sackett withdrew. Hobbs had lost only three men, Sackett's casualties were said to have been higher. The Abnaki warriors, some of whom still live up in the Swanton/Highgate area of northern Vermont, have never bothered Marlboro since then.

The Congregational church in Marlboro is well on its way to becoming a historic re-creation, it having been built in 1932 as an exact replica of the original meetinghouse. The real thing had burned to the ground in 1931 after serving the community faithful and faithfully since 1819.

Attractions, Recreational Pursuits

While many people still think of Hogback Mountain as being in Wilmington, it is actually in Marlboro Town. Hogback has the distinction of being the only family ski mountain that is poised every winter for skiers, and yet in the two decades we've driven by, we can't remember a time it was actually open.

Another distinction to this mountain is that it affords a 100-mile view a few yards beyond the now-defunct family ski area. On mornings in summer when the sun edges up over the distant mountains, the view of 100 miles fills with incredible colors that make even the most blasé local inhabitants stop for a moment and take a deep breath of near-magical morning. When the panorama is suffused in ground fog, or when the leaves ignite and glow in color, or when the snows turn everything simple black and white, the pull-off up here often proves unavoidably inviting.

There is a souvenir shop next to the view, and in the basement of this shop, to the left, is the Lymen Nelson Collection and Wildlife Museum. This is an odd, antique approach to displaying the kind of wildlife that inhabits the area. What Nelson collected was stuffed animals, and there are hundreds of animals and birds, both unusual and common to this area. We find this museum endlessly fascinating.

Across the highway, up on a knob that tops the 100-mile view, is the Skyline Restaurant, which serves breakfast, lunch, dinner, and that view, year-round. The Hamilton family, who have owned this establishment for four generations now, could boast the parking lot with the most incredible view in Vermont. It seems to extend even farther than 100 miles at road level. From the benches and chairs they set out in any season except winter, you can see the White Mountains, Mount Monadnock, and the Cathedral in the Pines in New Hampshire; Mount Grace, Wachusetts, and the Holyoke Range in Massachusetts; and every square inch of Vermont south of this section of Route 9.

The family-style, 100-seat restaurant has walls of windows facing the view, making any meal of the day at any one of the tables an experience of grandeur. If you want the breakfast specials of waffles and griddle cakes, topped with real Vermont maple syrup, at odd times of the day or night, it's available. The restaurant has a strong local, as well as tourist, clientele.

Just down the hill from that view is the Molly Stark State Park with 158 acres of woodlands for its 25 campsites and nine lean-tos. Located just five miles beyond Wilmington on State Route 9, the park features picnicking, camping, and hiking up to the fire tower on Mount Olga. It is a tidy little camp with such amenities as flush toilets, showers, fireplaces, picnic tables, and picnic shelter.

It is said Marlboro College saved Marlboro from becoming a ghost town. The college is a coeducational liberal arts school of high reputation and academic standards presided over by a president who came here after a full career as an international journalist. The curriculum includes field trips, study abroad, and a cooperative degree program with the School for International Training in Brattleboro.

The college provides a wonderfully scenic setting for the world-renowned Marlboro Music Festival. This summertime festival is under the artistic direction of Rudolf Serkin, pianist, and draws professional musicians from the world over to retreat into the hills of Marlboro, away from the demands of urban life where most musicians spend their professional lives, to play chamber and small orchestral pieces together. Directors say musicians come here to recharge their artistic batteries, to play music they choose, and to work with musicians with whom they feel artistically compatible.

The music school and festival have been touched by legendary names such as Pablo Casals, Alexander and Mischa Schneider, and Rudolf Serkin, continuing in his role as artistic mentor. The legendary Casals, who came here himself for 16 summers, called it a center "unlike that in any other place. . . . I don't know anything to equal it."

The wonderful bonus to area residents and visitors alike is that each week during this "musical retreat" the musicians gather at Perkins Hall, on the Marlboro campus, and perform the music they have been playing all week. Of course, the secret got out and many people now come from all over the country just to hear these musicians. Some who come to hear the music discover Vermont for the first time and begin to come back regularly. Some even relocate.

One such music lover is Jean Boardman, who with her husband, Harry, is owner of the Whetstone Inn, right in the center of Marlboro since 1787. Because there are only two or three other buildings here, a case can be made that the Whetstone is the center of Marlboro.

The inn is one of those old rambling affairs with nooks and crannies enough to keep the most curious visitor busy exploring it. The second-floor ballroom is sometimes used as such; the first-floor, old-fashioned kitchen, with a huge fireplace complete with cooking crane, is used as the dining room, a place people, not just guests mind you, gather to talk and/or eat especially when the winds are blowing and the warmth of a kitchen is inviting. The rooms are furnished to be lived in with woolen blankets, rocking chairs, old jug lanterns, and clean windows to look out on the hills, the stone walls, and the woodlands that surround the inn.

The view from the front rooms of the Whetstone Inn opens out onto cross-country ski terrain, with trails that start at the front door and wind around the town and the hills the inn is nestled into. If you take the Auger Hill Road, about a mile from here, you can get to Mount Snow in about 15 minutes. If you come in summer, you can hike the trails others may have skied upon. And when the Marlboro Music Festival is on, you cannot find a more convenient place from which to get to the concerts and open rehearsals.

Brattleboro North: Newfane, South Newfane, Townshend, Jamaica, and Putney

North of Brattleboro are some of the most picturesque towns in southern Vermont. Newfane on Route 30 with its magnificent nineteenth-century buildings surrounding the town green is worth a trip in any season. Its true New England charm has been photographed and sketched for many a magazine and postcard. It also boasts the granddaddy of all flea markets and not one, but three, award-winning restaurants for the gourmet diner. Farther north on Route 30 is Townshend, home to the Townshend State Park and Scott Bridge, one of the longest covered bridges in Vermont. Neighboring Jamaica is small but has a delightful mix of restaurants and stores for the locals and visitors and is home to Jamaica State Park, Hamilton Falls, and white water canoeing and kayaking.

On Route 5 north of Brattleboro is the pleasant town of Putney, a community with several shops and inns and an interesting history. Putney is home to the Yellow Barn Music Festival and the River Valley Playhouse and Arts Center, which presents year-round concerts and theater festivals.

Newfane, South Newfane

This is the village most people envision when searching for the "typical, charming" new England village, because it comes with the works. That includes a village greensward, or "common lands," on both sides of the highway, bevies of white-clapboard houses, a Union Hall (1832), a Congregational church (1839), both a revolutionary-period memorial and a Civil War statue, stone plaques for World War II and Korea/Vietnam fallen, a small fountain in front of the County Courthouse (1825), a brace of beautiful inns, and children with pink cheeks and bright smiles running around the common on summer or autumn days. The works!

To get to Newfane from Brattleboro, you drive the refreshingly scenic Route 30 along the banks of the West River for about 10 miles. When you think you've driven into a storybook, you will know you have arrived.

Another village of this ilk is Weston on Route 100 and, though it is not often touted, West Townshend, farther north on Route 30.

Historical Perspective

Newfane is a shire town, which means the courthouse is a real functioning courthouse that hears the legal problems of the people in the "north shire" of Windham County part of the year. The rest of the year, the legal center of the county moves to Brattleboro. Bennington and Manchester, in the western valleys of Vermont, have a similar shared legal "shire" arrangement.

The courthouse with its Greek Revival, four-pillared portico and rust-red-roofed tower is, along with the Old First Congregational Church in Old Bennington, one of the most photographed buildings in Vermont.

Newfane is a much named town. It started out as "Fane," for Thomas Fane who held the first charter. The village proper was then called Park's Flats after Jonathan Park, a pioneer settler. Then it became Fayetteville, following a visit by the revolutionary war General Lafayette who visited this village on his tour of the country following the war. Eventually, as if to finally get back to basics, the place was given the new name of Newfane, which stuck.

Across the street from the courthouse in Newfane is the former Windham County Jail, once notorious and popular because it was both a jail and an inn. Prisoners on good behavior dined with guests who often wrote about the experience on hotel stationery that read "Windham County Jail, Newfane, Vermont." Now called the Windham County Sheriff's Department, it no longer serves these two clienteles. Next to this symbol of curious hospitality is Windham Central Supervisory Union, which governs area schools.

Route 30, the main street here, is flanked by the village green, making that expanse of common lands larger than that of most New England villages. On the eastern side of the road is what is called the Park Memorial, erected in 1919 by the descendants of Jonathan Park to honor the Colonial settler who deeded the common lands to the town in perpetuity. It is a practical memorial, as would be suited to an old farmer, because it provides seats for people to occupy while watching the doings in front of the courthouse. It is without exaggeration that we can say that Park single-handedly assured the continuing beauty of this village. While the broad expanse of the common lands is usually just a park, it is also used for games of sandlot baseball, touch football, and outdoor art or pumpkin festivals.

Attractions, Recreational Pursuits

There is, as is true with most Vermont communities today, a mixture here of localized and visitor-oriented businesses. The Newfane Store, right on the northern edge of the greensward, is the real store that sells food, deli sandwiches, and hot coffee and also rents videos. The Newfane Country Store is quilts, fudge, and gifts that would be more attractive to visitors than locals.

The Four Columns Inn, which is next to the Congregational church and out behind the courthouse, is distinguished and prominently visible from the commons. It has been serving fine continental cuisine here since 1965. The building itself is distinguished by four Ionic columns in front.

This building was built in 1830 by General Pardon Kimball who, in a gesture of thoughtfulness, put in the Greek Revival columns to remind his wife, legend has it, of the Old South manse that had been her childhood home. The two-and-one-half story house was home to Newfane's prominent families for more than a century, until it became a restaurant and inn. All 17 rooms or suites located in the main house, or in the renovated barn where the inn's restaurant is also located, are furnished in antiques. No telephones, no TVs.

The pewter-top bar presides over the old tavern room; a huge, brick fireplace warms the dining room, and the fare served up is considered worth the trip here by many who have sampled it.

It is pleasant enough to have one inn/restaurant worth noting in a town this size, but three ranking, award-winning restaurants is like a landlord's flowing bowl overflowing. People have been known to come here just to eat at either the Four Columns Inn, the Newfane Inn, or the Inn at South Newfane.

The Newfane Inn, originally built in 1793, is an attractive Colonial building that sprawls along the north edge of the village's common lands and is said to be the second oldest in Vermont's hospitality business. The Dorset Inn and the Walloomsac Inn (1763) both claim to be first and, while we are not sure how many are vying to be second, it is still a historic distinction worth noting in Vermont. The cuisine is continental in flavor and enjoys an award-winning reputation.

The County Historical Society Museum is just south of the common and is marked by a large brass bell on a concrete pedestal out front. In a town with this much palpable history, this society is the revealer of secrets.

North of town, on what one writer called a "five-acre trove" of land, from the first Sunday in June to the last Sunday in October, the famed Newfane Flea Market goes into high gear as it has been doing regularly for more than 20 years. From 150 to 200 different dealers find a place to set up their stands and sell anything from hotdogs to coonskin hats, from dented milk cans to antique highboys. The regulars make a business out of it, the irregulars are just cleaning out their attics and hoping to tidy up the house a bit by selling some of the disposables, and the folks who come buy just about anything from what *Vermont Life* once called the state's greatest "collections of stuff." It has become an institution by now, and it is great fun.

As you head south of town, past the Dutton Farm Stand, Newfane Green House, and a few other shops, you will come to a side road, a gravel thing that has a sign indicating "Newfane Hill." This road, which doesn't stay dirt for long, by the way, leads to South Newfane and the inn that is located there. If you happen to miss that side road, a little farther on there is another road, this one properly paved with a sign pointing the way to South Newfane.

The Inn at South Newfane, where the Borst family presides, is another of those highlights on the road to good food. Once you find South Newfane itself, it should be easy to find the inn since the only other commercial establishment in the little village is a general store.

The Inn at South Newfane began as a vacation home for a well-to-do family who came here from Philadelphia to escape the hot and muggy summers. They usually brought five servants, and the place was considered one of the most beautiful estates in southern Vermont. Herb and Connie Borst bought the inn in 1984, when it was a "big, old, neglected house." They rolled up their sleeves and went to work. When they got ready to open, they offered their kitchen to their daughter, Lisa, who had studied art and art history in college and had — on a whim — signed up for and graduated from the CIA (Culinary Institute of America, of course) and had several chef positions under her belt. Herb, who used to call himself a "closet baker," makes the desserts; Lisa, who has since won a Vermont culinary award, takes care of everything else in the restaurant. They both agree if they can't do quantity in their cozy restaurant, "by golly we're going to do quality."

West Townshend, Townshend, and Jamaica

Townshend's claim to fame is that President William Howard Taft was born here in 1853. Townshend and its sister town, West Townshend on Route 30, are great places to explore, particularly in summer. West Townshend has a lovely town green and a charming inn and restaurant. Its neighbor to the north, Jamaica, boasts good eateries and small shops. Both towns have state parks, hiking trails, and other recreational pursuits.

Historical Perspective

Just east of Townshend, a Vermont Historical Society sign tells us that the Taft Homestead site is near here. It explains that "Generations of Tafts lived here. Two miles up the road is Taft Hill where Aaron Taft settled in 1799. His grandson, Alphonso, born here in 1810, was cabinet member and diplomat. Alphonso's son was William Howard (1853 – 1939), President of the United States and later Chief Justice of the U.S. Supreme Court. And his son, Robert A. Taft (1889 – 1953) was senator from Ohio."

A few miles farther down the road is the Townshend Dam, constructed between 1958 and 1961 to control flooding in the West River. This flood-control dam, 1,000 feet in length and 133 feet tall, was given a supreme test in 1987 when it was filled to 100 percent capacity in April. That meant the dam held back 10,900,000,000 gallons of raging water that otherwise would have wreaked havoc on the countryside. Most of the time this looks like a placid little lake way down in the valley below the dam.

In Jamaica the town hall, the banks, the white-clapboard churches are all fairly utilitarian eighteenth- and early-nineteenth-century stuff. The Congregational church (1808) was once rocked by an interesting scandal: The minister is said to have sold his wife to a parishioner; the wife, apparently happy with the arrangement, stayed to raise a family with the purchaser. Otherwise, the town has long since remained quiet.

The land upon which Jamaica State Park is sited has an interesting history. It is believed to have been an Abnaki Indian village. Archaeologists claim evidence of habitation here dates back 8,000 years. As settlers moved in, Vermont's original inhabitants either moved or died of European diseases. One incident indicates a little resistance to the encroachments when a Captain Eleazer Melvin and 18 soldiers, pursued from Lake Champlain by Abnaki warriors, were unable to defend themselves here. After a bruising exchange, Melvin and nine survivors escaped through the woods to Fort Dummer. Not long after that incident, settlers moved in, logged and farmed along the banks of the West River, harnessed its waters for power, and eventually laid out the West River Railroad. This became known, eventually, as "36 miles of trouble" and the tracks were eventually ripped up, leaving a wonderfully level pathway through the peaceful woods to, along with that solitude, the 125-foot-tall Hamilton Falls, about four miles in.

Attractions, Recreational Pursuits

Arriving in West Townshend, you'll notice the town green is the true center of this community. As you approach the Townshend Hardware Store, which has been here since 1895, and you glance to the left or northward, you look across a wonderfully beautiful village common accented in the middle by a hexagonal bandstand. Next to it is a towering elm, a rare creature indeed these days, and a fountain that is rather the worse for wear. The green is surrounded by small town landmarks — corner stores, churches, schools, and the tiny Grace Cottage Hospital, a complex of small, quaint buildings.

Although neighboring Newfane's greensward is considered one of the most beautiful, we have long thought that West Townshend's was every bit as beautiful, especially looking southward toward the mountains southwest of town.

Near the green, the Town Clerk's office has four huge Doric columns on front and the clock still tells the time. The main entrance is framed on both sides with plaques; one for "those who gave to the service of our country in the Civil War," another for the honor roll of World War I, a third plaque for World War II, and a fourth for those lost in Korea and Vietnam. This imposing building is where you go to buy your hunting and fishing licenses.

There are some signs of gentrification, but the town is not changing so rapidly the flavor is lost. The Chamberlane House is a relatively new inn, the post office looks like it's been here at the southern cuff of the town a century or two and, as does the library, has a white-clapboard simplicity under a smug tin roof.

The Townshend Country Inn and Restaurant is in a building that dates from circa 1775. Joe and Donna Peters have been here for five years and have settled into the routine of running a restaurant and inn successfully and are halfway through a "master plan" that will add 10 rooms to the existing 3 in the inn. The restaurant seats 60 in 2 comfortable rooms. The lounge has a small sit-down bar (5 seats), several tables, a piano, and a fireplace.

The Townshend Country Inn is becoming renowned also for its monthly wine tastings. From January to June, the last Thursday of each month, the Peters throw a party that includes great wines and cheeses and a special meal created just for the occasion.

The New England Division of the U.S. Army Corps of Engineers built the Townshend Dam and published a little brochure on the Ledges Overlook Hiking Trail that starts at the access road to the beach and dam. They call this a "relatively rugged climb" that goes through hardwood forests to the overlook. Then the trail follows the ridge past a woodland savannah and then back down through stands of beech, paper birch, and hemlock to the access road again. The whole hike takes about an hour and a half.

Townshend State Park is actually south of Townshend and has a Newfane address. With 856 acres, the 34 camping sites do not dominate the parklands. In addition to camping, the park offers picnic tables, fireplaces, a picnic shelter, and lots of woodlands to explore. Campers can hike to Townshend Dam or take trails to Bald Mountain.

The Scott Bridge, the longest covered bridge in Vermont, crosses the West River downstream from the dam. Its three spans extend 276 feet, overall, from shore to shore. There are a half dozen stone-arch bridges over this waterway that were built between 1894 and 1911 by James Otis Follett. These old stone bridges have stood tests of time and high water.

In Townshend itself, there is a small cluster of commercial enterprises dominated by the Mary Meyers Tender Toys Company Store, which offers 20 percent to 70 percent off on all products sold within. A large teddy bear sometimes sits in a lounge chair out front.

In addition to their own line of stuffed animals, they sell T-shirts, books, and other companies' toys, so this is not strictly a factory store. The company was started back in the 1930s by Mary's husband. The name on the label does belong to a real person whose son is now chairman of the board. At this writing, Mary still lived "in the red house out back there."

The town of Jamaica is where Ball Mountain Brook meets West River. It is home to Charlie and Eleanor Murray, owners of the wonderful Three Mountain Inn. This couple has inherited at least one unofficial town role. Eleanor Murray explained that there is no chamber of commerce or tourist information office here, "so when anything comes to the post office addressed to one, they give it to us to handle." The Murrays certainly know what to recommend in the area after running the most visible inn in town for a dozen plus years.

The Three Mountain Inn is in a valley surrounded by three mountains (the Murrays name Stratton, 10 minutes away; Big Bromley and Magic, each 25 minutes away in opposite directions), and it is comprised of three eighteenth-century buildings with 16 rooms and 2 comfortable dining rooms. The aroma of dill, banana, or sourdough breads baking makes the place smell like a good-old-time country home, and the excellent quality of Elaine's cooking has been reported in many an interested publication, including *Gourmet* magazine.

There are many small businesses in Jamaica, some designed for the people who have always lived there, like Dak's Jamaica Grocery, and others like Jamaica House, Bavaria Haus, and The Gallery at Jamaica, which have visitors in mind. The Jamaica House, by the way, serves excellent Italian food. In addition to the Three Mountain Inn, there is the Sunny Brook Lodge on the road to Jamaica State Park that serves hardy skiers in winter and hikers in other seasons.

You can browse around the shops in Jamaica or you can take long, lovely drives in the mountain valleys, which are wonderfully picturesque in summer and fall.

Or you can slip away to Jamaica State Park, just four blocks away, to obtain solitude. The road right next to the inn, with a sign stating "Jamaica School" and "Depot Street J-19," is the one to take to Jamaica State Park. While it is not always filled with solitude, trails lacing through 772 acres can probably lead you to more of it than you can find where you came from.

This park is becoming a busy place, at least on some weekends, in part because canoeists and kayakers have discovered the white water of the West River that skirts it. This is the site of the National Canoe and Kayak Championships in May. These are the Olympics and American time trials. At other times of the year, the water is still white enough for canoe groups to come in for the thrill. One mid-October weekend, not long ago, rangers helped carry 1,700 canoes and kayaks upriver on Friday and 1,500 of them up on Saturday. "It isn't always like that," a ranger assured us.

Jamaica State Park has 42 campsites, 17 lean-tos, and one group camp here. There is also an enclosed picnic shelter surrounded by a dozen or so tables for big outdoor parties. It offers a place where visitors can just sink into the natural world and forget whatever else they came from. A park ranger once said, "If you respect the woods and the animals you will respect yourself and others." Activities here include horseback riding, educational programs, and exploratory excursions under the guidance of a park naturalist.

Putney

Putney is a pleasant little town where many shops have sprung up over the years to serve visitors to the area. This is the headquarters of Basketville, a factory that makes and imports baskets of every kind from all over the world. People discovered the factory store and began to arrive in droves. And then other shops moved in to offer items other than baskets. Putney also boasts some good restaurants and an interesting history.

Historical Perspective

Putney resident John Humphrey Noyes lived a flower-child life of "free love" long before it was fashionable. In fact, because it was considered so *unfashionable* by his fellow Putneyites, he was more or less driven out of town in 1847. He and his entire commune of "Perfectionists" had to jump bail.

He founded the Perfectionists, his radical religious group, in 1835, based on the notion that Jesus Christ had established the Millennium that the rest of Christianity was still mistakenly waiting for. Noyes contended that humankind did not have to wait another thousand years to attain holiness or "perfection": They could have it now. Humankind could free itself of sin by living communally and sharing everything unselfishly. The philosophy he espoused was antislavery, antialcohol, and against any form of human bondage whatsoever. The group lived together communally and shared jobs. They ran a newspaper, a community farm, and a store (now the Putney Fruit Co. Café) and lived peaceably with their neighbors. Then the neighbors discovered that these folks considered marriage a form of human bondage and that they were "sharing wives" as well. The Perfectionists termed it communal marriage and based it on biblical teachings. Putneyites took offense; they termed the practice immoral, not to mention illegal.

When the group jumped bail and moved to New York, they established a long-lasting commune based on those same ideas as well as a company, Oneida Silver, that still bears the commune's name. The Oneida Community stayed together until 1879, when Noyes, then 68, no longer had the charismatic energy needed to serve as leader. He died seven years later, by which time the community had broken into monogamous families and no longer had any force.

Some 50 years ago the Experiment in International Living was created in Putney with the idea that people of the world need to learn to get along with one another and developed a curriculum to that end. Twenty-five years later, the School for International Training was created to prepare folks for the Peace Corps. Its campus is now in Brattleboro.

Attractions, Recreational Pursuits

Coming in from Interstate 91, you take exit 4 to Putney. Even as you drive off the interstate you can find places of interest.

Located right off that exit is the Green Mountain Spinnery, "the world's smallest spinning mill." It was formed in 1982 as a five-person cooperative to spin and sell yarns, knitting kits, and patterns and handmade gifts.

The Green Mountain Spinnery people offer guided tours of the little mill on the first and third Tuesday of each month for a token admission fee. They turn the wool of Dorset and rambouillet sheep into skeins of naturally dyed wools. They also create a mohair from young Angora goats. A true "factory outlet," you can buy here what they send off to 1,000 retail shops across the nation and sell by mail order.

Across from it is the Putney Inn Restaurant and Motel that houses part of its hospitality business in a 200-year-old farmhouse and part of it in a structure that mostly resembles a motel. It makes no pretense about being anything other than a motel with a restaurant that serves hearty stews and sandwiches and sautéed delicacies.

As you head westerly over the interstate highway to U.S. Route 5 and Putney, you will discover Curtis's All American Barbeque, the ninth wonder of the world.

Curtis's consists of two old school buses, painted blue, one of which has an awning affixed to the side to shade those coming up to the window to order. Curtis is the black man who stands out next to the bus at an open barbecue pit, covered by a corrugated roof but devoid of walls. He does all the ribs and chicken in great quantity in this open-air kitchen. All signs announcing this phenomenon and the prices attached to the various meals available are ferociously hand-painted.

This "wonder" closes the last weekend in October and opens as soon as Curtis gets his fires going in early summer. There are many picnic tables, some with umbrellas, where you can eat the best chicken or ribs in southern Vermont.

The Putney Nursery, right on the main drag, has a large and growing reputation, one writer has said, as "the wildflower capital of the region." Started by the late George Aiken, who now has a wilderness area named for him in Woodford, some of the wildflower arbors the nursery still uses were built by him back in 1937.

The late George Aiken, both a governor and the United States senator for Vermont, gained national notoriety during the height of the protests against the war in Vietnam when he advised the president to simply declare "victory" and pull out. Aiken didn't think of that idea as particularly radical, just practical.

The Putney Nursery is the place to buy seeds that will turn your backyard, or portions thereof, into a wildflower extravaganza (plant these seeds in the fall, because they need the winter cold to break their dormancy). Once you plant them, these flowers take care of themselves. They're wild!

The original draw to this community, Basketville, is just north of Putney's main intersection, where three roads meet at a small triangular green. This factory is packing 'em in more than ever with a factory store on one side and a factory sale, under a yellow-and-white awning tent, on the other. A policeman directs the traffic in either direction.

They claim to have the "largest and most amazing" collection of baskets. Period. Anywhere. Many of the baskets and wooden buckets and such are handmade right here in Putney, but the company imports enormous amounts of baskets from Europe and the Orient. The collection is rather awesome. This Putney company has an outlet in Sunderland, too.

Back down the hill, in the center of town, is the Putney Fruit Co. Café, in which you are "surrounded by fine music and fine art" as you eat. This building is where John Humphrey Noyes and his Perfectionists sold their farm produce. The name they used for their business is not known, but the Putney Fruit Company did occupy the building in the early decades of this century, long after the Perfectionists were a faded memory. While the outside looks antique and unassuming, the inside is modern, clean, and pleasant.

On another side of that triangular green is the Putney General Store, which is the real McCoy. It has been here continuously since 1843 and boasts an old-fashioned soda fountain. In addition to a full line of groceries, you can get sandwiches, beer, and wine to go.

The mix here is of real people and real stores juxtaposed to tourists and tourist stuff. The General Store is next to a jewelry store called the Silver Forest of Vermont; the Putney Woodshed deals with a different clientele than does Rod's Mobil.

Going up the hill beyond the Silver Forest, you can find The Putney School, a private prep school that espouses and practices the education of John Dewey, a Vermonter who thought it was a good idea to learn by doing. Not only do the students study the regular curriculum, they grow their own food and take care of farm animals that provide them with part of the necessities.

During the summer months, there is music in these hills, too. The Yellow Barn Music Festival is in its 20th year. This all started when internationally known cellist David Wells and his wife, concert pianist Janet Wells, came to Putney, were conquered by it, and tried to figure out a way to stay. They started teaching chamber music and holding concerts in the old yellow barn attached out back behind the house. It has become an institution around here.

Up on Westminster West Road is Putney Ridge Arabians, which specializes in boarding, training, and breeding Arabian horses. There is a place for the owners to stay for summer camp and winter weekend programs.

Also take this road up to Hickory Ridge Road, turn west there, and left at the fourth driveway to find the Hickory Ridge House, a bed-and-breakfast country inn. Built in 1808 by Theophilus and Annis Crawford of brick, alleged to have come all the way from Boston by ox cart, the building has been everything from a farmhouse to a college president's house. Seven guest rooms are furnished with antiques, six Rumford fireplaces grace the house, and exceptional care has been taken to keep the integrity of the beautiful building.

If you return to the center of town and take a left, heading northward out beyond Basketville is Landmark College, the only college in the country that is geared toward the learning problems of those suffering from dyslexia. The college grew out of a need discovered by the founder, who had already organized a prep school for dyslexics, only to discover there was no college to send his graduates to. So he created one here on the campus left by the now-defunct Windham College.

The River Valley Playhouse & Arts Center in Putney opened in 1986, taking over a building intended by Windham College as an arts center. With Windham College closed and Landmark College in its place, the arts center is doing what it was supposed to be doing after all.

You no longer park at the edge of campus for Landmark College, but drive about two-tenths of a mile farther on and pull into a gravel road that looks like a back alley but does lead to the center's gravel parking area. Because it is out behind and below the arts center, you get less than an impressive introduction to the arts in the area. The programs, created by the center's director, Susan Lamb, formerly of the Kennedy Center in Washington, are professional in quality.

With both a 100-seat studio theater and a 400-seat proscenium stage, the facility has been described as "elegant and well-equipped." A year-round variety of concerts, cinema, and theater festivals can be found here, as well as a dance studio, recording facilities, and gallery exhibits and conference space.

The Putney Summit Restaurant and Inn, on the west side of the highway, serves three hearty squares a day in a room full of antiques, hanging plants, and hand-hewn beams. Guests can stay in the guest rooms or cottages at the summit.

Beyond this along U.S. Route 5 is Harlow's Sugar House and Gift Shop. In early June, you can come here and pick your own strawberries. In July and August, blueberries and raspberries are here for the pickin'. In the fall, if you can take your eyes off the foliage, you can pick your own apples. And you can enjoy maple syrup and cheeses year-round.

One of the more magnificent views you will find in southern Vermont is at this farm, just three miles up the road from Putney, with an expanse out over the orchards, out over the Connecticut River valley, opening onto the White Mountains of New Hampshire.

But then, there is hardly a section of road along here that isn't worth the side trip just to see. Thoughtfully, the state has graded in many places to pull off the road and gather your thoughts should they have scattered, somehow, over the magnificent landscape.

For those interested in seeing the countryside from the seat of a bicycle, locals recommend the following bike tour that takes you over some scenic terrain. From the West Hill bike shop on Depot Road, turn left onto Route 5 and head south to avoid the uphill climbs. Take Route 5 down to Route 9 and the traffic light. Turn left and take Route 9, across the Connecticut River, and turn left onto Cross Road. Down a steep hill, Cross Road comes to a stop sign at Brook Street (no sign) where you turn left. At the next stop sign bear left onto Main Street, which becomes River Road. Follow the river on River Road, New Hampshire Route 63, then Route 12, and again River Road, and again Route 12. At the second blinking light, turn left onto New Hampshire Route 123 and head back across the river toward Westminster, Vermont. At the T at Westminster Station, turn right up a hill to a stop sign and bear right on U.S. Route 5. Turn left and at Arms Real Estate turn left again, toward I-91. Turn right just before the I-91 exit onto Westminster Heights Road, which becomes Patch Road. When you come to Westminster West Road, take it to Putney. Back down a steep hill in Putney, find Route 5. Turn right and soon find Depot Street, your starting point. It's a moderate 42 miles.

Santa's Land is, of course, north of the village of Putney on Route 5. This is a 1950s idea of a theme park still living in the time warp of Vermont, but most of the buildings are still brightly painted, and kids still come to visit Santa and pet the animals from May to Christmas Day (when it closes, because Santa has to work that day).

Another interesting attraction in the Putney area is the MG Museum located just north of the village of Westminster, which is lovely and rural with working farms all around, out behind the Peoples Car Company, a repair shop right on the road. It is in a long building, with fake Tudor exterior. The owner claims this is, with 27 MGs on display, the "world's largest private" exhibition of one single make of car. When the museum and shop are open from June to Columbus Day weekend, visitors can browse through an extensive library and buy artifacts and gifts. Call or check their flyer for hours.

Wilmington, West Dover

Hasn't changed that much since "the mountain came in." At least that's what some folks have said. Prices have though, we'd say. And traffic.

Obviously, Mohammed didn't cart a mountain in from somewhere else. It was always here. It just got a new name and a shave: Trails were razored and bush-hogged out in 1954 to allow ski enthusiasts to ski down what was to become known as Mount Snow, elevation 3,556 feet, about nine miles north of "the light" — there is only one in Wilmington. Right beside the Mount Snow ski slopes in West Dover, the Carinthia Ski Area, until recently a family owned ski slope, was also groomed out of the wooded mountain. And another whole mountain, Haystack, elevation 3,420 feet, in the town of Wilmington, also developed into a force to be reckoned with about that time.

The towns of Wilmington and West Dover on Route 100 have grown into a resort haven for the two ski areas within their boundaries. Each offers numerous lodgings, fine restaurants, and different shops to explore. Besides extensive Alpine skiing facilities, Mount Snow and Haystack Mountain have expanded over the years into summer recreation and now include golf courses, performing arts programs, mountain bike training, and professional golf tournaments. Pontoon boats with visitors aboard glide over the Harriman Reservoir, otherwise known as Lake Whitingham, in the warmer months, and members of the Living History Association, dressed in period garb, provide endless entertainment around Wilmington.

Wilmington

Main Street in Wilmington comes in three sections (East, West, and South), and all are lined on both sides with shops, most of them paying very close attention to the visitors to the area. During fall foliage you can expect the traffic to come to a halt a mile or two from town as the single light at the main intersection (Route 100 crosses/joins Route 9) slowly sorts the cars out. Another time you can expect traffic jams is late afternoons on Sunday in ski season, but that clot of cars comes down Route 100 north from Haystack and Mount Snow as skiers and weekenders try to rush home to New York or Boston before the traffic jams there run into one at the point where 100 north meets those three Main streets. Since these traffic problems in the two specific seasons are usually unavoidable in this popular area, it is better to be prepared. Bring soothing tapes to play, perhaps Windham Hill recordings, and a calming cup of tea-to-go to sip while waiting. The rest of the time, traffic's not that bad, really.

The Harriman Reservoir, which stretches from Whitingham to Wilmington, is an artificial lake that (1) is not named after Ambassador Averell Harriman or any other famous Harriman but after Joe Harriman, a power company engineer who found a suitable place for a dam 11 miles south of here, and (2) is also called Lake Whitingham, after a smaller lake that was enlarged when the water filled in behind the dam.

When the dam was finished in April 1924, the water backed up faster than anticipated and a town called Mountain Mills was hastily evacuated as it sank desolately into the lake. When the waters are let down in late winter to allow for spring runoff, from Route 9 you can still see a little evidence of the town that once was. However, during spring, summer, and fall, boats happily sail right over it.

Attractions, Recreational Pursuits

At a double curve on Route 9, a mile or so west of Wilmington, you can cruise in the warmer months on the M/V *Mt. Mills*, owned by Captain Dick Joyce, which plies the waters over the submerged town it is named after. This 50-passenger vessel and a clone named the *Heather Sue* are pontoon boats designed to remind one of stern-wheeler riverboats and tour all 11 miles of the lake. Over the years, both boats have tried dinners on board, entertainment, music, the works, so they do try to make it a pleasant as well as informative cruise.

The singularly most entertaining institution in town is called the Living History Association. The name sounds rather staid, rather scholarly. But the LHA is an association of groups from all over the United States and Canada that reenact great, usually military, moments in history. It is great fun!

The LHA claims to have a membership of 5,000. The executive director, Al Wurzberger, is the proprietor of the 1836 Country Store on West Main Street in Wilmington. His wife, Sue, is proprietor of the Norton House, which sells fabrics, and their daughter, Carolsue, runs the Ice Cream Parlor and Pancake House in the front building that also houses the classroom for the Living History Association.

When the LHA sponsors its International Time Line, you can meet people who have dressed up as knights in armor, ladies-in-waiting, Norman peasants, soldiers from the British (1648) Civil War, the French and Indian War (1750s), the War of 1812, the American Revolution (1770s), the American Civil War (1860s), and the two world wars as they wander around the Country Store complex acting as though they had never heard of the late twentieth century. Jim

Dassatti, the association's program director, explains that the LHA's goal is to "bring historical information to the public." But the goal of most of the reenactors seems to be to have a great time pretending to be living in a historical period other than the present. It is something akin to creatively avoiding reality.

The actual time line is held at the New England Plantation, 117 acres of farmland north of the village but in Wilmington Town on Route 100 where Coldbrook Road heads west toward Haystack Mountain. One recent time line had seven authentic tepees for Indian scouts and *couriers de bois*, dozens of white revolutionary and Civil War army tents, a German World War II mobile field headquarters compound, and a handful of medieval jousting tents. More than 300 reenactors were present for the weekend. The public is invited to attend; you can purchase period clothing and accessories. You can watch and cheer, or jeer, as knights joust over the honor of a maiden (very few dragons have attended these events), where both men and women model the fashions of their time, where segments of the American Revolution and Civil War are commonly fought again and again.

Before coming into Wilmington proper from the west, you'll see John McLeod's store. He started out making wonderfully simple, beautifully crafted, amazingly useful items out of wood. These items can hold tape cassettes, fine cheese or wine bottles, and keep hot pots from burning tables — and they do it in style. His work is now sold worldwide and he sells imported wooden items, making his shop a kind of international intersection of woodenware traffic. Part of his shop is also devoted to selling antique furnishings of top quality.

On the edge of the village at a sharp bend in the road is the Nutmeg Inn, which has 11 rooms all beautifully decorated with antiques. Another inn, right at the village edge on a hillside just before you plunge into the busy shopping section of Wilmington, is the Red Shutter Inn, which does have red shutters and a chef of reputation. The 1894 inn serves dinner in a candlelit dining room that locals, as well as visitors, frequent and recommend strongly.

On Main Street West, across from the 1836 Country Store complex, there is a most interesting shop: Klara Simpla. The name means "clear and simple" in universal Esperanto. Housed in what was once the village livery stable, some call this the health-food store. It is the center for alternative life-style items where you can buy crystals, homeopathic herbs and medicinals, study yoga (hatha or Kripalu), achieve body harmony, understand astral projection, and buy books on an amazingly wide variety of subjects in one of the most fascinating, small bookstores we know. You can also buy warm woolen clothing, hip boots, and other sundries. This place, in another way, seems to have settled into another time period itself. The proprietors are quietly friendly.

The Vermont House and Tavern, right next door to Klara Simpla, is both a good place for lunch and dinner, and it serves also as a kind of neighborhood pub. It is the impressive looking building with four enormous columns and an imposing presence. You would expect a county courthouse that serves up torts and suits in a place like this, rather than a pub that serves up tarts and soup.

A few doors closer to the light, you can find Quaigh Design, once home to Wilmington's hand-cranked telephone switchboard and now an upscale shop where Lilias Hart sells Irish woolens, jewelry, pottery, and art from her gallery upstairs. And beyond that, right next to the Deerfield River, you will find Dot's Restaurant. This is the real thing. No nonsense. She serves up good, stick-to-the-ribs breakfasts, starting at 5:30 A.M., and lunches at reasonable prices. She has added beer and wine to the menu now, claims to serve the "best buns in town," and is staying open Friday and Saturday nights. She has not tried to gussy the place up for the many new visitors; she still does just what she has done all these years: serve good food. Across from Dot's, the sprawling Craft's Inn, which contains time-share condominiums for regular visitors to the area, was named after the Craft family and has nothing to do with arts or crafts, really.

Poncho's Wreck, the self-proclaimed only certified shipwreck in Vermont, has become an institution in town. It is a little south of the light, on the east side of South Main Street, and it serves lunches and dinners of lobster, steak, and chicken, as well as some good Mexican food. It is casual, children are welcome, and entertainment is live and lively.

Two doors down, on the same side of South Main Street, is the Pettee Memorial Library, a tiny jewel of a building with two Ionic columns protecting a massive oak door crowned with a Colonial-style fan window, built in 1906. The library honors a doctor who served the community for 40 years, and its yard has several granite markers as well as a Civil War statue in front. If you follow the street past the library a few streets to Fairview Road and turn right (west), it will lead you to a New England Power Company boat landing and picnic area called Mountain Mill East Recreation Area. The road turns gravel before you get there and finally opens onto a parking area and a very pleasant, wooded park that edges Harriman Reservoir. There are no lifeguards on duty here, so boating and canoeing only is recommended.

New England Power Company owns all the land that shores up to the reservoir and offers two boat-launch areas and several picnic and swimming areas free of charge, one of which, Wards Cove, is still talked about in knowing tones because of its fading sixties and seventies reputation for bordering the local nude-bathing beach. Seems a cover-up has been going on since.

At the Mountain Mills West Picnic Area, hikers can follow an easy, seven-mile Harriman Trail with double yellow blazes down to the southern end of the reservoir, the dam, and the Glory Hole. Much of this trail follows the abandoned right-of-way for the old Hoosic Tunnel and Whitingham Railroad, known affectionately in its heyday in the 1890s to 1920s as Hoot, Toot, and Whistle. In order to get to the Mountain Mills West Picnic Area, cross the new bridge that is — oddly enough — right next to the old steel-truss bridge it replaced on the south side of Route 9 about a quarter mile east of the Searsburg/Wilmington line, and follow a gravel road to the left about one mile.

On East Main Street, a few doors up from Poncho's, you can see Wilmington's high-water mark on the white-clapboard building that houses the police station and town offices. The little black line indicates where the flood caused by the devastating hurricane of 1938 crested. When you cross the street at the light, stand on the bridge and look down at the babbling little Deerfield River a dozen feet below street level. You can marvel at just how rambunctious that stream must have gotten without the calming effect of the flood-control dam at the southern end of the Harriman Reservoir. While the water still rises menacingly during some spring runoffs, it never puffed itself up that high again.

If you took East Main Street, which is also Route 9/100, about 20 miles east, you would be in Brattleboro; 21 miles west takes you back to Bennington. On the north side of the street, in front of another white-clapboard building a modest city-block distance from the light, you will discover a sign for Thomas Politano, a lawyer. It is not that we recommend him, or think you need a lawyer at this juncture, but under his sign is another, smaller sign announcing the Wilmington Chamber of Commerce. This lower sign is closer to the ground and is, on some years when the flowers at its base are particularly abundant and cheerful, not easily visible — even when you are looking for it. A little parking lot out behind the law offices also serves the chamber, so you can pull off the main drag, drive in, and ask questions.

Just beyond the village's eastern edge, up a hill from Route 9, is The White House. Well, maybe not *The* White House. You do not have to be politically well connected to stay here, to dine here, to drink here, or for that matter to cross-country ski here. It is a 12-room, grand, beautiful inn with three public dining rooms seating 75 total, a sun-porch lounge, and an award-winning reputation. Sipping any concoction in that lounge, looking westward at sunset no matter the season, is worth the price of the drink.

This is another place that looks like a black-tie-and-tux affair with its stately antebellum columned front, its towering maple trees, and its expansive lawns spread out like bunting over a proud knoll. But it is fairly down-home. During winters, Bob Grinold, owner since 1976, has had his staff lay out cross-country ski trails. During summers volleyball nets go up. There are Jacuzzis, a sauna, a whirlpool, even a small indoor pool and other amenities, but none outweigh the warm hospitality here.

Wilmington's White House began life in 1915 as the private home of a Boston lumber baron named Martin Brown. Brown, apparently a romantic, dragged a huge boulder he fancied down from the top of the opposite hill, struggled it up toward the house, and deposited it next to a towering maple because, he said, that was the best place to watch the sun set. Those of us who have been there when the winter winds are bristling up the hill prefer the lounge.

Just down the hill beyond The White House, a horse barn away, is an open field that from Memorial Day through October's foliage season turns into the Wilmington Antiques & Flea Market, a new rival to other, older, more famous area flea markets (such as Newfane's — see Newfane section). It is right at the point where Routes 100 and 9 sort things out, with 100 heading south to Jacksonville and 9 heading eastward to Brattleboro.

The village of Jacksonville, part of Whitingham Town, is about nine miles south of Wilmington on Route 100 and is home to the North River Winery, which gives tours to the public. The winery is situated just south of the main intersection on Route 112 right in town, on the banks of the North River. It is devoted to producing palate-pleasing dinner wines from the fruits of Vermont.

The idea is that apples, pears, blueberries, and the like can result in a wine that is somewhat dry and nonfruity tasting. The winery also produces dessert wines, which are a bit sweeter. You can enter the winery via the retail shop/tasting room, the original winery room, take a tour — since you will see only nine huge stainless steel vats, it's brief — and then have a chance to taste the wines. Of the 50,000 bottles North River Winery sold in 1989, 25,000 of them went out these doors in the hands of those who came, who tasted, and who were conquered. The winery is open daily from May through December and Friday through Sunday, January to May. There are also other things to do and see here. The Engel House B&B is located in Jacksonville, along with Stone Soldier Pottery, the Carriage Shop Restaurant, and the Coombs' Family maple syrup operation.

The area north of Wilmington includes the Haystack Mountain Resort and several restaurants, inns, and other worthwhile stops on Route 100 north.

Haystack Mountain, two miles west of Route 100 north on Coldbrook Road, has 43 trails, 90 percent of which are covered by artificial snowmaking, with all levels of skills tested. Six lifts carry you to the top, which is 3,200 feet above sea level. The vertical drop is 1,400 feet, and some of the trails have an adrenaline-powered 40 to 45 percent grade. Haystack is now part of the Women's Pro Tour, holding the slalom and giant slalom events in January. Snowboarding, a relatively new sport, is coming to the mountain with snowboard competitions held here as well.

There is a base lodge for the lower, beginner slopes and another for the nerve-rattling upper mountain. Skiers six years of age and under ski free.

In summer, there is the nearby Haystack Golf and Country Club, as well as the annual "Art on the Mountain" held at the lower base lodge in August. The club, with its pro shop, is up Mann Road off Coldbrook Road (clearly marked) before you get to Haystack. You can play 18 holes with some spectacular views to slice, hook, or play through.

Just beyond Haystack is The Hermitage and the best wine cellar in this neck of the woods, more than 2,000 labels, if not southern Vermont. The Hermitage is a major enterprise created by Jim McGovern and his family since 1971, when he bought the place and began to expand its scope. He calls it a "working country inn." Not only is it now a 29-room, uppercase Inn, it is also a restaurant, with awards and recognition coming in regularly in both categories. The McGoverns also raise 7,000 game birds a year, as well as some ornamental birds and a few orange-colored Belten English setters.

In spring, as the sap starts running, McGovern taps 5,000 maple trees and throws sugar-on-snow parties where you throw the freshly rendered hot maple syrup in the snow and eat the congealed concoction.

In winter, The Hermitage also offers 55 kilometers of groomed cross-country ski trails and a ski school for those who have never been on cross-country skis before. One trail, the Ridge Trail, requires expert ability and involves a single-ride lift ticket to the top of Haystack. Since Haystack has none of its own trails, it sends all its cross-country enthusiasts over McGovern's way; his land abuts the mountain's.

Another accommodation up this road is the Nordic Hills Lodge, which began its life as a ski lodge and has developed into a pleasant inn that can comfortably accommodate a bus load of people in its 27 rooms. They often have skiers of both persuasions here in winters and summer visitors who like to tour the area or take boat rides on Lake Whitingham or just relax. They boast a fully stocked trout stream on the premises.

Back on Route 100, Michael's Theatre, which is just north of Wilmington's traffic light, around a very sharp turn in the highway where a stone wall seems to threaten your car's paint job as you round it, has been described as old-time fun and music. The two men who run this entertainment center can play a dozen instruments between them; they sing, they tell jokes, and everyone has a great time. It's open May through October.

A similar place, called Peaches Place, is open during the summer. It is a bit farther up Route 100. When it is called Peaches Place, it is a musical variety show offering up entertainment performed by a troupe of three men and a woman who direct their show to the "seniors" (not rock and roll). The facility is really a disco turned into a theater. During winters it becomes the North Country Fair and transforms back into a disco — complete with rock and roll music.

The Cup & Saucer, a bit farther up Route 100 north from Michael's, is a friendly little diner in the tradition of Dot's. The menus often have good coffee spilled on them, the specials are up on a chalkboard, and the stools at the counter are the shortest stools we have ever seen in a diner. The food is good, solid, stick-to-the-ribs, and reasonable.

Other good eating places along this road include Deerfield's, where you can get a good meal, all the time, every time, no matter what. It is a mainstay for the folks who live here and a find for those who are visiting. Out behind is the Cross Country Bicycle Shop, which is frequented by visitors more often than locals.

As you drive northward, the valley opens out toward the west. This valley is referred to as the Deerfield Valley by the locals and old-timers, because it is the valley that cradles the Deerfield River. Others call it the Mount Snow Valley after the ski mountain that has made it relatively famous. In the fields are Jersey cows grazing contentedly, not really knowing they are part of the only large dairy farm still remaining in the Deerfield Valley. The Wheeler family is still working the land here, rotating crops from corn to pasture and back to keep that land healthy, and they have a little stand up on the road to sell their maple syrup in the fall. The folks who own Wheeler Farm, unlike many others in southern Vermont, realized in time that once you plant condos, it is awfully hard to rotate your crops.

West Dover

Before the mountain came in, West Dover was a small, quiet village where the columned West Dover Inn towered sleepily over the smaller town offices and post office all on one side of Route 100. The few buildings that still keep these company are, and seemingly always have been, white clapboard.

Looking north from the town offices Mount Snow does loom; its white caps are a formidable presence. Having invited skiers to its slopes has made a huge impact on the town. Before there was not much needed here. Now the highway is lined with commercial establishments catering to these visitors. The year-round population still numbers only several hundred, while the skiers and other visitors, some of whom stay longer and longer, crowded in and number in the tens of thousands. The old farms that once lined the highway are gone, and in their place are such plazas as the North Commercial Center, Grampy's, and the Brookside Country Store plus hotels, motels, lodges, and furniture stores. It had become a very busy place by the late 1980s.

Historical Perspective

Carved out of the southern half of Wardsboro, Dover was incorporated in 1810, according to *Vermont Place-Names*. Determined residents struggled for 12 years prior to that time to have the Vermont legislature proclaim them as a separate entity. Over the years Dover languished, but West Dover and East Dover thrived, each with its own post office. Oddly enough, Mount Snow, a formidable and highly visible presence in this community, has had three different names. It started out as Somerset Mountain, apparently named because it separated the town of Dover from the town of Somerset, and was renamed Mount Pisgah before the final name, Mount Snow, was bestowed on its lofty white crown.

Attractions, Recreational Pursuits

As you drive north of Wilmington on Route 100 north before coming to the actual village of West Dover, you will find a building snugged right up close to the highway (the buildings built this way were built when traffic was horse-slow and no one worried about cars crashing into them) with a sign that seems to come out of a 1940s crime novel — The Road House. Jimmy and Diane Shipke own this establishment at the intersection of Old Ark Road and 100 north, and they serve excellent, consistently wholesome good food at dinnertime. No breakfasts, no lunches, no reservations.

A word about dinnertime. Vermonters have supper when others have dinner, and dinner is sometimes really lunch. So you might like to know the difference. When a Vermonter sits down to his midday meal, it is usually called a dinner; when a Vermonter sits down to his evening meal, that is called a supper. People who have moved up here to run inns and restaurants are not always aware of this nuance. And because some Vermonters are bilingual (speaking Yankee and

American), they sometimes refer to these meals the way visitors to the area do, but they are just being polite. At home, you can be sure, they know the difference; and they probably, if we can believe Robert Frost's definition of a real New Englander, have pie for breakfast.

Hobson's Choice sounds like a name for a tourists' place, but it is a vegetable stand. We know it looks larger than that, but this thing kind of grew out of hand. It started out, literally, as a little vegetable stand. But the demand for the very fresh, extremely varied assortment of vegetables these folks sold there seemed to draw in the customers. Instead of allowing the bins to empty out every day, they built bigger bins and put more in them. By now the building is pretty substantial for a roadside veggy stand, we all admit. And those fields out back, large as they are, only supply a small portion of what is sold there. The rest is imported from the flatlands south of Vermont. Hobson's is open year-round now.

Since July 4, 1981, Betty Hillman's Le Petit Chef has been presenting an elegant continental cuisine, at the junction of 100 north and an un-numbered road that heads off toward Dover, East Dover, and South Newfane. You enter in the back door, the way you would have had you been visiting the "old Cutter place" when it was still a farm. The place was deserted when Hillman found it and converted it into a restaurant of five dining rooms with a total of 60 seats. These rooms never seem crowded, even when bustling. On Mondays and Thursdays, in the lounge (to the left as you come in the door), you can relax in director's chairs at the tables scattered about or sit at a capacious bar and enjoy live entertainment. Hillman thought things were getting a little quiet in the valley along about midweek, and she had some friends who made music. . . .

The Inn at Quail Run and Trail's End Lodge are up Smith Road, which starts just across Route 100 north from Le Petit Chef. The Inn at Quail Run commands one of the most beautiful views of the mountains around here. The living room has a huge fieldstone fireplace, always cozy in winter, and large plate-glass windows that open onto the slopes of Mount Snow, carefully bracketed by stands of pine trees. Jacky and Jerry Bonney usually have a telescope positioned there so their guests can get a close look at the skiers before heading that way. Quail Run has 15 rooms furnished with family antiques and brass beds. Trails End has been gradually converted by Bill and Mary Kilburn from a ski lodge to a very comfortable 18-room inn with English flower gardens, a trout pond, and tea in the afternoon. These two neighboring inns are neighborly as they can be — to each other as well as their visitors. Maybe we should rename the road "hospitality lane."

Out behind the Inn at Quail Run are some cross-country ski trails, part of a system laid out by the folks at Sitzmark, which is kind of an ambitious, local phenomenon that fits in the land below Smith Road, between Route 100 north and the East Dover Road. It is single-handedly a four-season resort and inn. That means that during three seasons its guests play tennis on eight courts or golf on an 18-hole, par 3 course. During winters, the golf course is threaded with cross-country ski trails that wander up through the hills as well. All facilities are open to the public.

One of the most expensive dwelling places and, for that matter, eating places in the Mount Snow Valley is called the Inn at Sawmill Farm. Your host, Brill Williams, will lead you to an elegant dining room or to luxurious, antiques-furnished rooms or suites with fireplaces. It is quite formal — unapologetically so — and rather continental in scope and feeling. Across Route 100 north on the east side is the Snow Den inn, with eight, quaint little rooms, one of the cuter little B&B inns in the region. The building is a century old, five of the rooms have fireplaces, and a full New England breakfast is served to guests. Just up the hill from the Snow Den is Deer Hill Lodge, with 12 wonderfully furnished rooms, some with canopy beds; a lovely dining room overlooking the valley from a panoramic vantage; and huge fieldstone fireplaces to relax next to in the common rooms. The West Dover Inn, right on Route 110 north, is columned and balconied; it has looked like an inn should since 1846, has been an inn since 1889, and has been called by its current name since 1955. It has 10 rooms and an adjoining restaurant called The Capstone.

Up the road that runs westward alongside the Inn at Sawmill Farm is the Mount Snow Airport, where you land your small aircraft at 2,000 feet elevation. This is a smallish airport but growing as the demand grows; once it was a grass strip, now it is paved. You can sign up for flight instruction, for scenic rides, for aerial photography, and for charter tours. A year-round single-family home community is springing up around this facility.

The Brook House Country Store is set right along the side of a brook on the east side of Route 100 north in full view of Mount Snow. This store, under new management since 1988, has developed the reputation for having the best video rental service in the valley. It has always kept its ear open to the needs of those who are permanent residents, which explains hip boots, hunting vests, and the full line of groceries. The nearest full-line grocery store, other than this one, is back in Wilmington, nine miles south to the light and one mile east of the village. That makes the Brook House a very popular place. They also have a deli all year, good coffee, and soft ice cream during summers. You can order meals, created at Two Tannery Road, that you can heat up in your condo or efficiency.

Across from the Brook House is Grampy's, a convenience store that sells some of the same things the Brook House does, but they have a gas pump. The scuttlebut is that folks stop at the Brook House on the way into the mountain to stock up on groceries and at Grampy's on the way out to fill the tank and to buy coffees, sodas, and noshies for the trip back to urbanity. The scuttlebut is somewhat simplified, but both serve a purpose here and are thriving.

Next to Grampy's, on the west side of the highway, is Swe-Den-Nor, Ltd., a furniture extravaganza that features primarily Scandinavian-made furnishings. The name comes from Sweden-Norway-Denmark, the countries that supply most of the goods. They also carry a selection of contemporary and country furniture, lamps, paintings, and accessories. Another furnishing store is back in the North Country Stores Plaza, Green Mountain Interiors, which offers furniture and plans on how to use it most beautifully.

At the base of Mount Snow itself, a number of lodges have sprung up over the past three and a half decades to accommodate the skiers. They started out as elaborate bunkhouses for the hardy adventurers who came in the fifties when the slopes were still a bit rough at the edges and have tried to keep pace with the demands of the skiers who come to the more carefully groomed slopes of today. While the outsides of these lodges look much as they have over the years, the interior decorations and the amenities have been upgraded and retrofitted to a slightly higher level of luxury. It will be impossible, once you have found the mountain itself, to miss the several dozens of area lodges. We suggest you shop around, and ask visitors who have been here before for recommendations.

The mountain itself, visible from just about all parts of West Dover, towers 3,556 feet above sea level and has a vertical drop of 1,700 feet (to the base lodge, they say, at 1,878 — give or take a few — feet). A few years back, the mountain resort added to its slopes those of the family owned Carinthia Ski Area, which are now known simply as the Carinthia Slopes at Mount Snow. That brings the number of skiable trails up to 77, 80 percent of which are covered by snowmaking equipment, all of which are served by 17 lifts.

The mountain boasts skiing late into the spring. Places like Killington, a little farther up in Vermont, and Tuckerman's Ravine over in New Hampshire claim to be later, but even when the snow is long gone from the valley, the slopes on Mount Snow are still white. The latest skiing day on Mount Snow's record is May 15. Locals here think it a bit silly to be skiing into May, when others are golfing, but the snow does last.

The resort has three base lodges, counting Carinthia's, and one summit lodge with numerous cafeterias and lounges distributed among them. The lodge owned by Mount Snow is called Snow Lake Lodge, though the company manages several other lodges and inns in the area and has a complete accommodations service that serves most of the inns and lodges in the valley.

The Cupola and the Mount Snow Ski Shop are part of the ski resort and provide anything you need in skiwear and accessories, as well as repairs and rentals.

Skiing is the obvious draw to the mountain in winter, but during summer the Mount Snow Country Club & Public Golf Course, which is an 18-hole championship golf course with some pretty impressive views, keeps the resort viable. The New England Opens and New England PGA Championships are held here. And the Golf School at Mount Snow goes from mid-May to October 1. The course is public as is the Country Club, where the restaurant serves lunches and dinners to golfers and the nongolfing public alike.

Also in the so-called off-season, the Summer Fest at Mount Snow is held in the 400-seat Performing Arts Center. This is a large tentlike structure set up on extruded aluminum arches that span a freestanding area 60 feet by 105 feet. Sponsored jointly by Pepsi, National Endowment for the Arts, New England Foundation for the Arts, Vermont Council on the Arts, and the Arts Council of Windham County, the summer fest has included such groups as the Victoria Marks Performance Company, the Concert Dance Company of Boston, and the Berkshire Ballet, which have presented both performances and workshops during their two-week residencies. In addition, Gould & Stearn, a mime duo; the Mettawee Puppet Theater; the Kitchensink Mime Theater; the Paul Winter Consort; The Northeast Big Band; and The New England Symphony Orchestra have performed under this rather big top.

Mount Snow also sponsors the Fall Foliage Crafts Fair, usually scheduled the weekend prior to Columbus Day weekend. At the same time, the New England championship mountain bike races see folks on high-tech bikes riding furiously up to the summit via the various year-round access roads on the mountain, some in less than a half hour. If you are not up to this feat of strength and endurance, the mountain provides The Mountain Bike School to learn how to defy gravity. This area stays pretty busy almost year-round.

For the adventurous, Mount Snow bicycle tours take the hardy up to the top of Mount Snow on rugged mountain trails. For those who do not need to prove whatever that takes, start at the base lodge of Mount Snow and head south on the dirt road that wanders along the foot of the mountain for some tree-lined country biking and some breathtaking views when the woods are cleared away. You eventually come to a gradual turn to the left that becomes Cold Brook Road, which is paved, for the most part. This will take you back to Route 100. At that intersection, turn left and head north along the highway until you return to the base lodge, an easy 20 miles.

There used to be what was once called mud season in Vermont, when the dirt roads became quagmires of mud from the spring runoff. With fewer and fewer dirt roads, this is less of an issue, but there is a time between the last logical ski run and the first logical tee off that slows things down a bit here. The problem is that not everyone agrees as to the logic of those moments, so the off-season can't be pinned down very well.

A couple of public houses, Deacon's Den Tavern and Fennesseys, located along Route 100, need be mentioned because, we are told, they serve great sandwiches, burgers, seafood, chicken, and pizzas; they have live entertainment, and everybody goes there.

Another rather special place is called Two Tannery Row, because the view out back into what was once a deeryard is lovely, because the food is exceptional, and because the Roosevelt family used to summer here. Theodore Roosevelt's daughter-in-law bought the place in the early 1900s, and part of the building's legend is that Teddy himself visited here, sometimes arriving from Washington unannounced. The building is thought to be the oldest frame building in the valley, because it was built in Marlboro, Massachusetts, and moved to Vermont in the early 1800s. After the Roosevelts sold it in the 1940s, it was moved again, this time to its present site where a couple of sawmills and a tannery once stood.

Up the road, in the town of West Wardsboro, there's another good restaurant we recommend. It's called Brush Hill, and you need reservations. Actually, it is on the side of the long hill leading down to West Wardsboro. For those who have visited this area before, it used to be "since 1779 The Old Barn." It is small (25 seats) and looks more like a home than a restaurant, because back in 1955 a man bought the old barn and made it his home and then later converted it into a restaurant. It is now Michael and Lee Sylva's homey restaurant serving "contemporary cuisine." By that they mean everything from southeast Asian to Cajun to continental foods depending on availability of foodstuffs and the chef's mood. The beautiful, huge fireplace is cozy in wintertime.

At the north entrance to the Mount Snow Resort there are a lot of condominiums that regulars to these slopes buy or rent out. The so-called south entrance has up to now been considered the main entrance, but the traffic is picking up at both. The strange thing is that just north of that entrance, literally a half mile north, the countryside slips back to the quiet, undeveloped landscape that resembles what the whole valley must have looked like — before the mountain came in.

The Brattleboro/ Wilmington Area Essentials

Important Information

Municipal Services

Brattleboro Town Clerk: 254-4541.
Brattleboro Police: 254-2321.
Brattleboro Fire & Ambulance: 254-4543; 254-2010.
Dummerston Town Clerk: 257-1496.
Dummerston Police: 254-2382.
Dummerston Fire & Ambulance: (603) 352-1100; 254-2010.
Guilford Town Clerk: 254-6857.
Guilford Police: 254-2323.
Guilford Fire & Ambulance: 254-2636; 254-2010.
Jacksonville Town Clerk: 368-2838.
Jacksonville Police: 254-2382.
Jacksonville Fire & Ambulance: 368-2323.
Jamaica Town Clerk: 874-4681.
Jamaica Police: 254-2950.
Jamaica Fire & Ambulance: (603) 352-1100; 365-7676.
Marlboro Town Clerk: 254-2181.
Marlboro Police: 254-4122.
Marlboro Fire & Ambulance: 254-4122; 254-2010.
Newfane Town Clerk: 365-7772.
Newfane Police: 254-2382.
Newfane Fire & Ambulance: (603) 352-1100; 365-7676.
Putney Town Clerk: 387-5862.
Putney Police: 254-2950.
Putney Fire & Ambulance: (603) 352-1100; 254-2010.
Readsboro Town Clerk: 423-5405.

Readsboro Police: 254-2382.
Readsboro Fire & Ambulance: 423-5252; 368-2323.
Stamford Fire & Ambulance: 694-1314.
Townshend Town Clerk: 365-7300.
Townshend Police: 254-2382.
Townshend Fire & Ambulance: 365-7622; 365-7676.
Vernon Town Clerk: 257-0292.
Vernon Police: 254-6962.
Vernon Fire & Ambulance: (603) 352-1100; 254-2010.
Wardsboro Town Clerk: 896-6055.
Wardsboro Police: 874-4025.
Wardsboro Fire & Ambulance: (603) 352-1100; 365-7676.
West Dover Town Clerk: 464-8227.
West Dover Police: 254-2382.
West Dover Fire & Ambulance: 464-5653; 464-5335.
Westminster Town Clerk: 772-4091.
Westminster Police: 1-875-2112.
Westminster Fire & Ambulance: (603) 352-1100; 463-4223.
Whitingham Town Clerk: 368-2838.
Whitingham Police: 254-2382.
Whitingham Fire & Ambulance: 368-2323.
Wilmington Town Clerk: 464-5836.
Wilmington Police: 464-8593.
Wilmington Fire & Ambulance: 464-3737; 464-5335.

Medical Services

Brattleboro Memorial Hospital, 9 Belmont St., Brattleboro; 257-0341.
Deerfield Valley Health Center, Wilmington; 464-5311. A small clinic that takes care of minor injuries and some greater emergencies until they can be transported to Brattleboro.

Grace Cottage Hospital, Rte. 35, Townshend; 365-7676.
Vermont Poison Center, Medical Center Hospital, Burlington; 1-658-3456. They
   will follow through and call back to make sure everything is fine.

Veterinarians

Brattleboro Veterinary Clinic, Marlboro Rd., Brattleboro; 254-8140.
Grass, Albert (equine practitioner), Marlboro Rd., Brattleboro; 257-0790.
Pioneer Valley Veterinary Hospital, 571 Bernardston Rd., Greenfield, Mass.;
   (413) 773-7511. Small animal medicine and surgery.
Vermont/New Hampshire Veterinary Clinic, East Dummerston; 254-5422.
   Twenty-four-hour emergency service.
Westminster Animal Hospital, Rte. 5, Westminster Station; 722-4196.
Windham Veterinary Clinic, Putney Rd., Brattleboro; 254-9412.

Weather

24-Hour Weather Phone (West Dover): 464-2111.
WKVT Weather Hot Line (Brattleboro): 257-7117.

Tourist Information Services

Brattleboro Chamber of Commerce, 180 Main St., Brattleboro; 254-4565.
Mount Snow/Haystack Regional Chamber of Commerce, Rte. 9, Wilmington;
   464-8092. (Just west of the light, in Atty. Tom Politano's offices.)

Lodgings

Reservation Services

Mount Snow Vacation Services, 429 Mountain Rd., Mt. Snow; 464-8501 or (800)
   444-9404.
Vermont Bed & Breakfast Reservation Service, East Fairfield; 827-3827.
   Membership or booking fee required.

Inns and B&Bs

BRATTLEBORO
Dalem's Chalet, off Rte. 9 at 16 South St., West Brattleboro; 254-4323. Moderate.
   Comfortable rooms, some with balconies, color TV, pool, off the highway and
   quiet. You can try out your German in conversations with the owner. Authentic
   Swiss-German and Austrian specialties in the dining rooms.

DOVER
Cooper Hill Inn, Cooper Hill Rd., East Dover; 348-6333. Moderate. The most extraordinary view amongst many around here. They call it a "quiet, hilltop country
   inn," but you have to be there to understand how wonderful panoramic Vermont
   views can be. Cozy rooms. Family suites.

DUMMERSTON
Mapleton Farm Bed & Breakfast, Rd 2; 257-5252. Inexpensive/moderate. This
   homey 1803 building houses eight rooms, some sharing baths. Inexpensive/
   Moderate. The setting is rural, the dining room is for inn guests only.

JACKSONVILLE
Engel House, Rte. 112; 368-2974. Moderate. A village home, built in 1840, is now
   a B&B inn, right across the highway from the North River Winery.

JAMAICA

Jamaica House, Rte. 30 and Mechanic St. in the village; 874-4400. Moderate. An Italian restaurant, lounge, and inn with 12 European-style rooms (shared baths).

Sunny Brook Lodge, Town Rd., Jamaica; 874-4891. Inexpensive. Located just off Rte. 30, just this side of the West River. TV in lounge, private and shared baths.

Three Mountain Inn, Rte. 30; 874-4140. Moderate. In the center of the village. A total of 16 rooms in the 1780s main inn, the farmhouse across the road, and the house next door. Elaine Murray's work in the kitchen featured in *Gourmet* magazine. Hosts Charlie and Elaine Murray.

MARLBORO

Longwood Inn, Rte. 9; 257-1545. Moderate/expensive. Built in the late 1700s, this 15-room inn is set back off the road behind a quiet pond. The award-winning restaurant is open to the public as well as guests. Handy to ski slopes, handy to Marlboro Music Festival.

The Whetstone Inn, Marlboro village; 254-2500. Moderate/expensive. A 200-year-old inn that started as a tavern serving stagecoach travelers. Music lovers welcome, since the Marlboro Music School and Festival are just down the road.

NEWFANE

Four Columns Inn & Restaurant, 230 West St.; 365-7713. Expensive. The Allembert family presides over antiques-furnished rooms in an elegant "Old South" manse on the village green.

Inn at South Newfane, Dover Rd., South Newfane; 348-7191. Moderate/expensive. A family operation with Herb and Connie Borst in the inn and Lisa, their daughter, in the kitchen. A comfortable inn created in a turn-of-the-century mansion. Small dining room with large reputation. Award-winning chef.

Old Newfane Inn, On the Commons (Rte. 30); 365-4427. Expensive. Award-winning kitchen, continental cuisine. Luxurious inn rooms.

West River Lodge, Hill Rd.; 365-7745. Moderate. Antique furnishings in the rooms of the mid-nineteenth-century home in a rural setting. Some shared baths. Guest dining only.

PUTNEY

Hickory Ridge House Bed & Breakfast, Hickory Ridge Rd.; 387-5709. Moderate. Built in 1808 as a farmhouse, this B&B inn has seven rooms, some sharing baths. The living room has a fireplace. Guest dining only.

Putney Summit Restaurant and Inn, Rte. 5; 387-5806. Moderate. Emphasis is on the restaurant. Overnight guests welcome in guest rooms and cottages.

TOWNSHEND

Boardman House, on the green; 365-4086. Inexpensive/moderate. This bed & breakfast has seven rooms, most with private baths. Located within the village in a home built circa 1840.

Townshend Country Inn, Rte. 30, Townshend; 365-4141. Moderate. Only three rooms of this circa 1775 building are open to the public, the emphasis being on the restaurant. The rooms are comfortable and the food below is very good.

Windham Hill Inn, RR #1, West Townshend; 874-4080. Expensive. Fifteen antiques-furnished rooms with private baths in main 1826 building, with another five in the annex. Expensive. Dining for inn guests only.

WEST DOVER

Andirons Lodge, Rte. 100; 464-2114. Moderate. Sixty-one rooms from which you can keep an eye on Mt. Snow. A sauna, Jacuzzi, game room, cable color TV, two fireplaces, tennis, miniature golf. Kids free midweek (nonholiday). Dining room, two lounges. "We've got it all."

Austin Hill Inn, Rte. 100, West Dover; 464-5281. Expensive. Comfortable country inn, just up from Rte. 100. A dozen individually decorated rooms with private baths. Fireplaces in the two common rooms. Breakfast and dinner available.

Austrian Haus, Rte. 100; 464-3911. Moderate. Thirty-three rooms. Breakfast and dinner available. Indoor heated pool, whirlpool, sauna, game room, excellent food, BYOB lounge with fireplace.

Deerhill Inn & Restaurant, Valley View Rd.; 464-3100. Moderate. Sixteen individually decorated rooms with private baths. Some have canopy beds. Public rooms with mammoth fireplaces. Swimming pool, tennis. In-house restaurant for elegant candlelight dining.

Doveberry Inn, Rte. 100; 464-5652. Moderate/expensive. Sophisticated dining in candlelit dining rooms that are open to the public. Eight individually appointed rooms with private bath. Relax by a fireplace in the sitting room. Full country breakfast and afternoon tea.

Gray Ghost Inn, Rte. 100; 464-2474. Inexpensive/moderate. Family operated bed-&-breakfast inn, 26 attractive rooms with private baths. Dining room open to inn guests only. BYOB lounge, game room, sauna, and patio, open fireplace.

Inn at Sawmill Farm & Restaurant, Rte. 100; 464-5624, 464-8131. Expensive. The premiere place in the area. Elegant dining, luxurious master bedrooms, and fireplace suites. Antiques-filled public rooms. Gracious, traditional service.

Kitzhof Lodge, Rte. 100; 464-8310, 464-2342. Moderate. A "rustic Swiss chalet" in Vermont's ski country. Hearty, family dining in public dining room. Game room, cable TV, whirlpool, sauna, heated swimming pool, and fireplace lounge. Groups welcome. Twenty-five rooms.

Matterhorn of Dover, Rte. 100; 464-8011. Moderate. Color cable TV, private baths. Twenty-four guest rooms. Game room, sauna, bar, and lounge. Extensive menu and sleigh rides on premises.

Mountaineer Resort, Handle Rd.; 464-5404. Moderate/expensive. Right between Sundance and Carinthia base lodges. Twenty-six rooms at the base of Mt. Snow. Game room, cedar saunas, indoor pool.

North Branch Club, on Mt. Snow; 464-3319. Moderate. At the base of the mountain, folks renting the 18 rooms ski down to the lifts and ski back home.

Red Cricket Inn, Rte. 100; 464-8817. Moderate. From here it's a short hop to Mt. Snow, Haystack, Stratton, and Lake Whitingham. Twenty-six rooms, most with private baths, color TV in every room; a BYOB fireside lounge. Breakfast available. Dining room is open to the public, though they don't advertise it much.

Shield Inn, Rte. 100; 464-3984. Inexpensive/moderate. Six antiques-furnished rooms, with either fireplace or whirlpools. Hearty country breakfast and generous dinners. Cozy fireplace in lounge. TV and game room.

Snow Creek Inn, Rte. 100; 464-5632. Inexpensive. Efficiency apartments and rooms.

Snow Den Inn, Rte. 100; 464-9355 or 464-5852. Moderate. A restored 1885 country inn with eight rooms, each individually designed, five with fireplaces and sitting areas. Full New England breakfast served. Less than three miles to Mt. Snow.

The Weathervane, Dorr Fitch Rd.; 464-5426. Inexpensive. Enjoy the comforts of home. An old-fashioned family oriented ski lodge with some guests sleeping in nooks and crannies, some in deluxe accommodations, moderate. Full breakfast. Nine-room total. BYOB lounge with incredible fireplace. A find.

West Dover Inn, Rte. 100; 464-5207. Moderate. Historic country inn of 10 rooms in West Dover village. Beautifully restored, elegant rooms, and luxury suites. Candlelight dining in the attached Capstone Restaurant.

Whippletree, One Tannery Rd.; 464-5485. Inexpensive/moderate. A small country inn, seven rooms, almost at the foot of the mountain. Early reservations suggested.

Yankee Doodle Lodge, Rte. 100; 464-5591. Moderate. Two-, three-, four-, and five-day packages. Family rates. Twenty-five guest rooms at the lodge. Whirlpools, cable TV, BYOB lounge, ski movies, and mountain views.

WARDSBORO

The Whetstone, Rte. 100, West Wardsboro; 896-6544. Inexpensive/moderate. Bed & breakfast, five rooms (two with private bath and three shared).

WESTMINSTER

Blue Haven Bed & Breakfast Inn, Rte. 5; 463-9008. Moderate. Five antiques-furnished rooms with shared baths, Colonial public areas. Guest dining only.

Misty Meadow Bed & Breakfast, Rte. 5; 722-9517. Moderate. On 10 acres that roll down to the Connecticut River. Three guest rooms, a gazebo, a patio, a view, and personal attention lavished.

WHITINGHAM

Sadawga Lake House, Rte. 100; 368-2435. Inexpensive. Nine-room, old-fashioned country inn one-tenth of a mile east of the village right on Sadawga Lake. All shared baths. Breakfast and dinner is served to guests only.

WILLIAMSVILLE

Brook Acres, off Rte. 30; 348-7709. Moderate. Halfway between Newfane and South Newfane. Accommodations for six in a "spacious, gracious" old home. They offer scenic walks, tranquility, and a hearty breakfast.

Country Inn at Williamsville, Grimes Hill Rd.; 348-7148. Moderate. Six antiques-filled rooms in a building constructed circa 1795. Includes breakfast and dinner. Only inn guests are served in the dining room. Eight kilometers of ski trails.

Mugwump Farm, on the East Dover Rd. between Newfane and South Newfane, a mile from Rte. 30; 348-7761. Moderate. Three guest rooms with shared bath.

WILMINGTON

Beaver Brook Farmhouse, Rte. 9; 464-7607, 464-7474. Inexpensive/moderate. "A country guest house." Century-old restored farmhouse next to The White House. Six rooms. Bed and breakfast.

Birch Tree Inn, Rte. 100, Wilmington; 464-7717. Moderate. Small, friendly country inn. Large common room with fieldstone fireplace. Outdoor pool.

Darcroft's Schoolhouse, Rte. 100; 464-2631. Moderate. Cross-country skiing within walking distance, snowshoes on request.

Fjord Gate Inn & Farm, Higley Hill Rd.; 464-2783. Inexpensive/moderate. Rustic country inn with a comfortable fireplace and barn board comfort. They have Norwegian Fjord ponies and their foals. Sleigh rides. Hearty, satisfying meals at inexpensive rates.

The Hermitage, Coldbrook Rd.; 464-3511, 464-3759. Expensive. A "working country inn"; almost a self-contained resort unto itself. Award-winning restaurant and wine list, 29 luxurious rooms (11 with fireplaces), game bird farm, maple sugarhouse, hiking, outdoor pool, tennis, etc.

Horizon Inn, Rte. 9; 464-2131. Inexpensive. Family run lodge with 28 rooms, welcomes senior tours. Private baths, cable TV, sauna, and game room.

Inn at Quail Run, Smith Rd.; 464-3362. Moderate/expensive. The dining room, which is open to guests only, looks out on Mt. Snow; fantastic fieldstone fireplace. There are 15 rooms tastefully appointed with antiques, brass beds, and comforters; two, in the annex, share a bath. Heated pool.

Misty Mountain Lodge, Stowe Hill Rd.; 464-3961. Inexpensive. Small, cozy farmhouse inn with spectacular view. Nine guest rooms with shared baths. Family style dining with home cooking. Bring your own guitar and join in the fireside singing in the living room. The building dates from 1803.

Nordic Hills Lodge, 179 Coldbrook Rd.; 464-5130. Inexpensive/moderate. Family operated country inn with 27 guest rooms, color TV, heated swimming pool, ceiling fans, and a cozy BYOB lounge and dining room. No pets please. A few minutes from Haystack. Summers they arrange for tours of the area, including boat trips on Lake Whitingham. Dining room for guests only.

Nutmeg Inn, Rte. 9; 464-3351. Moderate. Right on a bend in the Molly Stark Trail, this is what country inns, especially if they were built in 1777, should look like. Eleven rooms with private baths and furnished with antiques. Dining room for guests only.

Old Red Mill, Rte. 100; 464-3700 or (800) 843-8483. Inexpensive/moderate. Clean comfortable rooms with private baths. In the village itself. Larger suites available.

Red Shutter Inn, Rte. 9; 464-3768. Moderate. This 1894 country inn is right on the edge of the village. Five beautiful, antiques-appointed rooms with private baths, Colonial public rooms with fireplace, comfortable dining room, good food.

Schroder Haus, Higley Hill Rd.; 464-2783. Inexpensive/moderate. Cross-country skiing, ice skating, sauna, fireplaces, TV room, BYOB lounge, dining room overlooking a mountain stream.

Sitzmark Lodge, East Dover Rd. (off Rte. 100, and five miles north of); 464-3384. Moderate. Full cross-country ski touring center with trails, rentals, lessons. Live entertainment on weekends. Mt. Snow and Haystack 10 minutes away. Thirteen rooms in the inn. They seem to have a little of everything.

Slalom Lodge, Shafter St.; 464-3783. Inexpensive. Victorian country B&B inn. Clean accommodations for 28 years. Five rooms. A skiing family.

Trail's End Lodge, Smith Rd.; 464-2727. Moderate. This has been in business since 1956 and provides lovely accommodations in 18 antiques-furnished rooms with private baths. They have a pond, a swimming pool, an English garden, and much hospitality to go with their two fireplaces.

The White House, Rte. 9; 464-2135. Moderate/expensive. Twelve rooms, 5 with fireplaces, are all elegant and have private baths. Extraordinary views, no matter the season. The White House has its own cross-country ski trails, volleyball net, 60-foot outdoor pool, as well as an indoor spa.

Resorts, Hotels, Condominiums

BRATTLEBORO

Latchis Hotel, 2 Flat St., Brattleboro; 254-4501. Moderate. 1930s art deco hotel with private baths, color TV, and phones. Renovated.

WEST DOVER

Dover Watch, Rte. 100, West Dover; 464-2270. Time-sharing townhouses in West Dover, in full view of Mt. Snow's slopes.

Encore, Handle Rd. (off Rte. 100), West Dover; 464-3392. Moderate. At the foot of Carinthia Slopes, can literally walk across the road to the slopes and ski home. Exercise room, game room, 48 guest rooms, and a large theater.

Greenspring Townhouses, Rte. 100, West Dover; 464-7111. Spacious two-, three-, and four-bedroom townhouses with views of Mt. Snow. Private clubhouse with indoor pool.

Inn at Mount Snow, Rte. 100, West Dover; 464-5550. Moderate. Walk 300 yards to the Beaver lift. Family atmosphere with hot tub, sauna, cocktail lounge, fireplace pit, video movies, and games. Twenty-two rooms. Dine in Orsini's Restaurant in the inn.

The Ironstone Lodge, Rte. 100, West Dover; 464-3796. Moderate. Right at the base of Mt. Snow. Former ski lodge, 33 rooms have been upgraded. Public dining rooms. Friendly and skilled chef.

Lodge at Mount Snow, Rte. 100, West Dover; 464-5112 or (800) 451-4289. Moderate. Forty-eight large rooms with private bath and TV. Cocktail lounge with fieldstone fireplace. "Roman" whirlpool. Three hundred yards from the lifts.

Mount Snow Village, Rte. 100, Mount Snow; 464-2407. Two hundred condominiums, two-bedroom, across from Conference Center. Resort center, hotel, and condominiums.

Snow Lake Lodge, Rte. 100, West Dover; 464-3333. Moderate/expensive. A comfortable 100-room ski lodge at the base of Mt. Snow. Lakeside dining, lounge with entertainment. Indoor leisure pools, game room, and shuttle to the lifts. Owned by Mt. Snow.

Tamarack Inn at Mt. Snow, Upper Handle Rd. (just off Rte. 100), West Dover; 464-8850. Moderate. Enviable location and view opening directly out onto Mt. Snow's slopes. Balcony rooms and in-room TV.

Timber Creek Luxury Townhouses, Rte. 100, West Dover; 464-2323 or (800) 437-7350. You can hardly get closer to the Mt. Snow slopes.

WILMINGTON

Crafts Inn, Main St., Wilmington; 464-2344 or (800) 445-7018. Expensive. Time-sharing in 29 suites with private baths. European plan. Indoor pool, racquetball court, hot tubs, saunas, gym. Right in the heart of Wilmington Village in an 1896 manse. The dining room, serving breakfast, lunch, and dinner, is open to the public as the Fiddleheads Restaurant.

Spyglass Hill Village, Mann Rd., Wilmington; 464-7458. Expensive. Luxurious two- and 3-bedroom condominiums on Haystack Mountain. Free shuttle to the mountain.

Motels, Cottages

BRATTLEBORO

Colonial Motel, Putney Rd., Brattleboro; 257-7733. Inexpensive.

Holly Motel, 243 Canal St., Brattleboro; 254-2360. Inexpensive. Forty-five rooms in the heart of Brattleboro.

Molly Stark Motel, Rte. 9, Brattleboro; 254-2440. Inexpensive. A 14-unit all-season motel. Skiers, hunters, businesspeople and tourists welcome.

Quality Inn, Rte. 5 (Putney Rd.), Brattleboro; 254-8701. Moderate. One hundred and nine-room inn in the business district.

Stoney Brook Motor Lodge, Marlboro Rd., Brattleboro; 254-8153. Inexpensive.

Super 8 Motel, Putney Rd., Brattleboro; 254-8889. Inexpensive/moderate. Sixty-four units in the business district.

Susse Chalet Motor Lodge, Putney Rd., Brattleboro; 254-6007. Moderate. Sixty-room motor lodge, part of a chain of Susse Chalets.

West River Motel & Cabins, 480 Western Ave., Brattleboro; 254-5610. Inexpensive. Fourteen-unit motel on Rte. 9, west of Brattleboro.

MARLBORO

Gold Eagle Motel, Rte. 9, Marlboro; 464-5540. Inexpensive. Restaurant on premises, reasonable rates, views. Short drive to the slopes and cross-country trails.

NEWFANE

River Bend Motel, Newfane; 365-7952. Inexpensive. Twenty-unit motel.

PUTNEY

Putney Inn & Motel, I-91, exit 4, Putney; 387-5517. Moderate. Charming motel rooms. Conveniently located just off I-91 exit 4. Old New England charm.

WILMINGTON

Viking Motel & Ski Lodge, Rte. 9, Wilmington; 464-5608. Moderate. Fourteen clean, comfortable rooms. Walking distance from village shops. Licensed bar and restaurant on premises. East of the village in the valley that leads up to The White House.

Vintage Motel, Rte. 9, West Wilmington; 464-8824. Inexpensive. Eighteen-unit motel in rural setting. Private baths, cable color TV, continental breakfast served in coffee lounge. Outdoor heated pool. A quarter century of pleasing people.

Campgrounds

BRATTLEBORO

Hidden Acres Camping Resort, Rte. 5, Brattleboro; 254-2098 or 257-2724. Swimming pool, 18-hole miniature golf course, shuffleboard, nature trails, horseshoes, volleyball, and more. Accepts credit cards.

Moss Hollow Campground, Jacksonville Rd., Brattleboro; 368-2418. Remote. Fifty-seven sites. Separate tent area.

NEWFANE

Kenolie Village, off Rte. 30, off Brookline Rd., Newfane; 365-7671. One hundred wooded and open sites. Beautiful West River Valley. Camp store, playground, and other amenities.

PUTNEY
Brookside Camping, off Rte. 5, Putney; 387-5331. RVs, tenting, cabins, hookups. Along a rustic brook.

TOWNSHEND
Bald Mountain Campground, on State Park Rd., Townshend; 365-7510. Our own private valley. Two hundred and twenty-eight sites. Hookups and related amenities.
Camperama, Family Camping, Depot Rd., Townshend; 365-4315. Member NCOA and VAPCO. Over 200 sites with hookups. On the West River. The works.

Dining

BRATTLEBORO
Backside Café, Midtown Mall; 254-5056. Moderate. Breakfast, Sunday brunch, lunch, and dinner. American cuisine. This is in the Harmony parking lot between Elliot and High streets.
Canton Restaurant, Putney Rd. (Rte. 5); 254-5318. Inexpensive. Authentic Chinese food. Take-out. In the North Brattleboro Shopping Plaza.
Chelsea Royal Restaurant, Rte. 9, West Brattleboro; 254-8399. Moderate. American cuisine.
Country Kitchen, Rte. 9, West Brattleboro; 257-0338. Moderate. Omelettes, sandwiches, meats and poultry, and seafood and pasta served at breakfast, lunch, and dinner. Casual dress. Children's menu.
Dalem's Chalet, off Rte. 9 at 16 South St., West Brattleboro; 254-4323. Moderate. Authentic Swiss-German and Austrian specialties. You can try out your German in conversations with the owner. Off the highway and quiet.
Fifth Season Restaurant, in the Main Street Gallery; 257-5015. Moderate. Mediterranean cuisine. Lunch, Sunday brunch, dinner. Full bar. Fine wines. Kebabs, Apple Plum Chicken, Seafood Past Carbonara, Hungarian Chicken to name a few entrées.
Greenhouse, North Putney Rd.; 254-8701. Inexpensive/moderate. Cajun, Tex Mex, Italian, charbroiled mixture of entrées and sandwiches. "Experience summer all year round in our all glass restaurant."
Jade Wah, 40 Main St.; 254-2392. Moderate/inexpensive. Old standby with newly decorated dining room. Chinese and American restaurant. Oriental food. Take-out orders available.
Jad's Family Restaurant, 107 Canal St.; 257-4559. Inexpensive/moderate. Homemade soups, chicken, prime ribs. Breakfast, lunch, and dinner. Between the car wash and the Laundromat.
Jolly Butcher, Rte. 9, West Brattleboro; 254-6043. Moderate. Steaks, prime ribs, live lobster. Healthy salad bar. Lunch and dinner. Children's menu.
Mole's Eye Café, High and Main Sts. (downstairs); 257-0771. Inexpensive. Soups, salads, sandwiches, and Mexican specialties. Entertainment every Wednesday, Friday, Saturday at 9 P.M.
Panda North, Rte. 5 north (I-91 exit 3); 257-4578, 257-4486. Inexpensive. "We bring Chinatown to you." Chinese restaurant and lounge. Take-out available.
Peter Haven's Restaurant, Elliot St. Moderate. Down-home cuisine.
Riverview Restaurant, Rte. 119, Bridge St.; 254-9841. Moderate. Panoramic view of the Connecticut River. Outside deck seats 40. A 14-foot-long salad bar. Seafood, steaks, burgers. Opens at 5 A.M.
Taft's, 142 Elliot St., 257-5222. Moderate/expensive. Lunch and dinner available in Brattleboro's only AAA three-star restaurant. Seafood, pasta, chicken. A taste of America. A lovely, comfortable place to dine. Claim to have a "devastating" dessert tray.
The Tavern, Putney Rd.; 257-1481. Soup and sandwiches and drinks. And then international cuisine of lamb, seafood, and veal. Also quiches and fondue. In addition a wine list. Moderate breakfast, lunch, and dinner.

T.J. Buckley's Uptown Dining, 132 Elliot St.; 257-4922. Moderate. American gourmet.

Upper Crust Bake House, Brooks House Mall; 257-1991. Inexpensive/moderate. "We're proud to be flaky." They serve sandwiches on their own baked bread and croissants. The desserts are all made here. But they serve soup and sandwiches, et al, daily.

Via Condotti Ristorante & Pizzeria, 69 Elliot St.; 257-0094. Inexpensive, family, affordable. Informal Italian restaurant. Lunch and dinner, wine, beer, and cocktails. Homemade Italian specialties, pasta, grinders, pizza. No reservations needed.

V.I.P., 228 Canal St.; 254-6264. Inexpensive. Vermont Inn Pizza, grinders, spaghetti. All available to go.

Walkers Restaurant, 132 Main St.; 254-6046. Moderate. Lunch and dinner. A very popular place in Brattleboro. They do a special thing with their chips.

Whetstone Café, 414 Western Ave., West Brattleboro; 254-5533. Moderate. Food that is no-nonsense, stick-to-your-ribs, honest-to-goodness home-style Vermont food. Serves "Mornings," "Mid-Day," and "Supper Time." Closed Tues.

JACKSONVILLE

The Carriage Stop, Main St.; 368-2882. Fine New England dining with an emphasis on practical good food. She serves her bakery goods with lunch and dinner as well as over the counter.

Jacksonville Tavern, Rte. 112. Moderate. Country dining. Open Tuesday – Saturday, 5 P.M. to 10 P.M.

JAMAICA

Jamaica House, Rte. 30 and Mechanic St. in the village; 874-4400. A restaurant and lounge specializing in Italian cuisine. They have satellite TV and all the games. Pizza is served in the lounge. Reservations appreciated on Saturday.

Three Mountain Inn, Rte. 30; 874-4140. Moderate. In the center of the village. The main inn, where the two small dining rooms are, was built in the 1780s. Elaine Murray's work in the kitchen featured in *Gourmet* magazine. She bakes her own sweets and her breads, makes her own salad dressings, and features such items as trout almandine, cornish hen, scallops maison, and Kahlua mocha fudge pie.

MARLBORO

Skyline Restaurant, Rte. 9; 464-5535. Inexpensive. The food is good enough, but the views are nonstop. The Skyline is the restaurant perched UP the hill from the 100-mile view at Hogback Mountain. They are famous for their waffles and griddle cakes. Lunches and dinners also served. And the same family has been cooking them for over 40 years. Even the great-grandchildren are beginning to come to work. Even if the food weren't good, hearty, stick-to-the-ribs good, people would come.

The Whetstone Inn, Marlboro Village; 254-2500. Moderate/expensive. A 200-year-old inn that started as a tavern serving stagecoach travelers. Nooks and crannies abound. Music lovers welcome, since the Marlboro Music School and Festival are just down the road. Jean and Harry Boardman your hosts.

Entertainment

Music & Stage

BRATTLEBORO

Actor's Theatre of Brattleboro, Guilford Center Rd.; 257-1129. Amateur and professional theater. Workshops and performances.

New England Bach Festival, 15 Walnut St.; 257-4523. Concertos, cantatas, and orchestral works performed at Marlboro College, the West Village Meeting House and First Baptist Church, and other locations in New York, Massachusetts, and Vermont. In September and October. Under the direction of Blanche Honegger Moyse.

Brattleboro Music Center, 15 Walnut St.; 257-4523. Various music groups and festivals are headquartered here, including the New England Bach Festival with Blanche Honegger Moyse.

MARLBORO
Marlboro Music Festival, Marlboro College; 254-2394 or 257-4333. Professional musicians migrate northward each summer to play in these hills. Public performances of chamber music in Persons Auditorium at the college are a special treat from mid-July to mid-August.

PUTNEY
River Valley Performing Arts Center, Rte. 5, Putney; 387-4355. A varied program of music and drama, workshops, as well as performances. Entrance, now a little obscure, two-tenths of a mile beyond the Landmark College entrance.
Yellow Barn Music Festival, Putney; 387-6637. Chamber music performed on a complicated schedule during July. Proven staying power in Putney.

WILMINGTON
Michael's Theatre, Rte. 100, Wilmington; 464-2893. Inexpensive. Several guys who play every instrument imaginable. Fun, entertaining, amazing.

Nightlife

BRATTLEBORO
Mole's Eye Café, High and Main sts. (downstairs), Brattleboro; 257-0771. Entertainment every Wednesday, Friday, and Saturday at 9 P.M.
Flat Street, 17 Flat St.; 254-8257. "Vermont's largest nightclub." Continuous entertainment, 10-x-12-foot video screen.

WEST DOVER
Cousins, in the Mount Snow Base Lodge. This is a popular bar, with live band in season. Hopping.
Deacons Den Tavern, Rte. 100; 464-9361. Dance, live bands, sandwiches, burgers, chicken, pizzas, subs, and a rocking bar.
Fennesseys, Rte. 100; 464-9361. Moderate. The place out back of Deacons Den. Serves prime ribs, kebabs, chicken, and fresh seafood. They have tables and alcoves for intimate dining. Classy.
Snow Barn, Rte. 100, Mt. Snow; 464-3333. Live entertainment. Live bands. Dancing, drinking, and general merrymaking. While it slows down a little when the snow comes off the hill, during ski season it is a huge rocking bar all week.

WILMINGTON
Le Petit Chef, Rte. 100, Wilmington; 464-8437. Betty Hillman's lounge takes over when business is slow in the restaurant on Monday and Thursday. Local musicians come in and sing and play into the wee hours.
North Country Fair. Huge live bands, comedian. Serves food, pizza. Cover charge. Peaches (a.k.a. North Country Fair) is what happens here in the summer months. It is live entertainment for seniors.

Movies

BRATTLEBORO
First Cinema, Putney Rd. (Rte. 5), Brattleboro; 254-8721, 254-8728.
Latchis Theatre, 48 Main St., Brattleboro; 254-5800.
Paramount Theatre, 167 Main St., Brattleboro; 254-4344.

PUTNEY
River Valley Playhouse and Arts Center, River Rd. (Rte. 5), Putney; 387-4355.

WILMINGTON
Michael's Playhouse, Rte. 100, Wilmington; 464-2893.
Pepsi-Mt. Snow Concert Series, Memorial Hall, West Main St., Wilmington; 464-3253.

Museums and Historical Sites

BRATTLEBORO
Brattleboro Museum & Art Center, Main and Vernon sts.; 257-0124. Changing art and historical exhibits, related adjunct programs, and Estey organs. Old railroad station.

MARLBORO
The Historical Society of Marlboro; 254-2839. The Ephraim Holland Newton House, 1814. Exhibits, reference room, library, special events. Adjacent one-room schoolhouse, colonial herb garden.
Luman Nelson Museum of New England Wildlife. Natural history museum with hundreds of stuffed animals and birds, a rare albino deer, moose hooves, odds and ends. Interesting, vaguely disturbing.

NEWFANE
The Historical Society of Windham; 365-4148, 365-7937. Exhibits of photos and artifacts and evidence of floods.

TOWNSHEND
Scott Covered Bridge, Rte. 30. Spanning the West River, the Scott Bridge is the longest, 165.7 feet, single-span bridge of its type in the state. Built in 1870.

WHITINGHAM
Brigham Young Birthplace, Rte. 100. A 14-foot granite monument is two miles from Whitingham off Rte. 100.

VERNON
School House Museum, at Rte. 142 and Pond Rd.; 257-0292. Summer and fall. Special schoolroom exhibit, farm and carpenter tool exhibit.

WESTMINSTER
The Westminster MG Car Museum, Rte. 5; 722-3708. July and August. Twenty-seven MG cars from the Goguen Collection on display, related artifacts, motorcar library.

WILMINGTON
The Living History Association is the international "chamber of commerce" for all eras of reenacted history. The New England Plantation is 117 acres of land that is used as a "theater" for the "performers" who come from the Living History Association to reenact fun, colorful, and usually military moments in history; from the Middle Ages to World War II.
Old Medbury Bridge, Rte. 9, west of Wilmington. This old double-intersection, Warren truss iron bridge is right next to a newer bridge that is functional. The flooring has been removed from the bridge, the ends have been fenced off, but you can view its detail.

Seasonal Events

BRATTLEBORO
Annual May Magic, Brattleboro; 254-4565. Early May. Fair, magic show, footraces.
Green Mountain Antique Arms Show, Union High School, Brattleboro; 257-7771. Early September.
Annual Apple Days, Brattleboro; 254-4565. First weekend in October. Craft fair, fiddlers' convention, auto rally, footrace.
Village Days, Brattleboro; 254-4565. Circus, raft regatta.

DUMMERSTON

Annual (for over 60 years) Strawberry Supper, Grange Hall, Dummerston Center. Late June.

GUILFORD

Labor Day Weekend Festival, Organ Barn, Guilford; 257-1961. Concerts on Labor Day weekend.
Guilford Fair, Weatherhead Hollow Rd., Guilford; 254-4339. Livestock, farm and garden products, arts and crafts, poultry and/or small animal competition, horse pulls, and games of chance.

JAMAICA

White Water Canoe & Kayak Races & Church Supper, Jamaica State Park, West River, Jamaica; 824-8178. First weekend in May. Recreational water sports races held the following weekend.

MARLBORO

Marlboro Music School & Festival, off Rte. 9 at Marlboro College, Marlboro; 254-8163.

NEWFANE

Bazaar & Flea Market, Rte. 30, Newfane; 254-2265. Saturdays, July to October. The granddaddy of all fleas. This one is legendary.
Annual Art Festival, on the common, Newfane; 365-4309. In Union Hall in case of rain. First weekend in October.
Annual Heritage Festival, on the common, Newfane; 257-0609. Second weekend in October.

PUTNEY

Vermont Composers Festival, River Valley Performing Arts Center, Putney; 257-1961. First weekend in November.

SAXTONS RIVER

Annual Organ Recital, Historical Society, Saxtons River; 869-2328. Mid-August.

TOWNSHEND

Annual "Now & Then" Antique Car Show & Flea Market, Townshend Family Park, Townshend; 365-7858. First weekend in June.
Annual Hospital Fair Day, Townshend; 365-7773. Early August. Parade, auction, barbecue, concerts on the common to benefit Grace Cottage Hospital.

WEST DOVER

Annual Attic Treasures & Bake Sale, Congregational Church, West Dover; 348-7765. Late May.
Air Show at the Mt. Snow Airport, on the top of Country Club Rd., West Dover; 464-2196. Early July. Scenic rides off a mountain airport, special group tours, aerial photography, and flight instructions.
Summerfest at Mt. Snow, Rte. 100, West Dover; 464-8501 or 464-3333. In July and August. The Summerfest has included modern, ballet, and concert dance companies; mime; comedy; music and puppeteering; symphony orchestras; big bands; folk singing; and Paul Winter Consort. Changing programs.
Grampy's New England Mountain Bike Championships, Mt. Snow, West Dover; 387-5718. A late-July race up Mt. Snow.
Annual Mt. Snow Craft Fair, Mt. Snow Base Lodge, West Dover; 464-3333. Second weekend in October. Music, entertainment, gourmet food.
Fall Foliage Summit Chair Lifts, Rte. 100, Mt. Snow, West Dover; 464-3333. Sporadically during summer, constantly during foliage. Take the Yankee Clipper quad to the 3,600-foot summit of Mt. Snow where you can see four states.

WILMINGTON

Antiques & Flea Market, where Rtes. 100 and 9 meet, Wilmington; 464-8092. Becoming the biggest flea on the block, rivaling the old guy in Newfane.

Art on the Mountain, Haystack Base Lodge, Coldbrook Rd., Wilmington; 464-5321. Late July to mid-August. Arts and crafts exhibition and sale. Benefits the local Deerfield Valley Health Center.

Deerfield Valley Farmer's Days, Baker Field, Wilmington; 464-5277 or 464-2028. Every year in mid-August. A long weekend of horse and pony pulls and taffy pulls, demonstrations of crafts and demolition derbies, arm wrestling, saw contests, children's pet shows, farm products, and old-fashioned community fun.

Children's Activities

BRATTLEBORO

Crowell Lot, Rte. 9 (High St.) in Brattleboro just west of the business district. A park with swings, slides, and benches from which to watch the kids.

Living Memorial Park, Rte. 9, Brattleboro; 254-6700. Swimming pool, softball, basketball, tennis courts, playgrounds, cookout facilities, and more; all two miles west of Brattleboro.

DUMMERSTON

Miniature Golf and Swimming at Hidden Acres, Rte. 5, Dummerston.

PUTNEY

Santa's Land, Rte. 5, Putney; 387-5550. It's Christmas all year long (except Christmas Day). Christmas theme park with petting zoo, carousel, train rides, exotic animals, picnic areas, Igloo Pancake House, and visits with the jolly old elf himself.

TOWNSHEND

Mary Meyer Stuffed Toy Factory Store, Rte. 30, Townshend; 365-7793. Vermont's largest toy manufacturer sells her stuffed toys at great discounts; along with hand puppets, penny candy, and so forth. A second factory store is in Brattleboro; 257-5846.

Townshend Family Park, Rte. 30, Townshend. A 14-acre park with kid's train rides, picnic tables, concert space, and room for family fun.

Shops

Art Galleries

BRATTLEBORO

Brattleboro Museum & Art Center, Main & Vernon sts., Brattleboro; 257-0124. Changing exhibits, related adjunct programs.

West Village Meeting House, West Brattleboro; 254-9377. Group and individual shows.

Windham Art Gallery, in the Latchis Hotel, Elliot St. Contemporary Vermont artists and artisans.

JACKSONVILLE

Stone Soldier Gallery, Mill Hill (off Rte. 100), Jacksonville; 368-7077. Contemporary artists on display. Across the street from the Stone Soldier Pottery, from which vantage Connie Burnell keeps her eye on things.

JAMAICA

Gallery at Jamaica, Rte. 30, Jamaica; 874-4478. Fine arts and crafts, paintings, ceramics, baskets, wood weaving, corn husk flowers, quilted items, hand-blown glass.

PUTNEY

River Valley Playhouse & Art Center, Rte. 5, Putney; 387-4355. At the eastern edge of Landmark College campus. Changing monthly exhibits.

TOWNSHEND

A. Richter Gallery, Rte. 30; 365-4549. Antique prints, original art, illustrative Americana, memorabilia, period prints, vintage posters, and conservation and custom framing.

WEST DOVER

Hayloft Gallery, Rte. 100, West Dover; 464-5525. Eclectic display of art, limited editions, lithographs, serigraphs, watercolors, oils, sculpture. Hayloft Gallery is also in West Wardsboro; 896-6058.

WILMINGTON

Craft-haus, Stowe Hill Rd., Wilmington; 464-2164. Fine art and craft gallery with cloisonné jewelry, art glass, pottery. Original paints, lithographs, and serigraphs.

Craft and Specialty Stores

BRATTLEBORO

Borter's Jewelry Studio-Gallery, 1 Harmony Pl., Brattleboro; 254-3452. You can see the artisans at work making jewelry as you browse through the wares. They handcraft original jewelry designs, limited editions, and one-of-a-kind pieces.

Brown & Roberts Hardware Store, 182 Main St., Brattleboro; 257-4566. This is an old-fashioned, family owned, if-we-don't-have-it-you-don't-need-it hardware store. They are reputed to have everything, including sporting goods.

Candle in the Night, 181 Main St. (Main Street Gallery), Brattleboro; 257-0471. Oriental rugs, decorative brass and hardware, ceramic tile, jewelry, ladies' clothing, and accessories.

Dancing Stone, 51 Elliot St., Brattleboro; 257-5716. Area's largest collection of crystals, native American books and crafts, ceremonial feathers, smudge sticks, Tibetan and crystal bowls, pentatonic harps.

Pam's Potpourri, Main St., Brattleboro. Collection of area crafts.

Vermont Artisan Designs, 115 Main St., Brattleboro; 254-4565. New England handcrafts for over 200 artisans. Jewelry, pottery, blown glass, weaving, candles, woodworking, porcelain, collectibles. Contemporary crafts.

Wilson's Ltd., 111 Main St., Brattleboro; 254-2499. Over 100 varieties of chocolate, gourmet jelly beans, teddy bears, cards, gifts.

DUMMERSTON

Botanical Castings, Rte. 30, West Dummerston; 375-1115. Dried flowers and artistic arrangements are cast in a polyester resin that preserves the natural color and form. These are sold here as sun catchers, cutting boards, lazy Susans, cheese plates, and so forth at the gift shop.

GUILFORD

Guilford Cheese Co., Rd #2, Guilford; 254-9182. Founded in 1984 by the Dixon family, the company produces Verde-mont and soft-ripened Brie and Mont-bert Camembert in the French tradition. Retail, wholesale, and mail order.

Guilford Country Store, Rte. 5, Guilford; 254-9898. In the historic 1817 Broad Brook House, this has groceries, gas, gifts, and the time to chat. You can buy hunting and fishing licenses here, and it is an official game reporting station in hunting season.

JAMAICA

American Country Designs, Rte. 30, Jamaica Village; 874-4222. Contemporary country accessories and gifts. Closed Tues.

JACKSONVILLE

Coombs Maple Products, located up the hill from Rte. 12, Jacksonville; 368-7301. The Coombs family has been making sweet syrup out of trees and maple cream, maple candies, and maple fudge out of the syrup since 1925. They will welcome you and show you how it's done, in season.

North River Winery, Rte. 12, Jacksonville; 368-7557. This is where Ed Metcalfe and family make 50,000 bottles of fine wine out of apples, blueberries, raspberries, and a little maple syrup. Tours, tasting, gift shop. Daily May through December; weekends January through April.

Stone Soldier Pottery, Mill Hill (off Rte. 100), Jacksonville; 368-7077. Pottery handcrafted by master craftsman Bob Burnell. Items include complete dinner sets, casseroles, and mugs. Also a year-round crafts shop featuring Vermont-made rugs, quilts, jewelry, blown glass, and baskets.

PUTNEY

Basketville, Rte. 5, Putney; 387-5509. Many of the baskets are made here, many others in New England, a few more are imported from the world over. Splint baskets, wicker ware, woven wood, and wood products.

Richard Bissell, Fine Wood Working, Putney; 387-4416. Handcrafted hardwood furniture. Custom work accepted.

Blossom Handweaving, Main St., Putney; 387-4189 or 387-5205. Fine handwoven rugs, clothing, table, and bed linen. Also children's books, cards, and crystals.

Casa del Sol, South Main St., Putney; 387-5318. Select Mexican gifts and crafts in a variety of materials including ceramics, onyx, wood, lacquer, clothing, and carved stone.

Green Mountain Spinnery, exit 4 off I-91, Putney; 387-4528. New England grown wool, yarns, mohair, knit kits, knitting goods. Tours to see how raw wool is milled into finished yarn (first and third Tuesday of month).

Mountain Paul's General Store, Main St., Putney; 387-4446. "Your everyday shopping center" right across from Basketville. Dairy bar features "real scoop" ice cream.

Oak Grove Handcrafted Yarns. Hand-spun or mill-spun yarns, hand-dyed mohair and angora. Sheepskins, hand-knit sweaters, and knitting accessories. Closed Tuesday and Wednesday.

Putney Consumers' Cooperative, Westminster West St., Putney; 387-5866. In business since 1944. Finest produce, meats, deli items, home-baked goods.

Putney General Store, Main St., Putney; 387-5842. This is the real thing. Continuous operation since 1843. Old-fashioned soda fountain. Everything conceivable. Almost.

Putney Woodshed, Main St., Putney; 387-4481. Works in wood, iron, pottery, fibers, cards, and prints by 100 area artists. Also wood stoves and accessories.

Sawmill Country Store, Main St., Putney; 387-4688. Factory-direct pine-crafted furniture. Pottery, cheese, maple products, etc.

Silver Forest of Vermont, next to the General Store, Putney; 387-4149. Imported and domestic clothing in natural fibers, jewelry, cards, and gifts.

Woodlot, Rte. 5, four miles north of Putney. Antiques and farm collectibles. Wagons, sleighs, buggies, pine tabletops and bottoms.

Woodzels by Wetzels Gifts, Westminster West Rd., Putney; 387-6642. Handpainted woodenware, antique roofing slate signs, switch plates and plaques, country folk art.

Zellmer, Jim & Nora, on Kimbel Hill, Putney; 387-5948. Custom cabinets, furniture, and wood carving.

WEST DOVER

Brookhouse Country Store, Rte. 100, West Dover; 464-3838. Fresh meats, deli counter, bagels, and "heat-and-serve" entrées from the chefs of Two Tannery Road Restaurant. General line of groceries. Hunting gear. Toys. You name it. You can get your morning coffee at 6:30 A.M. Largest video collection in West Dover.

Gourmet Galley, Rte. 100, West Dover; 464-7275. Top-quality foodstuffs, ad hoc catering, and carry-home cuisine. Jams, cheese, jellies, breads, pasta, coffee, tea, or a whole picnic basket.

Green Mountain Interiors, Rte. 100, West Dover; 464-3007. Home furnishings, window treatments, and accessories. In North Country Stores.

J.J. Hawkes of Vermont, Rte. 100, West Dover; 464-0988. Clothing and knitwear for the entire family. In the North Commercial Center.

Swe-Den-Nor, Rte. 100, West Dover; 464-2788. A collection of Scandinavian furniture and accessories. Much teaks. But more than that. They ship anywhere, they say.

Veronique's Ski Boutique, Rte. 100, West Dover; 464-5972. Fun and unique skiwear. Everything you need to look stylish on the slopes, which you can see from the store. Right across from North Country Stores.

WILLIAMSVILLE

Carriage House Comforters, Rte. 30, Brattleboro; 257-0407. The manufacturing shop, off Rte. 30, Williamsville; 348-6633. Goose-down comforters, bedding accessories, flannel nightshirts, cotton and terry robes.

WILMINGTON

Colanders, Rte. 9, Wilmington; 464-3138. Everything for the kitchen. Housewares of all kinds.

Down in the Valley, West Main St., Wilmington; 464-2211. Down-filled every-thing — jackets, vests, coats, mittens, and quilts. Other clothing and soft items.

1836 Country Store Village, West Main St., Wilmington; 464-7213. The 1836 Country Store sells decorative brass, historic flags, food products, and horse sup-plies. The 1760 Norton House sells over 2,000 calicos and solid fabrics and quilt-ing supplies, nonstop video lessons, and candles and gifts. The 1890 Restaurant, formerly the Lyman House, sells ice cream, cheeses, sandwiches, and pancakes. And behind the pancake kitchen is the classroom for the Living History Associa-tion (see Museums and Historical Sites).

For All Occasions, South Main St., Wilmington; 464-3525. Cards, gifts, party sup-plies, favors, and balloons. In the old church building.

Forever Lancelot, West Main St., Wilmington; 464-2439. Coin-cut jewelry. Look for the one-and-one-half-story-tall suit of armor.

Golden Bear Photo Co., East Main St., Wilmington; 464-6168. Quality photo finishing, cameras, film, fax service.

Incurable Romantic, West Main St., Wilmington; 464-3506. Linens, pillows, dresses, dried and silk flowers.

Klara Simpla, 10 West Main St., Wilmington; 464-5257. The health-food store carries a lot of other things too, including an incredibly interesting assortment of books.

John McLeod, Rte. 9, Wilmington. Manufactures fine woodenware west of town where he has a large showroom and shop where he sells his own woodenwares as well as beautifully crafted woodwork from around the world.

Quaigh Design Centre, West Main St., Wilmington; 464-2780. Lilias MacBean started out with fine Scottish woolens and weavings and has gone on from there. She also sells jewelry and has a small art gallery on the second floor. A special place.

Village Gardener, Main St., Wilmington; 464-3101. Specialty flower and gift shop. Fresh and dried flowers. By the stem, by the bouquet. Assortment of Hand-maiden Vermont gifts.

Antiques

BRATTLEBORO

Adam's What, 96 Elliot St., Brattleboro; 254-3636. Used furniture, many other collectibles.

Barry Kit Antiques, 143 Main St., Brattleboro; 254-3634. General merchandise.

Black Mountain Antique Center, Rte. 30, Brattleboro; 254-3848. Dealers from all over bring their wares to this central location.

JACKSONVILLE

Born Yesterday, Rte. 112, Halifax; (413) 624-3694. A 1792 homestead with primitives, art deco, cloth, paper, jewelry, collectibles, glassware, tools, books, gadgets. Six miles south of Jacksonville. May through October.

NEWFANE
Newfane Antiques Center, Rte. 30; 365-4482. Twenty dealers display a wide variety of antiques on three floors. Closed Wednesday.

Schommer Antiques, Rte. 30; 365-4482. Shirley and William Schommer concentrate on nineteenth-century furniture with some accessories, including china, glass, prints, kitchenware. Table settings a specialty. Call!

PUTNEY
The Unique Antique, Main St.; 387-4488. Jonathan Flaccus specializes in nineteenth-century art, unusual books, prints, paintings, photographs, and ephemera. Open 9 A.M.–6 P.M. year-round, but call ahead for appointment.

TOWNSHEND
Antique Boutique, Rte. 30; 365-4631. Quilts and linens, country furniture, general line. Open by chance and by appointment.

The Colt Barn, Rte. 35; 365-7574. Country furniture and accessories. Follow Vermont State signs up scenic mountain road.

WESTMINSTER
Larsons' Clock Shop, Main St. (Rte. 5); 722-4203. Lindy and Karen Larson have collected hundreds of antique clocks in many styles and prices. By chance and by appointment, year-round.

WILMINGTON
Antique & Flea Market, where Rtes. 100 and 9 meet; 464-8092. Becoming the biggest flea on the block, rivaling the old guy in Newfane.

Antiquarian Booksellers

The Bear Bookshop, off Rte. 9 on Butterfield Rd., Marlboro; 464-2260. General line of used and rare books, especially academic. Appointments always recommended. (Lists his mailing address as RD# 4, Box 466, West Brattleboro.)

Nu-tique Shop, Rte. 30, Newfane; 365-7677. Out-of-print books, town histories, poetry, novels, medical, Civil War, genealogy. Closed Thursday and Friday.

The Unique Antique, Main St., Putney; 387-4488. Old and unusual books, prints, paintings, photographs, and ephemera. Though open 9 A.M.–6 P.M., year-round, it is wise to call ahead for appointment.

Discount Outlets

BRATTLEBORO
Outlet Center, Canal St.; 254-4594. Twelve factory outlets including Van Heusen, Manhattan, Barbizo, Handbags, Kids Port, Dunhams, L'Eggs, Amherst Sportswear, Mary Meyer, Last Straw, Knitwits, Clothes Works.

Tom & Sally's Handmade Chocolates, 6 Harmony Pl.; 254-4200. Chocolate lovers' paradise is in the Harmony parking lot between Elliot and High sts. Watch them make what you can't resist. They sell ice cream when it gets warm.

PUTNEY
Green Mountain Spinnery, exit 4 off I-91; 387-4528. New England grown wool, yarns, mohair, knit kits, knitting goods. Tours to see how raw wool is milled into finished yarn (first and third Tuesday of month).

TOWNSHEND
Mary Meyer Stuffed Toy Factory Store, Rte. 30; 365-7793. Vermont's largest toy manufacturer sells her stuffed toys at great discounts, along with hand puppets, penny candy, and so forth. A second factory store in Brattleboro; 257-5846.

Sports and Recreation

Biking

BRATTLEBORO
Specialized Sports, Putney Rd., Brattleboro; 255-1017. In season, they sell and/or rent bicycles and accessories, skis, service, accessories.

PUTNEY
West Hill Shop, Depot Rd., Putney; 387-5718. Bike and ski touring. Speedy repairs on bikes. Rent touring bikes by half day, day, or longer.

WEST DOVER
Mountain Bike School, Mt. Snow Vacation Center; 464-7788, 464-3333, or (800) 451-4211. From May to October, learn the ins and outs of the strenuous sport of mountain biking at the school. Riding skills, bike maintenance and repair, map reading and orienteering. Rent handcrafted Cannondale mountain bikes by the hour, by the day, from the Mountain Bike Touring Center. Guided tours offered through some of the most exhilarating terrain in the area.

Golf

BRATTLEBORO
Brattleboro Country Club, Upper Dummerston Rd.; 257-7380. Semiprivate, visitors welcome. Eighteen holes, par 71, 6,265 yards.

WEST DOVER
Golf School at Mount Snow, Country Club Rd.; 464-3333. Intense, intimate lessons (four-to-one student to instructor ratio) in specially designed practice area. Lodging, all meals, and amenities included. From May through October. From October to May they move the operation to Florida.
Mt. Snow Country Club and Public Golf Course, Country Club Rd.; 464-3333. Site of recent New England Opens and the New England PGA Championships. Pro shop, clubhouse, and lounge. Eighteen holes, par 72, 6,443 yards.

WILMINGTON
Haystack Mountain Golf Club, Mann Rd.; 464-8301. It's right next to the ski mountain and is an 18-hole championship golf course. Open to the public. Pro shop, clubhouse, restaurant, and lounge.
Sitzmark Golf Course, East Dover Rd. (off Rte. 100 and five miles north of Wilmington); 464-3384. Eighteen holes, all par 3s. Fun little course. In addition there are eight all-weather tennis courts, cart and club rentals, an Olympic-sized pool with a bar and snack bar, and kilometers and kilometers of cross-country ski trails in winter.

WINDHAM
Tater Hill Club, Dungeon Rd., North Windham; 875-2517. One mile off Rte. 11. Open to the public; 9 holes, par 36, 3,346 yards.

Horseback Riding

Flame Stables, off Rte. 100, Wilmington; 464-8329. Trail rides, lessons, hay and sleigh rides in season.
West River Stables, Brookline, Newfane; 365-7745. Trail riding, lessons, and sleigh rides in season.

Sporting Goods Services

BRATTLEBORO

Southern Vermont Helicopter Service, West Brattleboro; 257-4354. Helicopter taxi, foliage rides. Marilyn George, owner.

WEST DOVER

The Cupola, Rte. 100, West Dover; 464-8010 or (800) 535-5013. Owned by Mt. Snow, this shop provides everything you need in skiing equipment and clothing. Since there are biking trails here, they handle that sport and just about any other that can be practiced in Vermont.

Frasers' Mountain Shop, Mt. Snow Access Rd., West Dover; 464-2222. All major brands of golf and ski equipment and clothing, rental, and certified mechanics.

Mt. Snow Airport, on the top of Country Club Rd., West Dover; 464-2196. Scenic rides off a mountain airport, special group tours, aerial photography, and flight instruction.

Tennis

BRATTLEBORO

Brattleboro Outing Club, Tennis, and General Information, Cedar St., Brattleboro; 254-3635. Six clay courts.

Living Memorial Park, Rte. 9, Brattleboro; 254-6700. Two outdoor courts, plus four covered courts (where the ice rink is in wintertime). All two miles west of Brattleboro.

WILMINGTON

Baker Field, Wilmington. Two municipal all-weather tennis courts.

Recreation area in Vernon. Two courts.

Sitzmark, East Dover Rd. (off Rte. 100), Wilmington; 464-3384. Eight all-weather tennis courts and an Olympic-sized pool with a bar and snack bar.

Alpine Ski Areas

DUMMERSTON

Maple Valley, Rte. 30, West Dummerston; 254-6083. A family ski area with a 1,000-foot drop over 13 trails serviced by three lifts. Snowmaking.

WEST DOVER

Mt. Snow, 429 Mountain Rd.; 464-3333. A 3,600-foot mountain with a 1,700-foot drop over 77 trails serviced by 17 lifts. Snowmaking covers 80 percent of skiable terrain on 58 trails on 296 acres.

WILMINGTON

Haystack Mountain, Coldbrook Rd.; 464-5321. A 3,200-foot mountain with 1,400-foot drop over 43 trails serviced by six lifts. Several of the trails have 40 percent to 45 percent grades. Snowmaking covers 90 percent of skiing terrain on 38 trails on 160 acres.

Nordic Ski Areas

BRATTLEBORO

Brattleboro Ski Hut, Upper Dummerston Rd., Brattleboro; 254-4081. With 20 kilometers of trails. Instruction available. No hot tubs. No ski fashion. No café or bar. No crowds. Simply skiing.

WILMINGTON

Hermitage, Coldbrook Rd.; 464-3511. Fifty kilometers of trails, one of which goes to top of Haystack. Instruction, rentals, retail shop, the works.

Sitzmark Golf Course, East Dover Rd. (off Rte. 100); 464-3384. In winter the 18 3-par hole golf course makes way for kilometers and kilometers of cross-country ski trails. Not only all over the course but up into the hills, past inns, and up toward some very nice views of the mountains around.

Timber Creek, Wilmington; 464-0999. Fourteen kilometers of trails. Instruction, rental, retail shop, restaurant.

White House, Rte. 9, Wilmington; 464-2136. Sets forty-five kilometers of trails. Instruction, rentals, restaurant, and lounge to greet you when you get back to the inn.

Fishing

Lake Whitingham, Lake Raponda, and Somerset Reservoir are home to trout, pickerel, bass, and panfish. The Townshend Reservoir has a few trout and panfish. Streams such as the Deerfield, Green, Saxtons, West, and Winhall rivers have brook and brown trout. The Connecticut River, in addition to the trout, has perch, walleye and northern pike, pickerel, bass, and panfish. The salmon, being reintroduced to the river system, are out of bounds.

Strictly Trout, RD #3, Westminster West; 869-3116. Arranges wading fly-fishing trips on any Vermont stream or river and accommodations.

You need a license to fish in Vermont if you are 15 years old or older. These can be purchased at the Brookhouse Country Store, the Dover Town Clerk, Guilford Country Store, and Jacksonville General Store.

Boating

BRATTLEBORO

Connecticut River Safari, Rte. 5, Brattleboro; 257-5008. Guided canoe tours of the Connecticut and West rivers. Rowboats, canoes, sailboats for hour, day, week, or month. Located at Putney Rd., next to the old truss bridge where the West River meets the Connecticut. Dock at marina, tie up for lunch or dinner.

JAMAICA

New England Sailboard Co., Jamaica; 874-4178. Sailboards for hour, day, week, month, or season. They arrange guided sailboard outings, too. Instruction.

West River Canoe Sailboard Center, Rte. 100, East Jamaica; 896-6209. Canoes, sailboards, paddleboats for hour, day, week, month, or season. Sailboard instruction.

SEARSBURG

Somerset Reservoir, Rte. 9, Searsburg. Five miles west of Wilmington. Nine miles long. Boat launch area at the end of a 10-mile dirt road. Picnic area provided by and cared for by New England Power Company.

WILMINGTON

Green Mountain Flagship Company, Rte. 9, Wilmington; 464-2975. One-and-one-half-hour cruises aboard M/V Mt. *Mills* on Harriman Reservoir (née Lake Whitingham) down to the Glory Hole and back. Group tours, dinner parties, moonlight cruises, individuals by reservation.

Heather Sue Tours, Rte. 9, Wilmington; 464-8011. A 55-foot pontoon boat, *Heather Sue,* takes a one-and-one-half-hour cruise of Harriman Reservoir. Group tours, dinner parties, live musical entertainment.

Lake Whitingham (Harriman Reservoir), Rte. 9, Wilmington. Eleven miles long. Boat launch at Mt. Mills. Maintained and provided by the New England Power Company.

Swimming

Colonial Inn & Spa. Olympic-size lap (shallow) pool and workout center. Saunas, steam baths, the works.

Lake Raponda, Higley Hill Rd., Wilmington. Small public beach and picnic area.

Lake Whitingham, Wilmington. Ward's Cove Beach (off Rte. 100 south toward Jacksonville) and Mt. Mills East (Off Castle Hill Rd., right onto Fairview Ave.). At the end of Fairview, NEPCO park provides a small swimming beach.

Living Memorial Park, Rte. 9, Brattleboro; 254-6700. Olympic-sized swimming pool and other sports facilities two miles west of Brattleboro.

Hiking and Nature Trails

BRATTLEBORO

Wantastiquet Mountain. Drive Rte. 119 across the Connecticut River into New Hampshire. Take the first dirt road on the left up to a parking lot. This is the base of an access road for the cable company. The road is the walking trail here. At the top of the mountain (40 minutes later), you have panoramic views of the river and Brattleboro.

JAMAICA

Jamaica State Park, Town Rd.; 874-4600. Has 772 acres to explore. The Railroad Bed Trail (three miles, one hour, 30 minutes) is along the river on the old railroad right-of-way out to Ball Mountain Dam and back. Hamilton Falls Trail is a spur of the Railroad Bed Trail that heads out to Hamilton Falls and back (additional one mile, 30 minutes). The Adam Pond Trail (two miles, one hour, 30 minutes) leaves from the campground and heads up into the forest, past the pond, and back down to the Railroad Bed Trail. The Overlook Trail (a .9-mile, one-hour side trip of the Adam Pond Trail) takes you to the top of Little Ball Mountain.

MARLBORO

Molly Stark State Park, Rte. 9; 464-5460. Thirty-four sites, hiking trails.

TOWNSHEND

Four Season Touring; 365-7937. Day hikes and guided ski tours featuring local history and lore. Old cemeteries, abandoned farms, and scenic wilderness in all seasons. Excursions last from two to five days. Guide: Charles Marchant.

Ledges Overlook Hiking Trail, Townshend Lake. Start at the access road to the beach and dam, and follow the trail through mature northern hardwood forest to the Ledges Overlook. Be careful at the overlook. Continue on through woodland savannah and back to the access road (1.7 miles, 1.5 hours).

Townshend State Forest. Starting at the state camping area, make a two-and-a-half-mile circle that includes Baled Mountain summit at 1,680 feet. Takes about three hours round-trip. Maintained by Vermont Department of Forests.

WEST DOVER

Thompson Nature Trail, Mt. Snow; 464-3333. This Mt. Snow trail is noted for historical, geologic, and natural points of interest.

State Parks

Dutton Pines State Park, Rte. 5, East Dummerston. Picnic area and shelter on 13 acres. Five miles north of Brattleboro.

Fort Dummer State Park, Old Guilford Rd., Brattleboro; 254-2610. Contains 61 sites, including 9 lean-tos, on 217 acres. Flush toilets, showers, public phone, picnic tables, and fireplaces. No hookups. Exit 1 from I-91; .1 mile north on Rte. 5, .5 mile east on Fairground Road, then 1 mile south on Main St. and Old Guilford Rd.

Jamaica State Park, Town Rd., Jamaica; 874-4600. Has 57 sites, including 17 lean-tos, on 772 acres. Flush toilets, showers, public phone, picnic tables, fireplaces. No hookups. Turn north at the Three Mountain Inn onto Town Rd., cross the bridge, and bear left. Half mile total. Kayak and canoe white-water time trials on the West River here in spring and summer.

Molly Stark State Park, Rte 9., Wilmington; 464-5460. Thirty-four sites, including 9 lean-tos on 158 acres at 1,900 feet elevation. Flush toilets, showers, public phone, playground, picnic tables, fireplaces, no hookups. Picnic, hike to Mt. Olga. Fifteen miles west of Brattleboro on Rte. 9.

Townshend State Park, off Rte. 30, Townshend; 365-7500. On 856 acres are 27 sites. Flush toilets, showers, picnic tables, fireplaces, picnic shelter. Fish, hike to Bald Mountain, visit Townshend Dam. Turn off Rte. 30 onto Town Rd., three miles in.

Foliage Vantage Points

Ames Hill in Marlboro is the road leading westward out of Brattleboro to Marlboro. Color-filled vistas all the way up (or down) in season.

Drive up Black Mountain Rd., up past The Experiment, for some panoramic views. This road connects both with Rtes. 5 and 30, which have some stunning foliage viewpoints too.

The East-West Rd. on the way to Dummerston Center brings you up past Millers Orchards, where you can pick your own and enjoy the foliage from there, on the way up and on the way down.

One-Hundred-Mile View, Hogback Mountain, Marlboro. From the pull-off from Rte. 9 (Molly Stark Trail), the view opens out from the Green Mountains in Vermont to the White Mountains in New Hampshire to Mt. Grace and the Holyoke Range in Massachusetts. When the foliage lights up these forested mountains, they become an irridescent carpet of color.

Best of Brattleboro Area

Country Inns: Four Columns Inn & Restaurant, 230 West St.; 365-7713.

Resort: Mt. Snow, Rte. 100, West Dover; 464-3333.

Breakfast: Skyline Restaurant, Rte. 9, Marlboro; 464-5535.

Lunch: Shin-La Restaurant, 57 Main St., Brattleboro; 257-5226.

Dinners (Moderately Priced): Panda North, Rte. 5 north (I-91 exit 3); 257-4578, 257-4486.

Dinners (Expensive): Le Petit Chef, Rte. 100, Wilmington; 464-8437.

Entertainment (Casual): The Living History Association, a "chamber of commerce" for all eras of reenacted history, Main St., Wilmington; 464-5102.

Entertainment (Stage): River Valley Performing Arts Center, River Rd. (Rte. 5), Putney; 387-4355.

Museum/Historical Site: Brattleboro Museum & Arts Center, Vernon St., Brattleboro; 257-0124.

Art Gallery: Vermont Artisan Designs, 115 Main St., Brattleboro; 257-7044.

Craft/Specialty Shop: Pam's Potpourri, Main St., Brattleboro.

Antiques Shops: Black Mountain Antiques Center, Rte. 30, two miles north of Brattleboro. Sixty dealers under one roof. Newfane Antiques Center, Rte. 30; 365-4482.

Discount Outlets: Factory Outlet Center at exit 1 off I-91.

Public Golf Course: Brattleboro Country Club, guests can play there. Nine holes.

Public Tennis Court: Brattleboro Outing Club, tennis & general information, Cedar St., Brattleboro; 254-3635. Six clay courts.

Hiking or Nature Trail: The walk up Wantastiquet Mountain, for the panoramic view of Brattleboro.

Camping: Ft. Dummer State Park, Old Guilford Rd., Brattleboro; 254-2610.

Children's Activities: Living Memorial Park, Rte. 9, Brattleboro; 254-6700.

Farm Stand: Albee's Farm Stand, Rte. 9, three miles west of Brattleboro.

Ice Cream: Pages Restaurant, Rte. 9, West Brattleboro; 257-7516.

Foliage Vantage Points: Up on Black Mountain Rd., up past The Experiment, for some panoramic views. That road connects with both Rtes. 5 and 30.

Ski Area (both): Brattleboro Ski Hut, Upper Dummerston Rd., Brattleboro; 254-4081. Twenty kilometers of ski trails.

PART III
Special Essays

Alpine Skiing

by MARY MCKHANN

"Vermont Is Skiing" reads a popular bumper sticker, and while Vermont is much more than that, to many winter visitors, skiing is the main attraction.

From colossal Killington to minute Maple Valley, southern Vermont offers a wide variety of ski experiences. Whether you are old or young, a hotshot or a bunny, single or married with a dozen kids, wealthy or just getting by, you can find a place for yourself at one of the area's many resorts.

I first experienced skiing in Vermont more than 20 years ago and knew then that this was a special place. Driving along narrow, snow-banked roads through picturesque villages, I could always feel a warm tingle of anticipation. Often in those days I would stay in old, converted Vermont farmhouses that always had wonderful baking smells and funky, tiny bedrooms. You shared the bathroom with at least a half dozen other people.

In those days, ski areas were usually just that. A simple base lodge, a couple of lifts, and minimally groomed trails were about the extent of it. There were ski schools, of course, but they were not the large, efficient organizations they are now. When you called skis "boards," you were being almost literal, and "bear traps" were what held the skis to your leather, lace-up boots.

Skiing in Vermont is a very different proposition these days. Ski areas have discovered that they cannot live by snow alone, and economic viability has dictated that most areas these days have to expand, build, and diversify. Real estate has become the bread and butter for resorts, and it is rare to find a ski area now that does not have condominiums sprouting like mushrooms in a damp summer. Base lodges have bars and restaurants as well as cafeterias. More, better, and faster lifts are installed to carry the ever-increasing numbers of skiers up the mountains. Parking lots proliferate, often served by shuttle buses due to their distance from the slopes.

Depending upon where you stay, the amenities may include discounted lift tickets at local ski areas as well as health club and/or spa facilities for the ultimate in après-ski relaxation. Most areas have package deals that may include just lodging and lift tickets or may cover every aspect of your ski vacation from airlines to rental cars to children's programs in one package.

One of the biggest boons to modern skiing has been the advances in the technology of snowmaking and grooming. While areas in the northern part of the state have, until quite recently, relied on natural snow, southern Vermont's quirky weather pushed forward-thinking ski area management into the forefront when it comes to man-made snow. Even in a winter like 1988–89, which would have been a total disaster in presnowmaking days, southern Vermont experienced good skiing all winter. The scenery wasn't quite as pretty, but if you came to ski, you weren't disappointed.

With 10 major ski areas in the southern part of the state, there is a lot of variety to choose from. Ski areas have their own personalities, and so do the skiers who go there. An area that is wonderful for a family of intermediate skiers with young children may not be so terrific for a young single who loves moguls. For one person, the quality of the ski school is an important priority; for another, it is the quality of the nightlife. While all ski areas have essentially the same services — day care, ski school, racing programs — the emphasis and quality of these programs may vary from area to area. Finding what you like may take a little time and effort.

One of the best ways to find an area that suits you is to try as many as possible. In southern Vermont, this is relatively easy to do. Within an hour's drive of Manchester, you can ski Killington, Pico, Bromley, Magic, Stratton, Haystack, and Mount Snow. If you stay in the Woodstock area, you can ski Pico, Killington, Suicide Six, Okemo, and Ascutney.

Most ski areas cater to beginners. After all, this is the new skier base that areas rely on to provide their future customers. The same is true of children's programs. While learning to ski, especially as an adult, is still intimidating, ski areas have gone to great lengths to take some of the fear out of the experience.

What can be harder to find are classes that cater to experts, but this need is being addressed at some ski areas. Killington offers Advanced Skier Workshops in racing and bump skiing, as well as a five-day Mountain Ski Week, which includes three hours of intensive instruction each day, videotape analysis, and ski tuning. Mount Snow has introduced EXCL (Express Customized Learning) for intermediate and advanced skiers, which features 45-minute workshops with three students per instructor where specific skills are addressed. Both Killington and Mount Snow also offer Race Weeks, where advanced skiers can pit their skills against the clock.

No matter what the conditions, one of the best things you can do to make your skiing here more enjoyable is to ski early — before the man-made snow gets scraped off or the sun softens the snow to the point where turning is nearly impossible. Skiing early has other advantages. Finding a parking spot is a lot more feasible, for one thing. Many accidents happen at the end of the day when skiers get tired and lose control; by starting when the lifts open and leaving at midafternoon, you reduce the risk of late-afternoon crash-and-burn syndrome.

Something else you should try to avoid is noontime in the cafeteria. Eat early or late. On weekends at most resorts, there isn't even likely to be a seat available, even if you are smart enough to brown-bag your lunch. A lot of ski area food is expensive and not necessarily very good or nutritious. A good breakfast is essential to start a hard day on the slopes, but a heavy, greasy lunch will do nothing to improve your afternoon performance. Soup, a sandwich, salad, and/or some fruit will give you energy without making you feel uncomfortable. After you eat, your body goes to work digesting the food and can't concentrate so well on keeping you warm. Don't overwork it.

Midwinter in Vermont — even southern Vermont — can be quite cold. Wind-chill factors below zero are not too unusual, so it is important to dress properly. Modern skiwear is designed to provide warmth and water repellency without the bulk of older designs. Layering is the key to keeping warm. A hat is essential in frigid weather because you can lose up to 80 percent of your body heat through your head. Neck gaitors, insulated gloves or mittens, goggles, and good long johns should all be part of your basic equipment. For kids, especially, it is important that clothes are water repellent, and that includes mittens. Frostbitten hands are no fun.

Keeping your equipment in good working order will add greatly to your enjoyment of your ski vacation in Vermont. Those familiar "hard" conditions are handled with relative ease on a pair of tuned and sharpened skis. On a pair of skis with rusty, dull edges, the same conditions can be a nightmare. A trip to your local ski shop to have your skis tuned and bindings checked before you leave for your ski trip can save not only frustration but possible hospital bills.

A duffle bag packed with extra gloves, scarves, goggles, and other necessities can save time and money when these items get lost or wet. Almost all ski areas have shops where you can pick up forgotten items, but generally the prices are high.

When you head out onto the slopes, be sure to pick up a trail map for each member of your party. Plan ahead where and when you will meet if you and your companions should become separated, especially at the larger ski areas. When you check out your map, look at the trails that are off to the sides of the mountain. Often, these get less traffic because they are less visible. Find a few that suit your ability and try them out.

Killington: If "Too Much is Not Enough" is your philosophy, Killington just might be the mountain. Killington talks in superlatives — the most, the biggest, the longest, the earliest, the latest. The largest ski area in the eastern United States, Killington generally opens in October and closes in late May or June, making for a season that is more than seven months long — pretty unusual for these parts. Some of my friends have been known to ski Killington in the morning and windsurf at Lake Bomoseen in the afternoon in the spring.

Killington is not *a* mountain; it is actually *six* mountains — Killington Peak, Snowdon, Rams Head, Skye Peak, Bear Mountain, and Sunrise Mountain (Northeast Passage). If you tell your friends you'll meet them in the Killington Base Lodge, make sure you know exactly what you are referring to. There are a total of six facilities, including a number of base lodges. Driving up the main access road off Route 4 in Sherburne, you first come to the Snowshed Novice and Learning Area on your left and Rams Head on your right. If you continue up the road, you come to what is actually the Killington Base Lodge. There are other base lodges at Northeast Passage and Bear Mountain. The facilities include a total of seven cafeterias, one full-service restaurant, a mountaintop restaurant, five retail shops, five ski rental and repair shops, four lounges, a children's center with child care and ski school, five first-aid stations, and a physician-staffed medical clinic.

Killington has more than 100 trails and 18 lifts. By getting on a lift to the top early, it is possible to spread out over the mountain and not have too much of a problem with lift lines. One veteran Killington skier recommends skiing the Glades Lift or Needle's Eye, which service slopes that can be enjoyed by intermediate to expert skiers. Or ski over to Bear Mountain and enjoy some fine cruising on Wildfire and Bear Claw, and when it starts getting crowded over there, work your way back.

If bumps, otherwise known as moguls, are your thing, Killington offers some long, challenging runs. In particular, Outer Limits at Bear Mountain is recognized as one of the finest, steepest bump runs in New England, but Lower Cascade also offers some good bump skiing. The Bear Mountain Base Lodge is relatively small and, in the spring, is a very busy place.

Although this may sound somewhat intimidating to beginning skiers, Killington also offers an excellent beginner area in Snowshed. There are "easier" trails interconnecting all six mountains, so even the new skier can enjoy the full scope of the ski area.

The Children's Center and Children's Ski School offer both indoor and skiing opportunities for all levels. The Children's Center takes care of children from 6 weeks to 8 years; there is an "Introduction to Skiing" program for ages 3 – 8 and "Young Skier" program for ages 4 – 6. There are also regular children's ski school lessons for ages 6 – 12. An all-day "Superstars" program is also available.

A couple of words of warning. Because Killington has such extensive snowmaking and opens so early in the season, a couple of problems can arise. Your favorite trail may be covered with snow guns, blasting frigid compressed water, which makes skiing those trails less than pleasant. Very early, and very late, skiing can be extremely limited, but everyone wants to say they skied the first or the last day of the season. It can, therefore, be extremely crowded.

Pico: Located on Route 4 just a few miles west of Killington, Pico has a smaller, more family oriented feeling. Now more than 50 years old, Pico is known as a friendly place to ski, and it is.

Over the past few years, Pico has seen a case of mushrooming condominiums and has added a small village in front of the base lodge. Even so, it retains its small-area atmosphere and is far more manageable for a family with children old enough to ski on their own but not quite old enough to deal with the possibility of ending up in an area miles from where they started. Pico caters to kids, with a very good junior racing program, fine ski school with special children's programs, and nursery located right at the base of the mountain.

Saturday nights and evenings during holiday periods, the Pico Children's Center holds a "Kid's Party" for youngsters ages 3 – 12, allowing Mom and Dad an evening on their own. Other Pico children's programs include "Explorers" and "Mountaineers" (ages 6 – 12).

For adults, Pico offers innovative one-on-one private lessons and a free (with a lift ticket) Beginner's Circle program. Their ski school has an excellent reputation, and classes run the gamut from beginner up to race camp.

The mountain has a nice layout. Basically, beginner slopes are on the right as you look up the mountain, with intermediate trails in the middle. The racing trails are on the left, and expert trails are on the upper mountain. A total of nine lifts — including two high-speed detachable quads — serving 35 trails make for few waits in lift lines, except on the busiest occasions.

There is some fine cruising for advanced skiers on Forty-Niner, Sunset '71, and Upper K.A. The Golden Express high-speed quad services a number of nice intermediate trails, and the Triple Slope (serviced by a triple chair) gives beginners their own, wide-open slope.

If you are in doubt about the conditions on any given day, Pico allows you to ski free from 8:30 to 9:30 A.M. before you decide to purchase a ticket. Another good reason to hit the slopes early! While many ski areas only offer half-day tickets in the afternoon, Pico has recognized that many visitors have to return home on Sunday afternoon, and you can buy a ticket here for Sunday morning only.

A relatively recent addition to the facilities at Pico is a sports center, complete with a 76-foot lap pool, fitness/cardiovascular area featuring Keiser air-resistance machines, Air-Dynes, Biocycles, Stairmasters, Nordic Trak, treadmill, rowing machines, and free weights. A special, suspended floor accommodates the activity of aerobic classes. There are saunas, Jacuzzis, tanning booths, and a nursery. Use of the sports center is free for those staying in Pico Village; daily rates are available for others.

Suicide Six: Suicide Six was founded in 1934, making it and Stowe the oldest ski areas in Vermont. Suicide is credited with having the first lift facilities — a rope tow — in the country.

The area may be old, but there is a comfortable new base lodge with a big stone fireplace and nice cafeteria.

With only 18 trails and three lifts, it might be easy to overlook this area, but don't. It has some good, steep skiing and a beautiful location on Route 12 near the picturesque town of Woodstock. The snowmaking coverage is not as good as at some other areas, so it is best to ski here when there has been some decent natural snow.

The area is frequented primarily by locals, although weekends now see a large influx of tourists. It is noted for its excellent junior racing program. A number of rising young superskiers have started on Suicide's slopes.

Okemo: Some of southern Vermont's ski areas have made dramatic reversals in the past decade, and Okemo is one example. From near bankruptcy in the early eighties, the resort has steadily grown in popularity and is now a favorite destination resort for many metropolitan skiers.

Okemo has three summit peaks. The Northwest Summit is the place to head for steeps and glades, while Northeast Summit and Solitude Peak Summit have long intermediate cruisers.

The emphasis is on family skiing here, and accommodations for children are excellent. The highly regarded SKIwee program for youngsters ages 4 – 8 is supplemented with Children's Ski School for those 7 and up and Young Mountain Explorers, for more accomplished young skiers ages 8 – 12. Day-care facilities are available for ages 12 months to 8 years, with an optional "Introduction to Skiing" for ages 3 and 4. As an added incentive to ski off-season, Okemo offers free day care from opening through December 22 and from March 19 through closing. They also provide evening child care from 6 to 10 P.M. during selected holiday periods.

Okemo has a "Beginners Learn-to-Ski Information Center," which provides all the personalized attention and information a newcomer to the sport could ask for, and for skiers of intermediate or better ability, a "Ski Tip" Station offers one run with an instructor from midmountain.

Bromley: Bromley is one of the oldest, and certainly the most rustic, of the major ski areas in southern Vermont. Founded in 1936 by beer baron Fred Pabst, the area remains a favorite for locals and young families. Although the ski facilities are thoroughly modern, the lodge is a throwback to earlier days with its moose and deer heads on the walls and large, stone fireplace. There is an upstairs, with its own minicafeteria, which generally does not get quite as much traffic, and on sunny days a large deck offers great views of the lower slopes.

Snowmaking and grooming have long been important at Bromley, and like most areas in this part of the state, they do an excellent job with these two important aspects of running a ski area.

The addition of a new quad chair lift on the East Side in the winter of 1988 – 89 has greatly improved Bromley's uphill capacity. The East Side has mainly intermediate and expert trails, and although the runs are relatively short, the lines over here are usually short and you can get plenty of skiing for your money. Trail names remind skiers of the mountain's founder: Pabst's Peril, Blue Ribbon, and Corkscrew are all fun runs that usually get some moguls. For those who prefer bigger bumps, Stargazer and the relatively new Havoc are your best bets.

Most of the trails on the front of the mountain are intermediate, with two long beginner trails that run from the top. Like many of the smaller areas, Bromley caters to families with young skiers. They have the first state-accredited day-care facility, caring for children ages one month to six years and considered one of the finest children's programs in the country. The ski school has excellent instruction for kids, and there are a number of special weekend programs for youngsters, as well as a good racing program. It also gives instruction in snowboarding.

Bromley and Magic mountains are under the same ownership, and lift tickets are interchangeable between the two areas.

Magic: When Hans Thorner discovered Magic Mountain, he knew he had something. Despite its relatively small size, Magic has some of the best steeps in southern Vermont. Unfortunately, Magic languished during some bad snow years, and many people just ignored this little gem. But in the past five or so years, new management has upgraded the snowmaking system, added to the village, acquired Timber Ridge on the back side of Magic, and voilà! Not a rabbit out of a hat, but an entirely revamped mountain to be reckoned with.

Now called Magicside and Timberside, the two areas of the mountain have been linked over the top, with Magicside having the expert terrain and Timberside the beginner and intermediate areas, generally speaking. On a crowded weekend, head for the small base lodge at Timberside and catch the lift over there. Once at the top, experts can enjoy several double black diamond trails and a number of glades on Magicside, while the less daring can cruise happily on either side of the mountain.

As with almost all ski areas, the steeper the trail, the harder it is to hold snow cover. Some to try are Maui and Sorcerer for bumps and Talisman for wide open, fast cruising.

Ascutney: Ascutney is another medium-size area and one that has something to offer for just about everyone. The challenging stuff is on top; the rest of the mountain is pretty much beginner and intermediate.

The area has a nice feeling, with an attractive base lodge and short lift lines. Under new ownership since the mideighties, Ascutney has begun to achieve some of its potential with 32 trails on a 1,530 vertical.

Ascutney also has a Sports and Fitness Center, which includes aerobics equipment and classes, weight room, racquetball court, sauna/whirlpool, and indoor swimming pool.

Like many of the smaller ski areas, Ascutney's lift prices tend to be lower than some of those at other larger, better-known resorts.

Stratton: Stratton has undergone some major changes, and it is a very different place than it was 10 years ago. It started with major development around the base lodge, which included condominiums, a hotel, parking facility, and its own village. It continued with the installation in 1988 of Starship XII, a 12-passenger high-speed gondola, Stratton's first bottom-to-top lift. And with Stratton's purchase by Victoria, USA — the American subsidiary of a large Japanese sporting goods chain — it has been topped off with expansion in the Sun Bowl.

The crowd here tends toward the trendy and expensive, with lots of Bogner and Head outfits in evidence. It is one of the first mountains that allowed snowboarding, so you'll also see some more radical chic.

Stratton is essentially an intermediate area with a few challenging trails. There are some very nice ego-inflating cruisers — the Supertrail can be handled by most and Standard has been widened to make for some easy turning. If bumps are your thing, Spruce can get a pretty good buildup, and World Cup (named for the race that was held at Stratton in 1978) has a short section that can test your mettle. (It also happens to be in plain view of those waiting in line for the Snow Bowl chair lift.)

The Snow Bowl is one of my favorite places to ski. The lines are generally not as long, and Liftline, which runs under the chair, is a trail that is lots of fun to ski for those at least at the intermediate level. It has a nice pitch, with a few steep spots, but watch out for the spots where other trails cut across it.

Stratton has an excellent ski school, with a number of instructors recruited from Europe. Their Little Cub and Big Cub programs for children have gotten many youngsters off to a good skiing start. They also have a good racing program for young people, some of whom go on to attend Stratton Mountain School, the acclaimed ski racing academy on the mountain.

Mount Snow: At one point, Mount Snow was more famous for its heated, outdoor swimming pool than for its slopes. But when SKI Limited, owners of Killington, took over the mountain sometime back, the area turned into the major resort it is today. It attracts skiers like honey attracts bees.

There are a lot of reasons. There is a good variety of slopes and trails, lots of programs for all ages, a multitude of slope-side condominiums and nearby lodging and entertainment, and a spacious (but often not spacious enough) base lodge.

Expert skiers will want to head for the top of the mountain and drop over onto the North Side, where a nice mix of mogul runs and steep, flat trails will challenge their prowess. Free Fall, Chute, Plummet, and Jaws of Death could certainly intimidate an intermediate but provide advanced skiers with a terrific playground. The steepest the North Side has to offer is Rip Cord, which also happens to be an awesome bump run.

There are also two beginner runs from the top, Deer Run and Long John. The main mountain has mainly intermediate trails, with some nice cruisers such as Snow Dance, South Bowl, and Ridge Run.

Corinthia is the beginner area and is also less crowded if all you need when you arrive at the mountain is lift tickets. Buy them here and save waiting in long lines at the main ticket offices.

People tend to take the line of least resistance, so lines for the lifts closest to the base lodge tend to be the longest. If the lift lines begin to jam up, head to your left from the lodge and take the Ego Alley lift, which goes three-quarters of the way up the mountain.

Mount Snow has an excellent ski school. For beginners, there is a five-day program that guarantees they will be skiing from the summit in that time period or the cost of lift tickets, lessons, and rental equipment will be refunded. For more advanced skiers, the new EXCEL program, at the same cost as regular two-hour class lessons, provides one instructor for a maximum of three students and will cover such advanced techniques as mogul skiing, carving, and long- and short-radius turns.

There are a number of theme weeks at Mount Snow, including special weeks for college students, racers, couples, and children. The mountain offers SKIwee for children ages 6 – 12 and PeeWee SKIwee for kids from 3 – 5. Day care is also available.

Haystack: This is another area that floundered rather badly and was actually shut down for a time, but Haystack, like Okemo, is a mountain that is making a dramatic comeback. Once considered a place for overflow traffic from Mount Snow, the area is finally coming into its own.

A new base lodge has been built, leaving the old one to service the beginner area and house the ski school. Since 1984, when the area reopened, Haystack has added four new lifts, several trails, and expanded snowmaking, as well as more slope-side condominiums.

The addition of a sports center is another plus for Haystack. An Olympic-size swimming pool, whirlpool, racquetball and squash courts, exercise and game rooms, and lounge and restaurant are some of the features of the new facility.

The main mountain has mainly intermediate trails, although novices can navigate Yellow Birch Lane and experts can play on the double black diamond Stump Jumper. The newest addition to the mountain is an area known as the Witches, served by its own triple chair lift. Gandolf, Merlin, and Cauldron are among the steepest on the mountain, and some are left ungroomed so mogul lovers will be happy. There are also some gentler trails that lead back into the main mountain's trail network from the top of the Witches' chair.

The ski school is using SyberVision to aid skiers, from never-evers to experts, in learning, and the Little Stack Nursery teaches children three to seven in either half- or full-day lessons that include lunch and rental equipment.

Anyone who is just learning can ski the lower mountain — which includes six slopes, a double chair lift, a T-bar, and its own base lodge — for $15.

Southern Vermont also has two very small ski areas — Prospect Mountain, on Route 9 eight miles east of Bennington, and Maple Valley Ski Area, on Route 30 seven miles north of Brattleboro. Frequented primarily by locals, the two areas offer an alternative to the crowds and high prices of larger areas. You won't find any frills here — there are no slope-side condos or health club facilities, and you are unlikely to find too many people wearing the latest in ski fashions — but you will get a taste of skiing the way it used to be.

Cross-Country Skiing

by ERIC EVANS

Utah has more sun, California has more trails, Montana has skiable snow in November, and in Colorado they never resort to using klister. But for diversity of cross-country skiing experiences, southern Vermont is unmatched. This diversity is manifested in the region's varied terrain, snow conditions and weather, and broad spectrum of trails and touring centers. Whether you're a shuffler or a hotshot skater, off the beaten path or on machine-groomed tracks, you'll find your type of skiing in the southern Green Mountains.

A Southern Vermont Tradition

Vermont boasts a rich and long skiing tradition. In the 1930s, the state's first formal ski trails were cut on Mount Mansfield, and the nation's first ski rope tow was built in 1936 in Woodstock. Ski jumping traces its ancestry back to the first years of this century, and by the 1920s there were three large jumps in the state: in Brattleboro, Barre, and Northfield.

Cross-country skiing in southern Vermont has been associated closely over the years with Windham County in general and The Putney School in particular. Since the latter's beginning in 1935, cross-country skiing has been an integral part of the Putney program. Putney graduate John Caldwell skied in the 1952 Olympics in Nordic Combined (jumping and cross-country skiing) and then returned to his alma mater to lead its skiing program. In 1964, his book on the sport of cross-country skiing was the first in this country. It was around that time that the Northeast's first track sled, pulled behind a Ski-Doo, was employed at Putney. Over the years, hundreds of tour skiers enjoyed the Putney School trails, while Olympians like Martha Rockwell, Bob Gray, Bill Koch, Tim Caldwell, and Willie Carow honed their skills. The school continues to host numerous cross-country events during the winter, including the annual George Washington's Birthday Ski Touring Race, which was held for the first time in Marlboro, Vermont, in 1963.

Today, southern Vermont has approximately 20 ski touring centers, miles of Forest Service trails, and many local golf courses open to cross-country skiers in the winter. The Bill Koch Ski League conducts low-key learning programs for elementary schoolchildren throughout the region. There is a strong circuit of high school racing today. On any winter afternoon you're liable to see all shapes, sizes, and ages "just puttering" on skinny skis over the countryside.

Varied Terrain

One of the major routes into southern Vermont is Interstate 91 in the eastern part of the state. Driving north through Massachusetts you travel along the valley floor of the wide Connecticut River — flat farmland for the most part — but as you approach Brattleboro, Vermont, the change in terrain is startling. Suddenly, there are hills — everywhere. The same dramatic change can also be experienced heading into Bennington in the western part of the state from the south and farther north going into Rutland from New York. The uphills are not particularly long (compared to mountains in the western United States) nor the downhills steep, but it's hard to get around southern Vermont without encountering ups and downs in terrain.

This is not to say, however, that southern Vermont cross-country skiing is always hills. Most touring centers have trails or loops that are benign. For extended tours, however, from point to point, at some time you are going to face vertical gain or loss or both.

Snow Conditions

Snow comes to stay in southern Vermont in mid- to late-December. We get teased with storms from Thanksgiving on, but it's really not until Christmas that we have sufficient snow to set tracks. And bare ground at Christmas is not uncommon. Those who push the season do so with their "rock" skis. Snow season dissolves into mud season in mid-March, but diehards can find skiing in north-facing pockets in April.

Spend a winter skiing in southern Vermont and you'll be a much more knowledgeable waxer in April than you were in December. That's a euphemistic way of saying you'll experience everything from ice to powder to wet corn snow. Recently we had a dearth of snow and people bemoaned the lack of skiing, but what snow did fall was granular and provided just enough of a surface for fast open-field skiing on golf courses or smoother logging roads. It was adequate for competent "skaters" out for exercise but not really suitable for beginners; diagonal skiers had their wax stripped quickly from their ski bases.

I try to base my skiing on the conditions. If it's thin cover or crusty, I go skating on open fields or the local golf course. During or just after a storm I like to tour on back roads or trails without tracks. A day or so later, after the snow has settled and compacted a bit, then it's diagonal skiing in prepared tracks.

Snow conditions will vary with altitude and location, too. We live on Putney Mountain at approximately 1,600 feet elevation. Our skiing in-laws live about a mile and a half away and 200 vertical feet lower. Often, that 200 feet is the difference between freezing rain and snow. No question, we have a longer winter and more powder, as we constantly like to remind them. The moral: Don't judge the skiing conditions by what you see in downtown Rutland or Windsor or Manchester — a few hundred feet up and the skiing may be quite different.

Logic would dictate that northern Vermont has more snow than southern Vermont and usually that's the case. However, it's not uncommon for storms coming up the East Coast to belt southern Vermont and then pass out to sea without going north of Route 4. Two winters ago the high schools in the north were canceling races because of no snow while we in the south had more than enough for good skiing.

Wait-A-Minute Weather

A key piece of every southern Vermont cross-country buff's ski equipment is the weather radio. Press a button and you get the crackling National Weather Service forecast for your region. In the winter I listen to it before going to bed and then again at breakfast the next day. Weather systems come in quickly and changes are rapid and frequent. Often it's just a few miles or hours between freezing rain and snow. If you are planning on skiing the next day, it behooves you to check the weather just before going to bed because the skiing may be good the next morning with a front passing through at midday. If you drive up Friday night, sleep late Saturday morning, and then putter around before deciding to go cross-country skiing, you may have missed the only good skiing available that day. If you don't own a weather radio, check for weather hot lines provided by the local radio station, or see the listings in each section of this guidebook for weather phone numbers.

Skiing the Back Country

There are hundreds of miles of trails not on private property or associated with a formal ski touring center. The problem is finding them. The best place to start is the innkeeper where you are staying or the folks at the nearest cross-country shop. I've recently discovered the United States Forest Service land around Somerset Reservoir in the west-central part of southern Vermont — great for mountain biking and short or long cross-country ski tours. Maps of this area and all Forest Service land in Vermont are available from USDA Forest Service, Box 1940, Manchester Center, Vermont 05255, or call 362-2307; or Forest Service Headquarters, Green Mountain National Forest, Federal Building, 1501 West Street, Rutland, Vermont. Bookstores or army-navy stores are also good sources for maps.

For years snowmobiles and cross-country skiers mixed like oil and water. That's changing: snowmobile-packed trails are great for skating and are sometimes the only packed trails in the area. Snowmobiles are maintaining trails throughout the state. The Vermont Association of Snow Travelers (VAST) has timely maps of its many routes; many of them are groomed with expensive sophisticated machinery. Write or call: VAST, Box 839, Montpelier, Vermont 05602, 229-0005.

In addition to the VAST network of trails that run throughout the state, there is another trail that runs the length of the state: the Catamount Trail. This trail traverses both public and private land and encompasses all types of terrain, conditions, and levels of accessibility. Some sections are well marked and maintained while other sections are overgrown and you need a map and compass to find the correct route. Dr. Eric Barradale of Guilford, one of the founding fathers of the George Washington Birthday Race (now in its 27th year), skied the Catamount Trail last winter. He and his wife averaged approximately 15 to 20 miles a day and stayed at inns at night.

It is essential that you obtain a map and/or guidebook for the Catamount Trail before attempting all or part of it. A set of maps is $8 while the guidebook is $6. Together they cost $12. Call or write Catamount Trail Association, Box 897, Burlington, Vermont, 864-5794.

Touring Centers

The best maintained trails are found at touring centers. "Center" is a catchall phrase that includes a range of facilities and resources, from a simple wood-stove-heated cabin next to a golf course to large lodges/inns that provide accommodations, lessons, child care, and rental gear. What they all have in common is trail maintenance, maps, and a fee structure. Here are some of the touring centers in southern Vermont where I have skied. It is always prudent to call ahead and inquire about the following:

1. What are the snow conditions? Ice is no fun for anyone.
2. What are the road conditions and weather forecast?
3. When were the trails last groomed? Keep in mind that a Pisten-Bully snow-grooming machine can transform hard granular into corn snow. A snowmobile dragging a track sled or a set of bedsprings cannot.
4. Is there rental equipment?

Hermitage Cross-Country Touring Center, Wilmington. It's located adjacent to Mount Snow and Haystack Alpine areas. Lessons and rentals are available. A complete inn sits atop the touring center. More of a center where the eating and drinking and relaxing are as important as the skiing. Trails are narrow and not wide enough in most places for skating. Snowmobile groomed so the best conditions are just after a storm. Good four-state view from the Ridge Trail.

Mountain Top Cross-Country Ski Resort, Chittenden. The name "resort" gives it away: superb and pricey accommodations and food, state-of-the-art grooming and snowmaking. Former U.S. Team Head Coach Mike Gallagher keeps the area at the cutting edge of the sport. Great views when you get there. Getting there involves a long climb up from Rutland.

Brattleboro Ski Touring Center, Brattleboro. There's no fancy inn, no bar, and no food. There's just a simple waxing/warming hut with a telephone. It has some grooming equipment and a great venue to ski on either the golf course or the woods next to it. Last winter I spent more time skiing at the Brattleboro Ski Touring Center than anywhere else: Three inches of snow goes a long way on a well-manicured fairway.

Wild Wings Ski Touring Center, Peru. A small unpretentious place in the Stratton/Bromley corridor. Last winter they didn't cater to any skating and took pride in saying so. Trails narrow and good for diagonal skiing. Get some good directions before you try to find Wild Wings, and then watch the signs carefully as you make your way over the dirt roads of Peru.

Stratton Mountain Ski Touring Center, Stratton. It's located on the golf course just below the Alpine area. There's a full ski shop and lessons, etc. It's easy terrain for the most part; good for beginners. This is a center more for the Alpine skier who wants a break from slope sliding than a place for the cross-country aficionado.

Sitzmark Ski Touring Center, Wilmington. Varsity off-snow facilities but junior varsity terrain, grooming, and diversity of trails. Again, like Stratton, more for the off-day Alpiner than for the true langlaufer.

Prospect Mountain Ski Touring Center, Bennington/Woodford. If there is snow in southern Vermont, then Prospect will have it. All vehicles head *up* Route 9 to this area, which is a combination modest Alpine area and a touring center. Great grooming equipment and very wide trails, and that last 100 feet of vertical to the parking lot ensures the best snow conditions around. Just down the road (to the east) is Woodford State Park, and also the VAST trails cross Route 9 at this point. All the Bennington school teams practice here. It's a low-key place where folks come to ski and the off-snow accoutrements are kept to a minimum.

Tater Hill Resort, Chester. There's that word again, resort. Fancy digs and a great restaurant and even its own airstrip. Trails are some of the flattest you'll find in this area. Good beginners' area.

There are three major ski touring centers in southern Vermont that I have not skied, but I checked with several locals who have skied there and they come highly recommended. One is Mountain Meadows Ski Touring Center near Killington. Located just five miles from the state's biggest Alpine area, Killington, there are plenty of lodging and eating facilities nearby. If you want to split your day between Alpine and cross-country skiing, this would be a good area to do that. Reinforcing this "cross-country area for Alpine skiers" theme is the moderate terrain at Mountain Meadows. Full rentals, waxing, and a warming hut are located at the center.

A second is the Woodstock Ski Touring Center in Woodstock. There isn't a town in Vermont with better recreational facilities than Woodstock. Indoors or out, this town has something for everybody. The ski touring includes easy golf course skiing (quite unlike the skiing at the Brattleboro golf course) and access to many miles of wooded trail skiing or mountain routes nearby. It has first-rate grooming facilities and a complete rental shop, lessons, and amenities.

A third is the Viking Ski Touring Centre in Londonderry. It not only has some really picturesque terrain but 40 kilometers of double-tracked trails for all ability levels. Viking also has a warming hut, ski rental equipment, lessons, equipment shop, and a small café. Backcountry tours and night skiing on a two-kilometer lighted course are also available.

Diversity has many benefits, but it does require preplanning and some flexibility. But the key point to remember: Don't judge the cross-country skiing by what you see out your window at home.

See you on the trails.

Golf

by DAVID RIHM

As the snow begins to melt and the spring days get warmer, the mountains and valleys of southern Vermont become a haven for the touring golfer. A wide variety of courses are available to play offering a great challenge to all-ability level golfers.

Golf has been established in Vermont since the turn of the century. In the midsixties and early seventies, the number of courses in the state almost doubled as the ski resort areas grew and began providing more varied activities for area visitors. In southern Vermont, there is a mixture of both the old and the new style of course architecture, which makes a trip to the area to play golf a lot of fun.

About 15 miles east of Manchester is the 27-hole Stratton Mountain Country Club. It is a Geoffrey Cornish-designed golf course that features tree-lined fairways and numerous mountain streams and ponds that require a golfer to play an accurate game. The original 18 holes (today the Lake and Mountain nines) were opened in 1964. In 1986, the Forest nine was added to make Vermont's only 27-hole golf course.

The golf course is open to the public, and advanced tee times may be made up to a week in advance for midweek play and 24 hours for weekends and holidays. There are a variety of golf packages available to guests of the Stratton Mountain Inn, Mountain Villas, Village Lodge, Lift Line Lodge, and Birkenhaus.

This course offers beautiful views of the surrounding mountains that are visible from every corner of the golf course. One of the most spectacular holes on the course is the 624-yard, par 5, fifth hole on the Mountain nine. From the elevated tee, the player must play three well-placed shots to avoid the stream on the right side of the driving area and two more smaller streams that traverse the fairway before the green is reached. Par on this long and difficult hole is a score to be proud of. The fourth hole of the Forest nine is another memorable hole. This 139-yard downhill par 3 is tricky because the long drop from tee to green makes club selection very difficult. A large stream runs close to the front edge of the green, so if in doubt on which club to hit, it is wise to play a little longer than to flirt with the water.

The Stratton Resort also boasts a superb golf school created by Arnold Palmer and Geoffrey Cornish. Designed expressly for golf instruction, this 22-acre site gives you ample opportunity to practice virtually every shot you may face on a golf course. Midweek and weekend sessions are available from mid-May until the end of September.

The Equinox Golf Course located in Manchester Village is a wonderful course that requires precise iron approaches to the small and undulating greens. Designed by famed architect Walter Travis in 1927, this course has ample driving areas and only a few water hazards. However, most of the greens are elevated and closely guarded by bunkers. Skilled iron shots are a must to score well. This valley golf course offers outstanding mountain scenery, and your ball seems to hang in the air with the steep mountains providing a picturesque backdrop for most of your shots.

The course is open to the public, and tee times can be made up to a week in advance. Packages are available to guests of the Equinox Hotel Resort and Spa located just a few hundred yards from the first tee.

The 13th hole of the Equinox Golf Course is one of the most difficult par 4 holes in the state. This uphill 426-yard hold is guarded in front by a grass bunker that must be 30 feet below the putting surface. Once on the green, a delicate touch is required on a steep, sloping surface. The 18th hole is also a memorable and scenic hole that is a great finish to this course. A dogleg left around a huge old tree requires a right-to-left play to have a shorter shot into this elevated, and extremely small, green. Normally played into a prevailing wind, two well-struck shots are needed to reach this green in regulation. Just north of Manchester on Route 7 is the Manchester Country Club. While this is a private club, there are approximately 15 motels and inns in the area that do have memberships that will allow you to play this well-kept Cornish-designed course. Opened in 1969, it is delightful to play and has a great variety of long and short holes.

The surprising factor of playing Manchester Country Club for the first time is the diversity between the front and the back nines. The first nine has a quite open rolling terrain featuring many mounds that can produce some awkward lies. The second nine is almost a complete opposite — extremely narrow holes carved from the woods starting up the hillside from the valley floor. All of the greens are large with subtle slopes to them, so if you can hit a straight ball, you can score well.

On the front nine, the 6th hole ranks as one of the more difficult par 3s in the state. At 220 yards, with a long carry over a large pond, a shot must be well struck to find the putting surface. On the back nine, the 402-yard 12th stands out as a truly great hole. The driving area is extremely narrow, and only the left half of the fairway affords you a clear, unobstructed shot to the green. A par on this hole will be a rewarding score and means you have played a couple of good golf shots.

Take Route 7 south to Bennington and you'll arrive at the Mount Anthony Golf and Tennis Club. Located on the edge of town just below the Bennington

Monument, this course will refresh your thoughts with spectacular views of the city below and the mountains rising up on the other side of town. Opened in 1897 as a 9-hole course, it is one of the oldest Vermont courses in operation. In 1963, J. C. Jerome, one of the state's finest amateur players, redesigned the course to the present 18-hole layout. While this is not a particularly long course, there are some hilly holes, and the ability to play from all types of hilly terrain will be an advantage to score well.

The 4th hole, at a mere 104 yards, appears to be an easy hole, but it has a very small green and is framed by four deep bunkers. Recovering for par on a shot that misses the green is difficult on this classic little par 3. The 17th hole is also a stern test of the players' golfing abilities. Normally played into the wind, this 415-yard par 4 is deceptively difficult. The tee shot must be straight and true as there are many trees close to the fairway on both sides. The green is slightly elevated, making chip shots tricky to get close to the pin.

The Mount Anthony Golf and Tennis Club is closed to the public until 2 P.M. on weekends and holidays. During the week and weekend afternoons, it is open for public play.

About a 20-minute ride from Bennington on Route 9 is the Wilmington area, which boasts two fine championship golf courses located at the Mount Snow and Haystack ski resorts.

The Mount Snow golf course, designed by Geoffrey Cornish and opened in 1967, features a nice variety of open and narrow driving holes. This moderately hilly course offers majestic views of the Green Mountains and is particularly beautiful in the fall when the hills come alive with color. The course is open to the public, and there are a variety of golf packages available through the Snowflake Lodge located within a mile of the golf course.

One of Mount Snow's unforgettable holes is the dogleg right 364-yard 4th hole. Position off the tee is very important as the fairway drops off steeply to the green, and a tee shot hit too long will leave a tricky downhill lie. On the back nine, the 12th hole is a gem of a par 3. It is 183 yards over water, and the green features three separate levels. Just hitting the ball on the green does not assure a par if the ball ends up on the wrong tier.

The Mount Snow resort also features a golf school that has both midweek and weekend packages for those who are looking to improve their games. The golf school has a low student-to-teacher ratio and is a great way for beginners to learn the game. The more experienced golfer can pick up those few pointers that may take a few strokes off his or her average game. The golf school has sessions available from mid-May through the end of September.

A short distance down Route 100 from the Mount Snow resort is the Haystack Golf Club. Designed by Desmond Muirhead in the early 1970s, the Haystack course is an interesting one. It has a challenging layout and features fairly large and contoured greens that make placement of the approach shot important if you want a good chance to make that birdie putt.

The two par 5 holes on the nine stand out as the most spectacular and challenging at the Haystack Golf Club. The 11th hole is a 533-yard par 5 that is steeply downhill the whole way. The view from the tee is a long one, and when a tee shot has been hit, it appears to hang in the air for an eternity. The second par 5, the 14th hole, calls for accurate shot placement and some thoughtful strategy to negotiate this difficult hole. There is a long hazard for the last 300 yards of this hole that cuts in and out of the fairway. After the drive, the player must decide to either lay up short of the water or try to hit over the hazard for a shorter third shot to the green. This is truly a great par 5 hole because the player can be faced with many options on how to play the hole depending on the placement of the tee shot.

The Haystack Golf Club is open to the public, and tee time reservations can be made up to 48 hours in advance. This is a medium-length golf course that twists through the woods, so be sure to bring your straight ball with you when you play this course!

The Sitzmark Golf and Tennis Club is located close to Haystack in the town of Wilmington. This 18-hole, par 3, executive layout is a great course to play for a quick round of golf. With holes ranging in distance from 90 to 165 yards, this exceptional course strengthens an iron game. The Sitzmark course requires extremely accurate shots, as all of the greens are quite small and guarded by some bunkers and natural contours of the land. Like most golf courses in Vermont, there is a mountain stream through the course that comes into play on a few of the holes that will catch the errant shots.

The Sitzmark golf course is open to the public, and no tee times are required. It is a really flat golf course, so it is also an enjoyable walk. So, if you're in a hurry and want a course you can scoot around quickly, give this executive course a try.

Just a short distance outside of Brattleboro on Route 30 is the Brattleboro Country Club. Originally opened in 1914, this lovely nine-hole course was rebuilt in the late twenties and over the years has not changed. The Brattleboro Country Club is typical of the older style golf course, which was fairly open in the driving areas but had small greens that placed a premium on accuracy with the player's iron approach shots.

The fifth hole is one of the best holes to challenge the golfer at this course. At 390 yards, it is not the length that is most demanding but the difficulty of hitting the green. The slightly elevated green has two grass bunkers to the right and a thick, heavy rough to the left and over the green, so getting on the putting surface in regulation is a must to assure a par. Making this hole even more difficult is the fact that the fifth green is tricky to read, so using only two putts can be a real challenge.

Brattleboro Country Club is open to the public, and tee times can be made two days in advance. It is a fun course to play and offers some great vistas. The view from the eighth tee is one of the most beautiful in southern Vermont.

Just outside of Springfield is the Crown Point Country Club, one of the best-kept secrets in Vermont. In previous years, it hosted both the Men's and Women's New England Amateur Championship, as well as the Vermont Amateur. The course takes advantage of the fine rolling terrain of the area to offer a superb test of golf. Adding to its beauty are the majestic long-distance mountain views.

Crown Point Country Club is a good mixture of open and tight golf holes. The 540-yard 15th hole, for instance, is one tough par 5 that requires both distance and accuracy. This hole has bunkers in the driving area and on both sides of the green, which demand straight shots. Being uphill most of the way, plays are even longer than the yardage indicates. The 222, par 3, 18th hole is the toughest of what many call the finest combination of par 3 holes of any course in the state. From the scenic, elevated tee, the player's shot must be struck long and straight to avoid bunkers on each side of the green to end up on the "dance floor."

Crown Point Country Club is a semiprivate club that will allow public play throughout the season. Although tee times are not taken, a call ahead should be placed to be sure there is no tournament activity going on the day you're interested in playing. This is a beautiful course and one all will enjoy.

Continuing our golfing trek around southern Vermont, we will travel a little farther north to the historic Woodstock area. No trip to this area would be complete without playing the impressive Woodstock Country Club course. Designed by Robert T. Jones in 1963, this par 69 layout will call for some true and accurate shot making on your part. While your first glimpse at the scorecard might give you the impression that this is an easy course since it is only 6,000 yards from the blue tees, don't be fooled. Crossing the Kendron Brook that winds through the course 11 times creates many problems for golfers.

The 4th and 12th holes are doglegs left, and both cross the brook in two places before you reach the green. While the 12th green is fairly large and easy to hit, if the drive has been positioned well, the 4th green is a long and narrow target closely guarded in front and to the right by the Kendron. Both holes have a very narrow landing area off the tee, and the straightest shot will be required to have any chance to reach either one of these holes in regulation.

Unlike the majority of golf courses in Vermont, the Woodstock Country Club is a relatively flat golf course. A number of the tees are elevated, but it is rare to have a hilly lie in any of the fairways. The greens are a nice variety of small and large targets, and most are carefully protected by bunkers that will require the golfer to be on his or her game to score well here.

Golf and lodging packages are available at the recently renovated Woodstock Inn, which is one of the most famous inns in all of New England. The Woodstock Country Club is available for public play, and tee times can be arranged by calling the pro shop on the day of play.

In Ludlow, just a short distance from Woodstock, is the Fox Run Golf Course. This is a nine-hole course that is not a demanding track. It features many short par 4s that give the player many options when on the tee to either drive close to the greens or lay back to have a full swing for their second shot. This is a nice little resort-type course, and it is rather flat.

The opening hole at Fox Run is probably the toughest hole on the course and tests the golfer right from the start. At 400 yards, with a closely bunkered green, two well-played shots will have to be executed in order to assure a par to start your round off. The par 3 ninth hole is also a picturesque and remarkable hole. This 160-yard short hole will require a tee shot over a pond that can be an intimidating feature to the less-accomplished golfer. While the water does not come too close to the green, any time a shot must be played over a body of water anything can happen!

The Fox Run Golf Course is semiprivate. Outside play is welcomed, and tee times can be arranged 24 hours in advance by calling the pro shop.

Located at the base of New England's largest ski resort, the Killington Golf Course is one of the newest golf courses in the state of Vermont. Opened in the summer of 1983, this Geoffrey Cornish designed layout has a great mixture of long and short holes. Cut through the wooded areas in the mountains, the course has no parallel fairways, which gives you the feeling that you have the whole course to yourself most of the time. As is the case with most of the Cornish-designed courses, the greens are ample targets, and they incorporate the many mountain streams to place a premium on shot selection and placement in order to score well.

The Killington Golf Course is open to the public, and tee times can be made one week in advance. There are a variety of golf packages offered through the lodging on the mountain that include greens fees, cart, and lodging. The lodging facilities are all close to the course.

My two favorite holes on the Killington Golf Course are the first and third. The first hole is a fairly short, easy hole that affords the player a good chance to "warm up" before getting into the tighter, more demanding holes found later on the course. The third hole is a nice, comfortable par 3 of 163 yards. Played from an elevated tee to the smallest green on the course, a precise shot is needed to get on the green and to avoid the bunkers that are near to the greens' edge. If the green is reached in regulation, there's a good chance for a birdie since this is such a small green.

The Rutland Country Club, located in the city of Rutland, has one of Vermont's finest layouts. The site of the 1989 New England Amateur, this finely conditioned course is a pleasure to play. While it is a fairly short course (5,761 yards from the white tees), the course plays much longer as the lush fairways do not afford a lot of roll. With very fast and sloping greens, placing the approach shots on the green below the pine is critical, or else there may be a lot of three putts! Adding to the difficulty of this beautiful course is that most of the greens are to some degree elevated and guarded closely up front by bunkers. Thus, all shots to the green must make it on a fly.

The two challenging and pretty holes on this course are the par 5 13th and the par 4 16th. Both holes have really sloping fairways, giving the player a tough sidehill lie for the fairway shots to the green. Compounding the difficulty of these two holes are the sloping greens, which makes putting an exceptional challenge. The 13th hole is 539 yards and, being slightly uphill on the drive and second shot, calls for the two of your best shots to be in good position for a shot to the green. The 365-yard 16th is a dogleg to the left, with the fairway sloping away to the right. A tee shot with a little draw is required here to keep the ball in the fairway to give you the best shot to the green.

Public play is welcomed at the Rutland Country Club, and tee times can be made the same day of play. Use of golf carts is required. A new clubhouse and pro shop facilities were built in 1988, and lunch can be enjoyed while watching the action on the course from the new clubhouse.

In Windham, there's a nice nine-hole course called Tater Hill. While this is a fairly wide-open golf course, the player is challenged by many uneven lies to fairly small greens that follow the terrain and often call for the bounce and run type of shot to stay on the green.

Tater Hill's fifth hole is a 439-yard par 4 that runs downhill to a very small green. The second shot must be played carefully to this green. The 575-yard ninth hole is also one that will challenge all levels of golfers as the fairway goes up and down all the way to the green. The key is to try to play to the flatter areas to give the player the best chance for a good swing on the next shot.

Tater Hill welcomes public play at all times of the season, and advance calls are recommended to check on course availability.

The Lake Saint Catherine Country Club Golf Course, located in Poultney, is another beautiful nine-hole track to play. While the course seems open and easy at first glance, there are a number of small streams and brooks strategically located that demand the player be accurate with his or her shot making. The course is a comfortable 6,000 yards from the white tees and is enjoyable for all levels of players.

The par 4, 416-yard fourth hole is my favorite hole on the course. From an elevated tee, a well-struck tee shot must be hit to a narrow landing area to set up your approach to the green. The green is closely guarded on both sides by bunkers that catch any shot that is off-line. The Lake Saint Catherine course is a moderately hilly course, and you will often be challenged by uneven lies and some uphill and downhill shots.

Lake Saint Catherine is open to the public, and tee times are only required on weekends. Reservations may be made three days in advance. If you are in the area, take the time to enjoy this pretty country course located in the rolling hills of the Poultney Valley.

That's the end of our tour of the great courses of southern Vermont. Any trip to this part of the state is much more fun if you remember to bring your clubs along and play a few of these fine courses. The variety of courses and the magnificent scenery will provide some of your fondest memories of southern Vermont.

Tennis

by GREG WORDEN

Harry always said that tennis was a lifetime sport. At that time, I didn't give it much thought. But, in retrospect, he was right.

He was in his 70s when he began to teach me the fundamentals of the sport that he loved. By that time, Harry's game was no longer a power game. He knew that his days of hard, crisp strokes were over, but he didn't let that stop him from enjoying his favorite sport.

Harry wasn't a Vermonter, but he would have fit in nicely with his dry sense of humor and eyes that twinkled when he doled out his challenges on the court.

"If you love the game, you'll always find someone to hit with," he used to say.

Harry taught by demonstration — the back-spinning drop shot, the twisting serve that seemed to dance out of the court as soon as it touched down inside the service box, the placement.

As he moved me around the court, he seemed to take great pleasure watching me scramble for shots off his old wooden racquet. And being young and agile and eager to accept a challenge, I took great pleasure in trying to return those shots. More often than not, when I reached the ball, I sent it back directly to Harry. And then he would send me scrambling again.

It's been about 30 years since Harry sent me scrambling for his Bobby Rigg-sian junk shots. But in the intervening years I've come to realize that he instilled in me an incurable desire to be on a tennis court — any place, any time.

Through the years I've found myself gasping for breath as I chased tennis balls under a high noon sun in the Rockies, on weakly-lit courts near Waikiki, and in a rare backyard court in Shirahama on the Kii Peninsula in Japan.

But it's here in Vermont that I've found the most consistent pleasure in play-ing tennis — practicing my drop shot and spin serve. To be sure, the times have changed since Harry taught me the basics of the game. Metal or composition racquets have almost completely replaced the wooden racquets of Harry's day. The all-white clothing rules of his day have given way to colorful combinations most everywhere, including Vermont.

Since the tennis boom in the 1970s, even Vermont has been blessed with numerous places to play the game.

However, in Vermont the game of tennis is still primarily a seasonal one. The outdoor courts far outnumber the indoor facilities, and that will likely be the case for some time to come. Indoor tennis centers are expensive to build and maintain and need a solid population base to keep them fiscally sound. Because of that, indoor tennis centers in sparsely populated Vermont are relatively few in number, and most are privately owned and operated by and for members only.

Nonetheless, if you're new to the southern Vermont area, or if you're just passing through, there are ample opportunities to play the game if you know where to look. Outdoor courts, however, are by far the easiest to find in this area that still caters to a multitude of seasonal sports.

In the following pages, I'll give you an idea of where you can expect to find a place to play; where to find good tennis racquets; where to find tennis clothes; and where to get your racquet strung in the southern Vermont area.

In the Brattleboro area, outdoor courts are definitely the easiest to come by. From late spring through fall, Living Memorial Park just off Route 9 west has eight courts — six lighted and under cover of the wintertime ice-skating rink and two unlighted outdoor courts adjacent to the indoor courts. All are hard courts and are open to the public on a first-come, first-served basis except when lessons are being given.

The local high school also has eight outdoor, hard-surface courts that are open to the public except when tennis team practice or meets are taking place.

The Brattleboro Outing Club on Cedar Street has six clay courts — four of which have been around since the early 1930s and two that have been in place since the 1970s. The two newest courts have been completely redone in the past year and are some of the best to be found in southern Vermont. The Outing Club offers tennis memberships for an annual fee, or one may play there as a guest for a minimal fee. A rustic clubhouse offers showers and a wonderful porch from which to watch matches on the various courts. The porch also serves as a place to pick up a game from one of the local players who frequent the club. Or, you may arrange a lesson from the club pro, who also offers tennis balls for sale.

If you're fortunate enough to find a member of the Brattleboro Tennis Club, a private indoor facility with two hard courts adjacent to the Outing Club, you may be able to arrange a match there, too. But, being a private facility, it's easier to schedule an outdoor match.

If you're looking for tennis racquets in Brattleboro, look at Burrows Sport Shop and Sam's Sporting Goods on Main Street. Both also carry tennis clothes and tennis balls. Burrows also will string racquets as will Holland Douglas, whose home is situated next to the Outing Club courts. Douglas also is a wellspring of information about tennis in the Brattleboro area.

Working our way across the southern tier, in Wilmington and Dover, outdoor hard courts can be found at several places. The high school behind the fire department has two hard courts that are open to the public. Up Route 100 five miles from the heart of Wilmington is the Sitzmark Lodge, which has eight hard courts and during the spring through late summer offers lessons, as well as courts, for the public as well as guests.

Other courts in the Wilmington-West Dover area open to the public include two hard courts at the Andirons Motor Lodge; six composition courts at Dover Watch on Route 100 across from the Mobil station; and a couple of hard courts at inns or condominiums at Mount Snow, which are mostly reserved for guests.

The Cupola Sports Shop on Route 100 is the best in the area for tennis racquets and gear, including racquet stringing. Although tennis gear is stowed away for the winter, the staff will be happy to dig a racquet out if needed during ski season.

Heading over Woodford Mountain into Bennington, courts are to be found at the recreation center on Gage Street, the Molly Stark School, and at Bennington College. Bennington College has two clay courts, the Molly Stark School has two hard courts, and the recreation center has four hard courts.

Other courts in the area include a hard court at the Ramada Inn and two hard courts at the Mount Anthony Country Club.

It's hard and nearly impossible to find either racquets or tennis clothes in Bennington; most people either go to Manchester, Vermont; Pittsfield, Massachusetts; or to Albany, New York.

Heading up Route 7 to Arlington, courts can be found at the high school and the town's park and recreation center.

Probably the nearest place to Bennington to find good tennis racquets and gear is in Manchester. The Manchester Sports Center, which carries a good selection of tennis equipment, has been the traditional spot to buy tennis goods. But a new store, Stratton Sports in Manchester's Equinox Square, plans to offer a wide selection of racquets and clothing as well.

Public courts in Manchester are limited to three outdoor hard courts at the Dana Thompson Memorial Park operated by the Manchester Recreation Department. Other courts can be found at various inns or at the Equinox Hotel but are usually limited to guests.

Taking a side tour from Manchester over to the Stratton Resort area, using Route 11 to Route 30, one finds perhaps the most well-known tennis center in Vermont.

For five years, Stratton was the home of the Volvo International Tennis Tournament, and in that time, many of the world's top players — including Ivan Lendl, Boris Becker, John McEnroe, Andre Agassi, and Yannick Noah — graced the courts at Stratton Mountain. In fact, it was at Stratton that Agassi first broke into the big-league ranks of the players. The site was more than once voted the professionals' favorite tour location, and indeed, it is one of the most picturesque settings for tennis in Vermont.

Before the Volvo came on the scene at Stratton, the Legends Tennis Tournament was held there for several years and featured such all-time stars as Ken Rosewall, Rod Laver, and John Newcombe.

In other words, if you're looking to play on courts that have seen some of the top players in the world, Stratton is the place to visit.

Private and group lessons are available at the Stratton Sports Center, which features 15 outdoor courts (8 Har-Tru and 7 Deco-Turf II) and 4 hard-surface indoor courts. Proper tennis attire is recommended, but there is no all-white rule. The pro shop offers a full line of tennis clothes and racquets as well as rental and demonstration racquets. Stringing is available, as well.

Also in the Stratton area, the Bear Creek condominiums on Route 30 offer five Har-Tru courts — two in view of the road and three others in back of the complex. The courts are available to the public as well as to the guests. Because of its accessibility to Stratton, the courts at Bear Creek also have seen their share of top pros who wanted a place to practice their strokes in preparation for the tournaments at Stratton.

From Bear Creek, it's not a far trip up Route 100 to South Londonderry and the West River Tennis Center, a small private club that opens its courts to the public when its members don't have reservations. The two indoor courts are Har-Tru, and although there is no formal dress code, normal tennis shoes are expected. The center also features an indoor fitness operation along with showers and dressing rooms. Racquets may be left at the center to be restrung.

Londonderry also has a hard court at the town's recreation area that is open to the public.

Backtracking to Route 7 and heading north to Rutland, courts can be found at the high school, at the town park, and at the Great Expectations Health and Racquet Club.

Great Expectations has recently undergone renovations to its facilities and offers three indoor hard courts to both members and the public. Eight outdoor clay courts also are available for play during the season.

Tennis balls and racquet restringing are also available at Great Expectations. Additionally, the facility offers four racquetball courts and a new fitness center.

Heading across Route 4 toward the Killington Resort area, one will find four clay and four hard courts at the Cortina Inn. The courts are open to guests and the public alike for a fee.

The Killington Tennis School operates on eight courts at the Village Motor Inn from May through September. Lessons are available during that time on both weekends and during the week. In season, a pro shop at the school offers racquet stringing as well as clothing and racquets. Eight other outdoor courts also are available for play at inns in the Killington complex for guests.

Continuing on Route 4 eastbound, the Woodstock Inn and Resort offers 10 outdoor courts and 2 indoor courts. The indoor courts are Deco-Turf II, and the outdoor courts include 6 clay, 2 Deco-Turf, and 2 hard surface. Platform tennis also is available. Towels, lockers, showers, and other amenities are offered.

The pro shop at the inn offers a good selection of racquets as well as a restringing service. Lessons are available, too. Two hard courts also can be found at Woodstock's town park.

Staying on Route 4 eastbound, the next tennis facility open to the general public is a hard court at the Fountain of Youth Health Center in the Howard Johnson's complex in White River Junction. Most people who play tennis in this area either belong to the private "Our Court" indoor facility or a similar one in nearby Quechee.

Heading south on Route 5, one comes to Windsor, the "birthplace of Vermont." Although it's famous for a number of things, tennis is not high on the list. Taking a turn on Route 44 will bring you to three outdoor hard courts that are open to the public free of charge.

Backtracking to Route 5 and continuing south will bring you to signs that will lead you to the Mount Ascutney Resort. There you will find five Har-Tru courts and two all-weather courts that are open to the public for a fee; all are outdoor courts. Once again, as in most areas of Vermont, the scenery around the courts is breathtaking.

Heading on down the line, in Springfield, four outdoor hard-surface courts are open to the public at the Riverside School Park on Route 11 westbound.

In Bellows Falls, hard courts are open to the public at the union high school (four) and at the playground (two).

That brings us back to Brattleboro, where I've been chasing tennis balls for the past 20 years. And where I'll probably be chasing tennis balls for at least 20 or 30 more years.

My friend Harry was right. Tennis is a sport for a lifetime. If you're not hooked already, I hope that this little tour of where you can play tennis in southern Vermont will get you hooked. You won't regret it!

Fishing

by JOHN MERWIN

After a while I was able to convince Sam, my four-year-old son, that when the red-and-white bobber went darting beneath the surface he should give a tug. Giggling, he lifted yet another sunfish flipping into the air from the sunny waters of Lake Saint Catherine near Wells, Vermont. After admiring its color and talking about its spiny fins, we carefully removed the hook and let it go.

That evening, familial duties taken care of, I put on my waders and stepped into the smooth Battenkill currents south of Manchester. As darkness fell, small yellow mayflies started hatching along the broken current, riding the water like tiny sailboats. Soon the spreading rings of rising trout were visible up and down the river, and my own dry fly disappeared in a swirl and a quick tug. The fish pulled hard into the pool's dark water and then surrendered at the net. It was a lovely wild brown trout of 14 inches or so that I carefully released, hoping that I or another angler would have the pleasure of catching him again.

On Saturday morning I had promises to keep, namely taking the two older kids bass fishing, so we loaded the canoe on the car and headed for Gale Meadows Pond in Winhall. As I paddled slowly along the shoreline, Emily used a spinning rod to flip a purple plastic worm in among the lily pads. We had already caught several small largemouth bass when her lure disappeared in a huge splash, and her rod was suddenly bent almost double into the water under the canoe.

A bass of six or seven pounds then jumped right next to the boat, throwing the hook free and splashing water all over. We sat in silence for a minute or two and then allowed as how bass fishing could be pretty dramatic.

As you may have gathered from these few examples, fishing in southern Vermont can be both varied and exciting for anglers of all ages and skill levels. Parents with toddlers can enjoy abundant panfishing for sunfish and perch with a minimum of skill or special equipment. Sophisticated bass fishermen can use a fully equipped bass boat to good advantage here. Kids will find easily caught brook trout in some mountain streams, while wild brook, brown, and rainbow trout will challenge, frustrate, and occasionally reward the most expert fly-fisherman on the area's larger rivers.

My family and I have fished this region week in and week out for more than 15 years, and I'll use this chapter to show you how, when, and where you can enjoy some of the things I've just described.

Before we actually go fishing, though, here are a few things you should know. Any individual older than sixteen will need a state (resident or nonresident) fishing license. For a short trip, a three- or seven-day license may be sufficient. This is less expensive than a season license, which is good for the whole calendar year in which it's purchased. In either case, licenses can be purchased from most town clerks in addition to numerous sporting goods stores. Town clerk offices, by the way, are usually closed on weekends. If you're trying to get a license on a Saturday, Sunday, or holiday and can't find a sporting goods store, your best bet is to find a police station and inquire.

Don't make the mistake of fishing without a license! Vermont's game wardens are extremely diligent and work all sorts of odd hours to better protect our fishing and game resources through law enforcement. Buying a license is much less expensive than having to pay a substantial fine because you didn't bother to get one.

You should take the time to review the small digest of Vermont's fish and game laws that you'll be given with your license. This will provide information as to limits on the numbers, size, and all kinds of fish you can catch and keep; general regulations as to open and closed seasons; plus some specific information on specially regulated waters. In general, Vermont's trout season opens on the second Saturday in April, while bass season (for largemouth and smallmouth both) starts on June 10. These dates are subject to change, so check your rule book.

While this chapter has enough information to get you started, there are many fishing opportunities I simply don't have space to describe here. Once again, find a sporting goods store and inquire. You'll find most such proprietors very helpful, all the more so if you buy something. You can obtain a free copy of the "Vermont Guide to Fishing" by writing the Vermont Fish and Wildlife Department, Montpelier, Vermont 05602. This is a large map of the state with rivers, streams, lakes, and ponds highlighted and marked as to the kinds of fish they contain. Roads and access areas are shown clearly, and I refer to mine every year.

Finally, if you're going into any sort of remote area where you'll be away from other people — and there are many such areas in southern Vermont — use a topographic map, take a compass, and make sure someone knows about where you'll be going and what time you expect to be back. That way help can arrive fairly quickly in the unlikely event you're stuck near a backcountry beaver pond with a broken leg.

I've organized the rest of this chapter into sections as follows: trout fishing, bass fishing, and a section for families with children. You can pick a section of particular interest or do what we do during the spring, summer, and fall: Try a little bit of everything.

Trout Fishing

Vermont relies on extensive populations of wild, naturally reproducing trout in most of its rivers. This is supplemented by limited stocking of catchable-size trout in a few cases, but many rivers — including the world-famous Battenkill — aren't stocked at all. Trout ponds and lakes are commonly stocked, either with fingerlings that will have to grow for a year or two before they're big enough to catch or else with catchable-size (nine inches, more or less) brown, brook, and/or rainbow trout — the species depending on the particular habitat requirements of a lake or pond.

Small Brook Fishing

Southern Vermont is crisscrossed by dozens of small brooks that are tributary to larger rivers and streams, and almost all of these small brooks hold brook trout. You'll even find them in the smallest trickles — only two or three feet wide — as long as running water is present all year. The farther away from the road you follow one of these brooks, the better the fishing will be.

The basic technique is simple: Use any lightweight fly or spinning rod, a fine four-pound-test monofilament leader, and a small size eight hook with a split-shot sinker about 12 inches above the hook. Use small garden worms for bait, or you can catch your own grasshoppers or crickets for bait in late summer when they're plentiful. Many general stores in the area sell small containers of garden worms that they get from bait distributors. Larger worms, so-called night crawlers, are much too big for this sort of fishing. Work your way upstream, dropping your baited hook into the deeper pockets of water above your position as you proceed. You really don't need to cast more than a few feet, since by working upstream you're sneaking up behind the fish's pool in a tumbling brook.

Fly-fishermen work these little brooks successfully, also, but more often by fishing downstream with a small wet fly or nymph imitation. Because the pools are small and often shallow, the spinning lures that work on bigger water aren't very effective here.

You can find these brooks by simply driving around and looking for them, or you can better your chances by getting a topographic map and picking one or two to explore. Some of the better-known (and harder fished) brooks include the Roaring Branch in Arlington along the Kelley Stand Road, the headwaters of the Deerfield River to the west of Somerset Reservoir and Wardsboro, Bromley Brook along Routes 11-30 east of Manchester, the Green River west of Route 313 in Sandgate, White Creek near Rupert, Mill Brook in Danby, and Big Brook in Mount Tabor.

These little brooks fish best early in the season shortly after the snow has melted from the mountains and before low water makes the fish harder to catch. If the big rivers are still too cold for good trout fishing, brook fishing is your best bet.

River Fishing

This area has two world-class trout rivers: the famous Battenkill and the lesser-known Mettawee. Both of these rivers start near my home in Dorset. The Battenkill flows south through Manchester and Arlington and then turns west into New York. The Mettawee flows generally north and west through Dorset, Rupert, and Pawlet before entering New York at Granville. Both are paralleled by roads and are easy to get to.

The Battenkill is world-famous as a fly-fishing river, partly because the Orvis Company has been making and selling fishing tackle in nearby Manchester continuously since 1856. Vermont's portion of the river hasn't been stocked for many years but sustains a large population of wild brook and brown trout in the face of heavy fishing pressure. The trout are just plain hard to catch. There are about twice as many brown trout in the river as brook trout, and they average somewhat larger — about nine inches. The average brook trout size is about seven inches.

Every year a few wise old browns of four and five pounds are taken here, usually on spinning tackle in May or June. My neighbors, however, recently took a six-and-a-half-pound brown trout on a dry fly, which would be recognized as a rare trophy on any stream in the world.

Fly-fishermen should look for the following fly hatches starting at these approximate dates: Hendricksons — May 1; Little Mahoganies — May 1; Tan Caddis — May 20; Blue-winged Olives — May 20; Sulphurs — June 1; Yellow Drakes — June 10; Mahogany Drakes — June 15; Gray Drakes — June 15; Tiny White-Winged Blacks — July 15; Flying Ants — September 10; and Minute Blue-winged Olives starting about September 20. There are, of course, many other hatches here as well. The dry-fly fishing is generally excellent from May through late October. I've spent so much time on this river that I finally wrote a book about it, so for more information you can check *The Battenkill* (Nick Lyons Books, New York, 1990).

Spin fishing on this river is generally most effective in May before the water starts to drop to summer levels. Most productive lures include gold Rapalas, Roostertails, and black-bladed Mepps spinners. Because the river is so clear and the trout so wary, bait fishing is usually less effective than other methods unless the water is briefly roiled by a thunderstorm.

The Mettawee River tumbles down out of Dorset Hollow and runs through a pastoral dairy-farmed valley on its way to Granville, New York, and beyond. Here there's a resident and naturally reproducing strain of rainbow trout that's unique in this part of the state. Mixed with the rainbows are a few larger brown trout and an even smaller number of native brook trout. The rainbows average seven to nine inches, but I've (rarely) caught them here to over two pounds.

Find the river by following Route 30 north of Dorset Village into Rupert and Pawlet. There are numerous bridge crossings that offer success. Places where fishermen have parked will be quite evident. There are a very few posted sections, so make sure you're not trespassing. When in doubt, ask the farmer's permission to park and fish.

Fly-fishing perhaps works better here than any other method, and beginners will be happy to note that you don't even have to cast: Just stand in a riffle above a pool, shake some line into the current, and let the current sweep your weighted nymph down into the pool. Chances are a rainbow will whack it. Of course, more skilled anglers who can stalk and cast to rising fish will generally have larger catches. This river has become increasingly popular in recent years. I let most of my fish go here so my family and others can have the fun of catching them again. I hope you do likewise.

Other trout streams worth your time include the Castleton River, near where it crosses under Route 4 west of Rutland. One of the biggest brown trout I've ever seen (and didn't catch) was swimming around one day right under the busy Route 4 bridge! Also worth a try are the Hoosic River in Pownal, Walloomsac River in Bennington, Winhall River in Winhall, and the upper end of the West River in Weston, which is a good brown trout stream.

Bass Fishing

Bass fishing opportunities are more limited in the southern part of the state than farther to the east (Connecticut River) and north in the central lakes district, but there is plenty of fishing to go around. While some bass fishing can be done successfully from the shore at times, most fishermen will do better with the added mobility of a boat or canoe. On large lakes such as Saint Catherine in Wells, a fully rigged bass boat with electronic fish-finding and bottom-scanning devices is a distinct advantage.

Bass fishermen know that lure color can be critical, and the best colors in this region are purple, chartreuse, and black — in that order. Day in and day out, a purple — or "grape" — six-inch plastic worm will outfish any other lure. Chartreuse spinner and buzz baits are effective in the early season shallows for largemouth bass, while smallmouths show a distinct preference for a three-inch clear chartreuse Mister Twister style jig on a 1/16- or 1/8-ounce lead head and fished with four-pound-test line. These fish are hard to fool, and the lighter line is important.

Lake Saint Catherine is a large bass (and trout) lake and is heavily fished. There are two sites maintained by the state where trailered boats can be launched: one at the south end of the lake and one at Lake Saint Catherine State Park at the north end. This lake has lots of boaters and water-skiers in summer, which makes daytime fishing tough. Fish early and late for best results and even after dark if your boat has running lights as required by law. My largest bass from this lake — about five pounds — was taken right in front of one of these launching areas after dark in midsummer on a jitterbug. Boats and/or canoes are sometimes available for hire at a small marina on Route 30 at the lake's north end. Because of the heavy fishing pressure here, those anglers fishing smaller lures on light line are by far the most successful.

Other bass waters in this area include Gale Meadows Pond in Winhall (lots of smaller fish); Lowell Lake (slow fishing but for larger-than-average largemouth bass); Somerset and Harriman reservoirs — north and south of Route 9, respectively, and east of Bennington — which are both good bets for smallmouths; and Emerald Lake State Park on Route 7 in East Dorset, which holds some big smallmouths that have seen and refused every lure known to man. The West River from Townshend Dam to Brattleboro is paralleled by Route 30 and is too warm for trout but offers excellent smallmouth bass fishing on flies, lures, or bait. Fish the deep holes and pay special attention to the water around very large boulders or ledges. I've seen (not caught) smallmouth bass to a trophy four pounds here.

The Connecticut River itself offers excellent fishing for white perch, yellow perch, walleye, shad, and some of the best smallmouth bass fishing in New England. A boat or canoe is required to make the most of this fishing, and numerous access points are noted on your "Vermont Guide to Fishing" state map. Anadromous shad runs can be fished in late spring below dams at Vernon, Bellows Falls, and Wilder (where the state record walleye of more than 12 pounds was caught), and these are also good spots for smallmouths. A large, shallow backwater just west of the state boat launching ramp on the river at Springfield is a hot spot for largemouths. Be careful of rapidly rising water levels when fishing this big river, as upstream hydroelectric generation can release large volumes of water without warning. Because the river is an interstate boundary, regulations are more complicated, and you may also need a nonresident New Hampshire license. Check your rule book.

Families with Children

Fishing in southern Vermont is a wonderful activity for small children. It's clean, inexpensive, and terrifically entertaining. Here are a couple of day trips that I've done often with my own kids and that might be fun for you and yours.

Take a picnic to Lake Saint Catherine State Park. Before you go, if you don't have *any* fishing tackle, find a general store that sells the rudiments. All you need is a simple cane pole (even a simple eight-foot, light stick will do), a spool of cheap six-pound-test monofilament line, a few small hooks (size six or eight), and some small garden-variety worms.

The park charges a nominal entrance fee, has wonderful picnic facilities, a sandy swimming beach (with lifeguard), and best of all has lots of willing sunfish and perch in easy reach of a shoreline toddler. Attach the bobber about 18 inches above the hook, put on a small piece of worm, and help your child swing the bait into the water. My kids have all started their fishing this way, and yours might, too.

For older children — those who can hike a woodland trail for about two miles — a walk up the Lye Brook Trail east of Manchester can be terrific. This is a great way of getting kids tired out so they go to bed early and fall asleep. Turn south on Richville Road off Route 11-30 in Manchester Depot. Then turn left on East Manchester Road and watch for signs on the right for "Lye Brook Wilderness Area." There's a parking area for your car. Don't forget your brook fishing tackle. Fish the brook for brook trout all the way up along the trail if you like. After a couple of miles, you'll come to a spectacular waterfall. This is a very popular outing among those of us who live here.

Don't forget that even though your children (under sixteen) are fishing and you're not, as an accompanying adult you need a fishing license.

Those are just a few of the fishing opportunities in this area. After many years here, I still haven't gotten to try all the places I've heard about and put on my list. The list is growing, too, as part of the fun is exploring and finding new spots. See you on the river!

Windsurfing

by MARY MCKHANN

People come to Vermont for a lot of reasons, many of them having to do with the natural beauty of the place and the opportunities to enjoy that beauty in the outdoors. For some, it is golf courses nestled in picturesque valleys or set among the mountains. For others, the cool, clean air is the perfect place to brush up on their serve and volley. Still others appreciate the quiet roads through towns long on charm and short on traffic for bicycling expeditions.

In winter, it is primarily skiing that attracts visitors to the Green Mountains. An abundance of downhill and cross-country areas cater to skiers of every taste, pocketbook, and ability.

When I moved to Vermont, it was for the skiing. I had spent too many years commuting every weekend from Manhattan to the Berkshires and wanted to be able to ski whenever the mood struck me. It didn't turn out quite that way, but close enough.

What I forgot was that I am an ocean person in the summer. Vermont has almost everything, but it does not have an ocean. It does have Lake Champlain, but that's in the northern part of the state. The question of what to do during the summer became a major issue in my life after I had survived my first mud season.

I happened to be skiing at Stratton one beautiful spring day when I overheard some instructors discussing windsurfing. Having been a sailor all my life, the conversation set off bells in my head. I had already toyed with the idea of getting a small sailboat but rejected the idea because it would involve getting a trailer and enlisting the aid of at least one other person every time I wanted to take it out.

Windsurfing. I liked the idea, even though I didn't know a whole lot about it. I had seen some people doing it on Cape Cod and had seen pictures of hotshots, and while it didn't look easy, it looked possible.

It was my good fortune that one of those ski instructors at Stratton was Jonathan Bischoff, who subsequently started New England Sailboard Company, which presently has stores in Rutland and Jamaica (that's Vermont, not the island). Bischoff sold me my first board and convinced me that windsurfing was not only possible but a lot of fun.

Unfortunately, that was before Bischoff started a sailboarding school at Stratton Lake, and my struggles during the first season or two learning the sport have convinced me that a lesson or two is time saved and money wisely invested. Even with good lessons, be prepared to spend a lot of time in the water, not necessarily on your sailboard.

Getting Started

For a beginner, the Stratton Windsurfing School is an ideal place to start. The lake is small — a bonus when you are learning and frequently don't end up back at exactly the same place you started from — and is free of motorboat traffic and wash — another plus for those just learning to stand on what seems a very tippy craft at the beginning.

The school starts beginners on a dryland trainer, which simulates the action of the board and teaches the basics of sailing and tacking (turning the board) without the added complication of constantly falling into the water. When students do venture onto the lake, they are tethered to their instructors until they have mastered the basic moves.

Sailing Winds at Lake Saint Catherine also offers lessons for beginners. They are located on Route 30 on the eastern shore of the lake and are on a small, protected inlet that allows students to practice before taking their boards into more open parts of the lake. Sailing Winds is open only late spring through early fall, and a call ahead is recommended to make sure the equipment you want is available. Both Sailing Winds and New England Sailboard rent equipment.

If, for whatever reasons, you choose not to take lessons, more than likely you can pick up some pointers on any light-air day at any of the local sailing spots. Two of the most popular are Lake Saint Catherine's State Park and Crystal Beach at Lake Bomoseen. A stop at either New England Sailboard store will yield a wealth of information on the best spot to sail that day, as well as good deals on new and used equipment. The shop also does repair work.

Vermont is not exactly a mecca for windsurfers — summer winds range from about 5 to 15 knots — but it gets its share of good days and is full of out-of-work skiers looking to emulate their winter thrills. Skiing and windsurfing come very close to giving the participant the same sense of exhilaration, and many of the moves are similar. And while we do not have Mount Hood and the Columbia River Gorge, on a good day in late spring you can ski Killington in the morning and sail Bomoseen in the afternoon.

Short boards are generally not a good bet in southern Vermont, and most local windsurfers choose "transition" or full-length fun boards. When the winds pick up, you can occasionally use a shorter slalom board. The smallest sail an average Vermont sailor might need is probably a 5.0, and there are plenty of days when most of the guys use 7.5 sails while the women are using something around a 6.5. Of course, there is always the chance that you will hit one of the days when it really blows....

If it's a good day, most of the brightly colored sails will be slashing across the water; on an okay day about half the sailors will be out practicing their jibes and other maneuvers while the "wind snobs" sit on the shore; and on a day when the wind never quite makes it, sailors sit on the beach and swap stories and tips on the latest in technology. Some local windsurfers have taken to bringing their mountain bikes as well as their boards on expeditions to the lakes, so they have the option to ride if there is no wind.

One of the problems for Vermont windsurfers is access to water, which is limited. Lake Saint Catherine and Lake Bomoseen both have state parks where windsurfers can be launched; Bomoseen also has Crystal Beach. These all have the advantage of having picnic areas, swings and play equipment for children, rest rooms, and refreshment stands. It costs a dollar per person for passenger cars at each of these facilities, but if you plan to use the state parks frequently, you can purchase season passes. The parks also have overnight camping facilities, but a call ahead is recommended as they tend to get crowded in the summer.

Popular Sailing Spots

Crystal Beach, just north of Castleton on Route 30, is a popular spot for windsurfers from the Rutland/Killington area but also attracts sailors from Manchester, Stratton, and Ludlow, among others. The parking lot is very close to the water, and even though the bank is fairly steep, it is the easiest place to launch. It is good in most winds, but when the wind is from the north, there is usually a dead-calm spot just in front of the launch area, which can make getting out and coming back in difficult and frustrating.

Like most other areas in Vermont, Crystal Beach has the advantage of large, grassy areas to rig. Sand is great to sunbathe on but not so nice when it gets into mast and boom parts and makes taking your rig apart impossible. Water temperatures in summer are quite warm, and in July, August, and early September, you are not likely to need a wet suit. Spring and fall can be very changeable, however, and a wet suit is a good idea. Dry suits come in handy if you plan to sail in the early spring or late fall. Personal flotation devices are legally required, although many windsurfers do not wear them.

Bomoseen is wide and open, and once you get away from shore, you can usually find some good sailing. Like many other lakes in Vermont, Bomoseen is suffering from an invasion of Eurasian milfoil — a rather nasty, indestructible weed that will wrap itself around skegs and dagger boards and cause incredible drag. There are skegs that are supposed to cut through the stuff, but most people just wait until they get to deep water, drop their sails, and clear the stuff off by hand.

Bomoseen State Park is located off Route 4 between Castleton and Fair Haven. It has all the amenities of a state park, but for some reason it has never proved as popular with windsurfers. This might be due to the fact that the park is located on an inlet, and getting in and out to the main part of the lake is somewhat difficult.

Islands, hills, and points of land tend to create shifty winds in most of Vermont's lakes, and, generally speaking, south to southwest winds tend to be the steadiest on both Bomoseen and Lake Saint Catherine.

Lake Saint Catherine State Park is also on Route 30, just south of Poultney. It is somewhat more of a hike to get your board to the water here but still not bad. Here, too, there are wide, grassy lawns to rig your board — in fact, this is probably the nicest place to rig of any of the lakes in southern Vermont. The launch area at Lake Saint Catherine is fairly small and is located just south of the swimming area. This can cause some problems for beginners when the wind is from the south, as they tend to blow into the swimming area. Here, too, milfoil can be an annoyance, and on weekends there is considerable motorboat traffic.

If you prefer something more pristine, head south to Somerset Reservoir near Wilmington. The reservoir is owned by the New England Power Company (NEPCO), but the only thing not allowed there is overnight camping. Somerset is located on a dirt road 10 miles off Route 9, just west of Wilmington. Getting there is definitely not half the fun in this case, but once you are there, it is a beautiful spot.

There are a number of nice picnic spots around the lake, and the water is very clear (so far, Somerset has avoided the milfoil invasion). There are a few private camps around, but for the most part, the reservoir is remote from civilization. It does tend to get somewhat crowded on holiday weekends, however. Sailing here tends to be best when the wind is blowing from the north.

Also in the Wilmington area is Lake Whitingham. It is a popular spot and gets a lot of powerboat traffic, as well as a fair number of windsurfers. Access is good, and the water is clear.

If you're looking for a different type of summer sport, you might want to try sailboarding in southern Vermont. It is a lot of fun.

Foliage Tours

by CRAIG WOODS

Nothing can be quite as relaxing and enjoyable as a ride in the country. This is something that has become an American tradition ever since Mr. Ford pioneered the mass production of automobiles early in this century, making them affordable to most families. Mom in her bonnet, dad in his straw hat, and the kids in the backseat cruising the countryside in a Model T on a Sunday afternoon is Americana as true as apple pie.

Today, in Vermont, taking a ride in the country is among the most popular of tourist activities. It's inexpensive, you travel at your own pace, stop only where you want to, and there are few, if any, highways that do not afford beautiful mountain vistas and panoramas of quaint New England villages and farms with rustic silos and white-clapboard church spires rising into the sky. Vermont is a small enough state that almost any town is not too far from any other Vermont town for a day trip.

And I think most residents and visitors alike will agree that the most spectacular time of year to take a ride in Vermont is during foliage season, which runs roughly from mid-September until the end of October in southern Vermont. At this time of year the leaves of the deciduous trees — the maples, beeches, birches, ashes, and others — turn color from green to autumn-bright yellow, gold, red, and orange, making the mountainsides look like the work of an impressionist artist. Add to this weather that is frequently clear, crisp, and dry along with the characteristically deep blue skies of autumn, and you have the makings of breathtaking scenery in an invigorating atmosphere. People come to Vermont from all over the United States and even from overseas to experience this natural phenomenon.

The phenomenon itself is quite easily understood. Leaves really don't *change* color. What happens is that in the autumn the hours of daylight diminish significantly. As a result, the photosynthetic process of trees — the process, briefly, by which they manufacture sustenance from sunlight — is affected. The trees produce less chlorophyll, a substance that gives leaves their green pigment. The bright colors that we see in the leaves in autumn have been there all along and are revealed with the withdrawal of chlorophyll.

And, interestingly enough, there is one species of evergreen, or pine, tree in southern Vermont whose needles do change color — to yellow brown — and drop to the ground in the fall. It is the tamarack.

Now, that's enough about Americana and natural history. Here's the straight scoop on three rides you can take in southern Vermont, each easily manageable as a one-day round-trip from the point of departure, which I have chosen as the popular resort town of Manchester, and each with its own special appeal.

But before taking off, stop at the local chamber of commerce (locations are listed elsewhere in this book) and pick up a copy of the official Vermont road map, published by the state of Vermont and free for the asking. Two other good regionalized road guides that include detailed maps as well as other helpful tourist information are the *Vermont Atlas and Gazetteer* (DeLorime Mapping Company, Box 298, Freeport, ME 04032; $11.95) and the *Vermont Road Atlas and Guide* (Northern Cartographic, Box 133, Burlington, VT 05402; $12.95), which are available at newsstands and in bookstores throughout southern Vermont. For my money, the Delorime *Atlas and Gazetteer* has a bit more to recommend itself than the Northern Cartographic book.

The West River Valley

My personal favorite foliage ride in southern Vermont is Route 30 between Manchester and Brattleboro. For most of this route, the road winds along the West River, which rises near Weston, Vermont, and flows southeast to join the Connecticut River in Brattleboro. The Connecticut River flows north-south and forms most of the boundary between Vermont and New Hampshire.

Leaving from Manchester, take Route 11-30 east toward Bromley Mountain Ski Area. Two miles before the ski area, Routes 30 and 11 part, the former heading south and the latter east. Make a right on Route 30, heading south.

Before you reach Bondville, which is the next town along the way, you will be afforded an expansive mountain vista to your left. To the west is Bromley Mountain, across a valley to Bromley's east is Magic Mountain, and to the south is Stratton Mountain (although you won't be able to actually see Stratton until you're much closer to Bondville, when Bromley and Magic are out of view). Each mountain is home to a popular ski area, and together local marketing types call them "Southern Vermont's Golden Triangle of Skiing."

After Bondville, the next town is Rawsonville, at the junction of Routes 30 and 100. After having driven through Rawsonville hundreds of times, I can only suggest that the sole reason to have created a town there and given it a name is that the spot lies at the junction of Route 100, a major north-south route, and Route 30, a major east-west route (when I say "major," bear in mind that everything's relative). Rawsonville: one gas station/general store, one inn and restaurant, one video store, one auto-repair shop, and one skiwear shop.

Beyond Rawsonville, Route 30 takes you over a few gentle ridges, winding its way to Jamaica. Jamaica is a cluster of white-clapboard storefronts and homes. There's a comfortable, rustic inn — the Jamaica House — that has been converted into a restaurant featuring excellent Italian food. There's another inn on the way out of town and an antiques shop — Antiques Anonymous — on the left at the edge of town that has some very nice things, if you can catch the owner around anywhere to let you in and show them to you (the owner is a friend of mine who is a musician by profession and jack-of-all-trades by temperament).

After passing through these several towns — which you will have covered in the space of about 20 miles — you begin about 25 miles of one of the most scenic foliage routes in the state. You are basically paralleling the West River now, passing through the small towns of West Townshend, Townshend, and Harmonyville, and the views open up as the road runs along the sides of ridges for much of the way. You can look down and see the West River, now large enough to be properly called a "river," as it wends its way southeast. Townshend was chosen as the location for filming Chevy Chase's recent movie, *Funny Farm*.

The postcard-perfect town of Newfane is the last stop before Brattleboro. Several stores and fine restaurants surround the spacious village green. The Newfane Inn and the Four Columns Inn are among two of the finest gourmet restaurants in New England. The village green itself, with its classic white gazebo, is lorded over by the county courthouse, a stately brick structure, tall white columns in front attesting to the importance of its purpose. Among the noteworthy figures who have or have had part-time places in or near Newfane are economist John Kenneth Galbraith and the late author Robert Penn Warren.

It is the last eight miles before Brattleboro, where Route 30 clings to a ridge to the west of the river, that is the climax. For the most part the river is well below the road, and its steady flow, disrupted here and there with small breaks of white water, is the perfect centerpiece for steeply rising ridges ablaze in the colors of autumn. Perhaps you will see an angler or two plying the currents for smallmouth bass. Before you reach Brattleboro, you'll pass the Dummerston covered bridge on your left.

Brattleboro is one of Vermont's largest cities, and it was once famous for being the largest manufacturer of musical organs in the world. Perched on the Connecticut River, at one time it was, of course, an active mill town, and its downtown streets are lined with the three- and four-story red-brick buildings typical of New England mill towns that flourished a century ago. There is plenty of good shopping, and there are good restaurants in the downtown area and even a museum where Main and Canal streets meet. The Book Cellar on Main Street is an excellent bookstore for browsing, and then there's Sam's Department Store, also on Main Street, with good prices on everything from pocketknives to shoes and clothing. Walker's Restaurant, just up the block from the Book Cellar, is a good place to have a sandwich before following Route 30 back to your home base in Manchester, which you will want to do before dark to take in the scenery from another angle — and perhaps to find my friend about his business at the antique shop in Jamaica.

Route 7 South to Bennington

Today there is a little bit of confusion about southern Vermont's section of U.S. Route 7, a north-south highway that runs from somewhere down in Connecticut to the Canadian border. You see, for a number of years, the state of Vermont has been creating a new highway paralleling Route 7 and stealing its name. The old highway has been renamed Route 7A — oops, actually, it is officially known as Historic Route 7A. I realize this is common practice when highway departments are rerouting roads, but those of us around here simply call the one New Route 7 and the other Old Route 7, stubborn as we are. But the great part is that on this particular day trip, you get to experience the best of both highways.

Again, departing from the Manchester area, take Route 7A/Old Route 7/Historic 7A heading south. Immediately, you will be leaving behind the venerable Equinox Hotel in Manchester, directly on Route 7A, that has been catering to the bluest of blood and the most fortunate of corporations since the middle of the nineteenth century. This hotel has had a varied past, at times welcoming such notables as presidents Lincoln and Taft, at other times housing corporate conventions and sales meetings, at still other times lying fallow for years on end. Restored, revitalized, and reopened in 1986 after more than a decade of uncertainty, the Equinox has once again become known as one of the important resort locations in southern Vermont.

Continuing south on Route 7A, you will pass through Sunderland, where there is the entrance to the Skyline Drive. This is a toll road that climbs to the top of Mount Equinox, the second highest mountain in Vermont (the highest is Mount Mansfield, up north near Stowe). At the top of Equinox is the Equinox Skyline Inn, which includes a restaurant. Save the Skyline Drive for another day and continue south through Sunderland to Arlington.

In Arlington, make a right at the junction of Routes 7A and 313. This is a short side trip. Follow Route 313 west for about eight miles. You are paralleling some of the most popular stretches of the Battenkill River, felt by many to be the finest trout stream in New England. It is a beautiful river here, just big enough to offer the angler variety but still small enough to be friendly. Serious fly-fishermen come from all over to fish this stream and to visit the Orvis Company showroom in Manchester. Orvis is a leading manufacturer of fine fishing tackle.

But you're not aiming to wet a line here, you're just out for a ride. So follow Route 313 until you see the red covered bridge — this bridge is the destination of our short side trip for the simple reason that it is so pretty, especially when the ridges of this gentle valley are in full foliage display. Cross the bridge and you'll be facing twin Colonial houses about 100 yards away. The one on the left was home to artist Norman Rockwell for a number of years. Many of his paintings from that period feature local residents who still live nearby. There's plenty of room to turn around once you've crossed the bridge, and now you can return to Arlington on Route 313 and go south again on Route 7A.

In Arlington itself, there is the beautiful Arlington Inn at the junction of Routes 7A and 313 that serves first-class gourmet food in a Victorian setting.

Just south of Arlington you'll be given an opportunity to access the new Route 7, but pass this up and stay on Route 7A south. Here, the vistas open up as you pass through broad fields and the towns of North Shaftsbury and Shaftsbury. Poet Robert Frost lived in Shaftsbury for a short period of time. As you approach Bennington, you will be given another opportunity to access the new Route 7, which you should do.

Once on the divided highway, it will deposit you at a traffic light on the way into town. Go through this light, staying on the same road, and you will hit a second traffic light in town. Go straight through this one, too. The third traffic light is smack in the middle of town at the junction of Route 7 (which is no longer a highway-sized road) and Main Street. There are numerous shops and restaurants on Bennington's Main Street, but two spots of interest in this town are the Bennington Battle Monument and the Bennington Museum.

To return to Manchester, retrace your route out of town, but when given the opportunity to take the new Route 7 north, do so. It is clearly marked. This is a very scenic ride, since the new highway is built for the most part on high ground, allowing vistas of the colorful mountains.

Cross-Country to Woodstock

I have made many trips to Woodstock, some on business and some just for fun. I have a favorite way to go that involves hopping over to several routes that keep you pretty much off the more heavily traveled highways but still on well-maintained roads.

Leaving from Manchester, take Route 11-30 toward Bromley Mountain Ski Area. Instead of going south toward Brattleboro where the two routes divide, continue on Route 11 to Londonderry. You will pass the ski area, which in the summer and fall operates its Alpine Slide. You might want to stop here if you're so inclined. You can take a chair lift ride up the mountain and then ride down in the Alpine Slide — a kind of slot car for people. It's fun and safe, and the views on the chair lift ride up and the slide ride down — looking straight across a valley to Stratton Mountain — are themselves worth the price of admission.

In Londonderry, there are stores and a couple of restaurants. Continue through Londonderry to Chester, a distance of about 10 miles on Route 11. Chester is a very scenic and delightful little town, and, like Londonderry, it has restaurants and shops you may want to explore. In Chester is where we get a bit off the beaten track.

Take Route 103 north for five miles until you hit Route 10, which you take four miles east until you reach Route 106, where you want to go north. Route 106 will take you the remaining 18 miles to Woodstock.

This route travels through or near such Vermont towns as Gassetts, Baltimore, Perkinsville, Downers, and, my favorite name, Felchville. As you can imagine, the countryside is varied, with most of it being woods and farmland.

When you reach Woodstock you will find one of the most popular Vermont destinations. Like the Manchester area with its Equinox Hotel, Woodstock has long been a favorite of the well-to-do, with a focus on the impressive Woodstock Inn. The Woodstock Inn is a Rockresort operation, and some time ago Laurence Rockefeller poured a lot of money into restoring the town. All in all, it's just about as charming a spot as you can imagine.

Naturally, there are lots of shops, boutiques, and restaurants in the center of town, some of them quite chic-chic. My favorite lunch spot is Bentley's, right in the middle of town, where you can get anything from hamburgers to gourmet entrées. The Woodstock Inn is a nice dining experience, too. And if you feel like having a simple grilled-cheese sandwich or cheeseburger at a counter, there's a classic, tiny diner on Route 4 east on the way out of town. Look closely or you'll miss it.

Among the things to do in Woodstock is to pay a visit to the Vermont Institute of Natural Science (VINS) and Raptor Center. Just outside of town are 77 acres of nature preserve with self-guided nature trails. VINS studies many forms of wildlife, and frequently some environmental project is going on at the institute. The Raptor Center, in a barn behind the institute, is one of only a handful in the world. Injured birds of prey — owls, hawks, eagles, and others — are brought to the Raptor Center and nursed back to health. Those birds that do not recover well enough to be returned to the wild are housed in large cages, which you can tour. VINS is located 1.5 miles from town on Church Hill Road. Admission is charged.

When you leave Woodstock, you can return to Manchester via another route. Take Route 4 west about eight miles to Bridgewater Corners, and then take Route 100A south to Plymouth, which is where Calvin Coolidge, 30th president of the United States, was born and lived as a boy. If it is before mid-September, you can visit the Coolidge home, which is now owned by the Vermont Board of Historic Sites. Unfortunately, it is closed from mid-September through mid-May.

Route 100A joins Route 100 just down the road from Plymouth, and you can follow Route 100 south all the way to Londonderry. You will pass through two very lovely towns — Ludlow and Weston — on the way, each with interesting shops and good restaurants. From Londonderry, you can retrace your path along Routes 11 and 11-30 back to Manchester.

Now, here are a few tips to help your ride go smoothly. Most are common sense, but Vermont sees a great deal of traffic on its highways during the foliage season, and enough motorists seem to act in certain predictable ways that the following seems worth mentioning.

First, many visitors from urban and suburban areas bring with them the driving habits they have developed in order to survive at home. Rarely are aggressive driving tactics needed in order to make left-hand turns or to pull into traffic. Exercise patience, and you'll be surprised that you didn't have to fight with the traffic to accomplish your objective — because even with foliage visitors, there's seldom a lot of traffic.

Second, many other out-of-state visitors do the opposite. That is, when they get to Vermont they act as though there is no one else on the road. After all, they must reason, we *are* in the country. So be aware of traffic — don't stop in the middle of the road to take pictures or to ask directions of someone if there are other vehicles on the road.

Third, many visitors, enjoying the foliage beauty, prefer to drive slowly. On our mountain roads, this can hold up traffic in a manner that is unsafe and inconvenient. There are other tourists on the roads as well as people going and coming from work or school. If you suspect you are holding someone up, pull over at a safe pull-off spot and let them pass.

Fourth, respect private roads. If someone has gone to the trouble to mark his or her road private, it's best to respect that.

The great thing about Vermont — at any time of the year — is that it is a small, manageable state with well-maintained highways that allow you to get from here to there with little trouble. Armed with a road map, you can chart just about any tour you'd like, tailoring it to your own schedule.

But you'll find that this little state is distinctly different from its neighbors — Massachusetts, New York, New Hampshire, and Quebec. The differences are architectural, topographic, and demographic. Who knows why things happened this way? We just know it is a great place in which to live and a great place to visit.

Index

369